T0062589

Machine Learning Engineering in Action

BEN WILSON

MANNING

SHELTER ISLAND

For online information and ordering of this and other Manning books, please visit www.manning.com. The publisher offers discounts on this book when ordered in quantity. For more information, please contact

> Special Sales Department
> Manning Publications Co.
> 20 Baldwin Road
> PO Box 761
> Shelter Island, NY 11964
> Email: orders@manning.com

©2022 by Manning Publications Co. All rights reserved.

No part of this publication may be reproduced, stored in a retrieval system, or transmitted, in any form or by means electronic, mechanical, photocopying, or otherwise, without prior written permission of the publisher.

Many of the designations used by manufacturers and sellers to distinguish their products are claimed as trademarks. Where those designations appear in the book, and Manning Publications was aware of a trademark claim, the designations have been printed in initial caps or all caps.

♾ Recognizing the importance of preserving what has been written, it is Manning's policy to have the books we publish printed on acid-free paper, and we exert our best efforts to that end. Recognizing also our responsibility to conserve the resources of our planet, Manning books are printed on paper that is at least 15 percent recycled and processed without the use of elemental chlorine.

The author and publisher have made every effort to ensure that the information in this book was correct at press time. The author and publisher do not assume and hereby disclaim any liability to any party for any loss, damage, or disruption caused by errors or omissions, whether such errors or omissions result from negligence, accident, or any other cause, or from any usage of the information herein.

Manning Publications Co.
20 Baldwin Road
PO Box 761
Shelter Island, NY 11964

Development editor:	Patrick Barb
Technical development editor:	Marc-Philippe Huget
Review editor:	Aleksandar Dragosavljević
Production editor:	Keri Hales
Copy editor:	Sharon Wilkey
Proofreader:	Melody Dolab
Technical proofreader:	Ninoslav Čerkez
Typesetter:	Dennis Dalinnik
Cover designer:	Marija Tudor

ISBN: 9781617298714

Printed and bound by CPI Group (UK) Ltd, Croydon, CR0 4YY

brief contents

contents

preface

Even as a young boy, I was stubborn. When people would suggest simple ways of doing things, I would ignore advice, choosing to always do things the hard way. Decades later, not much changed as I shifted through increasingly challenging careers, eventually landing in the realm of data science (DS) and machine learning (ML) engineering, and now ML software development. As a data scientist in industry, I always felt the need to build overly complex solutions, working in isolation to solve a given problem in the way that I felt was best.

I had some successes but many failures, and generally left a trail of unmaintainable code in my wake as I moved from job to job. It's not something that I'm particularly proud of. I've been contacted by former colleagues, years after leaving a position, to have them tell me that my code is still running every day. When I've asked each one of them why, I've gotten the same demoralizing answer that has made me regret my implementations: "No one can figure it out to make changes to it, and it's too important to turn off."

I've been a bad data scientist. I've been an even worse ML engineer. It took me years to learn why that is. That stubbornness and resistance to solving problems in the simplest way created a lot of headaches for others, both in the sheer number of cancelled projects while I was at companies and in the unmaintainable technical debt that I left in my wake.

It wasn't until my most recent job, working as a resident solutions architect at Databricks (essentially a vendor field consultant), that I started to learn where I had gone wrong and to change how I approached solving problems. Likely because I was now working as an advisor to help others who were struggling with data science problems, I was able to see my own shortcomings through the abstract reflection of what they were struggling through. Over the past few years, I've helped quite a few teams avoid many pitfalls that I've experienced (and created through my own stubbornness and hubris). I figured that writing down some of this advice that I give people regularly could benefit a broader audience, beyond my individual conversations with isolated teams in the context of my job.

After all, applying machine learning to a real-world use case is hard enough when following along with examples and books on the concepts of applied ML. When you introduce the staggering complexity of end-to-end project work (which is the focus of this book), it comes as little surprise that many companies fail to realize the potential of ML in their businesses. It's just hard. It's easier if you have a guide, though.

This book doesn't aim to be a guide to applied ML. We're not going to be covering algorithms or theories on why one model is better than another for a particular use case, nor will we delve into all the details to solve individual problems. Rather, this book is a guide to avoid the pitfalls that I've seen so many teams fall into (and ones that I've had to claw my way out of as a practitioner). It is a generalized approach to using DS techniques to solve problems in a way that you, your customers (the internal ones at your company), and your peers will not regret. It's a guide to help you avoid making some of the really stupid mistakes that I've made.

In the words of two of my relatively recently acquired favorite proverbs:

> *Ask the experienced rather than the learned.*
>
> —Arab proverb

> *It is best to learn wisdom by the experience of others.*
>
> —Latin proverb

acknowledgments

There's absolutely no way that this book would have been possible without the support of my truly staggeringly amazing wife, Julie. She's had to endure countless evenings of me toiling away in my office well past midnight, hammering away at drafts, edits, and code refactoring. I'm not sure if you'll ever get the chance to meet her, but she's truly incredible. Not only is she my soulmate, but she's one of the few people on this planet capable of making me genuinely laugh and is a constant inspiration to me. I could argue that most of the wisdom that I've learned about how to influence and interact with people in a positive manner comes directly from me observing her.

I'd like to thank Patrick Barb, my development editor at Manning, for this book. He's been invaluable in getting this into the state that it's in, consistently challenged me to reduce my verbosity, and has been a great resource for helping me distill the points I've tried to make throughout the book. Along with Brian Sawyer, my acquisitions editor, and Marc-Philippe Huget, my technical development editor, the three of them have been an immense help throughout this entire process. In addition, a sincere thank you to Sharon Wilkey, the copy editor for this book, for incredible insight and fantastic skill in making the tone and flow of the book much better, and to all of the Manning team for their hard work in producing this book.

I'd also like to thank the reviewers who have provided great feedback throughout the process of building this book: Dae Kim, Denis Shestakov, Grant van Staden, Ignacio A. Ruiz-Reyes, Ioannis Atsonios, Jaganadh Gopinadhan, Jesús Antonino Juárez Guerrero, Johannes Verwijnen, John Bassil, Lara Thompson, Lokesh Kumar, Matthias Busch, Mirerfan Gheibi, Ninoslav Čerkez, Peter Morgan, Rahul Jain, Rui Liu,

Taylor Delehanty, and Xiangbo Mao. Their candid and relevant opinions have been incredibly helpful in condensing a sprawling, tone-deaf, and overly verbose ramble into something that I'm fairly proud of.

I'd like to thank a few colleagues who have helped influence many of the stories and examples and who have been a sounding board for me during the development of this book: Jas Bali, Amir Issaei, Brooke Wenig, Alex Narkaj, Conor Murphy, and Niall Turbitt. I'd also like to acknowledge the creators and fantastic world-class engineers and product team members at Databricks ML engineering who have designed, built, and maintained much of the tech that is featured in parts of this book. It's an absolute honor to count you all as colleagues.

Finally, thank you to Willy, our dog, who is heavily featured in this book. Yes, his favorite food is my Bolognese. To the curious, yes, he gets enough treats (although he might argue with that statement), and is thanked, repeatedly, through the judicious offerings of such.

about this book

Machine Learning Engineering in Action is an extension of the recommendations, hard-earned wisdom, and general tips that I've been sharing with clients for the past few years. This isn't a book on theory, nor is it going to make you build the best models for a given problem. Those books have already been, and continue to be, written by great authors. This is a book focused on the "other stuff."

Who should read this book

This book is intended to reach a rather large audience in the ML community. It is neither too in the weeds to be exclusive to ML engineers, nor too high-level to be exclusively written for the benefit of a layperson. My intention in writing it in the way that I did is to make it approachable for anyone who is involved in the process of using ML to solve business problems.

I've been pleasantly surprised by some of the early-stage feedback during development of this book. One of the first questions that I ask people who have reached out is, "What do you do?" I've received a far wider range of job titles and industries than I ever would have imagined—venture capitalists with PhDs in economics, ML engineers with 20 years of industry experience at some of the most prestigious tech companies, product managers at Silicon Valley startups, and undergrad university students in their freshman year. This lets me know that the book offers a bit of something for everyone to learn in terms of using ML engineering to build something successful.

How this book is organized: A road map

This book has three main parts that address milestones in any ML project. From the initial scoping stages of "What are we trying to solve?" to the final stage of "How are we keeping this solution relevant for years to come?," the book moves through each of these major epochs in the same logical order that you would consider these topics while working through a project:

- Part 1 (chapters 1–8) is focused primarily on the management of ML projects from the perspective of a team lead, manager, or project lead. It lays out a blueprint for scoping, experimentation, prototyping, and inclusive feedback to help you avoid falling into solution-building traps.
- Part 2 (chapters 9–13) covers the development process of ML projects. With examples (both good and bad) of ML solution development, this section carries you through proven methods of building, tuning, logging, and evaluating an ML solution to ensure that you're building the simplest and most maintainable code possible.
- Part 3 (chapters 14–16) focuses on "the after": specifically, considerations related to streamlining production release, retraining, monitoring, and attribution for a project. With examples focused on A/B testing, feature stores, and a passive retraining system, you'll be shown how to implement systems and architectures that can ensure that you're building the minimally complex solution to solve a business problem with ML.

About the code

This book contains many examples of source code, both in numbered listings and inline with normal text. In both cases, source code is formatted in a `fixed-width font like this` to separate it from ordinary text.

In many cases, the original source code has been reformatted; we've added line breaks and reworked indentation to accommodate the available page space in the book. Code annotations accompany many of the listings, highlighting important concepts.

You can get executable snippets of code from the liveBook (online) version of this book at https://livebook.manning.com/book/machine-learning-engineering-in-action. The complete code for the examples in the book is available for download from the Manning website at www.manning.com/books/machine-learning-engineering-in-action, and from GitHub at https://github.com/BenWilson2/ML-Engineering.

liveBook discussion forum

Purchase of *Machine Learning Engineering in Action* includes free access to liveBook, Manning's online reading platform. Using liveBook's exclusive discussion features, you can attach comments to the book globally or to specific sections or paragraphs. It's a snap to make notes for yourself, ask and answer technical questions, and receive

help from the author and other users. To access the forum, go to https://livebook
.manning.com/book/machine-learning-engineering-in-action/discussion. You can also
learn more about Manning's forums and the rules of conduct at https://livebook
.manning.com/discussion.

Manning's commitment to our readers is to provide a venue where a meaningful
dialogue between individual readers and between readers and the author can take
place. It is not a commitment to any specific amount of participation on the part of
the author, whose contribution to the forum remains voluntary (and unpaid). We suggest you try asking the author some challenging questions lest his interest stray! The
forum and the archives of previous discussions will be accessible from the publisher's
website as long as the book is in print.

about the author

 **BEN WILSON** is an ML engineer who has served as a nuclear engineering technician, a semiconductor process engineer, and a data scientist. He's been solving problems with data and open source tooling for over a decade, helping others do the same for the last four years. He enjoys building ML framework code, helping people think through challenging DS problems, and having a good chuckle.

about the cover illustration

The figure on the cover of *Machine Learning Engineering in Action*, "Hiatheo ou Esclave Chinoise," or "Hia Theo, a Chinese servant," is taken from a collection by Jacques Grasset de Saint-Sauveur, published in 1788. Each illustration is finely drawn and colored by hand.

In those days, it was easy to identify where people lived and what their trade or station in life was just by their dress. Manning celebrates the inventiveness and initiative of the computer business with book covers based on the rich diversity of regional culture centuries ago, brought back to life by pictures from collections such as this one.

Part 1

An introduction to machine learning engineering

I'm sure you've seen, like most people in the data science field, the statistics on project failures. Based on my experience, the numbers thrown around for a project getting into production (namely, by vendors promising that their tooling stack will improve your chances if you just pay them!) are ridiculously grim. However, some element of truth exists in the hyperbolic numbers that are referenced in the rates of project failure.

Using machine learning (ML) to solve real-world problems is complex. The sheer volume of tooling, algorithms, and activities involved in building a useful model are daunting for many organizations. In my time working as a data scientist and subsequently helping many dozens of companies build useful ML projects, I've never seen the tooling or the algorithms be the reason a project fails to provide value to a company.

The vast majority of the time, a project that fails to make its way to production for sustained utility has issues that are rooted in the very early phases. Before even a single line of code is written, before a serving architecture is selected and built out, and long before a decision on scalable training is made, a project is doomed to either cancellation or unused obscurity if planning, scoping, and experimentation are not done properly.

From these early stages of project definition, subject-matter expertise review, and reasonable levels of research and testing validation, a coherent project plan and road map can be built that carries the idea of solving a problem to the phase in which an effective solution can be built. In part 1 of this book, we'll go through blueprints showing how to evaluate, plan, and validate a plan for determining the most likely low-risk solution for a problem by using (or not using!) ML.

What is a machine learning engineer?

This chapter covers

- The scope of knowledge and skills for machine learning engineers
- The six fundamental aspects of applied machine learning project work
- The functional purpose of machine learning engineers

Machine learning (ML) is exciting. It's fun, challenging, creative, and intellectually stimulating. It also makes money for companies, autonomously tackles overwhelmingly large tasks, and removes the burdensome task of monotonous work from people who would rather be doing something else.

ML is also ludicrously complex. From thousands of algorithms, hundreds of open source packages, and a profession of practitioners required to have a diverse skill set ranging from data engineering (DE) to advanced statistical analysis and visualization, the work required of a professional practitioner of ML is truly intimidating. Adding to that complexity is the need to be able to work cross-functionally with a wide array of specialists, subject-matter experts (SMEs), and business unit groups—communicating and collaborating on both the nature of the problem being solved and the output of the ML-backed solution.

ML engineering applies a *system* around this staggering level of complexity. It uses a set of standards, tools, processes, and methodology that aims to minimize the chances of abandoned, misguided, or irrelevant work being done in an effort to solve a business problem or need. It, in essence, is the road map to creating ML-based systems that can be not only deployed to production, but also maintained and updated for years in the future, allowing businesses to reap the rewards in efficiency, profitability, and accuracy that ML in general has proven to provide (when done correctly).

This book is, at its essence, that very road map. It's a guide to help you navigate the path of developing production-capable ML solutions. Figure 1.1 shows the major elements of ML project work covered throughout this book. We'll move through these proven sets of processes (mostly a "lessons learned" from things I've screwed up in my career) to give a framework for solving business problems through the application of ML.

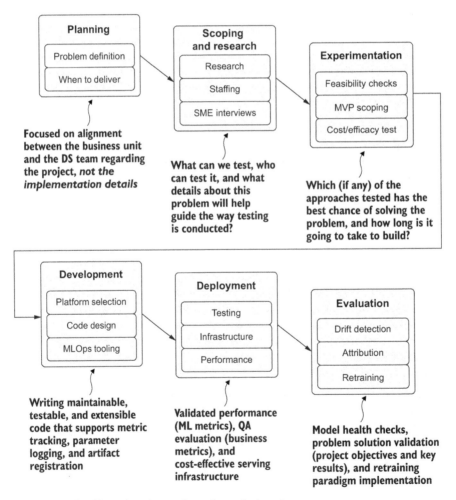

Figure 1.1   The ML engineering road map for project work

This path for project work is not meant to focus solely on the tasks that should be done at each phase. Rather, it is the methodology within each stage (the "why are we doing this" element) that enables successful project work.

The end goal of ML work is, after all, about solving a problem. The most effective way to solve those business problems that we're all tasked with as data science (DS) practitioners is to follow a process designed around preventing rework, confusion, and complexity. By embracing the concepts of ML engineering and following the road of effective project work, the end goal of getting a useful modeling solution can be shorter, far cheaper, and have a much higher probability of succeeding than if you just wing it and hope for the best.

1.1 Why ML engineering?

To put it most simply, ML is *hard*. It's even harder to do correctly in the sense of serving relevant predictions, at scale, with reliable frequency. With so many specialties existing in the field—such as natural language processing (NLP), forecasting, deep learning, and traditional linear and tree-based modeling—an enormous focus on active research, and so many algorithms that have been built to solve specific problems, it's remarkably challenging to learn even slightly more than an insignificant fraction of all there is to learn about the field. Understanding the theoretical and practical aspects of applied ML is challenging and time-consuming.

However, none of that knowledge helps in building interfaces between the model solution and the outside world. Nor does it help inform development patterns that ensure maintainable and extensible solutions.

Data scientists are also expected to be familiar with additional realms of competency. From mid-level DE skills (you have to get your data for your data science from somewhere, right?), software development skills, project management skills, visualization skills, and presentation skills, the list grows ever longer, and the volumes of experience that need to be gained become rather daunting. It's not much of a surprise, considering all of this, that "just figuring it out" in reference to all the required skills to create production-grade ML solutions is untenable.

The aim of ML engineering is not to iterate through the lists of skills just mentioned and require that a data scientist (DS) master each of them. Instead, ML engineering collects certain aspects of those skills, carefully crafted to be relevant to data scientists, all with the goal of increasing the chances of *getting an ML project into production* and making sure that it's not a solution that needs constant maintenance and intervention to keep running.

ML engineers, after all, don't need to be able to create applications and software frameworks for generic algorithmic use cases. They're also not likely to be writing their own large-scale streaming ingestion extract, transform, and load (ETL) pipelines. They similarly don't need to be able to create detailed and animated frontend visualizations in JavaScript.

ML engineers need to know *just enough software development skills* to be able to write modular code and implement unit tests. The don't need to know about the intricacies of non-blocking asynchronous messaging brokering. They need *just enough data engineering skills* to build (and schedule the ETL for) feature datasets for their models, but not to construct a petabyte-scale streaming ingestion framework. They need *just enough visualization skills* to create plots and charts that communicate clearly what their research and models are doing, but not to develop dynamic web apps that have complex user-experience (UX) components. They also need *just enough project management experience* to know how to properly define, scope, and control a project to solve a problem, but need not go through a Project Management Professional (PMP) certification.

A giant elephant remains in the room when it comes to ML. Specifically, *why*—with so many companies going all in on ML, hiring massive teams of highly compensated data scientists, and devoting enormous amounts of financial and temporal resources to projects—do so many endeavors end up failing? Figure 1.2 depicts rough estimates of what I've come to see as the six primary reasons projects fail (and the rates of these failures in any given industry, from my experience, are truly surprising).

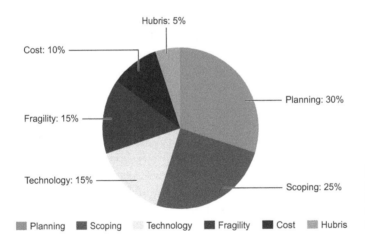

Figure 1.2 My estimation of why ML projects fail, from the hundreds I've worked on and advised others on

Throughout this first part of the book, we'll discuss how to identify the reasons so many projects fail, are abandoned, or take far longer than they should to reach production. We'll also discuss the solutions to each of these common failures and cover the processes that can significantly lower the chances of these factors derailing your projects.

Generally, these failures happen because the DS team is either inexperienced with solving a problem of the scale required (a technological or process-driven failure) or hasn't fully understood the desired outcome from the business (a communication-driven failure). I've never seen this happen because of malicious intent. Rather, most ML projects are incredibly challenging, complex, and composed of algorithmic software tooling that is hard to explain to a layperson—hence the breakdowns in communication with business units that most projects endure.

Adding to the complexity of ML projects are two other critical elements that are not shared by (most) traditional software development projects: a frequent lack of detail in project expectations and the relative industry immaturity in tooling. Both aspects are no different from the state of software engineering in the early 1990s. Businesses then were unsure of how to best leverage new aspects of technological capability, tooling was woefully underdeveloped, and many projects failed to meet the expectations of those who were commissioning engineering teams to build them. ML work is (from my biased view of working with only so many companies) at the same place now in the second decade of the 21st century that software engineering was 30 years ago.

This book isn't a doom-riddled treatise on the challenges of ML; rather, it's meant to show how these elements can be a risk for projects. The intent is to teach the processes and tools that help minimize this failure risk. Figure 1.3 shows an overview of

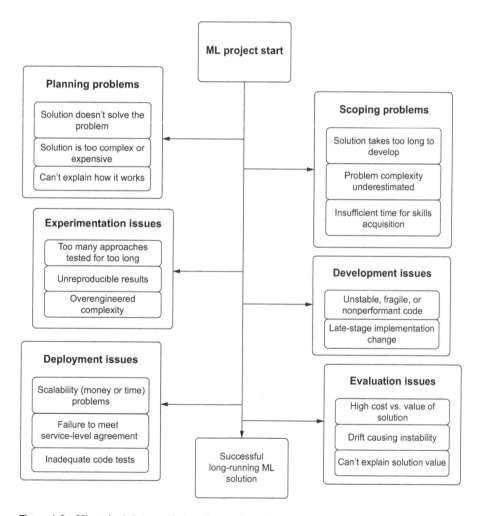

Figure 1.3 ML project detours that lead to project failure

the detours that can arise in the execution of a project; each brings a different element of risk to a project's successful execution.

The framework used in ML engineering is exactly dedicated to address each of these primary failure modes. Eliminating these chances of failure is at the heart of this methodology. It is done by providing the processes to make better decisions, ease communication with internal customers, eliminate rework during the experimentation and development phases, create code bases that can be easily maintained, and bring a best-practices approach to any project that is heavily influenced by DS work. Just as software engineers decades ago refined their processes from large-scale waterfall implementations to a more flexible and productive Agile process, ML engineering seeks to define a new set of practices and tools that will optimize the wholly unique realm of software development for data scientists.

1.2   *The core tenets of ML engineering*

Now that you have a general idea of what ML engineering is, we can focus in a bit on the key elements that make up those incredibly broad categories from figure 1.2. Each of these topics is the focus of entire chapter-length in-depth discussions later in this book, but for now we're going to look at them in a holistic sense by way of potentially painfully familiar scenarios to elucidate why they're so important.

1.2.1   *Planning*

> *Nothing is more demoralizing than building an ML solution that solves the wrong problem.*

By far the largest cause of project failures, failing to plan out a project thoroughly, is one of the most demoralizing ways for a project to be cancelled. Imagine for a moment that you're the first-hired DS for a company. On your first week, an executive from marketing approaches you, explaining (in their terms) a serious business issue that they are having. They need to figure out an efficient means of communicating to customers through email to let them know of upcoming sales that they might be interested in. With very little additional detail provided to you, the executive merely says, "I want to see the click and open rates go up on our emails."

If this is the only information supplied, and repeated queries to members of the marketing team simply state the same end goal of increasing the clicking and opening rate, the number of avenues to pursue seems limitless. Left to your own devices, do you

- Focus on content recommendation and craft custom emails for each user?
- Provide predictions with an NLP-backed system that will craft relevant subject lines for each user?
- Attempt to predict a list of products most relevant to the customer base to put on sale each day?

With so many options of varying complexity and approaches, and little guidance, creating a solution that is aligned with the expectations of the executive is highly unlikely. Instead, if a proper planning discussion delved into the correct amount of detail, avoiding the complexity of the ML side of things, the true expectation might be revealed. You'd then know that the only expectation is a prediction for when each user would most likely be open to reading email. The executive simply wants to know when someone is most likely to not be at work, commuting, or sleeping so that the company can send batches of emails throughout the day to different cohorts of customers.

The sad reality is that many ML projects start off in this way. Frequently, little communication occurs with regards to project initiation, and the general expectation is that the DS team *will just figure it out.* However, without the proper guidance on what needs to be built, how it needs to function, and what the end goal of the predictions is, the project is almost certainly doomed to failure.

After all, what would have happened if an entire content recommendation system were built for that use case, with months of development and effort wasted, when a simple analytics query based on IP address geolocation was what was really needed? The project would not only be cancelled, but many questions would likely come from on high as to why this system was built and why its development costed so much.

Let's look at the simplified planning discussion illustrated in figure 1.4. Even at the initial phase of discussion, we can see how just a few careful questions and clear answers

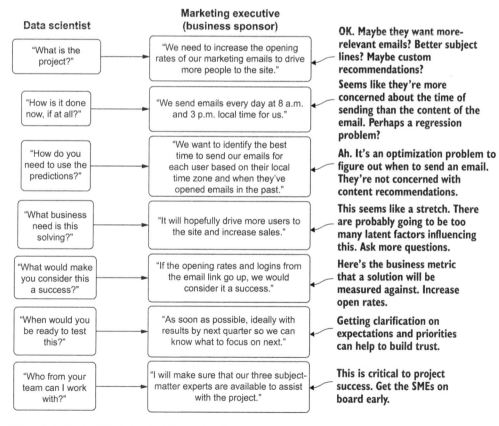

Figure 1.4   A simplified planning discussion diagram

can provide the one thing every data scientist should be looking for in this situation (especially as the first DS at a company working on the first problem): a quick win.

As you can see from the DS's internal monologue shown at the right, the problem at hand is not at all in the list of original assumptions that were made. There is no talk of email content, relevancy to the subject line, or the items in the email. It's a simple analytical query to figure out which time zone customers are in and to analyze historic opening in local times for each customer. By taking a few minutes to plan and understand the use case fully, weeks (if not months) of wasted effort, time, and money were saved.

By focusing on *what will be built* and *why it needs to be built*, both the DS team and the business are able to guide the discussion more fruitfully. Eschewing a conversation focused on *how it will be built* keeps the DS members of the group focused on the problem. Ignoring *when it will be built by* helps the business keep its focus aligned on the needs of the project.

Avoiding discussing implementation details at this stage of the project is not merely critical for the team to focus on the problem. Keeping the esoteric details of algorithms and solution design out of discussions with the larger team keeps the business unit members engaged. After all, they really don't care how many eggs go into the mix, what color the eggs are, or even what species laid the eggs; they just want to eat the cake when it's done. We will cover the processes of planning, having project expectation discussions with internal business customers, and general communications about ML work with a nontechnical audience at length and in much greater depth throughout the remainder of part 1.

1.2.2 Scoping and research

If you switch your approach halfway through development, you'll face a hard conversation with the business to explain that the project's delays are due to you not doing your homework.

After all, there are only two questions that your internal customers (the business unit) have about the project:

- Is this going to solve my problem?
- How long is this going to take?

Let's take a look at another potentially familiar scenario to discuss polar opposite ways that this stage of ML project development can go awry. Say we have two DS teams at a company, each being pitted against the other to develop a solution to an escalating incidence of fraud being conducted with the company's billing system. Team A's research and scoping process is illustrated in figure 1.5.

Team A comprises mostly junior data scientists, all of whom entered the workforce without an extensive period in academia. Their actions, upon getting the details of the project and the expectations of them, is to immediately go to blog posts. They search the internet for "detecting payment fraud" and "fraud algorithms," finding

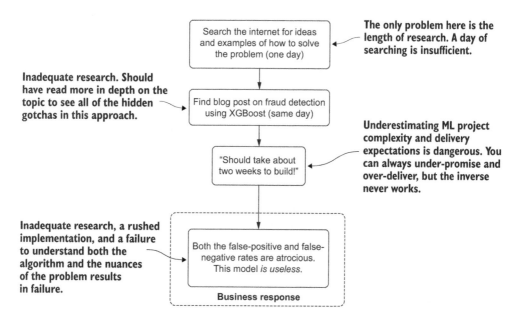

Figure 1.5 Research and scoping of a fraud-detection problem for a junior team of well-intentioned but inexperienced data scientists

hundreds of results from consultancy companies, a few extremely high-level blog posts from similar junior data scientists who have likely never put a model into production, and some rudimentary open source data examples.

Team B, in contrast, is filled with a group of PhD academic researchers. Their research and scoping is shown in figure 1.6.

With Team B's studious approach to research and vetting of ideas, the first actions are to dig into published papers on the topic of fraud modeling. Spending several days reading through journals and papers, these team members are now armed with a large collection of theory encompassing some of the most cutting-edge research being done on detecting fraudulent activity.

If we were to ask either team to estimate the level of effort required to produce a solution, we would get wildly divergent answers. Team A would likely estimate about two weeks to build its XGBoost binary classification model, while team B would tell a vastly different tale. Those team members would estimate several months for implementing, training, and evaluating the novel deep learning structure that they found in a highly regarded whitepaper whose proven accuracy for the research was significantly better than any Perforce-implemented algorithm for this use case.

The problem here with scoping and research is that these two polar opposites would both have their projects fail for two completely different reasons. Team A would fail because the solution to the problem is *significantly more complex than the example shown in the blog post* (the class imbalance issue alone is too challenging of a topic to

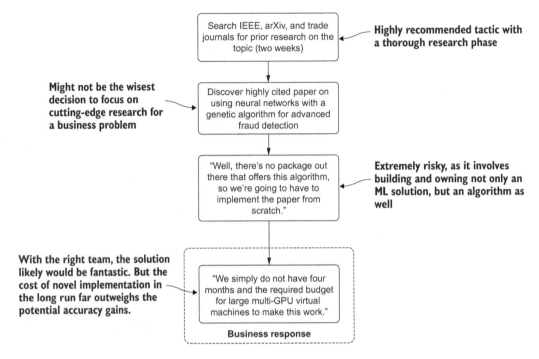

Figure 1.6   Research and scoping for an academia-focused group of researchers for the fraud-detection problem

effectively document in the short space of a blog). Team B, even though its solution would likely be extremely accurate, would *never be allocated resources to build the risky solution* as an initial fraud-detection service at the company.

Project scoping for ML is incredibly challenging. Even for the most seasoned of ML veterans, conjecturing how long a project will take, which approach is going to be most successful, and the amount of resources required is a futile and frustrating exercise. The risk associated with making erroneous claims is fairly high, but structuring proper scoping and solution research can help minimize the chances of being wildly off on estimation.

Most companies have a mix of the types of people in this hyperbolic scenario. Some are academics whose sole goal is to further the advancement of knowledge and research into algorithms, paving the way for future discoveries from within the industry. Others are "applications of ML" engineers who just want to use ML as a tool to solve a business problem. It's important to embrace and balance both aspects of these philosophies toward ML work, strike a compromise during the research and scoping phase of a project, and know that the middle ground here is the best path to trod upon to ensure that a project actually makes it to production.

1.2.3 Experimentation

Testing approaches is a Goldilocks activity; if you don't test enough options, you're probably not finding the best solution, while testing too many things wastes precious time. Find the middle ground.

In the experimentation phase, the largest causes of project failure are either the experimentation taking too long (testing too many things or spending too long fine-tuning an approach) or an underdeveloped prototype that is so abysmally bad that the business decides to move on to something else.

Let's use a similar example from section 1.2.2 to illustrate how these two approaches might play out at a company that is looking to build an image classifier for detecting products on retail store shelves. The experimentation paths that the two groups take (showing the extreme opposites of experimentation) are shown in figures 1.7 and 1.8.

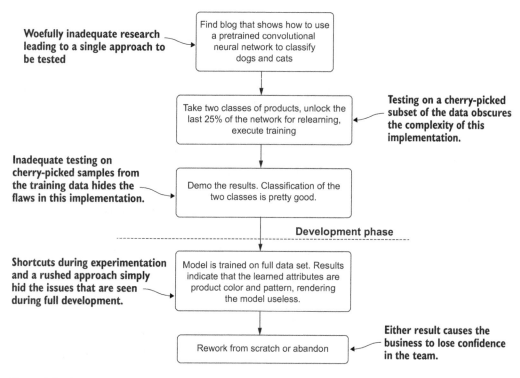

Figure 1.7   A rushed experimentation phase by a team of inexperienced data scientists

Team A embodies the example of wholly inadequate research and experimentation in the early phases of a project. A project that glosses over these critical stages of solution development runs the risk, as shown in figure 1.7, of having a result that is so woefully underdeveloped that it becomes irrelevant to the business. Projects like these erode the business's faith in the DS team, waste money, and needlessly expend precious resources of several groups.

These inexperienced DS team members, performing only the most cursory of research, adapt a basic demo from a blog post. While their basic testing shows promise, they fail to thoroughly research the implementation details required for employing the model on their data. By retraining the pretrained model on only a few hundred images of two of the many thousands of products from their corpus of images, their misleading results hide the problem with their approach.

This is the exact opposite situation to that of the other team. Team B's approach to this problem is shown in figure 1.8.

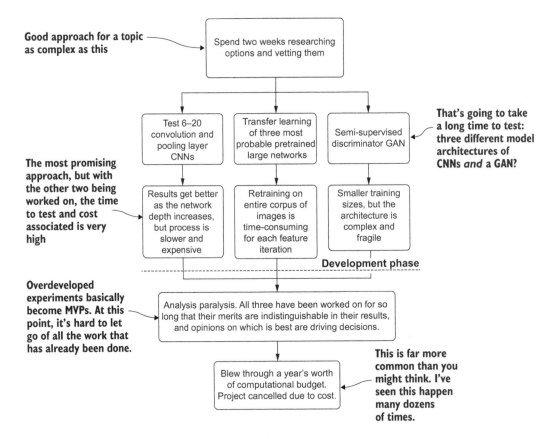

Figure 1.8   A case of too much testing in the experimentation phase of a project

Team B's approach to solving this problem is to spend weeks searching through cutting-edge papers, reading journals, and understanding the theory involved in various convolutional neural network (CNN) and generative adversarial network (GAN) approaches. They settle on three broad potential solutions, each consisting of several tests that need to run and be evaluated against the entire collection of their training image dataset.

It isn't the depth of research that fails them in this case, as it does for the other group. Team B's research is appropriate for this use case. The team members have an issue with their minimum viable product (MVP) because they are trying too many things in too much depth. Varying the structure and depth of a custom-built CNN requires dozens (if not hundreds) of iterations to get right for the use case that they're trying to solve. This work should be scoped into the development stage of the project, not during evaluation, after a single approach is selected based on early results.

While not the leading cause of project failure, an incorrectly implemented experimentation phase can stall or cancel an otherwise great project. Neither of these two extreme examples is appropriate, and the best course of action is a moderate approach between the two.

1.2.4 Development

No one thinks that code quality matters until it's 4 a.m. on a Saturday, you're 18 hours into debugging a failure, and you still haven't fixed the bug.

Having a poor development practice for ML projects can manifest itself in a multitude of ways that can completely kill a project. Though usually not as directly visible as some of the other leading causes, having a fragile and poorly designed code base and poor development practices can make a project harder to work on, easier to break in production, and far harder to improve as time goes on.

For instance, let's look at a rather simple and frequent modification situation that comes up during the development of a modeling solution: changes to the feature engineering. In figure 1.9, we see two data scientists attempting to make a set of changes in a monolithic code base. In this development paradigm, all the logic for the entire job is written in a single notebook through scripted variable declarations and functions.

Julie, in the monolithic code base, will likely have a lot of searching and scrolling to do, finding each individual location where the feature vector is defined and adding her new fields to collections. Her encoding work will need to be correct and carried throughout the script in the correct places as well. It's a daunting amount of work for any sufficiently complex ML code base (as the number of code lines for feature engineering and modeling combined can reach to the thousands if developed in a scripting paradigm) and is prone to frustrating errors in the form of omissions, typos, and other transcription mistakes.

Joe, meanwhile, has far fewer edits to do. But he is still subject to the act of searching through the long code base and relying on editing the hardcoded values correctly.

The real problem with the monolithic approach comes when they try to incorporate each of their changes into a single copy of the script. As they have mutual

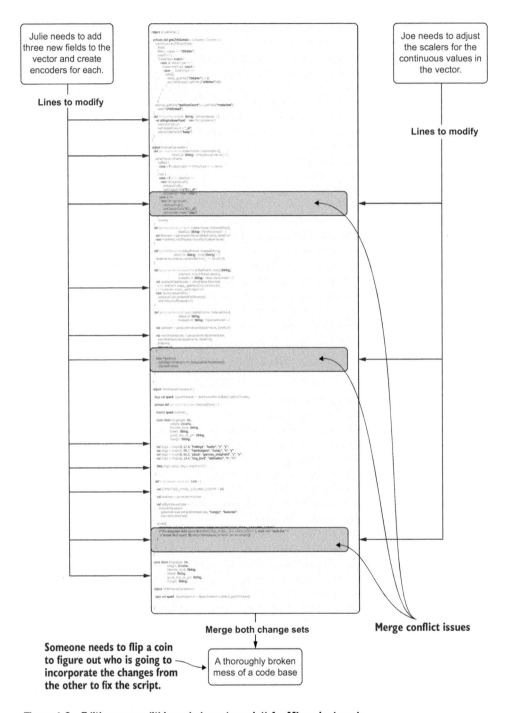

Julie needs to add three new fields to the vector and create encoders for each.

Lines to modify

Joe needs to adjust the scalers for the continuous values in the vector.

Lines to modify

Merge both change sets

Merge conflict issues

Someone needs to flip a coin to figure out who is going to incorporate the changes from the other to fix the script.

A thoroughly broken mess of a code base

Figure 1.9   Editing a monolithic code base (a script) for ML project work

dependencies on each other's work, both will have to update their code and select one of their copies to serve as a master for the project, copying in the changes from the other's work. This long and arduous process wastes precious development time and likely will require a great deal of debugging to get correct.

Figure 1.10 shows a different approach to maintaining an ML project's code base. This time, a modularized code architecture separates the tight coupling that is present within the large script from figure 1.9.

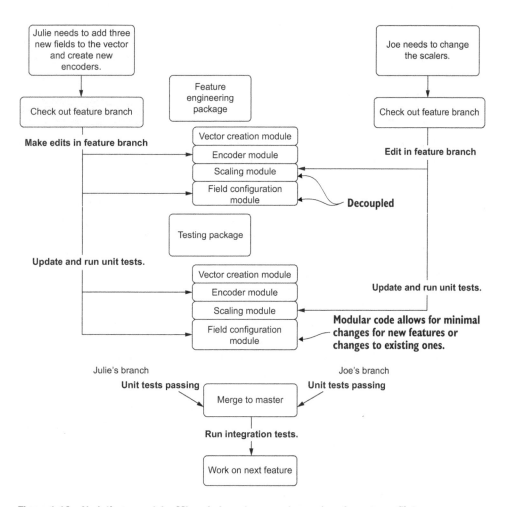

Figure 1.10   Updating a modular ML code base to prevent rework and merge conflicts

This modularized code base is written in an integrated development environment (IDE). While the changes being made by the two DSs are identical in their nature to those being made in figure 1.9 (Julie is adding a few fields to the feature vector and updating encodings for these new fields, while Joe is updating the scaler used on the feature vector), the amount of effort and time spent getting these changes working in concert with one another is dramatically different.

With a fully modularized code base registered in Git, each of them can check out a feature branch from the master, make small edits to the modules that are part of their features, write new tests (if needed), run their tests, and submit a pull request. Once their work is complete—because of the configuration-based code and the capability of the methods in each module class to act upon the data for their project through leveraging the job configuration—each feature branch will not impact the other and should just work as designed. Julie and Joe can cut a release branch of both of their changes in a single build, run a full integration test, and safely merge to the master, confident that their work is correct. They can, in effect, work efficiently together on the same code base, greatly minimizing the chance of errors and reducing the amount of time spent debugging code.

1.2.5 *Deployment*

> *Not planning a project around a deployment strategy is like having a dinner party without knowing how many guests are showing up. You'll either be wasting money or ruining experiences.*

Perhaps the most confusing and complex part of ML project work for newer teams is in how to build a cost-effective deployment strategy. If it's underpowered, the prediction quality doesn't matter (since the infrastructure can't properly serve the predictions). If it's overpowered, you're effectively burning money on unused infrastructure and complexity.

As an example, let's look at an inventory optimization problem for a fast-food company. The DS team has been fairly successful in serving predictions for inventory management at region-level groupings for years, running large batch predictions for the per-day demands of expected customer counts at a weekly level, and submitting forecasts as bulk extracts each week. Up until this point, the DS team has been accustomed to an ML architecture that effectively looks like that shown in figure 1.11.

This relatively standard architecture for serving up scheduled batch predictions focuses on exposing results to internal analytics personnel who provide guidance on quantities of materials to order. This prediction-serving architecture isn't particularly complex and is a paradigm that the DS team members are familiar with. With the scheduled synchronous nature of the design, as well as the large amounts of time between subsequent retraining and inference, the general sophistication of their technology stack doesn't have to be particularly high (which is a good thing; see the following sidebar).

As the company realizes the benefits of predictive modeling over time with these batch approaches, its faith in the DS team increases. When a new business opportunity arises that requires near-real-time inventory forecasting at a per-store level, company executives ask the DS team to provide a solution for this use case.

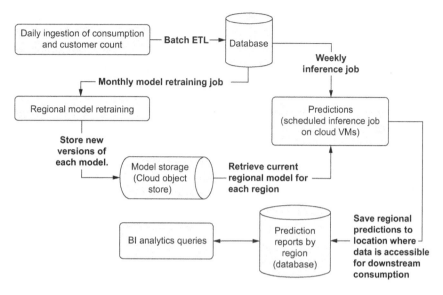

Figure 1.11 A basic batch-prediction-serving architecture

A brief note on simplistic architecture

In the world of ML, always strive for the simplest design possible when building an architecture. If the project requires a periodicity of inference of one week, use a batch process (not real-time streaming). If the data volumes are in the megabytes, use a database and a simple virtual machine (not a 25-node Apache Spark cluster). If the runtime of training is measured in minutes, stick to CPUs (not GPUs).

Using complex architecture, platforms, and technology simply for the sake of using them will create a condition that you will inevitably regret, as it introduces unnecessary complexity to an already complex solution. With each new complexity introduced, the chances rise that something is going to break (usually in a spectacularly complex manner). Keeping the technology, the stack, and the architecture as simple as is needed to solve the imminent business needs of the project is always a recommended best practice in order to deliver a consistent, reliable, and effective solution to a business.

The ML team members understand that their standard prediction-serving architecture won't work for this project. They need to build a REST application programming interface (API) to the forecasted data to support the request volume and prediction updating frequency. To adapt to the granular level of a per-store inventory prediction (and the volatility involved in that), the team knows that they need to regenerate predictions frequently throughout the day. Armed with these requirements, they enlist the help of some software engineers at the company and build out the solution.

It isn't until after the first week of going live that the business realizes that the implementation's cloud computing costs are more than an order of magnitude higher than the cost savings seen from the more-efficient inventory management system. The new architecture, coupled with autoregressive integrated moving average (ARIMA) models needed to solve the problem, is shown in figure 1.12.

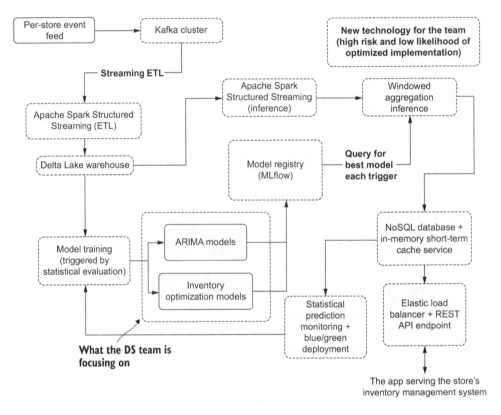

Figure 1.12   The far more complex pseudo-real-time serving architecture required to meet the business needs for the project

It doesn't take long for the project to get cancelled and a complete redesign of the architecture for this implementation to be commissioned to keep the costs down. This is a story that plays out time and again at companies implementing ML to solve new and interesting problems (and to be fair, one that I've personally caused three times in my career).

Without focusing on the deployment and serving at the start of a project, the risk of building a solution that is under-engineered—doesn't meet service-level agreement (SLA) or traffic-volume needs—or is overengineered—exceeds technical specifications at an unacceptably high cost—is high. Figure 1.13 shows some (not all, by

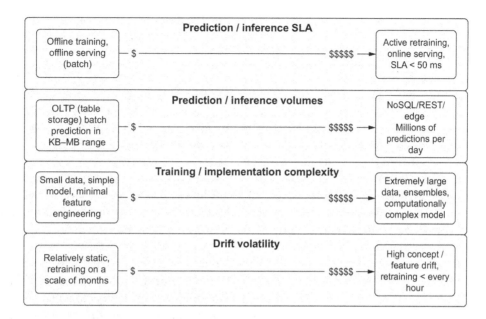

Figure 1.13 Deployment cost considerations

any stretch of the imagination) elements to think about with regards to serving prediction results and the costs associated with the extremes of the ranges of those paradigms.

It may not seem particularly exciting or important to think about cost when faced with a novel problem to solve in a clever way with an algorithm. While the DS team might not be thinking of total cost of ownership for a particular project, rest assured that executives are. By evaluating these considerations early enough in the process of building a project, analyses can be conducted to determine whether the project is worth it.

It's better to cancel a project in the first week of planning than to shut off a production service after spending months building it, after all. The only way to know whether a relatively expensive architecture is worth the cost of running it, however, is by measuring and evaluating its impact to the business.

1.2.6 Evaluation

> *If you can't justify the benefits of your project being in production, don't expect it to remain there for very long.*

The worst reason for getting an ML project cancelled or abandoned is budget. Typically, if the project has gotten into production to begin with, the up-front costs associated with developing the solution were accepted and understood by the leadership at the company. Having a project cancelled after it's already in production because of a lack of visibility of its impact to the company is a different matter entirely. If you can't prove the worth of the solution, you face the real possibility of someone telling you to turn it off to save money someday.

Imagine a company that has spent the past six months working tirelessly on a new initiative to increase sales through the use of predictive modeling. The DS team members have followed best practices throughout the project's development—making sure that they're building exactly what the business is asking for and focusing development efforts on maintainable and extensible code—and have pushed the solution to production.

The model has been performing wonderfully over the past three months. Each time the team has done post hoc analysis of the predictions to the state of reality afterward, the predictions turn out to be eerily close. Figure 1.14 then rears its ugly head with a simple question from one of the company executives who is concerned about the cost of running this ML solution.

The one thing that the team forgot about in creating a great ML project is thinking of how to tie their predictions to some aspect of the business that can justify its existence. The model that they've been working on and that is currently running in production was designed to increase revenue, but when scrutinized for the cost of using it, the team realized that they hadn't thought of an attribution analytics methodology to prove the worth of the solution.

Can they simply add up the sales and attribute it all to the model? No, that wouldn't be even remotely correct. Could they look at the comparison of sales versus last year? That wouldn't be correct either, as far too many latent factors are impacting sales.

The only thing that they can do to give attribution to their model is to perform A/B testing and use sound statistical models to arrive at a revenue lift calculation (with estimation errors) to show how much additional sales are due to their model. However, the ship has already sailed, as the solution has already been deployed for all customers. The team lost its chance at justifying the continued existence of the model. While the project might not be shut off immediately, it certainly will be on the chopping block if the company needs to reduce its budgetary spending.

It's always a good idea to think ahead and plan for this case. Whether it's happened to you yet or not, I can assure you that at some point it most certainly will (it took me two very hard lessons to learn this little nugget of wisdom). It is far easier to defend your work if you have the ammunition at the ready in the form of validated and statistically significant tests showing the justification for the model's continued existence. Chapter 11 covers approaches to building A/B testing systems, statistical tests for attribution, and associated evaluation algorithms.

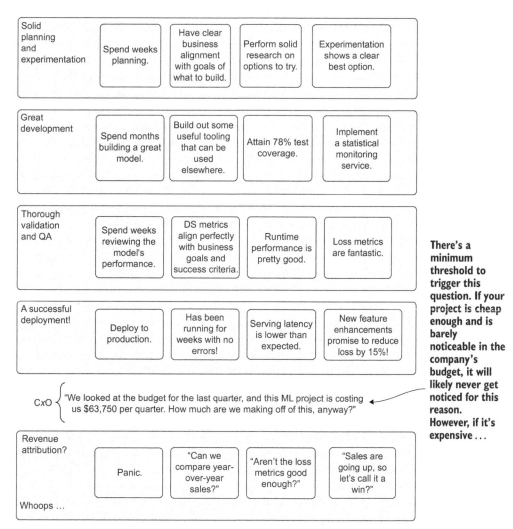

There's a minimum threshold to trigger this question. If your project is cheap enough and is barely noticeable in the company's budget, it will likely never get noticed for this reason. However, if it's expensive ...

If metrics for attribution and measurement are not agreed upon during project planning, data is not collected, and a thorough statistical analysis is not performed routinely on the efficacy of the model, *even a great solution could be turned off one day.*

Figure 1.14   A nearly flawless ML project getting cancelled because of a lack of A/B testing and statistically valid attribution measurement

1.3   *The goals of ML engineering*

In the most elemental sense, the primary goal of any DS is to solve a difficult problem through the use of statistics, algorithms, and predictive modeling that is either too onerous, monotonous, error-prone, or complex for a human to do. It's not to build the fanciest model, to create the most impressive research paper about their approach to a solution, or to search out the most exciting new tech to force into their project work.

We're all here in this profession to solve problems. Among a vast quantity of tools, algorithms, frameworks, and core responsibilities that a DS has at their disposal to solve those problems, it's easy to become overwhelmed and focus on the technical aspects of the job. Without a process guide to wrangle the complexity of ML project work, it's incredibly easy to lose sight of the real goal of solving problems.

By focusing on the core aspects of project work highlighted in section 1.2 and covered in greater detail throughout this book, you can get to the true desired state of ML work: seeing your models run in production and having them solve a real business problem.

> **You can do this**
>
> An entire industry out there is designed to convince you that you can't—that you need to hire them to do all of this complex work for you. They make a great deal of money doing this.
>
> But trust me, you can learn these core concepts and can build a team that follows a methodology for approaching ML work that can dramatically increase the success rate of a project. The work may be complex and rather confusing at first, but following the guidelines and using the right tooling to help manage the complexity can help any team develop sophisticated ML solutions that won't require massive budgets or consume all the free time that a DS team has to keep the lights on for poorly implemented solutions. You've got this.

Before delving into the finer details of each of these methodologies and approaches for ML engineering work, see the outline detailed in figure 1.15. This is effectively a process flow plan for production ML work that I've seen prove successful for any project with any team.

Throughout this book, we'll cover these elements, focusing not only on discussions and implementations of each, but also on why they're so important. This path—focusing on the people, processes, and tools to support successful ML projects—is paved over the corpses of many failed projects I've seen in my career. However, by following the practices that this book outlines, you will likely see fewer of these failures, allowing you to build more projects that not only make their way to production, but get used and stay in production.

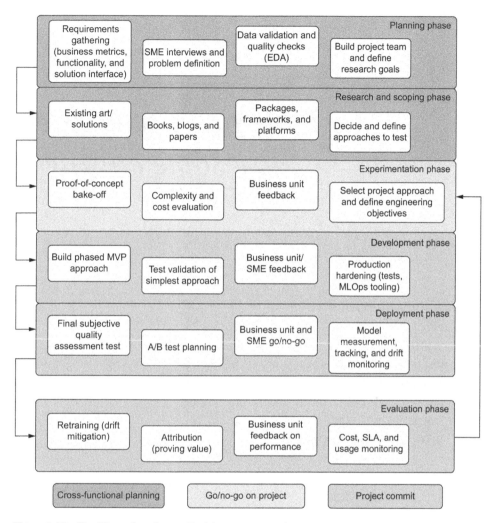

Figure 1.15 The ML engineering methodology component map

Summary

- ML engineers need to know aspects of data science, traditional software engineering, and project management to ensure that applied ML projects are developed efficiently, focus on solving a real problem, and are maintainable.
- Focusing on best practices throughout the six primary project phases of applied ML work—planning, scoping and research, experimentation, development, deployment, and evaluation—will greatly help a project minimize risk of abandonment.
- Shedding concerns about technical implementation details, tooling, and novelty of approaches will help focus project work on what really matters: solving problems.

Your data science could use some engineering

This chapter covers

- Elucidating the differences between a data scientist and an ML engineer
- Focusing on simplicity in all project work to reduce risk
- Applying Agile fundamentals to ML project work
- Illustrating the differences and similarities between DevOps and MLOps

In the preceding chapter, we covered the components of ML engineering from the perspective of project work. Explaining what this approach to DS work entails from a project-level perspective tells only part of the story. Taking a view from a higher level, ML engineering can be thought of as a recipe involving a trinity of core concepts:

- Technology (tools, frameworks, algorithms)
- People (collaborative work, communication)
- Process (software development standards, experimentation rigor, Agile methodology)

The simple truth of this profession is that project work that focuses on each of these elements are generally successful, while those that omit one or many of them tend to fail. This is the very reason for the hyperbolic and oft-quoted failure rates of ML projects in industry (which I find to be rather self-serving and panic-fueled when coming from vendor marketing materials).

This chapter covers, at a high level, this trio of components for successful projects. Employing the appropriate balance of each, focused on creating maintainable solutions that are co-developed with internal customers in a collaborative and inclusive fashion, will greatly increase the chances of building ML solutions that endure. After all, the *primary focus of all DS work is to solve problems.* Conforming work patterns to a proven methodology that is focused on maintainability and efficiency translates directly to solving more problems with much less effort.

2.1   Augmenting a complex profession with processes to increase project success

In one of the earliest definitions of the term *data science,* as covered in *Data Science, Classification, and Related Methods* (Springer, 1996), compiled by C. Hayashi et al., the three main focuses are as follows:

- *Design for data*—Specifically, the planning surrounding how information is to be collected and in what structure it will need to be acquired to solve a particular problem
- *Collection of data*—The act of acquiring the data
- *Analysis on data*—Divining insights from the data through the use of statistical methodologies to solve a problem

A great deal of modern data science is focused mostly on the last of these three items (although in many cases, a DS team is forced to develop its own ETL), as the first two are generally handled by a modern data engineering team. Within this broad term, *analysis on data,* a large focus of the modern DS resides: applying statistical techniques, data manipulation activities, and statistical algorithms (models) to garner insights from and to make predictions upon data.

The top portion of figure 2.1 illustrates (in an intentionally brief and high-level manner) the modern data scientist's focus from a technical perspective. These are the elements of the profession that most people focus on when speaking about what we do: from data access to building complex predictive models utilizing a dizzying array of algorithmic approaches and advanced statistics. It isn't a particularly accurate assessment of what a data scientist actually does when doing project work, but rather focuses on some of the tasks and tools that are employed in solving problems. Thinking of data science in this manner is nearly as unhelpful as classifying the job of a software developer by listing languages, algorithms, frameworks, computational efficiency, and other technological considerations of their profession.

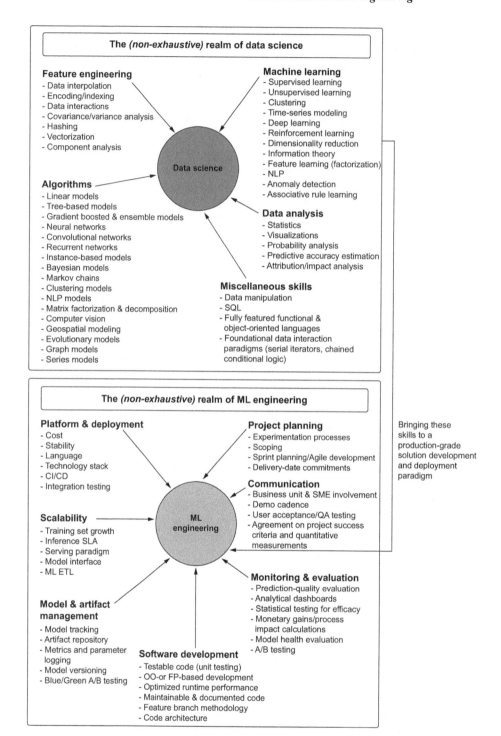

Figure 2.1   The merging of software engineering skills and DS into the ML engineer role

We can see in figure 2.1 how the technological focus of DS from the top portion (which many practitioners focus on exclusively) is but one aspect of the broader system shown in the bottom portion. It is in this region, ML engineering, that the complementary tools, processes, and paradigms provide a framework of guidance, foundationally supported by the core aspects of DS technology, to work in a more constructive way.

ML engineering, as a concept, is a paradigm that helps practitioners focus on the only aspect of project work that truly matters: providing solutions to problems that actually work. Where to start, though?

2.2 *A foundation of simplicity*

When it comes down to truly explaining what data scientists do, nothing can be more succinct than, "They solve problems through the creative application of mathematics to data." As broad as that is, it reflects the wide array of solutions that can be developed from recorded information (data).

Nothing is prescribed regarding expectations of what a DS does regarding algorithms, approaches, or technology while in the pursuit of solving a business problem. Quite the contrary, as a matter of fact. *We are problem solvers*, utilizing a wide array of techniques and approaches.

Unfortunately for newcomers to the field, many data scientists believe that they are providing value to a company only when they are using the latest and "greatest" tech that comes along. Instead of focusing on the latest buzz surrounding a new approach catalogued in a seminal whitepaper or advertised heavily in a blog post, a seasoned DS realizes that the only thing that really matters is the act of solving problems, regardless of methodology. As exciting as new technology and approaches are, the effectiveness of a DS team is measured in the quality, stability, and cost of a solution it provides.

As figure 2.2 shows, one of the most important parts of ML work is navigating the path of complexity when facing any problem. By approaching each new ask from a business with this mindset as the veritable cornerstone of ML principles (focusing on the simplest solution possible that solves the business's problem), the solution itself can be focused on, rather than a particular approach or fancy new algorithm.

Having a focus built around this principle—of pursuing the simplest possible implementation to solve a problem—is the foundation upon which all other aspects of ML engineering are built. It is by far the single most important aspect of ML engineering, as it will inform all other aspects of project work, scoping, and implementation details. Striving to exit the path as early as possible can be the single biggest driving factor in determining whether a project will fail.

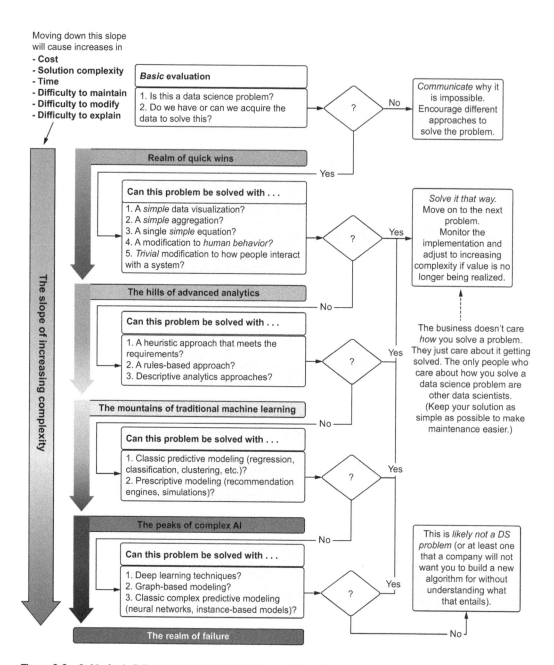

Figure 2.2   Guide for building the simplest solution to an ML problem

"But it's not data science work if the solution doesn't use AI"

I never entered this career path with expectations of using technology, a specific algorithm, framework, or methodology. I've met plenty of people who have, and many I've known throughout their career journeys have ended up being amazed at how little they've ended up using a particular oft-mentioned framework or library for their work. Most of them have been especially surprised at how much time they've spent writing SQL, performing statistical analyses of their data, and cleaning messy data to solve a problem.

I suppose that I never had that seemingly demoralizing experience that many of my peers have had regarding their infrequent application of cutting-edge approaches in the "real world" because I started in analytics before moving into ML much later. I learned early in my time transitioning to this field that the simplest solutions to problems were always the best approach.

The unsophisticated reason for this is quite simple: I had to maintain the solution. Whether monthly, daily, or in real time, my solution and code were things that I would need to debug, improve, troubleshoot inconsistencies in, and frankly, just keep running. The more sophisticated a given solution, the longer it took to diagnose failures, the harder it was to troubleshoot, and the more frustrating it was to change its internal logic for added features.

The point of pursuing simplicity in solutions (the simplest design and approach that still solves the problem, that is) translates directly to less time spent maintaining solutions to problems that you've solved. That frees you up to solve more problems, bring more value to your company, and generally give you exposure to more problems.

I've seen the passion that people have for using exciting algorithms play out poorly many times. One of the more notable ones was a GAN for image-resolution upscaling that took a team of 12 data scientists 10 months to get to a state that was production ready and scalable. When talking with their C-level staff, they said that they were hiring the consultants on staff to build a churn model, a fraud model, and a revenue-forecasting model. They felt that they had to hire outside consultants to do the important critical modeling work because their internal team was too busy working on an R&D project. Within the 12 weeks of working with that company, they entire DS team was let go, and the image project was abandoned.

Sometimes working on the basic things that bring incredible value to a company can help you keep your job (which isn't to say that forecasting, churn, and fraud modeling are simple, even if they don't seem particularly interesting).

2.3 Co-opting principles of Agile software engineering

Development operations (DevOps) brought guidelines and a demonstrable paradigm of successful engineering work to software development. With the advent of the Agile Manifesto, seasoned industry professionals recognized the failings of the way software had been developed. Some of my fellow colleagues and I took a stab at adapting these guiding principles to the field of data science, shown in figure 2.3.

DQ 355 2164

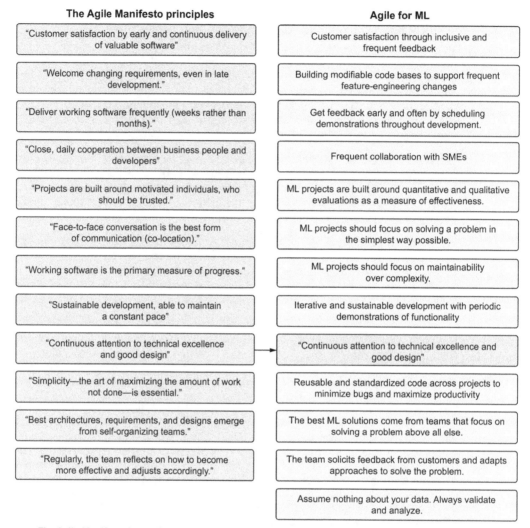

The Agile Manifesto is credited to the original team of 17 developers who met in Snowbird, Utah in 2001 to draft these principles, recorded in *"Manifesto for Agile Software Development."*

Figure 2.3   Agile Manifesto elements adapted to ML project work

With this slight modification to the principles of Agile development, we have a base of rules for applying DS to business problems. We'll cover all of these topics, including why they are important, and give examples of how to apply them to solve problems throughout this book. While some are a significant departure from the principles of Agile, the applicability to ML project work has provided repeatable patterns of success for us and many others.

However, two critical points of Agile development can, when applied to ML project work, dramatically improve the way that a DS team approaches its work: communication and cooperation, and embracing and expecting change. We'll take a look at these next.

2.3.1 Communication and cooperation

As discussed many times throughout this book (particularly in the next two chapters), the core tenets of successful ML solution development are focused on people. This may seem incredibly counterintuitive for a profession that is so steeped in mathematics, science, algorithms, and clever coding.

The reality is that quality implementations of a solution to a problem are never created in a vacuum. The most successful projects that I've either worked on or have seen others implement are those that focus more on the people and the communications regarding the project and its state rather than on the tools and formal processes (or documentation) surrounding the development of the solution.

In traditional Agile development, this rings very true, but for ML work, the interactions between the people coding the solution and those for whom the solution is being built are even more critical. This is due to the complexity of what is involved in building the solution. Since the vast majority of ML work is rather foreign to the general layperson, requiring years of dedicated study and continual learning to master, we need to engage in a much greater effort to have meaningful and useful discussions.

The single biggest driving factor in making a successful project that has the least amount of rework is *collaborative involvement* between the ML team and the business unit. The second biggest factor to ensure success is communication *within the ML team.*

Approaching project work with a lone-wolf mentality (as has been the focus for most people throughout their academic careers) is counterproductive to solving a difficult problem. Figure 2.4 illustrates this risky behavior (which I've done early in my career and seen done dozens of times by others).

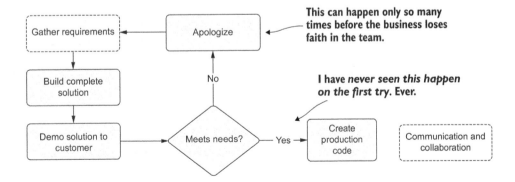

Figure 2.4 The hard-learned lesson of working on a full ML solution in isolation. It rarely ends well.

The reasons for this development style can be many, but the end result is typically the same: either a lot of rework, or a lot of frustration on the part of the business unit. Even if the DS team has no other members (a "team" of a single person), it can be helpful to ask for peer reviews and demonstrate the solution to other software developers, an architect, or SMEs from the business unit department that the solution is being built for.

The absolute last thing that you want to do (trust me, I've done it, and it's ugly) is to gather requirements and head off to a keyboard to solve a problem without ever talking to anyone. The chances of meeting all of the project requirements, getting the edge cases right, and building what the customer is expecting are so infinitesimally small that, should it work out well, perhaps you should look into buying some lottery tickets with all of the excess luck that you have to spare.

A more comprehensive and Agile-aligned development process for ML bears a close resemblance to Agile for general software development. The only main difference is the extra levels of internal demonstrations that won't necessarily be required for software development (a peer review feature branch typically suffices there). For ML work, it's important to show the performance as a function of how it affects the data being passed into your code, demonstrate functionality, and show visualizations of the output. Figure 2.5 shows a preferable Agile-based approach to ML work, focused heavily on collaboration and communication, both internally and externally.

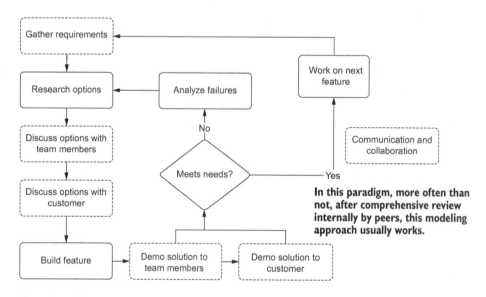

Figure 2.5 ML Agile feature creation process, focusing on requirement gathering and feedback

The greater level of interaction among team members will nearly always contribute to more ideas, perspectives, and challenges to assumed facts, leading to a higher-quality solution. If you choose to leave either your customers (the business unit requesting your help) or your peers out of the discussions (even around minute details in development choices), the chances that you're building something that they weren't expecting, or desiring, go up.

2.3.2 Embracing and expecting change

It is of utmost importance, not only in experimentation and project direction, but also in project development, to be prepared and expect inevitable changes to occur. In nearly every ML project I've worked on, the goals defined at the beginning of the project never turned out to be exactly what was built by the end. This applies to everything from specific technologies, development languages, and algorithms, to assumptions or expectations about the data—and, sometimes, even to the use of ML to solve the problem in the first place (a simple aggregation dashboard to help people solve a problem more efficiently, for example).

If you plan for the inevitable change, you can help focus on the most important goal in all DS work: solving problems. This expectation can also help remove focus from the insignificant elements (which fancy algorithm, cool new technology, or amazingly powerful framework to develop a solution in).

Without expecting or allowing for change to happen, decisions about a project's implementation may be made that make it incredibly challenging (or impossible) to modify without a full rewrite of all work done up to that point. By thinking about how the direction of the project could change, the work is forced more into a modular format of loosely coupled pieces of functionality, reducing the impact of a directional pivot on other parts of the already completed work.

Agile embraces this concept of loosely coupled design and a strong focus on building new functionality in iterative sprints so that even in the face of dynamic and changing requirements, the code still functions. By applying this paradigm to ML work, abrupt and even late-coming changes can be relatively simplified—within reason, of course. (Moving from a tree-based algorithm to a deep learning algorithm can't happen in a two-week sprint.) While simplified, this *doesn't guarantee simplicity*, though. The fact simply stands that anticipating change and building a project architecture that supports rapid iteration and modification will make the development process much easier.

2.4 The foundation of ML engineering

Now that you've seen the bedrock of DS work in the form of adapting Agile principles to ML, let's take a brief look at the entire ecosystem. This system of project work has proven to be successful through my many encounters in industry with building resilient and useful solutions to solve problems.

As mentioned in the introduction to this chapter, the idea of ML operations (MLOps) as a paradigm is rooted in the application of similar principles that DevOps has to software development. Figure 2.6 shows the core functionality of DevOps.

Comparing these core principles, as we did in section 2.3 to Agile, figure 2.7 shows the data science version of DevOps: MLOps. Through the merging and integration of

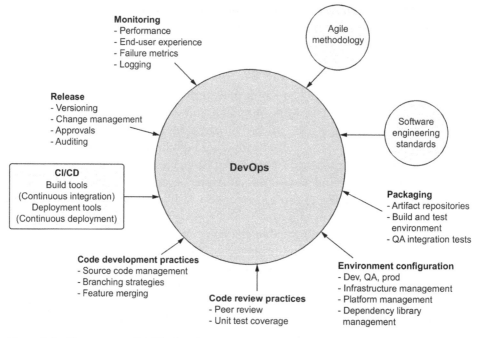

Figure 2.6   The components of DevOps

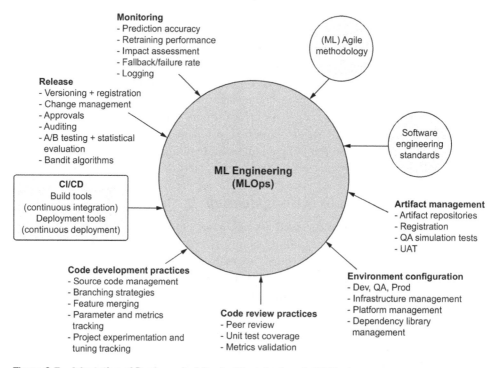

Figure 2.7   Adaptation of DevOps principles to ML project work (MLOps)

each of these elements, the most catastrophic events in DS work can be completely avoided: the elimination of failed, cancelled, or non-adopted solutions.

Throughout this book, we'll cover not only why each of these elements is important, but also show useful examples and active implementations that you can follow along with to further cement these practices in your own work. The goal of all of this, after all, is to make you successful. The best way to do that is to help you make your business successful by giving a guideline of how to address project work that will get used, provide value, and be as easy as possible to maintain for you and your fellow DS team members.

Summary

- ML engineering brings the core functional capabilities of a data scientist, a data engineer, and a software engineer into a hybrid role that supports the creation of ML solutions focused on solving a problem through the rigors of professional software development.
- Developing the simplest possible solution helps reduce development, computational, and operational costs for any given project.
- Borrowing and adapting Agile fundamentals to ML project work helps shorten the development life cycle, forces development architectures that are easier to modify, and enforces testability of complex applications to reduce maintenance burdens.
- Just as DevOps augments software engineering work, MLOps augments ML engineering work. While many of the core concepts are the same for these paradigms, additional aspects of managing model artifacts and performing continuous testing of new versions introduce nuanced complexities.

Before you model: Planning and scoping a project

This chapter covers

- Defining effective planning strategies for ML project work
- Using efficient methods to evaluate potential solutions to an ML problem

The two biggest killers in the world of ML projects have nothing to do with what most data scientists ever imagine. These killers aren't related to algorithms, data, or technical acumen. They have absolutely nothing to do with which platform you're using, nor with the processing engine that will be optimizing a model. The biggest reasons for projects failing to meet the needs of a business are in the steps leading up to any of those technical aspects: the planning and scoping phases of a project.

Throughout most of the education and training that we receive leading up to working as a DS at a company, emphasis is placed rather heavily on independently solving complex problems. Isolating oneself and focusing on showing demonstrable skill in the understanding of the theory and application of algorithms trains us to have the expectation that the work we will do in industry is a solo affair. Given a problem, we figure out how to solve it.

The reality of life in a DS capacity couldn't be further than the academic approach of proving one's knowledge and skill in solving problems alone. This profession is, in actuality, far more than just algorithms and amassing knowledge of how to use them. It's a highly collaborative and peer-driven field; the most successful projects are built by integrated teams of people working together, communicating throughout the process. Sometimes this isolation is imposed by company culture (intentionally walling off the team from the rest of the organization under the misguided intention of "protecting" the team from random requests for projects), and other times it is self-imposed.

This chapter covers why this paradigm shift that has ML teams focusing less on the *how* (algorithms, technology, and independent work) and more on the *what* (communication about and collaboration in what is being built) can make for a successful project. This shift helps reduce experimentation time, focus the team on building a solution that will work for the company, and plan out phased project work that incorporates SME knowledge from cross-functional teams to help dramatically increase the chances of a successful project.

The start of this inclusive journey, of bringing together as many people as possible to create a functional solution that works to solve a problem, is in the scoping phase. Let's juxtapose an ML team's workflow that has inadequate or absent scoping and planning (figure 3.1) with a workflow that includes proper scoping and planning (figure 3.2).

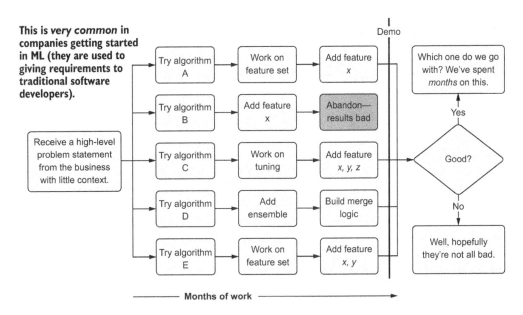

Figure 3.1 A lack of planning, improper scoping, and a lack of process around experimentation

Through absolutely no fault of their own (unless we want to blame the team for not being forceful with the business unit to get more information, which we won't), these

ML team members do their best to build several solutions to solve the vague require-ments thrown their way. If they're lucky, they'll end up with four MVPs and several months of effort wasted on three that will never make it to production (a lot of wasted work). If they're terribly unlucky, they'll have wasted months of effort on nothing that solves the problem that the business unit wants solved. Either way, no good outcome results.

With the adequate scoping and planning shown in figure 3.2, the time spent build-ing a solution is *reduced considerably*. The biggest reason for this change is that the team has fewer total approaches to validate (and all are time-boxed to two weeks), mostly because "early and often" feedback is received by the internal customer. Another rea-son is that at each phase of new feature development, a quick meeting and demonstra-tion of the added functionality is shown for acceptance testing by the SMEs.

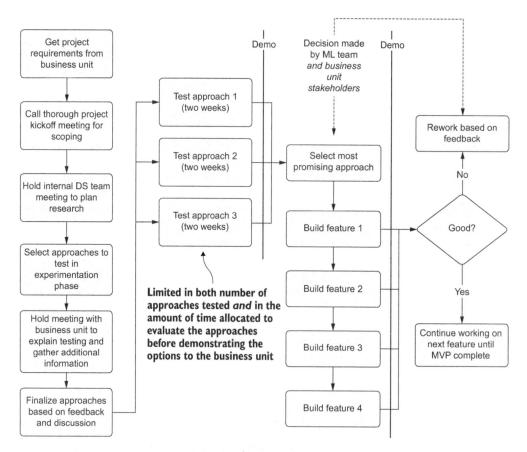

Figure 3.2　A thoroughly scoped, planned, and collaborative ML MVP project road map

To add to the substantial efficiency improvement, the other large benefit to this methodology of inclusiveness with the internal customer is a significantly increased probability of the end solution meeting the business's expectations. Gone is the extreme risk shown in figure 3.1: delivering demonstrations of multiple solutions after months of work, only to find that the entire project needs to be restarted from scratch.

Isn't planning, scoping, brainstorming, and organizing meetings a project manager thing?

Some ML practitioners may balk at including planning, communication, brainstorming, and other project-management-focused elements in a discussion on ML projects. In response, I can only muster another piece of anecdotal evidence: in the most successful projects that I've been involved in, the ML team lead has worked closely with not only any other involved team leads and the project manager, but also representatives of the department requesting the solution.

Because the leads are involved with the project management aspects of the solution, the team(s) typically endure far less work-related churn and rework. Team members can focus on development with a holistic approach to get the best possible solution shipped to production.

Comparatively, teams that operate in silos typically struggle to make a project work. That struggle may be due to a failure to keep discussions in abstract terms, thereby isolating others from contributing ideas to the solution (for example, the ML team focusing discussions around implementation details or getting too far into the weeds about algorithms during meetings). Additionally, an attitude of "we're not PMs . . . our job is to build models" may play a role. The end result of working in a cross-functional team without proper and effective communication patterns invariably leads to scope creep, confusion, and a general social antagonism among the warring factions of sub-teams within a project.

By approaching these early phases with an open mind (and a very open set of ears and eyes to the opinions and thoughts of others, regardless of their technical acumen) and a generous embrace of all of the myriad viewpoints in a cross-functional team, you may find that a far simpler solution to the problem at hand can arise. As I will state ad nauseam (for it bears repetition as a general words-to-live-by mantra for ML practitioners), the simplest approach is the best approach. Most of the time, I've found, these revelations happen in the early planning and scoping phases.

Throughout this chapter (and the next), we'll go through approaches to help with these discussions, a rubric that I've used to guide these phases, and some lessons that I've learned after messing up this phase so many times.

But what if all of our tests are garbage?

I received some pretty consistent feedback on figure 3.2. Nearly everyone who has ever worked on a real-world ML project asked this exact question: "OK, Ben, limiting the scope of testing is definitely a good idea. But what if none of it works? What then?"

(continued)

I responded to everyone in the same way: "What else could you be working on?"

This may seem like the most obtuse answer possible, but it opens up the larger meta-question around the project. If all of the research into the most promising testing approaches runs into unsuccessful results, the problem that you're trying to solve is probably going to be rather expensive in terms of development effort and time. If the project is sufficiently important, the business is adamant about incurring the delays associated with additional testing, and the team has sufficient bandwidth to support this additional work, then go for it. Start a new round of testing. Figure it out. Ask for help if need be.

If the project doesn't meet those requirements, however, it is of paramount importance to explain to the business that a monumental amount of risk is being taken on by continuing the work. This stage of evaluation is critical for no greater reason than to make this adjudication: "Can we actually build this?" or "Do we even know if we can build this?"

If the answer isn't a resounding "yes" with quantitative evidence to support that assertion, it's time for a whole lot of honesty with the business unit, further proof-of-concept work, and a risk-focused discussion held collaboratively with the project owner about any unknown elements surrounding the project.

3.1   *Planning: You want me to predict what?!*

Before we get into how successful planning phases for ML projects are undertaken, let's go through a simulation of a typical project's genesis at a company that doesn't have an established or proven process for initiating ML work. Let's imagine that we work at an e-commerce company that is just getting a taste for wanting to modernize its website.

After seeing competitors tout massive sales gains by adding personalization services to their websites for years, the C-level staff is demanding that the company needs to go all in on recommendations. No one in the C-suite is entirely sure of the technical details about how these services are built, but they all know that the first group to talk to is the ML nerds. The business (in this case, the sales department leadership, marketing, and product teams) calls a meeting, inviting the entire ML team, with little added color to the invitation apart from the title, "Personalized Recommendations Project Kickoff."

Management and the various departments that you've worked with have been happy with the small-scale ML projects that your team has built (fraud detection, customer valuation estimation, sales forecasting, and churn probability risk models). Each of the previous projects, while complex in various ways from an ML perspective, were largely insular—handled within the ML team, which came up with a solution that could be consumed by the various business units. None of these projects required subjective quality estimations or excessive business rules to influence the results. The mathematical purity of these solutions simply was not open to argument or interpretation; either they were right, or they were wrong.

Victims of your own success, the team is approached by the business with a new concept: modernizing the website and mobile applications. The executives have heard about the massive sales gains and customer loyalty that comes along with personalized recommendations, and they want your team to build a system for incorporation to the website and the apps. They want each and every user to see a unique list of products greet them when they log in. They want these products to be relevant and interesting to the user, and, at the end of the day, they want to increase the chances that the user will buy these items.

After a brief meeting during which examples from other websites are shown, they ask how long it will be before the system will be ready. You estimate about two months, based on the few papers that you've read in the past about these systems, and set off to work. The team creates a tentative development plan during the next scrum meeting, and everyone sets off to try to solve the problem.

You and the rest of the ML team assume that management is looking for the behavior shown in so many other websites, in which products are recommended on a main screen. That, after all, is personalization in its most pure sense: a unique collection of products that an algorithm has predicted will have relevance to an individual user. This approach seems pretty straightforward, you all agree, and the team begins quickly planning how to build a dataset that shows a ranked list of product keys for each of the website's and mobile app's users, based solely on the browsing and purchase history of each member.

Hold up a minute. Isn't planning a project at odds with Agile?

Well, yes, and no. To quote Scott Ambler (one of the most prolific writers on foundational processes for Agile), "A project plan is important, but it must not be too rigid to accommodate changes in technology or the environment, stakeholders' priorities, and people's understanding of the problem and its solution" (http://www.ambysoft.com/essays/agileManifesto.html).

I've seen the misinterpretation of this sentiment come up rather frequently in my career. Ambler and the original creators of the Agile Manifesto were pointing out that a project should not be dictated by a preplanned and immutable script of elements that need to be constructed. The intention is not, and never was, to not plan at all. It is simply to be flexible in the plans that are created, to enable them to be changed when the needs arise.

If a simpler way to implement something arises, a better way that reduces complexity while still achieving the same end result, then a project plan should change. In the world of ML, this is a frequent occurrence.

Perhaps, at the start of the project (before a thorough research phase is completed), the cross-functional team determines that the only possible solution is a highly complex and complicated modeling approach. After conducting experiments, however, the team finds that a simple linear equation could be developed to solve the problem with acceptable accuracy at a fraction of the development time and cost. Although the initial plan was to use, say, deep learning to solve the problem, the team can, should, and must shift directions to the much simpler approach. The plan changed,

(continued)

certainly, but without a plan in the first place, the research and experimentation phase would be like a ship lost in the night—unguided, directionless, and chaotically moving about in the dark.

Planning is good in ML. It's just critical to not set those plans in stone.

For the next several sprints, *you all studiously work in isolation.* You test dozens of implementations that you've seen in blog posts, consume hundreds of papers' worth of theory on different algorithms and approaches to solving an implicit recommendation problem, and finally build out an MVP solution using alternating least squares (ALS) that achieves a root mean squared error (RMSE) of 0.2334, along with a rough implementation of ordered scoring for relevance based on prior behavior.

Brimming with confidence that you have something amazing to show the business team sponsor, you head to the meeting armed with the testing notebook, graphs showing the overall metrics, and sample inference data that you believe will truly impress the team. You start by showing the overall scaled score rating for affinity, displaying the data as an RMSE plot, as shown in figure 3.3.

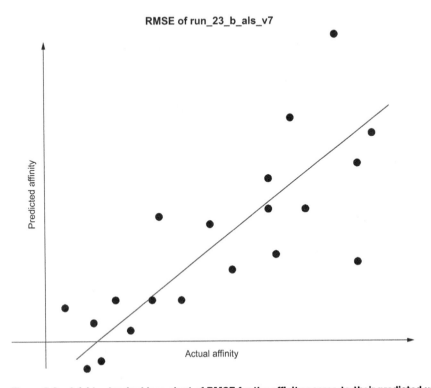

Figure 3.3   A fairly standard loss chart of RMSE for the affinity scores to their predicted values

The response to showing the chart is lukewarm at best. A bevy of questions arise, focused on what the data means, what the line that intersects the dots means, and how the data was generated. Instead of a focused discussion about the solution and the next phase you'd like to be working on (increasing the accuracy), the meeting begins to devolve into a mix of confusion and boredom. In an effort to better explain the data, you show a quick table of rank effectiveness using non-discounted cumulative gain (NDCG) metrics to illustrate the predictive power of a single user chosen at random, as shown in figure 3.4.

User ID	Item ID	Actual ranking	Predicted ranking	DCG value
38873	25	1	3	3.0
38873	17	2	2	1.26186
38873	23	3	6	3.0
38873	11	4	1	0.403677
38873	19	5	5	1.934264
38873	3	6	4	1.424829

Figure 3.4 NDCG calculations for a recommendation engine for a single user. With no context, presenting raw scores like this will do nothing beneficial for the DS team.

The first chart created a mild sense of perplexity, but the table brings complete and total confusion. No one understands what is being shown or can see the relevance to the project. The only thing on everyone's mind is, "Is this really what weeks of effort can bring? What has the data science team been doing all this time?"

During the DS team's explanation of the two visualizations, one of the marketing analysts begins looking up the product recommendation listing for one of the team members' accounts in the sample dataset provided for the meeting. Figure 3.5 illustrates the results along with the marketing analyst's thoughts while bringing up the product catalog data for each recommendation in the list.

The biggest lesson that the DS team learns from this meeting is not, in fact, the necessity of validating the results of its model in a way that would simulate the way an end user of the predictions would react. Although an important consideration, and one that is discussed in the following sidebar, it is trumped quite significantly by the realization that the reason that the model was received so poorly is that the team didn't properly plan for the nuances of this project.

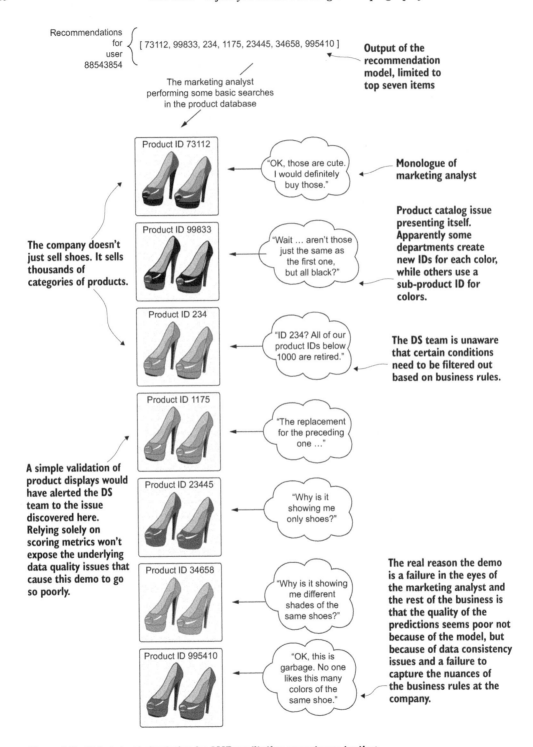

Figure 3.5   Using visual simulation for SME qualitative acceptance testing

> **Don't blindly trust your metrics**
>
> When doing particularly large-scale ML, relying heavily on error metrics and validation scores for models is incredibly tempting. Not only are they the only truly realistic means of measuring objective quality for predictions on large datasets (which many of us deal with frequently these days), but they're often the only real, valid quantitative means of adjudicating the predictive quality of a particular implementation.
>
> However, it is important to not rely on these model-scoring metrics alone. Do use them (the appropriate ones for the work at hand, that is), but supplement them with additional means of getting subjective measurements of the prediction's efficacy. As shown in figure 3.5, a simple visualization of the predictions for an individual user uncovered far more objective and subjective quality assessments than any predictive ordering scoring algorithm or estimation of loss could ever do.
>
> Keep in mind that this additional end-use simulation sample evaluation shouldn't be done by the DS team members, unless they are adjudicating the prediction quality for data for which they themselves are considered SMEs. For the use case that we're discussing, it would behoove the DS team to partner with a few of the marketing analysts to do a bit of informal quality assurance (QA) validation before showing results to the larger team.

The DS team simply hadn't understood the business problem from the perspective of the other team members in the room who knew where all of the proverbial "bodies were buried" in the data and who have cumulative decades of knowledge around the nature of the data and the product. The onus of this failure doesn't rest solely on the project manager, the DS team lead, or any single team member. Rather, this is a collective failure of every member of the broader team in not thoroughly defining the scope and details of the project. How could they have done things differently?

The analyst who looked up their own predictions for their account uncovered a great many problems that were obvious to them. They saw the duplicated item data due to the retiring of older product IDs and likewise instantly knew that the shoe division used a separate product ID for each color of a style of shoe, both core problems that caused a poor demo. All of the issues found, causing a high risk of project cancellation, were due to improper planning of the project.

3.1.1 Basic planning for a project

The planning of any ML project typically starts at a high level. A business unit, executive, or even a member of the DS team comes up with an idea of using the DS team's expertise to solve a challenging problem. While typically little more than a concept at this early stage, this is a critical juncture in a project's life cycle.

In the scenario we've been discussing, the high-level idea is *personalization*. To an experienced DS, this could mean any number of things. To an SME of the business unit, it could mean many of the same concepts that the DS team could think of, but it may not. From this early point of an idea to before even basic research begins, the first thing everyone involved in this project should be doing is having a meeting. The subject of this meeting should focus on one fundamental element: *Why are we building this?*

It may sound like a hostile or confrontational question to ask. It may take some people aback when hearing it. However, it's one of the most effective and important questions, as it opens a discussion into the true motivations for why people want the project to be built. Is it to increase sales? Is it to make our external customers happier? Or is it to keep people browsing on the site for longer durations?

Each of these nuanced answers can help inform the goal of this meeting: *defining the expectations of the output of any ML work.* The answer also satisfies the measurement metric criteria for the model's performance, as well as attribution scoring of the performance in production (the very score that will be used to measure A/B testing much later).

In our example scenario, the team fails to ask this important *why* question. Figure 3.6 shows the divergence in expectations from the business side and the ML side because neither group is speaking about the essential aspect of the project and is instead occupied in mental silos of their own creating. The ML team is focusing entirely on how to solve the problem, while the business team has expectations of what would be delivered, wrongfully assuming that the ML team will "just understand it."

Figure 3.6 sums up the planning process for the MVP. With extremely vague requirements, a complete lack of thorough communication about expectations for

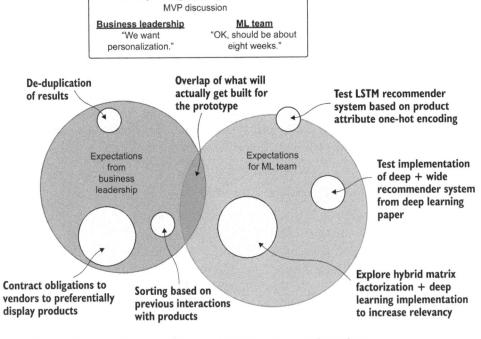

Figure 3.6 Project expectation gap driven by ineffective planning discussions

the prototype's minimum functionality, and a failure to reign in the complexity of experimentation, the demonstration is considered an absolute failure. Preventing outcomes like this can be achieved only in these early meetings when the project's ideas are being discussed. Widening the overlap between these regions of expectation gap is the responsibility of the DS team lead and project manager. At the conclusion of planning meetings, an ideal state is alignment of everyone's expectations (without anyone focusing on implementation details or specific out-of-scope functionality to potentially be added in the future).

Continuing with this scenario, let's look at the MVP demonstration feedback discussion to see the sorts of questions that could have been discussed during that early planning and scoping meeting. Figure 3.7 shows the questions and the underlying root causes of the present misunderstandings.

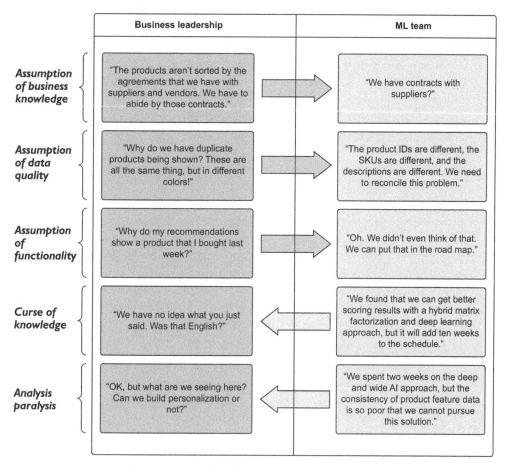

Figure 3.7   The results of the MVP presentation demo. Questions and their subsequent discussions could have happened during the planning phase to prevent all five core issues that are shown.

Although this example is intentionally hyperbolic, I've found elements of this confusion present in many ML projects (those outside of primarily ML-focused companies), and this is to be expected. The problems that ML is frequently intended to solve are complex, full of details that are specific and unique to each business (and business unit within a company), and fraught with disinformation surrounding the minute nuances of these details.

It's important to realize that these struggles are going to be an inevitable part of any project. The best way to minimize their impact is to have a thorough series of discussions that aim to capture as many details about the problem, the data, and the expectations of the outcome as possible.

ASSUMPTION OF BUSINESS KNOWLEDGE

Assumption of business knowledge is a challenging issue, particularly for a company that's new to utilizing ML, or for a business unit at a company that has never worked with its ML team before. In our example, the business leadership's assumption was that the ML team knew aspects of the business that the leadership considered widely held knowledge. Because no clear and direct set of requirements was set out, this assumption wasn't identified as a clear requirement. With no SME from the business unit involved in guiding the ML team during data exploration, there simply was no way for them to know this information during the process of building the MVP either.

An assumption of business knowledge is often a dangerous path to tread for most companies. At many companies, the ML practitioners are insulated from the inner workings of a business. With their focus mostly in the realm of providing advanced analytics, predictive modeling, and automation tooling, scant time can be devoted to understanding the nuances of how and why a business is run. While some obvious aspects of the business are known by all (for example, "we sell product x on our website"), it is not reasonable to expect that the modelers should know that a business process exists in which some suppliers of goods would be promoted on the site over others.

A good solution for arriving at these nuanced details is to have an SME from the group that is requesting a solution be built for them (in this case, the product marketing group) explain how they decide the ordering of products on each page of the website and app. Going through this exercise would allow for everyone in the room to understand the specific rules that may be applied to govern the output of a model.

ASSUMPTION OF DATA QUALITY

The onus of duplicate product listings in the demo output is not entirely on either team. While the ML team members certainly could have planned for this to be an issue, they weren't aware of it precisely in the scope of its impact. Even had they known, they likely would have wisely mentioned that correcting for this issue would not be a part of the demo phase (because of the volume of work required and the request that the prototype not be delayed for too long).

The principal issue here is in *not planning for it*. By not discussing the expectations, the business leaders' confidence in the capabilities of the ML team erodes. The objective measure of the prototype's success will largely be ignored as the business members focus solely on the fact that for a few users' sample data, the first 300 recommendations show nothing but 4 products in 80 available shades and patterns.

For our use case, the ML team believed that the data they were using was, as told to them by the DE team, quite clean. Reality, for most companies, is a bit more dire than what most would think when it comes to data quality. Figure 3.8 summarizes two industry studies, conducted by IBM and Deloitte, indicating that thousands of companies are struggling with ML implementations, specifically noting problems with data cleanliness. Checking data quality before working on models is pretty important.

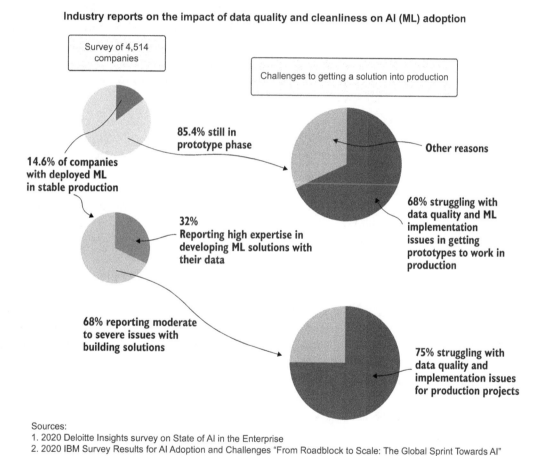

Industry reports on the impact of data quality and cleanliness on AI (ML) adoption

Survey of 4,514 companies

Challenges to getting a solution into production

85.4% still in prototype phase

Other reasons

14.6% of companies with deployed ML in stable production

68% struggling with data quality and ML implementation issues in getting prototypes to work in production

32% Reporting high expertise in developing ML solutions with their data

68% reporting moderate to severe issues with building solutions

75% struggling with data quality and implementation issues for production projects

Sources:
1. 2020 Deloitte Insights survey on State of AI in the Enterprise
2. 2020 IBM Survey Results for AI Adoption and Challenges "From Roadblock to Scale: The Global Sprint Towards AI"

Figure 3.8 The impact of data quality issues on companies engaging in ML project work. Data quality issues are common, and as such, should always be vetted during the early stages of project work.

It's not important to have "perfect" data. Even the companies in figure 3.8 that are successful in deploying many ML models to production still struggle with data quality issues regularly (75% as reported). These problems with data are just a byproduct of the frequently incredibly complex systems that are generating the data, years (if not decades) of technical debt, and the expense associated with designing "perfect" systems that do not allow an engineer to generate problematic data. The proper way to handle these known problems is to anticipate them, validate the data that will be involved in any project before modeling begins, and ask questions about the nature of the data to the SMEs who are most familiar with it.

For our recommendation engine, the ML team members failed to not only ask questions about the nature of the data that they were modeling (namely, "Do all products get registered in our systems in the same way?"), but also validate the data through analysis. Pulling quick statistical reports may have uncovered this issue quite clearly, particularly if the unique product count of shoes was orders of magnitude higher than any other category. "Why do we sell so many shoes?," posed during a planning meeting, could have instantly uncovered the need to resolve this issue, but also resulted in a deeper inspection and validation of all product categories to ensure that the data going into the models was correct.

ASSUMPTION OF FUNCTIONALITY

In this instance, the business leaders are concerned that the recommendations show a product that was purchased the week before. Regardless of the type of product (consumable or not), the planning failure here is in expressing how off-putting this would be to the end user to see this happen.

The ML team's response of ensuring that this key element needs to be a part of the final product is a valid response. At this stage of the process, while it is upsetting to see results like this from the perspective of the business unit, it's nearly inevitable. The path forward in this aspect of the discussion should be to scope the feature addition work, make a decision on whether to include it in a future iteration, and move on to the next topic.

To this day, I have not worked on an ML project where this has not come up during a demo. Valid ideas for improvements always come from these meetings—that's one of the primary reasons to have them, after all: to make the solution better! The worst things to do are either dismiss them outright or blindly accept the implementation burden. The best thing to do is to present the cost (time, money, and human capital) for the addition of the improvement and let the internal customer decide if it's worth it.

CURSE OF KNOWLEDGE

The ML team, in this discussion point, instantly went "full nerd." Chapter 4 covers the curse of knowledge at length, but for now, realize that, when communicating, the inner details of things that have been tested will always fall on deaf ears. Assuming that everyone in a room understands the finer details of a solution as anything but a random collection of pseudo-scientific buzzword babble is doing a disservice to yourself as an ML practitioner (you won't get your point across) and to the audience (they will feel ignorant and stupid, frustrated that you assume that they would know such a specific topic).

The better way to discuss your numerous attempts at solutions that didn't pan out: simply speak in as abstract terms as possible: "We tried a few approaches, one of which might make the recommendations much better, but it will add a few months to our timeline. What would you like to do?"

Handling complex topics in a layperson context will always work much better than delving into deep technical detail. If your audience is interested in a more technical discussion, gradually ease into deeper technical aspects until the question is answered. It's never a good idea to buffalo your way through an explanation by speaking in terms that you can't reasonably expect them to understand.

ANALYSIS PARALYSIS

Without proper planning, the ML team will likely just experiment on a lot of approaches, likely the most state-of-the-art ones that they can find in the pursuit of providing the best possible recommendations. Without focusing on the important aspects of the solution during the planning phase, this chaotic approach of working solely on the model purity can lead to a solution that misses the point of the entire project.

After all, sometimes the most accurate model isn't the best solution. Most of the time, a good solution is one that incorporates the needs of the project, and that generally means keeping the solution as simple as possible to meet those needs. Approaching project work with that in mind will help alleviate the indecisions and complexity that can arise from trying to choose the best model.

3.1.2 *That first meeting*

As we discussed earlier, our example ML team approached planning in a problematic way. How did the team get to that state of failing to communicate what the project should focus on, though?

While everyone on the ML team was quietly thinking about algorithms, implementation details, and where to get the data to feed into the model, they were too consumed to ask the questions that should have been posited. No one was asking details about the way the implementation should work, the types of restrictions needing to be in place on the recommendations, or whether products should be displayed in a certain way within a sorted ranked collection. They were all focused on the *how* instead of the *why* and *what*.

> ### Focusing on the "how" during cross-functional meetings
> While it may be tempting to discuss potential solutions during the planning and scoping phases of a project, I urge you to resist. It's not that the discussion is dangerous to have in front of your internal customers. Far from it. It's just that they don't care (nor should they). For some ML practitioners (I'm speaking to you, younger me), the idea that people wouldn't want to immediately discuss all of the cool algorithms and fancy feature engineering that will be involved in the *how* of the project solution is just unthinkable. Surely, everyone must find these topics as exciting as we do, right?

(continued)

Wrong. If you don't believe me, I challenge you to discuss your next project with your spouse, significant other, children, friends, non-DS colleagues, hairstylist (or barber), mailperson, or dog. I can assure you that the only one interested would be your dog.

And that's only if you're eating something while telling them. Especially if it's a cheeseburger. Dogs love cheeseburgers. Especially my dog.

The time to discuss the how is internally, later, within the DS team. Have brainstorming sessions. Debate with one another (civilly). But for your sake, and the sake of your business unit members, I recommend not doing it while they are in the room.

Conversely, the internal marketing team members bringing the project to the ML team did not clearly discuss their expectations. With no malicious intent, their ignorance of the methodology of developing this solution, coupled with their intense knowledge of the customer and the way they want the solution to behave, created a perfect recipe for a perfect implementation disaster.

How could this have been handled differently? How could that first meeting have been orchestrated to ensure that the greatest number of hidden expectations that the business unit team members hold (as we discussed in section 3.1.1) can be openly discussed in the most productive way? It can be as easy as starting with a single question: "What do you do now to decide which products to display in which places?" In figure 3.9, let's look at what posing that question may have revealed and how it could have informed the critical feature requirements that should have been scoped for the MVP.

As you can see, not every idea is a fantastic one. Some are beyond the scope of budget (time, money, or both). Others are simply beyond the limits of our technical capabilities (the "things that look nice" request). The important thing to focus on, though, is that two key critical features were identified, and a potential additive future feature that can be put in the backlog for the project.

Although this figure's dialogue may appear to be quite caricatural, this is a nearly verbatim transcription of an actual meeting I was part of. Although I was stifling laughter a few times at some of the requests, I found the meeting to be invaluable. Spending a few hours discussing all of the possibilities that SMEs see was able to give me and my team a perspective that we hadn't considered, in addition to revealing key requirements about the project that we never would have guessed or assumed without hearing them from the team.

The one thing to make sure to avoid in these discussions is speaking about the ML solution. Keep notes so that you and fellow DS team members can discuss later. It's critical that you don't drag the discussion away from the primary point of the meeting (gaining insight into how the business solves the problem currently).

One of the easiest ways to approach this subject is, as shown in the following sidebar, by asking how the SMEs currently solve the problem. Unless the project is an

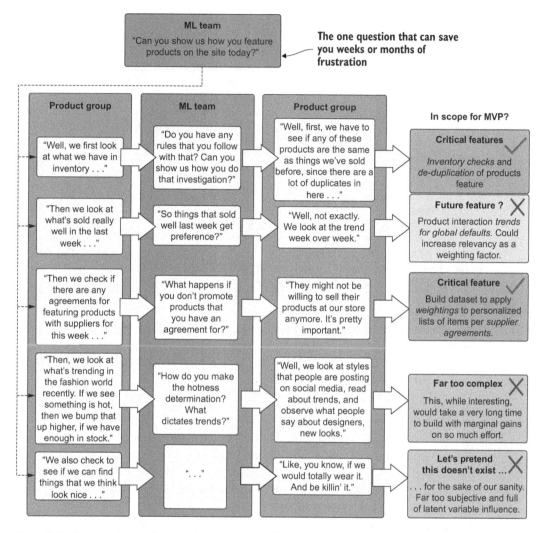

Figure 3.9 An example scoping and planning meeting that focuses on the problem to define features

entirely greenfield moon-shot project, someone is probably solving it in some way or another. You should talk to them. This methodology is precisely what informed the line of questioning and discussion in figure 3.9.

Explain how you do it so I can help automate this for you

Although not every piece of ML is a direct replacement for boring, error-prone, or repetitive work done by humans, I've found that the overwhelmingly vast majority of it is. Most of these solutions are either being done to replace this manual work, or, at the very least, do a more comprehensive job at what people have been attempting to do without the aid of algorithms.

(continued)

For this recommendation engine we've been discussing, the business had been attempting to work on personalization; it was just personalization by way of attempting to appeal to as many people (or themselves) as much as they could when selecting products for prominent feature and display. This applies to ML projects as far ranging as from supply-chain optimization to sales forecasts. At the root of most projects that will come your way is likely someone at the company who is making their best effort to accomplish the same thing (albeit without the benefit of an algorithm that can sift through billions of data points and draw an optimized solution from relationships that are far too complex for our minds to recognize in an acceptable amount of time).

I've always found it best to find those people and ask them, "Teach me how you do it now, please." It's truly staggering how a few hours of listening to someone who has been working through this problem can eliminate wasted work and rework later. Their wealth of knowledge about the task that you're going to be modeling and the overall requirements for the solution will help to not only get a more accurate project-scoping assessment, but also to ensure that you're building the right thing.

We'll discuss the process of planning and examples of setting periodic ideation meetings later in this chapter in much more depth.

3.1.3   *Plan for demos—lots of demos*

Yet another cardinal sin that the ML team members violated in presenting their personalization solution to the business was attempting to show the MVP only once. Perhaps their sprint cadence was such that they couldn't generate a build of the model's predictions at times that were convenient, or they didn't want to slow their progress toward having a true MVP to show to the business. Whatever the reason, the team members actually wasted time and effort while trying to save time and effort. They were clearly in the top portion of figure 3.10.

In the top scenario (frequent demonstrations of each critical feature), some amount of rework is likely associated with each feature after the demonstrations. Not only is this to be expected, but the amount of time required to adjust features when approached in this Agile methodology is reduced, since fewer tightly coupled dependencies exist when compared with the rework needed for the bottom develop-in-a-vacuum approach.

Even though Agile practices were used within the ML team, to the marketing team, the MVP presentation was the first demo that they had seen in two months of work. At no point in those two months did a meeting take place to show the current state of experimentation, nor was any plan communicated about the cadence of seeing results from the modeling efforts.

Without frequent demos as features are built out, the team at large is simply operating in the dark with respect to the ML aspect of the project. The ML team, meanwhile,

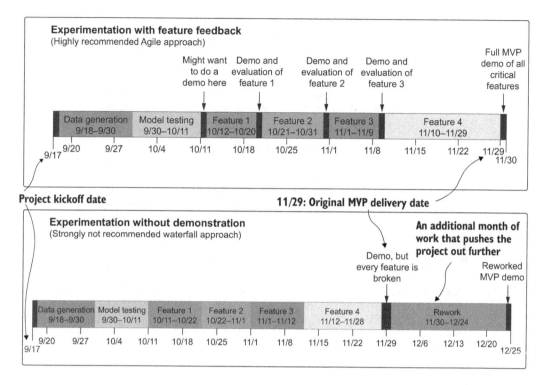

Figure 3.10   Timeline comparison of feedback-focused demo-heavy project work and internal-only focused development. While the demonstrations take time and effort, the rework that they save is invaluable.

is missing out on valuable time-saving feedback from SME members who would be able to halt feature development and help refine the solution.

For most projects involving ML of sufficient complexity, far too many details and nuances exist to confidently approach building out dozens of features without having them reviewed. Even if the ML team is showing metrics for the quality of the predictions, aggregate ranking statistics that "conclusively prove" the power and quality of what they're building, the only people in the room who care about that are the ML team. To effectively produce a complex project, the SME group—the marketing group—needs to provide feedback based on data it can consume. Presenting arbitrary or complex metrics to that team is bordering on intentional obtuse obfuscation, which will only hinder the project and stifle the critical ideas required to make the project successful.

By planning for demos ahead of time, at particular cadences, the ML-internal Agile development process can adapt to the needs of the business experts to create a more relevant and successful project. The ML team members can embrace a true Agile approach: testing and demonstrating features as they are built, adapting their future work, and adjusting elements in a highly efficient manner. They can help ensure that the project will actually see the light of day.

But I don't know frontend development. How can I build a demo?

There's a phrase I've used before.

If you do happen to know how to build interactive lightweight apps that can host your ML-backed demos, that's awesome. Use those skills. Just don't spend too much of your time building that portion. Keep it as simple as possible and focus your energy and time on the ML problem at hand.

For the other 99% of us ML practitioners out there, you don't need to mock up a website, app, or microservice to show content. If you can make slides (notice I'm not asking if you want to—we all know that all of us hate making slides), then you illustrate how your project will work by displaying a simulation of what something will look like to the end user. Copy and paste images. Make a basic wireframe diagram. Anything that can approximate what the end result will look like to a user of your generated data will be sufficient.

If you clearly communicate that the final design of the UX team and frontend developers or application designers will be completely different from your presentation and that you're just here to show the data, then something as simple as a slide deck or PDF of a layperson-friendly layout will work just fine. I can promise you that converting arrays of primary keys or matplotlib area-under-ROC curves into something that tells the story of how the model performs in a digestible way will always go over better in meetings involving nontechnical audiences.

3.1.4   *Experimentation by solution building: Wasting time for pride's sake*

Looking back at the unfortunate scenario of the ML team members building a prototype recommendation engine for the website personalization project, their process of experimentation was troubling, but not only for the business. Without a solid plan in place for what they would be trying and how much time and effort they would be spending on the different solutions they agreed on pursuing, a great deal of time (and code) was unnecessarily thrown away.

Coming out of their initial meeting, they went off on their own as a team, beginning their siloed ideation meeting by brainstorming about which algorithms might best be suited for generating recommendations in an implicit manner. About 300 or so web searches later, they came up with a basic plan of doing a head-to-head comparison of three main approaches: an ALS model, a singular value decomposition (SVD) model, and a deep learning recommendation model. Having an understanding of the features required to meet the minimum requirements for the project, three separate groups began building what they could in a good-natured competition.

The biggest flaw in approaching experimentation in this way is in the sheer scope and size of the waste involved in doing bake-offs like this. Approaching a complex problem by way of a hackathon-like methodology might seem fun to some, not to mention being far easier to manage from a process perspective by the team lead (you're all on your own—whoever wins, we go with that!), but it's an incredibly irresponsible way to develop software.

This flawed concept, solution building during experimentation, is juxtaposed with the far more efficient (but, some would argue, less fun) approach of prototype experimentation in figure 3.11. With periodic demos, either internally to the ML team or to the broader external cross-functional team, the project's experimentation phase can

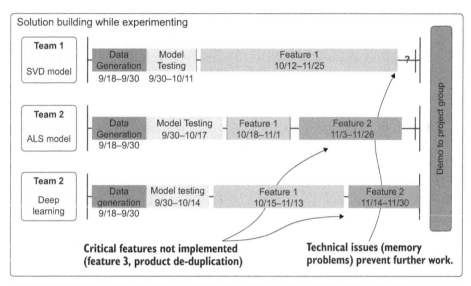

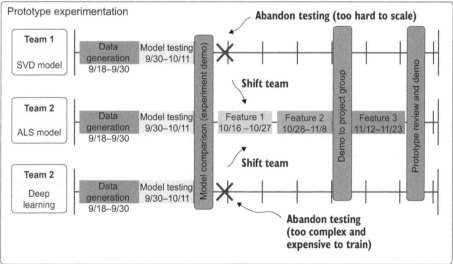

Figure 3.11 Comparison of multiple-MVP development (top) and experimentation culling development (bottom). By culling options early, more work (at a higher quality and in less time) can get done by the team.

be optimized to have more hands (and minds) focused on getting the project as successful as it can be as fast as possible.

As shown in the top section of figure 3.11, approaching the problem of a model bake-off without planning for *prototype culling* runs two primary risks. First, in the top portion, Team A had difficulty incorporating the first primary feature that the business dictated was critical.

Since no evaluation was done after the initial formulation of getting the model to work, a great deal of time was spent trying to get the feature built out to support the requirements. After that was accomplished, when moving on to the second most critical feature, the team members realized that they couldn't implement the feature in enough time for the demo meeting, effectively guaranteeing that all of the work put into the SVD model would be thrown away.

Teams using the other two approaches, both short-staffed on the implementation of their prototypes, were unable to complete the third critical feature. As a result, none of the three approaches would satisfy the critical project requirements. This delay to the project, due to its multidiscipline nature, affects other engineering teams. What the team should have done instead was follow the path of the bottom Prototype Experimentation section.

In this approach, the teams met with the business units early, communicating ahead of time that the critical features wouldn't be in at this time. They chose instead to make a decision on the raw output of each model type that was under testing. After deciding to focus on a single option, the entire ML team's resources and time could be focused on implementing the minimum required features (with an added check-in demo between the presentation of the core solution to ensure that they were on the right track) and get to the prototype evaluation sooner.

Focusing on early and frequent demos, even though features weren't fully built out yet, helped both maximize staff resources and get valuable feedback from the SMEs. In the end, all ML projects are resource-constrained. By narrowly focusing on the fewest and most potentially successful options as early as possible, even a lean set of resources can create successful complex ML solutions.

3.2 *Experimental scoping: Setting expectations and boundaries*

We've now been through planning of the recommendation engine. We have the details of what is important to the business, we understand what the user expects when interacting with our recommendations, and we have a solid plan for the milestones for our presentations at certain dates throughout the project. Now it's time for the fun part for most of us ML nerds. It's time to plan our research.

With an effectively limitless source of information at our fingertips on the topic, and only so much time to do it, we really should be setting guidelines on what we're going to be testing and how we're going to go about it. This is where scoping of experimentation comes into play.

The team should, by this time, having had the appropriate discovery sessions with the SME team members, know the critical features that need to get built:

- We need a way to de-duplicate our product inventory.
- We need to incorporate product-based rules to weight implicit preferences per user.
- We need to group recommendations based on product category, brand, and specific page types in order to fulfill different structured elements on the site and app.
- We need an algorithm that will generate user-to-item affinities that won't cost a fortune to run.

After listing out the absolutely critical aspects for the MVP, the team can begin planning the work estimated to be involved in solving each of these four critical tasks. Through setting these expectations and providing boundaries on each of them (for both time and level of implementation complexity), the ML team can provide the one thing that the business is seeking: *an expected delivery date and a judgment call on what is or isn't feasible.*

This may seem a bit oxymoronic to some. "Isn't experimentation where we figure out how to scope the project from an ML perspective?" is likely the very thought that is coursing through your head right now. We'll discuss throughout this section why, if left without boundaries, the research and experimentation on solving this recommendation engine problem could easily fill the entire project-scoping timeline. If we plan and scope our experimentation, we'll be able to focus on finding, perhaps not the best solution, but hopefully a good enough solution to ensure that we'll eventually get a product built out of our work.

Once the initial planning phase is complete (which certainly will not happen from just a single meeting), and a rough idea of what the project entails is both formulated and documented, there should be no talk about scoping or estimating how long the actual solution implementation will take, at least not initially. Scoping is incredibly important and is one of the primary means of setting expectations for a project team as a whole, but even more critical for the ML team. However, in the world of ML (which is very different from other types of software development because of the complexity of most solutions), two distinct scopings need to happen.

For people who are accustomed to interactions with other development teams, the idea of experimental scoping is completely foreign, and as such, any estimations for the initial phase scoping will be misinterpreted. With this in mind, however, it's certainly not wise to not have an internal target scoping for experimentation.

3.2.1 What is experimental scoping?

Before you can begin to estimate how long a project is going to take, you need to research not only how others have solved similar problems but also potential solutions from a theoretical point of view. With the scenario that we've been discussing, the initial project planning and overall scoping (the requirements gathering), a number of potential approaches were decided on. When the project then moves into the phase of research and experimentation, it is *absolutely critical* to set an expectation with the larger team of how long the DS team will spend on vetting each of those ideas.

Setting expectations benefits the DS team. Although it may seem counterproductive to set an arbitrary deadline on something that is wholly unknowable (which is the best solution), having a target due date can help focus the generally disorganized process of testing. Elements that under other circumstances might seem interesting to explore are ignored and marked as ""will investigate during MVP development" with the looming deadline approaching. This approach simply helps focus the work.

The expectations similarly help the business and the cross-functional team members involved in the project. They will gain not only a decision on project direction that has a higher chance of success in the end, but also a guarantee of progress in the near-term future. Remember that *communication is absolutely essential to successful ML project work*, and setting delivery goals even for experimentation will aid in continuing to involve everyone in the process. It will only make the end result better.

For relatively simple and straightforward ML use cases (forecasting, outlier detection, clustering, and conversion prediction, for example), the amount of time dedicated to testing approaches should be relatively short. One to two weeks is typically sufficient for exploring potential solutions for standard ML; remember, this isn't the time to build an MVP, but rather to get a general idea of the efficacy of different algorithms and methodologies.

For a far more complex use case, such as this scenario, a longer investigation period can be warranted. Two weeks alone may be needed to devote simply to the research phase, with an additional two weeks of "hacking" (roughshod scripting of testing APIs, libraries, and building crude visualizations).

The sole purpose of these phases is to decide on a path, but to make that decision in the shortest amount of time practicable. The challenge is to balance the time required to make the best adjudication possible for the problem against the timetable of delivery of the MVP.

No standard rubric exists for figuring out how long this period should be, as it is dependent on the problem, the industry, the data, the experience of the team, and the relative complexity of each option being considered. Over time, a team will gain the wisdom that will make for more accurate experimental ("hacking") estimates. The most important point to remember is that this stage, and the communication to the business unit of how long it will take, *should never be overlooked*.

3.2.2 *Experimental scoping for the ML team: Research*

In the heart of all ML practitioners is the desire to experiment, explore, and learn new things. With the depth and breadth of all that exists in the ML space, we could spend a lifetime learning only a fraction of what has been done, is currently being researched, and will be worked on as novel solutions to complex problems. This innate desire shared among all of us means that it is of the utmost importance to set boundaries around how long and how far we will go when researching a solution to a new problem.

In the first stages following the planning meetings and general project scoping, it's now time to start doing some actual work. This initial stage, experimentation, can vary quite significantly among projects and implementations, but the common theme for the ML team is that it *must be time-boxed*. This can feel remarkably frustrating for many of us. Instead of focusing on researching a novel solution to something from the ground up, or utilizing a new technique that's been recently developed, sometimes we are forced into a "just get it built" situation. A great way to meet that requirement of time-bound urgency is to set limits on how much time the ML team has to research possibilities for solutions.

For the recommendation engine project that we've been discussing in this chapter, a research path for the ML team might look something like figure 3.12.

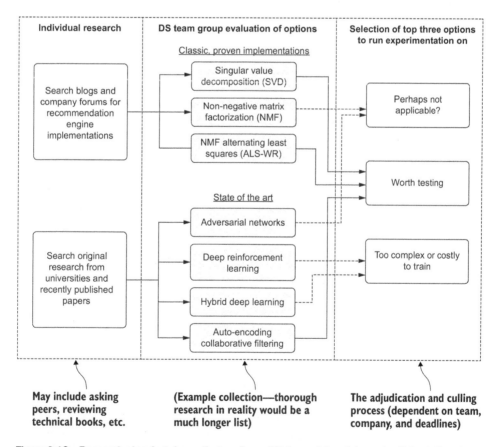

Figure 3.12   Research planning phase diagram for an ML team determining potential solutions to pursue testing. Defining structured plans such as this can dramatically reduce the time spent iterating on ideas.

In this simplified diagram, effective research constrains the options available to the team. After a few cursory internet searches, blog readings, and whitepaper consultations, the team can identify (typically in a day or so) the "broad strokes" for existing solutions in industry and academia.

Once the common approaches are identified (and individually curated by the team members), a full list of possibilities can be researched in more depth. Once this level of applicability and complexity is arrived at, the team can meet and discuss its findings

As figure 3.12 shows, the approaches that are candidates for testing are culled during the process of presenting findings. By the end of this adjudication phase, the team should have a solid plan of two or three options that warrant testing through prototype development.

Note the mix of approaches that the group selects. Within the selections is sufficient heterogeneity that will help aid the MVP-based decision later (if all three options are slight variations on deep learning approaches, for instance, it will be hard to decide which to go with in some circumstances).

The other key action is whittling down the large list of options to help prevent the chances of either over-choice (a condition in which making a decision is almost paralyzing to someone because of the overabundance of options) or the Tyranny of Small Decisions (in which an accumulation of many small, seemingly insignificant choices made in succession can lead to an unfavorable outcome). It is always best, in the interests of both moving a project along and in creating a viable product at the end of the project, to limit the scope of experimentation.

The final decision in figure 3.12, based on the team's research, is to focus on three separate solutions (one with a complex dependency): ALS, SVD, and a deep learning (DL) solution. Once these paths have been agreed upon, the team can set out to attempt to build prototypes. Just as with the research phase, the experimentation phase is time-boxed to permit only so much work to be done, ensuring that a measurable result can be produced at the conclusion of the experimentation.

3.2.3 *Experimental scoping for the ML team: Experimentation*

With a plan in place, the ML team lead is free to assign resources to the prototype solutions. At the outset, it is important to be clear about the expectations from experimentation. The goal is to produce a simulation of the end product that allows for an unbiased comparison of the solutions being considered. There is no need for the models to be tuned, nor for the code to be written in such a way that it could ever be considered for use in the final project's code base. The name of the game here is a balance between two primary goals: speed and comparability.

A great many things need to be considered when deciding which approach to take, and these are discussed at length in several later chapters. But for the moment, the critical estimation at this stage is about the performance of the solutions as well as the difficulty of developing the full solution. Estimates for total final code complexity can be created at the conclusion of this phase, thereby informing the larger team of the estimated development time required to produce the project's code base. In addition to the time commitment associated with code complexity, this can also help inform the total cost of ownership for the solution: the daily run cost to retrain the models, generate inferences of affinity, host the data, and serve the data.

Before setting out to plan the work that will be done through the generally accepted best methodology (Agile) by writing stories and tasks, it can be helpful to create a testing plan for the experimentation. This plan, devoid of technical implementation details and the verbose nature of story tickets that will be accomplished throughout the testing phases, can be used to not only inform the sprint planning but also track the status of the bake-off that the ML team will be doing. This can be shared and utilized as a communication tool to the larger team, helping to show the tasks completed and the results, and can accompany a demo of the two (or more!) competing implementations being pursued for options.

Figure 3.13 shows a staged testing plan for the experimentation phase of the recommendation engine.

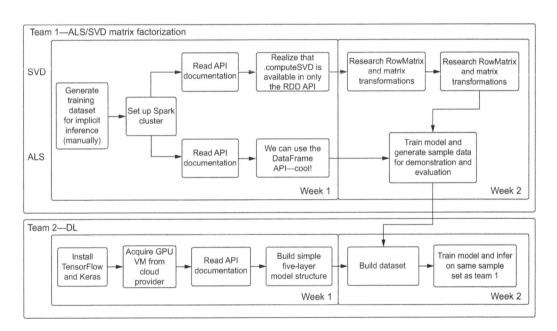

Figure 3.13 An experimentation tracking flow chart for two of the prototyping phases for the recommendation engine project

These testing paths clearly show the results of the research phase. Team 1's matrix factorization approach shows a common data source that needs to be manually generated (not through an ETL job for this phase of testing). Based on the team members' research and understanding of the computational complexity of these algorithms (and the sheer size of the data), they've chosen Apache Spark to test out solutions.

From this phase, both teams had to split their efforts to research the APIs for the two models, coming to two very different conclusions. For the ALS implementation, the high-level DataFrame API implementation from SparkML makes the code architecture far simpler than the lower-level RDD-based implementation for SVD. The team can define these complexities during this testing, bringing to light for the larger team that the SVD implementation will be significantly more complex to implement, maintain, tune, and extend.

All of these steps for team 1 help define the development scope later. Should the larger team as a whole decide that SVD is the better solution for their use case, they should weigh the complexity of implementation against the proficiency of the team. If the team isn't familiar with writing a Scala implementation that utilizes Breeze, can the project and the team budget time for team members to learn this technology? If the experimentation results are of significantly greater quality than the others being tested (or are a dependency for another, better solution), the larger team needs to be aware of the additional time that will be required to deliver the project.

Team 2's implementation is significantly more complex and requires as input the SVD model's inference. To evaluate the results of two approaches such as this, it's important to assess the complexity.

ASSESSING COMPLEXITY RISK

If the results for team 2 are significantly better than those of the SVD on its own, the team should be scrutinizing a complex solution of this nature. The primary reason for scrutiny is the level of increased complexity in the solution. Not only will it be more costly to develop (in terms of time and money), but the maintenance of this architecture will be much harder.

The gain in performance from added complexity should always be of such a significant level that the increased cost to the team is negligible in the face of such improvement. If an appreciable gain isn't clearly obvious to everyone (including the business), an internal discussion should take place about resume-driven development (RDD) and the motive for taking on such increased work. Everyone just needs to be aware of what they're getting into and what they'll potentially be maintaining for a few years should they choose to pursue this additional complexity.

TRACKING EXPERIMENTATION PHASES

An additional helpful visualization to provide to the larger team when discussing experimental phases is a rough estimate of what the broad strokes of the solution will be from an ML perspective. A complex architectural diagram isn't necessary, as it will change so many times during the early stages of development that creating anything of substantial detail is simply a waste of time at this point of the project.

However, a high-level diagram, such as the one shown in figure 3.14 that references our personalization recommendation engine, can help explain to the broader team what needs to be built to satisfy the solution. Visual "work architecture" guides like this (in an actual project it would have a great deal more detail) can also help the ML team keep track of current and upcoming work (as a complement to a scrum board).

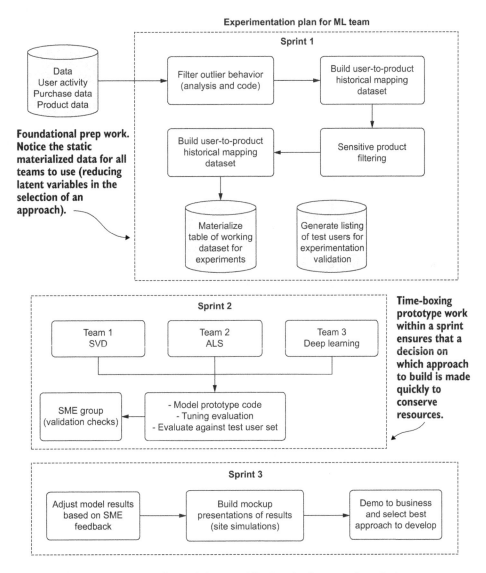

Figure 3.14   A high-level experimental phase architecture for the scenario project

These annotations can help communicate with the broader team at large. Instead of sitting in a status meeting that could include a dozen or more people, working diagrams like this one can be used by the ML team to communicate efficiently with everyone. Various explanations can be added to answer questions about what the team is working on and why at any given time, as well as to provide context to go along with chronologically focused delivery status reports (which, for a project as complex as this, can become difficult to read for those not working on the project).

UNDERSTANDING THE IMPORTANCE OF SCOPING A RESEARCH (EXPERIMENT) PHASE

If the ML team members working on the personalization project had all the time in the world (and an infinite budget), they might have the luxury of finding an optimal solution for their problem. They could sift through hundreds of whitepapers, read through treatises on the benefits of one approach over another, and even spend time finding a novel approach to solve the specific use case that their business sees as an ideal solution. Not held back by meeting a release date or keeping their technical costs down, they could easily spend months, if not years, just researching the best possible way to introduce personalization to their website and apps.

Instead of just testing two or three approaches that have been proven to work for others in similar industries and use cases, they could work on building prototypes for dozens of approaches and, through careful comparison and adjudication, select the absolutely best approach to create the optimal engine that would provide the finest recommendations to their users. They may even come up with a novel approach that could revolutionize the problem space. If the team were allowed to be free to test whatever they wanted for this personalized recommendation engine, the ideas whiteboard might look something like figure 3.15.

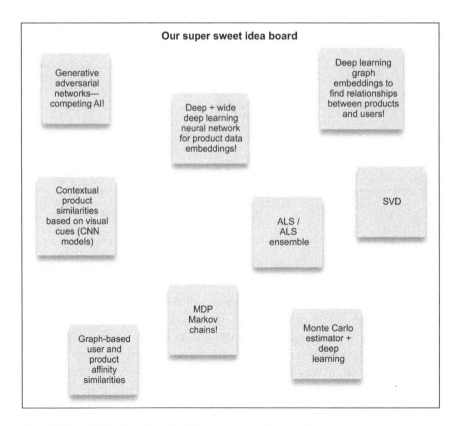

Figure 3.15 Coming up with potential ways to solve the problem

After a brainstorming session that generated these ideas (which bears striking resemblance to many ideation sessions I've had with large and ambitious DS teams), the next step that the team should take collectively is to start making estimations of these implementations. Attaching comments to each alternative can help formulate a plan of the two or three most likely to succeed within a reasonable time of experimentation. The commentary in figure 3.16 can assist the team with deciding what to test out to meet the needs of *actually shipping a product to production.*

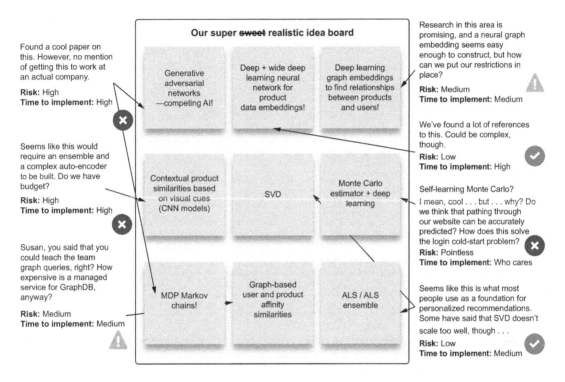

Figure 3.16 **Evaluating and rating options discussed during a brainstorming session. This is an effective way to generate the two or three approaches to test against one another during experimentation.**

After the team goes through the exercise of assigning risk to the different approaches, as shown in figure 3.16, the most likely and least risky options can be decided on that fit within the scope of time allocated for testing. The primary focus of evaluating and triaging the various ideas is to ensure that plausible implementations are attempted. To meet the goals of the project (accuracy, utility, cost, performance, and business problem-solving success criteria), pursuing experiments that can achieve all of those goals is of the utmost importance.

SOME ADVICE The goal of experimentation is to find the most promising and simplest approach that solves the problem, not to use the most technologically sophisticated solution. Focusing on solving the problem and not on which tools you're going to use to solve it will always increase the chances of success.

Take a look at figure 3.17. This is a slightly modified transposed time-based representation of the experimentation plan for two of the teams working on the experimentation phase. The most critical part to notice is at the top: the time scale.

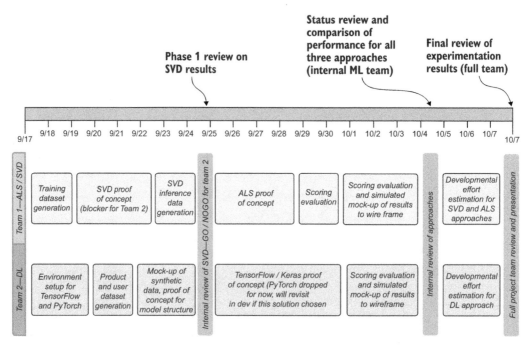

Figure 3.17 Chronological representation for two of the teams working on the experimentation phase of the project

This critical factor—time—is the one element that makes establishing controls on experimentation so important. Experimentation takes time. Building a proof of concept (PoC) is a grueling effort of learning new APIs, researching new ways of writing code to support the application of a model, and wrangling all the components together to ensure that at least one run succeeds. This can take a staggering amount of effort (depending on the problem).

Were the teams striving to build the best possible solution to do a bake-off, this time scale would stretch for many months longer than figure 3.17 shows. It's simply not in the company's interest to spend so many resources on trying to achieve perfection through two solutions that will never see the light of day. However, by limiting the total expenditure of time and accepting that the comparison of implementation strategies will be significantly less than perfect, the team can make an informed decision that weighs the quality of prediction against the total cost of ownership for the direction being chosen.

Total cost of ownership

While an analysis of the cost to maintain a project of this nature is nigh impossible to estimate accurately at the experimentation stage, it is an important aspect to consider and make an educated guess at.

During the experimentation, elements inevitably will be missing from the overall data architecture of the business. Services will likely need to be created for capturing data. Serving layers will need to be built. If the organization has never dealt with modeling around matrix factorization, it will need to potentially use a platform that it has never used before.

What if data can't actually be acquired to satisfy the needs of the project, though? This is the time to identify show-stopping issues. Identify them, ask if solutions are going to be provided to support the needs of the implementation, and, if not, alert the team that without investment to create the needed data, the project should be halted.

Provided that there aren't issues as severe as that, here are some questions to think about during this phase when gaps and critical issues are discovered:

- What additional ETL do we need to build?
- How often do we need to retrain models and generate inferences?
- What platform are we going to use to run these models?
- For the platform and infrastructure that we need, are we going to use a managed service or are we going to try to run it ourselves?
- Do we have expertise in running and maintaining services for ML of this nature?
- What is the cost of the serving layer plans that we have?
- What is the cost of storage, and where will the inference data live to support this project?

You don't have to answer each of these before development begins (other than the platform-related questions), but they should always be kept in mind as elements to revisit throughout the development process. If you don't have sufficient budget to run one of these engines, perhaps a different project should be chosen.

We time-block each of these elements for a final reason as well: to move quickly into making a decision for the project. This concept may well be significantly insulting to most data scientists. After all, how could someone adequately gauge the success of an implementation if the models aren't fully tuned? How could someone legitimately claim the predictive power of the solution if all of its components aren't completed?

I get it. Truly, I do. I've been there, making those same arguments. In hindsight, after having ignored the sage advice that software developers gave me during those early days of my career about why running tests on multiple fronts for long periods of time is a bad thing, I realize what they were trying to communicate to me.

> *If you had just made a decision earlier, all that work that you spent on the other things would have been put into the final chosen implementation.*
>
> —A lot of good engineers

Even though I knew what they were telling me was true, it still was a bit demoralizing to hear, realizing that I wasted so much time and energy.

An anecdote on morale

The time blocking isn't intended to force unrealistic expectations on the team, but rather to prevent the team from wasting time and energy on shelfware. Restricting time spent on potential solutions also helps with team morale with respect to such never-to-be-realized implementations—after all, you can really build only one solution for a project.

Setting restrictions on the amount of time people can work on a solution is valuable because throwing away their work becomes far less painful if they've been working on it for only a week. If they've been working on it for months, though, it's going to feel rather demoralizing when they're informed that their solution is not going to be used.

One of the most toxic things that can happen when testing implementations is for tribes to form within a team. Each team has spent so much time researching its solution and has been blinded by factors that might make it less than desirable for using as a path to solve the problem. If the experiments are allowed to go from the PoC phase to materialize as a true MVP (and, to be honest, if given enough time, most ML teams will build an MVP instead of a PoC), when it comes to deciding on which implementation to use, tensions will arise. Tempers will flare, lunches will disappear from fridges, arguments will break out during standups, and the general morale of the team will suffer. Save your team, save yourself, and make sure that people don't get attached to a PoC.

Time blocking is also critical if the project is entirely new. Moon-shot projects may not be common in companies with an established ML presence, but when they do arise, it's important to limit the amount of time spent in the early phases. They're risky, have a higher probability of going nowhere, and can end up being remarkably expensive to build and maintain. It's always best to fail fast and early for these projects.

The first time anyone approaches a new problem that is foreign to their experience, a lot of homework is usually required. Research phases can involve a lot of reading, talking to peers, searching through research papers, and testing code in Getting Started guides. This problem compounds itself many times over if the only available tooling to solve the problem is on a specific platform, uses a language that no one on the team has used before, or involves system designs that are new to the team (for example, distributed computing).

With the increased burden of research and testing that such a situation brings, it's even more of a priority to set time limits on research and experimentation. If the team members realize that they need to get up to speed on a new technology to solve the business problem, this is fine. However, the project's experimentation phase should be adapted to support this. The key point to remember, should this happen, is to communicate this to the business leaders so that they understand the increase in scope before the project work commences. It is a risk (although we're all pretty smart and can learn new things quickly) that they should be made aware of in an open and honest fashion.

The only exception to this time-blocking rule occurs if a simple and familiar solution can be utilized and shows promising results during experimentation. If the problem can be solved in a familiar and easy manner but new technology could (maybe) make the project better, then taking many months of learning from failures while the team gets up to speed on a new language or framework is, in my opinion, unethical. It's best to carve out time in the schedules of a DS team for independent or group-based continuing education and personal project work to these ends. During the execution of a project for a business is not the time to learn new tech, unless there is *no other option.*

HOW MUCH WORK IS THIS GOING TO BE, ANYWAY?

At the conclusion of the experimental phase, the broad strokes of the ML aspect of the project should be understood. It is important to emphasize that they should be understood, *but not implemented yet.*

The team should have a general view of the features that need to be developed to meet the project's specifications, as well as any additional ETL work that needs to be defined and developed. The team members should reach a solid consensus about the data going into and coming out of the models, how it will be enhanced, and the tools that will be used to facilitate those needs.

At this juncture, risk factors can begin to be identified. Two of the largest questions are as follows:

- How long will this take to build?
- How much will this cost to run?

These questions should be part of the review phase between experimentation and development. Having a rough estimate can inform the discussion with the broader team about why one solution should be pursued over another. But should the ML team be deciding alone which implementation to use? Inherent bias will be present in any of the team's assumptions, so to assuage these factors, it can be useful to create a weighted matrix report that the larger team (and the project leader) can use to choose an implementation.

Owner bias in ML

We all love what we build, particularly if it's clever. However, one of the most toxic things that can happen to a project after an experimentation phase is latching onto something that's clever and unique simply because you built it.

If someone else on the team has something that is of a similar prediction quality but far more boring or standard, that should be embraced as the better option. Remember that everyone else on the team is going to have to maintain this solution, contribute to it, improve it over time, and perhaps one day upgrade it to work in a new ecosystem. The clever custom solution can be a horrible burden on a team if it's too complicated to maintain.

This is why I've always found it useful to enlist the assistance of a peer to draft a comparative analysis. It's important to find someone familiar with gauging the cost and benefit of different approaches—someone who has enough experience to have lived through the difficult times of maintaining fragile approaches. I typically find someone who hasn't been involved in the project up to this point in order to ensure that they have no bias about a decision. Their objective opinion, without bias, can help ensure that the data contained in the report is accurate so that the larger team can evaluate options honestly.

When my clever solution has been thrown out because of its complexity, I've quickly moved on. I've always been fine with a "cool" solution being discarded, regardless of how much I may have, at the time, wanted to build it. The team, the company, and the project are far more important than my pride, after all.

Figure 3.18 shows an example of one such weighted matrix report (simplified for brevity) to allow for active participation by the greater team. The per-element ratings are locked by the expert reviewer who is doing the unbiased assessment of the relative attributes of different solutions, but the weights are left free to modify actively in a meeting. Tools like this matrix help the team make a data-driven choice after considering the various trade-offs of each implementation.

If this matrix were to be populated by ML team members who had never built a system this complex, they might employ heavy weightings to Prediction Quality and little else. A more seasoned team of ML engineers would likely overemphasize Maintainability and Implementation Complexity (no one who has ever endured them likes never-ending epics and pager alerts at 2 a.m. on a Friday). The director of data science might only care about Cost to Run, while the project lead may only be interested in Prediction Quality.

The important point to keep in mind is that this is a balancing act. With more people who have a vested interest in the project coming together to debate and explain their perspectives, a more informed decision can be arrived at that can help ensure a successful and long-running solution.

At the end of the day, as the cliché goes, there is no free lunch. Compromises will need to be made, and they should be agreed upon by the greater team, the team leader, and the engineers who will be implementing these solutions as a whole.

	Weights	SVD		ALS		DL + SVD	
		Base score	Weighted score	Base score	Weighted score	Base score	Weighted score
Implementation complexity	5	2	10	4	20	1	5
Cost to run	1	2	2	3	3	1	1
Estimated development time	2	3	6	5	10	2	4
Maintainability	4	5	20	5	20	2	8
Prediction quality	5	3	15	4	20	5	25
Weighted scores		53		73		43	

Per item scoring is set to a scale from 1 (worst) to 5 (best). Higher aggregate scores are better.

Figure 3.18 Weighted decision matrix for evaluating the experimental results, development complexity, cost of ownership, ability to maintain the solution, and comparative development time of the three tested implementations for the recommendation engine

Summary

- Spending time at the beginning of projects focused solely on how best to solve a given problem leads to great success. Gathering the critical requirements, evaluating approaches without introducing technical complexity or implementation details, and ensuring that communication with the business is clear helps avoid the many pitfalls that would necessitate rework later.
- Using principles of research and experimentation from Agile methodologies, ML projects can dramatically reduce the time to evaluate approaches and determine feasibility of the project much faster.

Before you model: Communication and logistics of projects

This chapter covers

- Structuring planning meetings for ML project work
- Soliciting feedback from a cross-functional team to ensure project health
- Conducting research, experimentation, and prototyping to minimize risk
- Including business rules logic early in a project
- Using communication strategies to engage nontechnical team members

In my many years of working as a data scientist, I've found that one of the biggest challenges that DS teams face in getting their ideas and implementations to be used by a company is rooted in a failure to communicate effectively. This isn't to say that we, as a profession, are bad at communicating.

It's more that in order to be effective when dealing with our internal customers at a company (a business unit or cross-functional team), a *different form of communication* needs to be used than the one that we use within our teams. Here are some of the biggest issues that I've seen DS teams struggle with (and that I have had personally) when discussing projects with our customers:

- Knowing which questions to ask at what time
- Keeping communication tactically targeted on essential details, ignoring insignificant errata that has no bearing on the project work
- Discussing project details, solutions, and results in layperson's terms
- Focusing discussions on the problem instead of the machinations of the solution

Since this field is so highly specialized, no common layperson's rubric exists that distills our job in the same way as for other software engineering fields. Therefore, an extra level of effort is required. In a sense, we need to learn a way of translating what it is that we do into a different language in order to have meaningful conversations with the business.

We also need to work hard at quality communication practices in general as ML practitioners. Dealing with complex topics that are inevitably going to be frustratingly confusing for the business requires a certain element of empathetic communication.

> ### Having difficult conversations with angry or frustrated people
>
> I have a lot of difficult conversations with people in my current line of work. Sometimes people are frustrated that a solution isn't making progress. Other times, people are angry that a solution isn't interpretable. In rare instances, people are dead set against using an ML solution because of their perception that it's going to replace their job.
>
> After each one of these difficult conversations, someone inevitably approaches me afterward and asks for tips on how to do what I just did during the meeting. In years past, I was confused about this question. It made little sense to me. All I did, after all, was listen to the complaints, have an open discussion that focused on their concerns, and come to a mutual understanding about what is important to address in order to move forward. These days, however, I think I know why people ask this question.
>
> As an expert in a highly esoteric field, DS practitioners can easily lose sight of what a layperson knows or doesn't know. This is gradually changing in industry as AI is becoming increasingly part of today's zeitgeist. It doesn't necessarily mean that every person you're talking to will understand what your solutions can and cannot do, though.
>
> The answer that I give to people who ask me how I manage to defuse difficult discussions is simple: just listen. Talk less. Don't talk at the business unit. Listen to their concerns and communicate clearly in terms that they understand. Above all else, be honest. Don't promise magical solutions or delivery dates that are beyond your ability to execute. They will appreciate being listened to and having an honest discussion. Having an empathetic mindset of truly listening to their grievances can help de-escalate hostile discussions far better than any other method I'm aware of.

Figure 4.1 shows a generic conversation path that I've always found to work well, one that we will apply throughout this chapter.

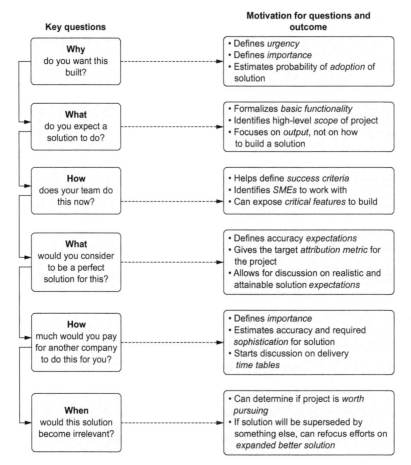

Notice the lack of discussion on *how the solution will be built*. The conversation is on *what should be built* and how important it is to the business.

Figure 4.1   Critical questions to have with a business unit during a first planning meeting, followed by the critically important answers that will inform what, how, and when to build the solution

By using a clear, to-the-point communication style that focuses on outcomes, those project outcomes can be more closely aligned with business expectations of the work. A pointed discussion with this as the primary goal helps define *what to build, how to build it, when to have it done by, and what the success criteria is.* It's effectively the entire recipe outlined for every further stage of the project up to and including flipping the switch to On in production.

4.1   *Communication: Defining the problem*

As covered in chapter 3, we're going to continue discussing the product recommendation system that our DS team was tasked with building. We've seen a juxtaposition of ineffective and effective ways of planning a project and setting scoping for an MVP, but we haven't seen *how* the team got to the point of creating an effective project plan with a reasonable project scope.

The first example meeting, as we discussed in section 3.1, revolved around the end goal in highly abstract terms. The business wanted personalization of its website. The DS team's first error during that conversation was in not continuing the line of questioning. The single most important question was never asked: "Why do you want to build a personalization service?"

Most people, particularly technical people (likely the vast majority of the people who will be in a room discussing this initial project proposal and brainstorming session), prefer to focus on the *how* of a project. How am I going to build this? How is the system going to integrate to this data? How frequently do I need to run my code to solve the need?

For our recommendation engine project, if anyone had posed this question, it would have opened the door to an open and frank conversation about what needs to be built, what the expected functionality should be, how important the project is to the business, and when the business wants to start testing a solution. Once those key answers are received, all of the details surrounding logistics can be conducted.

The important thing to keep in mind with these kickoff meetings is that they're effective when both sides—customer and supplier of the solution—are getting what they need. The DS team is getting its research, scoping, and planning details. The business is getting a review schedule for the work to be conducted. The business gets the inclusiveness that's paramount to the project success, which will be exercised at the various presentations and ideation sessions scheduled throughout the project (more on these presentation boundaries is covered in section 4.1.2). Without a directed and productive conversation, as modeled in figure 4.1, the respective people in the meeting would likely be engaged in the thought patterns shown in figure 4.2.

By focusing the meeting on a common purpose, the areas of individual responsibility and expectation of each persona in figure 4.2 can be collaboratively directed toward defining the project and helping to ensure its success.

The other primary benefit to collectively discussing the project's key principles is to help define the *simplest possible solution that solves the problem*. By having buy-in from the business unit, feedback from SMEs, and input from fellow software engineers, the end solution can be crafted to meet the exact needs. It can also be adapted to new functionality at each subsequent phase without causing frustration for the larger team. After all, everyone discussed the project *together* from the start.

A GREAT RULE OF THUMB FOR ML DEVELOPMENT   Always build the simplest solution possible to solve a problem. Remember, you have to maintain this thing and improve it to meet changing needs as time goes on.

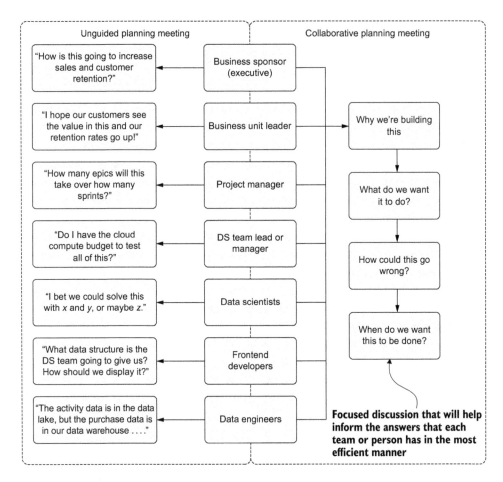

Figure 4.2   Comparison of unguided and guided planning meetings

4.1.1   *Understanding the problem*

In our scenario, the unguided nature of the planning meeting(s) resulted in the DS team members not having a clear direction on *what to build*. Without any real definition from the business of the desired end state, they focused their effort solely on building the best collection of recommendations for each user that they could prove with scoring algorithms. What they had done was effectively missed the plot.

At its core, the problem is a fundamental breakdown in communication. Without asking what the business wanted from their work, they missed the details that meant the most to the business unit (and to the external "real" customers). You'll always want to avoid situations like this. These breakdowns in communication and planning can play out in multiple ways, ranging from slow, simmering passive-aggressive hostility to outright shouting matches (usually one-sided) if the realization is made toward the end of a project.

What we have here is a failure to communicate

In the many dozens of ML projects that I've been a part of as a developer, data scientist, architect, or consultant, the one consistent, common theme among all projects that never make it to production has been a lack of communication. This isn't a reference to a communication failure in the engineering team (although I have certainly witnessed that more than enough for my liking in my career thus far).

The worst sort of breakdown is the one that happens between the DS team and the business unit requesting the solution. Whether it's a long, slow, drawn-out entropy of communication or a flat-out refusal to speak in a common form of dialogue that all parties can understand, the result is always the same when the customers (internal) aren't being listened to by the developers.

The most destructive time for a lack of communication to become apparent to everyone involved in the project is around the final release to production. End users consuming the predictions come to the conclusion that not only does something seem a bit off about the results coming from the predictive model, but that it's just fundamentally broken.

Breakdowns in communication aren't restricted only to production release, though. They typically happen slowly during the development of the solution or when going through user acceptance testing. Assumptions on all sides are made; ideas are either unspoken or ignored, and commentary is dismissed as either being irrelevant or simply a waste of time during full team meetings.

Few things are as infinitely frustrating as a project failure that is due to communication breakdown among a team, but it can be avoided completely. These failures, resulting in enormous wastes of time and resources, can be attributed to the very early stages of the project—before a single line of code is written—when the scoping and definition of the problem happens. These failures are entirely preventable with a conscious and determined plan of ensuring that open and inclusive dialogue is maintained at every phase of the project, starting at the first ideation and brainstorming session.

WHAT DO YOU WANT IT TO DO?

The *what* for this recommendation is far more important to everyone on the team than the *how*. By focusing on the functionality of the project's goal (the "What will it do?" question), the product team can be involved in the discussion. The frontend developers can contribute as well. The entire team can look at a complex topic and plan for the seemingly limitless number of edge cases and nuances of the business that need to be thought of for building not just the final project, but the MVP as well.

The easiest way for the team that's building this personalization solution to work through these complex topics is by using simulation and flow-path models. These can help identify the entire team's expectations for the project in order to then inform the DS team about the details needed to limit the options for building the solution.

The best way for the team working on this project to go through this conversation is to borrow liberally from the best practices of frontend software developers. Before a

What do you mean, you don't care about my struggles?

Yes, my fellow ML brethren, I can admit it: the *how* is complex, involves the vast majority of the work for the project, and is incredibly challenging. However, the *how* is what we get paid to figure out. For some of us, it's the very thing that brought us to this profession. The "how to solve problems" question occupies a lot of the nerd-focused talk that many of us engage in while speaking with one another. It's fun stuff, it's complex, and it's fascinating to learn.

But the rest of the team doesn't care about which modeling approaches are going to be used; trust me, even if they feign interest, they're asking questions about it only so they can make it seem like they care—they don't really care. Keep these details out of group discussions if you want to have meaningful, collaborative, and inclusive meetings. It's only when the discussion is kept in this welcoming tone of teamwork that you'll get the insights, creative ideas, and identification of seemingly innocuous details that need to be handled in order to make the project as successful as it can be.

single feature branch is cut, before a single Jira ticket is assigned to a developer, front-end dev teams utilize wireframes that simulate the final end state.

For our recommendation engine, figure 4.3 shows what a high-level flow path might look like initially for a user journey on the website with personalization features applied. Mapping even simplistic architectural user-focused journeys like this can help the entire team think about how all of these moving parts will work. This process also open up the discussion to the nontechnical team members in a way that is far

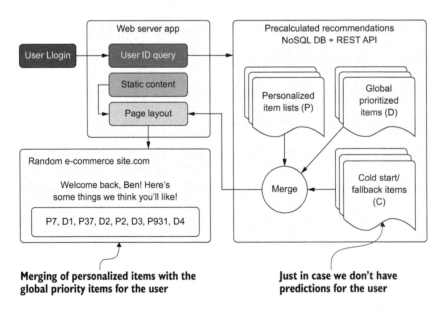

Figure 4.3   A simplified, basic overview of the personalization recommendation engine to aid in planning requirements and features of a personalization project. This is the core, minimal functionality to start an ideation session from.

less confusing than looking at code snippets, key-value collections, and accuracy metrics plotted in highly confusing representations that they are unfamiliar with.

> **NOTE** Even if you're not going to be generating a prediction that is interfacing with a user-facing feature on a website (or any ML that has to integrate with external services), it is incredibly useful to block out the end-state flow of the project's aims while in the planning stage. This doesn't expressly mean to build out a full architectural diagram for sharing with the business unit, but a line diagram of the way the pieces of the project interact and the way the final output will be utilized can be a great communication tool.

Diagrams such as this one are helpful for conducting a planning discussion with a broader team. Save your architecture diagrams, modeling discussions, and debates on the appropriateness of scoring metrics for a recommendation system to internal discussions within the DS team. Breaking out a potential solution from the perspective of a user not only enables the entire team to discuss the important aspects, but also opens the discussion to the nontechnical team members who will have insights into points to consider that will directly impact both the experimentation and the production development of the actual code.

Because the diagram is so incredibly simple and facilitates seeing the bare-bones functionality of the system, while hiding the complexity contained inside the Precalculated Recommendations section in particular, the discussion can begin with every person in the room being engaged and able to contribute to the ideas that will define the project's initial state. As an example, figure 4.4 shows what might come from an initial meeting with the broader team, discussing what *could be built* in a thorough ideation session.

Figure 4.4, when compared with figure 4.3, shows the evolution of the project's ideation. It is important to consider that many of the ideas presented would likely have *not been considered* by the DS team had the product teams and SMEs not been part of the discussion. Keeping the implementation details out of the discussion allows for everyone to continue to focus on the biggest question: "Why are we talking about building this, and how should it function for the end user?"

What is a user-experience journey?

Borrowed liberally from the field of product management in the business-to-customer (B2C) industry, a *user-experience journey* (or *journey map*) is a simulation of a product, exploring how a new feature or system will be consumed by a particular user. It's a form of a map, of sorts, beginning with the user interacting with your system initially (logging in, in the example in figure 4.4), and then following them through the user-facing interactions that they will have with elements of the system.

I've found that these are useful for not only e-commerce and application-based implementations that ingest ML to serve a feature, but can also be quite helpful in designing even internal-facing systems. At the end of the day, you want your predictions to be used by someone or something. Many times, drawing a map of the way that person, system, or downstream process will interact with the data that you're producing can

(continued)
aid in designing the ML solution to best meet the needs of the customer. The mapping process can help find areas to inform the design of not only the serving layer, but also elements that may need to be considered as critical features during the development of the solution.

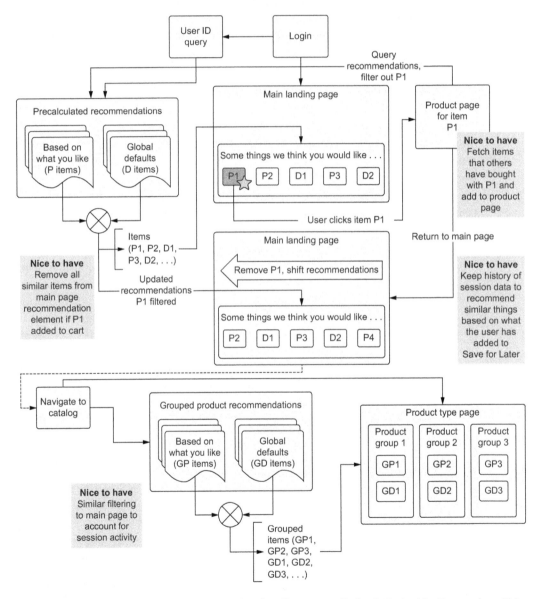

Figure 4.4   Additions made to the core minimal functionality as a result of an inclusive ideation session within a cross-functional team

In figure 4.4, notice the four items marked *Nice to have*. This is an important and challenging aspect of initial planning meetings. Everyone involved wants to brainstorm and work toward making the best possible solution to the problem. The DS team should welcome all of these ideas but add a caveat to the discussion that a *cost is associated with each addition*.

A sincere focus should be made on the essential aspects of the project (the MVP). Pursuit of an MVP ensures that only the most critical aspects will be built first. The other requirement is that they function correctly before including any additional features. Ancillary items should be annotated as such; ideas should be recorded, referenceable, modified, and referred to throughout the experimentation and development phases of the project. What once may have seemed insurmountably difficult could prove to be trivial later as the code base takes shape, and it could be worthwhile to include these features even in the MVP.

The only bad ideas are those that get ignored. Don't ignore ideas, but also don't allow every idea to make it into the core experimentation plan. If the idea seems far-fetched and incredibly complex, simply revisit it later, after the project is taking shape and the feasibility of implementation can be considered when the total project complexity is known to a deeper level.

Keeping the engineering out of ideation meetings

I've been a part of many planning meetings in my career. They typically fall into one of three categories. The examples in figures 4.2 and 4.3 represent the planning events that I've seen and had the most success using.

The ones that are least useful (where follow-up meetings, off-line discussions, and resulting chaos ensues) are those that focus either entirely on the ML aspect of the project or on the engineering considerations of making the system work.

If the model is the main point of concern, many of the people in the group will be completely alienated (they won't have the knowledge or frame of reference to contribute to a discussion of algorithms) or annoyed to the point that they disengage from the conversation. At this point, it's just a group of data scientists arguing about whether they should be using ALS or deep learning to generate the raw recommendation scores and how to fold in historical information to the prediction results. Discussing these things in front of a marketing team is pointless.

If the engineering aspects are the focus, instead of creating a diagram of a user-experience flow path, the diagram will be an architectural one that will be alienating an entirely different group of people. Both an engineering and a modeling discussion are important to have, but they can be conducted without the broader team and can be iteratively developed later—after experimentation is completed.

While walking through this user-experience workflow, it could be discovered that team members have conflicting assumptions about how one of these engines work. The marketing team assumes that if a user clicks something, but doesn't add it to their cart, we can infer dislike of the product. Those team members don't want to see that product in recommendations again for the user.

How does this change the implementation details for the MVP? The architecture is going to have to change.

It's a whole lot easier to find this out now and be able to assign scoped complexity for this feature while in the planning phase than before a model is built; otherwise, the change has to be monkey-patched to an existing code base and architecture. The defined functional architecture also may, as shown in figure 4.4, start adding to the overall view of the engine: what it's going to be built to support and what will not be supported. Functional architecture design will allow the DS team, the frontend team, and the DE team to begin to focus on what they respectively will need to research and experiment with in order to prove or disprove the prototypes that will be built. Remember, all of this discussion happens *before a single line of code is written*.

Asking the simple question "How should this work?" and avoiding focusing on the standard algorithmic implementations is a habit that can help ensure success in ML projects more so than any technology, platform, or algorithm. This question is arguably the most important one to ask to ensure that everyone involved in the project is on the same page. I recommend asking this question along with the necessary line of questioning to eke out the core functionality that needs to be investigated and experimented on. If there is confusion or a lack of concrete theories regarding the core needs, it's much better to sit in hours of meetings to plan things out and iron out all of the business details as much as possible in the early stages, rather than waste months of your time and effort in building something that doesn't meet the project sponsor's vision.

WHAT DOES THE IDEAL END-STATE LOOK LIKE?

The ideal implementation is hard to define at first (particularly before any experimentation is done), but it's incredibly useful to the experimentation team to hear all aspects of an ideal state. During these open-ended stream-of-consciousness discussions, a tendency of most ML practitioners is to instantly decide what is and isn't possible based on the ideas of people who don't understand what ML is. My advice is to simply listen. Instead of shutting down a thread of conversation immediately as being out of scope or impossible, let the conversation happen.

You may find an alternative path during this creative ideation session that you otherwise would have missed. You might just find a simpler, less unique, and far more maintainable ML solution than what you may have come up with on your own. The most successful projects that I've worked on over the years have come from having these sorts of creative discussions with a broad team of SMEs (and, when I've been lucky, the actual end users) to allow me to shift my thinking into creative ways of getting as close as possible to their vision.

Discussing an ideal end state isn't just for the benefit of a more amazing ML solution, though. Engaging the person asking for the project to be built allows their perspective, ideas, and creativity to influence the project in positive ways. The discussion also helps build trust and a feeling of ownership in the development of the project that can help bring a team together.

Learning to listen closely to the needs of your ML project's customer is one of the most important skills of an ML engineer—far more than mastering any algorithm, language, or platform. It will help guide what you're going to try, what you're going to research, and how to think differently about problems to come up with the best solution that you possibly can.

In the scenario shown in figure 4.4, the initial planning meeting results in a rough sketch of the ideal state. This likely *will not be the final engine* (based on my experience, that most certainly is never the case). But this diagram will inform how to convert those functional blocks into systems. It will help inform the direction of experimentation, as well as the areas of the project that you and the team will need to research thoroughly to minimize or prevent unexpected scope creep, as shown in figure 4.5.

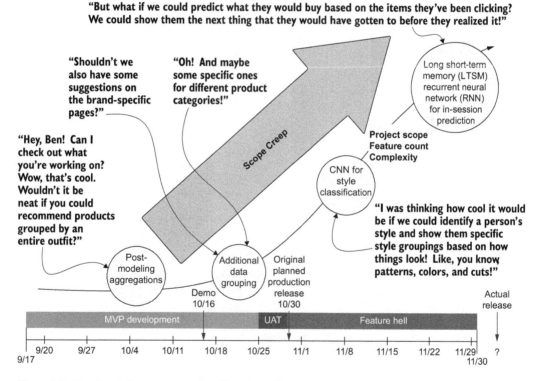

Figure 4.5 The dreaded scope creep of an ML project. Be clear at the outset of planning that this will not be tolerated, and you shouldn't have to worry about it.

Figure 4.5 should be familiar to any reader who has ever worked at a startup. The excitement and ideas that flow from driven and creative people who want to do something amazing is infectious and can, with a bit of tempering, create a truly revolutionary company that does a great job at its core mission. However, without that tempering and focus applied, particularly to an ML project, the sheer size and complexity of a solution can quite rapidly spiral out of control.

> **NOTE** I've never, not even once, in my career allowed a project to get to the level of ridiculousness shown in figure 4.5 (although a few have come close). However, on nearly every project that I've worked on, comments, ideas, and questions like this have been posed. My advice: thank the person for their idea, gently explain in nontechnical terms that it's not possible at this time, and move on to finish the project.

Scope creep: An almost guaranteed assassination of a project

Improper planning (or planning without involving the team that the project is being built for) is a perfect recipe for one of the most frustrating ways of having a project die a slow, whimpering death. Also known as *ML death by a thousand requests*, this concept materializes at later stages of development, particularly when a demo is shown to a team that is uninformed about the details that went into building the project. If the customer (the internal business unit) was not party to the planning discussions, they inevitably will have questions, and many of them, about what the demo does.

In nearly every case that I've seen (or caused in my earlier days of trying to "hero my way through" a project without asking for input), the result of the demo session is going to be dozens of requests for additional features and requirements to be added. This is expected (even in a properly designed and planned project), but if the implementation is unable to easily include critical features that relate to immutable business operation "laws," a potential full reimplementation of the project could be required. That leaves decision makers with the difficult choice of whether to delay the project because of the decision that the DS team (or individual) made, or to scrap the project entirely to prevent the chances of a repeat of the initial failure.

Few things are more devastating to hear in the world of ML than intensely negative feedback immediately after something goes live in production. Getting a flood of email from executive-level staff indicating that the solution you just shipped is recommending cat toys to a dog owner is laughable, but one that is recommending adult-themed products to children is about as bad as it can get. The only thing worse is realizing, right before the project is shipped, during user-acceptance testing (UAT), that an insurmountable list of changes needs to be made to satisfy the urgent requirements of the business and that it would take less time to start the project over from scratch than to make the changes to the existing solution.

Identifying scope creep is important, but its magnitude can be minimized, and in some cases eliminated. The appropriate level of discussion needs to be reached, and critical aspects of a project included in sometimes excruciating recursive and painful detail well before a single character is typed in an experimentation notebook or IDE.

WHO IS YOUR CHAMPION FOR THIS PROJECT THAT I CAN WORK WITH ON BUILDING THESE EXPERIMENTS?

The most valuable member of any team I've worked with has been the SME—the person assigned to work with me or my team in order to check our work, answer every silly question that we had, and provide creative ideation that helped the project grow in ways that none of us had envisioned. While usually not a technical person, the SME has a deep connection and expansive knowledge of the problem. Taking a little bit of extra time to translate between the world of engineering and ML to layperson's terms has always been worth it, primarily because it creates an inclusive environment that enables the SME to be invested in the success of the project since they see that their opinions and ideas are being considered and implemented.

I can't stress enough that the *last person* you want to fill this role is the actual executive-level project owner. While it may seem logical at first to assume that being able to ask the manager, director, or VP of a group for approval of ideation and experimentation will be easier, I can assure you that this will only stagnate a project. These people are incredibly busy dealing with dozens of other important, time-consuming tasks that they have delegated to others. Expecting this person—who may or may not be an expert in the domain that the project is addressing—to provide extensive and in-depth discussions on minute details (all ML solutions are all about the small details, after all) will likely put the project at risk. In that first kick-off meeting, make sure to have a resource from the team who is an SME and has the time, availability, and authority to deal with this project and the critical decisions that will need to be made throughout.

WHEN SHOULD WE MEET TO SHARE PROGRESS?

Because of the complex nature of most ML projects (particularly ones that require so many interfaces to parts of a business as a recommendation engine), meetings are critical. However, not all meetings are created equally.

While it is incredibly tempting for people to want to have cadence meetings on a certain weekly prescribed basis, project meetings should coincide with milestones associate with the project. These project-based milestone meetings should

- Not be a substitute for daily standup meetings
- Not overlap with team-focused meetings of individual departments
- Always be conducted with the full team present
- Always have the project lead present to make final decisions on contentious topics
- Be focused on presenting the solution as it stands at that point and nothing else

Well-intentioned but toxic external ideation

It's incredibly tempting for discussions to happen outside these structured presentation and data-focused meetings. Perhaps people on your team who are not involved in the project are curious and would like to provide feedback and additional brain

(continued)

storming sessions. Similarly, it could be convenient to discuss a solution to something that you're stuck on with a small group from the larger team.

I cannot stress strongly enough how much disruption can, and likely will, arise from these outside-of-the-team discussions. Any decisions made in a large-scale project (even in the experimentation phase) by the team members should be considered sacrosanct. Involving outside voices and people who are "trying to help" erodes the inclusive communication environment that has been built collectively.

Outside ideation also typically introduces an *uncontrollable chaos* to the project that is difficult for everyone involved in the implementation to manage. If the DS team decides in a vacuum, for instance, to change the delivery method of the predictions (reusing a REST endpoint with additional payload data, for instance), it would affect the entire project. Even though it may save the DS team a week's worth of work by not having to create another REST endpoint, it would be disastrous for any work that the frontend engineers are working on. This could potentially cause weeks of rework for the frontend team.

Introducing changes without notifying and discussing them in the larger group risks wasting a great deal of time and resources, which in turn erodes the confidence that the team and the business at large has in the process. It's a fantastically effective way of having the project become shelfware or introducing silo behavior among microcosm groups of business units.

At the early meetings, it is imperative for the DS team to communicate to the group the need for these event-based meetings. You want to let everyone know that changes that might seem insignificant to other teams could have rework risks associated with them that could translate to weeks or months of extra work by the DS team. Similarly, DS changes could have dramatic impacts on the other teams.

To illustrate the interconnectedness of the project and how hitting different deliveries can impact a project, let's take a look at figure 4.6. This chart shows what this solution would look like in a relatively large company (let's say over 1,000 employees) with the roles and responsibilities divided among various groups. In a smaller company (a startup, for instance), many of these responsibilities would fall either on the frontend or DS team rather than separate DE teams.

Figure 4.6 shows how dependencies from the ML experimentation, for instance, affect the future work of both the DE and frontend development teams. Adding excessive delays or required rework results in not only the DS team reworking its code, but also potentially weeks of work being thrown away by an entire engineering organization. This is why planning, frequent demonstrations of the state of the project, and open discussions with the relevant teams are so critical.

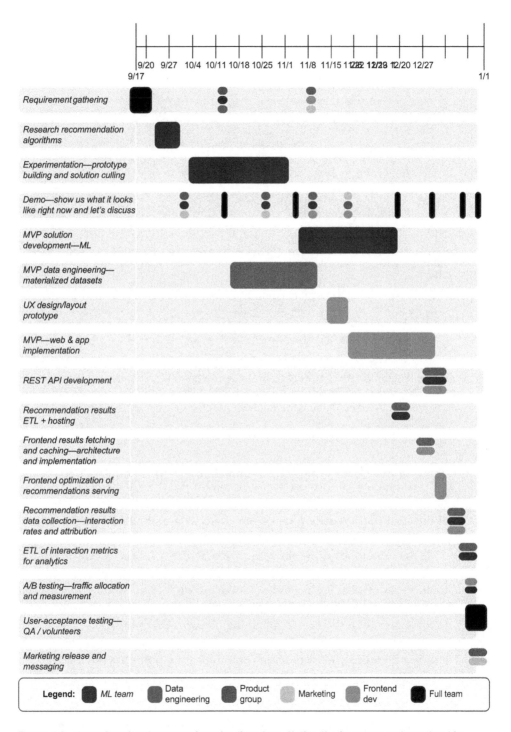

Figure 4.6 Cross-functional team project timeline chart. Notice the frequency and membership requirements for each demo and discussion (most are for the full team).

But when is it going to be done?

Honesty is always the best policy. I've seen a lot of DS teams think that it's wise to under-promise and over-deliver during project planning. This isn't a wise move.

Many times, this policy of giving wiggle room to a project is employed to protect against unforeseen complexities that arise during project development. But factoring those into estimated delivery dates doesn't do the team any favors. It's dishonest and can erode trust that the business has in the team. The better approach is to just *be honest* with everyone. Let them know that ML projects have a lot of unknown factors baked into them.

The only thing this practice will result in is frustrated and angry internal business unit customers. They won't like continually getting results weeks earlier than promised and will quickly catch on to your antics. *Trust is important.*

The other side of this factual omission coin relates to setting unrealistic expectations in deliveries. By not telling the business that things can go sideways during many of the phases of project work and setting an aggressive delivery date for iterative design, everyone will expect something useful to be delivered on that date. Failing to explain that these are general targets that may need slight adjustment means that the only way to accommodate unforeseen complications is by forcing the DS team to work long and grueling hours to hit those goals.

Only one result is guaranteed: team burnout. If the team is completely demotivated and exhausted from striving to meet unreasonable demands, the solution will never be very good. Details will be missed, bugs will proliferate in code, and the best members on the team will be updating their resumes to find a better job once the solution is in production.

Figure 4.7 illustrates a high-level Gantt chart of the milestones associated with a general e-commerce ML project, focusing solely on the main concepts. Using charts like this as a common focused communication tool can greatly improve the productivity of all the teams and reduce a bit of the chaos in a multidisciplinary team, particularly across the walls of department barriers.

As the milestone arrows along the top of figure 4.7 show, at critical stages, the *entire team* should be meeting together to ensure that all team members understand the implications of what has been developed and discovered so that they may collectively adjust their own project work. Most teams that I've worked with hold these meetings on the same day as their sprint planning, for what that's worth.

These breakpoints allow for demos to be shown, basic functionality to be explored, and risks identified. This common communication point has two main purposes:

- Minimizing the amount of time wasted on rework
- Making sure that the project is on track to do what it set out to do

While spending the time and energy to create Gantt charts for each and every project is not absolutely necessary, creating at least something to track progress and milestones

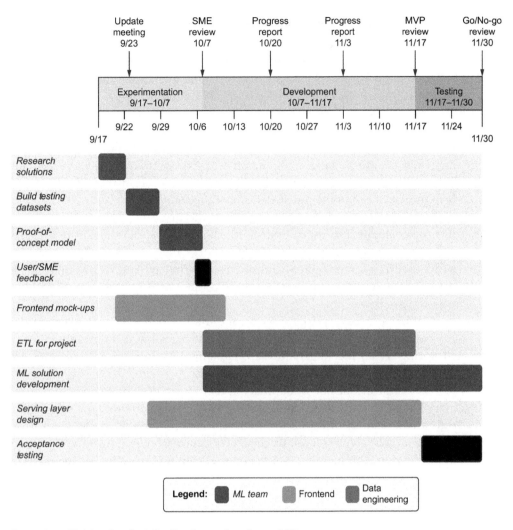

Figure 4.7   High-level project timeline for engineering and DS

against is advisable. Colorful charts and interdisciplinary tracking of systems development certainly doesn't make sense for solo outings led by a single ML engineer handling the entire project. But even when you may be the only person putting fingers to keyboard, figuring out where major boundaries exist within the project's development and scheduling a bit of a show-and-tell can be extremely helpful.

Do you have a demonstration test set from a tuned model that you want to make sure solves the problem? Set a boundary at that point, generate the data, present it in a consumable form, and show it to the team that asked for your help in solving the problem. Getting feedback—the right feedback—in a timely manner can save you and your customer a great deal of frustration.

4.1.2   *Setting critical discussion boundaries*

The next question that begs to be asked is, "Where do I set these boundaries for my project?" Each project is completely unique with respect to the amount of work required to solve the problem, the number of people involved in the solution, and the technological risks surrounding the implementation.

But a few general guidelines are helpful for setting the minimum required meetings. Within the confines of the recommendation engine that we're planning on building, we need to set some form of a schedule indicating when we will all be meeting, what we will be talking about, what to expect from those meetings, and most important, how the active participation from everyone involved in the project will help minimize risk in the timely delivery of the solution.

Let's imagine for a moment that this is the first large-scale project involving ML that the company has ever dealt with. It's the first time that so many developers, engineers, product managers, and SMEs have worked in concert, and none of them have an idea of how often to meet and discuss the project. You realize that meetings do have to happen, since you identified this in the planning phase. You just don't know *when* to have them.

Within each team, people have a solid understanding of the cadence with which *they* can deliver solutions—assuming they're using some form of Agile, they're likely all having scrum meetings and daily stand-ups. But no one is really sure what the stages of development look like in other teams.

The simplistic answer is, naturally, a frustrating one for all involved: "Let's meet every Wednesday at 1 p.m." Putting a "regularly scheduled program" meeting in place, with a full team of dozens of people, will generally result in the team not having enough to talk about, demo, or review. Without a pointed agenda, the importance and validity of the meeting can become questioned, resulting in people failing to show up when something critical needs review.

The best policy that I've found is to set deliverable date meetings with tangible results to review, a strong agenda, and an expectation of contribution from everyone who attends. That way, everyone will realize the importance of the meeting, everyone's voice and opinions will be heard, and precious time resources will be respected as much as is practicable.

A note on pointless meetings for DS teams

Everyone wants to talk to the DS team when something interesting is being worked on. That may be because of the general excitement about the project's progress or because the business leaders are simply scared that you're going to go full prison riot on a project, with an inmates-running-the-asylum style of development (hopefully, that isn't the case).

These are understandable reasons to want to meet and discuss the project's status. (Well, hopefully if your company is worried that you're going to go full cowboy/girl, you can assuage their fears in time with some successfully delivered projects.) However, holding many meetings that serve little purpose other than to state a progress report that hasn't changed since the last meeting is detrimental to the team.

I emphatically suggest that this concept be communicated at the start of the project: to meet the agreed-upon delivery goals for each presentation and demo, the team needs to be left largely alone to do its work. Questions, thoughts, helpful conversations being held face-to-face are welcome (and are part of the cornerstone of Agile). But status meetings, progress reports, and repetitive bean counting serve no purpose and should be summarily eliminated from the team's burden.

This can be a difficult conversation to have, particularly if the company is wary of ML because of its novelty at the company. But the issue should be brought up so you can communicate clearly why it hurts, rather than helps, meeting deadlines for deliverable results.

The more logical, useful, and efficient use of everyone's time is to meet to review the solution-in-progress *only when something new needs review*. But when are those decision points? How do we define these boundaries in order to balance the need to discuss elements of the project with the exhaustion that comes with reviewing minor changes with too-frequent work-disrupting meetings?

It depends on the project, the team, and the company. The point I'm making is that it's different for every situation. The conversation about these expectations of meeting frequency, the meeting agenda, and the people who are to be involved simply needs to happen to help control the chaos that could otherwise arise and derail progress toward solving the problem.

POST-RESEARCH PHASE DISCUSSION (UPDATE MEETING)

For the sake of example within our scenario, let's assume that the DS team identifies that two models must be built to satisfy the requirements from the planning phase user-journey simulation. Based on the team members' research, they decide that they want to pit both collaborative filtering and frequent-pattern-growth (FP-growth) market-basket analysis algorithms against deep learning implementations to see which provides a higher accuracy and lower cost of ownership for retraining.

The DS lead assigns two groups of data scientists and ML engineers to work on these competing implementations. Both groups generate simulations of the model results on the exact same synthetic customer dataset, providing mock product images to a wireframe of the pages displaying these recommendations for the actual website.

This meeting should not focus on any of the implementation details. Instead, it should focus solely on the results of the research phase: the whittling down of nigh-infinite options that have been read about, studied, and played with. The team has found a lot of great ideas and an even larger group of potential solutions that won't work based on the data available, and has reduced the list of great ideas to a bake-off of two implementations that they'll pit against each other. Don't bring up all of the options that you've explored. Don't mention something that has amazing results but will likely take two years to build. Instead, distill the discussion to the core details required to get the next phase going: experimentation.

Show these two options to the SMEs, solely within the confines of presenting what can be done with each algorithmic solution, what is impossible with one or both, and when the SMEs can expect to see a prototype in order to decide which they like better. If no discernable difference exists in the quality of the predictions, the decision of which to go with should be based on the drawbacks of the approaches, leaving the technical complexity or implementation details out of the discussion.

Keep the discussion in these dense meetings focused on relatable language and references that your audience will comprehend and associate with. You can do the translating in your head and leave it there. The technical details should be discussed only internally by the DS team, the architect, and engineering management.

In many cases that I've been involved with, the experimental testing phase may test out a dozen ideas but present only the two most acceptable to a business unit for review. If the implementation would be overly onerous, costly, or complex, it's best to present options that will *guarantee the greatest chance of project success*—even if they're not as fancy or exciting as other solutions. Remember: the DS team has to maintain the solution, and something that sounds really cool during experimentation can turn into a nightmare to maintain.

POST-EXPERIMENTATION PHASE (SME/UAT REVIEW)

Following the experimentation phase, the subteams within the DS group build two prototypes for the recommendation engine. In the previous milestone meeting, the options for both were discussed, with their weaknesses and strengths presented in a way that the audience could understand. Now it's time to lay the prediction cards out on the table and show off what a prototype of the solution looks like.

Before, during reviews of the potential solutions, some pretty rough predictions were shown. Duplicate products with different product IDs were right next to one another, endless lists of one product type were generated for some users (there's no way that anyone likes belts that much), and the list of critical issues with the demo were listed out for consideration. In those first early pre-prototypes, the business logic and feature requirements weren't built out yet, since those elements directly depended on the models' platform and technology selection.

The goal of the presentation that completes the experimentation phase should be to show a mock-up of the core features. Perhaps elements need to be ordered based on relevancy. Special considerations may require recommending items based on price point, recent non-session-based historical browsing, and the theory that certain customers have implicit loyalty to certain brands. Each of these agreed-upon features should be shown to the entire team. The full implementation, however, should not be done by this point, but merely simulated to show what the eventual designed system would look like.

The results of this meeting should be similar to those from the initial planning meeting: additional features that weren't recognized as important can be added to the development planning, and if any of the original features are found to be unnecessary, they should be removed from the plan. Revisiting the original plan, an updated user experience might look something like figure 4.8.

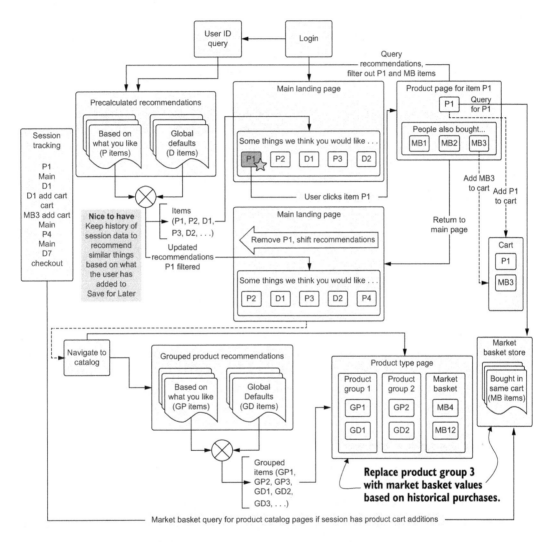

Figure 4.8 The final wireframe design of the recommendation engine resulting from the review of the experimentation results

With the experimentation phase out of the way, the DS team can explain that the nice-to-have elements from earlier phases are not only doable but can be integrated without a great deal of extra work. Figure 4.8 shows the integration of those ideas (market-basket analysis, dynamic filtering, and aggregated filtering), but also maintains one idea as a "nice to have." If it is found that, during development, the integration of this feature would be attainable, it is left as part of this living planning document.

The most important part of this stage's meeting is that everyone on the team (from the frontend developers who will be handling the passing of event data to the server to conduct the filtering, to the product team) is aware of the elements and moving pieces involved. The meeting ensures that the team understands which elements need to be scoped, as well as the general epics and stories that need to be created for sprint planning. Arriving at a collaborative estimation of the implementation is critical.

DEVELOPMENT SPRINT REVIEWS (PROGRESS REPORTS FOR A NONTECHNICAL AUDIENCE)

Conducting recurring meetings of a non-engineering-focused bent are useful for more than just passing information from the development teams to the business. They can serve as a bellwether of the state of the project and help indicate when integration of disparate systems can begin. These meetings should still be a high-level project-focused discussion, though.

The temptation for many cross-functional teams that work on projects like this is to turn these update meetings into either an über-retrospective or a super sprint-planning meeting. While such discussions can be useful (particularly for integration purposes among various engineering departments), those topics should be reserved for the engineering team's meetings.

A full-team progress report meeting should make the effort to generate a current-state demonstration of progress up to that point. Simulations of the solution should be shown to ensure that the business team and SMEs can provide relevant feedback on details that might have been overlooked by the engineers working on the project. These periodic meetings (either every sprint or every other sprint) can help prevent the aforementioned dreaded scope creep and the 11th-hour finding that a critical component that wasn't noticed as necessary is missing, causing massive delays in the project's delivery.

MVP REVIEW (FULL DEMO WITH UAT)

Code complete can mean different things to different organizations. In general, it is widely accepted to be a state in which

- Code is tested (and passes unit/integration tests).
- The system functions as a whole in an evaluation environment using production-scale data (models have been trained on production data).
- All agreed-upon features that have been planned are complete and perform as designed.

This doesn't mean that the subjective quality of the solution is met, though. This stage simply means the system will pass recommendations to the right elements on the page for this recommendation engine example. The MVP review and the associated UAT that goes into preparing for this meeting is the stage at which subjective measures of quality are done.

What does this mean for our recommendation engine? It means that the SMEs log in to the UAT environment and navigate the site. They look at the recommendations based on their preferences and make judgments on what they see. It also means that high-value accounts are simulated, ensuring that the recommendations that the SMEs are looking at through the lens of these customers are congruous to what they know about those types of users.

For many ML implementations, metrics are a wonderful tool (and most certainly should be heavily utilized and recorded for all modeling). But the best gauge of determining whether the solution is qualitatively solving the problem is to use the breadth of knowledge of internal users and experts who can use the system before it's deployed to end users.

At meetings evaluating the responses to UAT feedback of a solution developed over a period of months, I've seen arguments break out between the business and the DS team about how one particular model's validation metrics are higher, but the qualitative review quality is much lower than the inverse situation. This is exactly why this particular meeting is so critical. It may uncover glaring issues that were missed in not only the planning phases, but in the experimental and development phases as well. Having final sanity checks on the results of the solution can only make the end result better.

There is a critical bit of information to remember about this meeting and review period dealing with estimates of quality: nearly every project carries with it a large dose of *creator bias*. When creating something, particularly an exciting system that has a sufficient challenge to it, the creators can overlook and miss important flaws because of familiarity with and adoration of it.

> *A parent can never see how ugly or stupid their children are. It's human nature to unconditionally love what you've created.*
>
> —Every rational parent, ever.

If, at the end of one of these review meetings, the only responses are overwhelmingly positive praise of the solution, the team should have concerns. One of the side effects of creating a cohesive cross-functional team of people who all share in a collective feeling of project ownership is that emotional bias for the project may cloud judgment of its efficacy.

If you ever attend a summarization meeting about the quality of a solution and hear nary an issue, it would behoove you and the project team to pull in others at the company who have no stake in the project. Their unbiased and objective look at the solution could pay dividends in the form of actionable improvements or modifications that the team, looking through its bias of nigh-familial adoration of the project, would have completely missed.

PREPRODUCTION REVIEW (FINAL DEMO WITH UAT)

The final preproduction review meeting is right before "go time." Final modifications are complete, feedback from the UAT development-complete tests have been addressed, and the system has run without blowing up for several days.

The release is planned for the following Monday (pro tip: never release on a Friday), and a final look at the system is called for. System load testing has been done, responsiveness measured through simulation of 10 times the user volume at peak traffic, logging is working, and the model retraining on synthetic user actions has shown that the models adapt to the simulated data. Everything from an engineering point has passed all tests.

> *So why are we meeting again?*
>
> —Everyone who is exhausted by countless meetings

This final meeting before release should review a comparison to original plans, the features rejected for being out of scope, and any additions. This can help inform expectations of the analytics data that should be queried upon release. The systems required to collect the data for interactions for the recommendations have been built, and an A/B testing dataset has been created that can allow for analysts to check the performance of the project.

This final meeting should focus on where that dataset will be located, how engineers can query it, and which charts and reports will be available (and how to access them) for the nontechnical members of the team. The first few hours, days, and weeks of this new engine powering portions of the business is going to receive a great deal of scrutiny. To save the sanity of the analysts and the DS team, a bit of preparation work to ensure that people can have self-service access to the project's metrics and statistics will ensure that critical data-based decisions can be made by everyone in the company, even those not involved in creating the solution.

A note on patience

Releasing an ML project as significantly business-impacting as a recommendation engine for an e-commerce company is scary for the business. Business leaders are going to want to know what today's numbers are yesterday. Heck, they probably want to know what tomorrow's sales figures are going to be yesterday as well. With this level of anticipation and fear, it is important to communicate the virtue of patience in the analysis of the results. It's important to remind people to breathe.

Many latent factors can affect the perceived success or failure of a project, some of them potentially within the control of the design team, and others completely out of that control and wholly unknown. Because of this abundance of latent factors, any judgment about the design's efficacy needs to be withheld until a sufficient quantity of data is collected about the solution's performance in order to make a statistically valid adjudication.

Waiting, particularly for a team that has spent so much time and effort in seeing a project shift into production use, is challenging. People will want to check the status constantly, tracking the results of interactions in broad aggregations and trends with the speed and ferocity of laboratory mice pressing a lever for cheese to be dispensed.

It is in the best interests of the DS team to provide a crash course in statistical analysis for the decision makers in charge of this project. For a project such as a recommendation engine, explaining topics such as analysis of variance (ANOVA); degrees of freedom in complex systems; recency, frequency, monetary (RFM) cohort analysis; and confidence intervals at a relatively high level (focusing mostly on how confident an analysis will be at short time-intervals—well, specifically, how confident it will not be) will help those people make informed decisions. Depending on the number of users, the number of platforms you're serving, and the frequency at which customers arrive at your site, it may take several days or weeks to collect enough data to make an informed decision about the project's impact on the company.

In the meantime, work studiously to assuage worries and tamp down expectations that seeing a substantial rise in sales may or may not be directly attributable to the project. Only with careful and conscientious analysis of the data will anyone know what lift in engagement and revenue the new features may have.

4.2 Don't waste our time: Meeting with cross-functional teams

Chapter 3, in discussing the planning and experimentation phases of a project, noted that one of the most important aspects to keep in mind (aside from the ML work itself) is the communication *during those phases*. The feedback and evaluation received can be an invaluable tool to ensure that the MVP gets delivered on time and is as correct as can be so that the full development effort can proceed.

Let's take another look at our Gantt chart from figure 4.7 for keeping track of the high-level progress of each team's work throughout the phases. For the purposes of communication, however, we're concerned with only the top portion, shown in figure 4.9.

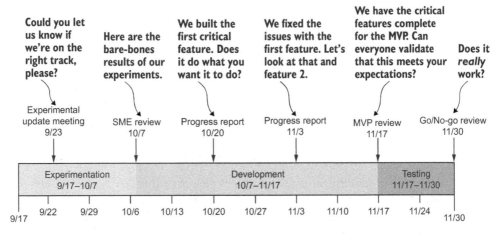

Figure 4.9 A translation of the critical meeting boundaries during the project

Depending on the type of project being built, countless more meetings may be spread throughout the phases (as well as follow-up meetings for months after release to review metrics, statistics, and estimations of the resiliency of the solution). Even if the development phase takes nine months, for instance, the biweekly progress report meetings are just repetitive discussions on the progress of accomplishments during the previous sprint. We're going to break down these phases in detail next.

4.2.1 Experimental update meeting: Do we know what we're doing here?

The *experimental update meeting* is the one that the DS team dreads more than any other, and the meeting that everyone else is incredibly excited for. The meeting interrupts the DS team in the midst of half-baked prototype implementations and unfinished research. The state of elements in flux is at nearly peak entropy.

This meeting is perhaps the second most important meeting in a project, though. This is the second-to-last time for the team members to have the ability to graciously raise a white flag in surrender if they've discovered that the project is untenable, will end up taking more time and money than the team has allocated, or is of such complexity that technologies will not be invented within the next 50 years to meet the requirements set forth. This is a time for honesty and reflection. It's a time to set one's ego aside and admit defeat, should the situation call for it.

The overriding question dominating this discussion should be, "Can we actually figure this out?" Any other discussions or ideations about the project are completely irrelevant at this point. It is up to the DS team to report on the status of its discoveries (without getting into the weeds of model-specific details or additional algorithms that they will be employing for testing, for example). The most critical discussion points for this meeting should be the following:

- How is the progress toward the prototype coming along?
  - Have you figured out any of the things that you're testing yet?
  - Which one looks like it's the most promising so far?
  - Are you going to stop pursuing anything that you had planned to test?
  - Are we on track to have a prototype by the scheduled due date?
- What risks have you uncovered so far?
  - Are there challenges with the data that the DE team needs to be made aware of?
  - Are we going to need a new technology, platform, or tooling that the team isn't familiar with?
  - As of right now, do you feel as though this is a solvable problem for us?

Aside from these direct questions, there really isn't much else to discuss that will do anything other than waste the time of the DS team at this point. These questions are all designed to evaluate whether this project is tenable from a personnel, technology, platform, and cost perspective.

Raising a white flag: When admitting defeat is acceptable

Few serious DS people ever like to admit defeat. For a junior person, fresh out of a PhD program in which research and experimentation can last months or even years, the concept of admitting that the problem is unsolvable will not ever enter their mind. That's a good thing, too, for these are the people who invent new algorithms! (Note: they get approval from their companies to do this and don't just choose to solve a problem in a novel way for the sake of it.)

When developing an ML solution for a company, however, the question of whether "this is a solvable problem for us" is not whether it is actually possible to solve the problem, but whether we can create a solution in a short enough time so as not to waste too much money and resources. Eagerness to arrive at a solution can cloud the estimation of capabilities for even the most skilled ML practitioner.

With enough experience in struggling through maintaining fragile or unstable solutions, a degree of temperance is gained. Desire for solving "all the things" can be suppressed with the knowledge that the solution might not be right for this particular project, the company, or the teams involved in maintaining it. Not every project, team, or company needs to tackle the most demanding and complex problems. Everyone has limits, after all. I can assure you that even if that white flag of defeat is raised, more than enough DS projects will remain to be worked on by the team and company for the next few centuries.

The earlier this is realized, the better. As mentioned earlier, creators' reluctance to abandon their creations only grows as time and energy expenditure toward that creation increases. If you can call a halt to a project early enough (and hopefully recognize the signs that this is not worth pursuing), you will be able to move onto something more worthwhile, instead of wading blindly through solutions that will end up creating little more than frustration, regret, and a complete loss of faith in the team—and in the worst case, ML in general at your company.

Provided that the answers are all positive in this meeting, work should commence in earnest. (Hopefully, no further interruptions to the work of the DS team members occur so that they can meet the next deadline and present at the next meeting.)

4.2.2 SME review/prototype review: Can we solve this?

By far the most important of the early meetings, the *SME review* is one you really don't want to skip. This is the point at which a resource commit occurs. It's the final decision on whether this project is going to happen or will be put into the backlog while a simpler problem is solved.

During this review session, the same questions should be asked as in the preceding meeting with the SME group. The only modification is that they should be tailored to answering whether the capability, budget, and desire exist for developing the full solution, now that the full scope of the work is more fully known.

The main focus of this discussion is typically on the mocked-up prototype. For our recommendation engine, the prototype may look like a synthetic wireframe of the website with a superimposed block of product image and labels associated with the product being displayed. It is always helpful, for the purposes of these demonstrations, to use real data. If you're showing a demonstration of recommendations to a group of SME members, show their data. Show the recommendations for their account (with their permission, of course!) and gauge their responses. Record each positive—but more important, each negative—impression that they give.

What if it's terrible?

Depending on the project, the models involved, and the general approach to the ML task, the subjective rating of a prototype being "terrible" can be either trivial to fix (properly tune the model, augment the feature set, and so forth) or can be a complete impossibility (the data doesn't exist to augment the additional feature requests, the data isn't granular enough to solve the request, or improving the prediction to the group's satisfaction would require a healthy dose of magic since the technology to solve that problem doesn't exist yet).

It's critical to quickly distill the reasons that any identified issues are happening. If the reasons are obvious and widely known as elements that can be modified by the DS team, simply answer as such. "Don't worry, we'll be able to adjust the predictions so that you don't see multiple pairs of sandals right next to one another" is perfectly fine. But if the problem is of an intensely complex nature, "I really don't want to see bohemian maxi dresses next to grunge shoes" (hopefully, you will be able to quickly search what those terms mean during the meeting), the response should be either thoughtfully articulated to the person, or recorded for a period of additional research, capped in time and effort to such research.

At the next available opportunity, the response may be along the lines of either, "We looked into that, and since we don't have data that declares what style these shoes are, we would have to build a CNN model, train it to recognize styles, and create the hundreds of thousands of labels needed to identify these styles across our product catalog. That would likely take several years to build." or "We looked into that, and because we have the labels for every product, we can easily group recommendations by style type to give you more flexibility around what sort of product mixing you would like."

Make sure that you know what is and is not possible before the prototype review session. If you encounter a request that you're not sure of, use the eight golden words of ML: "I don't know, but I'll go find out."

At the end of the demonstration, the entire team should have the ability to gauge whether the project is worth pursuing. You're looking for *consensus* that the recommended approach is something that everyone in the group (regardless of whether they know how it works) is *comfortable with as an appropriate direction* that the project is about to take.

Unanimity is not absolutely critical. But the team will be more cohesive if everyone's concerns are addressed and an unbiased and rational discussion is had to assuage their fears.

4.2.3   Development progress review(s): Is this thing going to work?

The *development progress reviews* are opportunities to "right the ship" during development. The teams should be focusing on milestones, such as these that show off the current state of the features being developed. Using the same wireframe approach used in the experimentation review phase is useful, as well as using the same prototype data so that a direct comparison between earlier stages can be seen by the entire team. Having a common frame of reference for the SMEs is helpful in order for them to gauge the subjective quality of the solution in terms that they fully understand.

The first few of these meetings should be reviews of the actual development. While the details should never go into the realm of specific aspects of software development, model tuning, or technical details of implementation, the overall progress of feature development should be discussed in abstract terms.

If, at a previous meeting, the quality of the predictions was determined to be lacking in one way or another, an update and a demonstration of the fix should be shown to ensure that the problems were solved to the satisfaction of the SME group. It is not simply sufficient to claim that "the feature is complete and has been checked into master." Prove it instead. Show them the fix with the same data that they had to originally identify the problem.

As the project moves further and further along, these meetings should become shorter and more focused on integration aspects. By the time the final meeting comes along for a recommendation project, the SME group should be looking at an actual demo of the website in a QA environment. The recommendations should be updating as planned through navigation, and validation of functionality on different platforms should be checked. As the complexity grows in these later stages, it can be helpful to push out builds of the QA version of the project to the SME team members so that they can evaluate the solution on their own time, bringing their feedback to the team at a regularly scheduled cadence meeting.

Unforeseen changes: Welcome to the world of ML

To say that most ML projects are complex is a sad understatement. Some implementations, such as a recommendation engine, can be among the most complex code bases that a company has. Setting aside the modeling, which can be relatively complex, the interrelated rules, conditions, and usages of the predictions can be complex enough to almost guarantee that things will be missed or overlooked even in the most thorough planning phases.

The sometimes fitful, but frequently fungible, nature of ML projects means that things will change. This is OK. Applying Agile to ML should allow for change to be as small of a disruption to the work (and the code) as possible.

Perhaps the data doesn't exist or is too costly to create to solve a particular problem in the framework of what has been built up to that point. With a few changes in approach, the solution can be realized, but it will be at the expense of an increase in

(continued)

complexity or cost for another aspect of the solution. This is, both fortunately and unfortunately (depending on what needs to be changed), a part of ML.

The important point to realize, while understanding that things change, is that when a blocker arises, it should be communicated clearly to everyone who needs to know about the change. Is it something affecting the API contract for the serving layer? Talk to the frontend team; don't call a full team-wide meeting to discuss technical details. Is it something that affects the ability to filter out gender-specific recommendations? That's a big deal (according to the SMEs), and talking through solutions could benefit having every bright mind in the group together to solve the problem and explore alternatives.

When problems arise (and they will), just ensure that you're not doing a "ninja-solve." Don't silently hack a solution that seems like it will work and not mention it to anyone. The chances that you create unforeseen issues later is incredibly high, and the impacts to the solution should be reviewed by the larger team.

4.2.4   *MVP review: Did you build what we asked for?*

By the time you're having the *MVP review*, everyone should be both elated and quite burned out on the project. It's the final phase; the internal engineering reviews have been done, the system is functioning correctly, the integration tests are all passing, latencies have been tested at large burst-traffic scale, and everyone involved in development is ready for a vacation.

The number of times I've seen teams and companies release a solution to production right at this stage is astounding. Each time that it's happened, they've all regretted it. After an MVP is built and agreed upon, the next several sprints should focus on code hardening (creating production-ready code that is testable, monitored, logged, and carefully reviewed—we'll get to all of these topics in parts 2 and 3 of this book).

Successful releases involve a stage after the engineering QA phase is complete in which the solution undergoes UAT. This stage is designed to measure the subjective quality of the solution, rather than the objective measures that can be calculated (statistical measures of the prediction quality) or the bias-laden subjective measure of the quality done by the SMEs on the team who are, by this point, emotionally invested in the project.

UAT phases are wonderful. It's at this point when the solution finally sees the light of day in the form of feedback from a curated group of people who were external to the project. This fresh, unbiased set of eyes can see the proposed solution for what it is, not for the toil and emotion that went into building it.

While all of the other work in the project is effectively measured via the Boolean scale of works/doesn't work, the ML aspect is a sliding scale of quality dependent on the interpretations of the end consumer of the predictions. For something as subjective as the relevancy of recommendations to an end user, this scale can be remarkably broad. To gather relevant data to create adjustments, one effective technique is a survey (particularly for a project as subjective as recommendations). Providing feedback based on a controlled test with a number ranking of effective quality can allow for standardization in the analysis of the responses, giving a broad estimation of any additional elements that need to be added to the engine or settings that need to be modified.

The critical aspect of this evaluation and metric collection is to ensure that the members evaluating the solution are not in any way vested in creating it, nor are they aware of the inner workings of the engine. Having foreknowledge of the functionality of any aspect of the engine may taint the results, and certainly if any of project team members were to be included in the evaluation, the review data would be instantly suspect.

When evaluating UAT results, it is important to use appropriate statistical methodologies to normalize the data. Scores, particularly those on a large numeric scale, need to be normalized within the range of scores that each user provides to account for review bias that most people have (some tending to either score maximum or minimum, others gravitating around the mean value, and others being overly positive in their review scores). Once normalized, the importance of each question and how it impacts the overall predictive quality of the model can be assessed and ranked, and a determination of feasibility to implement be conducted. Provided that there is enough time, the changes are warranted, and the implementation is of a low-enough risk to not require an additional full round of UAT, these changes may be implemented in order to create the best possible solution upon release.

Should you ever find yourself having made it through a UAT review session without a single issue being found, either you're the luckiest team ever, or the evaluators are completely checked out. This is quite common in smaller companies, where nearly everyone is fully aware and supportive of the project (with an unhealthy dose of confirmation bias). It can be helpful to bring in outsiders in this case to validate the solution (provided that the project is not something, for instance, akin to a fraud detection model or anything else of extreme sensitivity).

Many companies that are successful in building solutions for external-facing customers typically engage in alpha or beta testing periods of new features for this exact purpose: to elicit high-quality feedback from customers who are invested in their products and platforms. Why not use your most passionate end users (either internal or external) to give feedback? After all, they're the ones who are going to be using what you're building.

4.2.5 *Preproduction review: We really hope we didn't screw this up*

The end is nigh for the project. The final features have been added from UAT feedback, the development has been finished, the code hardened, QA checks have all passed, and the solution has been running for over a week without a single issue in a stress-testing environment. Metrics are set up for collecting performance, and analytics reporting datasets have been created, ready to be populated for measuring the success of the project. The last thing to do is to ship it to production.

It's best to meet one final time, but not for self-congratulations (definitely do that later, though, as a full cross-functional team). This final *preproduction review* meeting should be structured as a project-based retrospective and analysis of features. Everyone at this meeting, regardless of area of expertise and level of contribution to the final product, should be asking the same thing: "Did we build what we set out to build?"

To answer this question, the original plans should be compared to the final designed solution. Each feature that was in the original design should be gone through and validated that it functions in real time from within the QA (testing) environment. Do the items get filtered out when switching between pages? If multiple items are added to the cart in succession, do all of those related products get filtered or just the last one? What if items are removed from the cart—do the products stay removed from the recommendations? What happens if a user navigates the site and adds a thousand products to the cart and then removes all of them?

Hopefully, all of these scenarios have been tested long before this point, but it's an important exercise to engage in with the entire team to ensure that the functionality is conclusively confirmed to be implemented correctly. After this point, there's no going back; once it's released to production, it's in the hands of the customer, for better or for worse. We'll get into how to handle issues in production in later chapters, but for now, think of the damage to the reputation of the project if something that is fundamentally broken is released. It's this last preproduction meeting where concerns and last-minute fixes can be planned before the irrevocable production release.

4.3   Setting limits on your experimentation

We've gone through the exhausting slog of preparing everything that we can up until this point for the recommendation engine project. Meetings have been attended, concerns and risks have been voiced, plans for design have been conducted and based on the research phase, and we have a clear set of models to try out. It's finally time to play some jazz, get creative, and see if we can make something that's not total garbage.

Before we get too excited, though, it's important to realize that, as with all other aspects of ML project work, we should be doing things in moderation and with a thoughtful purpose behind what we're doing. This applies more so to the experimentation phase than any other aspect of the project—primarily because this is one of the few completely siloed-off phases.

What might we do with this personalized recommendation engine if we had all the time and resources in the world? Would we research the latest whitepaper and try to implement a completely novel solution? (You may, depending on your industry and company.) Would we think about building a broad ensemble of recommendation models to cover all of our ideas? (Let's do a collaborative filtering model for each of our customer cohorts based on their customer lifetime value scores for propensity and their general product-group affinity, and then merge that with an FP-growth market-basket model to populate sparse predictions for certain users.) Perhaps we would build a graph-embedding to a deep learning model that would find relationships in product and user behavior to potentially create the most sophisticated and accurate predictions achievable.

All of these are neat ideas and could be worthwhile if the entire purpose of our company was to recommend items to humans. However, these are all *very expensive to develop* in the currency that most companies are most strapped for: time.

We need to understand that time is a finite resource, as is the patience of the business unit requesting the solution. As we discussed in section 3.2.2, the scoping of the experimentation is tied directly to the resources available: the number of data scientists on the team, the number of options we are going to attempt to compare, and, most critically, the time that we have to complete this. The final limitations that we need to control for, knowing that there are limited constraints on time and developers, is that only so much can be built within an MVP phase.

It's tempting to want to fully build out a solution that you have in your head and see it work exactly as you've designed it. This works great for internal tools that are helping your own productivity or projects that are internal to the DS team. But pretty much every other thing that an ML engineer or data scientist is going to work on in their careers has a customer aspect, be it an internal or external one. This means that you will have someone else depending on your work to solve a problem. They will have a nuanced understanding of the needs of the solution that might not align with your assumptions.

Not only is it, as mentioned earlier, incredibly important to include them in the process of aligning the project to the goals, but it's potentially dangerous to fully build out a tightly coupled and complex solution without getting their input on the validity of what you're building to the issue of solving the problem. The way of solving this issue of involving the SMEs in the process is to set boundaries around prototypes that you'll be testing.

4.3.1 Set a time limit

Perhaps one of the easiest ways to stall or cancel a project is by spending too much time and effort on the initial prototype. This can happen for any number of reasons, but most of them, I've found, are due to poor communication within a team, incorrect assumptions by non-DS team members about how the ML process works (refinement through testing with healthy doses of trial, error, and reworking mixed in), or an inexperienced DS team assuming that they need to have a "perfect" solution before anyone sees their prototypes.

The best way to prevent this confusion and complete wasting of time is to set limits on the time allotted for experimentation surrounding vetting of ideas to try. By its very nature, this limitation will eliminate the volume of code written at this stage. It should be clear to all members of the project team that the vast majority of ideas expressed during the planning stages are not going to be implemented for the vetting phase; rather, in order to make the crucial decision about which implementation to go with, the bare minimum amount of the project should be tested.

Figure 4.10 shows the most minimalistic amount of implementation required to achieve the goals of the experimentation phase. Any additional work, at this time, does not serve the need at the moment: to decide on an algorithm that will work well at scale and at cost, and that meets objective and subjective quality standards.

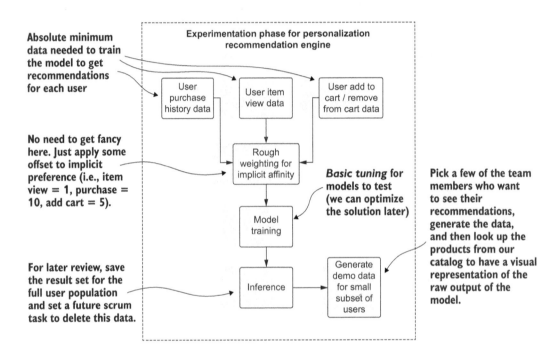

Figure 4.10   Mapping the high-level experimentation phase for the teams testing ideas

In comparison, figure 4.11 shows a simplified view of some potential core features based on the initial plan from the planning meeting.

By comparing figure 4.10 and figure 4.11, it should be easy to imagine the increasing scope of work involved in the transition from the first plan to the second. Entirely new models need to be built, a great deal of dynamic run-specific aggregations and filtering need to be done, custom weighting must be incorporated, and potentially dozens of additional datasets need to be generated. None of these elements solves the core problem at the boundary of experimentation: which model should we go with for developing?

Limiting the time to make this decision will prevent (or at least minimize) the natural tendency of most ML practitioners to want to build a solution, regardless of plans that have been laid out. Sometimes forcing less work to get done is a good thing for the cause of reducing churn and making sure the right elements are being worked on.

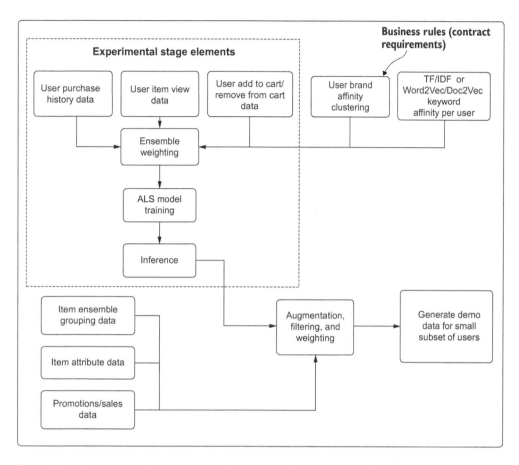

Figure 4.11 **A pseudo architectural plan for the expanded features involved in the development phase, realized by conducting effective experimentation and getting feedback from the larger team**

A note on experimental code quality

Experimental code should be a little "janky." It should be scripted, commented out, ugly, and nigh-untestable. It should be a script, filled with charts, graphs, print statements, and all manner of bad coding practices.

It's an experiment, after all. If you're following a tight timeline to get an experimental decision-of-action to be made, you likely won't have time to be creating classes, methods, interfaces, enumerators, factory builder patterns, couriering configurations, and so forth. You're going to be using high-level APIs, declarative scripting, and a static dataset.

Don't worry about the state of the code at the end of experimentation. It should serve as a reference for development efforts in which proper coding is done (and under no circumstances should experimental code be expanded upon for the final solution),

> **(continued)**
>
> wherein the team is building maintainable software, using standard software development practices.
>
> But for this stage, and only this stage, it's usually OK to write some pretty horrible-looking scripts. We all do it sometimes.

4.3.2   Can you put this into production? Would you want to maintain it?

While the primary purpose of an experimentation phase, to the larger team, is to make a decision on the predictive capabilities of a model's implementation, one of the chief purposes internally, among the DS team, is to determine whether the solution is tenable for the team. The DS team lead, architect, or senior DS person on the team should be taking a close look at what is going to be involved in this project, asking difficult questions, and producing honest answers. Some of the most important questions are as follows:

- How long is this solution going to take to build?
- How complex is this code base going to be?
- How expensive is this going to be to train based on the schedule it needs to be retrained at?
- Does my team have the skill required to maintain this solution? Does everyone know this algorithm/language/platform?
- How quickly will we be able to modify this solution should something dramatically change with the data that it's training or inferring on?
- Has anyone else reported success with using this methodology/platform/language/API? Are we reinventing the wheel or are we building a square wheel?
- How much additional work will the team have to do to make this solution work while meeting all of the other feature goals?
- Is this going to be extensible? When the inevitable version 2.0 of this is requested, will we be able to enhance this solution easily?
- Is this testable?
- Is this auditable?

Innumerable times in my career, I've been either the one building these prototypes or the one asking these questions while reviewing someone else's prototype. Although an ML practitioner's first reaction to seeing results is frequently, "Let's go with the one that has the best results," many times the "best" one ends up being either nigh-impossible to fully implement or a nightmare to maintain.

It is of paramount importance to weigh these future-thinking questions about maintainability and extensibility, whether regarding the algorithm in use, the API that calls the algorithm, or the very platform that it's running on. Taking the time to properly evaluate the production-specific concerns of an implementation, instead of simply the predictive power of the model's prototype, can mean the difference between a successful solution and vaporware.

4.3.3 *TDD vs. RDD vs. PDD vs. CDD for ML projects*

We seem to have an infinite array of methodologies to choose from when developing software. From waterfall to the Agile revolution (and all of its myriad flavors), each has benefits and drawbacks.

We won't discuss the finer points of which development approach might be best for particular projects or teams. Absolutely fantastic books have been published that explore these topics in depth, and I highly recommend reading them to improve the development processes for ML projects. *Becoming Agile in an Imperfect World* by Greg Smith and Ahmed Sidky (Manning, 2009) and *Test Driven: TDD and Acceptance TDD for Java Developers* by Lasse Koskela (Manning, 2007) are notable resources. Worth discussing here, however, are four general approaches to ML development (one being a successful methodology, the others being cautionary tales).

TEST-DRIVEN DEVELOPMENT OR FEATURE-DRIVEN DEVELOPMENT

Pure *test-driven development* (*TDD*) is incredibly challenging to achieve for ML projects (and certainly unable to achieve the same test coverage in the end that traditional software development can), mostly due to the nondeterministic nature of models themselves. A pure *feature-driven development* (*FDD*) approach can cause significant rework during a project.

But most successful approaches to ML projects embrace aspects of both of these development styles. Keeping work incremental, adaptable to change, and focused on modular code that is not only testable but focused entirely on required features to meet the project guidelines is a proven approach that helps deliver the project on time while also creating a maintainable and extensible solution.

These Agile approaches will need to be borrowed from and adapted in order to create an effective development strategy that works not only for the development team, but also for an organization's general software development practices. In addition, specific design needs can dictate slightly different approaches to implementing a particular project.

Why would I want to use different development philosophies?

When discussing ML as a broad topic, we run the risk of oversimplifying an incredibly complex and dynamic discipline. Since ML is used for such a wide breadth of use cases (as well as having such a broad set of skills, tools, platforms, and languages), the magnitude of difference in complexity among various projects is truly astounding.

For a project as simple as "we would like to predict customer churn," a TDD-heavy approach can be a successful way of developing a solution. A model and inference pipeline for implementations of churn-prediction models is typically rather simple (the vast majority of the complexity is in the data engineering portion). Therefore, modularizing

(continued)

code and building the code base in such a way that each component of the data acquisition phase can be independently tested can be beneficial to an efficient implementation cycle and an easier-to-maintain final product.

On the other hand, a project that is as complex as, say, an ensemble recommender engine may use real-time prediction serving, have hundreds of logic-based reordering features, employ the predictions from several models, and have a large multidiscipline team working on it. This type of project could greatly benefit from using the testability components of TDD, but throughout the project, use the principles of FDD to ensure that only the most critical components are developed as needed to help reduce feature sprawl.

Each project is unique. The team lead or architect in charge of the implementation from a development perspective should set the expectations of work velocity with respect to testing and general code architecture that is adapted to the project's needs. With the proper balance in place of best practices from these proven standards of development, a project can hit its required feature-complete state at its lowest-risk-to-failure point so that the solution is stable and maintainable while in production.

PRAYER-DRIVEN DEVELOPMENT

At one point, all ML projects resulted from *prayer-driven development* (*PDD*). In many organizations that are new to ML development, projects still do. Before the days of well-documented high-level APIs to make modeling work easier, everything was a painful exercise in hoping that what was being scratched and cobbled together would work at least well enough that the model wouldn't detonate in production. That hoping (and praying) for things to "just work, please" isn't what I'm referring to here, though.

What I'm facetiously alluding to is rather the act of frantically scanning for clues for solving a particular problem by following bad advice from either internet forums or someone who likely has no more actual experience than the searcher. The searcher may find a blog covering a technology or application of ML that seems somewhat relevant to the problem at hand, only to find out, months later, that the magical solution that they were hoping for is nothing more than fluff.

Prayer-driven ML development is the process of handing over problems that one doesn't know how to solve into the figurative hands of some all-knowing person who has solved it before, all in the goal of eliminating the odious tasks of proper research and evaluation of technical approaches. Taking such an easy road rarely ends well. With broken code bases, wasted effort ("I did what they did—why doesn't this work?") and, in the most extreme cases, project abandonment, this is a problem and a development antipattern that is growing in magnitude and severity.

The most common effects that I see happen from this approach of ML "copy culture" are that people who embrace this mentality want to either use a single tool for every problem (Yes, XGBoost is a solid algorithm. No, it's not applicable to every supervised learning task) or try only the latest and greatest fad ("I think we should use TensorFlow and Keras to predict customer churn").

If all you know is XGBoost, everything looks like a gradient boosting problem.

When limiting yourself in this manner—not doing research, not learning or testing alternate approaches, and restricting experimentation or development to a narrow set of tools—the solution will reflect those limitations and self-imposed boundaries. In many cases, latching onto a single tool or a new fad and forcing it onto every problem creates suboptimal solutions or, more disastrously, forces you to write far more lines of unnecessarily complex code in order to fit a square peg into a round hole.

A good way of detecting whether the team (or yourself) is on the path of PDD is to see what is planned for a project's prototyping phase. How many models are being tested? How many frameworks are being vetted? If the answer to either of these is "one," and no one on the team has solved that particular problem several times before, you're doing PDD. And you should stop.

CHAOS-DRIVEN DEVELOPMENT

Also known as *cowboy development* (or hacking), *chaos-driven development* (*CDD*) is the process of skipping experimentation and prototyping phases altogether. It may seem easier at first, since not much refactoring is happening early on. However, using such an approach of building ML on an as-needed basis during project work is fraught with peril.

As modification requests and new feature demands arise through the process of developing a solution, the sheer volume of rework, sometimes from scratch, slows the project to a crawl. By the end (if it makes it that far), the fragile state of the DS team's sanity will entirely prevent any future improvements or changes to the code because of the spaghetti nature of the implementation.

If there is one thing that I hope you take away from this book, it's to avoid this development style. I've not only been guilty of it in my early years of ML project work, but have also seen it become one of the biggest reasons for project abandonment in companies that I've worked with. If you can't read your code, fix your code, or even explain how it works, it's probably not going to work well.

RESUME-DRIVEN DEVELOPMENT

By far the most detrimental development practice—designing an overengineered, show-off implementation to a problem—is one of the primary leading causes of projects being abandoned after they are in production. These *resume-driven development* (*RDD*) implementations are generally focused on a few key characteristics:

- A *novel algorithm* is involved.
  - Unless it's warranted by the unique nature of the problem
  - Unless multiple experienced ML experts agree that no alternative solution is available

- A new (*unproven in the ML community*) framework for executing the project's job is involved (with features that serve no purpose in solving the problem).
  - There's not really an excuse for this nowadays.
- A blog post, or series of blog posts, about the solution are being written *during development* (after the project is done is fine, though!).
  - This should raise a healthy suspicion among the team.
  - There will be time to self-congratulate after the project is released to production, has been verified to be stable for a month, and impact metrics have been validated.
- An overwhelming amount of the code is devoted to the ML algorithm as opposed to feature engineering or validation.
  - For the vast majority of ML solutions, the ratio of feature engineering code to model code should always be > 4x.
- An abnormal level of discussion in status meetings is about the model, rather than the problem to be solved.
  - We're here to *solve a business problem*, aren't we?

This isn't to say that novel algorithm development or incredibly in-depth and complex solutions aren't called for. They most certainly can be. But they should be pursued only if all other options have been exhausted.

For the example that we've been reviewing throughout this chapter, if someone were to go from a position of having nothing in place at all to proposing a unique solution that has never been built before, objections should be raised. This development practice and the motivations behind it are not only toxic to the team that will have to support the solution but will poison the well of the project and almost guarantee that it will take longer, be more expensive, and do nothing apart from pad the developer's resume.

4.4   *Planning for business rules chaos*

As part of our recommendation engine that we've been building throughout this chapter (or, at least, speaking of the process of building), a great many features crept up that were implemented and that augmented the results of the model. Some of these were to solve particular use cases for the end result (collection aggregations to serve the different parts of the site and app for visualization purposes, for instance), while others were designed for contractual obligations to vendors.

The most critical ones protect users from offense or filter inappropriate content. I like to refer to all of these additional nuances to ML as *business rules chaos*. These specific restrictions and controls are incredibly important but also frequently the most challenging aspects of a project to implement correctly.

Failing to plan for them accordingly (or failing to implement them entirely) is an *almost guarantee* that your project will be shelved before it hits its expected release date. If these restrictions are not caught before release, they could damage the brand of your company.

4.4.1 Embracing chaos by planning for it

Let's pretend for a moment that the DS team working on the MVP for the recommendation engine doesn't realize that the company sells sensitive products. This is understandable, since most e-commerce companies sell a lot of products, and the DS team members are not product specialists. They may be users of the site, but certainly aren't all likely to be intimately familiar with everything that's sold. Since they aren't aware that items could be offensive as part of recommendations, they fail to identify these items and filter them out of their result sets.

There's nothing wrong with missing this detail. In my experience, details like this always come up in complex ML solutions. The only way to plan for them is to expect things like this to come up, and to architect the code base in such a way that it has proverbial "levers and knobs"—functions or methods that can be applied or modified through passed-in configurations. Then, implementing a new restriction doesn't require a full code rewrite or weeks of adjustments to the code base to implement.

When in the process of developing a solution, a lot of ML practitioners tend to think mostly about the quality of the model's predictive power above all other things. Countless hours of experimentation, tuning, validating, and reworking of the solution is done in the pursuit of attaining a mathematically optimal solution that will solve the problem best in terms of validation metrics. Because of this, it can be more than slightly irritating to find out that, after having spent so much time and energy in building an ideal system, additional constraints need to be placed onto the model's predictions.

These constraints exist in almost all systems (either initially or eventually if the solution is in production for long enough) that have predictive ML at their core. There may be legal reasons to filter or adjust the results in a financial system. There could, perhaps, be content restrictions on a recommendation system based on preventing a customer from taking offense to a prediction (trust me, you don't want to explain to anyone why a minor was recommended an adult-oriented product). Whether for financial, legal, ethical, or just plain old common-sense reasons, inevitably something is going to have to change with the raw predictions from most ML implementations.

It's definitely a best practice to understand potential restrictions before you start spending too much time in development of a solution. Knowing restrictions ahead of time can influence the overall architecture of the solution and the feature engineering, and allow for controlling the method in which an ML model learns the vector. It can save the team countless hours of adjustment and eliminate costly-to-run and difficult-to-read code bases filled with never-ending chains of `if/elif/else` statements to handle post hoc corrections to the output of the model.

For our recommendation engine project, a lot of rules likely need to be added to a raw predictive output from an ALS model. As an exercise, let's revisit the earlier development phase work component diagram. Figure 4.12 shows the elements of the planned solution specifically intended to enforce constraints on the output of the recommendations. Some are absolutely required—contract requirement elements, as

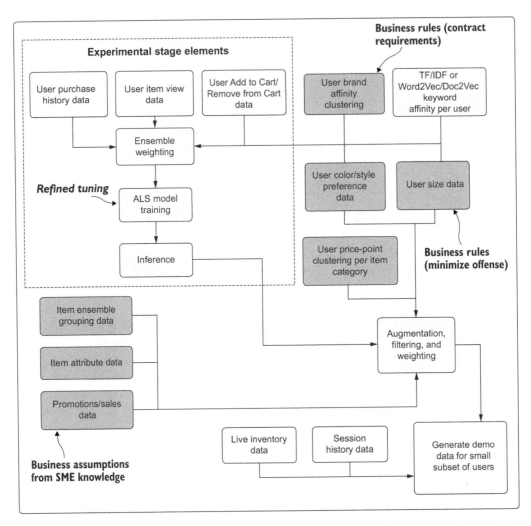

Figure 4.12   Identifying business contextual requirements for the recommendation engine project—a risk-detection diagram, in other words

well as filters intended to cull products that are inappropriate for certain users. Others are ideas that the project team suspects are going to be heavily influential in getting the user to engage with the recommendation.

This diagram shows the locations, but more important, the *type of business restriction* to the model. In the planning phases, after experimentation and before full development begins, it is worthwhile to identify and classify each of these features.

The absolutely required aspects, shown in figure 4.12 as Business Rules, *must be planned within the scope* of the work and built as an integral part of the modeling process. Whether they're constructed in such a way as to be tune-able aspects of the solution (through weights, conditional logic, or Boolean switches) is up to the needs of the team, but they should be considered essential features, not optional or testable features.

The remaining aspects of rules, marked in figure 4.12 as Business Assumptions, can be handled in various ways. They could be prioritized as testable features (configurations will be built that allow for A/B testing different ideas for fine-tuning the solution). Alternatively, they could be seen as future work that is not part of the initial MVP release of the engine, simply implemented as placeholders within the engine that can be easily modified at a later time.

4.4.2 Human-in-the-loop design

Whichever approach works best for the team (and particularly for the ML developers working on the engine), the important fact to keep in mind is that these sorts of restrictions to the model output should be identified early and allowances be made for them to be mutable for the purposes of changing their behavior, if warranted. The last thing that you want to build for these requirements, though, is hardcoded values in the source code that would require a modification to the source code in order to test.

It's best to approach these items in a way that you can empower the SMEs to modify the performance, to rapidly change the behavior of the system without having to take it down for a lengthy release period. You also want to ensure that controls are established that restrict the ability to modify these without going through appropriate validation procedures.

4.4.3 What's your backup plan?

What happens when there's a new customer? What happens with recommendations for a customer that has returned after having not visited your site in more than a year? What about for a customer who has viewed only one product and is returning to the site the next day?

Planning for sparse data isn't a concern just for recommendation engines, but it certainly impacts their performance more so than other applications of ML.

All ML projects should be built with an expectation of data-quality issues arising, necessitating the creation of fallback plans when data is malformed or missing. This safety mode can be as complex as using registration information or IP geolocation tracking to pull aggregated popular products from the region that the person is logging in from (hopefully, they're not using a virtual private network, or VPN), or can be as simple as generic popularity rankings from all users. Whichever methodology is chosen, it's important to have a safe set of generic data to fall back to if personalization datasets are not available for the user.

This general concept applies to many use cases, not just recommendation engines. If you're running predictions but don't have enough data to fully populate the feature vector, this could be a similar issue to having a recommendation engine cold-start problem. There are multiple ways to handle this issue, but at the stage of planning, it's important to realize that this is going to be a problem and that a form of fallback should be in place in order to produce some level of information to a service expecting data to be returned.

4.5 *Talking about results*

Explaining how ML algorithms work to a layperson is challenging. Analogies, thought-experiment-based examples, and comprehensible diagrams to accompany them are difficult at the best of times (when someone is asking for the sake of genuine curiosity). When the questions are posed by members of a cross-functional team who are trying to get a project released, it can be even more challenging and mentally taxing, since they have expectations regarding what they want the black box to do. When those same team members are finding fault with the prediction results or quality and are aggravated at the subjectively poor results, this adventure into describing the functionality and capabilities of the chosen algorithms can be remarkably stressful.

In any project's development, whether at the early stages of planning, during prototype demonstrations, or even at the conclusion of the development phase while the solution is undergoing UAT assessment, questions will invariably come up. The following questions are specific to our example recommendation engine, but I can assure you that alternative forms of these questions can be applied to any ML project, from a fraud-prediction model to a threat-detection video-classification model:

- "Why does it think that I would like that? I would never pick something like that for myself!"
- "Why is it recommending umbrellas? That customer lives in the desert. What is it thinking?!"
- "Why does it think that this customer would like t-shirts? They only buy haute couture."

The flippant answer to all of these questions is simple: "It doesn't think. The algorithm only 'knows' what we 'taught' it." (Pro tip: if you're going to use this line, don't; for the sake of further tenure in your position, place emphasis on those quoted elements when delivering this line. On second thought, don't talk to colleagues like this, even if you're annoyed at having to explain this concept for the 491st time during the project.) The acceptable answer, conveyed in a patient and understanding tone, is one of simple honesty: "We don't have the data to answer that question." It's best to exhaust all possibilities of feature-engineering creativity before claiming that, but if you have, it's really the only answer that is worth giving.

What has been successful for me is to explain this issue and its root cause through articulating the concept of cause and effect, but in a way that relates to the ML aspect of the problem. Figure 4.13 shows a helpful visualization for explaining what ML can, but also, more important, what it cannot do.

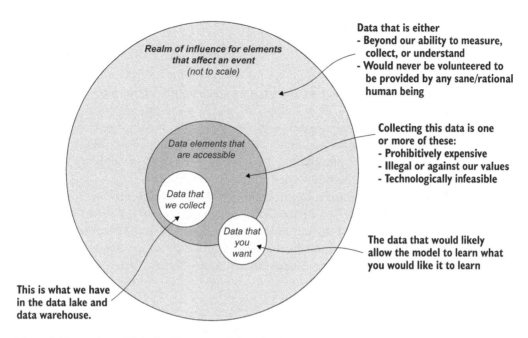

Figure 4.13 Realms of data for ML—we can't have it all

As figure 4.13 shows, the data that the person in the review meeting is asking for is simply beyond the capability to acquire. Perhaps the data that would inform someone's subjective preference for a pair of socks is of such a personal nature that there is simply no way to infer or collect this information. Perhaps, in order to have the model draw the conclusion that is being asked for, the data to be collected would be so complex, expensive to store, or challenging to collect that it's simply not within the budget of the company to do so.

When an SME at the meeting asks, "Why didn't this group of people add these items to their cart if the model predicted that these were so relevant for them?," there is absolutely no way you can answer that. Instead of dismissing this line of questioning, which will invariably lead to irritation and frustration from the asker, simply posit a few questions of your own while explaining the view of reality that the model can "see." Perhaps the user was shopping for someone else. Perhaps they're looking for something new that they were inspired by from an event that we can't see in the form of data. Perhaps they simply just weren't in the mood.

There is a staggering infiniteness to the latent factors that can influence the behavior of events in the "real world." Even if you were to collect all of the knowable information and metrics about the observable universe, you would still not be able to predict, reliably, what is going to happen, where it's going to happen, and why it will or will not happen as such. It's understandable for that SME to want to know why the model behaved a certain way and the expected outcome (the user giving us money for our goods) didn't happen; as humans, we strive for explainable order.

Relax. We, like our models, can't be perfect.

The world's a pretty chaotic place. We can only hope to guess right at what's going to happen more than we guess wrong.

Explaining limitations in this way (that we can't predict something that we don't have information to train on) can help, particularly at the outset of the project, to dispel assumed unrealistic capabilities of ML to laypeople. Having these discussions within the context of the project and including how the data involved relates to the business can be a great tool in eliminating disappointment and frustration later as the project moves forward through milestones of demos and reviews.

Explaining expectations clearly, in plain-speak, particularly to the project leader, can be the difference between an acceptable risk that can be worked around in creative ways and a complete halt to the project and abandonment due to the solution not doing what the business leader had in mind. As so many wise people have said throughout the history of business, "It's always best to under-promise and over-deliver."

> ### Explain it to me like I'm a five-year-old, please
>
> At times it can feel as though, when speaking about models, data, machine learning, algorithms, and so forth, you are living through the Allegory of the Cave. Although it may feel like you're the one who's been in the sun and are trying to convince everyone what daylight is like, nothing could be further from the truth.
>
> The goal in communication that we've been discussing in the last two chapters is simple: to be understood. Resist the urge to think of yourself or your team as the members of the cave dwellers who have "stepped into the light" and are merely returning to the cave to show the miraculous imagery of full color and the "real world." You may know more about ML than the uninitiated, but taking the stance of being "the enlightened" and adopting a superior tone when explaining concepts to other team members will only breed derision and anger, just as with the returning group that attempted to drag the others to the light.
>
> You will always have more success explaining concepts in familiar terms to your audience and approaching complex topics through allegory and examples rather than defaulting to exclusionary dialogue that will not be fully understood by others on the team who are not familiar with the inner workings of your profession.

Summary

- Focusing cross-functional team communication on objective, nontechnical, solution-based, and jargon-free speech will aid in creating a collaborative and inclusive environment that ensures an ML project meets its goals.
- Establishing specific milestones for project functionality demonstrations to a broad team of SMEs and internal customers will dramatically reduce rework and unexpected functionality shortcomings in ML projects.

- Approaching the complexities of research, experimentation, and prototyping work with the same rigor that is applied to Agile development can reduce the time to arrive at a viable option for development.
- Understanding, defining, and incorporating business rules and expectations early in a project will help ensure that ML implementations are adapted and designed around these requirements, rather than shoehorning them in after a solution is already built.
- Avoiding discussion about implementation details, esoteric ML-related topics, and explanations about how the internals of an algorithm work will help deliver a clear and focused discussion of the performance of a solution, allowing for creative discourse from all team members.

Experimentation in action: Planning and researching an ML project

This chapter covers

- The details of a project's research phase
- The process and methodology of conducting solution experimentation for a project

We spent the preceding two chapters focusing on the processes surrounding planning, scoping of work, and communication among a team working on an ML project. This chapter and the next two focus on the next most critical aspects of ML work as it pertains to data scientists: research, experimentation, prototyping, and MVP development.

Once a project's requirements have been thoroughly captured from planning meetings (as much as can be realistically achieved) and the goal of the modeling solution has been defined, the next phase of creating an ML solution is to begin *experimentation and research*. These processes, conducted without an appropriate level of structure, can easily result in a cancelled project.

Projects may be cancelled because of a seemingly endless experimentation phase, wherein no clear direction for finalizing an approach to a solution is decided on. Stalled projects may also be the result of poor predictive capabilities. Whether due to indecision or an inability to meet accuracy expectations, the prevention of stalled and cancelled projects that have data and algorithm issues starts in the experimentation phase.

No concrete rule set exists for estimating exactly how long an experimentation phase should last, because a myriad of complexities may arise from each unique project. However, the methodologies in this chapter guarantee a reduction in the amount of time to reach a favorable MVP state and a marked reduction in the amount of duplicate effort that a team would face were they to approach experimentation without such methods.

This chapter covers the first phase of ML experimentation, as shown in figure 5.1. We will go through a proven method for setting up an effective experimentation environment, evaluating a dataset through the creation of reusable visualization functions, and conducting research and modeling approach validations in a controlled and efficient manner to help get to the MVP phase earlier with less rework.

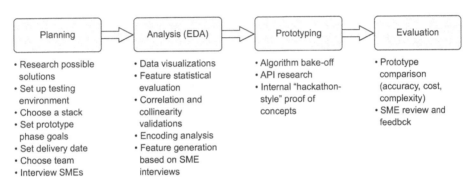

Figure 5.1   The ML experimentation process

We'll see how to organize and plan appropriate research, set expectations and rules within the planning phase, properly analyze the scenario that we'll be solving in this chapter to inform our model selection and experimentation, and finally, conduct our experiments and build useful utilities for the project at hand. All of these stages and processes are designed to maximize the opportunity to have an easier development period and to minimize not only the risk of creating technical debt from the start of the project, but also the risk of project abandonment.

We spent the previous chapters working through the pre-experimentation phases of a recommendation engine for an e-commerce company. We're going to use a much simpler example in these next few chapters in the interests of brevity. While this time-series modeling project is much simpler than many ML implementations, the aspects that we're covering are generally universally applicable to all ML work; when they are not, I provide additional comments in sidebar discussions. As with all things in software development, a quality project starts with planning.

5.1   *Planning experiments*

Let's pretend for this chapter that we work for a company that is in the business of supplying peanuts (specifically, those individual-serving wrapped peanuts that are handed out on most major airlines throughout the world, coupled with a square napkin, a ridged plastic cup engineered to tip beverages into laps when a seatmate adjusts to a more comfortable position, and a twice-pasteurized can of carbonated beverage). The business unit in charge of logistics for the peanuts has requested a project to be developed that can forecast demand of these sad in-flight snacks because of the increased pressure that they are getting from airlines about the excessive quantities of bulk-shipped dry-roasted legumes that they continually have to throw away when their expiration dates strike.

The meetings have been conducted, the requirements have been gathered, and the ML team has internally discussed the project. The general consensus is that we're looking at a simple demand forecast time-series prediction problem. But where do we start, now that we know the problem that we're trying to solve? We also have two weeks to come up with a rough MVP to show that we have a proven approach to solving this problem. Best get to it.

What we're going to be getting to is illustrated in figure 5.2: the planning phase of ML experimentation. In this phase, a lot of things will be read, most will hopefully be retained in our heads, and many browser bookmarks will be created.

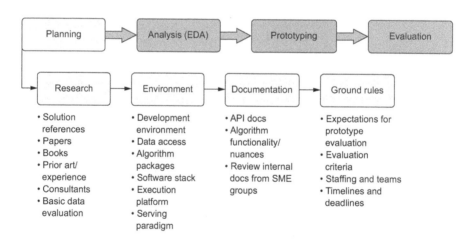

Figure 5.2   The ML experimentation planning phase road map

5.1.1   *Perform basic research and planning*

The first thing that the team members are going to do, once they get back to their desks after the planning meeting, is look at the data available. Since we're a peanut manufacturer, and not in any partnership with major airlines, we're not going to get ticket sales forecasting data. We certainly don't have time to build web scrapers to attempt to see flight capacity for each airport (nor would anyone want to do this who has ever attempted to build a scraper before). What we do have available, though, is historic passenger capacity that the airport transit authorities provide freely.

We know from figure 5.2 that one of the first actions that we should be doing to understand the nature of the data is to visualize it and run a few statistical analyses we have available. Most people would simply load the data into their local computer's environment and begin working in a notebook.

This is a recipe for disaster, though. A default Python environment that is running on the main operating system of your primary computer is anything but pristine. To minimize the amount of time wasted on struggling with a development environment (and help prepare for a smooth transition to the development phase later), we need to create a clean environment for our testing. For guidance on getting started with Docker and Anaconda to create a development environment for the code listings in this chapter and all subsequent chapters, see appendix B at the end of this book.

Now that we have an isolated environment (with persistence of the notebook storage location on the container mapped to a local filesystem location), we can get the sample data into this location and create a new notebook for experimentation.

A QUICK VISUALIZATION OF THE DATASET

The first thing that should be done before choosing an ML approach to solving the problem is the most trivial (but frequently overlooked) aspect of data science: getting to know your data. For the airport forecasting, let's take a look at the data available to us. Listing 5.1 demonstrates a scripted approach to quickly visualize one of the time series (JFK domestic passengers) that needs to be forecasted.

> **NOTE** To follow along exactly with this example, you can acquire this dataset by cloning a repo maintained by the Alan Turing Institute. Navigate to the local notebook directory that was synced in the steps outlined in appendix B and run through the command-line statement `git clone https://github.com/alan-turing-institute/TCPD.git`.

Listing 5.1 Visualizing the data

Makes a shallow copy of the DataFrame so we can use mutable modifications to it

Converts the Month column to a datetime object so we can assemble the date from it. (Currently, it's a string three-letter abbreviation of the month.)

```
import pandas as pd
import numpy as np
import matplotlib.pylab as plt

ts_file = '/opt/notebooks/TCPD/datasets/jfk_passengers/air-passenger-
    traffic-per-month-port-authority-of-ny-nj-beginning-1977.csv'
raw_data = pd.read_csv(ts_file)
raw_data = raw_data.copy(deep=False)
raw_data['Month'] = pd.to_datetime(raw_data['Month'], format='%b').dt.month
raw_data.loc[:, 'Day'] = 1
raw_data['date'] = pd.to_datetime(raw_data[['Year', 'Month', 'Day']])
```

Adds a constant literal column so we can assemble a date column

Assembles the date column for our row-based index for each airport

```
jfk_data = raw_data[raw_data['Airport Code'] == 'JFK']
jfk_asc = jfk_data.sort_values('date', ascending=True)
jfk_asc.set_index('date', inplace=True)
plt.plot(jfk_asc['Domestic Passengers'])
plt.show()
```

Filters the DataFrame so we're looking at only a single airport (in this case, JFK)

Sorts the DataFrame by date so the time series is ordered correctly for plotting (and future activities)

Sets the index of the filtered DataFrame to the date column

After executing listing 5.1 in the notebook read-eval-print loop (REPL), we'll get a simple visualization of the time-series trend, showing the monthly passengers who have made domestic flights inside the United States from 1977 to 2015. The matplotlib window is shown in figure 5.3.

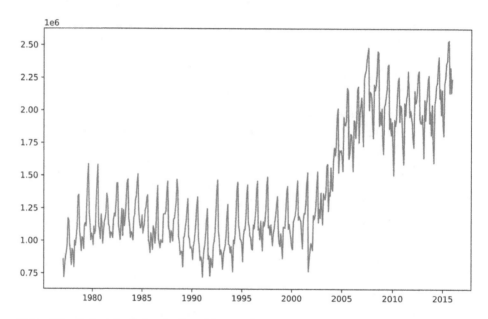

Figure 5.3   Basic default visualization of the raw data

Seeing this raw data displayed, we can start thinking through our plans for the experimentation phase. First, we come up with questions that should be answered to inform not only the research that we'll need to do in order to understand our options for forecasting, but also the platform decisions (which are covered in depth in section 5.2). Here are our data observations and questions:

- Latent factors are influencing the trend. The data doesn't look stationary.
- The data seems to have a strong seasonality component.
- We have thousands of airports to model. We need to think about scaling the approach that we choose.
- What models are good for this use case?

- We have two weeks to come up with a direction for approaching this. Can we get this done?

Both the questions for this phase of data visualization and the answers can help create a more effective experimentation phase for the project. Jumping directly to creating the model and testing random ideas too early can create a great deal of wasted work that sets the delivery for an MVP back in terms of meeting the deadlines. It will always be an effective use of time to understand the nature of your dataset and uncover any hidden issues prior to researching potential solutions, as this phase can help reduce the amount of testing and additional research by culling options early.

RESEARCH PHASE

Now that we know some of the concerns with the data—it's highly seasonal, with trends influenced by latent factors that are wholly unknown to us—we can start researching. Let's pretend for a moment that no one on the team has ever done time-series forecasting. Where, without the benefit of expert knowledge on the team, should research begin?

Internet searches are a great place to start, but most search results show blog posts of people offering forecasting solutions that involve a great deal of hand-waving and glossing over of the complexities involved in building out a full solution. White-papers can be informative but generally don't focus on the applications of the algorithms that they're covering. Lastly, script examples from Getting Started guides for different APIs are wonderful for seeing the mechanics of the API signature but are intentionally simplistic to serve as nothing more than a basic starting point, as the name indicates.

So, what should we be looking at to figure out how to predict future months of passenger demand at airports? The short answer is books. Quite a few great ones exist on time-series forecasting. In-depth blogs can help as well, but they should be used exclusively as an initial approach to the problem at hand, rather than as a repository from which to directly copy code.

> **NOTE** The seminal work *Time Series Analysis* by G. E. P. Box and G. M. Jenkins (Holden-Day, 1970) is widely considered the foundation of all modern time-series forecasting models. The Box-Jenkins methodologies are the basis for nearly all forecasting implementations today.

After a bit of research into time-series forecasting, we find a few options that seem commonly used enough to warrant some effort in implementing a rough scripted approach. The short list that we decide to try out is as follows:

- Linear regression (OLS, ridge, lasso, elastic net, and ensemble)
- ARIMA (autoregressive integrated moving average)
- Exponential smoothing (Holt-Winters)
- VAR (vector autoregression)
- SARIMA (seasonal autoregressive integrated moving average)

With that list of things to test out, the next step is to figure out which packages have these algorithms and read through their API documentation. A good rule to live by in the ML world is to establish a healthy library and a team budget to continuously expand that library. Having a collection of in-depth guides in the form of technical books can help a great deal with new challenges that the team will face and ensure that the nuanced complexity of applications of ML can be done with the right information.

5.1.2   *Forget the blogs—read the API docs*

Project failure is almost guaranteed when a team—typically, a rather junior team— believes so thoroughly in the veracity of a blog post that it bases an entire project around the methodology (and sometimes the exact code) of that blog. While almost always well-intentioned, authors of short blog posts on ML topics are not able, because of the format of the medium, to cover in the depth necessary all the information required to be garnered for a real-world production ML solution.

Let's look at what a blog post might have for our time-series problem. If we were to search for "time series forecasting example," we'd likely find more than a few results. Forecasting, after all, has been around for quite some time. What we'll likely find, though, are code snippets that are highly scripted, using the API defaults, and omit many of the finer details needed to make the exercise repeatable.

If you choose to follow along with the example (provided that it has convinced you of the approach), you'll likely end up spending a few hours looking up API documentation and getting frustrated with something that the author made look simple, only to find out that they left out all the complex details in an effort to hit that magic 10-minute read that people of low attention spans are so hungry for. The following listing is an example snippet from a fictional blog on elastic net regression (scikit-learn example) for demonstration purposes.

> **Listing 5.2   A blog example for elastic net from scikit-learn**

```
import pandas as pd
import numpy as np
from sklearn.model_selection import train_test_split
from sklearn import datasets
from sklearn.linear_model import ElasticNet        Uses the built-in datasets—
from sklearn import metrics                          a solid move for a
boston_data = datasets.load_boston()            ←    reproducible demo
boston_df = pd.DataFrame(boston_data.data, columns=boston_data.feature_names)
boston_df['House_Price'] = boston_data.target
x = boston_df.drop('House_Price', axis=1)
y = boston_df['House_Price']
train_x, test_x, train_y, test_y = train_test_split(x, y, test_size=0.3,
    random_state=42)
lm_elastic = ElasticNet()         ←    Sure hope the defaults are OK . . .
lm_elastic.fit(train_x, train_y)
predict_lm_elastic = lm_elastic.predict(test_x)      I guess we don't need a
print("My score is:")                                reference to the fit model?
```

Random sample split → (pointing to `train_x, test_x, train_y, test_y = train_test_split` line)

```
np.round(metrics.mean_squared_error(test_y, predict_lm_elastic)
>> My score is:
>> 25.0
```

> **A single metric? Surely, we can do better than that. . . .**

What are the issues in using this code? Setting aside the atrocious formatting and wall of text, let's enumerate the problems with using an example like this as a foundation for performing a time-series regression:

- It's a demo. A fairly poor one at that. But it's meant to be as *simple as possible*, showing the broad strokes of the APIs.
- The train-test split uses random sampling. This will not bode well for predicting a time series. (Keep in mind that the blog is intended to show elastic net regression, not a time-series problem.)
- The model uses default hyperparameters. This is, for the purposes of a blog, entirely understandable for the sake of brevity, but doesn't help out the reader much in knowing what they might need to change in order to make it applicable to their use case.
- It is method chaining and printing to stdout in such a way that the objects are not usable for further processing

Don't get me wrong here. Blogs are good. They help teach new concepts and provide inspiration for alternate solutions for problems that you may be working on. The primary reason I always tell people to not rely on them too much is that they're meant to be digestible, concise, and simple. To achieve those three goals, along with the overarching mission of maximum brevity, the finer details absolutely have to be omitted.

A note about blogs

I don't want to make it seem like I'm knocking them. They're great. They provide a wonderful introduction to concepts and potential solutions that are absolutely invaluable. If you're a blog writer, please, keep up the amazing work. It really does help out. If you're a blog reader, just, you know, proceed with caution.

Some truly great blog posts surrounding ML are on the internet. Unfortunately, these are drowned out by blogs filled with overly simplistic proofs-of-concept, broken code, or unintentionally horrific programming practices. If you're using blogs as a primary point of basic research when starting a project, just keep in mind that basing your prototype directly off example code from a blog might be OK, but you will have to completely rewrite the solution when building an MVP.

My best advice, if using blogs as a primary reference tool, is to vet the ideas by quorum. Do you see multiple people writing about similar (but not identical) solutions using a particular approach? Then it's probably a safe bet to test the approach on your data.

Do you see a particular solution that has the exact same code examples in multiple blogs? It's likely this is a copy-paste job to get advertising revenue or some other nefarious ruse. The more blogs you look at, the more that you'll be able to sniff bad

WR 933 6842

> **(continued)**
>
> code and poor implementation, and determine whether the author knows what they're talking about and can be trusted.
>
> Just remember: the one thing that you never want to do is base your implementation directly off code copied from a blog post. Blogs are written for brevity and usually focused on covering only a narrow topic. This short-form writing does not lend itself to realistic examples of production code, and as such, should always be seen for what it actually is: a means of communicating a single topic in the shortest span of text and time possible.

Instead of blindly trusting a blog post by basing the project around something that seems like it will work, you need to check and vet additional sources of information. These include academic papers, API tutorials, published books on the subject, and, most critically, an effective testing and validation phase of the team's approach. Having a project cancelled because the copied (or copied in essence) work from a blogger's informative post about something new that they've learned recently is not only detrimental to the business's opinion of the DS team, but also potentially dangerous.

NO, SERIOUSLY, READ THE API DOCS

Once we have the list of modeling approaches that we want to test, we should head over to the API documentation for the module that we're using. If we do that for elastic net, as an example, we'll find that the hyperparameters for this model have a few options that are pretty important to test and tune, as reflected in the following listing.

Listing 5.3   The full API signature for elastic net on scikit-learn

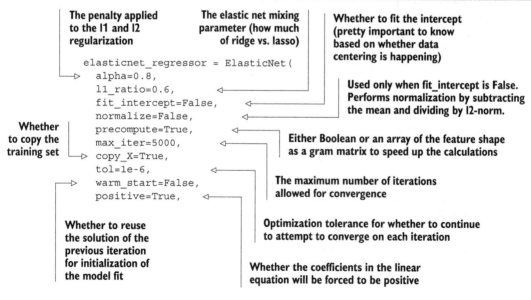

The penalty applied to the l1 and l2 regularization

The elastic net mixing parameter (how much of ridge vs. lasso)

Whether to fit the intercept (pretty important to know based on whether data centering is happening)

```
elasticnet_regressor = ElasticNet(
    alpha=0.8,
    l1_ratio=0.6,
    fit_intercept=False,
    normalize=False,
    precompute=True,
    max_iter=5000,
    copy_X=True,
    tol=1e-6,
    warm_start=False,
    positive=True,
```

Whether to copy the training set

Whether to reuse the solution of the previous iteration for initialization of the model fit

Used only when fit_intercept is False. Performs normalization by subtracting the mean and dividing by l2-norm.

Either Boolean or an array of the feature shape as a gram matrix to speed up the calculations

The maximum number of iterations allowed for convergence

Optimization tolerance for whether to continue to attempt to converge on each iteration

Whether the coefficients in the linear equation will be forced to be positive

```
    random_state=42
    selection='random'
)
```

Seed value if the selection type is "random"

Selection type for coefficient selection (cyclic is default and loops over the feature vector, while random utilizes random coefficient selection for a different feature each iteration)

For many ML algorithms, the options (hyperparameters) specified as defaults are occasionally good for some common data structures being passed into them. But it's always best to verify what those options are and what they are used for, and identifying ones that should be tuned is an essential part of building an effective model. Many times, these options are specified simply as placeholders, with the API developer fully intending for the end user to override those values.

> **TIP** Like anything else in the world of DS, don't assume anything. Assumption results in problems coming to haunt you later in your project work.

Based on the list of models that the team has agreed to test out, everyone on the team should head off to familiarize themselves with the options available for the signatures of each model's API. This is important to handle early so that when the results of each quick-and-dirty experiment are run, the maintainability and complexity of the model can be weighed in concert with the accuracy metrics that are typically the sole point of judgment.

No, really, you should read the docs

I've always been a bit surprised when I see someone using a particular API, sometimes for a production use case, without having ever read the documentation surrounding that API (including myself, in hindsight). I've been surprised in the sense that most people would be surprised to see a cabin crew member step into the cockpit of an airplane and start flying the aircraft. Can they keep it aloft? Sure (well, hopefully). Do they know how the aircraft works and the dynamics of flight? Probably not. Let's hope that the skies stay clear and blue.

This isn't to say that you should be reading every single developer API doc for each module you're ever going to use. That's untenable and a bit ridiculous. However, in the world of ML, where the number of available algorithms is seemingly endless (not to mention the inner workings of the code powering those algorithms are exceedingly complex and lengthy), it's quite important to read the API docs from at least the main interface level.

This means becoming familiar with the classes that you're using, their signatures, and the methods that you're using within those classes. There's no need to reverse engineer the package. However, at the very least, you should become familiar with the doc string descriptions of the class, know which attributes to pass in or override, and understand the basic functionality of the methods that you're going to be calling and interfacing with.

The implementation of most of these algorithms has nuances (particularly the higher-level meta-algorithms whose entire behavior is determined by configuration).

(continued)

Understanding which knobs need to be turned, how to turn them, and the implications of spinning those knobs can help reduce risk during testing. It will save you a lot of time and frustration, particularly once you move on to the full development of the solution, knowing which default values are placeholders and which are generally good values to leave as is.

We'll discuss these concepts in greater detail later this book, but for now, you have an understanding of why all the settings are specified for the APIs throughout this MVP simulation in this chapter.

A critical function of API docs is in informing a user of the options available for controlling the behavior of the software (and in turn, for ML use cases, the algorithms' learning patterns). Without understanding how to control the model's learning behavior, we run the risk of building models that are unable to generalize well because of overfit, or are so fragile that even a slight change in the baseline variability of the feature inputs will make the solution absolutely useless to a business.

When a model becomes useless, performing worse than a manual human-centric solution, it's usually abandoned by the business (even if it is still running in production by the ML team). Understanding how to tune and control the behavior of the model properly in the early stages of experimentation is critical, even though the act of fine-tuning it is not necessary during this phase.

QUICK TESTING AND ROUGH ESTIMATES

Perhaps the only time in ML project work that extensive evaluation of appropriate hyperparameter tuning can be ignored is at this point. During the rapid evaluation period, we're not particularly interested in seeing how well we can optimize a model's fit to our data. Rather, we're interested in measuring the general sensitivity of a group of disparate algorithms, trying to gauge how stable a particular approach will be later when we're fine-tuning our models and maintaining them through drift situations.

The previous section covered why it's important to know how to tune each model by reading through the API docs (and perhaps the source code as well). But for the rapid testing phase, it simply isn't tenable to tune all of these (see the following sidebar on overbuilding). While going through the process of whittling down those nine possible implementations to something more manageable for MVP implementation and full testing, it can be helpful to just use most of the defaults and see what the results look like. It is also a useful practice, however, to either explicitly mark the instantiation blocks with the provided default conditions or to just leave a TODO in the code to make sure, when ready to move toward full tuning of a model for the MVP phase, that the API documentation is checked and the optional settings that are part of the API are validated and tested.

> **A note on overbuilding a rapid prototype test**
>
> The focus in the early smoke test experimentation for candidate solutions should be on speed and not accuracy. Keep in mind that you work for a company, results are expected, and there are likely other projects to work on.
>
> I mentioned in previous chapters some of the dangers of overdeveloping a prototype (it makes it harder to decide what to choose for an MVP). Looking at the bigger picture, though, the more detrimental effect of unnecessary work is on the business. Every day that the team is working on proving out different solutions is a day that's not available to work on the next project.
>
> Efficiency, objective selection based on common criteria, and moving to developing an MVP should always be the primary focus of prototyping. Nothing else. There will be time during the MVP phase to build out better accuracy, clever feature engineering, and creative approaches to the problem.

We'll go through testing examples for our forecasting problem in the next chapter. For now, just know that for the initial round of exploratory work and evaluating solutions, the predictions don't have to be perfect. Your time will be much better spent focusing your energy on culling the list of possibilities so that you have one or two candidate solutions, rather than spending an inordinate amount of time fine-tuning nine (or more) approaches.

5.1.3 *Draw straws for an internal hackathon*

Setting boundaries around testing is incredibly critical, particularly as a team grows in number and project complexity grows as the team matures in experience. In pursuit of efficiency (and the aforementioned critical *time* aspect of picking a direction for building an MVP), it can be absolutely detrimental to the success of a project if testing isn't assigned to individuals or pair-programming teams.

If everyone is left to just figure out the best solution, duplicated work and excessive effort will undoubtedly be placed on particular solutions. By focusing on a single approach, with consistent status updates on its progress, the team can minimize the chance of missing the delivery date for the MVP.

Now that we've come up with a list of potential solutions for our forecasting model, how do we go about testing them? Whether the team includes a single person or a dozen data scientists, the approach should be the same:

- Block off a set amount of time to do the testing. Giving an end-time deadline to this phase will impart a sense of urgency so that a decision can be made quickly on the efficacy of the solution.
- Set some rules, just as you would for a hackathon:
  - Everyone must use the same dataset.
  - Everyone must use the same evaluation metrics.
  - Each evaluation needs to forecast over the same time period.

  – Visualizations of the forecast, along with metrics, need to be provided.
  – The experimentation code needs to be re-runnable from scratch.
- Make sure that the language chosen is supportable by the team and that the platform it's running on is available for the team to use if the business decides to move forward with the solution.

If we set up the experimentation in this way, for this problem, we would likely have the following rules based on this dataset:

- One week of testing—starting on Thursday after the scrum meeting, the presentations are due on the following Thursday morning for review by the entire team.
- The data to be modeled is for JFK domestic passengers.
- The eval metrics will be as follows:
  – Mean absolute error (MAE)
  – Mean absolute percentage error (MAPE)
  – Mean squared error (MSE)
  – Root mean square error (RMSE)
  – R-squared
- The forecast period for evaluation will be the last five years of the dataset.
- Experimentation will be done in Jupyter notebooks running Python 3, utilizing the standard Anaconda build in a Docker container.

With the rules established, the team (if count(team) > 1 else you) can set about figuring out solutions. Before we get into looking at how that would be done in an efficient way, we have just one more thing to cover: standards.

5.1.4   *Level the playing field*

For our experimentation to be meaningful with these nine separate approaches, we need to ensure that we're playing fairly. This means that we're not only comparing using the same dataset, but also evaluating the test data against the predictions with the exact same error metrics. The core issue that we need to prevent is indecision and chaos among the team when measuring the effectiveness of a solution (which wastes time that, as we've mentioned before, we simply don't have if we want to move to the MVP phase of the project).

Since we're looking at a time-series problem, we're going to evaluate a regression problem. We know that, to do a true comparison, we need to control the data splits (which we will explore throughout the code examples in section 5.2), but we also need to agree on an evaluation metric that each model is going to record to do the comparison of goodness of fit of the prediction. Since we're eventually going to need to build thousands of these models, and the raw prediction values are of wildly different orders of magnitude (just slightly more people fly through JFK and ATL than do through, say, Boise), the team members have agreed to use MAPE as the comparison metric. In a wise decision, though, they have also agreed to capture as many regression metrics as are applicable to a time-series regression problem, should they choose to switch to a different metric during tuning later for the per model optimizations.

For this reason, we'll agree to collect metrics on MAPE, MAE, MSE, RMSE, explained variance, and R-squared. This way, we'll have the flexibility to discuss the benefits of the different metrics as they relate to the data and to the project.

The metric wars and how to solve them

A lot of opinions exist on the best metrics to use for different ML solutions. Innumerable hours have been wasted in ridiculous arguments over whether to use MSE or RMSE, whether an F1 score is appropriate versus area under ROC, and whether a normalization of MAE should be applied, turning it into MAPE.

There's definitely a great argument to be made for selecting the appropriate metric for each use case. However, calculating errors is usually pretty cheap and fast. It doesn't hurt to calculate all of the applicable ones and record them all. Obviously, don't record categorical metrics for a regression problem (that would be incredibly ill-advised) or vice versa, but slapping down MAE, MSE, and R-squared calculations for a model to ensure that the benefits of each method can be utilized for determination can prove helpful.

It is likewise similarly invaluable to record them all in case, while building out a solution and tuning it, the team decides to utilize a different metric. Having each metric there from the beginning can give a historical reference for each run that was attempted without having to go back to rerun old experiments just to collect additional metrics (which is both costly and time-consuming).

The only notable exception to collecting all the metrics exists if the metric evaluation is so expensive (computationally) that the benefit that it provides outweighs the cost of calculating it. For instance, in chapter 4's recommendation engine, a calculation for NDCG involves a window function over a large corpus of data (the implicit scoring data), which can take hours to execute on a relatively large Apache Spark cluster. Calculating these scores in a relational database management system (RDBMS) involves expensive Cartesian joins, which can take even longer. If the metric is not critical and takes periods of time to execute that don't justify its collection, then it's best not to waste time with it.

5.2 *Performing experimental prep work*

After the planning and research phase is completed by a team focused on building an ML solution to a business problem, the next phase, preparation for experimental testing, is one of the most oft-omitted activities in the DS community (speaking from personal experience here). Even with a solid plan of who is going to test what, an agreed-upon series of metrics, an evaluation of the dataset, and an agreed-upon methodology of how far into experimentation each team will be going, this preparatory phase, if ignored, will create more inefficiencies that can lead to a project being delayed. This preparatory phase is focused on doing a deep analysis of the datasets, creating common tools that the entire team can use in order to increase the speed at which they can evaluate their experimental attempts.

At this point, we've decided on some models to try, set the ground rules for the experimentation phase, and selected our language (Python, mostly because of the statsmodels library) and our platform (Jupyter Notebook running on Docker containers so we don't waste our time with library compatibility issues and can rapidly prototype tests and see visualizations directly). Before we start firing off a bunch of modeling tests, it's important to understand the data as it relates to the problem at hand.

For this forecasting project, that means going through a thorough analysis of stationarity tests, a decomposition of the trend, identification of severe outliers, and building basic visualization tooling that will aid in the rapid phases of model testing that the subteams will be doing. As shown in figure 5.4, we'll cover each of these key stages of preparation work to ensure that each of our hacking teams will have an efficient development process and won't be focused on creating nine different copies of the same way of plotting and scoring their results.

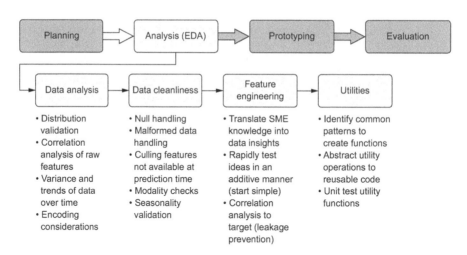

Figure 5.4   The analysis phase, focusing on evaluating the data to inform the prototyping work

This analysis pathing is highly dependent on the type of ML project being undertaken. For this time-series forecasting, these are a good set of items to accomplish prior to building prototype solutions to evaluate. Each step is fairly applicable to any supervised ML problem. For an NLP project, however, you would have slightly different actions to perform in this stage.

The point of showing these processes and the order in which they need to be done is to illustrate that a plan needs to be developed before working on model prototyping.

Without one, the evaluation phase will be guaranteed to be long, arduous, chaotic, and likely inconclusive.

5.2.1 Performing data analysis

In the course of researching possible solutions, a lot of people seem to find trend visualizations pretty helpful. Not only does this activity prepare for baseline visualizations of the data to the broader business unit team that will be the consumers of the project solution, but it can help minimize unforeseen issues with the data that might be uncovered much later in the project; these issues could require a complete rework of the solution (and potentially a cancellation of the project if the rework is too expensive from a time and resources perspective). To marginalize the risk associated with finding out too late about a serious flaw in the data, we're going to build a few analytics visualizations.

Based on the initial raw data visualization built in listing 5.1 (and shown in figure 5.3), we notice a great deal of noise in the dataset. Having a great deal of noise in a trend can certainly help visualize the general trend line, so let's start by applying a smoothing function to the raw data trend for the domestic passengers at JFK. The script that we're going to be executing is in the following listing, utilizing basic matplotlib visualizations.

Listing 5.4 Moving average trend with two-sigma error

Generates a rolling average series based on a year's period of smoothing

Generates the standard deviation series on the same rolling time period as the smoothed rolling average

```
rolling_average = jfk_asc['Domestic Passengers'].rolling(12,
    center=False).mean()
rolling_std = jfk_asc['Domestic Passengers'].rolling(12, center=False).std()
plt.plot(jfk_asc['Domestic Passengers'], color='darkblue', label='Monthly
    Passenger Count')
plt.plot(rolling_average, color='red', label='Rolling Average')
plt.plot(rolling_average + (2 * rolling_std), color='green', linestyle='-.',
    label='Rolling 2 sigma')
plt.plot(rolling_average - (2 * rolling_std), color='green', linestyle='-.')
plt.legend(loc='best')
plt.title('JFK Passengers by Month')
plt.show(block=False)
```

Applies the rolling average series to the plot

Displays the plot in stdout

Puts a title to the plot so exported images from this are instantly identifiable

Applies the rolling stddev series at two-sigma to the plot by adding and subtracting the values from the rolling average series

Initializes the plot with the raw data (domestic passengers) and creates a label for the legend box

---

> **NOTE** The code shown here and throughout section 5.2 is for rapid experimentation only. Section 5.22 covers more effective ways to write MVP code.

Running this code in our Jupyter notebook will generate the plot shown in figure 5.5. Note how the general trend of the data looks when smoothed and realize that a definite

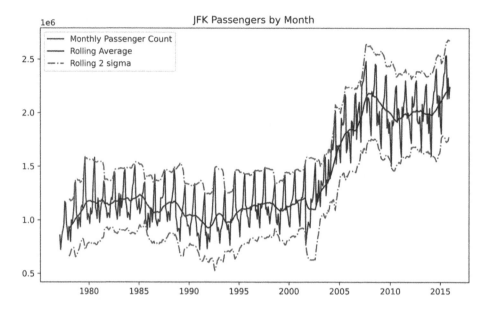

Figure 5.5 Baseline smoothing and sigma fits from listing 5.4

step function occurs around 2002. Also note that the stddev varies widely during different time periods. After 2008, the variance becomes much broader than it had been historically.

The trend is OK, and somewhat useful for understanding the potential problems that might arise from building training and validation datasets that don't reflect the trend change. (Specifically, we can see what might happen if we train up to the year 2000 and expect that a model will accurately predict from 2000 to 2015.)

During the research and planning phase, however, we found a great many mentions of stationarity in time series and how certain model types can really struggle with predicting a nonstationary trend. We should take a look at what that is all about.

For this, we're going to use an augmented Dickey-Fuller stationarity test, provided in the statsmodels module. This test will inform us of whether we need to provide stationarity adjustments to the time series for particular models that are incapable of handling nonstationary data. If the test comes back with a value indicating that the time series is stationary, essentially all models can use the raw data with no transformations applied to it. However, if the data is nonstationary, extra work will be required. The script to run this test for the JFK domestic passengers series is shown next.

Listing 5.5 Stationarity test for a time series

Instantiates the adfuller (augmented Dickey-Fuller test) and sets the autolag to automatically minimize the information criterion for lag count determination

```
from statsmodel.tsa.stattools import adfuller
dickey_fuller_test = adfuller(jfk_asc['Domestic Passengers'], autolag='AIC')
```

```
test_items = dickey_fuller_test[:4]
report_items = test_items + (("not " if test_items[1] > 0.05 else "") +
    "stationary",)
df_report = pd.Series(report_items, index=['Test Statistic', 'p-value',
    '# Lags', '# Observations', 'Stationarity Test'])
for k, v in dickey_fuller_test[4].items():
    df_report['Critical Value(%s)' % k] = v
print(df_report)
```

Grabs the first elements of the test results ─▷

Generates an indexed series of the information ◁─

Creates a Boolean yes/no stationarity test. (In practice, it's best to compare the test statistic to the critical values to make a true determination of stationarity.)

Extracts the critical values from the test statistics

Upon running this code, we get the result in figure 5.6, printed to stdout.

```
Test Statistic             -0.0498716
p-value                      0.954208
# Lags                             13
# Observations                    454
Stationarity Test      not stationary
Critical Value(1%)           -3.44484
Critical Value(5%)           -2.86793
Critical Value(10%)          -2.57017
dtype: object
```

Figure 5.6   Results of the augmented Dickey-Fuller test for stationarity. This is what we will see by running the code in listing 5.5.

OK, so that's cool. But what does all of that mean?

The *test statistic* (always negative) is a measure of the adjacency a time series has to containing a unit root. (If multiple unit roots—for example, a number of differencing functions—must be applied to the time series to make it essentially flat, then the less stationary it is.) In non-math terms, if the test statistic is less than the critical values, the series will be determined as stationary. In this case, our test statistic value is much higher than the critical values, thus giving us a null-accepting p-value where we can quite confidently state, "This is not stationary" (H0 of the `adfuller` test is that the time series is *nonstationary*).

> **NOTE** If you're curious about the theory and math behind the test, I highly encourage you to search for the original research papers: "Efficient Tests for an Autoregressive Unit Root" by Graham Elliot et al. (1996) as well as the foundational unit root theory espoused in the journal publication "Distribution of the Estimators for Autoregressive Time Series with a Unit Root" by D. A. Dickey and W. A. Fuller (1979).

Other interesting data is also in there—specifically, the number of lags discovered. We can look at this value in an additional way, which can help us figure out settings that we should be using when we get to the modeling phase with ARIMA-based models. The number 13 seems a bit odd, considering that we're looking at monthly data here. If we were to blindly just use that value as a seasonality (period) component in our models, we would probably get some pretty terrible results. We can validate this, though, by looking at some trend decompositions in figure 5.7.

We're going to see if we can effectively decompose the trend, seasonality, and residuals in the signal with the built-in functionality in statsmodels, helping to inform some of the settings that we will need to use in the modeling experiments. Thankfully, the authors of the package have built out not only the decomposition methods, but also a nice visualization that we can easily plot out, as shown in the following listing. Let's see what happens if we use the lag count from the `adfuller` report for the seasonality period.

Listing 5.6   Trend decomposition for seasonality

Performs the seasonal decomposition with the adfuller lag value of 13

```
from statsmodels.tsa.seasonal import seasonal_decompose
decomposed_trends = seasonal_decompose(jfk_asc['Domestic Passengers'], period=13)  ⟵
trend_plot = decomposed_trends.plot()        ⟵
plt.savefig("decomposed13.svg", format='svg')  ⟵
```

Saves the plot for later reference

Gets a reference to the plot for storing. (It will automatically display inline as well.)

Figure 5.7 shows what that chart looks like when the code from listing 5.6 is executed.

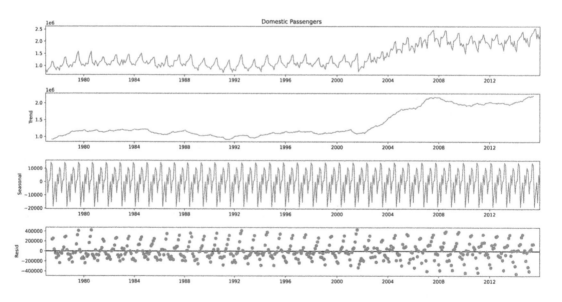

Figure 5.7   The trend decomposition plot consisting of (from top to bottom): the raw data, the extracted trend, the seasonality component, and the residuals. This doesn't seem to be right.

Not exactly the most compelling data, is it? The residuals (the bottom pane) seem to have a signal in there. A residual should be the unexplained noise that is left over after the general trend and the seasonality are extracted from the data. But here, it seems as though quite a bit of actual repeatable signal is still in there. Let's try a different run of this, but specifying the period as 12, as shown in figure 5.8.

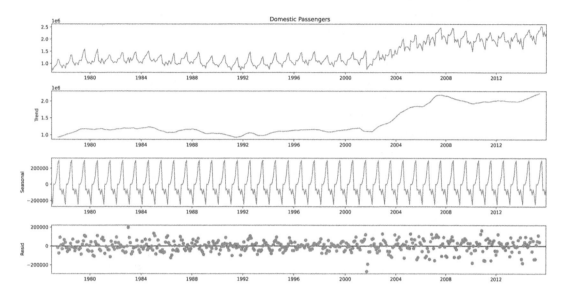

Figure 5.8 The trend decomposition plots with the period set to 12 instead of 13. That's a bit better.

The evaluation in figure 5.8 with the period value of 12 looks significantly better than the earlier test of 13. Our trend is nice and smooth, our seasonality looks well matched to the periodicity of the repeated pattern in the data, and the residuals are (mostly) random. We'll remember this value when we do testing in chapter 6.

The importance of doing this prep work ahead of time is to *inform our testing*. It is to guide the testing in such a way that we can rapidly iterate on experiments from a position of knowledge about the data, thereby getting to answers about approaches and their applicability to this problem faster.

Keep in mind that we're going to be evaluating nine approaches to forecasting during the testing phase. The faster we can determine which of those nine are the two most promising candidates, the faster we can ignore the other seven and, collectively as a team, make progress toward our deadline for an MVP for the business.

How clean is our data?

Data cleanliness issues are one of the prime reasons for an MVP extending much longer than was promised to a business. Identifying bad data points is crucial not only for the purposes of modeling training effectiveness, but also to help tell a story to the business about why certain outputs of the model might be less than accurate at times. Building a series of visualizations that can communicate the complexities of latent factors, data-quality issues, and other unforeseen elements that can affect the solution can serve as a powerful tool during discussions with the project's business unit.

One of the most important points that we'll have to explain about the forecasting from this project is that it will not, and cannot, be an infallible system. Many unknowns remain in our dataset—elements of influence to the trend that are either too complex to track, too expensive to model, or nearly impossible to predict—that need to feed into the algorithm. For the case of univariate time-series models, nothing is going into the model other than the trending data itself. In the case of more complex implementations, such as windowed approaches and deep learning models like long short-term memory (LSTM) recurrent neural networks (RNNs), even though we can create vectors that contain much more information, we don't always have the capability or the time to collate all of the features that could influence the trend.

To aid in having this conversation, we can take a look at a simple method of identifying outlier values that are dramatically different from what we would otherwise expect from a seasonally influenced trend. A relatively easy way to do this with series data is to use a differencing function on the sorted data. This can be accomplished as shown in the following listing.

Listing 5.7   Time-series differencing functions and visualizations

Gets a per-unit differencing of each position's value compared to the lag specified. Here, we're looking at the immediately preceding value.

Generates the plot structure so we can create a single image of these three separate plots

Gets the logarithm of the raw data to reduce the magnitude of difference for subsequent steps

```python
from datetime import datetime
jfk_asc['Log Domestic Passengers'] = np.log(jfk_asc['Domestic Passengers'])
jfk_asc['DiffLog Domestic Passengers month'] = jfk_asc['Log Domestic
    Passengers'].diff(1)
jfk_asc['DiffLog Domestic Passengers year'] = jfk_asc['Log Domestic
    Passengers'].diff(12)
fig, axes = plt.subplots(3, 1, figsize=(16,12))
boundary1 = datetime.strptime('2001-07-01', '%Y-%m-%d')
boundary2 = datetime.strptime('2001-11-01', '%Y-%m-%d')
axes[0].plot(jfk_asc['Domestic Passengers'], '-', label='Domestic Passengers')
axes[0].set(title='JFK Domestic Passengers')
axes[0].axvline(boundary1, 0, 2.5e6, color='r', linestyle='--', label='Sept 11th
    2001')
axes[0].axvline(boundary2, 0, 2.5e6, color='r', linestyle='--')
axes[0].legend(loc='upper left')
axes[1].plot(jfk_asc['DiffLog Domestic Passengers month'], label='Monthly diff
    of Domestic Passengers')
axes[1].hlines(0, jfk_asc.index[0], jfk_asc.index[-1], 'g')
axes[1].set(title='JFK Domestic Passenger Log Diff = 1')
```

Always plot the raw data if generating graphics to share to the rest of the business. It will save you from having to craft horrifically complex slides later.

Displaying the highlighted aberrations in data in multiple ways can help communicate the impact of latent factors more clearly.

Plots the static boundaries we want to highlight about why unforeseen latent factors affected the trend

Gets the differencing of the 12th preceding value (difference from last year, since our data is monthly)

Creates x-axis reference points that illustrate abnormality periods in the series data (to aid in explanations to business unit members who will ask questions about why predictions failed)

```
axes[1].axvline(boundary1, 0, 2.5e6, color='r', linestyle='--',
    label='Sept 11th 2001')
axes[1].axvline(boundary2, 0, 2.5e6, color='r', linestyle='--')

axes[1].legend(loc='lower left')
axes[2].plot(jfk_asc['DiffLog Domestic Passengers year'], label='Yearly diff of
    Domestic Passengers')
axes[2].hlines(0, jfk_asc.index[0], jfk_asc.index[-1], 'g')
axes[2].set(title='JFK Domestic Passenger Log Diff = 12')
axes[2].axvline(boundary1, 0, 2.5e6, color='r', linestyle='--', label='Sept 11th
    2001')
axes[2].axvline(boundary2, 0, 2.5e6, color='r', linestyle='--')
axes[2].legend(loc='lower left')
plt.savefig("logdiff.svg", format='svg')   ◁──── Regardless of platform, visualization
                                                 technology, or process, it's a good
                                                 habit to save all of our generated
                                                 plots for later reference.
```

When we execute this, we get the plot shown in figure 5.9 (as well as an SVG image saved to our shared notebook directory).

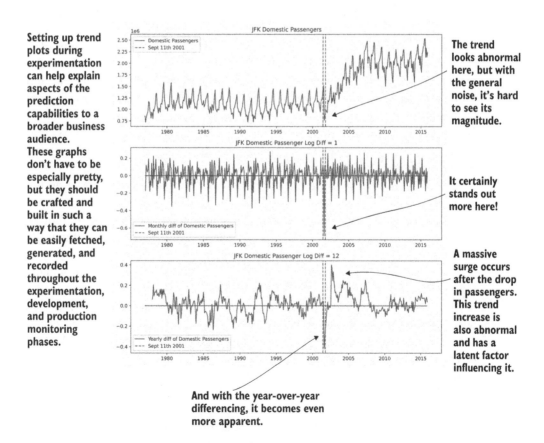

Setting up trend plots during experimentation can help explain aspects of the prediction capabilities to a broader business audience.

These graphs don't have to be especially pretty, but they should be crafted and built in such a way that they can be easily fetched, generated, and recorded throughout the experimentation, development, and production monitoring phases.

The trend looks abnormal here, but with the general noise, it's hard to see its magnitude.

It certainly stands out more here!

A massive surge occurs after the drop in passengers. This trend increase is also abnormal and has a latent factor influencing it.

And with the year-over-year differencing, it becomes even more apparent.

Figure 5.9   Outlier analysis demonstration from listing 5.7

We now have some insight into what the data looks like. We've created demonstration plots and basic trend decompositions, and collected data about what these trends look like. The code has been a bit rough and reads like a script. If we don't take a little time to make this code reusable through the use of utility functions, we will likely find that each time someone wants to generate such visualizations, they will be employing Chef Boyardee levels of copy-pasta throughout their code base.

5.2.2   *Moving from script to reusable code*

Returning to the theme of timeliness, the urgency of making decisions about directions for the project can be lessened if we focus on employing reusable code. It not only makes for a cleaner code base (and fewer versions of the exact same thing being created by multiple people), but also helps standardize elements of the project in preparation for the MVP (and development) phases. Reducing confusion, speeding time to decision making, and creating less chaos in notebooks and scripts are all in an effort to maximize the chances of the business having enough faith in the project to continue development efforts on it.

We've been doing an awful lot of scripting here with the trend analysis and the visualizations of our JFK domestic passenger data. That's perfectly fine for doing a quick check on things and certainly understandable for the early stages of experimentation (we all do it, and anyone who says otherwise is a liar). However, when the team breaks off to work on modeling activities, it will be incredibly wasteful for everyone to be building their own visualizations, their own implementations of similar tests, and code that can be relatively easily rolled into standard functions. The last thing we (should) want is to have a disparate collection of notebooks that have multiple copies of the exact same code, just slightly modified, spread everywhere. While using the magical copy and paste commands might seem expedient, it ends up wreaking havoc on both productivity and sanity. The better thing to do is to create functions.

I'm certainly not recommending, at this stage, to build a package-level project for these utility functions. That work will come later, in the actual development phase of the project, during the long and arduous road to production release.

For now, let's take these useful and repeatable code snippets for manipulating the raw data, visualizing the trends, and extracting information from them into a standardized collection of basic functions. This work will save us dozens of hours, particularly when different implementations are going to be tested against other airports' data. The absolutely last thing that we want to do is copy and paste a block of script in order to present a visualization and analysis, which will leave everyone wondering which methodology is the best, cause massive amounts of duplicated work, and generate code sprawl that will be untenable to maintain.

Let's take a look at the dataset ingestion script from listing 5.1 and see what a function to acquire the data and format it correctly might look like. To make the ingestion function useful, we need to get a list of the airports included with this file, be able to apply filtering to get a single airport, and specify the time-series periodicity associated with the data. The following listing shows each of these functions.

Listing 5.8 Data ingestion and formatting functions

Defines a static variable for the column that contains the key for the airports (to minimize string replacements within code, should this need to be changed)

Function for setting the time-series frequency for the index of the DataFrame

```
AIRPORT_FIELD = 'Airport Code'

def apply_index_freq(data, freq):
    return data.asfreq(freq)

def pull_raw_airport_data(file_location):
    raw = pd.read_csv(file_location)
    raw = raw.copy(deep=False)
    raw['Month'] = pd.to_datetime(raw['Month'], format='%b').dt.month
    raw.loc[:, 'Day'] = 1
    raw['date'] = pd.to_datetime(raw[['Year', 'Month', 'Day']])
    raw.set_index('date', inplace=True)
    raw.index = pd.DatetimeIndex(raw.index.values,
      freq=raw.index.inferred_freq)
    asc = raw.sort_index()
    return asc

def get_airport_data(airport, file_location):
    all_data = pull_raw_airport_data(file_location)
    filtered = all_data[all_data[AIRPORT_FIELD] == airport]
    return filtered

def filter_airport_data(all_data, airport):
    filtered_data = all_data[all_data[AIRPORT_FIELD] == airport]
    return filtered_data

def get_all_airports(file_location):
    all_data = pull_raw_airport_data(file_location)
    unique_airports = all_data[AIRPORT_FIELD].unique()
    return sorted(unique_airports)
```

Primary data acquisition and formatting function

Sets a copy of the ingested data so it can be safely mutated

Extracts the month from the string date value in the original data

Sets the index of the DataFrame to the date column (useful for plotting and modeling)

Sets the properties of the index to the inferred frequency

Generates the date field in appropriate NumPy datetime format (required for time-series modeling)

Utility function for returning a list of all airports contained within the data

Creates a day field (first day of the month) so the encoding to a date object can happen

Ensures that the DataFrame has been sorted by the date index to prevent issues with series extraction of data later

With these functions established, they can be used by each subteam that will be testing out solutions to the forecasting project throughout the experimental phase. With a little bit more work, these can all be modularized into a class later, during the development phase, to create a standardized and testable implementation for the production-grade final project (covered in chapters 9, 10, and 14). The usage of these can be as simple as the next listing.

Listing 5.9   Ingesting data by using a reusable function

```
DATA_PATH = '/opt/notebooks/TCPD/datasets/jfk_passengers/air-passenger-
    traffic-per-month-port-authority-of-ny-nj-beginning-1977.csv'
jfk = get_airport_data('JFK', DATA_PATH)        ◁
jfk = apply_index_freq(jfk, 'MS')      ◁
```

Uses the function get_airport_data() to acquire the data as a date-indexed pandas DataFrame

Applies the correct time periodicity to the date index on the DataFrame (MS is for "month start frequency")

Let's look at one additional modification that we can do, focused on the outlier visualization script created in listing 5.7 and demonstrated in figure 5.9. We'll see how this script could be adapted to a one-line use that greatly simplifies the generation of these plots without having to make it fully generic (which would take a great deal of time and effort). Even though the function representation of this visualization logic is a bit more complex, and requires a few more lines of code, the end result will be worth it in no small part because we can generate plots with a single line of code.

Listing 5.10   Reusable function for visualizing outlier data

Functions generally don't have quite this many arguments. The * tuple packing operator and the ** dictionary packing operator allow for passing multiple arguments. For this example, I name them explicitly to minimize confusion.

Uses string interpolation to build static references to dynamically created fields in the DataFrame

```
from datetime import datetime
from dateutil.relativedelta import relativedelta

def generate_outlier_plots(data_series, series_name, series_column,
        event_date, event_name, image_name):
    log_name = 'Log {}'.format(series_column)            ◁
    month_log_name = 'DiffLog {} month'.format(series_column)
    year_log_name = 'DiffLog {} year'.format(series_column)
    event_marker = datetime.strptime(event_date, '%Y-%m-%d').replace(day=1)
    two_month_delta = relativedelta(months=2)
    event_boundary_low = event_marker - two_month_delta
    event_boundary_high = event_marker + two_month_delta
    max_scaling = np.round(data_series[series_column].values.max() * 1.1, 0)  ◁
    data = data_series.copy(deep=True)      ◁
```

Creates a date differencing so we can get a uniform scaling based on the frequency of the time-series index of the DataFrame

Creates a maximum bound on the vertical lines being drawn that is based on the range of the data

Converts the passed-in date to something that will match up with the datetime index of the DataFrame. For this example, it's OK to convert passed-in values. In general practice (particularly for libraries), the correct action is to raise an exception for invalid passed-in configurations (a validation that the value exists in the index could be one method to employ) so that the end user of the function doesn't get an unexpected result.

Makes a deep copy (object replication in different memory address) for the series of mutations we will be doing to the data. This is a useful operation, particularly for ML, wherein we may want to change this so subsequent calls to this function won't be mutating the source data, allowing us to loop or map/lambda over a collection that calls this data.

```
data[log_name] = np.log(data[series_column])
data[month_log_name] = data[log_name].diff(1)
data[year_log_name] = data[log_name].diff(12)
fig, axes = plt.subplots(3, 1, figsize=(16, 12))
axes[0].plot(data[series_column], '-', label=series_column)
axes[0].set(title='{} {}'.format(series_name, series_column))
axes[0].axvline(event_boundary_low, 0, max_scaling, color='r',
 linestyle='--', label=event_name)
axes[0].axvline(event_boundary_high, 0, max_scaling, color='r',
 linestyle='--')
axes[0].legend(loc='best')
axes[1].plot(data[month_log_name], label='Monthly diff of
 {}'.format(series_column))
axes[1].hlines(0, data.index[0], data.index[-1], 'g')
axes[1].set(title='{} Monthly diff of {}'.format(series_name,
 series_column))
axes[1].axvline(event_boundary_low, 0, max_scaling, color='r',
 linestyle='--', label=event_name)
axes[1].axvline(event_boundary_high, 0, max_scaling, color='r',
 linestyle='--')
axes[1].legend(loc='best')
axes[2].plot(data[year_log_name], label='Year diff of
 {}'.format(series_column))
axes[2].hlines(0, data.index[0], data.index[-1], 'g')
axes[2].set(title='{} Yearly diff of {}'.format(series_name,
 series_column))
axes[2].axvline(event_boundary_low, 0, max_scaling, color='r',
 linestyle='--', label=event_name)
axes[2].axvline(event_boundary_high, 0, max_scaling, color='r',
 linestyle='--')
axes[2].legend(loc='best')
plt.savefig(image_name, format='svg')
return fig
```

Performs the same log and diff functions performed earlier in the scripted version, except these are parameterized by the interpolated names so that no hardcoding is required

All the code from here to the bottom is identical to our previous scripted version, with the exception that we're using dynamic variables from the passed-in arguments to construct everything in a flexible manner.

These values could also be arguments to this function (the figsize value) in case you want the user to have flexibility in the size of the plots. For this example, we're leaving them hardcoded.

Interpolation is your friend

In the realm of ML, a lot of what we do involves passing around string references. It can get a bit tedious. The only thing that I've found to be more tedious than dealing with strings in configurations is manually overwriting those strings for different uses in code.

Interpolation is a remarkably powerful tool that, once you learn how to use it correctly, can save you no end of frustration and typo-induced failures. As great as it is, however, there are ways that people use it correctly, and then there are the "lazy" implementations.

> **(continued)**
>
> How do you do string building in a lazy fashion? By using the concatenation operator.
>
> Let's say we want to build one of those strings from listing 5.10, the title for `axes[1]`. In a lazy implementation of concatenation, we might do something like this:
>
> ```
> axes[1].set(title=series_name + ' Monthly diff of ' + series_column)
> ```
>
> While technically correct (it will assemble the string correctly), it's ugly, hard to read, and incredibly error-prone. What if you forgot to put the leading and trailing spaces into the middle statically defined string? What if someone comes in later and needs to change that string? What if the title needs to be added onto to provide a dozen different strings? At a certain point, the code will start to look amateurish and impossible to read.
>
> Using the `'{}'.format()` syntax (bonus points for declaring variables and type formatting in there as well) will save you from annoying bugs and make your code look cleaner, which should be the end goal for maintainability's sake. If you don't like the format syntax, you can always use f-strings, which are an optimized and much more shorthand means of interpolating values into strings. Throughout this book, I stick to the older format to make the code more approachable to people who are familiar with that, but in practice I use f-strings.

Executing the code from listing 5.10 and building a visualization (which can also be stored for later reference) is as simple as the following code.

Listing 5.11   Usage of the outlier visualization function

```
irrelevant_outlier = generate_outlier_plots(jfk, 'JFK', 'International
    Passengers', '2003-10-24', 'Concorde Retired', 'irrelevant_outlier.svg')
```

If we execute this, we get the visualization shown in figure 5.10. Notice that we don't have to specify date windows, formatting, or any other boilerplate since it is all dynamically generated based on the function's configuration arguments. We can even plot the international passenger counts with this function instead of hardcoding all the values into the script, as we did in listing 5.7 (and the subsequent visualization).

To demonstrate the benefits of taking a little bit of extra time and building a function out of even experimental validation code, let's see what we can do with the data generation from a completely different airport, LaGuardia (LGA). If we scripted out our original outlier plotting and wanted to generate the same plot for LGA, we'd have to copy the JFK script, go through the painstaking process of overwriting each reference to JFK, change the plotting and analysis field from International Passengers to Domestic Passengers, and hope that we get all of the references replaced to prevent the wrong time series or values from being plotted. (Since the Python REPL has the concept of object constancy, all references are held

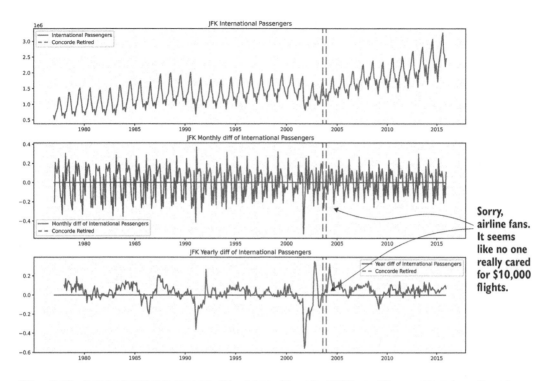

Figure 5.10 Using a function to generate this plot provides adaptability, and its reusable nature allows for rapid validation of data anomalies, saving time.

in memory until the kernel REPL is stopped.) The code with the function implementation of the plotting is shown next.

Listing 5.12 Experimental phase function use for outlier analysis

Pulls the data for LaGuardia. (This is for demonstration purposes only. In a properly developed solution, we would load the data only once and apply a filter directly on the in-memory DataFrame.)

Sets the index frequency of "beginning of month" in the same way that we did for JFK data

```
laguardia = get_airport_data('LGA', DATA_PATH)
laguardia = apply_index_freq(laguardia, 'MS')
useful_outlier = generate_outlier_plots(laguardia, 'LGA', 'Domestic
    Passengers', '2001-09-11', 'Domestic Passenger Impact of 9/11',
    'lga_sep_11_outlier.svg')
```

Generates the visualizations and saves them to disk. The arguments for this function make generating these plots trivial, but more important, repeatable.

With these three brief lines, we can get a new visualization that is stored to disk, labeled appropriately for the indicated outlier period that we discovered, without the need to reimplement all the code originally used to build the dataset and the visualizations. Figure 5.11 shows the resulting visualization.

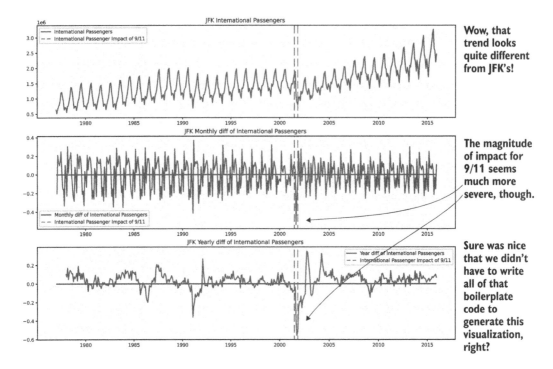

Wow, that trend looks quite different from JFK's!

The magnitude of impact for 9/11 seems much more severe, though.

Sure was nice that we didn't have to write all of that boilerplate code to generate this visualization, right?

Figure 5.11   Plot result from listing 5.12

NOTE   The functions shown here are for illustrative purposes only. Later chapters cover proper ways of building functions and methods for ML so that fewer actions are taken in a single function or method. For now, the point is simply to illustrate the benefit of reusable code even in the early stages of a project.

When functions should be created

In the course of experimentation, in addition to the immediate focus of solving a problem, we should consider which elements of the code need to be modularized for reuse. Not every aspect of a solution needs to be production-ready, particularly in the early stages, but it is helpful to start thinking about which aspects of the project will need to be referenced or executed many times over.

Stepping aside from rapid prototyping to build functions can sometimes feel like a temporary derailment of what you're trying to get done. It's important to realize that, by taking an hour or so to create a generic reference to a repeatable task, you could be saving yourself dozens of hours later.

These hours are mostly saved by the simple fact that when you're working to convert your scripted solution into a properly developed ML code base, you won't have to review so many implementations. Instead of dozens of visualizations and scoring functions littered throughout the code, you will be left with a group of single-purpose functions that will need to be looked at and evaluated as only a single unit.

Some elements that I typically look to create functions for as early as possible in the ML space are as follows:

- Data ingestion and data cleansing
- Scoring and error calculations
- General data visualizations
- Validation and prediction visualizations
- Model performance reports (for example, ROC curves and confusion matrices)

Many other instances are eligible for "function treatment" early in the process of building an ML solution. The important point to keep in mind when building even the earliest phases of a project is to either set aside the time to create reusable code immediately, or to at least flag the code for implementation in such a way that makes it easy to identify for action as soon as is practicable.

WHY ARE WE TALKING ABOUT THE BENEFITS OF FUNCTIONS? SURELY EVERYONE KNOWS WHEN TO USE THEM, RIGHT?

The reality of experimentation in predictive modeling is that most ML practitioners end up spending the vast majority of their efforts working on feature engineering, data validation, and modeling. The process of constant code rewrites and testing inures us all to the fact that the project experimentation code that we're building can rapidly devolve into a half-implemented, commented-out, and generally unreadable sprawl of chaos.

Sometimes it feels as if, in the process of wanting to test something new, it's easier to copy a block of code from a notebook cell far above just to simply get something to work quickly. This ends up causing a complete disjointed mess of mangled code that is going to require a monumental undertaking to fashion into something eligible for further development.

Most of the time, when I've seen (or done, in the past) such greenfield experimentation, all the original testing code is simply abandoned when an approach is decided upon. It doesn't have to be that way, though. If a little care is taken during this phase, the subsequent development phases can be much more efficient.

If you're working on a team, these problems only compound themselves. Imagine if this project were being undertaken by six subteams of data scientists. By the time the testing phase of ideas was complete, dozens of implementations would exist of the data ingestion alone, paired with at least a dozen ways of plotting the data and running statistical analysis on the time-series data. Standardization and using functions can help reduce this redundant code.

5.2.3   *One last note on building reusable code for experimentation*

Before we move on to the modeling phase of this project's experimentation, let's look at another function. This function will help us get a useful snapshot of a particular time series (one of the passenger series of data) from one of the airports in the list of comparison locations for each of the models.

Earlier we took a look at plotting outliers (section 5.2.2) and getting trend decomposition plots (section 5.2.1). Two additional plots, if we had them, would be invaluable in helping inform us of the initial settings we should use for some of the model types that we'll be testing. Those two plots are of autocorrelation and partial autocorrelation.

Autocorrelation is an algorithm that will run a Pearson's test between the time series and lagged values of the same series (previous steps of the same data series), giving results in a range of –1 to +1, indicating the relative correlation between these lags. A value of +1 is a maximum positive correlation, indicating a perfect synchronicity between the values at that specified lag position throughout the data series (if there is a repeatable pattern every 10 values along the time series, this will show up as a maximum positive correlation of +1). The graph plotted from an autocorrelation test will show each lag value that has been calculated, and a blue cone stretching out from 0 in a logarithmic curve, denoting a confidence interval (defaulted at 95%). The points that extend outside this blue cone are considered statistically significant. The autocorrelation test includes direct dependence information in the lag measurement as well as indirect effects.

Because of this impact of the nature of the autocorrelation test, it can be slightly misleading when looked at on its own. Along with the autocorrelation test, a useful additional plot, the *partial autocorrelation test*, is also used when analyzing time-series data. This additional test evaluates each lag position in a similar way that autocorrelation does, but it goes one step further by removing the effects that previous lag values introduced to the independent lag being measured. By removing these effects, the direct lag relationship at that particular value can be measured.

WHY IS THIS IMPORTANT?

We can use the values uncovered in these charts as starting points for our modeling (the models that are designed for autoregression, that is). We'll get more into that in chapter 6.

For now, we should make sure that before anyone starts off on modeling, we have a standardized way of generating these charts in one shot so that all the teams can rapidly generate these visualizations to help guide their tuning. Let's create a simple function to plot most of what we need to analyze the series that we'll be forecasting.

> Listing 5.13   **Standardized time series visualization and analysis for model preparation**

```
from statsmodels.graphics.tsaplots import plot_acf, plot_pacf
def stationarity_tests(time_df, series_col, time_series_name, period,
image_name, lags=12, cf_alpha=0.05, style='seaborn', plot_size=(16, 32)):
```

Wrapper around matplotlib.pyplot.plot to allow for setting graph styling and a more efficient rendering of plot cells

Slight adjustment for rendering the plots to ensure that the titles and axis labels don't overlap

Extracts the start and end values of the index to allow for plotting horizontal lines

Calculates the log differencing data for the outlier plot

Decomposes the series to get the trend component, seasonality component, and the residuals as NumPy series

```
log_col_name = 'Log {}'.format(series_col)
diff_log_col_name = 'LogDiff {}'.format(series_col)
time_df[log_col_name] = np.log(time_df[series_col])
time_df[diff_log_col_name] = time_df[log_col_name].diff()          ◄
decomposed_trend = seasonal_decompose(time_df[series_col], period=period)
df_index_start = time_df.index.values[0]
df_index_end = time_df.index.values[len(time_df)-1]
with plt.style.context(style=style):
    fig, axes = plt.subplots(7, 1, figsize=plot_size)
    plt.subplots_adjust(hspace=0.3)                                ◄
    axes[0].plot(time_df[series_col], '-', label='Raw data for
        {}'.format(time_series_name))
    axes[0].legend(loc='upper left')
    axes[0].set_title('Raw data trend for {}'.format(time_series_name))
    axes[0].set_ylabel(series_col)
    axes[0].set_xlabel(time_df.index.name)
    axes[1].plot(time_df[diff_log_col_name], 'g-', label='Log Diff for
        {}'.format(time_series_name))
    axes[1].hlines(0.0, df_index_start, df_index_end, 'r', label='Series
        center')
    axes[1].legend(loc='lower left')
    axes[1].set_title('Diff Log Trend for outliers in
        {}'.format(time_series_name))
    axes[1].set_ylabel(series_col)
    axes[1].set_xlabel(time_df.index.name)
    fig = plot_acf(time_df[series_col], lags=lags, ax=axes[2])      ◄
    fig = plot_pacf(time_df[series_col], lags=lags, ax=axes[3])     ◄
    axes[2].set_xlabel('lags')
    axes[2].set_ylabel('correlation')
    axes[3].set_xlabel('lags')
    axes[3].set_ylabel('correlation')
    axes[4].plot(decomposed_trend.trend, 'r-', label='Trend data for
        {}'.format(time_series_name))
    axes[4].legend(loc='upper left')
    axes[4].set_title('Trend component of decomposition for
        {}'.format(time_series_name))
    axes[4].set_ylabel(series_col)
    axes[4].set_xlabel(time_df.index.name)
    axes[5].plot(decomposed_trend.seasonal, 'r-', label='Seasonal data for
        {}'.format(time_series_name))
    axes[5].legend(loc='center left', bbox_to_anchor=(0,1))
    axes[5].set_title('Seasonal component of decomposition for
        {}'.format(time_series_name))
    axes[5].set_ylabel(series_col)
    axes[5].set_xlabel(time_df.index.name)
```

Plot of the raw data to have a visual reference for all the other plots

Outlier data plot (log diff)

Autocorrelation plot to provide insight for tuning (along with the partial autocorrelation) for autoregressive models

Partial autocorrelation plot to provide insight for tuning autoregressive models

Plot of the extracted trend from the series

Plot of the seasonality signal from the series

Plot of the residuals from the series ⟶

```
axes[6].plot(decomposed_trend.resid, 'r.', label='Residuals data for
    {}'.format(time_series_name))
axes[6].hlines(0.0, df_index_start, df_index_end, 'black',
    label='Series Center')
axes[6].legend(loc='center left', bbox_to_anchor=(0,1))
axes[6].set_title('Residuals component of decomposition for
    {}'.format(time_series_name))
axes[6].set_ylabel(series_col)
axes[6].set_xlabel(time_df.index.name)
plt.savefig(image_name, format='svg')          ⟵⎯⎯  Saves the figure for
plt.tight_layout()                                    later reference and
return fig   ⟵⎯⎯                                      for presentations
```

Returns the composed figure in case additional processing is desired

Now let's see what that code produces. Figure 5.12 is the result of executing the following code.

Listing 5.14   Trend visualization for Newark domestic passengers

From the original source dataset, acquires the data for EWR (Newark International Airport)

```
ewr = get_airport_data('EWR', DATA_PATH)
ewr = apply_index_freq(ewr, 'MS')          ⟵⎯⎯  Applies the frequency
ewr_plots = stationarity_tests(ewr, 'Domestic Passengers', 'Newark Airport',    on the date index of
    12, 'newark_domestic_plots.svg', 48, 0.05)    ⟵⎯⎯⎯⎯⎯⎯⎯⎯   the DataFrame
```

Generates the snapshot charts for the time series specified (domestic passengers) for Newark

Now we're finally ready to start model evaluations. We have some standard visualizations that are wrapped up nicely in reusable functions, we know which airports are going to be adjudicated for the test, and the tooling that we've developed will ensure that each experimental test will be using the same set of visualizations and data processing steps. We've eliminated much of the boilerplate code that might have been developed, and reduced the time to get started on the core problem that we're trying to solve: forecasting.

We'll be building additional standard visualizations for the modeling phase when we start that in the next chapter. For now, we can guarantee one thing: the teams won't be reinventing the wheel or using copy and paste too much.

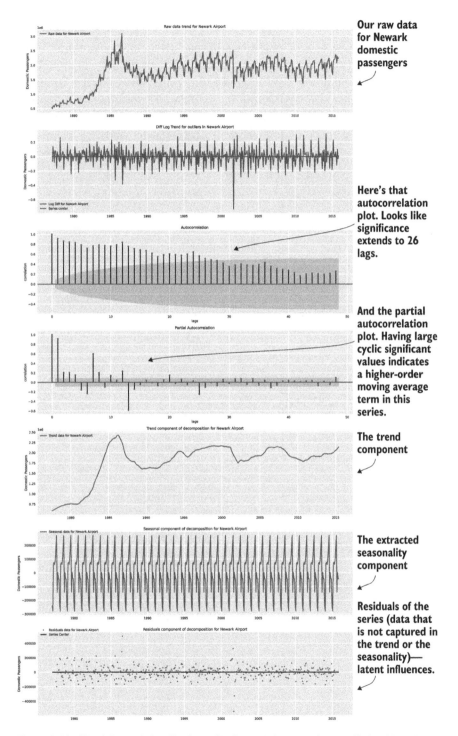

Figure 5.12 The full trend visualization suite for model preparation, applied to Newark International Airport domestic passenger travel data

Summary

- Thorough research of potential approaches to solve a problem involves time-constrained evaluation through dataset statistical analysis, model API review, API documentation perusal, rapid prototyping, and objective comparison.
- Gaining a deep understanding of candidate feature data through appropriate statistical evaluation and visualization will help uncover issues early. Starting with a clean and well-defined state of familiarity with the training data for a project will eliminate costly rework later in the project's development cycle.

Experimentation in action: Testing and evaluating a project

This chapter covers
- Evaluating potential approaches for an ML project
- Objectively selecting an approach for a project's implementation

The preceding chapter covered all the preparatory actions that should be taken to minimize the risks associated with an experimentation phase of a project. These range from conducting research that informs the options available for solving the problem to building useful functions that the team members can leverage during the prototyping phase. We will continue the previous scenario throughout this chapter, a time-series modeling project for airport passenger demand forecasting, while focusing on methodologies to be applied to experimental testing that will serve to reduce the chances of project failure.

We will spend time covering testing methodologies simply because this stage of project development is absolutely crucial for two primary reasons. First, at one extreme, if not enough approaches are tested (evaluated critically and objectively), the chosen approach may be insufficient to solve the actual problem. At the other extreme, testing too many options to too great a depth can result in an experimental prototyping phase that risks taking too long in the eyes of the business.

By following a methodology that aims to rapidly test ideas, using uniform scoring methods to achieve comparability between approaches, and focusing on evaluation of the performance of the approaches rather than the absolute accuracy of the predictions, the chances of project abandonment can be reduced.

Figure 6.1 compares the two extremes of prototyping within an ML project. The middle ground, the moderate approach, has shown the highest success rates with the teams that I've either led or worked with.

As this diagram shows, the extreme approaches on either side frequently result in polar opposite problems. On the left side, there exists an extremely high probability for project cancellation due to a lack of faith on the part of the business the business in the DS team's ability to deliver a solution. Barring a case of extreme good luck, the solution that the team haphazardly selected and barely tested is likely not going to be even remotely optimal. Their implementation of their solution is equally likely to be poor, expensive, and fragile.

On the other side of the diagram, however, there exists a different problem entirely. The academic-influenced thoroughness on display here is admirable and would work well for a team conducting original research. For a DS team working in industry, though, the sheer volume of time required to thoroughly evaluate all possible solutions to a problem will delay the project far longer than most companies have patience for. Customized feature engineering for each approach, full evaluation of available models in popular frameworks, and, potentially, the implementation of novel algorithms are all sunk costs. While they are more scientifically rigorous as a series of actions to take, the time spent building each of these approaches in order to properly vet which is most effective means that other projects aren't being worked on. As the old adage goes, time is money, and spending time building out fully fledged approaches to solve a problem is expensive from both a time and a money perspective.

For the purposes of exploring an effective approach in an applications-focused manner, we will continue with the preceding chapter's scenario of time-series modeling. In this chapter, we'll move through the middle ground of figure 6.1 to arrive at the candidate approach that is most likely to result in a successful MVP.

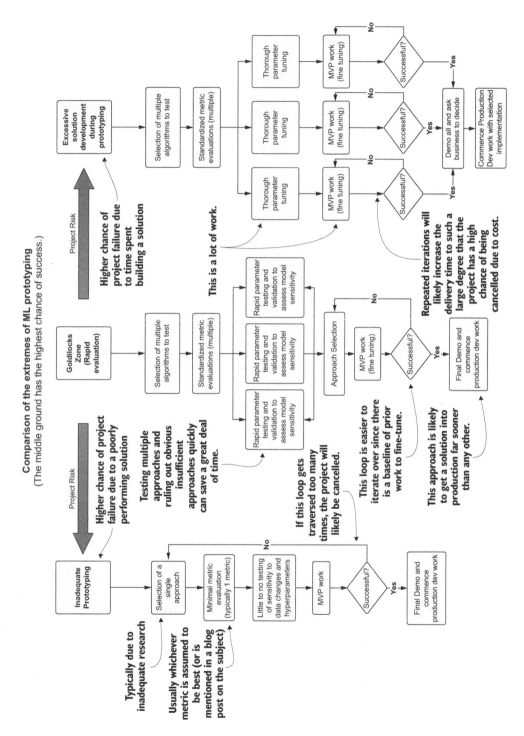

Figure 6.1   The sliding scale of approaches to ML solution prototyping work

Resist the temptation to achieve perfection at this stage

As data scientists, our natural inclination in all of our work is to build solutions that are as optimal and mathematically correct as possible. This is an important drive to have, but it should be the goal for the project as a whole. During early testing phases, having a drive for perfection can actually be a detriment to the success of a project.

While the project's business sponsors share the same desire to have the best possible solutions, their visibility into this solution is focused only on the eventual approach that you decide upon. They are also focused on the time required to develop this solution (as well as its cost). They have no visibility into what you're doing to figure out the best solution, and don't really care how many things you've tested on the way to discovering an optimal solution.

It is best, at this stage of prototyping and testing approaches, to eschew your innate desire to fully explore all options to solve a problem and instead focus on efficient means of finding the most probable approach. By adjusting focus in this way and shifting your paradigm to thinking of the time to deliver as the second-most important factor in the project, you will ensure a higher chance of the solution being allowed to progress further along the path to production.

6.1 *Testing ideas*

At the conclusion of chapter 5, we were left at a stage where we were ready to evaluate the different univariate modeling approaches for forecasting passengers at airports. The team is now ready to split into groups; each will focus on implementations of the various researched options that have been discovered, putting forth their best efforts not only to produce as accurate a solution as they can, but also to understand the nuances of tuning each model.

Before everyone goes off to hack through the implementations, a few more standard tooling functions need to be developed to ensure that everyone is evaluating the same metrics, producing the same reports, and generating the appropriate visualizations that can easily show the benefits and drawbacks of the disparate approaches. Once these are completed, the teams can then get into the task of evaluating and researching each of their assigned modeling tasks, all using the same core functionality and scoring. Figure 6.2 gives an overview of typical utilities, functionality, and standards that should be adhered to during the model prototyping phase of a project.

As mentioned in section 5.2, this path of actions is generally focused on supervised learning project work. A prototyping phase for, say, a CNN would look quite a bit different (with far more front-loaded work in building human-readable evaluations of the model performance, particularly if we're talking about a classifier). But in general, these pre-work actions and approaches to prototyping different solutions will save weeks of frustrating rework and confusion if adhered to.

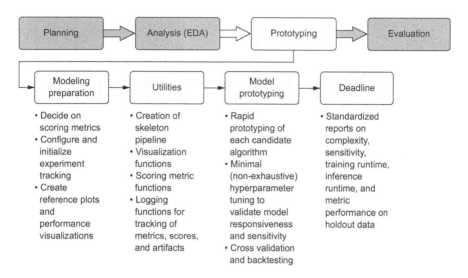

Figure 6.2   The prototyping phase work elements and their functions

6.1.1   Setting guidelines in code

In chapter 5, we looked at and developed a set of visualization tools and basic data ingestion and formatting functions that each team can use. We built these for two primary purposes:

- *Standardization*—So that each team is generating identical plots, figures, and metrics to allow for a coherent comparison between the different approaches
- *Communication*—So that we can generate referenceable visualizations to demonstrate to the business how our modeling efforts are solving the problem

It is critically important to meet these two needs starting at this phase of project work. Without standardization, we run the risk of making poor decisions on which approach to go with for the MVP (and the subsequent fully developed solution). In addition, we risk wasting time by multiple teams that, instead of testing their approaches, are building implementations that are effectively identical to a visualization that in essence does the same thing. Without the communication aspect, we would be left with either confusing metric score values to report, or, in the worst case, raw code to show to the business. Either approach would be a recipe for disaster in a demonstration meeting.

Always be prepared with non-confusing plots

One of the earliest lessons that I learned as a fledgling data scientist (back before we were called that) was that not every person in a company has an appetite for statistics. There is no better way to learn this than by spouting off the veracity of a solution that you've spent months working on by claiming some obscure (to them, not to

(continued)

us) accuracy score, confidence interval, or other mathematical metric to an executive who is providing funding for a project.

As a species, we yearn for order and patterns in the world. *Negentropy* (a term coined by Leon Brillouin) is a natural evolutionary tendency that is effectively programmed into us. Because of this, visual representations of data, particularly when crafted to simplify a highly complex system, are always going to be more effective as a communications tool.

I can't recommend strongly enough that for any particular solution that a data scientist is working on, a great deal of thought and energy should be spent thinking of, and building, the most effective and easy-to-comprehend visualization that conveys the respective predictive power of the algorithms in use (or developed from scratch) to solve the targeted business problem. This isn't to say that everyone in the business units is going to be ignorant of the metrics used; rather, the point is that a visual representation is always going to be more powerful in conveying information about an ML solution than any other means.

To quote the original conveyer of the idea, Henrik Ibsen, "A thousand words leave not the same deep impression as does a single deed." In other words, conveniently adapted by Fred R. Barnard, "a picture is worth a thousand words."

Before the teams break out and start developing their assigned solutions too intensely in their respective silos, we could stand to have one final analysis done by the larger team to help inform how well their predictions are performing in a visual sense. Keep in mind that, as we discussed in chapter 4, at the conclusion of this phase of experimentation the team will need to present its findings in a way that can be easily digested by a non-ML and nontechnical audience.

One of the most effective ways of achieving this communication is through simple visualizations. Focusing on showing the results of the approach's output with clear and simple annotations can not only benefit the early phases of testing but also can be used to report on performance of the solution later, when it is in production. Avoiding confusing reports and tables of metrics with no visual cue to explain what they mean will ensure clear and concise communication with the business.

BASELINE COMPARISON VISUALIZATION

To have a basic reference for more-complex models, it can be beneficial to see what the simplest implementation produces; then we can see if whatever we come up with can do better than that. This baseline, for the purposes of time-series modeling, can take the form of a simple moving average and an exponentially smoothed average. Neither of these two approaches would be applicable for the forecasting needs of the project, but their output results can be used to see, within the holdout period for validation, if our more sophisticated approaches will be an improvement.

To create a visualization that the teams can use to see these relationships for simpler algorithms, we first have to define an exponential smoothing function, as shown in the next listing. Keep in mind that this is all designed both to standardize the work of each team and to build an effective communication tool for conveying the success of the project to the business.

Listing 6.1 Exponential smoothing function to generate a comparison forecast

alpha is the smoothing parameter, providing dampening to the previous values in the series. (Values close to 1.0 have strong dampening effects, while conversely, values near 0.0 are not dampened as much.)

Adds the starting value from the series to initiate the correct index positions for the traversal

Iterates through the series, applying the exponential smoothing formula to each value and preceding value

```
def exp_smoothing(raw_series, alpha=0.05):
    output = [raw_series[0]]
    for i in range(1, len(raw_series)):
        output.append(raw_series[i] * alpha + (1-alpha) * output[i-1])
    return output
```

A complementary function is needed for additional analytics purposes to generate a metric and error estimation for these simple modeling fits for the time series. The following listing provides a method for calculating the mean absolute error for the fit, as well as for calculating the uncertainty intervals (`yhat` values).

Listing 6.2 Mean absolute error and uncertainty

Instantiates a dictionary to place the calculated values in for the purposes of currying

Calculates the standard deviation of the series differences to calculate the uncertainty threshold (yhat)

```
from sklearn.metrics import mean_absolute_error
def calculate_mae(raw_series, smoothed_series, window, scale):
    res = {}
    mae_value = mean_absolute_error(raw_series[window:],
        smoothed_series[window:])
    res['mae'] = mae_value
    deviation = np.std(raw_series[window:] - smoothed_series[window:])
    res['stddev'] = deviation
    yhat = mae_value + scale * deviation
    res['yhat_low'] = smoothed_series - yhat
    res['yhat_high'] = smoothed_series + yhat
    return res
```

Uses the standard sklearn mean_absolute_error function to get the MAE between the raw data and the smoothed series

Calculates the standard baseline yhat value for the differenced series

Generates a low and high yhat series centered around the smoothed series data

NOTE Throughout these code listings, `import` statements are shown where needed above functions. This is for demonstration purposes only. All `import` statements should always be at the top of the code, whether writing in a notebook, a script, or in an IDE as modules.

Now that we've defined the two functions in listings 6.1 and 6.2, we can call them in another function to generate not only a visualization, but a series of both the moving average and the exponentially smoothed data. The code to generate this reference data and an easily referenceable visualization for each airport and passenger type follows.

Listing 6.3   Generating smoothing plots

```
def smoothed_time_plots(time_series, time_series_name, image_name,
    smoothing_window, exp_alpha=0.05, yhat_scale=1.96, style='seaborn',
    plot_size=(16, 24)):
    reference_collection = {}              ⟵──  Currying dictionary for
    ts = pd.Series(time_series)                  data return values
    with plt.style.context(style=style):
        fig, axes = plt.subplots(3, 1, figsize=plot_size)
        plt.subplots_adjust(hspace=0.3)
        moving_avg = ts.rolling(window=smoothing_window).mean()    ⟵─┘
        exp_smoothed = exp_smoothing(ts, exp_alpha)
        res = calculate_mae(time_series, moving_avg, smoothing_window,
            yhat_scale)
        res_exp = calculate_mae(time_series, exp_smoothed, smoothing_window,
            yhat_scale)
        exp_data = pd.Series(exp_smoothed, index=time_series.index)    ⟵─
        exp_yhat_low_data = pd.Series(res_exp['yhat_low'],
            index=time_series.index)
        exp_yhat_high_data = pd.Series(res_exp['yhat_high'],
            index=time_series.index)
        axes[0].plot(ts, '-', label='Trend for {}'.format(time_series_name))
        axes[0].legend(loc='upper left')
        axes[0].set_title('Raw Data trend for {}'.format(time_series_name))
        axes[1].plot(ts, '-', label='Trend for {}'.format(time_series_name))
        axes[1].plot(moving_avg, 'g-', label='Moving Average with window:
            {}'.format(smoothing_window))
        axes[1].plot(res['yhat_high'], 'r--', label='yhat bounds')
        axes[1].plot(res['yhat_low'], 'r--')
        axes[1].set_title('Moving Average Trend for window: {} with MAE of:
            {:.1f}'.format(smoothing_window, res['mae']))
        axes[1].legend(loc='upper left')
        axes[2].plot(ts, '-', label='Trend for {}'.format(time_series_name))
        axes[2].legend(loc='upper left')
        axes[2].plot(exp_data, 'g-', label='Exponential Smoothing with alpha:
            {}'.format(exp_alpha))
        axes[2].plot(exp_yhat_high_data, 'r--', label='yhat bounds')
        axes[2].plot(exp_yhat_low_data, 'r--')
        axes[2].set_title('Exponential Smoothing Trend for alpha: {} with MAE
            of: {:.1f}'.format(exp_alpha, res_exp['mae']))
        axes[2].legend(loc='upper left')
        plt.savefig(image_name, format='svg')
        plt.tight_layout()
        reference_collection['plots'] = fig
        reference_collection['moving_average'] = moving_avg
        reference_collection['exp_smooth'] = exp_smoothed
        return reference_collection
```

Calls the function defined in listing 6.1

Calls the function defined in listing 6.2 for the simple moving average series

Calls the function defined in listing 6.2 for the exponentially smoothed trend

Simple time-series moving average calculation

Applies the pandas index date series to the non-indexed exponentially smoothed series (and the yhat series values as well)

Uses string interpolation with numeric formatting so the visualizations are more legible

We call this function in the next listing. With this data and the visualization prebuilt, the teams can have an easy-to-use and standard guide to reference throughout their modeling experimentation.

Listing 6.4 Calling the reference smoothing function for series data and visualizations

```
ewr_data = get_airport_data('EWR', DATA_PATH)
ewr_reference = smoothed_time_plots(ewr_data['International Passengers'],
    'Newark International', 'newark_dom_smooth_plot.svg', 12, exp_alpha=0.25)
```

When it's executed, this code will give the subteams a quick reference visualization (and the series data to compare with from the moving average and exponentially weighted moving average smoothing algorithm), shown in figure 6.3.

The goal in wrapping this boilerplate visualization code into a function (as shown in listing 6.3 and used in listing 6.4) at this stage is twofold:

- *Portability*—Each team can be given this function as a referenceable bit of code that can be used as a dependency to its work, ensuring that everyone is generating the exact same visualizations.
- *Preparing for production*—This code, as a function, can be easily ported into a visualization class as a method that can be used for not only this project, but also other forecasting projects in the future.

The focus on spending a marginal amount of time at creating reusable code may not seem worthwhile at this point, particularly with the focus that we've been giving to timeliness of delivery for the solution prototype. But rest assured, as projects grow in scope and the complexity extends far beyond a simple forecasting problem, the relatively small effort made at this point to prepare for modularized code now will save a great deal of time later.

STANDARD METRICS

The last thing the team needs to implement before moving to the model experimentation is the standardized measurement of the forecasting predictions to holdout validation data. This effort is to eliminate any chance of debate regarding the effectiveness of each implementation. We're effectively streamlining the adjudication of each implementation's merits by way of standardization, which will not only save time in meetings, but also provide a strong scientific methodology to the comparison of each.

If were we to leave each team to determine its own optimal evaluation metrics, comparing them to one another would be nigh impossible, leading to rework of tests and further project delays. If we were to accumulate enough of these avoidable delays, we could dramatically increase the possibility of project abandonment.

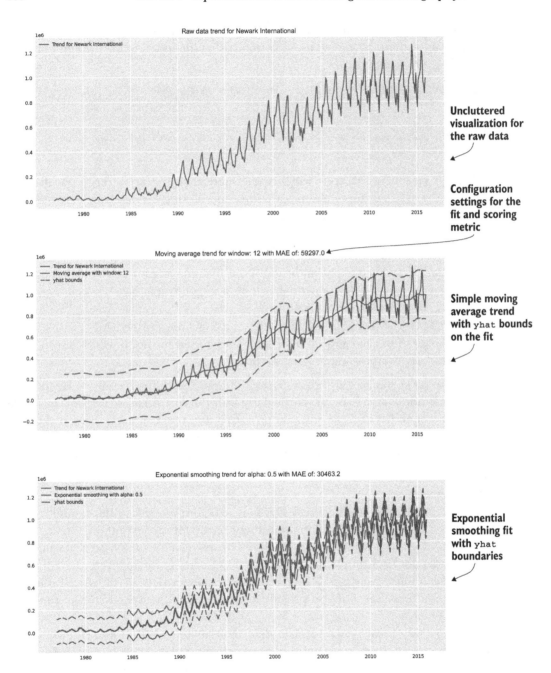

Figure 6.3   Reference trends visualization based on the usage of the `smoothed_time_plots()` **function, as shown in listing 6.4**

Arguing over metrics sounds silly, right?

Yes. Yes, it most certainly does.

Have I seen it done? Yes, I have.

Have I done it? Shamefully, yes, and I wish I had those hours of my life back to use more fruitfully.

Have I endured it as a recipient? I most certainly have.

Have I seen it be the cause of a project being cancelled? No, that's ridiculous.

What needs to be mentioned is that time is finite. When building a solution to solve a business problem, only so many delays can be allowed to occur before the business unit will either continue doing what it's been doing up until the DS team was involved, or will flat-out call for a cancellation of the project and basically refuse to ever work with the team again.

Avoidable and superfluous delays surrounding sustained arguments about which metric to use to evaluate a model are flat-out silly, particularly when we consider that it's such a trivial investment of time to calculate all the metrics for a model evaluation and have their referenceable scores preserved for post hoc evaluation at any time in the future. Just collect all that are relevant to the problem you're trying to solve (with the notable exception mentioned earlier—if the metric is of such computational complexity to prove noticeably expensive to acquire, make sure it's worthwhile to capture before writing the code for it). Adapting the code to support such flexibility is in alignment with Agile principles, permitting a rapid pivot without requiring a large refactoring to change the functionality.

In section 5.1.3, we covered the agreed-upon metrics that the team will be using to score models: R-squared, MSE, RMSE, MAE, MAPE, and explained variance. To save a great deal of time for each subteam that will be focused on implementing the modeling tests, we should build a few functions that will make scoring and standardized reporting of the results much easier.

First, we need to actually implement MAPE, as it is not readily available as a scoring metric in Python libraries (at the time of this writing). This metric is of critical importance to assessing the overall quality of predictions across so many different time series, as it is a scaled and standardized value that can be used to compare against different forecasts without having to account for the magnitude of the series values.

It shouldn't, however, be used as the only measurement metric, as we discussed earlier in planning for our experimentation. Having multiple metrics recorded for each experiment being conducted is going to pay dividends if we need to evaluate previous experiments based on a different metric. The following listing shows a basic MAPE implementation.

> **Listing 6.5**   Simple MAPE implementation

```
def mape(y_true, y_pred):
    return np.mean(np.abs((y_true - y_pred) / y_true)) * 100
```

Now that we have that defined, we can create a simple series scoring function that will calculate all the agreed-upon metrics without having to litter all of the experimentation code bases with manual implementations of each calculation. This function will also allow us to embed these calculations into our visualizations without having to constantly redefine standard metric calculations throughout the code. The standard metric function that we'll be using is shown next.

> **Listing 6.6**   Standard error calculations for scoring forecast data

Imports and utilizes as many standard scoring implementations as possible that are available. There's no reason to reinvent the wheel.

```
from sklearn.metrics import explained_variance_score, mean_absolute_error,
        mean_squared_error, r2_score
def calculate_errors(y_true, y_pred):          ◁─── Passes in the actual series and the
    error_scores = {}                               predicted series for the forecasting
    mse = mean_squared_error(y_true, y_pred)        validation time period
    error_scores['mae'] = mean_absolute_error(y_true, y_pred)
    error_scores['mape'] = mape(y_true, y_pred)    ◁─── Calculation and usage of the mape
    error_scores['mse'] = mse                           calculation defined in listing 6.5
    error_scores['rmse'] = sqrt(mse)
    error_scores['explained_var'] = explained_variance_score(y_true, y_pred)
    error_scores['r2'] = r2_score(y_true, y_pred)
    return error_scores
```

Local variable declaration (since the mse value will be stored and used for the rmse metric)

Instantiates a dictionary construct for storing the scores for use elsewhere (notice the absence of print statements)

Conspicuously absent from this function is a `print` statement. This is by design for two distinctly different reasons.

First, we want to use the dictionary-encapsulated score metrics for the visualization we're going to build for the teams to use; therefore, we don't want to have the values simply printed to stdout. Second, it's a bad practice to have stdout reporting in functions and methods, as this will create more work for you later when developing a solution.

Digging through code prior to a release to production to scrub out `print` statements (or convert them to logging statements) is tedious, error-prone, and if missed, can have performance impacts on production solutions (particularly in lazily evaluated languages). In addition, in production, *no one will ever read* stdout, leaving the `print` statements as nothing more than needlessly executed code.

Print statements and why they're terrible for ML

Honestly, `print` statements are bad for all software. The only notable exception is for temporary debugging of code. If you want to check the state of something complex during runtime, they can be a great help. Aside from that specific use case, they should be avoided at all costs.

The problem is that I see them everywhere: printed row counts, printed scoring metrics, printed lengths of arrays and lists, printed hyperparameters being tested, printed sources and sinks for I/O operations, and printed configurations for arguments supplied to methods. They're all equally useless (and most are actively detrimental to your team's infrastructure budget).

Blog posts, hello worlds, and basic Getting Started guides for APIs use them liberally to showcase an immediate and gratifying result for those getting into a new language, topic, or API, but once you've become marginally familiar with the syntax and usage, these should always be removed from code. The reason is simple: you're never going to look at those `print` statements ever again outside of experimentation and development. Littering them around in code will leave confusing and hard-to find references within stdout, indicating where the code is going to be running in production, which generally means that once a run is over, the information is lost forever.

The better approach for information associated with an ML run is to persist the data to a location that can be easily queried or visually referenced. That way, the information that you painstakingly collect for the purpose of the `print` statement can be stored for later reference, plotting, or for system control for automated processes.

Do yourself a favor and, if you really need to print things during experimentation, make sure that `print` statements are present only in experimental script code. The better alternative is to log the results in code, or, as we will cover in the next chapter, a service like MLflow.

For the final pre-modeling work, we need to build a quick visualization and metric-reporting function that will give each team a standard and highly reusable means of evaluating the prediction performance for each model. The following listing shows a simple example, which we will be utilizing during the model experimentation phase in section 6.1.2.

Listing 6.7 Prediction forecast plotting with error metrics

Calls the function created in listing 6.6 to calculate all of the agreed-upon error metrics for the project

Sets the inputs to be indexed series values instead of a DataFrame input with field names to keep the function more generic

```
def plot_predictions(y_true, y_pred, time_series_name, value_name,
    image_name, style='seaborn', plot_size=(16, 12)):
    validation_output = {}
    error_values = calculate_errors(y_true, y_pred)
    validation_output['errors'] = error_values
    text_str = '\n'.join((
        'mae = {:.3f}'.format(error_values['mae']),
        'mape = {:.3f}'.format(error_values['mape']),
```

Adds the error metrics to the output dictionary for use outside of simply producing a visualization

```
                  'mse = {:.3f}'.format(error_values['mse']),
                  'rmse = {:.3f}'.format(error_values['rmse']),
                  'explained var = {:.3f}'.format(error_values['explained_var']),
                  'r squared = {:.3f}'.format(error_values['r2']),
              ))
          with plt.style.context(style=style):
              fig, axes = plt.subplots(1, 1, figsize=plot_size)
              axes.plot(y_true, 'b-', label='Test data for
                  {}'.format(time_series_name))
              axes.plot(y_pred, 'r-', label='Forecast data for
                  {}'.format(time_series_name))
              axes.legend(loc='upper left')
              axes.set_title('Raw and Predicted data trend for
                  {}'.format(time_series_name))
              axes.set_ylabel(value_name)
              axes.set_xlabel(y_true.index.name)
              props = dict(boxstyle='round', facecolor='oldlace', alpha=0.5)
              axes.text(0.05, 0.9, text_str, transform=axes.transAxes, fontsize=12,
                  verticalalignment='top', bbox=props)
              validation_output['plot'] = fig
              plt.savefig(image_name, format='svg')
              plt.tight_layout()
          return validation_output
```

Generates the string that will be applied to a bounding box element superimposed on the graph

Plots the overlays of the actual and forecasted prediction data onto the same graph with different colors

Creates a text box that shows all error scores along with the plotted data

Writes the text contents into the text bounding box

Now, after creating these basic functions to accelerate our experimentation work, we can finally begin the process of testing various forecasting algorithms for our time-series work.

6.1.2   *Running quick forecasting tests*

The rapid testing phase is by far the most critical aspect of prototyping to get right. As mentioned in this chapter's introduction, it is imperative to strive for the middle ground—between not testing enough of the various approaches to determine the tuning sensitivity of each algorithm, and spending inordinate amounts of time building a full MVP solution for each approach. Since *time is the most important aspect of this phase*, we need to be efficient while making an informed decision about which approach shows the most promise in solving the problem in a robust manner.

Freshly armed with useful and standardized utility functions, each team can work on its respective approaches, rapidly testing to find the most promising model. The team has agreed that the airports under consideration for modeling tests are JFK, EWR, and LGA (each team needs to test its model and tuning paradigms on the same datasets so a fair evaluation of each approach can occur).

Let's take a look at what the teams will be doing with the different model approaches during rapid testing, what decisions will be made about the approaches, and how the teams can quickly pivot if they find that the approach is going nowhere. The exploratory phase is going to not only uncover nuances of each algorithm but also illuminate aspects of the project that might not have been realized during the preparatory phase (covered in chapter 5). It's important to remember that this is to be expected and that during this rapid testing phase, the teams should be in frequent communication with one another when they discover these problems (see the following sidebar for tips on effectively managing these discoveries).

A call for a referee during hackathons

Some of my most exciting DS work has occurred in the rapid prototyping phase of a project. It's exciting to see the creativity that's generated and the intensity of groups of brilliant minds working together to build a solution to a business problem previously thought to be unsolvable.

With all of the chaos of the day (or days, depending on the complexity of the problem) of a hackathon, it is important to have a moderator for the event. Whether it be the team lead, manager, lead data scientist, or the most senior individual technical contributor to the group, the important thing is to set one person aside from the work to serve as a communicator among the groups.

This person's role is to discuss what is being worked on, provide advice, and transfer knowledge that has been gained among the groups. This person shouldn't be actively working on any of the solutions because of the importance of the arbiter role. They should be spending time moving from group to group, asking brief but pointed questions, and helping provide advice on alternate strategies in case a team gets stuck.

We'll see throughout this exercise of rapid prototyping in this section that findings that come up in one team can apply to other teams. Having a neutral technical party available to disperse this information is key.

Whether the prototyping phase is gamified or not, the important point to remember is that the entire team is, after all, working for the same company. Everyone will eventually be focused on the approach that wins out through the MVP, development, and production phases of the solution. There's really nothing to be gained by having an aggressive and highly competitive competition.

Wait a minute . . . how are we going to create a validation dataset?

One group drew the proverbial short straw in the model-testing phase with a forecasting approach to research and test that isn't particularly well understood by the team. Someone on the team found mention of using a VAR to model multiple time series together (multivariate endogenous series modeling), and thus, this group sets out to research what this algorithm is all about and how to use it.

The first thing that they do is run a search for "vector autoregression," which results in a massive wall of formulaic theory analysis and mathematical proofs centered primarily around macro-econometrics research and natural sciences utilizations of the model. That's interesting, but not particularly useful if they want to test out the applications of this model to the data quickly. They next find the statsmodels API documentation for the model.

The team members quickly realize that they haven't thought about standardizing one common function yet: the split methodology. For most supervised ML problems, they've always used pandas split methodologies through DataFrame slicing or utilizing the high-level random split APIs, which use a random seed to select rows for training and test datasets. However, for forecasting, they realize that they haven't had to do datetime splitting in quite some time and need a deterministic and chronological split method to get accurate forecast validation holdout data. Since the dataset has an index set from the ingestion function's formatting of the DataFrame, they could probably craft a relatively simple splitting function based on the index position. What they come up with is in the following listing.

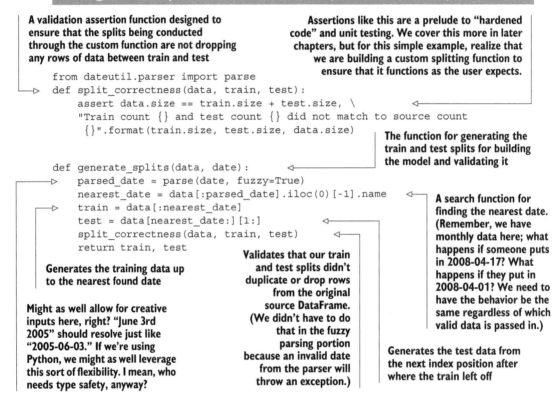

Listing 6.8 Time split for train and test datasets (with validation check)

A validation assertion function designed to ensure that the splits being conducted through the custom function are not dropping any rows of data between train and test

Assertions like this are a prelude to "hardened code" and unit testing. We cover this more in later chapters, but for this simple example, realize that we are building a custom splitting function to ensure that it functions as the user expects.

```
from dateutil.parser import parse
def split_correctness(data, train, test):
    assert data.size == train.size + test.size, \
    "Train count {} and test count {} did not match to source count
    {}".format(train.size, test.size, data.size)


def generate_splits(data, date):
    parsed_date = parse(date, fuzzy=True)
    nearest_date = data[:parsed_date].iloc(0)[-1].name
    train = data[:nearest_date]
    test = data[nearest_date:][1:]
    split_correctness(data, train, test)
    return train, test
```

The function for generating the train and test splits for building the model and validating it

A search function for finding the nearest date. (Remember, we have monthly data here; what happens if someone puts in 2008-04-17? What happens if they put in 2008-04-01? We need to have the behavior be the same regardless of which valid data is passed in.)

Generates the training data up to the nearest found date

Validates that our train and test splits didn't duplicate or drop rows from the original source DataFrame. (We didn't have to do that in the fuzzy parsing portion because an invalid date from the parser will throw an exception.)

Might as well allow for creative inputs here, right? "June 3rd 2005" should resolve just like "2005-06-03." If we're using Python, we might as well leverage this sort of flexibility. I mean, who needs type safety, anyway?

Generates the test data from the next index position after where the train left off

This team's members, being the wonderful stewards of teamwork and comradery that they know themselves to be, immediately send this function snippet to the other teams so that they can have an easy single-line methodology for splitting their data. They even put in a creative fuzzy matching parser in case people want to use different date formats.

Just to be sure that they've written it correctly, they're going to do some testing of their implementation. They want to make sure that they're actually getting exceptions raised if the data doesn't match up correctly. Let's see what they test in figure 6.4.

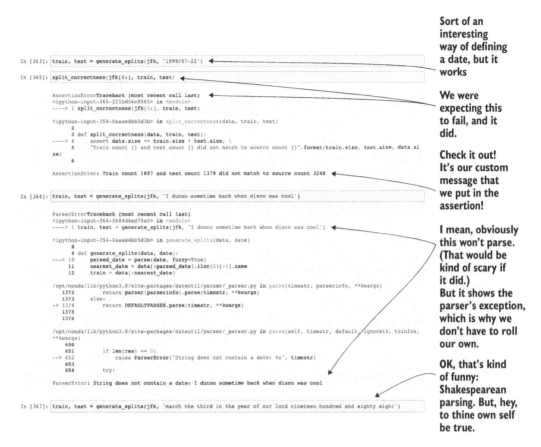

Annotations (right margin, top to bottom):

- Sort of an interesting way of defining a date, but it works
- We were expecting this to fail, and it did.
- Check it out! It's our custom message that we put in the assertion!
- I mean, obviously this won't parse. (That would be kind of scary if it did.) But it shows the parser's exception, which is why we don't have to roll our own.
- OK, that's kind of funny: Shakespearean parsing. But, hey, to thine own self be true.

Figure 6.4 This function validation for custom logic ensures that listing 6.8 functions the way we expect.

RAPID TESTING OF THE VAR MODEL APPROACH

Now that we have a way to split data into train and test, let's check back in with the team that was set up with testing out a VAR model. Without getting into excruciating detail about what this model can do, the goal of a VAR model is for simultaneous modeling of multiple time series in a single pass.

> **NOTE** If you are interested in learning more about these advanced approaches, there is no better resource than *New Introduction to Multiple Time Series Analysis* (Springer, 2006) by Helmut Lütkepohl, the creator of this algorithm.

The team looks at the example on the API docs page and starts to implement a simple test, shown next.

Listing 6.9 A rough first pass at a VAR model

There's our vector autoregressor that we've been talking about!

```
from statsmodels.tsa.vector_ar.var_model import VAR
jfk = get_airport_data('JFK', DATA_PATH)
```

Configures the **VAR** model with a vector of
time-series data. We can model both at the
same time! Cool? I guess?

Uses our super-sweet split function that
can read all sorts of nonsense that
people want to type in as dates

```
jfk = apply_index_freq(jfk, 'MS')
train, test = generate_splits(jfk, '2006-07-08')
var_model = VAR(train[['Domestic Passengers', 'International Passengers']])
var_model.select_order(12)
var_fit = var_model.fit()
lag_order = var_fit.k_ar
var_pred = var_fit.forecast(test[['Domestic Passengers', 'International
    Passengers']].values[-lag_order:], test.index.size)
var_pred_dom = pd.Series(np.asarray(list(zip(*var_pred))[0],
    dtype=np.float32), index=test.index)
var_pred_intl = pd.Series(np.asarray(list(zip(*var_pred))[1],
    dtype=np.float32), index=test.index)
var_prediction_score = plot_predictions(test['Domestic Passengers'],
    var_pred_dom,
    "VAR model Domestic Passengers JFK",
    "Domestic Passengers",
    "var_jfk_dom.svg")
```

Let's call fit() on the model and see
what equation it comes up with.

Generates the predictions. This was a bit tricky to
figure out because the documentation was super
vague and apparently few people use this model.
We noodled around and figured it out, though.
Here, we're starting the forecast on the test dataset
for both series, extracting the pure series from
them, and forecasting out the same number of
data points as are in the test dataset.

Let's finally use that
prediction plot code
created in listing 6.7 to see
how well our model did!

The documentation said to do this. It's
supposed to get the AIC-optimized lag
order from the fit model.

We don't even use this for plotting (reasons
forthcoming), but this obnoxious copy-pasta is
to be expected from experimental code.

The VAR class has an optimizer based on minimizing
the Akaike information criterion (AIC). This function
attempts to set a limit on the ordering selection to
optimize for goodness of fit. We learned this by
reading the API documentation for this module.
Optimizing for AIC will allow for the algorithm to test a
bunch of autoregressive lag orders and select the one
that performs the best (at least it's supposed to).

This hurts my head, and I wrote it. Since we get a
vector of forecasts (a tuple of domestic passenger
predictions and international passenger
predictions), we need to extract the values from
this array of tuples, put them into a list, convert
them to a NumPy array, and then generate a
pandas series with the correct index from the test
data so we can plot this. Whew.

The resulting forecast plot in the preceding code, comparing the predicted to actual
data within the holdout validation period, is shown in figure 6.5.

> **PRO TIP** If I had a penny for every time I've either created a hot mess like
> that shown in figure 6.5 in a prediction (or in algorithm development code),
> I wouldn't be employed right now. I'd be relaxing somewhere with my gor-
> geous wife and a half dozen dogs, sipping on a well-chilled cocktail and listen-
> ing to the sweet sounds of the ocean lapping at a crystalline shore. Don't get
> discouraged when you generate garbage. We all do it. It's how we learn.

OK, so that was bad. Not as bad as it could have been (it didn't predict that there would
be more passengers than the number of humans that had ever lived, for instance), but
it's pretty much a garbage prediction. Let's pretend that the team's constitutional forti-
tude and wisdom are high enough that they are up for digging through the API documentation and Wikipedia articles to figure out what went wrong.

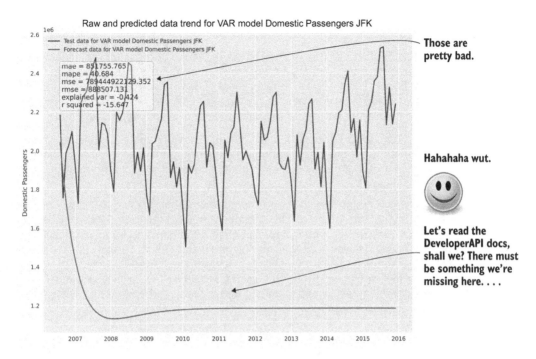

Figure 6.5 **Probably should have read the API documentation**

The most important aspect to remember here is that *poor results are an expected part of the rapid testing phase.* Sometimes you get lucky and things just work, but the vast majority of the time, things aren't going to work out well on the first try. The absolute worst thing to do, after seeing results similar to figure 6.5, would be to classify the approach as untenable and move on to something else. With some tuning and adjustments to the approach, this model could be the best solution. If it's abandoned after a first attempt of just using default configurations on a raw series of data, the team would never know that it could be a viable solution.

Bearing that extreme in mind, however, the other extreme is just as damaging to the project's success. If the team members were to spend days (or weeks) reworking the approach hundreds of times to get the absolute best result from the model, they would no longer be working on a prototype; rather, they would be building out an MVP and sinking a great deal of resources into this single approach. The goal at this stage is getting a quick answer in a few hours as to whether this one out of many approaches is worth risking the success of the project.

Let's get ready to screw some things up

Throughout this chapter, we've been looking at building up experiments from a state of terrible results to something that is pretty OK. This is to be expected in ML. For any problem that is approached with the tools of ML, many possible avenues could

(continued)

solve it. Some are easier to implement than others. For those others, hidden levels of complexity may not instantly be apparent when reading through API docs, blogs, and even books. It is inevitable that, for most of us who are naturally fallible humans, the perfect solution is not going to be found initially. In fact, the first dozen or so attempts at solving a problem are probably going to be embarrassingly bad.

My general guide to ML development is that for every successful model that I've brought to a production state, I've thrown away over a hundred attempts (and generally a similar factor of the lines of code of the final solution is thrown away in the process of building it).

It's critical as a professional ML engineer to realize that, in the early stages of experimentation, you'll have some truly (perhaps amusing) failures. Some can be pretty frustrating, but most give an incredible sense of satisfaction when you finally figure out the issue and have a less-than-horrible prediction result. Simply embrace the failures, learn from them, and get a solid feel for how much API documentation you need to read before writing even your first attempt, to strike the balance between hacking through a problem blindly and spending weeks learning the API to the same level of detail as the original authors.

During this next round of testing, the team discovers that the `fit()` method *actually takes parameters.* The example that they saw and used as a baseline for the first attempt didn't have this defined, so they were unaware of these arguments until they read the API documentation. They discovered that they can set the lag periodicity to help the model understand how far back to look when building its autoregressive equations, which, according to the documentation, should help with building the autoregressive model's linear equations.

Looking back to what they remembered (and recorded, saved, and stored) from the time-series analysis tasks that they did before starting on modeling, they knew that the trend decomposition had a period of 12 months (that was the point at which the residuals of the trend line became noise and not some cyclic relationship that didn't fit with the seasonality period). They gave it another go, shown in the next listing.

Listing 6.10   Let's give VAR another shot after we read the docs

There's the key. Let's try to set that correctly and see if we get something that's not so embarrassingly bad.

To be thorough, let's take a look at the other time series as well (international passengers).

```
var_model = VAR(train[['Domestic Passengers', 'International Passengers']])
var_model.select_order(12)
var_fit = var_model.fit(12)
lag_order = var_fit.k_ar
var_pred = var_fit.forecast(test[['Domestic Passengers', 'International
    Passengers']].values[-lag_order:], test.index.size)
var_pred_dom = pd.Series(np.asarray(list(zip(*var_pred))[0], dtype=np.float32),
    index=test.index)
var_pred_intl = pd.Series(np.asarray(list(zip(*var_pred))[1], dtype=np.float32),
    index=test.index)
```

```
var_prediction_score = plot_predictions(test['Domestic Passengers'],
                                         var_pred_dom,
                                         "VAR model Domestic Passengers JFK",
                                         "Domestic Passengers",
                                         "var_jfk_dom_lag12.svg")
var_prediction_score_intl = plot_predictions(test['International Passengers'],
                                         var_pred_intl,
                                         "VAR model International Passengers JFK",
                                         "International Passengers",
                                         "var_jfk_intl_lag12.svg")
```

Let's plot the international passengers as well to see how well this model predicts both. ⊳

After running this slightly adjusted test, the team looks at the results, shown in figure 6.6. They look better than before, certainly, but they're still just a bit off. Upon a final review and a bit more research, they find that the VAR model is designed to handle stationary time-series data only.

At this point, this team is done with its evaluations. The team members have learned quite a few things about this API:

- The acquisition of a forecast from this API is complex.
- Running multiple time series through this model seems to have a complementary effect to the vector passed in. This could prove problematic for divergent series at the same airport.
- With a vector being required of a similar shape, will this handle airports that began offering international flights only after they were a domestic hub?
- The loss of resolution in seasonality components means that fine detail in the predicted trend will be lost if the forecast runs too far in the future.
- The algorithm seems sensitive to the `fit()` method's `maxlags` parameter. This will require extensive testing and monitoring if used in production.
- The VAR model is not designed to handle nonstationary data. From the earlier tests, we know that these time series are not stationary, based on the Dickey-Fuller tests from section 5.2.1 when running code listing 6.10.

Now that this team has finished testing and has a solid understanding of the limitations of this model family (namely, the stationarity issue), it's time to look into a few other teams' progress (don't worry, we won't be going through all nine models). Perhaps they're having more luck.

On second thought, let's just give it one last shot. The team has a day to draw conclusions on this model, and a few more hours are still left before the internal deadline for each team, after all.

Let's figure out that stationarity issue quickly and see if we can make the predictions just a little bit better. To convert the time series to a stationary series, we need to normalize the data by applying a natural log to it. Then, to remove the nonstationary trend associated with the series, we can use a differencing function to get the rate of change as the series moves along the timescale. Listing 6.11 is the full code for converting to a differenced scale, running the model fit, and uncompacting the time series to the appropriate scale.

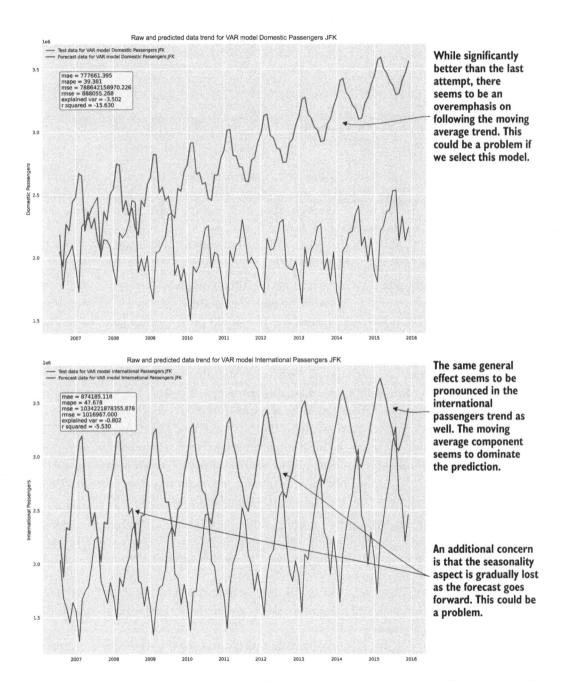

While significantly better than the last attempt, there seems to be an overemphasis on following the moving average trend. This could be a problem if we select this model.

The same general effect seems to be pronounced in the international passengers trend as well. The moving average component seems to dominate the prediction.

An additional concern is that the seasonality aspect is gradually lost as the forecast goes forward. This could be a problem.

Figure 6.6   Just because this result of executing listing 6.10 is an order of magnitude better than before doesn't mean that it's good.

Listing 6.11 Stationarity-adjusted predictions with a VAR model

We also have to do the same thing to the other vector position series data for international passengers.

Takes a differencing function of the log of the series to create a stationary time series (remember, this is just as we did for the outlier analysis)

```
jfk_stat = get_airport_data('JFK', DATA_PATH)
jfk_stat = apply_index_freq(jfk, 'MS')
jfk_stat['Domestic Diff'] = np.log(jfk_stat['Domestic Passengers']).diff()
jfk_stat['International Diff'] = np.log(jfk_stat['International
    Passengers']).diff()
jfk_stat = jfk_stat.dropna()
train, test = generate_splits(jfk_stat, '2006-07-08')
var_model = VAR(train[['Domestic Diff', 'International Diff']])
var_model.select_order(6)
var_fit = var_model.fit(12)
lag_order = var_fit.k_ar
var_pred = var_fit.forecast(test[['Domestic Diff', 'International
    Diff']].values[-lag_order:], test.index.size)
var_pred_dom = pd.Series(np.asarray(list(zip(*var_pred))[0], dtype=np.float32),
    index=test.index)
var_pred_intl = pd.Series(np.asarray(list(zip(*var_pred))[1], dtype=np.float32),
    index=test.index)
var_pred_dom_expanded = np.exp(var_pred_dom.cumsum()) * test['Domestic
    Passengers'][0]
var_pred_intl_expanded = np.exp(var_pred_intl.cumsum()) * test['International
    Passengers'][0]
var_prediction_score = plot_predictions(test['Domestic Passengers'],
                            var_pred_dom_expanded,
                            "VAR model Domestic Passengers JFK Diff",
                            "Domestic Diff",
                            "var_jfk_dom_lag12_diff.svg")
var_prediction_score_intl = plot_predictions(test['International Passengers'],
                            var_pred_intl_expanded,
                            "VAR model International Passengers JFK
                             Diff",
                            "International Diff",
                            "var_jfk_intl_lag12_diff.svg")
```

Trains the model on the stationary representation of the data

Converts the stationary data back to the actual scale of the data by using the inverse function of a diff(), a cumulative sum. Then converts the log scale of the data back to linear space by using an exponential. This series is set as a diff, though, so we have to multiply the values by the starting position value (which is the actual value at the start of the test dataset series) in order to have the correct scaling.

Compares the test series with the expanded prediction series

What's with all of this copying and pasting?

In all of the examples in this section, we've been seeing the same lines of code pasted over and over above each of our iterations of model improvement. Including all of this in these snippets is not merely to demonstrate a fully built-out code block that can execute. Rather, it's a simulation of what many experimental notebooks (or, if writing Python scripts, the copies of such scripts) will end up looking like as implementations are tested, individual ideas are iterated upon, and eventually a functional script of code will produce results that are measurable

(continued)

This is normal. This is expected in experimentation.

A generally good guideline is to ensure that your experimentation and evaluation code is relatively well organized, easy to read and follow, and documented with enough comments that can explain anything particularly complex. Whichever solution is selected, keeping the code clean enough will facilitate the next phase in development. Clean up as you go, delete dead code, and keep a salient structure.

What you certainly don't want to do is have out-of-order cells, broken variable dependency chains, and large amounts of commented-out nonfunctional code in a state of pure distilled chaos littered about a notebook. Trying to piece together a chaotic experiment is an exercise in frustration and futility, raising the difficulty of an already complex process (formulating encapsulation design and architecture of production-grade code) to levels that, in many cases, make it easier to just rewrite everything from scratch rather than try to salvage what has already been developed.

Having fully functional and cell-level encapsulation isn't necessarily a bad thing while in this phase of a project. Provided that the code is cleanly written and correctly formatted, this encapsulation can be easier than sifting through dozens (or hundreds!) of cells to figure out how to get an experiment to run as it did during the rapid prototyping phase. It also makes conversion to a class-based or functional programming-based implementation quite a bit easier.

Figure 6.7 shows the final state that this team finds itself in, after having iterated on the model implementation, gone back to read the documentation fully, and done a bit of research about how the model works (at an "applications of ML level" at least). This visualization results from running the code in listing 6.11.

The first part of the experimentation phase is done. The team has a model that shows promise and, more important, understands the application of the model and can tune it properly. The visualizations have been recorded for them to show the results, and clean example code is written in a notebook that can be referenced for later use.

The people working on this particular model implementation, provided that they have finished their prototyping before the other groups, can be spread to other teams to impart some of the wisdom that they have gained from their work. This sharing of information will also help speed the progress of all the experiments so that a decision can be made on what approach to implement for the actual project work.

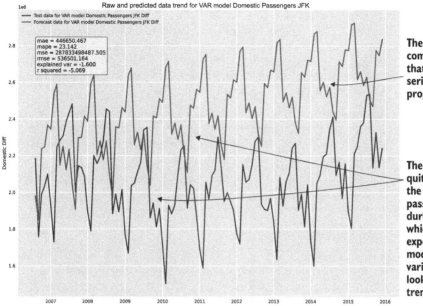

The seasonality component here, now that we've made the series stationary, is properly modeled.

The general trend is quite linear with the dip in domestic passenger traffic during the recession, which is to be expected (we're not modeling these latent variables and are looking at only the trends themselves).

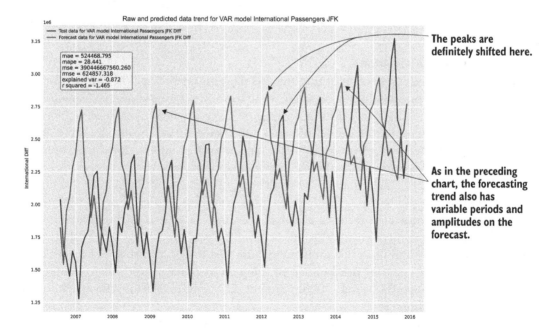

The peaks are definitely shifted here.

As in the preceding chart, the forecasting trend also has variable periods and amplitudes on the forecast.

Figure 6.7   Result of executing listing 6.11

Wow, that was unpleasant . . .

It's important to note how difficult it is for a particular approach to get an acceptable result. Whether it requires an abnormally large amount of feature engineering for a model to produce something other than garbage, or has extreme sensitivity to hyperparameters, or even uses a confusing and poorly designed API, the difficulties presented during this phase need to be noted by the team.

As we will review in section 6.2, the challenges faced in implementing the various solutions will have a strong bearing on the complexity of developing a production-capable solution. In addition, these challenges will directly influence the team's ability to maintain the solution when it is in production.

It's good to think about the following topics while going through this phase and to take notes during the process so that they can be referenced when evaluating the complexity later:

- Sensitivity to parameter changes.
- Quantity of hyperparameters. (This will affect the optimization of models.)
- Fluency of the API. (Is it standard? Can it be placed into a pipeline?)
- Amount of feature-engineering work that had to be done to get an acceptable result.
- Adaptability to changes in training and test data volumes. (Did the predictions fall apart when the split boundary was changed?)

RAPID TESTING FOR ARIMA

Let's pretend for a moment that the ARIMA team members don't get any tips from the VAR team when getting started, aside from the train and test split methodology for the series data to perform scoring of their predictions against holdout data. They're beginning the model research and testing phases, using the same function tools that the other teams are using for data preprocessing and formatting of the date index, but aside from that, they're in greenfield territory.

The team realizes that one of its first big obstacles is in the required settings for the ARIMA model, specifically the p (autoregressive parameters), d (differences), and q (moving average) variables that need to be assigned during model instantiation. Reading through the documentation, the team members realize that the pre-experimentation work that everyone contributed to already provides a means of finding a place to start for these values. By using the stationarity test visualization function built in chapter 5's listing 5.14, we can get the significance values for the autoregressive (AR) parameters.

To get the appropriate autocorrelation and partial autocorrelation measurements, we're going to have to perform the same difference function on the logarithm of the time series as the VAR team did in its final model for testing (the VAR team members were being especially nice and shared their findings) so that we can remove as much of the noise as we can. Figure 6.8 shows the resulting trend plots.

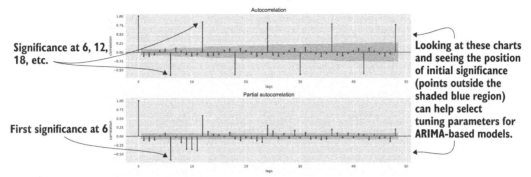

Figure 6.8 Executing the stationarity tests for the lag-diff of the JFK domestic passenger series

Much like the VAR team before them, the ARIMA team members spend a few iterations trying different parameters to get results that aren't tragically poor. We won't cover all those iterations (this isn't a book on time-series modeling, after all). Instead, let's look at the final result that they came up with.

Listing 6.12 Final state of the ARIMA experimentation

```
from statsmodels.tsa.arima.model import ARIMA
jfk_arima = get_airport_data('JFK', DATA_PATH)
jfk_arima = apply_index_freq(jfk_arima, 'MS')
train, test = generate_splits(jfk_arima, '2006-07-08')
arima_model = ARIMA(train['Domestic Passengers'], order=(48,1,1),
        enforce_stationarity=False, trend='c')
arima_model_intl = ARIMA(train['International Passengers'], order=(48,1,1),
        enforce_stationarity=False, trend='c')
arima_fit = arima_model.fit()
arima_fit_intl = arima_model_intl.fit()
arima_predicted = arima_fit.predict(test.index[0], test.index[-1])
arima_predicted_intl = arima_fit_intl.predict(test.index[0], test.index[-1])
arima_score_dom = plot_predictions(test['Domestic Passengers'],
                                    arima_predicted,
                                    "ARIMA model Domestic Passengers JFK",
                                    "Domestic Passengers",
                                    "arima_jfk_dom_2.svg"
                                    )
arima_score_intl = plot_predictions(test['Domestic Passengers'],
                                    arima_predicted_intl,
                                    "ARIMA model International Passengers JFK",
                                    "International Passengers",
                                    "arima_jfk_intl_2.svg"
                                    )
```

The ordering parameters of (p,d,q). The p (period) value was derived from the autocorrelation and partial autocorrelation analyses as a factor of the significant values calculated.

Of particular note is the absence of the stationarity-forcing log and diff actions being taken on the series. While these stationarity adjustments were tested, the results were significantly worse than the forecasting that was done on the raw data. (We won't be looking at the code, as it is nearly identical to the approaches in listing 6.11.)

Figure 6.9 shows the validation plots and scores for a few of their tests; the log diff attempt is on the left (obviously inferior), and the unmodified series being used for training is on the right. While the right grouping of charts is by no means ideal for the project solution as is, it certainly gives the broader team an idea of the nuances and capabilities of an ARIMA model for forecasting purposes.

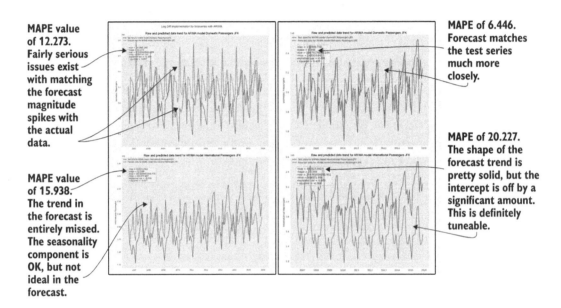

MAPE value of 12.273. Fairly serious issues exist with matching the forecast magnitude spikes with the actual data.

MAPE of 6.446. Forecast matches the test series much more closely.

MAPE value of 15.938. The trend in the forecast is entirely missed. The seasonality component is OK, but not ideal in the forecast.

MAPE of 20.227. The shape of the forecast trend is pretty solid, but the intercept is off by a significant amount. This is definitely tuneable.

Figure 6.9   Comparison of enforcing stationarity (left) and using the raw data (right) for ARIMA modeling

These results from their testing show promise in both approaches (raw data and stationarity-enforced manipulations), illustrating that an opportunity exists for better tuning to make this algorithm's implementation better. Armed with this knowledge and the results, this team can be ready to present its findings to the larger team in an adjudication without spending more precious time on attempting to improve the results at this stage.

RAPID TESTING OF THE HOLT-WINTERS EXPONENTIAL SMOOTHING ALGORITHM

We're going to be much briefer with this one (sorry, fans of time-series modeling). For this model evaluation, the team members wanted to wrap their implementation of the Holt-Winters exponential smoothing model in a function so that they didn't have to keep copying the same code throughout their notebook cells.

The reasons that this approach is the preferred way to write even experimental code will become more obvious in the next chapter. For now, let's just say that this team has a few more senior DS members. The next listing shows what they eventually came up with.

Listing 6.13 Holt-Winters exponential smoothing function and usage

```
from statsmodels.tsa.holtwinters import ExponentialSmoothing
def exp_smoothing(train, test, trend, seasonal, periods, dampening, smooth_slope,
    damping_slope):
    output = {}
    exp_smoothing_model = ExponentialSmoothing(train,
                                               trend=trend,
                                               seasonal=seasonal,
                                               seasonal_periods=periods,
                                               damped=dampening
                                               )
    exp_fit = exp_smoothing_model.fit(smoothing_level=0.9,
                                      smoothing_seasonal=0.2,
                                      smoothing_slope=smooth_slope,
                                      damping_slope=damping_slope,
                                      use_brute=True,
                                      use_boxcox=False,
                                      use_basinhopping=True,
                                      remove_bias=True
                                      )
    forecast = exp_fit.predict(train.index[-1], test.index[-1])
    output['model'] = exp_fit
    output['forecast'] = forecast[1:]
    return output
jfk = get_airport_data('JFK', DATA_PATH)
jfk = apply_index_freq(jfk, 'MS')
train, test = generate_splits(jfk, '2006-07-08')
prediction = exp_smoothing(train['Domestic Passengers'], test['Domestic
    Passengers'], 'add', 'add', 48, True, 0.9, 0.5)
prediction_intl = exp_smoothing(train['International Passengers'],
    test['International Passengers'], 'add', 'add', 60, True, 0.1, 1.0)
exp_smooth_pred = plot_predictions(test['Domestic Passengers'],
                                   prediction['forecast'],
                                   "ExponentialSmoothing Domestic Passengers JFK",
                                   "Domestic Passengers",
                                   "exp_smooth_dom.svg"
                                   )
exp_smooth_pred_intl = plot_predictions(test['International Passengers'],
                                   prediction_intl['forecast'],
                                   "ExponentialSmoothing International Passengers
                                    JFK",
                                   "International Passengers",
                                   "exp_smooth_intl.svg"
                                   )
```

In development, if this model is chosen, all of these settings (as well as the others available to this fit method) will be parameterized and subject to auto-optimization with a tool like Hyperopt.

Slightly different from the other models tested, this model requires at least the last element of the training data to be present for the range of predictions.

Removes the forecast made on the last element of the training data series

Uses a longer periodicity for the autoregressive element (seasonal_periods) because of the nature of the time series of that group. In development, if this model is chosen, these values will be automatically tuned through a grid search or more elegant auto-optimization algorithm.

In the process of developing this, this subteam discovers that the API for Holt-Winters exponential smoothing changed fairly dramatically between versions 0.11 and 0.12

(0.12.0 was the most recent documentation on the API doc website, and as such, shows up by default). As a result, team members spend quite a bit of time trying to figure out why the settings that they try to apply are constantly failing with exceptions that are the result of renamed or modified parameters.

Eventually, they realize that they need to check the version of statsmodels that was installed to get the correct documentation. (For further reading on versioning in Python, see the following sidebar.) Figure 6.10 shows the results of this group's work, reflecting the most promising metrics yet from any of the groups.

How to quickly figure out the version of a module without a huge fuss

The package manager that we're using for these examples, Anaconda, has quite a few modules available. In addition to the base Python itself, hundreds of incredibly useful tools have been included for ML work. Each has been meticulously collated such that the respective dependencies are all aligned to work together.

Because of this, some of the modules may not be as recent as the "stable release" that the API documentation might have (particularly for projects that are under active development and do frequent releases). As a result, the docs may not reflect the version of the module that you are interacting with.

This isn't just a Python problem either. Any large open source ecosystem will have this issue. You'll encounter this in Java, Scala, R, TensorFlow, Keras, and more. In Python, however, we can relatively easily get the version information from within the Python REPL (or a notebook cell).

For the purposes of our examples, let's check the versioning information for statsmodels. To acquire it, you simply have to figure out the method name (usually a pseudo-private method) and call it. You can find what these method names might be called (typically, a variant of `__VERSION__`, `__version`, `_version`, or the like) by importing the base package, performing a `dir(<package name>)`, and seeing the naming of it.

For statsmodels, the method name is `_version`. To print the version information, we simply type the following in a cell, and it will print to stdout:

```
import statsmodels
statsmodels._version.get_versions()
```

At the time of this writing, the latest stable version of statsmodels is 0.12.0, with some significant changes to the APIs that we've been using. Luckily, each release of an open source software package typically retains older versions of its documentation on its web page. Just be sure that the correct version is selected when you're looking at the docs to make sure that you're not wasting time implementing something incompatible with the installed version of the package that you're running against.

The version that we're using in this build of Anaconda, though, is 0.11.1. We need to make sure that we're looking at that version of the API docs to see the options with each class that we're importing for modeling.

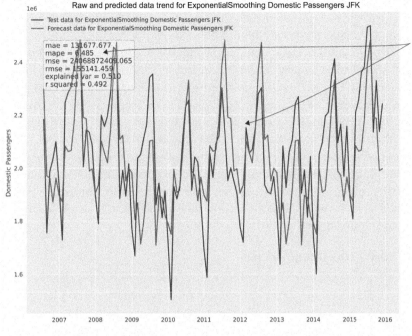

MAPE of 6.485.
Best result yet
for the Domestic
Passengers at JFK.
The seasonality,
periodicity, and
general magnitude
trend shifts are much
more in line with the
test data.

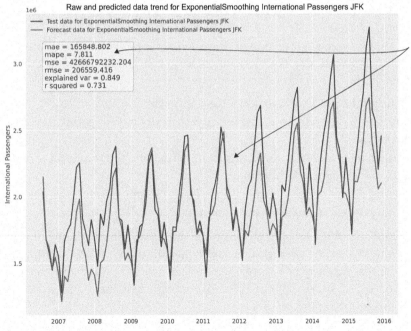

MAPE of 7.811 is by
far the best result
that's been seen of
any of the tests for
the international
passenger data. This
is likely going to be a
strong contender to
consider for the
project.

Figure 6.10   Results of the Holt-Winters exponential smoothing tests from listing 6.13. We have a clear contender!

After completing their day-long mini hackathon, the teams collate their results into simple and easy-to-digest reports on the efficacy of the algorithms' abilities to forecast this data. Then the teams meet for a bit of a show-and-tell.

Applying the preparation steps defined throughout section 6.1, we can efficiently, reliably, and objectively compare different approaches. The standardization means that the team will have a true baseline comparison to adjudicate each approach, while the time-boxed nature of the evaluations ensures that no team spends too much time building out an MVP solution (wasting both time and computing resources) without knowing whether the approach that they're building is actually the best one.

We've reduced the chances of picking a poor implementation to solve the business need and have done so quickly. Even though the business unit that is asking for an answer to their problem is blind to these internal processes, the company will have a better product by the end because of this methodical approach, as well as one that meets the project's deadline.

6.2   *Whittling down the possibilities*

How does the team as a whole decide which direction to go in? Recall that in chapters 3 and 4, we discussed that after experimentation evaluation is complete, it's time to involve the business stakeholders. We'll need to get their input, subjective as it may be, to ensure that they're going to feel comfortable with the approach and included in the direction choice, and that their expertise of deep subject area knowledge is weighed heavily in the decision.

To ensure a thorough adjudication of the tested potential implementations for the project, the broader team needs to look at each approach that has been tested and make a judgment that is based on the following:

- Maximizing the predictive power of the approach
- Minimizing the complexity of the solution as much as is practicable to still solve the problem
- Evaluating and estimating the difficulty in developing the solution for purposes of realistic scoping for delivery dates
- Estimating the total cost of ownership for (re)training and inference
- Evaluating the extensibility of the solution

By focusing on each of these aspects during the evaluation phase, the team can dramatically reduce risk in the project, collectively deciding on an MVP approach that will reduce the vast majority of reasons ML projects fail, end up abandoned, or get cancelled. Figure 6.11 shows each of these criteria and how they fit into the overall prototyping phase of ML project work.

Now that you have a solid idea of *what* a team should be looking at when evaluating an approach, let's look at *how* this team will arrive at a decision on which approach to implement.

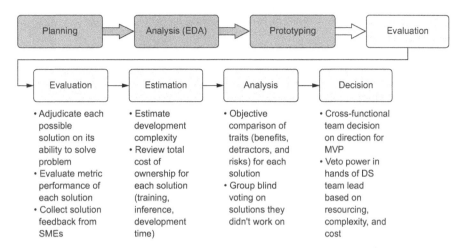

Figure 6.11 Elements of the evaluation phase to guide the path for building the MVP

6.2.1 *Evaluating prototypes properly*

It's at this point that most ML teams can let themselves be led astray, specifically in the sense of presenting only the accuracy that a particular solution brings. We've discussed previously in section 6.1.1 (and listing 6.7) the importance of creating compelling visualizations to illustrate in an easy-to-consume format for both the ML teams and the business unit, but that's only part of the story for deciding on one ML approach versus another. The predictive power of an algorithm is certainly incredibly important, but it is merely one among many other important considerations to weigh. As an example, let's continue with these three implementations (and the others that we didn't show for brevity's sake) and collect data about them so that the full picture of building out any of these solutions can be explored.

The team meets, shows code to one another, reviews the different test runs with the various parameters that were tested, and assembles an agreed-upon comparison of relative difficulty. For some models (such as the VAR model, elastic net regressor, lasso regressor, and RNN), the ML team decides to not even include these results in the analysis because of the overwhelmingly poor results generated in forecasting. Showing abject failures to the business serves no useful purpose and simply makes an already intellectually taxing discussion longer and more onerous. If a full disclosure about the amount of work involved to arrive at candidates is in order, simply state, "We tried 15 other things, but they're really not suited for this data" and move on.

After deliberating over the objective merits of each approach, the internal DS team arrives at an evaluation matrix similar to figure 6.12. While relatively generic, the evaluation elements in this matrix can be applied to most project implementations. In the past, I've used selection criteria that are far more detailed and customized to the type of problem the project is aiming to solve, but a generic one is a good place to start.

Airport demand forecasting project
Model evaluation matrix

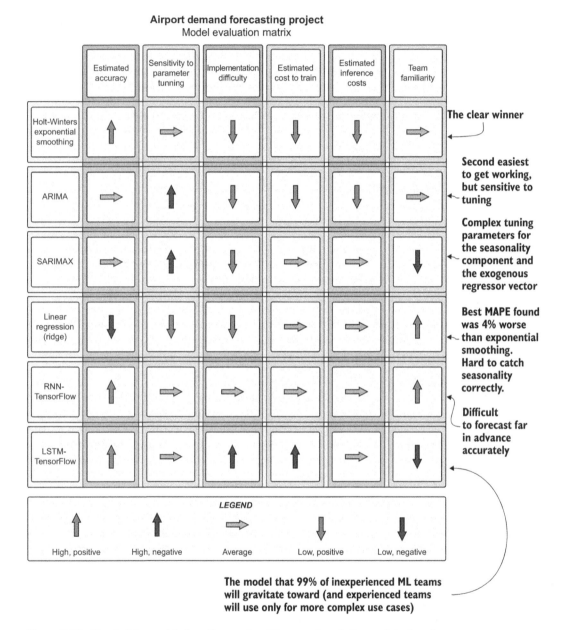

Figure 6.12　The decision matrix from the results of the experimentation prototyping phase

As you can see, it's incredibly important to holistically evaluate an approach on elements other than its predictive power. After all, the chosen solution will need to be developed for production, monitored, modified, and maintained for (hopefully) a long time. Failing to take the maintainability factors into account can land a team with an incredibly powerful solution that is nearly impossible to keep running.

It's worthwhile, at the stage after prototyping is done, to think deeply about what it's going to be like to build this solution, as well as what total life-cycle ownership will be like. Is anyone going to want to improve upon it? Will they be able to? Is this something that will be relatively straightforward to troubleshoot should the predictions start to become poor? Can we explain why the model made the decisions that it did? Can we afford to run it?

If you're unsure of any of these aspects of the proposed group of solutions, it's best to either discuss these topics among the team until consensus is arrived at, or, at the very least, don't propose it as a potential solution to the business. The absolutely last thing that you want from the conclusion of a project is to realize that you've built an abomination that you wish would just silently fade away into nothingness, never to return and rear its ugly head, pervading your waking and sleepless nights like a haunting fever dream. Choose wisely at this point, because once you commit, it's going to be expensive to pivot to another approach.

6.2.2 *Making a call on the direction to go in*

Now that the data about the relative strengths and weaknesses of each approach has been assembled and the modeling approach has been decided upon, the real fun begins. Since everyone came to the conclusion that Holt-Winters exponential smoothing seems like the safest option for building these forecasts, we can start talking about architecture and code.

Before any code is written, though, the team needs to have another planning session. This is the time for the *hard questions*. The most important thing to keep in mind about these is that *they should be answered before committing to a development direction*.

QUESTION 1: HOW OFTEN DOES THIS NEED TO RUN?

"How often does this need to run?" is quite possibly the most important question, considering the type of model that everyone selected. Since this is an autoregressive model, if the model is not retrained at a high frequency (probably each inference run), the predictions will not adapt to new factual data coming in. The model looks at only a univariate series to make its forecasts, so having training that's as up-to-date as possible can ensure that the forecasts adapt to the changing trend accurately.

> **TIP** Don't ever ask the business or any frontend developer, "So, how often do you need the predictions?" They will usually spout off some ridiculously short time period. Instead, ask, "At what point will the predictions become irrelevant?" and work back from there. The difference between a 4-hour SLA and a 10-millisecond SLA is several hundred thousand dollars of infrastructure and about six months of work.

The business is going to need to provide a minimum and maximum service-level agreement (SLA) for the "freshness" of these predictions. Give rough estimates of how long it will take to develop a solution that supports these SLA requirements, as well as how expensive the solution will be to run in production.

QUESTION 2: WHERE IS THE DATA FOR THIS RIGHT NOW?

Since the data is provided by an external data feed, we need to be conscientious about how to create a stable and reliable ETL ingestion for both the training data and the imputation (prediction) data. The freshness of this data needs to meet the requirements of question 1's answer (the SLA being requested).

We need to bring in the DE team members to ensure that they are prioritizing the acquisition of this feed long before we're thinking of going into production for this project. If they are unable to commit to an acceptable date, we will have to write this ETL and populate the source tables with this data ourselves, increasing our project scope, cost, and risk.

QUESTION 3: WHERE ARE THE FORECASTS GOING TO BE STORED?

Are the users going to be issuing business intelligence (BI) style queries to the predictions, fueling analytics visualizations in an ad hoc manner? Then we can probably write the data to an RDBMS source that we have in-house.

Is this going to be queried frequently by hundreds (or thousands) of users? Is the data going to be made available as a service for a web frontend? If so, we're going to have to think about storing the predictions as sorted arrays in a NoSQL engine or perhaps an in-memory store such as Redis. We'll need to build a REST API in front of this data if we're going to be serving to a frontend service, which will increase the scope of work for this project by a few sprints.

QUESTION 4: HOW ARE WE SETTING UP OUR CODE BASE?

Is this going to be a new project code base, or are we going to let this code live with other ML projects in a common repo? Are we pursuing a full object-oriented (OO) approach with the modular design, or will we be attempting to do functional programming (FP)?

What is our deployment strategy for future improvements? Are we going to use a continuous integration/continuous deployment (CI/CD) system, GitFlow releases, or standard Git? Where are our metrics associated with each run going to live? Where are we going to log our parameters, auto-tuned hyperparameters, and visualizations for reference?

It's not *absolutely critical* to have answers to all of those questions regarding development immediately at this point, but the team lead and architect should be carefully considering all of these aspects of the project development *very soon* and should be making a well-considered set of decisions regarding these elements (we'll cover this in the next chapter at length).

QUESTION 5: WHERE IS THIS GOING TO RUN FOR TRAINING?

We ~~probably~~ *really shouldn't run this on our laptops.* Seriously. Don't do it.

With the number of models involved in this project, we'll be exploring options for this in the next chapter and discussing the pros and cons of each.

QUESTION 6: WHERE IS THE INFERENCE GOING TO RUN?

We ~~really~~ *definitely shouldn't be running this on our laptops.* Cloud service provider infrastructure, on-premises data centers, or ephemeral serverless containers running on either the cloud or on-prem are really the only option here.

QUESTION 7: HOW ARE WE GOING TO GET THE PREDICTIONS TO THE END USERS?

As stated in the answer to question 3, getting the predictions to the end users is by far the most overlooked and yet most critical part of any ML project that strives to be actually useful. Do you need to serve the predictions on a web page? Now would be a good time to have a conversation with some frontend and/or full-stack developers.

Does it need to be part of a BI report? The DE and BI engineering teams should be consulted now.

Does it need to be stored for ad hoc SQL queries by analysts? If that's the case, you've got this. That's trivial.

QUESTION 8: HOW MUCH OF OUR EXISTING CODE CAN BE USED FOR THIS PROJECT?

If you have utility packages already developed that can make your life easier, review them. Do they have existing tech debt that you can fix and make better while working on this project? If yes, then now's the time to fix it. If you have existing code and believe it has no tech debt, you should be more honest with yourself.

If you don't have an existing utility framework built up or are just getting started with ML engineering practices for the first time, worry not! We'll cover what this sort of tooling looks like in many of the subsequent chapters.

QUESTION 9: WHAT IS OUR DEVELOPMENT CADENCE, AND HOW ARE WE GOING TO WORK ON FEATURES?

Are you dealing with a project manager? Take some time now to explain just how much code you're going to be throwing away during this development process. Let the project manager know that entire stories and epics are going to be dead code, erased from the face of the earth, never to be seen again. Explain to them the chaos of ML project work so that they can get through those first four stages of grief and learn to accept it before the project starts. You don't need to give them a hug or anything, but break the news to them gently, for it will shatter their understanding of the nature of reality.

ML feature work is a unique beast. It is entirely true that huge swaths of code will be developed, only to be completely refactored (or thrown away!) when a particular approach is found to be untenable. This is a stark contrast to "pure" software development, in which a particular functionality is rationally defined and can be fairly accurately scoped. Unless part of your project is the design and development of an entirely new algorithm (it probably shouldn't be, for your information, no matter how much one of your team members is trying to convince you that it needs to be), there is no guarantee of a particular functionality coming out of your code base.

Therefore, the pure Agile approach is usually not an effective way of developing code for ML simply because of the nature of changes that might need to be made (swapping out a model, for instance, could incur a large, wholesale refactoring that could consume two entire sprints). To help with the different nature of Agile as applied to ML development, it's critical to organize your stories, your scrums, and your commits accordingly.

6.2.3   So . . . what's next?

What's next is actually building the MVP. It's working on the demonstrable solution that has fine-tuned accuracy for the model, logged testing results, and a presentation to the business showing that the problem can be solved. What's next is what puts the *engineering* in *ML engineering*.

We'll delve heavily into these topics in the next chapter, continuing with this peanut-inventory-optimization problem, watching it go from a hardcoded prototype with marginal tuning to the beginnings of a code base filled with functions, the support for automatically tuned models, and full logging for each model's tuning evaluations into MLflow. We'll also be moving from the world of single-threaded sequential Python into the world of concurrent modeling capabilities in the distributed system of Apache Spark.

Summary

- A time-boxed and holistic approach to testing APIs for potential solutions to a problem will help ensure that an implementation direction for a project is reached quickly, evaluated thoroughly, and meets the needs of the problem in the shortest possible time. Predictive power is not the only criteria that matters.
- Reviewing all aspects of candidate methods for solving a problem encourages evaluating more than predictive power. From maintainability, to implementation complexity, to cost, many factors should be considered when selecting a solution to pursue to solve a problem.

Experimentation in action: Moving from prototype to MVP

This chapter covers
- Techniques for hyperparameter tuning and the benefits of automated approaches
- Execution options for improving the performance of hyperparameter optimization

In the preceding chapter, we explored the scenario of testing and evaluating potential solutions to a business problem focused on forecasting passengers at airports. We ended up arriving at a decision on the model to use for the implementation (Holt-Winters exponential smoothing) but performed only a modicum of model tuning during the rapid prototyping phases.

Moving from experimental prototyping to MVP development is challenging. It requires a complete cognitive shift that is at odds with the work done up to this point. We're no longer thinking of how to *solve a problem* and get a good result. Instead, we're thinking of how to *build a solution* that is good enough to solve the problem in a way that is robust enough so that it's not breaking constantly. We need to shift focus to monitoring, automated tuning, scalability, and cost. We're moving from scientific-focused work to the realm of engineering.

The first priority when moving from prototype to MVP is ensuring that a solution is tuned correctly. See the following sidebar for additional details on why it's so critical to tune models and how these seemingly optional settings in modeling APIs are actually important to test.

Hyperparameters are important—very important

One of the most frustrating things to see in ML code bases is an *untuned model* (a model that will be generated by using the placeholder defaults provided by the API). With all of the advanced feature engineering, ETL, visualization work, and coding effort that is involved in building the rest of the solution, seeing a bare model using defaults is like buying a high-performance sports car and filling it with regular gas.

Will it run? Sure. Will it perform well? Nope. Not only will it underperform, but the chances of it breaking are high once you take it out into the "real world" (in reference to a model, using it on heretofore unseen data to make predictions).

Some algorithms automatically handle their methodologies in arriving at an optimized solution, thus requiring no hyperparameters to be overridden. However, the vast majority have anywhere from a single to dozens of parameters that influence not only the core functionality of the algorithm's optimizer (for example, the `family` parameter in generalized linear regression will directly influence the predictive performance of such a model more dramatically than any other hyperparameter), but the way the optimizer executes its search to find the minimum objective function. Some of these hyperparameters apply only to specific applications of an algorithm—the hyperparameters are applicable only if the variance within the feature vector is extreme or if a particular distribution is associated with the target variable. But for most of them, the influence of their set values over the manner in which the algorithm will "learn" an optimal fit to the data is exceptionally important.

The following graphs are simplified examples of two such critical hyperparameters for linear regression models. It is impossible to guess where these values should be set, as each feature vector collection and problem will generally have dramatically different optimal hyperparameter settings from others.

Note that these examples are for demonstration purposes only. The effects on models for different values set for hyperparameters is not only highly dependent on the algorithm type being used, but also on the nature of the data contained in the feature vector and the attributes of the target variable. This is why every model needs to be tuned.

As you can see, the seemingly optional settings associated with each ML algorithm actually do matter a great deal in the way the training process executes. Without changing any of these values and optimizing them, there is little chance of having a successful ML-based solution to a problem.

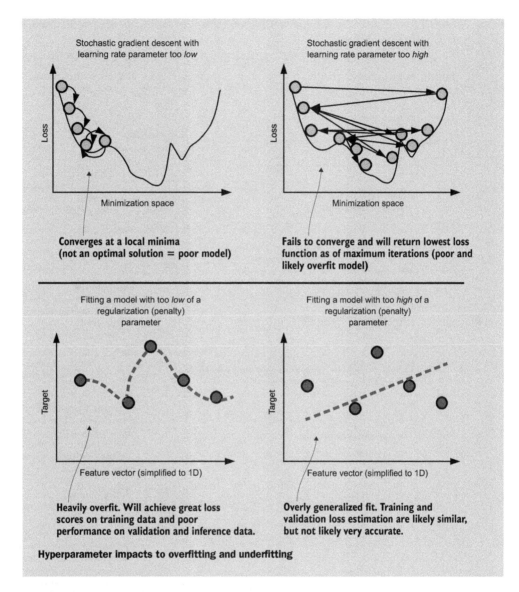

Hyperparameter impacts to overfitting and underfitting

7.1 Tuning: Automating the annoying stuff

Throughout the last two chapters, we've been focusing on a peanut forecasting problem. At the end of chapter 6, we had a somewhat passable prototype, validated on a single airport. The process used to adjust and tune the predictive performance of the model was manual and not particularly scientific, and left a large margin between what is possible for the model's predictive ability and what we had manually tuned.

In this scenario, the difference between OK and very good predictions could be a large margin of product that we want to stage at airports. Being off in our forecasts, after all, could translate to many millions of dollars. Spending time manually tuning by just trying a bunch of hyperparameters simply won't scale for predictive accuracy or for timeliness of delivery.

If we want to come up with a better approach than tribal-knowledge guessing for tuning the model, we need to look at our options. Figure 7.1 shows various approaches

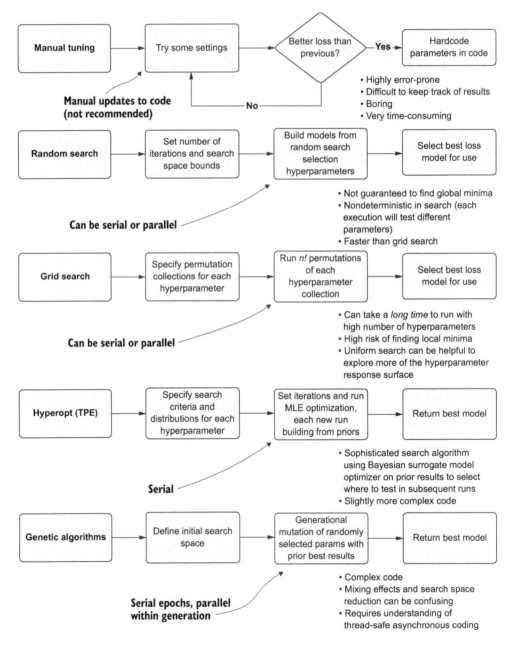

Figure 7.1 Comparison of hyperparameter tuning approaches

that DS teams use to tune models, progressing in order from simple (less powerful and maintainable) to complex (custom framework).

The top section, manual tuning, is typically how prototypes are built. Manually testing values of hyperparameters, when doing rapid testing, is an understandable approach. The goal of the prototype, as mentioned in chapter 6, is getting an approximation of the tunability of a solution. At the stage of moving toward a production-capable solution, however, more maintainable and powerful solutions need to be considered.

7.1.1 Tuning options

We know that we need to tune the model. In chapter 6, we saw clearly what happens if we don't do that: generating a forecast so laughably poor that pulling numbers from a hat would be more accurate. However, multiple options could be pursued to arrive at the most optimal set of hyperparameters.

MANUAL TUNING (EDUCATED GUESSING)

We will see later, when applying Hyperopt to our forecasting problem, just how difficult it will be to arrive at the optimal hyperparameters for each model that needs to be built for this project. Not only are the optimized values unintuitive to guess at, but each forecasting model's optimal hyperparameter set is different from that of other models.

Getting even remotely close to optimal parameters with a manual testing methodology is unlikely. The process is inefficient, frustrating, and an incredible waste of time to attempt, as shown in figure 7.2.

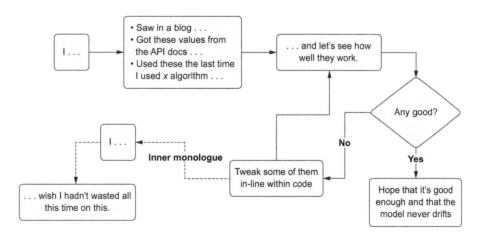

Figure 7.2   The acute pain of manual hyperparameter tuning

TIP Don't try manual tuning unless you're working with an algorithm that has a very small number of hyperparameters (one or two, preferably Boolean or categorical).

The primary issue with this method is in tracking what has been tested. Even if a system was in place to record and ensure that the same values haven't been tried before, the sheer amount of work required to maintain that catalog is overwhelming, prone to errors, and pointless in the extreme.

Project work, after the rapid prototyping phase, should always abandon this approach to tuning as soon as is practicable. You have so many better things to do with your time, believe me.

GRID SEARCH

A cornerstone of ML techniques, the brute-force-search approach of grid-based testing of hyperparameters has been around for quite some time. To perform a grid search, the DS will select a set collection of values to test for each hyperparameter. The grid search API will then assemble collections of hyperparameters to test by creating permutations of each value from each group that has been specified. Figure 7.3 illustrates how this works, as well as why it might not be something that you would entertain for models with a lot of hyperparameters.

As you can see, with high hyperparameter counts, the sheer number of permutations that need to be tested can quickly become overwhelming. The trade-off, clearly,

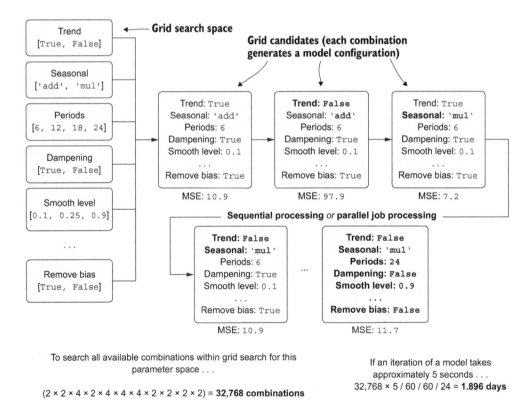

Figure 7.3 Brute-force grid search approach to tuning

is between the time required to run all of the permutations and the search capability of the optimization. If you want to explore more of the hyperparameter response surface, you're going to have to run more iterations. There's really no free lunch here.

RANDOM SEARCH

With all of the grid search's limitations that hamper its ability to arrive at an optimized set of hyperparameters, using it can be prohibitively expensive in terms of both time and money. Were we interested in thoroughly testing all continuously distributed hyperparameters in a forecasting model, the amount of time to get an answer, when running on a single CPU, would be measured in *weeks* rather than minutes.

An alternative to grid search, to attempt to simultaneously test the influencing effects of different hyperparameters at the same time (rather than relying on explicit permutations to determine the optimal values), is using random sampling of each of the hyperparameter groups. Figure 7.4 illustrates random search; compare it to figure 7.3 to see the differences in the approaches.

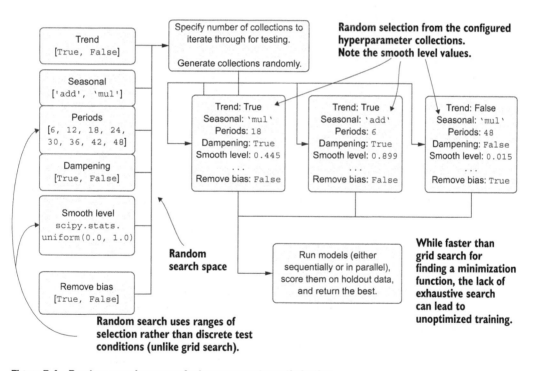

Figure 7.4   Random search process for hyperparameter optimization

As you can see, the selection of candidates to test is random and is controlled not through the mechanism of permutations of all possible values, but rather through a maximum number of iterations to test. This is a bit of a double-edged sword: although the execution time is dramatically reduced, the search through the hyperparameter space is limited.

Nerdy arguments about parameter searching

Numerous arguments can be made for why random search is superior to grid-based search, many of them quite valid. However, the vast majority of examples presented in online references, examples, and blog posts are still using grid search as a means to perform model tuning.

There's a clear reason for this: it's fast. No package developer blogger wants to create an example that is incredibly complex or time-consuming for their readers to run. This doesn't make it a good practice to follow, though.

Seeing so many grid searches employed in examples has generated the mistaken impression in many practitioners that it is far more effective at finding good parameters, more so than other approaches. We may also have general entropic aversion, collectively as humans (we abhor randomness, so a random search must be bad, right?). I'm not entirely sure.

I can't emphasize enough, however, how limiting grid search is (and expensive, if you want to be thorough). I'm not alone in this either; see "Random Search for Hyper-Parameter Optimization" by James Bergstra and Yoshua Bengio (2012) at www.jmlr .org/papers/volume13/bergstra12a/bergstra12a.pdf. I generally agree with their conclusion that grid search is essentially flawed as an approach; since some hyperparameters are far more influential in the overall quality of a particular trained model, those with greater effect get the same amount of coverage as those with negligible influence, limiting the effective search because of computation time and the cost of more expansive testing. Random search is, in my opinion, a better approach than grid search, but it still isn't the most effective or efficient approach.

Bergstra and Bengio agree: "Our analysis of the hyperparameter response surface suggests that random experiments are more efficient because not all hyperparameters are equally important to tune. Grid search experiments allocate too many trials to the exploration of dimensions that do not matter and suffer from poor coverage in dimensions that are important." In the next section, we talk about how they did something about it by creating a novel algorithm that is truly brilliant.

MODEL-BASED OPTIMIZATION: TREE-STRUCTURED PARZEN ESTIMATORS (HYPEROPT)

We face a complex search for hyperparameters in our time-series forecasting model—11 total hyperparameters, 3 continuously distributed and 1 ordinal—confounding the ability to effectively search the space. The preceding approaches are either too time-consuming (manual, grid search), expensive (grid search), or difficult to achieve adequate fit characteristics for validation against holdout data (all of them).

The same team that brought the paper arguing that random search is a superior methodology to grid search also arrived at a process for selecting an optimized hyperparameter response surface: using Bayesian techniques in a model-based optimization relying on either Gaussian processes or tree of Parzen estimators (TPEs). The results of their research are provided in the open source software package Hyperopt. Figure 7.5 shows at a high level how Hyperopt works.

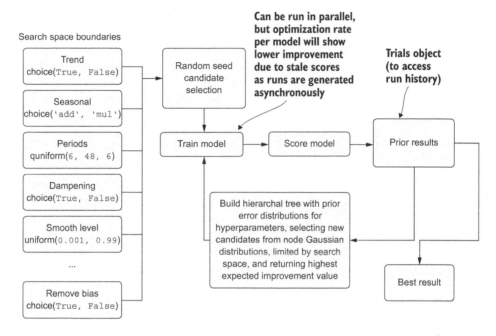

Figure 7.5   A high-level diagram of how Hyperopt's tree-structured Parzen estimator algorithm works

This system is nearly guaranteed to outperform even the most experienced DS working through any of the earlier mentioned classical tuning approaches. Not only is it remarkably capable of exploring complex hyperparameter spaces, but it can do so in far fewer iterations than other methodologies. For further reading on this topic, I recommend perusing the original 2011 whitepaper, "Algorithms for Hyper-Parameter Optimization" by James Bergstra et al. (http://mng.bz/W76w) and reading the API documentation for the package for further evidence of its effectiveness (http://hyperopt .github.io/hyperopt/).

MORE ADVANCED (AND COMPLEX) TECHNIQUES

Anything more advanced than Hyperopt's TPE and similar automated tuning packages typically means doing one of two things: paying a company that offers an automated-ML (autoML) solution or building your own. In the realm of building a custom tuner solution, you might look into a mixture of genetic algorithms with Bayesian prior search optimization to create search candidates within the n-dimensional hyperparameter space that have the highest likelihood of giving a good result, leveraging the selective optimization that genetic algorithms are known for.

Speaking from the perspective of someone who has built one of these autoML solutions (https://github.com/databrickslabs/automl-toolkit), I cannot recommend going down this path unless you're building out a custom framework for hundreds (or more) different projects and have a distinct need for a high-performance and lower-cost optimization tool specifically customized to solve the sorts of problems that your company is facing.

AutoML is definitely not a palatable option for most experienced DS teams, however. The very nature of these solutions, being largely autonomous apart from a configuration-driven interface, forces you to relinquish control and visibility into the decision logic contained within the software. You lose the ability to discover the reasoning behind why some features are culled and others are created, why a particular model was selected, and what internal validations may have been performed on your feature vector to achieve the purported best results.

Setting aside that these solutions are black boxes, it's important to recognize the target audience for these applications. These full-featured pipeline-generation toolkits are not designed or intended for use by seasoned ML developers in the first place. They're built for the unfortunately named *citizen data scientist*—the SMEs who know their business needs intimately but don't have the experience or knowledge to handcraft an ML solution by themselves.

Building a framework to automate some of the more (arguably) boring and rudimentary modeling needs that your company faces may seem exciting. It certainly can be. These frameworks aren't exactly simple to build, though. If you're going down the path of building something custom, like an autoML framework, make sure that you have the bandwidth to do so, that the business understands and approves of this massive project, and that you can justify your return on a substantial investment of time and resources. During the middle of a project is not the time to tack on months of cool work.

7.1.2 *Hyperopt primer*

Going back to our project work with forecasting, we can confidently assert that the best approach for tuning the models for each airport is going to be through using Hyperopt and its TPE approach.

> **NOTE** Hyperopt is a package that is external to the build of Anaconda we've been using. To use it, you must perform a pip or conda install of the package in your environment.

Before we get into the code that we'll be using, let's look at how this API works from a simplified implementation perspective. To begin, the first aspect of Hyperopt is in the definition of an objective function (listing 7.1 shows a simplified implementation of a function for finding a minimization). This objective function is, typically, a model that is fit on training data, validated on testing data, scored, and returns the error metric associated with the predicted data as compared to the validation data.

Listing 7.1 Hyperopt fundamentals: The objective function

Defines the objective function to minimize

A one-dimensional fourth-order polynomial equation that we want to solve for

Loss estimation for the minimization optimization

```
import numpy as np
def objective_function(x):
    func = np.poly1d([1, -3, -88, 112, -5])
    return func(x) * 0.01
```

Why Hyperopt?

I'm using Hyperopt for this discussion simply because it's widely used. Other tools perform similar and arguably more advanced versions of what this package is designed to do (optimize hyperparameters). Optuna (https://optuna.org) is a rather notable continuation of the work of the original research that went into building Hyperopt. I highly encourage you to check it out.

The point of this book isn't about technology. It's about the processes that surround the use of technology. At some point in the not so distant future, a better tech will come out. A more optimal way of finding optimized parameters will come along. Furtherance of the field is something that is constant, inevitable, and rapid. I'm not interested in discussing how one technology is better than another. Plenty of other books do that. I'm interested in discussing why it's important to use something to solve this problem. Feel free to the choose the *something* that feels right for you.

After we have declared an objective function, the next phase in using Hyperopt is to define a space to search over. For this example, we're interested in only a single value to optimize for, in order to solve the minimization of the polynomial function in listing 7.1. In the next listing, we define the search space for this one x variable for the function, instantiating the `Trials` object (for recording the history of the optimization), and running the optimization with the minimization function from the Hyperopt API.

Listing 7.2 Hyperopt optimization for a simple polynomial

Instantiates the Trials object to record the optimization history

Defines the search space—in this case, a uniform sampling between −12 and 12 for the seed and bounded Gaussian random selection for the TPE algorithm after the initial seed priors return

```
optimization_space = hp.uniform('x', -12, 12)
trials = Trials()
trial_estimator = fmin(fn=objective_function,
                space=optimization_space,
                algo=tpe.suggest,
                trials=trials,
                max_evals=1000
)
```

The objective function as defined in listing 7.1, passed in to the fmin optimization function of Hyperopt

The optimization algorithm to use—in this case, tree-structured Parzen estimator

The space to search, defined above (−12 to 12, uniformly)

The number of optimization runs to conduct. Since hpopt is iterations-bound, we can control the runtime of the optimization in this manner.

Passes the Trials object into the optimization function to record the history of the run

Once we execute this code, we will receive a progress bar (in Jupyter-based note-books) that will return the best loss that has been discovered throughout the history of the run as it optimizes. At the conclusion of the run, we will get as a return value from `trial_estimator` the optimal setting for x to minimize the value returned from the polynomial defined in the function `objective_function`. The following listing shows how this process works for this simple example.

Listing 7.3 Hyperopt performance in minimizing a simple polynomial function

Generates a range of x values for plotting the function defined in listing 7.1

Retrieves the corresponding y values for each of the x values from the rng collection

Plots the function across the x space of rng

Plots the optimized minima that Hyperopt finds based on our search space

```
rng = np.arange(-11.0, 12.0, 0.01)
values = [objective_function(x) for x in rng]
with plt.style.context(style='seaborn'):
    fig, ax = plt.subplots(1, 1, figsize=(5.5, 4))
    ax.plot(rng, values)
    ax.set_title('Objective function')
    ax.scatter(x=trial_estimator['x'], y=trials.average_best_error(),
        marker='o', s=100)
    bbox_text = 'Hyperopt calculated minimum value\nx:
        {}'.format(trial_estimator['x'])
    arrow = dict(facecolor='darkblue', shrink=0.01,
        connectionstyle='angle3,angleA=90,angleB=45')
    bbox_conf = dict(boxstyle='round,pad=0.5', fc='ivory', ec='grey', lw=0.8)
    conf = dict(xycoords='data', textcoords='axes fraction', arrowprops=arrow,
        bbox=bbox_conf, ha='left', va='center', fontsize=12)
    ax.annotate(bbox_text, xy=(trial_estimator['x'],
        trials.average_best_error()), xytest=(0.3, 0.8), **conf)
    fig.tight_layout()
    plt.savefig('objective_func.svg', format='svg')
```

Adds an annotation to the graph to indicate the minimized value

Running this script results in the plot in figure 7.6.

Linear models frequently have "dips" and "valleys" between parameters and their loss metrics. We use the terms *local minima* and *local maxima* to describe them. If the parameter search space isn't explored sufficiently, a model's tuning could reside in a local, instead of the global, minima or maxima.

7.1.3 *Using Hyperopt to tune a complex forecasting problem*

Now that you understand the concepts behind this automated model-tuning package, we can apply it to our complex forecasting modeling problem. As we discussed earlier in this chapter, tuning this model is going to be complex if we don't have some assistance. Not only are there 11 hyperparameters to explore, but the success that we had in chapter 6 at manually tuning was not particularly impressive.

We need something to help us. Let's let Thomas Bayes lend a hand (or, rather, Pierre-Simon Laplace). Listing 7.4 shows our optimization function for the Holt-Winters exponential smoothing (HWES) model for passengers at airports.

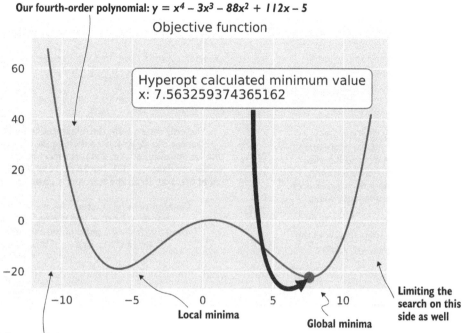

Our fourth-order polynomial: $y = x^4 - 3x^3 - 88x^2 + 112x - 5$

Objective function

Hyperopt calculated minimum value
x: 7.563259374365162

Local minima

Global minima

Limiting the search on this side as well

We have to limit our search space here (for the sake of plotting *and* for efficiency of search) since this equation goes to very big numbers of y rather quickly.

Figure 7.6 Using Hyperopt to solve for the minimal value of a simple polynomial

---

Listing 7.4 Minimization function for Holt-Winters exponential smoothing

Instantiates the ExponentialSmoothing class as an object, configured with the values that Hyperopt will be selecting for each model iteration to test

selected_hp_values is a multilevel dictionary. Since we have two separate sections of hyperparameters to apply and some of the parameter names are similar, we separate them between "model" and "fit" to reduce confusion.

```
def hwes_minimization_function(selected_hp_values, train, test, loss_metric):
    model = ExponentialSmoothing(train,
                    trend=selected_hp_values['model']['trend'],
                    seasonal=selected_hp_values['model']['seasonal'],
                    seasonal_periods=selected_hp_values['model'][
                      'seasonal_periods'],
                    damped=selected_hp_values['model']['damped']
                    )
    model_fit = \
    model.fit(smoothing_level=selected_hp_values['fit']['smoothing_level'],
                    smoothing_seasonal=selected_hp_values['fit'][
                      'smoothing_seasonal'],
                    damping_slope=selected_hp_values['fit']['damping_slope'],
                    use_brute=selected_hp_values['fit']['use_brute'],
                    use_boxcox=selected_hp_values['fit']['use_boxcox'],
```

The fit method has its own set of hyperparameters that Hyperopt will be selecting for the pool of models it will generate and test.

A utility function to get the number of parameters (viewable in the book's GitHub repository)

```
                                  use_basinhopping=selected_hp_values['fit'][
                                    'use_basinhopping'],
                                  remove_bias=selected_hp_values['fit']['remove_bias']
                                  )
        forecast = model_fit.predict(train.index[-1], test.index[-1])
        param_count = extract_param_count_hwes(selected_hp_values)
        adjusted_forecast = forecast[1:]
        errors = calculate_errors(test, adjusted_forecast, param_count)
        return {'loss': errors[loss_metric], 'status': STATUS_OK}
```

Calculates all of the error metrics—Akaike information criterion (AIC) and Bayesian information criterion (BIC), newly added metrics, requires the hyperparameter count

The only return from the minimization function for Hyperopt is a dictionary containing the metric under test for optimization and a status report message from within the Hyperopt API. The Trials() object will persist all of the data about the runs and a tuned best model.

Generates the forecast for this run of the model to perform validation and scoring against. We are forecasting from the point of the end of the training set to the last value of the test set's index.

Removes the first entry of the forecast since it overlaps with the training set's last index entry

As you may recall from chapter 6, when creating the prototype for this algorithm, we hardcoded several of these values (smoothing_level, smoothing_seasonal, use_brute, use_boxcox, use_basin_hopping, and remove_bias) to make the prototyping tuning a bit easier. In listing 7.4, we're setting all of these values as tunable hyperparameters for Hyperopt. Even with such a large search space, the algorithm will allow us to explore the influence of all of them over the predictive capabilities of the holdout space. If we were using something permutations-based (or, worse, human-short-term-memory-based) such as a grid search, we likely wouldn't want to include all of these for the sole reason of factorially increasing runtime.

Now that we have our model-scoring implementation done, we can move on to the next critical phase of efficiently tuning these models,: defining the search space for the hyperparameters.

Listing 7.5   Hyperopt exploration space configuration

For readability's sake, we're splitting the configuration between the class-level hyperparameters (model) and the method-level hyperparameters (fit) since some of the names for the two are similar.

hp.quniform chooses a random value uniformly in a quantized space (in this example, we're choosing a multiple of 12, between 12 and 120).

```
        hpopt_space = {
            'model': {
                'trend': hp.choice('trend', ['add', 'mul']),
                'seasonal': hp.choice('seasonal', ['add', 'mul']),
                'seasonal_periods': hp.quniform('seasonal_periods', 12, 120, 12),
                'damped': hp.choice('damped', [True, False])
            },
            'fit': {
                'smoothing_level': hp.uniform('smoothing_level', 0.01, 0.99),
                'smoothing_seasonal': hp.uniform('smoothing_seasonal', 0.01, 0.99),
```

hp.choice is used for Boolean and multivariate selection (choose one element from a list of possible values).

hp.uniform selects randomly through the continuous space (here, between 0.01 and 0.99).

```
        'damping_slope': hp.uniform('damping_slope', 0.01, 0.99),
        'use_brute': hp.choice('use_brute', [True, False]),
        'use_boxcox': hp.choice('use_boxcox', [True, False]),
        'use_basinhopping': hp.choice('use_basinhopping', [True, False]),
        'remove_bias': hp.choice('remove_bias', [True, False])
    }
}
```

The settings in this code are the total sum of hyperparameters available for the
ExponentialSmoothing() class and the fit() method as of statsmodels version 0.11.1.
Some of these hyperparameters may not influence the predictive power of our model.
If we had been evaluating this through grid search, we would likely have omitted them
from our evaluation. With Hyperopt, because of the manner in which its algorithm
provides greater weight to influential parameters, leaving them in for evaluation
doesn't dramatically increase the total runtime.

The next step for automating away the daunting task of tuning this temporal
model is to build a function to execute the optimization, collect the data from the
tuning run, and generate plots that we can use to further optimize the search space as
defined in listing 7.5 on subsequent fine-tuning runs. Listing 7.6 shows our final execution function.

> **NOTE** Please refer to the companion repository to this book at https://github
> .com/BenWilson2/ML-Engineering to see the full code for all of the func-
> tions called in listing 7.6. A more thorough discussion is included there in a
> downloadable and executable notebook.

Listing 7.6   Hyperopt tuning execution

Because of the volume of configurations used to execute the tuning
run and collect all the visualizations and data from the optimization,
we'll use named dictionary-based argument passing (**kwargs).

```
def run_tuning(train, test, **params):
    param_count = extract_param_count_hwes(params['tuning_space'])
    output = {}
    trial_run = Trials()
    tuning = fmin(partial(params['minimization_function'],
                          train=train,
                          test=test,
                          loss_metric=params['loss_metric']
                         ),
```

fmin() is the main method for initiating a Hyperopt
run. We're using a partial function as a wrapper
around the per-model static attributes so that the
sole differences between each Hyperopt iteration is
in the variable hyperparameters, keeping the other
attributes the same.

To calculate AIC and BIC, we need the
total number of hyperparameters
being optimized. Instead of forcing
the user of this function to count
them, we can extract them from the
passed-in Hyperopt configuration
element tuning_space.

The Trials() object records each of the, well, trials of
different hyperparameter experiments and allows
us to see how the optimization converged.

```
                            params['tuning_space'],
                            algo=params['hpopt_algo'],
                            max_evals=params['iterations'],
                            trials=trial_run
                        )
    best_run = space_eval(params['tuning_space'], tuning)
    generated_model = params['forecast_algo'](train, test, best_run)
    extracted_trials = extract_hyperopt_trials(trial_run,
     params['tuning_space'], params['loss_metric'])
    output['best_hp_params'] = best_run
    output['best_model'] = generated_model['model']
    output['hyperopt_trials_data'] = extracted_trials
    output['hyperopt_trials_visualization'] = \
      generate_hyperopt_report(extracted_trials, params['loss_metric'],
      params['hyperopt_title'], params['hyperopt_image_name'])
    output['forecast_data'] = generated_model['forecast']
    output['series_prediction'] = build_future_forecast(
                                 generated_model['model'],
                                 params['airport_name'],
                                 params['future_forecast_
                                         periods'],
                                 params['train_split_cutoff_
                                         months'],
                                 params['target_name']
                                 )

    output['plot_data'] = plot_predictions(test,
                                 generated_model['forecast'],
                                 param_count,
                                 params['name'],
                                 params['target_name'],
                                 params['image_name'])

    return output
```

The number of models to test and search through to find an optimal configuration

Extracts the best model from the Trials() object

Plots the trial history)

Pulls the tuning information out of the Trials() object for plotting

Rebuilds the best model to record and store

The optimization algorithm for Hyperopt (random, TPE, or adaptive TPE), which can be automated or manually controlled

The tuning space defined in listing 7.5

Plots the forecast over the holdout validation period to show test vs. forecast (updated version from chapter 6 visualization)

Builds the future forecast for as many points as specified in the future_forecast_periods configuration value

NOTE   To read more about how partial functions and Hyperopt work, see the Python documentation at https://docs.python.org/3/library/functools.html #functools.partial and the Hyperopt doc and source code at http://Hyperopt .github.io/Hyperopt/.

NOTE   Listing 7.6's custom plot code is available in the companion repository for this book; see the Chapter7 notebook at https://github.com/BenWilson2/ ML-Engineering.

Executing the call to `plot_predictions()` from listing 7.6 is shown in figure 7.7. Calling `generate_hyperopt_report()` from listing 7.6 results in the plot shown in figure 7.8.

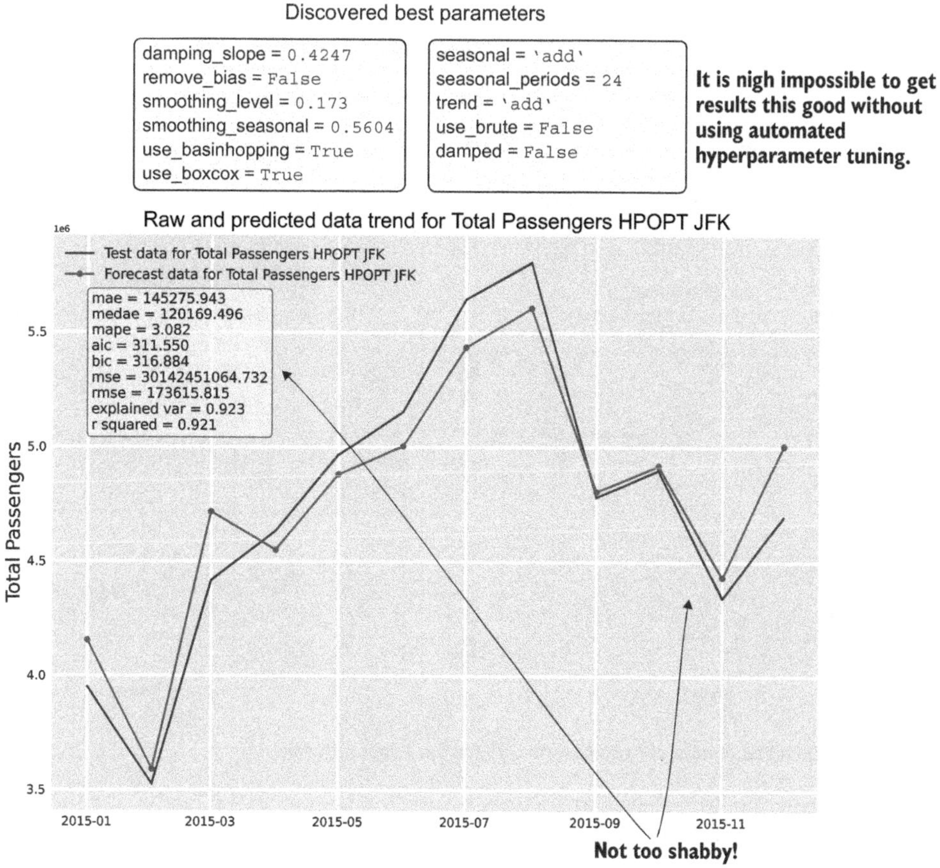

Discovered best parameters
damping_slope = 0.4247
remove_bias = False
smoothing_level = 0.173
smoothing_seasonal = 0.5604
use_basinhopping = True
use_boxcox = True
seasonal = 'add'
seasonal_periods = 24
trend = 'add'
use_brute = False
damped = False
It is nigh impossible to get results this good without using automated hyperparameter tuning.
Raw and predicted data trend for Total Passengers HPOPT JFK
1e6
Test data for Total Passengers HPOPT JFK
Forecast data for Total Passengers HPOPT JFK
mae = 145275.943
medae = 120169.496
mape = 3.082
aic = 311.550
bic = 316.884
mse = 30142451064.732
rmse = 173615.815
explained var = 0.923
r squared = 0.921
Total Passengers
5.5
5.0
4.5
4.0
3.5
2015-01
2015-03
2015-05
2015-07
2015-09
2015-11
Not too shabby!

Figure 7.7 Prediction backtesting on the most recent data from the total time series (x-axis zoomed for legibility)

By using Hyperopt to arrive at the best predictions on our holdout data, we've optimized the hyperparameters to a degree that we can be confident of having a good projection of the future state (provided that no unexpected and unknowable latent factors affect it). Thus, we've addressed several key challenging elements in the optimization phase of ML work by using automated tuning:

- *Accuracy*—The forecast is as optimal as it can be (for each model, provided that we select a reasonable search space and run through enough iterations).
- *Timeliness in training*—With this level of automation, we get well-tuned models in minutes instead of days (or weeks).

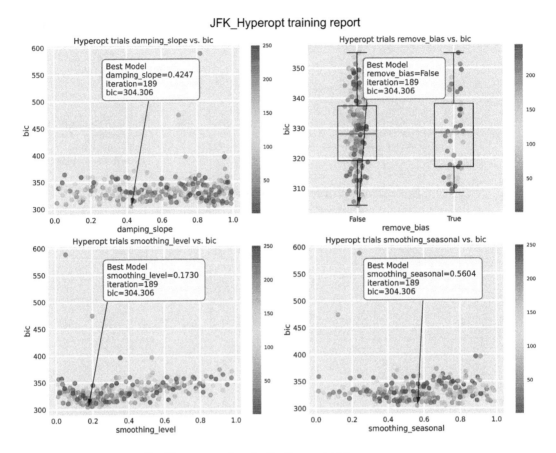

Figure 7.8 **Sampled results of hyperparameters for the Hyperopt trials run**

- *Maintainability*—Automating tuning keeps us from having to manually retrain models as the baseline shifts over time.
- *Timeliness in development*—Since our code is pseudo-modular (using modularized functions within a notebook), the code is reusable, extensible, and capable of being utilized through a control loop to build all the models for each airport with ease.

NOTE The extracted code samples that we've just gone through with Hyperopt are part of a much larger end-to-end example hosted within the book's repository in the Notebooks section for chapter 7. In this example, you can see the automated tuning and optimization for all airports within this dataset and all utility functions that are built to support this effective tuning of models.

7.2   *Choosing the right tech for the platform and the team*

The forecasting scenario we've been walking through, when executed in a virtual machine (VM) container and running automated tuning optimization and forecasting for a single airport, worked quite well. We got fairly good results for each airport. By using Hyperopt, we also managed to eliminate the unmaintainable burden of manually tuning each model. While impressive, it doesn't change the fact that we're not looking to forecast passengers at just a single airport. We need to create forecasts for thousands of airports.

Figure 7.9 shows what we've built, in terms of wall-clock time, in our efforts thus far. The synchronous nature of each airport's models (in a `for` loop) and Hyperopt's Bayesian optimizer (also a serial loop) means that we're waiting for models to be built one by one, each next step waiting on the previous to be completed, as we discussed in section 7.1.2.

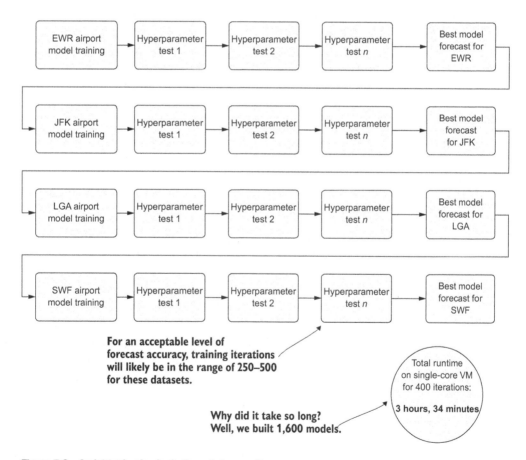

Figure 7.9   Serial tuning in single-threaded execution

This problem of ML at scale, as shown in this diagram, is a stumbling block for many teams, mostly because of complexity, time, and cost (and is one the primary reasons why projects of this scale are frequently cancelled). Solutions exist for these scalability issues for ML project work; each involves stepping away from the realm of serial execution and moving into the world of distributed, asynchronous, or a mixture of both of these paradigms of computing.

The standard structured code approach for most Python ML tasks is to execute in a serial fashion. Whether it be a list comprehension, a lambda, or a `for` (`while`) loop, ML is steeped in sequential execution. This approach can be a benefit, as it reduces memory pressure for many algorithms that have a high memory requirement, particularly those that use recursion, which are many. But this approach can also be a handicap, as it takes much longer to execute, since each subsequent task is waiting for the previous to complete.

We will discuss concurrency in ML briefly in section 7.4 and in more depth in later chapters (both safe and unsafe ways of doing it). For now, with the issue of scalability with respect to wall-clock time for our project, we need to look into a *distributed approach* to this problem in order to explore our search spaces faster for each airport. It is at this point that we stray from the world of our single-threaded VM approach and move into the distributed computing world of Apache Spark.

7.2.1   Why Spark?

Why use Spark? In a word: speed.

For the problem that we're dealing with here, forecasting each month the passenger expectations at each major airport in the United States, we're not bound by SLAs that are measured in minutes or hours, but we still need to think about the amount of time it takes to run our forecasting. There are multiple reasons for this, chiefly

- *Time*—If we're building this job as a monolithic modeling event, any failures in an extremely long-running job will require a restart (imagine the job failing after it was 99% complete, running for 11 days straight).
- *Stability*—We want to be very careful about object references within our job and ensure that we don't create a memory leak that could cause the job to fail.
- *Risk*—Keeping machines dedicated to extremely long-running jobs (even in cloud providers) risks platform issues that could bring down the job.
- *Cost*—Regardless of where your virtual machines are running, someone is paying the bill for them.

When we focus on tackling these high-risk factors, distributed computing offers a compelling alternative to serial looped execution, not only because of cost, but mostly because of the speed of execution. Were any issues to arise in the job, unforeseen issues with the data, or problems with the underlying hardware that the VMs are running on, these dramatically reduced execution times for our forecasting job will give us flexibility to get the job up and running again with predicted values returning much faster.

A brief note on Spark

Spark is a large topic, a monumentally large ecosystem, and an actively contributed-to open source distributed computing platform based on the Java Virtual Machine (JVM). Because this isn't a book about Spark per se, I won't go too deep into the inner workings of it.

Several notable books have been written on the subject, and I recommend reading them if you are inclined to learn more about the technology: *Learning Spark* by Jules Damji et al. (O'Reilly, 2020), *Spark: The Definitive Guide* by Bill Chambers and Matei Zaharia (O'Reilly, 2018), and *Spark in Action* by Jean-Georges Perrin (Manning, 2020).

Suffice it to say, in this book, we will explore how to effectively utilize Spark to perform ML tasks. Many examples from this point forward are focused on leveraging the power of the platform to perform large-scale ML (both training and inference).

For the current section, the information covered is relatively high level with respect to how Spark works for these examples; instead, we focus entirely on how we can use it to solve our problems.

But how is Spark going to help us with this problem? We can employ two relatively straightforward paradigms, shown in figure 7.10. We could use more than just these two, but we're going to start with the straightforward and less complex ones for now; the more advanced approaches are mentioned in section 7.4.

The first approach is to leverage the workers within the cluster to execute parallel evaluation of the hyperparameters. In this paradigm, our time-series dataset will need to be collected (materialized in full) from the workers to the driver. Limitations exist (serialization size of the data is currently limited to 2 GB at the time of this writing), and for many ML use cases on Spark, this approach shouldn't be used. For time-series problems such as this one, this approach will work just fine.

In the second approach, we leave the data on the workers. We utilize `pandas_udf` to distribute concurrent training of each airport on each worker by using our stand-alone Hyperopt `Trials()` object, just as we did in chapter 6 when running on a single-core VM.

Now that we've defined the two paradigms for speeding up hyperparameter tuning from a high-level architectural perspective, let's look at the process execution (and trade-offs of each) in the next two subsections.

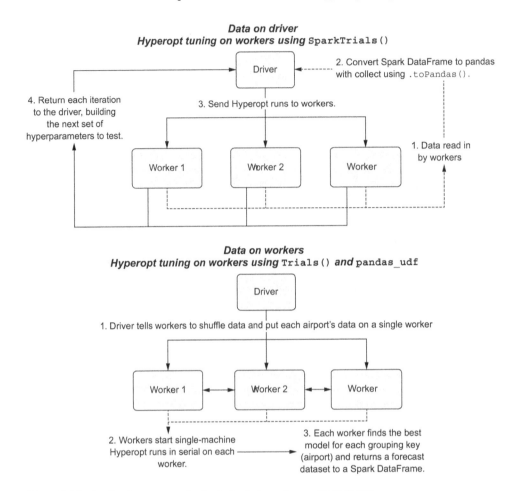

Figure 7.10   Scaling hyperparameter tuning using `pandas_udf` on Spark

7.2.2   *Handling tuning from the driver with SparkTrials*

While figure 7.10 shows the physical layout of the operations occurring within a Spark cluster for handling distributed tuning with `SparkTrials()`, figure 7.11 shows the execution in more detail. Each airport that needs to be modeled is iterated over on the driver, its optimization handled through a distributed implementation wherein each candidate hyperparameter collection is submitted to a different worker.

This approach works remarkably well with a minimal amount of modification to achieve a similar level of hyperparameter space searching as compared to the single-core approach, needing only a small increase to the number of iterations as the level of parallelism is increased.

NOTE Increasing the number of iterations as a factor of the parallelism level is not advisable. In practice, I generally increase the iterations by a simple

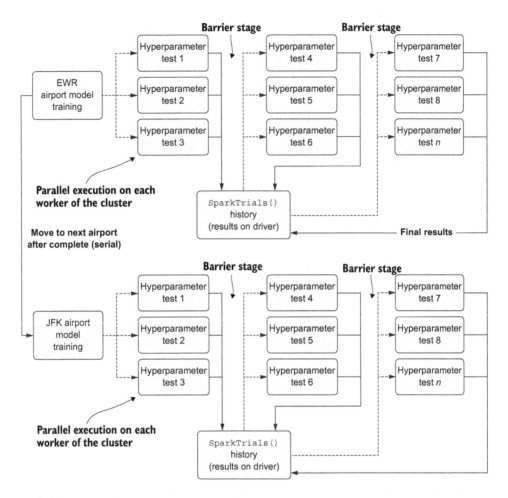

Figure 7.11   Logical architecture of utilizing Spark workers to distribute Hyperopt test iterations for hyperparameter optimization

adjustment of the number of single-core iterations + (parallelism factor / 0.2). This is to give a larger pool of prior values to pull from. With parallel runs executing asynchronously, each boundary epoch that is initiated will not have the benefit of in-flight results that a synchronous execution would.

This is so critical to do because of the nature of the optimizer in Hyperopt. Being a Bayesian estimator, the power of its ability to arrive at an optimized set of parameters to test lies directly in its access to prior data. If too many runs are executing concurrently, the lack of data on their results translates to a higher rate of searching through parameters that have a lower probability to work well. Without the prior results, the optimization becomes much more of a random search, defeating the purpose of using the Bayesian optimizer.

This trade-off is negligible, though, particularly when compared to the rather impressive performance achievable by utilizing *n* workers to distribute each iteration to. To port our functions over to Spark, only a few changes need to happen for this first paradigm.

> **NOTE** To follow along fully with a referenceable and executable example of distributed hyperparameter optimization with Apache Spark, please see the companion Spark notebook in the book's repository entitled Chapter8_1, which we will be using throughout the next chapter as well.

The first thing that we'll need to do is to import the module `SparkTrials` from Hyperopt. `SparkTrials` is a tracking object that allows for the cluster's driver to maintain a history of all the experiments that have been attempted with different hyperparameter configurations executed on the remote workers (as opposed to the standard `Trials` object that tracks the history of runs conducted on the same VM).

Once we have the import completed, we can read in our data by using a native Spark reader (in this instance, our data has been stored in a Delta table and registered to the Apache Hive Metastore, making it available through the standard database and table name identifiers). Once we have the data loaded onto the workers, we can then collect the series data to the driver, as shown in the following listing.

> **Listing 7.7 Using Spark to collect data to the driver as a pandas DataFrame**

Defines the name of the Delta table that we've written the airport data to

Defines the name of the Hive database that the Delta table is registered to

```
delta_table_nm = 'airport'
delta_database_nm = 'ben_demo'
delta_full_nm = "{}.{}".format(delta_database_nm, delta_table_nm)
local_data = spark.table(delta_full_nm).toPandas()
```

Interpolates the database name and the table name into standard API signature for data retrieval

Reads in the data with the workers from Delta (there is no ability to directly read in data to the driver from Delta), and then collects the data to the driver node as a pandas DataFrame

> **WARNING** Be careful about collecting data in Spark. With the vast majority of large-scale ML (with a training dataset that could be in the tens or hundreds of gigabytes), a `.toPandas()` call, or any collect action at all, in Spark will fail. If you have a large collection of data that can be iterated through, simply filter the Spark `DataFrame` and use an iterator (loop) to collect chunks of the data with a `.toPandas()` method call to control the amount of data being processed on the driver at a time.

After running the preceding code, we are left with our data residing on the driver, ready for utilizing the distributed nature of the Spark cluster to conduct a far more scalable tuning of the models than what we were dealing with in our Docker container VM from section 7.1. The following listing shows the modifications to listing 7.6 that allow us to run in this manner.

Listing 7.8 Modifying the tuning execution function for running Hyperopt on Spark

Configures Hyperopt to use SparkTrials() instead of Trials(), setting the number of concurrent experiments to run on the workers in the cluster and the global time-out level (since we're using Futures to submit the tests)

```
def run_tuning(train, test, **params):
    param_count = extract_param_count_hwes(params['tuning_space'])
    output = {}
    trial_run = SparkTrials(parallelism=params['parallelism'],
      timeout=params['timeout'])
    with mlflow.start_run(run_name='PARENT_RUN_{}'.format(params[
      'airport_name']), nested=True):
        mlflow.set_tag('airport', params['airport_name'])
        tuning = fmin(partial(params['minimization_function'],
                              train=train,
                              test=test,
                              loss_metric=params['loss_metric']
                      ),
                  params['tuning_space'],
                  algo=params['hpopt_algo'],
                  max_evals=params['iterations'],
                  trials=trial_run,
                  show_progressbar=False
                  )
        best_run = space_eval(params['tuning_space'], tuning)
        generated_model = params['forecast_algo'](train, test, best_run)
        extracted_trials = extract_hyperopt_trials(trial_run,
          params['tuning_space'], params['loss_metric'])
        output['best_hp_params'] = best_run
        output['best_model'] = generated_model['model']
        output['hyperopt_trials_data'] = extracted_trials
        output['hyperopt_trials_visualization'] =
          generate_Hyperopt_report(extracted_trials,
                                params['loss_metric'],
                                params['hyperopt_title'],
                                params['hyperopt_image_name'])
        output['forecast_data'] = generated_model['forecast']
        output['series_prediction'] = build_future_forecast(
                                generated_model['model'],
                                params['airport_name'],
                                params['future_forecast_periods'],
                                params['train_split_cutoff_months'],
                                params['target_name'])
        output['plot_data'] = plot_predictions(test,
                                generated_model['forecast'],
                                param_count,
                                params['name'],
                                params['target_name'],
                                params['image_name'])
        mlflow.log_artifact(params['image_name'])
        mlflow.log_artifact(params['hyperopt_image_name'])
    return output
```

Logs the airport name to MLflow to make it easier to search through the results of the tracking service

Configures MLflow to log the results of each hyperparameter test within a parent run for each airport

The minimization function remains largely unchanged with the exception of adding in MLflow logging of both the hyperparameters and the calculated loss metrics that are being tested for the iteration within the child run.

Logs the generated prediction plots for the best model to the parent MLflow run

Logs the Hyperopt report for the run, written to the parent MLflow run ID

Little modification needed to happen to the code to get it to work within the distributed framework of Spark. As a bonus (which we will discuss in more depth in section 7.3), we can also log information with ease to MLflow, solving one of our key needs for creating a maintainable project: provenance of tests for reference and comparison.

Based on the side-by-side comparison of this methodology to that of the run conducted in our single-core VM, this approach meets the goals of timeliness that we were searching for. We've reduced the optimization phase of this forecasting effort from just over 3.5 hours to, on a relatively small four-node cluster, just under 30 minutes (using a higher Hyperopt iteration count of 600 and a parallelization parameter of 8 to attempt to achieve similar loss metric performance).

In the next section, we will look at an approach that solves our scalability problem in a completely different way by parallelizing the per airport models instead of parallelizing the tuning.

7.2.3   *Handling tuning from the workers with a pandas_udf*

With the previous section's approach, we were able to dramatically reduce the execution time by leveraging Spark to distribute individual hyperparameter-tuning stages. However, we were still using a sequential loop for each airport. As the number of airports grows, the relationship between total job execution time and airport count is still going to increase linearly, no matter how many parallel operations we do within the Hyperopt tuning framework. Of course, this approach's effectiveness has a limit, as raising Hyperopt's concurrency level will essentially negate the benefits of running the TPE and turn our optimization into a random search.

Instead, we can parallelize the actual model phases themselves, effectively turning this runtime problem into a horizontally scaling problem (reducing the execution time of all airports' modeling by adding more worker nodes to the cluster), rather than a vertically scaling problem (iterator-bound, which can improve runtime only by using faster hardware). Figure 7.12 illustrates this alternative architecture of tackling our many-model problem through the use of pandas_udf on Spark.

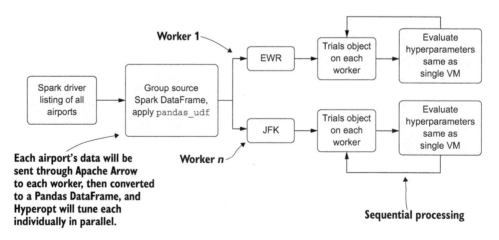

Figure 7.12   Using Spark to control a fleet of contained VMs to work on each forecast asynchronously

Here, we're using Spark DataFrames—a distributed dataset based on resiliently distributed dataset (rdd) relations residing on different VMs—to control the grouping-by of our primary modeling key (in this case, our Airport_Code field). We then pass this aggregated state to a pandas_udf that will leverage Apache Arrow to serialize the aggregated data to workers as a pandas DataFrame. This creates a multitude of concurrent Python VMs that are all operating on their own airport's data as if they were a single VM.

A trade-off exists here, though. To make this approach work, we need to change some things with our code. Listing 7.9 shows the first of these changes: a movement of the MLflow logging logic to within our minimization function, the addition of logging arguments to our function arguments, and the generation of the forecast plots for each iteration from within the minimization function so that we can see them after the modeling phase is completed.

Listing 7.9 Modifying the minimization function to support a distributed model approach

Adds arguments to support MLflow logging

Initializes each iteration to its own MLflow run with a unique name to prevent collisions

Searchable tags for the collection of all models that have been built for a particular execution of the job

Records the hyperparameters for a particular iteration

Adds searchable tags for the MLflow UI search functionality

Records the iteration number of Hyperopt

Logs the loss metrics for the iteration

```python
def hwes_minimization_function_udf(selected_hp_values, train, test,
    loss_metric,  airport, experiment_name, param_count, name, target_name,
    image_name, trial):
    model_results = exp_smoothing_raw_udf(train, test, selected_hp_values)
    errors = calculate_errors(test, model_results['forecast'],
      extract_param_count_hwes(selected_hp_values))
    with mlflow.start_run(run_name='{}_{}_{}_{}'.format(airport,
        experiment_name,str(uuid.uuid4())[:8], len(trial.results))):
      mlflow.set_tag('airport', airport)
      mlflow.set_tag('parent_run', experiment_name)
      mlflow.log_param('id', mlflow.active_run().info.run_id)
      mlflow.log_params(selected_hp_values)
      mlflow.log_metrics(errors)
      img = plot_predictions(test,
                             model_results['forecast'],
                             param_count,
                             name,
                             target_name,
                             image_name)
      mlflow.log_artifact(image_name)
    return {'loss': errors[loss_metric], 'status': STATUS_OK}
```

Saves the image (in PNG format) generated from the plot_predictions function that builds the test vs. forecast data

Since we're going to be executing a pseudo-local Hyperopt run from directly within the Spark workers, we need to create our training and evaluation logic directly within a new function that will consume the grouped data passed via Apache Arrow to the workers for processing as a pandas DataFrame. The next listing shows the creation of this user-defined function (udf).

Listing 7.10   Creating the distributed model `pandas_udf` **to build models concurrently**

Since Spark is a strong-typed language, we need to provide expectations to the udf of
what structure and data types pandas will be returning to the Spark DataFrame. This is
accomplished by using a StructType object defining the field names and their types.

```
output_schema = StructType([
  StructField('date', DateType()),
  StructField('Total_Passengers_pred', IntegerType()),
  StructField('Airport', StringType()),
  StructField('is_future', BooleanType())
])
```

> Defines the type of the
> pandas_udf (here we
> are using a grouped
> map type that takes in
> a pandas DataFrame
> and returns a pandas
> DataFrame) through
> the decorator applied
> above the function

```
@pandas_udf(output_schema, PandasUDFType.GROUPED_MAP)
def forecast_airports(airport_df):

  airport = airport_df['Airport_Code'][0]
  hpopt_space = {
    'model': {
        'trend': hp.choice('trend', ['add', 'mul']),
        'seasonal': hp.choice('seasonal', ['add', 'mul']),
        'seasonal_periods': hp.quniform('seasonal_periods', 12, 120, 12),
        'damped': hp.choice('damped', [True, False])
    },
    'fit': {
        'smoothing_level': hp.uniform('smoothing_level', 0.01, 0.99),
        'smoothing_seasonal': hp.uniform('smoothing_seasonal', 0.01, 0.99),
        'damping_slope': hp.uniform('damping_slope', 0.01, 0.99),
        'use_brute': hp.choice('use_brute', [True, False]),
        'use_boxcox': hp.choice('use_boxcox', [True, False]),
        'use_basinhopping': hp.choice('use_basinhopping', [True, False]),
        'remove_bias': hp.choice('remove_bias', [True, False])
    }
  }

  run_config = {'minimization_function': hwes_minimization_function_udf,
                'tuning_space': hpopt_space,
                'forecast_algo': exp_smoothing_raw,
                'loss_metric': 'bic',
                'hpopt_algo': tpe.suggest,
                'iterations': 200,
                'experiment_name': RUN_NAME,
                'name': '{} {}'.format('Total Passengers HPOPT', airport),
                'target_name': 'Total_Passengers',
                'image_name': '{}_{}.png'.format('total_passengers_
                  validation', airport),
                'airport_name': airport,
                'future_forecast_periods': 36,
                'train_split_cutoff_months': 12,
                'hyperopt_title': '{}_hyperopt Training
                  Report'.format(airport),
                'hyperopt_image_name': '{}_{}.png'.format(
                  'total_passengers_hpopt', airport),
                'verbose': True
              }
```

> We need to extract the airport name
> from the data itself since we can't pass
> additional values into this function.

> We need to define
> our search space
> from within the
> udf since we can't
> pass it into the
> function.

> Sets the run
> configuration for the
> search (within the udf,
> since we need to name
> the runs in MLflow by
> the airport name,
> which is defined only
> after the data is
> passed to a worker
> from within the udf)

```
airport_data = airport_df.copy(deep=True)
airport_data['date'] = pd.to_datetime(airport_data['date'])
airport_data.set_index('date', inplace=True)
airport_data.index = pd.DatetimeIndex(airport_data.index.values,
    freq=airport_data.index.inferred_freq)
asc = airport_data.sort_index()
asc = apply_index_freq(asc, 'MS')          ◄─────────

train, test = generate_splits_by_months(asc,
    run_config['train_split_cutoff_months'])

tuning = run_udf_tuning(train['Total_Passengers'],
    test['Total_Passengers'], **run_config)    ◄─────

return tuning        ◄──────────
```

The airport data manipulation of the pandas DataFrame is placed here since the index conditions and frequencies for the series data are not defined within the Spark DataFrame.

The only modification to the "run tuning" function is to remove the MLflow logging created for the driver-based distributed Hyperopt optimization and to return only the forecasted data instead of the dictionary containing the run metrics and data.

Returns the forecast pandas DataFrame (required so that this data can be "reassembled" into a collated Spark DataFrame when all the airports finish their asynchronous distributed tuning and forecast runs)

With the creation of this `pandas_udf`, we can call the distributed modeling (using Hyperopt in its single-node `Trials()` mode).

Listing 7.11   Executing a fully distributed model-based asynchronous run of forecasting

A modification of the airport filtering used in the single-node code, utilizing PySpark filtering to determine whether enough data is in a particular airport's series to build and validate a forecasting model

```
def validate_data_counts_udf(data, split_count):
    return (list(data.groupBy(col('Airport_Code')).count()
        .withColumn('check', when(((lit(12) / 0.2) < (col('count') * 0.8)),
            True)
        .otherwise(False))
        .filter(col('check')).select('Airport_Code').toPandas()[
            'Airport_Code']))

RUN_NAME = 'AIRPORT_FORECAST_DEC_2020'
raw_data = spark.table(delta_full_nm)        ◄─────
filtered_data =
    raw_data.where(col('Airport_Code').isin(validate_data_counts_udf(raw_
    data, 12))).repartition('Airport_Code')
grouped_apply =
    filtered_data.groupBy('Airport_Code').apply(forecast_airports)    ◄─────
display(grouped_apply)
```

Reads the data from Delta (raw historical passenger data for airports) into the workers on the cluster

Groups the Spark DataFrame and sends the aggregated data to the workers as pandas DataFrames for execution through the udf

Forces the execution (Spark is lazily evaluated)

Filters out insufficient data wherein a particular airport does not have enough data for modeling

Defines a unique name for the particular execution of a forecasting run (this sets the name of the MLflow experiment for the tracking API)

When we run this code, we can see a relatively flat relationship between the number of airport models being generated and the number of workers available for processing our optimization and forecasting runs. While the reality of modeling over 7,000 airports in the shortest amount of time (a Spark cluster with thousands of worker nodes) is more than a little ridiculous (the cost alone would be astronomical), we have a queue-able solution using this paradigm that can horizontally scale in a magnitude that any other solution cannot.

Even though we wouldn't be able to get an effective O(1) execution time because of cost and resources (that would require one worker for each model), we can start a cluster with 40 nodes that would, in effect, run 40 airport modeling, optimizing, and forecasting executions concurrently. This would dramatically reduce the total runtime to 23 hours for all 7,000 airports, as opposed to either running them in a VM through a sequential loop-within-a-loop (> 5,000 hours), or collecting the data to the driver of a Spark cluster and running distributed tuning (> 800 hours).

When finding options for tackling large-scale projects of this nature, the scalability of the execution architecture is just as critical as any of the ML components. Regardless of how much effort, time, and diligence went into crafting the ML aspect of the solution, if solving the problem takes thousands (or hundreds) of hours, the chances that the project will succeed are slim. In the next chapter, section 8.2, we will discuss alternative approaches that can reduce the already dramatically improved 23 hours of runtime down to something even more manageable.

7.2.4 *Using new paradigms for teams: Platforms and technologies*

Starting on a new platform, utilizing a new technology, and perhaps learning a new programming language (or paradigm within a language you already know) is a daunting task for many teams. In the preceding scenarios, it was a relatively large leap to move from a Jupyter notebook running on a single machine to a distributed execution engine like Spark.

The world of ML provides a great many options—not only in algorithms, but also in programming languages (R, Python, Java, Scala, .NET, proprietary languages) and places to develop code (notebooks for prototyping, scripting tools for MVPs, and IDEs for production solution development). Most of all, a great many places are available to run the code that you've written. As we saw earlier, it wasn't the language that caused the runtime of the project to drop so dramatically, but rather the platform that we chose to use.

When exploring options for project work, it is absolutely critical to do your homework. It is critical to test different algorithm approaches to solve a particular problem, and it is arguably more critical to find a place to run the solutions that fits within the needs of that project.

To maximize the chances of a solution being adopted by the business, the right platform should be chosen to minimize execution cost, maximize the stability of the solution, and shorten the development cycle to meet delivery deadlines. The important point to keep in mind about where to run ML code is that it is like any other aspect of this profession: time spent learning the framework used to run your models and analyses will be well spent, enhancing your productivity and efficiency for future work. Without knowing how to actually use a particular platform or execution paradigm, as mentioned in section 7.2.3, this project could have been looking at hundreds of hours of runtime for each forecasting event initiated.

A bit of advice on learning new things

Early in my DS career, I was a bit intimidated and reluctant to learn languages other than Python. I mistakenly thought that my language of choice could "do all the things" and that I had no need for any other language, because the algorithms I used were all there (as far as I was aware at the time) and I was familiar with the nuances of manipulating data in pandas and NumPy. I was sorely mistaken when I had to build my first extremely large-scale ML solution involving a prediction-delivery SLA that was simply too short to allow for looped inference processing of terabytes of data.

Over the years following my exposure to Hadoop, I've become proficient in Java and Scala, used both to build custom algorithms and frameworks for ML use cases, and expanded my knowledge of concurrent asynchronous programming to allow me to leverage as much computational power in solutions as is available to me. My advice? Make learning new technologies part of a regular habit.

DS and ML work is not about a single language, a single platform, or anything that is set in stone. It is a mutable profession of discovery, focused on solving problems in whatever is the best manner to solve them in. Learning new ways to solve problems will only benefit you and whatever company you work for, and may one day help you contribute back to the community with the knowledge that you've gained along your journey.

Summary

- Relying on manual and prescriptive approaches for model tuning is time-consuming, expensive, and unlikely to produce quality results. Utilizing model-driven parameter optimization is preferred.
- Selecting an appropriate platform and implementation methodology for time-consuming CPU-bound tasks can dramatically increase the efficiency and lower the cost of development for an ML project. For processes like hyperparameter tuning, maximizing parallel and distributed system approaches can reduce the development timeline significantly.

Experimentation in action: Finalizing an MVP with MLflow and runtime optimization

This chapter covers

- Approaches, tools, and methods to version-control ML code, models, and experiment results
- Scalable solutions for model training and inference

In the preceding chapter, we arrived at a solution to one of the most time-consuming and monotonous tasks that we face as ML practitioners: fine-tuning models. By having techniques to solve the tedious act of tuning, we can greatly reduce the risk of producing ML-backed solutions that are inaccurate to the point of being worthless. In the process of applying those techniques, however, we quietly welcomed an enormous elephant into the room of our project: tracking.

Throughout the last several chapters, we have been required to retrain our time-series models each time that we do inference. For the vast majority of other supervised learning tasks, this won't be the case. Those other applications of modeling, both supervised and unsupervised, will have periodic retraining events, between which each model will be called for inference (prediction) many times.

Regardless of whether we'll have to retrain daily, weekly, or monthly (you really shouldn't be letting a model go stale for longer than that), we will have versions of not only the final production model that will generate scoring metrics, but also the optimization history of automated tuning. Add to this volume of modeling information a wealth of statistical validation tests, metadata, artifacts, and run-specific data that is valuable for historical reference, and you have yourself a veritable mountain of critical data that needs to be recorded.

In this chapter, we'll go through logging our tuning run data to MLflow's tracking server, enabling us to have historical references to everything that we deem important to store about our project's solution. Having this data available is valuable not merely for tuning and experimentation; it's also critical for monitoring the long-term health of your solution. Having referenceable metrics and parameter search history over time helps inform ways to potentially make the solution better, and also gives insight into when the performance degrades to the point that you need to rebuild the solution.

> **NOTE** A companion Spark notebook provides examples of the points discussed in this chapter. See the accompanying GitHub repository for further details, if interested.

8.1 *Logging: Code, metrics, and results*

Chapters 2 and 3 covered the critical importance of communication about modeling activities, both to the business and among a team of fellow data scientists. Being able to not only show our project solutions, but also have a provenance history for reference, is just as important to the project's success, if not more so, than the algorithms used to solve it.

For the forecasting project that we've been covering through the last few chapters, the ML aspect of the solution isn't particularly complex, but the magnitude of the problem is. With thousands of airports to model (which, in turn, means thousands of models to tune and keep track of), handling communication and having a reference for historical data for each execution of the project code is a daunting task.

What happens when, after running our forecasting project in production, a member of the business unit team wants an explanation as to why a particular forecast was so far off from the eventual reality of the data that is collected? This is a common question from many companies that rely on ML predictions to inform the business about actions that should be taken in running the business. The very last thing that you would want to have to deal with if a black swan event occurs and the business is asking questions about why the modeled forecast solution didn't foresee it, is having to try to regenerate what the model might have forecasted at a certain point in time in order to fully explain how unpredictable events cannot be modeled.

> **NOTE** A black swan event is an unforeseeable and many times catastrophic event that changes the nature of acquired data. While rare, they can have disastrous effects on models, businesses, and entire industries. Some recent black swan events include the September 11th terrorist attacks, the financial collapse of 2008, and the Covid-19 pandemic. Due to the far-reaching and entirely unpredictable nature of these events, the impact to models can be absolutely devastating. The term "black swan" was coined and popularized in

reference to data and business in the book *The Black Swan: The Impact of the Highly Improbable* by Nassim Nicholas Taleb (Random House, 2007).

To solve these intractable issues that ML practitioners have had to deal with historically, MLflow was created. The aspect of MLflow that we're going to look at in this section is the Tracking API, giving us a place to record all of our tuning iterations, our metrics from each model's tuning runs, and pre-generated visualizations that can be easily retrieved and referenced from a unified graphical user interface (GUI).

8.1.1 *MLflow tracking*

Let's look at what is going on with the two Spark-based implementations from chapter 7 (section 7.2) as they pertain to MLflow logging. In the code examples shown in that chapter, the initialization of the context for MLflow was instantiated in two distinct places.

In the first approach, using `SparkTrials` as the state-management object (running on the driver), the MLflow context was placed as a wrapper around the entire tuning run within the function `run_tuning()`. This is the preferred method of orchestrating the tracking of runs when using `SparkTrials` so that a parent run's individual children runs can be associated easily for querying from within the tracking server's GUI as well as from REST API requests to the tracking server that involve filter predicates.

Figure 8.1 shows a graphical representation of this code when interacting with MLflow's tracking server. The code records not only the metadata of the parent

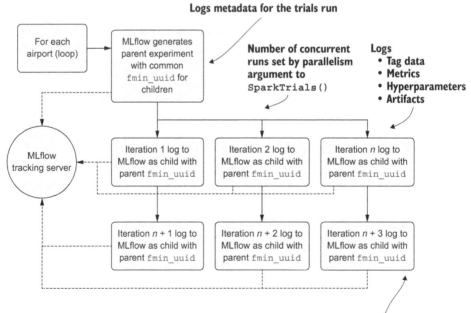

Figure 8.1   MLflow tracking server logging using distributed hyperparameter optimization

encapsulating run, but the per iteration logging that occurs from the workers as each hyperparameter evaluation happens.

When looking at the actual code manifestation within the MLflow tracking server's GUI, we can see the results of this parent-child relationship, shown in figure 8.2.

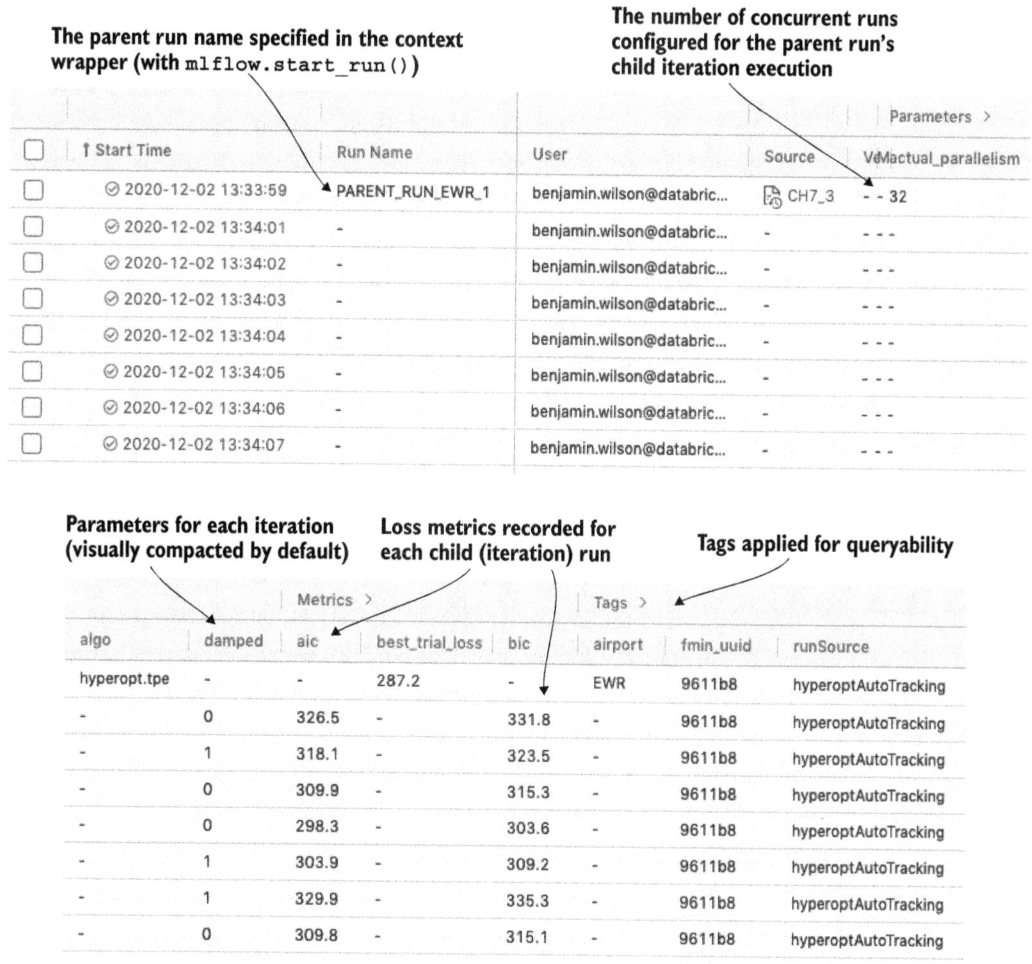

The parent run name specified in the context wrapper (with `mlflow.start_run()`)

The number of concurrent runs configured for the parent run's child iteration execution

	↑ Start Time	Run Name	User	Source	VdMactual_parallelism
☐	⊘ 2020-12-02 13:33:59	PARENT_RUN_EWR_1	benjamin.wilson@databric...	CH7_3	- - 32
☐	⊘ 2020-12-02 13:34:01	-	benjamin.wilson@databric...	-	- - -
☐	⊘ 2020-12-02 13:34:02	-	benjamin.wilson@databric...	-	- - -
☐	⊘ 2020-12-02 13:34:03	-	benjamin.wilson@databric...	-	- - -
☐	⊘ 2020-12-02 13:34:04	-	benjamin.wilson@databric...	-	- - -
☐	⊘ 2020-12-02 13:34:05	-	benjamin.wilson@databric...	-	- - -
☐	⊘ 2020-12-02 13:34:06	-	benjamin.wilson@databric...	-	- - -
☐	⊘ 2020-12-02 13:34:07	-	benjamin.wilson@databric...	-	- - -

Parameters for each iteration (visually compacted by default)

Loss metrics recorded for each child (iteration) run

Tags applied for queryability

algo	damped	aic	best_trial_loss	bic	airport	fmin_uuid	runSource
hyperopt.tpe	-	-	287.2	-	EWR	9611b8	hyperoptAutoTracking
-	0	326.5	-	331.8	-	9611b8	hyperoptAutoTracking
-	1	318.1	-	323.5	-	9611b8	hyperoptAutoTracking
-	0	309.9	-	315.3	-	9611b8	hyperoptAutoTracking
-	0	298.3	-	303.6	-	9611b8	hyperoptAutoTracking
-	1	303.9	-	309.2	-	9611b8	hyperoptAutoTracking
-	1	329.9	-	335.3	-	9611b8	hyperoptAutoTracking
-	0	309.8	-	315.1	-	9611b8	hyperoptAutoTracking

Figure 8.2 Example of the MLflow tracking UI

Conversely, the approach used for the `pandas_udf` implementation is slightly different. In chapter 7's listing 7.10, each individual iteration that Hyperopt executes requires the creation of a new experiment. Since there is no child-parent relationship to group the data together, the application of custom naming and tagging is required to allow for searchability within the GUI and—more important for production-capable code—the REST API. The overview of the logging mechanics for this alternative (and more scalable implementation for this use case of thousands of models) is shown in figure 8.3.

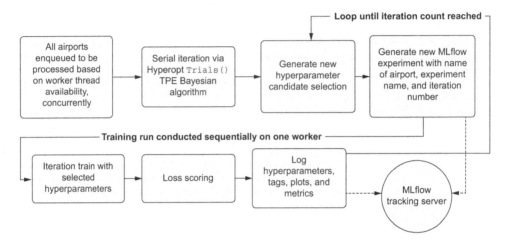

Figure 8.3   MLflow logging logical execution for the `pandas_udf` distributed model approach.

Regardless of which methodology is chosen, the important aspect of all of this discussion is that we've solved a large problem that frequently causes projects to fail. (Each methodology has its own merits for different approaches; for a single-model project, `SparkTrials` is by far the better option, while for the scenario of forecasting that we've shown here, with thousands of models, the `pandas_udf` approach is far superior.) We've solved the historical tracking and organization woes that have hamstrung ML project work for a long time. Having the ability to readily access the results of not only our testing, but also the state of a model currently running in production as of the point of its training and scoring, is simply an essential aspect of creating successful ML projects.

8.1.2   *Please stop printing and log your information*

Now that we've seen a tool that we can use to keep track of our experiments, tuning runs, and pre-production training for each prediction job that is run, let's take a moment to discuss another best-practice aspect of using a tracking service when building ML-backed projects: logging.

The number of times that I've seen `print` statements in production ML code is truly astonishing. Most of the time, it's due to forgotten (or intentionally left-in for future debugging) lines of debugging script to let the developer know that code is being executed (and whether it's safe to go get a coffee while it runs). At no point outside of coffee breaks during solution development will these `print` statements ever be seen by human eyes again. The top of figure 8.4 shows the irrelevance of these `print` statements within a code base.

Figure 8.4 compares methodologies that are frequent patterns in ML project code, particularly in the top two areas. While the top portion (printing to stdout in notebooks that get executed on some periodicity) is definitely not recommended, it is, unfortunately, the most frequent habit seen in industry. For more sophisticated teams that are writing packaged code for their ML projects (or using languages that can be compiled, like Java, Scala, or a C-based language), the historical recourse has been to log information about the run to a logging daemon. While this does maintain a historical reference for the data record, it also involves a great deal of either ETL or, more commonly, ELT in order to extract information in the event that something goes wrong. The final block in figure 8.4 demonstrates how utilizing MLflow solves these accessibility concerns, as well as the historical provenance needs for any ML solution.

To be explicit, I'm not saying to never use `print` or `log` statements. They have a remarkable utility when debugging particularly complex code bases, and are incredibly useful while developing solutions. This utility begins to fade as you transition to production development. The `print` statements are no longer looked at, and the

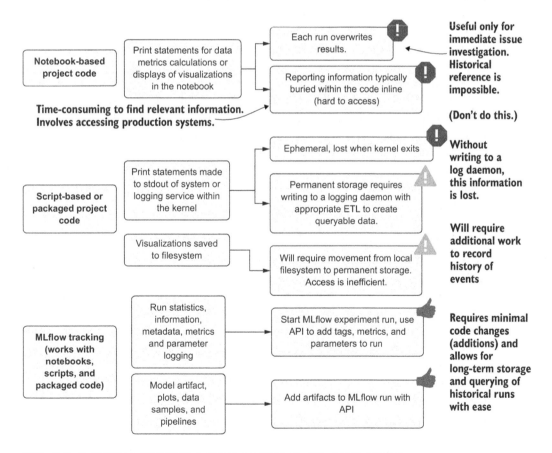

Figure 8.4   Comparison of information storage paradigms for ML experimentation

desire to parse logs to retrieve status information becomes far less palatable when you're busy with other projects.

If critical information needs to be recorded for a project's code execution, it *should be logged and recorded for future reference at all times.* Before tools like MLflow solved this problem, many DS teams would record this critical information for production purposes to a table in an RDBMS. Larger-scale groups with dozens of solutions in production may have utilized a NoSQL solution to handle scalability. The truly masochistic would write ELT jobs to parse system logs to retrieve their critical data about their models. MLflow simplifies all of these situations by creating a cogent unified framework for metric, attribute, and artifact logging to eliminate the time-consuming work of ML logging.

As we saw in the earlier examples running on Spark, we were recording additional information to these runs outside of the typical information that would be associated with a tuning execution. We logged the per airport metrics and parameters for historical searchability, as well as charts of our forecasts. If we had additional data to record, we could simply add a tag through the API in the form of `mlflow.set_tag(<key>, <value>)` for run information logging, or, for more complex information (visualizations, data, models, or highly structured data), we can log that information as an artifact with the API `mlflow.log_artifact(<location and name of data on local filesystem>)`.

Keeping a history of all information surrounding a particular model tuning and training event in a single place, external to the system used to execute the run, can save countless hours of frustrating work when trying to re-create the exact conditions that the model may have seen when it was trained and you are asked to explain what happened to a particular build. Being able to quickly answer questions about the business's faith in your model's performance can dramatically reduce the chances of project abandonment, as well as save a great deal of time in improving an underperforming model.

8.1.3   Version control, branch strategies, and working with others

One of the biggest aspects of development work that can affect a timely and organized delivery of a project to the MVP phase is in the way a team (or an individual) interacts with a repository. In our example scenario, with a relatively sizeable ML team working on individual components of the forecasting model, the ability for everyone to contribute to pieces of the code base in a structured and controlled manner is absolutely critical for eliminating frustrating rework, broken code, and large-scale refactoring. While we haven't been delving into what the production version of this code would look like (it wouldn't be developed in a notebook, that's for certain), the general design would look something like the module layout in figure 8.5.

As the project progresses, different team members of the project will be contributing to different modules within the code base at any given time. Some, within the sprint, may be tackling tasks and stories surrounding the visualizations. Others on that

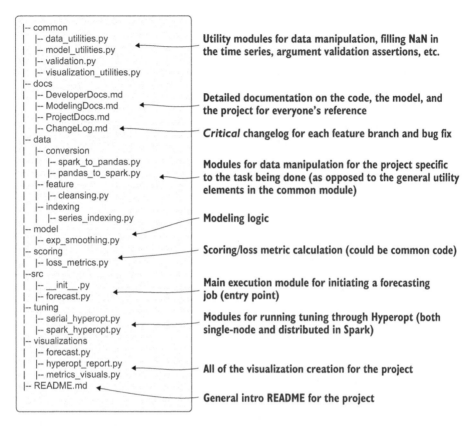

Figure 8.5 An initial repository structure for the forecasting project

sprint may be working on the core modeling classes, while the common utility functions will be added to and refined by nearly everyone on the team.

Without the use of not only a strong version-control system but also a foundational process surrounding the committing of code to that repository, the chances of the code base being significantly degraded or broken is high. While most aspects of ML development are significantly different from traditional software engineering development, the one aspect that is completely identical between the two fields is in version-control and branched development practices.

To prevent issues arising from incompatible changes being merged to a master branch, each story or task that is taken from a sprint for a DS to work on should have its own branch cut from the current build of the master branch of the repo. It is within this branch that the new features should be built, updates to common functionality made, and the addition of new unit tests to assure the team that the modifications are not going to break anything should all be done. When it comes time to close out the story (or task), the DS who developed the code for that story will need to ensure that the entire project's code passes both unit tests (especially for modules and functionality that they did not modify) and a full-run integration test before submitting their peer review request to merge their code into the master.

Figure 8.6 shows the standard approach for ML project work when dealing with a repository, regardless of the repository technology or service used. Each has its own nuances, functionality, and commands, which we won't get into here; what's important is the way the repository is used, rather than how to use a particular one.

By following a paradigm for code merging like this one, a great deal of frustration and wasted time can be completely avoided. It will simply leave more time for the DS

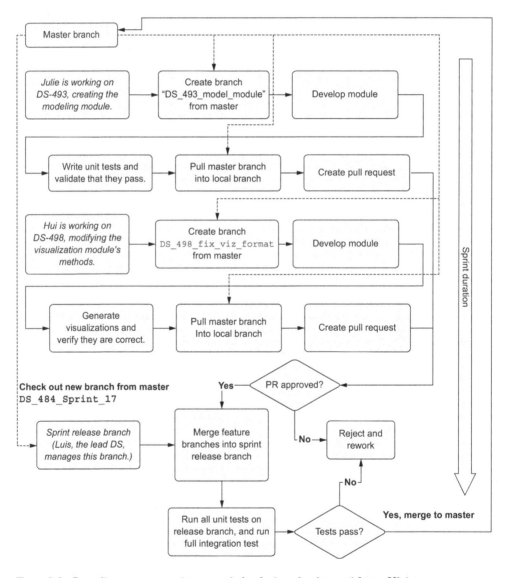

Figure 8.6   Repository management process during feature development for an ML team

team members to solve the actual problem of the project, rather than solving merge-hell problems and fixing broken code resulting from a bad merge. Effective testing of code-merge candidates brings a higher level of project velocity that can dramatically reduce the chances of project abandonment by creating a more reliable, stable, and bug-free code base for a project.

8.2 Scalability and concurrency

Throughout this project that we've been working on, the weightiest and most complex aspect of the solution has been in scalability. When we talk about scalability here, we're actually referring to *cost*. The longer that VMs are running and executing our project code, the more the silent ticker of our bill is going up. Anything that we can do to maximize resource utilization of that hardware as a function of time is going to keep that bill in a manageable state, reducing the concern that the business will have about the total cost of the solution.

Throughout the second half of chapter 7, we evaluated two strategies for scaling our problem to support modeling many airports. The first, parallelizing the hyper-parameter evaluation over a cluster, scaled down the per-model training time significantly as compared to the serial approach. The second, parallelizing the actual per-model training across a cluster, scaled the solution in a slightly different way (which is more in favor of the many models/reasonable training iterations approach), reducing our cost footprint for the solution in a much larger manner.

As mentioned in chapter 7, these are but two ways of scaling this problem, both involving parallel implementations that distribute portions of the modeling process across multiple machines. However, we can add a layer of additional processing to speed these operations up even more. Figure 8.7 shows an overview of our options for increasing the throughput for ML tasks to reduce the wall-clock time involved in building a solution.

Moving down the scale in figure 8.7 brings a trade-off between simplicity and performance. For problems that require a scale that distributed computing can offer, it is important to understand the level of complexity that will be introduced into the code base. The challenges with these implementations are no longer relegated to the DS part of the solution and instead require increasingly sophisticated engineering skills in order to build.

Gaining the knowledge and ability to build large-scale ML projects that leverage systems capable of handling distributed computation (for example, Spark, Kubernetes, or Dask) will help ensure that you are capable of implementing solutions requiring scale. In my own experience, my time has been well spent learning how to leverage concurrency and the use of distributed systems to accelerate the performance and reduce the cost of projects by monopolizing available hardware resources as much as I can.

For the purposes of brevity, we won't go into examples of implementing the last two sections of figure 8.7 within this chapter. However, we will touch on examples of concurrent operations later in this book.

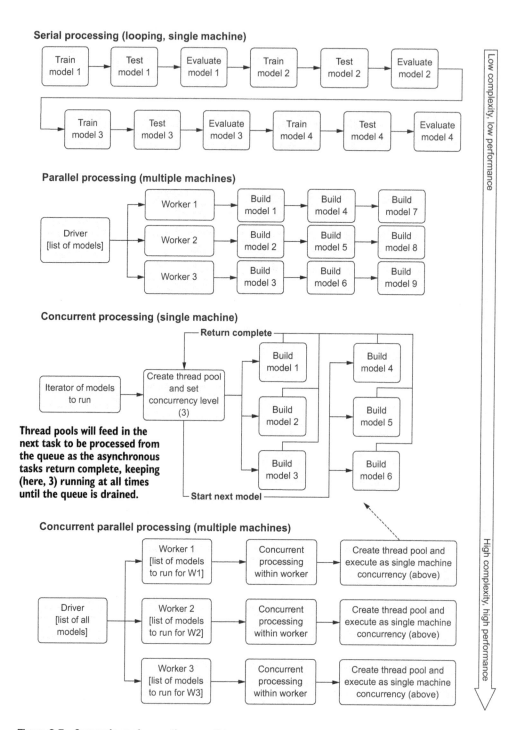

Figure 8.7   Comparison of execution paradigms

8.2.1 What is concurrency?

In figure 8.7, you can see the term *concurrency* listed in the bottom two solutions. For most data scientists who don't come from a software engineering background, this term may easily be misconstrued as *parallelism*. It is, after all, effectively doing a bunch of things at the same time.

Concurrency, by definition, is the act of executing many tasks at the same time. It doesn't imply ordering or sequential processing of tasks simultaneously. It merely requires that a system and the code instructions being sent to it be capable of running more than one task at the same time.

Parallelism, on the other hand, works by dividing tasks into subtasks that can be executed in parallel, simultaneously, on discrete threads and cores of a CPU or GPU. Spark, for instance, executes tasks in parallel on a distributed system of discrete cores in executors.

These two concepts can be combined in a system that can support them, one of multiple machines, each of which has multiple cores available to it. This system architecture is shown in the final bottom section of figure 8.7. Figure 8.8 illustrates the differences between parallel execution, concurrent execution, and the hybrid parallel-concurrent system.

Leveraging these execution strategies for the appropriate type of problem being solved can dramatically improve the cost of a project. While it may seem tempting to utilize the most complex approach for every problem (parallel concurrent processing in a distributed system), it simply isn't worth it. If the problem that you're trying to solve can be implemented on a single machine, it's always best to reduce the infrastructure complexity by going with that approach. It's advisable to move down the path of greater infrastructure complexity only when you need to. This is particularly true when the data, the algorithm, or the scale of tasks is so large that a simpler approach is not possible.

8.2.2 What you can (and can't) run asynchronously

For a final note on improving runtime performance, it is important to mention that not every problem in ML can be solved through the use of parallel execution or on a distributed system. Many algorithms require maintaining state to function correctly, and as such, cannot be split into subtasks to execute on a pool of cores.

The scenario that we've gone through in the past few chapters with univariate time series could certainly benefit from parallelizing. We can parallelize both the Hyperopt tuning and the model training. The isolation that we can achieve within the data itself (each airport's data is self-contained and has no dependency on any other's) and the tuning actions means that we can dramatically reduce the total runtime of our job by appropriately leveraging both distributed processing and asynchronous concurrency.

When selecting opportunities for improving performance of a modeling solution, you should be thinking about the dependencies within the tasks being executed. If there is an opportunity to isolate tasks from one another, such as separating model

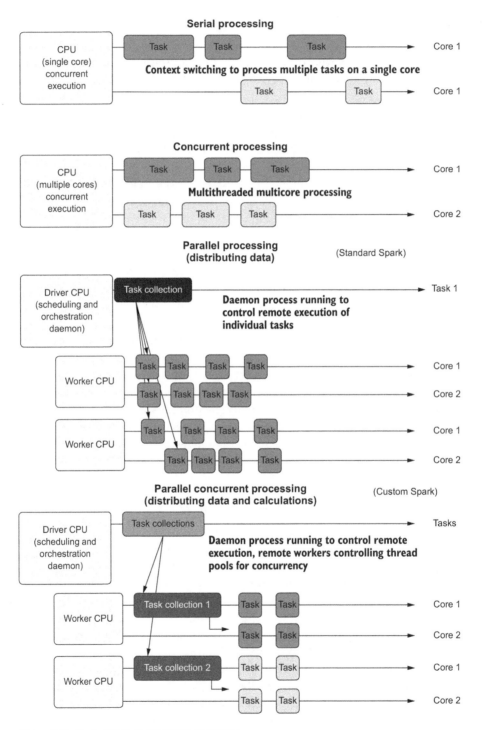

Figure 8.8   Comparison of execution strategies

evaluation, training, or inference based on filters that can be applied to a dataset, it could be worthwhile to leverage a framework that can handle this processing for you.

However, many tasks in ML cannot be distributed (or, at least, cannot be distributed easily). Models that require access to the entirety of a feature training set are poor candidates for distributed training. Other models may have the capability to be distributed but simply have not been because of either demand or the technological complexity involved in building a distributed solution. The best bet, when wondering whether an algorithm or approach can leverage concurrency or parallelism through distributed processing, is to read the library documentation for popular frameworks. If an algorithm hasn't been implemented on a distributed processing framework, there's likely a good reason. Either simpler approaches are available that fulfill the same requirements of the model you're looking into (highly likely), or the development and runtime costs for building a distributed solution for the algorithm are astronomically high.

Summary

- Utilizing an experimentation tracking service such as MLflow throughout a solution's life cycle can dramatically increase auditability and historical monitoring for projects. Additionally, utilizing version control and logging will enhance production code bases with the ability to reduce troubleshooting time and allow for diagnostic reporting of the project's health when in production.
- Learning to use and implement solutions in a scalable infrastructure is incredibly important for many large-scale ML projects. While not appropriate for all implementations, understanding distributed systems, concurrency, and the frameworks that enable these paradigms is crucial for an ML engineer.

Part 2

Preparing for production: Creating maintainable ML

Now that you've worked through part 1 of this book, you have a feel for a pattern of validating project ideas that borrows heavily from the approaches set in modern software development. Once an idea has been properly vetted and a (rough) prototype built, the next step in building a maintainable solution is to focus on building it properly.

In the introduction to part 1, I mentioned that a lot of ML projects fail because of lackluster planning and scoping. Following closely on the heels of those reasons is the failure mode of shutting off a project that's in production because it's either an unsalvageable broken mess or because the business doesn't realize the value of it and is unwilling to keep paying for it to run. These are solvable problems, provided that a specific methodology of project development is applied to avoid these pitfalls.

In part 2, we'll go through some of the lessons I've learned through my own project work, those I've seen in others' work (for better or worse), and standards of applied ML code development that will help you build the following:

- Code that runs well
- Code that is testable and able to be debugged
- A solution that can be modified easily
- A solution that can be evaluated for performance (based on whether it solves the problem well and continues to solve the problem it set out to solve)
- A solution that you don't regret building

With these guidelines in place, you'll be in a much better place to ship your solution to production, comforted in the knowledge that you'll be supporting a software deployment that you and your team can maintain.

Modularity for ML: Writing testable and legible code

This chapter covers

- Demonstrating why monolithic script-coding patterns make ML projects more complex
- Understanding the complexity of troubleshooting non-abstracted code
- Applying basic abstraction to ML projects
- Implementing testable designs in ML code bases

Precious few emotions are more soul-crushing than those forced upon you when you're handed a complex code base that someone else wrote. Reading through a mountain of unintelligible code after being told that you are responsible for fixing, updating, and supporting it is demoralizing. The only worse situation when inheriting a fundamentally broken code base to maintain occurs when your name is the one on the commit history.

This isn't to say that the code doesn't work. It may run perfectly fine. The fact that code *runs* isn't the issue. It's that a human can't easily figure out *how* (or, more disastrously, *why*) it works. I believe this problem was most eloquently described by Martin Fowler in 2008:

> *Any fool can write code that a computer can understand. Good programmers write code that humans can understand.*

A large portion of ML code is not aligned with good software engineering practices. With our focus on algorithms, vectors, indexers, models, loss functions, optimization solvers, hyperparameters, and performance metrics, we, as a profession of practitioners, generally don't spend much time adhering to strict coding standards. At least, most of us don't.

I can proudly claim that I was one such person for many years, writing some truly broken code (it worked when I released it, most of the time). Focused solely on eking the slightest of accuracy improvements or getting clever with feature-engineering tasks, I would end up creating a veritable Frankenstein's monster of unmaintainable code. To be fair to that misunderstood reanimated creature, some of my early projects were far more horrifying. (I wouldn't have blamed my peers if they chased me with torches and pitchforks.)

This chapter and the next are devoted to the lessons in coding standards that I've learned over the years. It is by no means an exhaustive treatise on the topic of software engineering; there are books for that. Rather, these are the most important aspects that I've learned in order to create simpler and easier-to-maintain code bases for ML project work. We will cover these best practices in five key areas, as shown in figure 9.1.

The sections in this chapter, reflected in figure 9.1, demonstrate examples of the horrible things that I've done, the terrifying elements that I've seen in others' code, and, most important, ways to address them. Our goal in this chapter is to avoid the Frankenstein's monster of convoluted and overly complex code.

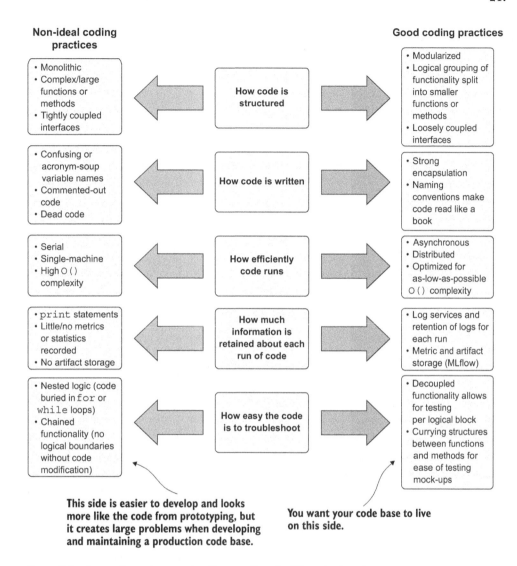

Figure 9.1   Comparing extremes of coding practices for ML project work

Complicated vs. complex code

This phrase *complicated vs. complex* may seem like a poor interpretation of grammar—the two terms seem to mean the same thing, after all. But, applied to code, each is markedly different. A *complex code base* is an empirical assessment of the branching paths that a particular piece of encapsulated code (think: function or method) can traverse. The `for` loops, conditional statements, matching switch statements, and passed-in argument-functionality state changes are all elements that add to the complexity of code. With many "things" that a bit of contained code can do, the number

(continued)

of results that could come out of that code is very high. Code bases that are complex typically require a great deal of testing to ensure that they function correctly under all conditions possible. This complexity also makes the code base more difficult to understand than those that have fewer branching paths of functionality.

A *complicated code base*, however, is one that is written in such a way that makes it difficult to ascertain how the code functions. This highly subjective assessment of "how hard it is to read and figure out" is a measurement that depends heavily on the person reading the code. Be that as it may, a general consensus can be agreed upon by most experienced developers on what constitutes a complicated code base as compared to an uncomplicated one.

A highly complicated code base may have gotten to that state after repeated patching of the code (retrofitting code to fix deferred technical debt). This code may be chained, use poor naming conventions, include repeated use of conditional logic in a difficult-to-read manner, or just liberally use uncommon shorthand notation (I'm looking at you, Scala wildcard, _).

A code base can be a mixture of these elements:

- *Complex and not complicated*—A challenging but acceptable state for ML code bases.
- *Not complex and not complicated*—Also acceptable, but typically not seen outside of analytics use cases in DS work.
- *Not complex and complicated*—We'll see an example in section 9.1.1.
- *Complex and complicated*—The bane of our existence as ML practitioners when inheriting a code base.

The goal in developing ML projects is to focus first on keeping the measure of *complicated* for the code base as low as possible, while also focusing on reducing the complexity as much as is practicable. The lower the measure of both of these concepts, the greater the chances that the project you're working on will not only get to production but stay as a maintainable and extensible solution to a business need.

To make things easier, we're going to look at a single relatively simple example throughout this chapter, something that we should all be rather familiar with: a distribution estimation for univariate data. We'll stick with this example because it is simple and approachable. We'll look at the same effective solution through the lens of different programming problems, discussing how important it is to focus on maintainability and utility above all other considerations.

9.1 *Understanding monolithic scripts and why they are bad*

Inheritance, in the world of computing, can mean a few different things. The topic first comes to mind when thinking of crafting extensible code through abstraction (code reuse in object-oriented design to reduce copied functionality and decrease complexity). While this type of inheritance is undeniably good, a different type of inheritance can range from good to nightmarish. This is the inheritance we get when assuming responsibility for someone else's code base.

Let's imagine that you start at a new company. After indoctrination is done, you're given a token to access the DS repository (repo). This moment of traversing the repo for the first time is either exciting or terrifying, depending on the number of times you've done this before. What are you going to find? What have your predecessors at this company built? How easy is the code going to be to debug, modify, and support? Is it filled with technical debt? Is it consistent in style? Does it adhere to language standards?

At first glance, you feel a sinking in your stomach as you look through the directory structure. There are dozens of directories, each with a project name. Within each of these directories is a single file. You know you are in for a world of frustration in figuring out how any of these monolithic and messy scripts work. Any on-call support you'll be tasked with providing for these is going to be incredibly challenging. Each issue that comes up, after all, will involve reverse engineering these confusing and complicated scripts for even the most trivial of errors that occur.

9.1.1 How monoliths come into being

If we were to dig into the commit history of our new team's repository, we'd likely find a seamless transition from prototype to experimentation. The first commit would likely be the result of a bare-bones experiment, filled with TODO comments and placeholder functionality. As we move through the commit history, the script begins to take shape, piece by piece, finally arriving at the production version of the code that you see in the master branch.

The problem here is not that scripting was used. The vast majority of professional ML engineers, myself included, do our prototyping and experimentation in notebooks (scripts). The dynamic nature of notebooks and the ability to rapidly try out new ideas makes them an ideal platform for this stage of work. Upon accepting a prototype as a path to develop, however, all of that prototype code is thrown out in favor of creating modularized code during MVP development.

The evolution of a script from a prototype is understandable. ML development is notorious for having countless changes, needing rapid feedback of results, and pivoting dramatically in approaches during the MVP phase. Even during early phases, however, the code can be structured such that it is much easier to decouple functionality, abstract away complexity, and create a more testable (and debug-friendly) code base.

The way a monolithic production code base comes into being is by shipping a prototype to production. This is never advisable.

9.1.2 Walls of text

If there was one thing that I learned relatively early in my career as a data scientist, it was that I truly hate debugging. It wasn't the act of tracking down a bug in my code that frustrated me; rather, it was the process that I had to go through to figure out what went wrong in what I was telling the computer to do.

Like many DS practitioners at the start of their career, when I began working on solving problems with software, I would write a lot of declarative code. I wrote my solutions much in the way that I logically thought about the problem ("I pull my data, then I do some statistical tests, then I make a decision, then I manipulate the data, then I put it in a vector, then into a model . . . "). This materialized as a long list of actions that flowed directly, one into another. What this programming model meant in the final product was a massive wall of code with no separation or isolation of actions, let alone encapsulation.

Finding the needle in the haystack for any errors in code written in that manner is an exercise in pure, unadulterated torture. The architecture of the code was not conducive to allowing me to figure out which of the hundreds of steps contained therein was causing an issue.

Troubleshooting *walls of text* (*WoT*, pronounced *What?!*) is an exercise in patience that bears few parallels in depth and requisite effort. If you're the original author of such a display of code, it's an annoying endeavor (you have no one to hate other than yourself for creating the monstrosity), depressing activity (see prior comment), and time-consuming slog that can be so easily avoided—provided you know how, what, and where to isolate elements within your ML code.

If written by someone else, and you're the unfortunate heir to the code base, I extend to you my condolences and a hearty "Welcome to the club." Perhaps a worthy expenditure of your time after fixing the code base would be to mentor the author, provide them with an ample reading list, and help them to never produce such rage-inducing code again.

To have a frame of reference for our discussion, let's take a look at what one of these WoTs could look like. While the examples in this section are rather simplistic, the intention is to imagine what a complete end-to-end ML project would look like in this format, without having to read through hundreds of lines. (I imagine that you wouldn't like to flip through dozens of pages of code in a printed book.)

A quick note about the code in listing 9.1

The last thing that I'd like to infer by putting this example in this book is that I've never created code like this. I can assure you that I've written far more horrifying code early in my career. I've written scripts, functions, and entire classes filled with methods that are so horrifically bad and impossible or confusing to read that upon revisiting my "work" less than two weeks after having written it, I couldn't follow along with what I had created.

It's a terrifying feeling when this happens, since for all intents and purposes, the original author of code should be the singular person on the planet who can figure out how it works. When that fails, whether through complexity or just the sheer mountain of code that needs to be modified to make an improvement to the code base, I've frequently started over from scratch.

My intention in showing these examples is to illuminate things that I learned the hard way, why they made my life very difficult at the time (missing deadlines, angering others

> when I realized I needed to completely rewrite hundreds upon hundreds of lines of code), and how you can learn my hard-earned lessons in a much simpler way. Bask in the glory, dear reader, of my previous ineptitude and ignorance, and please don't repeat my mistakes. I promise that you'll end up thanking me—and your future self will thank your present self as well.

Listing 9.1 presents a relatively simple block of script that is intended to be used to determine the nearest standard distribution type to a passed-in series of continuous data. The code contains some normalcy checks at the top, comparisons to the standard distributions, followed by the generation of a plot.

NOTE The code examples in this chapter are provided in the accompanying repository for this book. However, I do *not* recommend that you run them. They take a very long time to execute.

Listing 9.1   A wall-of-text script

pval? That's not a standard naming convention. It should be p_value_shapiro or something similar.

Mutating the variable pval makes the original one from shapiro inaccessible for future usage. This is a bad habit to adopt and makes more complex code bases nigh impossible to follow.

String concatenation is difficult to read, can create issues in execution, and requires more things to type. Don't do it.

With such a general variable name, we have to search through the code to find out what this is for.

Mutating x here makes sense, but again, we have no indication of what this is for.

bl? What is that?! Abbreviations don't help the reader understand what is going on.

```python
import warnings as warn
import pandas as pd
import numpy as np
import scipy.stats as stat
from scipy.stats import shapiro, normaltest, anderson
import matplotlib.pyplot as plt
from statsmodels.graphics.gofplots import qqplot

data = pd.read_csv('/sf-airbnb-clean.csv')
series = data['price']
shapiro, pval = shapiro(series)
print('Shapiro score: ' + str(shapiro) + ' with pvalue: ' + str(pval))
dagastino, pval = normaltest(series)
print("D'Agostino score: " + str(dagastino) + " with pvalue: " + str(pval))
anderson_stat, crit, sig = anderson(series)
print("Anderson statistic: " + str(anderson_stat))
anderson_rep = list(zip(list(crit), list(sig)))
for i in anderson_rep:
    print('Significance: ' + str(i[0]) + ' Crit level: ' + str(i[1]))
bins = int(np.ceil(series.index.values.max()))
y, x = np.histogram(series, 200, density=True)
x = (x + np.roll(x, -1))[:-1] / 2.
bl = np.inf
bf = stat.norm
bp = (0., 1.)
with warn.catch_warnings():
    warn.filterwarnings('ignore')
    fam = stat._continuous_distns._distn_names
```

```
for d in fam:
    h = getattr(stat, d)
    f = h.fit(series)
    pdf = h.pdf(x, loc=f[-2], scale=f[-1], *f[:-2])
    loss = np.sum(np.power(y - pdf, 2.))
    if bl > loss > 0:
        bl = loss
        bf = h
        bp = f
start = bf.ppf(0.001, *bp[:-2], loc=bp[-2], scale=bp[-1])
end = bf.ppf(0.999, *bp[:-2], loc=bp[-2], scale=bp[-1])
xd = np.linspace(start, end, bins)
yd = bf.pdf(xd, loc=bp[-2], scale=bp[-1], *bp[:-2])
hdist = pd.Series(yd, xd)
with warn.catch_warnings():
    warn.filterwarnings('ignore')
    with plt.style.context(style='seaborn'):
        fig = plt.figure(figsize=(16,12))
        ax = series.plot(kind='hist', bins=100, normed=True, alpha=0.5,
    label='Airbnb SF Price', legend=True)
        ymax = ax.get_ylim()
        xmax = ax.get_xlim()
        hdist.plot(lw=3, label='best dist ' + bf.__class__.__name__,
    legend=True, ax=ax)
        ax.legend(loc='best')
        ax.set_xlim(xmax)
        ax.set_ylim(ymax)
qqplot(series, line='s')
```

All of these single-letter variable names are impossible to figure out without reverse engineering the code. It may make for concise code, but it's really hard to follow. With a lack of comments, this shorthand becomes difficult to read.

All of these hardcoded variables (the bins in particular) mean that if this needs to be adjusted, the source code needs to be edited. All of this should be abstracted in a function.

My most sincere apologies for what you just had to look at. Not only is this code confusing, dense, and amateurish, but it's written in such a way that its style is approaching intentional obfuscation of functionality.

The variable names are horrific. Single-letter values? Extreme shorthand notation in variable names? *Why?* It doesn't make the program run faster. It just makes it harder to understand. Tunable values are hardcoded, requiring modification of the script for each test, which can be exceedingly prone to errors and typos. No stopping points are set in the execution that would make it easy to figure out why something isn't working as intended.

9.1.3   Considerations for monolithic scripts

Aside from being hard to read, listing 9.1's biggest flaw is that it's monolithic. Although it is a script, the principles of WoT development can apply to both functions and methods within classes. This example comes from a notebook, which increasingly is the declarative vehicle used to execute ML code, but the concept applies in a general sense.

Having too much logic within the bounds of an execution encapsulation creates problems (since this is a script run in a notebook, the entire code is one encapsulated block). I invite you to think about these issues through the following questions:

- What would it look like if you had to insert new functionality in this block of code?
- Would it be easy to test if your changes are correct?
- What if the code threw an exception?
- How would you go about figuring out what went wrong with the code from an exception being thrown?
- What if the structure of the data changed? How would you go about updating the code to reflect those changes?

Before we get into answering some of these questions, let's look at what this code actually does. Because of the confusing variable names, dense coding structure, and tight coupling of references, we would have to run it to figure out what it's doing. The next listing shows the first aspect of listing 9.1.

Listing 9.2   Stdout results from listing 9.1 `print` statements

These pvalue elements are potentially confusing. Without some sort of explanation of what they signify, a user has to look up these tests in the API documentation to understand what they are.

That is, perhaps, a few too many significant digits to be useful.

```
Shapiro score: 0.33195996284484863 with pvalue: 0.0
D'Agostino score: 14345.798651770001 with pvalue: 0.0
Anderson statistic: 1022.1779688188954
Significance: 0.576 Crit level: 15.0
Significance: 0.656 Crit level: 10.0
Significance: 0.787 Crit level: 5.0
Significance: 0.917 Crit level: 2.5
Significance: 1.091 Crit level: 1.0
```

With no explanation about these significances and critical levels, this data is meaningless to anyone unfamiliar with the Anderson-Darling test.

This code is doing normalcy tests for a univariate series (a column within a `Data-Frame` here). These are definitely worthwhile tests to conduct on a target variable for a regression problem. The image shown in figure 9.2 is the result of the first of the plots that are generated by the remainder of the script (apart from the very last line).

> **NOTE** Chapter 8 covered the power of logging information to MLflow and other such utilities, and how bad of an idea it is to print important information to stdout. However, this example is the exception. MLflow stands as a comprehensive utility tool that aids in model-based experimentation, development, and production monitoring. For our example, in which we are performing a one-off validation check, utilizing a tool like MLflow is simply not appropriate. If the information that we need to see is relevant for only a short period of time (while deciding a particular development approach, for instance), maintaining an indefinite persistence of this information is confusing and pointless.

Figure 9.3 shows the last plot that is generated from listing 9.1.

BD 732 7981

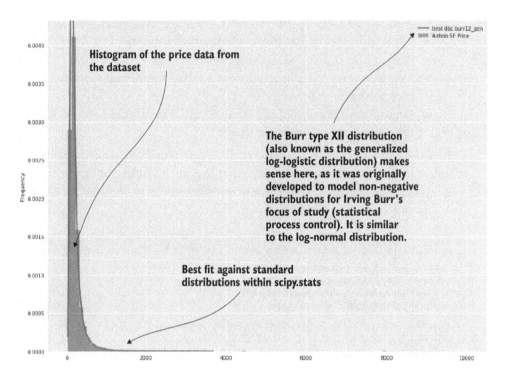

Figure 9.2   The first plot that is generated from listing 9.1

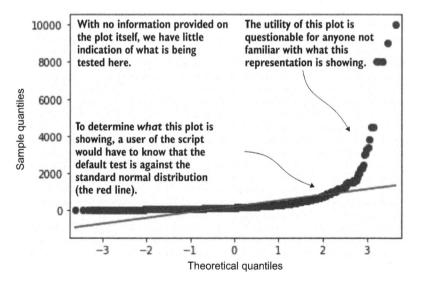

Figure 9.3   The tacked-on-at-the-end plot generation from listing 9.1

This quantile-quantile plot is a similarly useful exploratory aid in determining the normalcy (or goodness of fit to different distributions) by plotting the quantile values from a series against those of another series. In this example, the quantiles of the price series from the dataset are plotted against those of the standard normal distribution.

With no callout in the code or indication of what this plot is, however, the end user of this script can be left a bit confused about what is going on. It's rarely ever a good practice to place evaluations into code in this manner; they are easily overlooked, and users may be perplexed about why they are included in that location in the code.

Let's pretend for a moment that we aren't restricted to the medium of print here. Let's say that instead of a simple statistical analysis of a single target variable example, we are looking at a full project written as a monolithic script, as was shown in listing 9.1. Something on the order of, say, 1,500 lines. What would happen if the code broke? Can we clearly see and understand everything that's happening in the code in such a format? Where would we begin to troubleshoot the issue?

Isn't encapsulation of actions just moving around complexity, though?

Well, yes, and no.

It's undebatable that if we wrap common functionality of code from within the script into functions or methods, the refactoring doesn't do much for the code complexity (the same logic will be processed in the same order as the CPU sees it, after all). The refactoring will, however, dramatically reduce the complicated nature of the code. It will allow us, the human developers, to see smaller chunks of the code, allow us to debug functionality, test that the isolated (encapsulated) groupings of code function as we intend them to, and dramatically increase our ability to modify the code in the future.

Converting a script into functional (FP) or object-oriented (OO) code may seem like it's adding complexity: the code will have more lines, will have more elements to keep track of, and may be harder for those unfamiliar with FP or OO concepts to read the code initially. But once those team members become more fluent with the design practices of these paradigms, it will be far easier to maintain a structured and isolation-of-functionality design than a giant WoT code base.

9.2 Debugging walls of text

If we fast-forward a bit in our theoretical new job, after having seen the state of the code base, we'd eventually be in the position of maintaining it. Perhaps we were tasked with integrating a new feature into one of the preexisting scripts. After reverse engineering the code, and commenting it for our own understanding, we progress to putting in the new functionality. The only way, at this point, to test our code is to run the entire script.

We're inevitably going to have to work through some bugs in the process of changing the script to accommodate the new features. If we're dealing with a script or notebook environment with a long list of actions being taken in succession, how can we troubleshoot what went wrong with the code? Figure 9.4 shows the troubleshooting process that would have to happen to correct an issue in the WoT in listing 9.1.

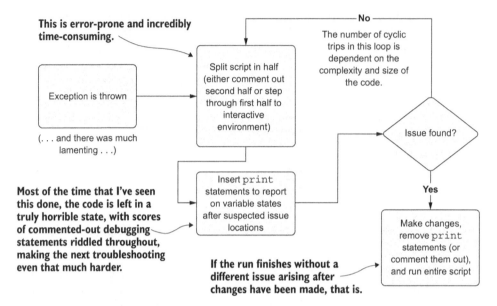

Figure 9.4   The time-consuming and patience-testing process of binary troubleshooting complicates (not necessarily complex) monolithic code bases.

This process, as frustrating as it is to go through, is complicated enough without having poor variable names and confusing shorthand notation as in listing 9.1. The more difficult the code is to read and follow, the deeper the cognitive load required, both to select binary boundary points for isolation while testing the code and to figure out which variable states will need to be reported out to stdout.

This halving process of evaluating and testing portions of the code means that we're having to actually *change the source code to do our testing.* Whether we're adding print statements, debugging comments, or commenting out code, a lot of work is involved in testing faults with this paradigm. Mistakes will likely be made, and there is no guarantee that you won't add in a new issue through manipulating the code in this way.

A note on monolithic code

Listing 9.1 may seem as though it's a hyperbolic example of poor development practices. You might read through it, scoffing, and think that no one would ever write an entire ML solution to a problem in such a way. Before I entered consulting, I probably would have thought the same thing.

The truth, based on seeing how hundreds of companies' ML teams develop solutions, is that writing code in monolithic blocks is remarkably common. Typically, this arises from an isolated DS department that has no outside contact with other members of the engineering teams within the company and no one on the team who has worked with software developers before. These teams are effectively shipping their prototype PoC solutions (which, from an algorithm implementation perspective, do solve the problem) to production.

In actuality, I've seen code bases (which are, for lack of a better term, "running" in production with frequent errors and failures) that are far more difficult to read than what was shown in listing 9.1. The large majority of these companies that have ML code that looks like this end up doing one of two things:

- Hire an expensive consulting firm to refactor the code and make it production ready. Your mileage may vary here with respect to the maintainability of their solution, the technical sophistication of the consultants, and the total cost to hire a quality team to do this.
- Keep the code limping along until resourcing limitations (do you really want your team constantly fixing the same project code to keep it running?) and the cost of constantly fixing it outweighs the benefits that the solution brings, thereupon abandoning the project completely.

The intention of calling out these practices is to illuminate the issues with developing code like this and to help those who are not aware of why writing code like this is a bad idea.

Surely, there must be a better way to organize code (complex or not) to reduce the levels of complication. Listing 9.3 shows an alternative in the form of an OO version of the script from listing 9.1.

9.3 Designing modular ML code

After going through such a painful exercise of finding, fixing, and validating our change to this massive script, we've hit our breaking point. We communicate to the team that the code's technical debt is too high, and we need to pay it down before any other work continues. Accepting this, the team agrees to breaking up the script by functionality, abstracting the complexity into smaller pieces that can be understood and tested in isolation.

Before we look at the code, let's analyze the script to see its main groupings of functionality. This functionality-based analysis can help inform what methods to create in order to achieve functionality isolation (aiding our ability to troubleshoot, test, and insert new features in the future). Figure 9.5 illustrates the core functionality contained within the script and how we can extract, encapsulate, and create single-purpose code groupings to define what belongs in our methods.

This structural and functional analysis of the code helps us rationalize the elements of common functionality. From this inspection, elements are identified, isolated, and encapsulated to aid in both legibility (to help us, the humans) and

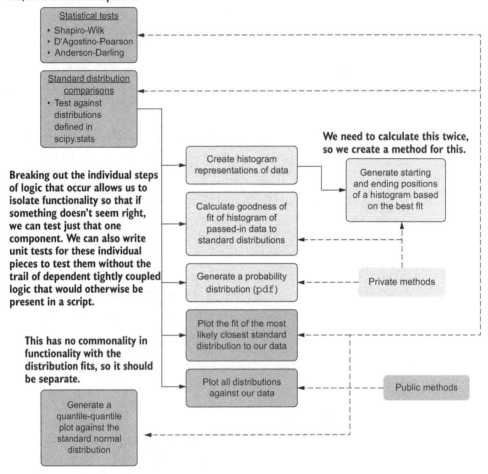

Figure 9.5   Code architecture refactoring for listing 9.1

maintainability (troubleshooting and extensibility) of the code. Notice the private (internal functionality that the end user doesn't need to use to get value from the module) and public (the user-facing methods that will generate specific actions from the code based on what they need) methods. Hiding internal functionality from users of this module will help reduce the cognitive load placed on the user, while minimizing the code complexity as much as possible.

Now that we have a plan for refactoring the code from the nigh-unintelligible script into something easier to follow and maintain, let's look at the final product of the refactoring and modularization in the next listing.

Listing 9.3 An object-oriented version of the scripted code from listing 9.1

Passes in a **kwargs argument so defined defaults within the class initialization method can be overridden with a key-value combination (the script had these all hardcoded)

Encapsulates the entire module as a class since all of the functionality within is focused on distribution analysis

Version checks switch statement since the SciPy API changed (a frequent occurrence in Python open source libraries as these libraries are improved over time). Newer versions of SciPy have protected the access to the distribution listing and have created an access method to retrieve them.

A static method is effectively an encapsulated function; no references to the initialized arguments are passed into the class, nor are there dependencies on any other methods. Most code bases have quite a few of these, and it's considered a better practice than defining global functions to prevent issues with mutable state in a global context.

```python
import warnings as warn
import pandas as pd
import numpy as np
import scipy
import scipy.stats as stat
from scipy.stats import shapiro, normaltest, anderson
import matplotlib.pyplot as plt
from statsmodels.graphics.gofplots import qqplot


class DistributionAnalysis(object):

    def __init__(self, series, histogram_bins, **kwargs):
        self.series = series
        self.histogram_bins = histogram_bins
        self.series_name = kwargs.get('series_name', 'data')
        self.plot_bins = kwargs.get('plot_bins', 200)
        self.best_plot_size = kwargs.get('best_plot_size', (20, 16))
        self.all_plot_size = kwargs.get('all_plot_size', (24, 30))
        self.MIN_BOUNDARY = 0.001
        self.MAX_BOUNDARY = 0.999
        self.ALPHA = kwargs.get('alpha', 0.05)

    def _get_series_bins(self):
        return int(np.ceil(self.series.index.values.max()))

    @staticmethod
    def _get_distributions():
        scipy_ver = scipy.__version__
        if (int(scipy_ver[2]) >= 5) and (int(scipy_ver[4:]) > 3):
            names, gen_names = stat.get_distribution_names(stat.pairs,
    stat.rv_continuous)
        else:
            names = stat._continuous_distns._distn_names
        return names


    @staticmethod
    def _extract_params(params):
        return {'arguments': params[:-2], 'location': params[-2], 'scale':
            params[-1]}
```

These values are left as static but could be wrapped into kwargs overrides if needed.

Private utility method to keep the callee locations cleaner and easier to read

Method for extracting the parameters from a distribution fit, putting them into a dictionary structure (this is known as currying, an eponymous reference to Haskell Curry, which condenses complex return types into a single reference to make code much cleaner).

Recall that this exact reference logic was copied multiple times throughout listing 9.1. Providing a single reference to extract this information reduces the chances of typo-induced bugs in code, which are frustrating to troubleshoot.

Private method for building the probability density function (pdf) based on the fit parameters found. The switch conditional is due to the varying number of arguments among the distribution families.

Private method to generate the starting and ending points of the generated standard histograms through the percent point function (the inverse of the cumulative distribution function) for a distribution

```python
@staticmethod
def _generate_boundaries(distribution, parameters, x):
    args = parameters['arguments']
    loc = parameters['location']
    scale = parameters['scale']
    return distribution.ppf(x, *args, loc=loc, scale=scale) if args else
  distribution.ppf(x, loc=loc, scale=scale)

@staticmethod
def _build_pdf(x, distribution, parameters):
    if parameters['arguments']:
        pdf = distribution.pdf(x, loc=parameters['location'],
            scale=parameters['scale'], *parameters['arguments'])
    else:
        pdf = distribution.pdf(x, loc=parameters['location'],
            scale=parameters['scale'])
    return pdf

def plot_normalcy(self):
    qqplot(self.series, line='s')

def check_normalcy(self):
    def significance_test(value, threshold):
        return "Data set {} normally distributed from".format('is' if value
            > threshold else 'is not')
    shapiro_stat, shapiro_p_value = shapiro(self.series)
    dagostino_stat, dagostino_p_value = normaltest(self.series)
    anderson_stat, anderson_crit_vals, anderson_significance_levels =
        anderson(self.series)
    anderson_report = list(zip(list(anderson_crit_vals),
        list(anderson_significance_levels)))
    shapiro_statement = """Shapiro-Wilk stat: {:.4f}
Shapiro-Wilk test p-Value: {:.4f}
{} Shapiro-Wilk Test""".format(
        shapiro_stat, shapiro_p_value, significance_test(shapiro_p_value,
            self.ALPHA))
    dagostino_statement = """\nD'Agostino stat: {:.4f}
D'Agostino test p-Value: {:.4f}
{}  D'Agostino Test""".format(
        dagostino_stat, dagostino_p_value,
  significance_test(dagostino_p_value, self.ALPHA))
```

Switch logic to handle some distributions requiring only two arguments (location and scale), while others require additional arguments

A public method for generating the Q-Q plot comparing the series against the standard normal distribution. For future work, this could be expanded or refactored to allow plotting against any distribution within scipy.stats.

A method-private method. Since this functionality is solely intended to make the code easier to read and less dense, and has no external uses, making it private within this method is a preferred methodology.

The stdout print functions for reporting on normalcy tests to the three primary families. The interpolation here is a bit different than in the script, and the human-readable nature of the decision of normalcy based on a passed-in alpha significance level makes the final report more interpretable and less prone to error in making assumptions about the series.

Private method to score the fit of the histogram of the data series under test to the standard histograms in scipy.stats, using SSE

```
        anderson_statement = '\nAnderson statistic: {:.4f}'.format(anderson_stat)
        for i in anderson_report:
            anderson_statement = anderson_statement + """
        For signifance level {} of Anderson-Darling test: {} the evaluation.
          Critical value: {}""".format(
                i[1], significance_test(i[0], anderson_stat), i[0])
        return "{}{}{}".format(shapiro_statement, dagostino_statement,
          anderson_statement)
```

Private method for generating the pdf and converting it to a series of data points to compare against the raw passed-in data series

```
    def _calculate_fit_loss(self, x, y, dist):
        with warn.catch_warnings():
            warn.filterwarnings('ignore')
            estimated_distribution = dist.fit(x)
            params = self._extract_params(estimated_distribution)
            pdf = self._build_pdf(x, dist, params)
        return np.sum(np.power(y - pdf, 2.0)), estimated_distribution

    def _generate_probability_distribution(self, distribution, parameters, bins):
        starting_point = self._generate_boundaries(distribution, parameters,
          self.MIN_BOUNDARY)
        ending_point = self._generate_boundaries(distribution, parameters,
          self.MAX_BOUNDARY)
        x = np.linspace(starting_point, ending_point, bins)
        y = self._build_pdf(x, distribution, parameters)
        return pd.Series(y, x)

    def find_distribution_fit(self):
        y_hist, x_hist_raw = np.histogram(self.series, self.histogram_bins,
          density=True)
        x_hist = (x_hist_raw + np.roll(x_hist_raw, -1))[:-1] / 2.
        full_distribution_results = {}
        best_loss = np.inf
        best_fit = stat.norm
        best_params = (0., 1.)
        for dist in self._get_distributions():
            histogram = getattr(stat, dist)
            results, parameters = self._calculate_fit_loss(x_hist, y_hist,
              histogram)
            full_distribution_results[dist] = {'hist': histogram,
                                       'loss': results,
                                       'params': {
                                           'arguments': parameters[:-2],
                                           'location': parameters[-2],
                                           'scale': parameters[-1]
                                       }}
```

Primary raw method for finding the closest (and all other) standard distributions to the series passed in. From an end-user perspective, exposing the raw data from the results of a module is sometimes worthwhile (often marked as a developer API) so that the user can use such data to perform additional actions.

Currying again so we don't have to return a complex n-valued tuple as a return statement. Dictionaries in Python (and case classes in Scala) are preferable to positional-encoded return statements to make debugging and end-user experiences much more seamless, even if it means more typing for the developer of the module.

```
            if best_loss > results > 0:
                best_loss = results
                best_fit = histogram
                best_params = parameters
        return {'best_distribution': best_fit,
                'best_loss': best_loss,
                'best_params': {
                    'arguments': best_params[:-2],
                    'location': best_params[-2],
                    'scale': best_params[-1]
                },
                'all_results': full_distribution_results
                }
```

Public method for plotting the best fit found to the series data passed in for evaluation to the class

```
    def plot_best_fit(self):
        fits = self.find_distribution_fit()
        best_fit_distribution = fits['best_distribution']
        best_fit_parameters = fits['best_params']
        distribution_series =
    self._generate_probability_distribution(best_fit_distribution,
    best_fit_parameters,
    self._get_series_bins())
        with plt.style.context(style='seaborn'):
            fig = plt.figure(figsize=self.best_plot_size)
            ax = self.series.plot(kind='hist', bins=self.plot_bins, normed=True,
                                  alpha=0.5, label=self.series_name,
                                  legend=True)
            distribution_series.plot(lw=3,
    label=best_fit_distribution.__class__.__name__, legend=True, ax=ax)
            ax.legend(loc='best')
        return fig

    def plot_all_fits(self):
```

Additional method to plot all the distributions against the passed-in series data as an aid to visualize similarities between standard distributions

```
        fits = self.find_distribution_fit()
        series_bins = self._get_series_bins()

        with warn.catch_warnings():
            warn.filterwarnings('ignore')
            with plt.style.context(style='seaborn'):
                fig = plt.figure(figsize=self.all_plot_size)
                ax = self.series.plot(kind='hist',
                                      bins=self.plot_bins,
                                      normed=True,
                                      alpha=0.5,
                                      label=self.series_name,
                                      legend=True)
                y_max = ax.get_ylim()
                x_max = ax.get_xlim()
                for dist in fits['all_results']:
                    hist = fits['all_results'][dist]
                    distribution_data = self._generate_probability_distribution(
                        hist['hist'], hist['params'], series_bins)
                    distribution_data.plot(lw=2, label=dist, alpha=0.6, ax=ax)
                ax.legend(loc='best')
```

```
            ax.set_ylim(y_max)
            ax.set_xlim(x_max)
        return fig
```

This code is functionally identical to that of the script. It produces the same results in the same amount of runtime and will just-in-time (JIT) compile to the exact same byte code as the script in listing 9.1 (minus the additional method for plotting all standard reference distributions against the series data). The primary difference in this code is in its utility.

While there are significantly more lines of code here than in the script, we now have isolation in the processing of the core logic of the code. We can walk through the code, method by method, to trace any issues that might arise, aiding any troubleshooting that may need to be done by a very large degree. We also now have the ability to unit test the code. With data mock-ups of predictable and readily understandable data, we can verify each of these methods against known functionality as a sort of litmus test.

The benefit of writing code in this manner means that we can, after a single up-front investment in slightly more complex development actions, potentially save ourselves countless frustrating hours of troubleshooting faults in the code. This frees us up to do what we should be doing: *solving business problems.*

NOTE If this solution were for a real code base, the statistical calculations would be put into their own class in a statistics module, while the visualization code would be put in another module. All of the methods shown in listing 9.3 are collapsed into a single class to make them easier to read in this book.

Machine-readable vs. human-readable code

An important point to bring up about code design and structure is that it's primarily for the benefit of humans and not the machine executing the code. While it may seem as though it is more efficient for execution to chain operations together in dense and complicated blocks, the truth is that, to the computer, provided that the executable logic is the same, the manner in which code is written (with respect to functional versus object-oriented versus scripted) is purely for the benefit of the people maintaining the code.

A high-quality code base should read like written text. It should be clear, concise, and easy enough to follow by looking at variable, function, method, class, and module names and the standard manipulation actions within the language. Someone proficient in that programming language should be able to understand the functionality of the code as easily as if they were reading a written-text description of the code base.

Shorthand notations, confusing acronyms, and overly dense control flows do no one any favors in helping to indicate how code works. After all, to the computer executing the byte code that is compiled from your high-level language code, a variable named `h` means the same as `standard_distribution_histogram` when referring to the same object in memory. The same can't be said about a human evaluating the code.

An entire design philosophy exists for writing code, which is applicable to ML project work. Known as *test driven development* (*TDD*), it can help structure code solutions in an efficient manner. In the next section, we'll go through the principles of TDD as it applies to ML development.

9.4   *Using test-driven development for ML*

As part of the follow-up to the refactoring work that we did for a problematic script with our new team, we should probably discuss how to work through MVP development in a different way. Many philosophies and patterns of software development have been developed over the years, and one that I've used and seen work remarkably well for ML project work is TDD.

TDD, as a principle, is great for general software development. At its core, TDD approaches development efforts by focusing on writing tests first, followed by creating a functional and elegant code base to support the passing of those tests. It approaches the creation of minimal functionality from the viewpoint of, "I need to perform operation x that I expect to generate result y, so I will create a test that asserts y and then build the code for x that makes the y test pass." For most software engineering done today, TDD is considered one of the foundational approaches to developing software in an Agile paradigm.

While pure TDD is incredibly challenging as a development strategy for ML use cases (particularly if trying to test results from non- or semi-non-deterministic algorithms), the basic principles, when applied to ML project work, can dramatically improve the functionality, readability, and stability of your code. Your assertions may change from the way a traditional software developer would write theirs, but the intentions and foundation remain the same. It's all about having intentional and predictable behavior that can be confirmed as functioning correctly during your development process.

When looking at the refactoring that happened between code listings 9.1 and 9.3, the decisions on where to split out functionality were informed more by the question, "How can I test this block of code?" than by, "What looks nice?" Figure 9.6 covers the thought process that I went through in creating listing 9.3.

Each of the boxes to the right of the leftmost column in figure 9.6 represents distinct logical operations that have been separated out for the purposes of testing. Breaking up the components in this way enables us to have fewer places that we have to search through. We also reduce the code complexity by isolating individual functionality, making a complicated series of actions little more than a path of complex actions, each stage capable of being checked and validated for proper functionality independent of one another.

> **NOTE** While writing these examples, I actually wrote listing 9.3 first, and then later adapted listing 9.1 from that code. Writing from the perspective of generating unit-testable code from the start helps keep your solutions

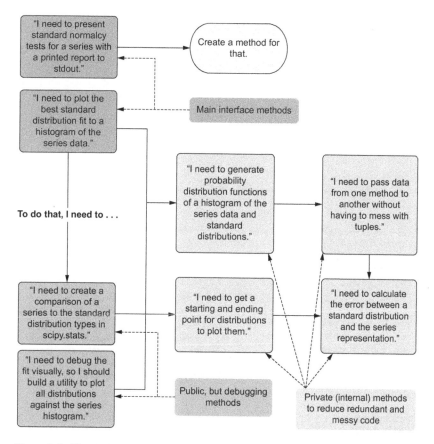

Figure 9.6 The design process for listing 9.3, focusing on testability and isolable code structure

easier to read, modify, and, of course, test (or, in this case, convert into a hard-to-read script). When getting started in writing abstract code, the process of creating abstraction may seem foreign. As with anything else in this profession, you will naturally gravitate toward more efficient methods over time. Don't be discouraged if you feel that you are going from script to abstraction in refactoring. Before you know it, you'll be leaving the world of scripting behind.

To further explain how the thought process in figure 9.6 translates from structural design into creating testable code in succinct and isolable groupings of functionality, let's take a look at the private method `_generate_boundaries()` as an example. The following listing shows what a simple unit test for this private method would look like.

Listing 9.4   An example unit test for the `_generate_boundaries()` **method**

Static test values that we're expecting as
a result to ensure proper functionality

A unit test definition
function for testing the
_generate_boundaries()
method

```
def test_generate_boundaries():
    expected_low_norm = -2.3263478740408408
    expected_high_norm = 2.3263478740408408
    boundary_arguments = {'location': 0, 'scale': 1, 'arguments': ()}
    test_object = DistributionAnalysis(np.arange(0,100), 10)
    normal_distribution_low = test_object._generate_boundaries(stat.norm,
                                        boundary_arguments,
                                        0.01)
    normal_distribution_high = test_object._generate_boundaries(stat.norm,
                                        boundary_arguments,
                                        0.99)
    assert normal_distribution_low == expected_low_norm, \
        'Normal Dist low boundary: {} does not match expected: {}' \
        .format(normal_distribution_low, expected_low_norm)
    assert normal_distribution_high == expected_high_norm, \
        'Normal Dist high boundary: {} does not match expected: {}' \
        .format(normal_distribution_high, expected_high_norm)

if __name__ == '__main__':
    test_generate_boundaries()
    print('tests passed')
```

Allows for all tests for the module to be run
(in practice, multiple unit test functions will
be called here). If all tests pass (assertions
don't throw assertion exceptions), this script
will exit, printing that tests passed.

Asserts that the return from the
_generate_boundaries method
equals our expected value

Object instantiation of our
class DistributionAnalysis()

Calls the protected method
_generate_boundaries with the
lower boundary value of 0.01

In this approach, we're testing several conditions to ensure that our method works as we expect. It's important to note from this example that, if this block of code were not isolated from the remainder of the actions going on in this module, it would be incredibly challenging (or impossible) to test. If this portion of the code was causing a problem (if one arose) or another tightly coupled action that preceded or followed this code, we wouldn't have any way of determining the culprit without modifying the code. However, by separating out this functionality, we can test at this boundary and determine whether it is behaving correctly, thereby reducing the number of things we need to evaluate if the module does not do what it is intended to do.

NOTE   Many Python unit-test frameworks exist, each with its own interface and behavior (pytest, for instance, relies heavily on fixture annotations). JVM-based languages generally rely on standards set by xUnit, which look dramatically different from those in Python. The point here is not to use one particular style, but rather to write code that is testable and stick to a particular standard of testing.

To demonstrate what this paradigm will do for us in practice, let's see what happens when we switch the second assertion statement from equality to non-equality. When we run this test suite, we get the following output as an `AssertionError`, detailing exactly what (and where) things went wrong with our code.

Listing 9.5 An intentional unit-test failure

```
=================================== FAILURES ===================================
_____ test_generate_boundaries _____

    def test_generate_boundaries():
        expected_low_norm = -2.3263478740408408
        expected_high_norm = 2.3263478740408408
        boundary_arguments = {'location': 0, 'scale': 1, 'arguments': ()}
        test_object = DistributionAnalysis(np.arange(0, 100), 10)
        normal_distribution_low = test_object._generate_boundaries(stat.norm,
                                                            boundary_arguments,
                                                            0.01)
        normal_distribution_high = test_object._generate_boundaries(stat.norm,
                                                            boundary_arguments,
                                                            0.99)
        assert normal_distribution_low == expected_low_norm, \
            'Normal Dist low boundary: {} does not match expected: {}' \
                .format(normal_distribution_low, expected_low_norm)
>       assert normal_distribution_high != expected_high_norm, \
            'Normal Dist high boundary: {} does not match expected: {}' \
                .format(normal_distribution_high, expected_high_norm)
E       AssertionError: Normal Dist high boundary: 2.3263478740408408 does not match
            expected: 2.3263478740408408
E       assert 2.3263478740408408 != 2.3263478740408408

ch09/UnitTestExample.py:20: AssertionError
========================== 1 failed in 0.99 seconds ==========================
Process finished with exit code 0
```

The caret at the edge of this report shows the line in our unit test that failed.

The actual evaluation that the assertion attempted to perform

The return of the top-level exception (the AssertionError) and the message that we put within the test to ensure we can track down what went wrong

Designing, writing, and running effective unit tests is absolutely critical for production stability, particularly when thinking of future code refactoring or extending the functionality of this utility module, since additional work may change the way that this method or others that feed data into this module function. We do, however, want to know before we merge code into the master (or main) branch that the changes being made will not introduce issues to the rest of the methods in this module (as well as giving us direct insight into where a problem may lie since the functionality is isolated from other code in the module). By having this security blanket of knowing that things work as originally intended, we can confidently maintain complex (and hopefully not complicated) code bases.

NOTE   For more information on TDD, I highly encourage you to check out Kent Beck's book, *Test-Driven Development by Example* (Addison-Wesley Professional, 2002).

Summary

- Monolithic scripts are not only difficult to read but also force inefficient and error-prone debugging techniques.
- Large, eagerly evaluated scripts are incredibly challenging in terms of modifying behavior and introducing new features. Troubleshooting failures in these becomes an exercise in frustration.
- Defining logical separation of tasks by using abstraction within an ML code base greatly aids legibility for other team members who will need to maintain and improve a solution over time.
- Designing project code architecture to support discrete testable interfaces to functionality greatly helps in debugging, feature enhancement work, and continued maintenance updates to long-lived ML projects.

Standards of coding and creating maintainable ML code

10

This chapter covers

- Identifying ML code smells and how to correct them
- Reducing code complexity in ML projects
- Currying for cleaner and more understandable code
- Applying proper exception handling in ML code bases
- Understanding side effects and how they can create bugs
- Simplifying nested logic to improve comprehension

In the preceding chapter, we covered the broad strokes of a code foundation. Focusing on breaking up complex structure by utilizing refactoring and basic software-engineering best practices was important to pave the way for further discussion of the more detailed aspects of software development for ML. Without laying the foundation of basic best-practices, the code architecture and design elements that follow simply don't matter.

Early in anyone's career in software development (ML or otherwise), the ability to identify potential issues with an implementation is effectively nonexistent. This is understandable, as the wisdom of knowing what works and what doesn't comes directly from experience. Everyone who works in developing software eventually learns that just because you can do something doesn't mean that you should do it in code. These lessons are typically gained by messing things up a great deal.

Projects that have too many of the aforementioned mistakes run the risk of being abandoned. After all, if no one can troubleshoot the code, let alone read it, the chance that the technical-debt-riddled solution will be permitted to run for very long in production is slim.

The goal of this chapter is to identify the most common issues that I see in ML code bases that directly affect the *stability of the solution* (and the general mental well-being of those required to maintain it).

10.1 ML code smells

Sometimes you look at a code base and just know something is not right. The mistakes you see in formatting, collection handling, lack of appropriate recursion, or quantity of dead code can give you a sense of the overall health of a code base. If they're bad enough, even the most junior members of a team can identify them.

More insidious problems might be much harder for a junior DS to identify but can be clear to more senior members of the team. These "smells" within the code (a term famously coined by Martin Fowler) are indicative of potentially crippling problems that may arise elsewhere, directly impacting production stability or making the code nigh-impossible to debug if a problem happens.

Table 10.1 lists some of the more common code smells that I see in ML code bases. While the ones listed are not catastrophic, per se, they typically are the first sign that I have that "all is not well in Denmark." Finding one of these code smells generally means that one of the more insidious issues that will likely affect production stability is contained somewhere in the code base. Learning to recognize these issues, setting plans to address the technical debt of them, and working to learn techniques to avoid these in ML projects can significantly reduce the refactoring and repair work that the ML team will have to do in the future.

Table 10.1 Common "nontoxic" code smells in ML code bases

Code smell	Example	Why it stinks
Wildcard imports	`from scipy import *`	It brings in all of the top-level functions in a package. It may create namespace collisions among other imported libraries or within the project's code base.
Multiple imports	`import numpy as np`	Confusing, mixed bag of usage throughout code.

Table 10.1 Common "nontoxic" code smells in ML code bases *(continued)*

Code smell	Example	Why it stinks
	`from numpy import add`	Makes the code harder to read.

Too many parameters	`def my_method(df, name,`
	`source, fitting, metric,`
	`score, value, rename,`
	`outliers, train, valid)`
		Hard to read, hard to maintain, and confusing. Indicative of deeper issues in abstraction and encapsulation throughout the code base.

Copied boiler-plate	Having feature-engineering code for training, test, and inference defined in three separate places	Aka *shotgun surgery*— changes need to be identically matched in all places, increasing the chances of making a mistake and having inconsistencies.

Default Hyperparameters	`km = Kmeans()`
	
	`km.fit(train)`
		The defaults are generally not ideal.
		
		Seeing untuned models outside of rapid prototyping is dangerous.

Variable reuse	`pred = lr.predict(test)`
	`pred.to_parquet('/<loc>')`
	`pred = rf.predict(test)`
	`pred.to_parquet('/<loc2>')`
		Violates the single-responsibility principle. Makes the code hard to follow and debug. Can create stateful bugs that are hard to fix. Adding new functionality can create spaghetti code.

Use of literals	`profit = 0.72 * revenue`	Literals are "magic numbers" that, when littered throughout code, can make updating them a nightmare. These should always be defined as named constants.
In-line comments explaining how the code works	`<some abhorrently complex chained code>`	If you need to write comments to explain how code works, you are doing it wrong. Anytime the code becomes so complicated that you need a reminder of how it works, you should assume that no one else will be able to figure out what you wrote. Refactor it to reduce complexity.
SQL without common table expressions (CTEs)	`<chained joins with no encapsulated interim table definitions>`	CTEs help readability of SQL. Having hundreds (or thousands) of lines of SQL that have a single dependency chain means that any modification (adding or dropping a column) can take hours and is nearly impossible to debug.
SQL walls	`<no upper casing to functions, no indentation or line-wrap SQL>`	All three of these are impossible to read.

Constant recasting	`age = int(age)`
	`height = float(height)`
	`seniority = int(`
	`retirement) \`
	`- int(age)`
		Typing doesn't change. Cast it once. This is indicative of naïve programming ("It threw an exception once for not being an int, so I will make sure all integers are cast as int.") It's pointless.

This chapter is focused on the five most frequent "deadly" errors. These are the crippling problems that create fundamentally broken ML code bases. Seeing these sorts of issues would likely mean a pager duty call at least once per week.

If a project contains a small number of the issues described in this chapter, it's not guaranteed to fail. The project may be onerous and confusing to continue developing, or incredibly unpleasant to maintain, but that doesn't mean it won't run and serve its intended purpose.

However, if the code base is riddled with multiple instances of each type of problem, the chances that you're going to sleep well through your on-call week are pretty grim. Figure 10.1 shows the relationship between the severity of these issues and their potential effect on the outcome of the final project.

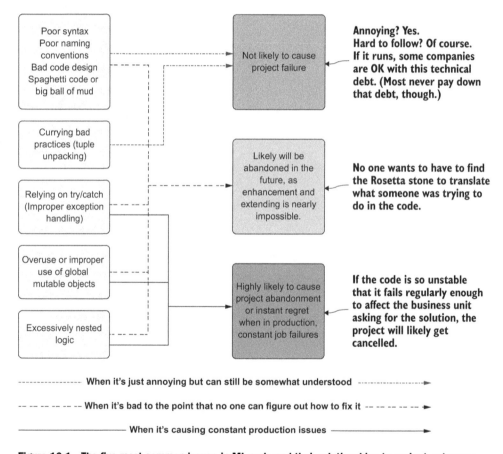

Figure 10.1 The five most common issues in ML code and their relationships to project outcomes

We'll take a look at these five main bad practices throughout the rest of this chapter. We'll focus on how to fix them and discuss why they can be so detrimental to ML project work.

10.2 Naming, structure, and code architecture

Someone who is on on-call support experiences few more exhausting and panic-inducing scenarios than realizing that the job that just broke and requires investigation is "that one" This code is so overly confusing, complicated, and monkey-patched that when it breaks, the original author is usually called in to fix it. What makes it even worse is knowing that person left the company—two months ago. And now you have to fix their code.

Digging into it, all you see are obscure acronyms as variable names, massive walls of code within functions, classes with dozens of unrelated methods thrown in haphazardly, unhelpful inline comments, and thousands of lines of commented-out code. It's basically the worst of both worlds: both a bowl of *spaghetti code* (control flow in the code organized as well as noodles in a bowl of spaghetti) and a *ball of mud* (effectively a morass of individual bowls of spaghetti with duplicated code, global references, dead code, and no seeming architectural design for maintainability).

A lot of ML code tends to look like this, unfortunately, and it can be remarkably frustrating to diagnose and refactor. Let's take a look at a few bad habits regarding naming, structure, and architecture, as well as better alternatives to those bad practices.

10.2.1 Naming conventions and structure

Naming variables can be a bit of a tricky exercise. Some schools of thought subscribe to the "less is more" philosophy, where the most succinct (shortest) code is best. Others, including myself, when writing non-ML code, tend to stick to more verbose naming conventions. As mentioned in chapter 9, the computer doesn't care at all how you name things (provided that you're not, as shown in listing 10.1, using a reserved keyword for a structure as a variable name).

Let's look at a dense representation of some naming issues. From lazy abbreviations (shorthand placeholder variable names) to unintelligible cipher-like names and a reserved function name, this listing has more than a few problems.

Listing 10.1   Bad naming conventions

Defines a tuple using the built-in language function tuple() that takes an iterable (here, a list). The variable definition sheds no light on what this is used for, though.

Generates a list of numbers. The variable name "abc" is just laziness.

Creates a merged list of each of the other lists. Defining the list in this statement is hard to read and increases code complexity. The variable name is acronym soup and provides zero insight to anyone reading the code.

```
import functools
import operator
import math
gta = tuple([1,2,3,4])
abc = list(range(100))
REF_IND_24G_88A = list(zip(abc, list(range(0, 500, 5))))
tuple = [math.pow(x[0] - x[1],2) for x in REF_IND_24G_88A]
rtrn = math.sqrt(functools.reduce(operator.add, tuple) / len(tuple))
```

Calculates the squared error of the two lists of numbers. The variable name is dangerous because it's a reserved function name that will now get overwritten for this context.

Calculates the root mean squared error (RMSE), but the variable defined is just a shortened name for a reserved language feature ("return")

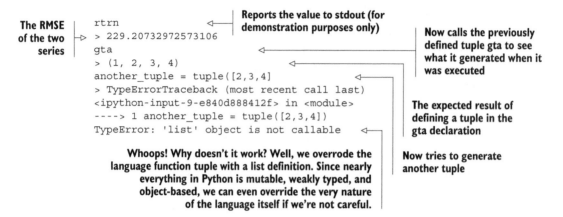

The RMSE of the two series

```
rtrn
> 229.20732972573106
gta
> (1, 2, 3, 4)
another_tuple = tuple([2,3,4]
> TypeErrorTraceback (most recent call last)
<ipython-input-9-e840d888412f> in <module>
----> 1 another_tuple = tuple([2,3,4])
TypeError: 'list' object is not callable
```

Reports the value to stdout (for demonstration purposes only)

Now calls the previously defined tuple gta to see what it generated when it was executed

The expected result of defining a tuple in the gta declaration

Now tries to generate another tuple

Whoops! Why doesn't it work? Well, we overrode the language function tuple with a list definition. Since nearly everything in Python is mutable, weakly typed, and object-based, we can even override the very nature of the language itself if we're not careful.

This is clearly meant to be an exaggerated example of multiple bad practices condensed into a single block. You have little chance of seeing something like this "in the wild," but each and every one of these issues has been in code bases that I've seen.

Of all of the issues presented here, the reserved name usage is perhaps the most insidious. Not only is it incredibly hard to detect in a large code base, but it can wreak havoc on future feature development. I can't stress strongly enough how important it is to *avoid using nonspecific variable names*, particularly in a language like Python, because you can override core functionality with seemingly innocuous shortcut naming.

While this isn't a problem in compiled languages directly (the compiler will not allow reassignment of a protected method to something that you define, after all), it can be introduced by unintentionally overriding methods that have dependencies. While JVM languages will detect and not permit mixing in of improperly overridden traits from a superclass, having poorly named methods during development can lead to wasting countless hours tracking down why a build fails.

10.2.2 *Trying to be too clever*

There is no award, nor will there ever be, for developing software with the fewest keystrokes. Trying to be clever by seeing how compact and concise code can be written does nothing for the runtime efficiency of the code in an interpreted language. The only thing it achieves is raising the ire of others who have to read the code.

> **NOTE** Code styling and comprehensible structure benefits humans. The computer doesn't care how fancy your chained operations are, but other humans will. And they will hate you for this form of cleverness.

Listing 10.2 exemplifies an attempt at creating the most dense and efficient code achievable. While it is technically correct and will result in the calculation of a root mean squared error, it's nearly impossible to read.

Writing code like this *does nothing for performance*. The author may feel smarter by writing what they see as efficient code, but nothing could be further from the truth.

The code makes it hard for others to figure out what is going on, will be incredibly challenging to modify, and limits the ability to debug.

Listing 10.2   Complex one-liner

```
rmse = math.sqrt(functools.reduce(operator.add, [math.pow(x[0] - x[1], 2) for
    x in list(zip(list(range(100)), list(range(0,500,5))))]) / 100)    ◁
```

Borderline intentionally obfuscated functionality. Writing code like this does no one, including yourself, any favors. It's dense, hard to read, and requires a lot of mental effort to figure out what it's doing (even if it is named correctly).

This style of efficient one-line coding requires paying far too much attention to each element in order to piece together all of the actions occurring. Thankfully, a simple set of logic is being performed in this example. I have seen one-liners span dozens of lines in an IDE before, and it does no one any favors by writing code like this.

The following is a cleaner and more straightforward way to write this block of functionality. While still not ideal, it achieves a higher degree of legibility.

Listing 10.3   Properly named and structured version

Much clearer variable names that explain, in plain text, the values that the variable is pointing to

By describing what is happening within the variable name, the code can be scanned much more easily. Instead of a confusing name that bears no meaning to the state of the operations at this point, stating what is being done makes reading the code much easier.

```
first_series_small = list(range(100))
larger_series_by_five = list(range(0, 500, 5))
merged_series_by_index = list(zip(first_series_small, larger_series_by_five))  ◁
merged_squared_errors = [math.pow(x[0] - x[1],2) for x in
    merged_series_by_index]
merged_rmse = math.sqrt(functools.reduce(operator.add, merged_squared_errors)
    / len(merged_squared_errors))    ◁
```

Naming the final action properly as a specific calculated value based on the defined logic makes this entire block much easier to figure out.

However, the proper way to write this code is shown in listing 10.4. Not only are the variable names clear, but we're not reimplementing functionality that already exists within standard packages. To keep code as simple and legible as possible, don't try to reinvent the wheel.

Listing 10.4   How it should be written

The RMSE equation is graciously provided and maintained for you by the scikit-learn contribution team. They certainly know what they're doing, and you should trust that their modules work correctly.

Hardcoding values within functions or methods is an antipattern (except for in the mean_squared_error function, we're forcing a particular functionality with the flag setting to False), so here we're allowing the generator to calculate different values of generated sequences by passed-in configuration.

```
import numpy as np
from sklearn.metrics import mean_squared_error

def calculate_rmse_for_generated_sequences(**kwargs):
    first_sequence = np.arange(kwargs['seq_1_start'], kwargs['seq_1_stop'],  ◁
        kwargs['seq_1_step'], float)
```

```
    second_sequence = np.arange(kwargs['seq_2_start'], kwargs['seq_2_stop'],
        kwargs['seq_2_step'], float)
    return mean_squared_error(first_sequence, second_sequence, squared=False)    ◁──┐

calculate_rmse_for_generated_sequences(**{'seq_1_start': 0, 'seq_1_stop': 100,
                                          'seq_1_step': 1, 'seq_2_start': 0,
                                          'seq_2_stop': 500, 'seq_2_step': 5})
> 229.20732972573106
```

**Sets the mean square error function's (MSE) squared
argument flag to False, and you have RMSE**

10.2.3 *Code architecture*

Code architecture is a contentious subject. While many people tout that they have an
ideal approach, the only valid answer to what makes a good layout of logic within a
code base is the *one that the team can maintain*. I've lost count of the number of times
that I've worked on or seen someone's ideal repository structure that is so ridiculously
overengineered that the team ends up struggling to merge code to it before the project is done.

The inevitable result of defining a well-intentioned but overly complex repository
structure for a project is a breakdown in proper abstraction. As the process of development moves along in an ML project, and additional features are created to solve the
needs of the solution, new functionality ends up getting shoehorned in places that it
would not have otherwise been placed. By the time the development cycle is complete, the code base is impossible to navigate, as shown in figure 10.2.

In this example, a series of three major feature updates need to be added to the
code. Each contributor attempts to figure out where their feature branch code needs
to be placed, based on the existing wireframe built at the start of the project. The first
improvement that adds more features to the vector isn't confusing. The repository
structure has clearly defined modules dedicated to this.

The second change, modifications to the model family, involves replacing the
model that had been used earlier. As long as the original model's core code, which
was in existence before the change, gets completely removed from the code base, and
the dead code is removed and not just commented out, this form of refactoring is perfectly fine. However, as part of this model change, new functionality is required in the
form of a validation check. Where should this go?

The contributor ends up slapping this new functionality into the feature-validation
statistics class. This now creates a tight coupling of functionality between feature-
related statistics and the new target-related statistics.

While it's true that both operations are doing statistical validation of data, the algorithms, validations, and operations being performed have nothing to do with one
another. Furthermore, in order to fit this functionality into the existing class, the signature needs to be changed to adapt to both use cases. This is a clear case of code spaghetti:
completely unrelated code and modifications used to "monkey-patch" functionality
together end up leaving the code more fragile, more confusing, and harder to modify
in the future. Tests on this class will similarly become far more difficult to write as the

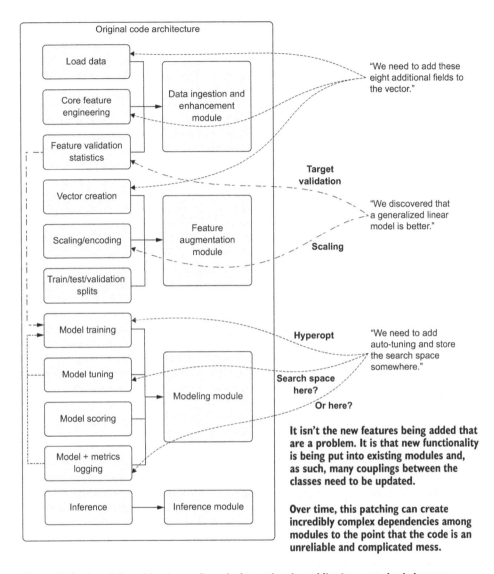

Figure 10.2 A well-thought-out repository design and code architecture can slowly become a tangled and confusing mess.

new functionality has to be considered. It's simply more work than it's worth. What the contributor should have done with this new functionality is create a *new module* with a class (or classes) that support the target's statistical validation needs.

The final change required, adding Hyperopt for auto-tuning of the model, forces the team members to perform a highly complex refactoring. They updated the model-training module to support this, which is reasonable. However, the search space configuration should have been externalized to a different module. Loading down the metrics, parameters, and monitoring module with unrelated functionality will only create a sloppy code base. It will make the peer review (PR) process more complicated, make future feature work more challenging, and force more-complex unit tests to be written to ensure proper code coverage.

To be crystal clear here, I'm not advocating rigid adherence to a particular code architecture, nor sticking with whatever design the repository was in at the conclusion of the MVP phase of a project. Code should always organically grow; the process of refactoring, improving, adding features, removing features, and maintaining a code base should be embraced by all who work in software development.

However, there are ways to add features that make a code base maintainable, and there are ways that make it a broken, complicated, and confusing mess. If you're changing existing functionality or adding a new feature that is isolated to the encapsulation defined by a current class or module, you should be writing your feature within that module. However, if the change is extremely large (an entirely new functionality that can be abstracted away into its own module) or involves communication with many other classes and modules spread throughout your code base, do yourself and your team a favor and just create a new module.

10.3 Tuple unpacking and maintainable alternatives

Let's suppose for a moment that we're working on a relatively complex ML code base that's in production. We've created our feature branch and are ready to implement the improvement. The ticket we're working on, adding a statistical test to a core module, requires adding another return value to a scoring method.

Looking at the method that exists, we see that the return is a tuple of values, currently three of them. After adding in the additional logic and updating the return tuple with the additional variable, we move to the portion of the code that needs the new return value. After updating the return structure where our feature branch is targeting consumption of this method, we run a test on our feature branch.

Everything breaks. The other places in the code base that didn't specifically need the new variable, even though they don't use it, still need to capture the added return value. Thankfully, there's a solution to this issue of currying return values by position reference: tuple unpacking.

10.3.1 Tuple unpacking example

Let's take a look at a simple data generator in listing 10.5. In this code, we're using the logistic map function to generate a series of data, visualizing it, and returning both the plot object and the series (so we can do some statistical analysis on it based on the configured values).

> **Listing 10.5   Logistic map data generator with tuple return**

```
import matplotlib.pyplot as plt
import numpy as np
```

```
def logistic_map(x, recurrence):
    return x * recurrence * (1 - x)
```

The logistic map function for use in recursing over prior values

```
def log_map(n, x, r, collection=None):
    if collection is None:
        collection = []
    calculated_value = logistic_map(x, r)
    collection.append(calculated_value)
    if n > 0:
        log_map(n-1, calculated_value, r, collection)
    return np.array(collection[:n])
```

The tail-recursive function for generating the series by applying the logistic map equation over each previous value

```
def generate_log_map_and_plot(iterations, recurrence, start):
    map_series = log_map(iterations, start, recurrence)
    with plt.style.context(style='seaborn'):
        fig = plt.figure(figsize=(16,8))
        ax = fig.add_subplot(111)
        ax.plot(range(iterations), map_series)
        ax.set_xlabel('iterations')
        ax.set_ylabel('logistic map values')
        ax.set_title('Logistic Map with recurrence of:
    {}'.format(recurrence))
    return (map_series, fig)
```

Function for generating the series and a plot to show what the particular recurrence value does to the series

```
log_map_values_chaos, log_map_plot_chaos = generate_log_map_and_plot(1000,
    3.869954, 0.5)
```

Calls the function with tuple unpacking of the return values, assigning them to variables directly

The tuple return type. This is not a particularly egregious demonstration of complexity in passing a result out of a function, but it still requires knowledge of the function signature to use. It also requires positional reference for each place this function will be called (creating a tightly coupled structure between this function's return type and each place that it is used in code).

NOTE For the results of these examples, see the Jupyter notebook for this chapter in the companion repository for this book at https://github.com/ BenWilson2/ML-Engineering.

With the two return values specified with the generate_log_map_and_plot() function, it's not an overly complex burden from a usage and maintainability perspective to keep the correct references when using it. However, when the size and complexity of the return values grow, using the function becomes increasingly difficult.

As an example of a complex return type from a function, see listing 10.6. This simple statistical analysis of a univariate series generates a complex output. While the intention of making it easier to use is there with the utilization of grouped tuples, it's still too complex.

Listing 10.6 Statistical analysis function with a nightmarish tuple unpacking

```
def analyze_series(series):
    minimum = np.min(series)
    mean = np.average(series)
    maximum = np.max(series)
```

Function for collecting statistics on a series of data

```
q1 = np.quantile(series, 0.25)
median = np.quantile(series, 0.5)
q3 = np.quantile(series, 0.75)
p5, p95 = np.percentile(series, [5, 95])
std_dev = np.std(series)
variance = np.var(series)
return ((minimum, mean, maximum), (std_dev, variance), (p5, q1, median,
    q3, p95))
```

The complex grouped nested tuple return type that will force positional (or complex defined returns) on the caller side of this function

```
get_all_of_it = analyze_series(log_map_values_chaos)
mean_of_chaos_series = get_all_of_it[0][1]
mean_of_chaos_series
> 0.5935408729262835
```

Uses an object to hold the entire return structure in a single variable

```
((minimum, mean, maximum), (std_dev, variance), (p5, q1, median, q3, p95)) =
    analyze_series(log_map_values_chaos)
```

Uses positional notation and nesting to return a particular element from the return structure. This is extremely fragile and difficult to use. Most of the time, when approach is utilized, if this function changes, these values are overlooked when refactoring, leading to confusing exceptions or incorrect calculations.

The alternative access pattern for expanding the tuples. This is just ugly code and difficult to maintain. When the underlying function changes, this tightly coupled signature will throw a ValueError Exception with unpacking counts being off from expected.

Writing code in this way is problematic for reasons other than simply having to look at source code to use it, though. What happens when this function needs to change? What if, instead of needing to evaluate the 95th percentile of the series, we also need to calculate the 99th percentile? Where do we put that within the structure?

If we update the return signature, we then have to update every single place that this function is used. It's simply not a usable form of currying data from the function for use elsewhere. It also increases the complicated levels of the code in a way that makes the entire code base more fragile, harder to maintain, and frustrating to troubleshoot and test.

10.3.2 *A solid alternative to tuple unpacking*

Listing 10.7 shows a solution to this problem, using a structure and approach that is similar to that used for another dominant ML language: Scala (through the use of case classes). In this listing, we're using *named tuples* to handle the return type structure, allowing us to use named references to get to the underlying data within the structure.

This approach enables future-proofing since any modification of the return structure will not require defining consumption patterns at place of use. It's also far easier to implement. Using these structures is like using dictionaries (using similar underlying structures), but they have a more syntax-sugar feel than dictionaries because of the positional named entity notation.

Listing 10.7　Refactoring the series and plot generator with named tuples

**Imports the standard collections library
to have access to named tuples**

```
from collections import namedtuple

def generate_log_map_and_plot_named(iterations, recurrence, start):
    map_series = log_map(iterations, start, recurrence)
    MapData = namedtuple('MapData', 'series plot')
    with plt.style.context(style='seaborn'):
        fig = plt.figure(figsize=(16,8))
        ax = fig.add_subplot(111)
        ax.plot(range(iterations), map_series)
        ax.set_xlabel('iterations')
        ax.set_ylabel('logistic map values')
        ax.set_title('Logistic Map with recurrence of:
    {}'.format(recurrence))
    return MapData(map_series, fig)

other_chaos_series = generate_log_map_and_plot_named(1000, 3.7223976, 0.5)
other_chaos_series.series

> array([0.9305994 , 0.24040791, 0.67975427, 0.81032278, 0.57213166,
        0.91123186, 0.30109864, 0.78333483, 0.63177043, 0.86596575, …])
```

**Defines the named tuple
we'll be using for named
access to the data within
our tuple return type**

**The individual values contained within the return variable
are accessed through the named elements that we defined
as part of the named tuple collection definition.**

**Creates a new instance of our named tuple MapData
and places the objects to be returned from the
function within the named tuple defined structure**

**The return signature is now a
single element (keeping the
code looking much cleaner
when using the function), but
it no longer requires
positional notation to
access the elements.**

Now that we have a simple example of the refactoring of the series generation and plotting from listing 10.5, let's take a look at how a named tuple approach with defined structure can aid us with the far more complicated return type from listing 10.6, as shown in the next listing.

Listing 10.8　Refactoring the statistical attribute function with named tuples

**Defines
named
tuples
for each
component
of the
analysis**

```
def analyze_series_legible(series):
    BasicStats = namedtuple('BasicStats', 'minimum mean maximum')
    Variation = namedtuple('Variation', 'std_dev variance')
    Quantiles = namedtuple('Quantiles', 'p5 q1 median q3 p95')
    Analysis = namedtuple('Analysis', ['basic_stats', 'variation', 'quantiles'])
    minimum = np.min(series)
    mean = np.average(series)
    maximum = np.max(series)
    q1 = np.quantile(series, 0.25)
    median = np.quantile(series, 0.5)
    q3 = np.quantile(series, 0.75)
    p5, p95 = np.percentile(series, [5, 95])
    std_dev = np.std(series)
```

**Named tuples can be nested
to aggregate similar data
return types together.**

```
        variance = np.var(series)
        return Analysis(BasicStats(minimum, mean, maximum),
                        Variation(std_dev, variance),
                        Quantiles(p5, q1, median, q3, p95))
```

Calls the function and passes in the name-referenced series data from the generator function return

Generates series data

```
    bi_cycle = generate_log_map_and_plot_named(100, 3.564407, 0.5)
    legible_return_bi_cycle = analyze_series_legible(bi_cycle.series)
    legible_return_bi_cycle.variation.std_dev
    > 0.21570993929353727
```

Extracts a nested named tuple variable's data

By using named structures, you create less work for yourself and others when refactoring code, because you don't have to change all calling instances of a function or a method. In addition, the code is far easier to read. Increasing legibility of the code may not reduce the complexity of what your code is doing, but it is guaranteed to make your code *far less complicated.*

A great many ML APIs leverage tuple unpacking. Typically, the tuple is restricted to no more than three elements to reduce end-user confusion. Keeping track of three elements doesn't seem very complex (for the most part). But using positional references to return elements from a function or a method becomes a nuisance, since the code has to reflect these positional returns *each place that the code is called.*

Tuple unpacking ends up increasing the level of confusion in people reading and maintaining the code and raises the overall level of complexity of the code base. By moving to encapsulated return types (named tuples in Python, case classes in Scala), we can minimize the number of lines of code that need to be changed in a feature branch and reduce the confusion in interpreting the code.

10.4   *Blind to issues: Eating exceptions and other bad practices*

Let's continue our scenario of walking into a code base that we're unfamiliar with by focusing on running a full test of our first feature branch. As part of this branch, we have to use a data loader module that was written for interfacing with the object-storage data lake. Because of the poor documentation and difficult-to-read code of this module, we mistakenly pass the wrong authentication token. Stderr and stdout, upon executing our branch, merely have a single line printed out: `Oops. Couldn't read data.`

Not only is this incredibly annoying (cute error messages are not useful), but it doesn't provide any guidance as to *why* the data couldn't be read. Was the data not present? Did we pass in an invalid path? Do we have access to this data? Is something in the new feature branch's usage of the method within the data loader class malformed?

We simply won't know without loading and parsing the logs on the system. We will have to trace, modify our code, insert debug statements, and spend hours digging into our code and the utility module code to figure out what's going on. We've become an unwitting victim of *exception eating*: a misguided intention to "just make it work" by the inappropriate use of a try/catch block.

10.4.1 Try/catch with the precision of a shotgun

One of the more dangerous bad habits to get into when developing ML code is in exception handling. This area of software development is typically foreign to the way most DS practitioners write code when trying to solve a problem.

Generally, when an error happens while writing code, the issue is fixed for the problem at hand, and then work continues on solving the problem. However, in the realm of production code, many things can go wrong in a code base. Perhaps the data being passed in is malformed, the scale of the data changes to such a degree that calculations are no longer valid, or one of the other millions of things that can go wrong might go wrong.

I've seen many people slap a try/catch around where a seemingly innocuous fault occurs. Not fully understanding how to implement handling of a specific exception, however, could lead to using a *blind catch*, which can create a situation that makes the code base incredibly challenging to debug.

> **NOTE** For step-by-step examples of how exception handling, when done incorrectly, can cause problems, see the companion repository to this book and follow along with the Jupyter notebook CH09_1.ipynb.

Listing 10.9 illustrates this concept. In this simple example, we're taking an integer and dividing it by a list of integers. What we want out of this function is a new collection that represents the quotient of the base number divided by each member of the passed-in collection. The results below the function show the inevitable result of executing the code: a ZeroDivisionError.

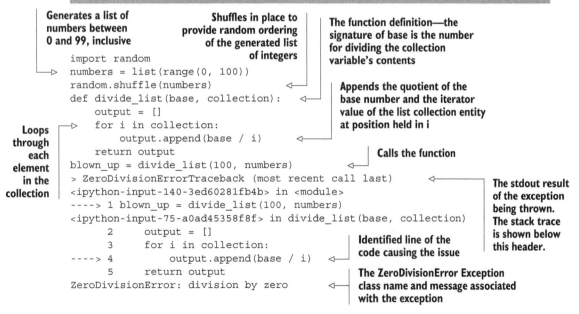

Listing 10.9 A simple collection division function that will throw an exception

Generates a list of numbers between 0 and 99, inclusive

Shuffles in place to provide random ordering of the generated list of integers

The function definition—the signature of base is the number for dividing the collection variable's contents

```
import random
numbers = list(range(0, 100))
random.shuffle(numbers)
def divide_list(base, collection):
    output = []
    for i in collection:
        output.append(base / i)
    return output
blown_up = divide_list(100, numbers)
> ZeroDivisionErrorTraceback (most recent call last)
<ipython-input-140-3ed60281fb4b> in <module>
----> 1 blown_up = divide_list(100, numbers)
<ipython-input-75-a0ad45358f8f> in divide_list(base, collection)
      2         output = []
      3         for i in collection:
----> 4             output.append(base / i)
      5         return output
ZeroDivisionError: division by zero
```

Appends the quotient of the base number and the iterator value of the list collection entity at position held in i

Loops through each element in the collection

Calls the function

The stdout result of the exception being thrown. The stack trace is shown below this header.

Identified line of the code causing the issue

The ZeroDivisionError Exception class name and message associated with the exception

The *blind catch* (aka *eating* all of the exceptions) solution that many DSs I've seen use to address this problem might look something like the following listing. To be clear, this should *never* be done.

Listing 10.10 Unsafe exception-handling example

```
def divide_list_unsafe(base, collection):
    output = []
    for i in collection:
        try:
            output.append(base / i)
        except:
            pass
    return output
```

The try block attempts to perform the encapsulated action, but if an exception is thrown (raised), it will move to the except blocks.

The except block(s) that contain handling code for specific exceptions. This implementation (blind catch) is dangerous, inadequate, and will cause stability and troubleshooting problems (this is effectively writing a bug directly into code).

The dangerous "pass" (do nothing) command can be useful for stateless transaction systems (think web apps) but should never be used in ML code.

When we execute this code against our list, we will get a return of a list filled with 99 numbers, minus the 0 value that threw an exception and was ignored because of the pass keyword. While this might seem like it solves the problem and lets the execution continue, this is a *truly terrible solution*. The following listing illustrates why.

Listing 10.11 Example of why blind exception handling is bad

Since we're catching all exceptions and just moving on (the pass keyword), no exceptions are thrown to warn us that something didn't work properly.

Passes in a string to be divided by. This obviously will not work (it will throw a TypeError).

```
broken = divide_list_unsafe('oops', numbers)
len(broken)
> 0
```

The list is empty. That will likely break things downstream.

When we pass something that is not a number into this function, we get no errors. Not a single exception is thrown to warn us that the return value is an empty list. What we can try to do is catch the exact exception instead so that situations like this won't happen, making us effectively blind to issues.

Issues with catching all exceptions

While the example in listing 10.11 is obvious, rather simple, and somewhat pointless in its functionality, real-world instances of this sort of pattern rear themselves in truly ugly ways.

Suppose that you have a series of blind try/catch statements written around the vast majority of the code within an ML project. From reading in the source data, performing feature-engineering tasks, model tuning, validation, and logging, each major step is wrapped in a try, except, and then pass statement. What would happen if there was an issue with the data that failed in an encoding step? What about an expired authentication token to read the source data? What if the data was moved, and the location that you're reading from is now empty? What if the model failed to converge?

The point I'm trying to make is that those scenarios, to the person investigating why the job didn't produce any output, all look identical. The only indication that something went wrong is that the job didn't do what it was supposed to do. Since all of the exceptions have been eaten, there is absolutely no indication of where to even begin looking to find the culprit.

It's for this reason that blind catching of exceptions is so inherently dangerous. At some point in the future of any long-running project code base, problems will arise. The job will fail for one reason or another. If you're handicapping your ability to figure out the issue, you're going to have to step through the code manually or perform some sort of binary search to track down what's going on. Figuring out problems in this way wastes effort and time.

Even though it may seem like more work to write proper exception handling, it's the right thing to do. When the code eventually blows up—and it will, trust me, because given enough time, all code bases do—you'll be grateful to have spent an extra 30 minutes writing proper handling code when it gets you to the source of the issue in minutes rather than days.

10.4.2 Exception handling with laser precision

The next listing shows the proper way to catch an exception by type.

Listing 10.12 Catching and handling a single exception safely

Catches the exact exception that we want (ZeroDivisionError) and gets a reference to the exception object (e)

A less-than-ideal handling of the exception (we're still effectively ignoring it by printing it to stdout whenever it occurs, but at least we're doing something with it). A proper handling would be to log the error to a logging service or to MLflow.

```
def divide_list_safer(base, collection):
    output = []
    for i in collection:
        try:
            output.append(base / i)
        except ZeroDivisionError as e:
            print("Couldn't divide {} by {} due to {}".format(base, i, e))
    return output

safer = divide_list_safer(100, numbers)
> Couldn't divide 100 by 0 due to division by zero
len(safer)
> 99
```

Calling the function results in no thrown interruptible exceptions, but it does let us know what happened.

It dropped one of the elements (the zero integer), but processed the remaining 99 elements of the input list.

This introduces a new problem, though. We have the warning message that was generated, but it's printed to stdout. This doesn't help us in a production system where we will need, in order to troubleshoot issues, a historical record of the conditions under which this problem happened.

We will instead need to have a centralized place to see the details of the *what*, the *where*, and the *when* for the times that these issues happen. We also need to ensure that, at a minimum, we have a parse-able standard format for our logs that can reduce the time spent searching through log files to track down an issue.

10.4.3 Handling errors the right way

The following listing shows the final implementation of this exception-handling scenario, replete with a custom exception, logging, and control handling for the zero-division error.

Listing 10.13   **Final implementation with proper exception handling and logging**

Creates a custom exception class with the ability to inherit properties from the standard ValueError exception, as well as providing *args to allow another developer to extend or customize this exception class

These three lines are required only for Jupyter Notebook functionality. In an .egg file, you would simply instantiate a new logging instance (Jupyter, however, starts one for you when you initialize a session).

```
from importlib import reload
from datetime import datetime
import logging
import inspect

reload(logging)
log_file_name = 'ch9_01logs_{}.log'.format(datetime.now().date().strftime(
    '%Y-%m-%d'))
logging.basicConfig(filename=log_file_name, level=logging.INFO)

class CalculationError(ValueError):
    def __init__(self, message, pre, post, *args):
        self.message = message
        self.pre = pre
        self.post = post
        super(CalculationError, self).__init__(message, pre, post, *args)

def divide_values_better(base, collection):
    function_nm = inspect.currentframe().f_code.co_name
    output = []
    for i in collection:
        try:
            output.append(base / i)
        except ZeroDivisionError as e:
            logging.error(
                "{} -{}- Couldn't divide {} by {} due to {} in {}".format(
                    datetime.now(), type(e), base, i, e, function_nm)
            )
            output.append(0.0)
        except TypeError as e:
            logging.error(
                "{} -{}- Couldn't process the base value '{}' ({}) in {}".format(
```

Retrieves the current function name for logging purposes (prevents having to hand-type the name in multiple places)

Catches the divide-by-zero exception, logs it, and then provides a placeholder value

Catches the TypeError for mathematically invalid operations based on the data passed in

```
                    datetime.now(), type(e), base, e, function_nm)
            )
        raise e
    input_len = len(collection)
    output_len = len(output)
    if input_len != output_len:
        msg = "The return size of the collection does not match passed in
      collection size."
        e = CalculationError(msg, input_len, output_len)
        logging.error("{} {} Input: {} Output: {} in {}".format(
            datetime.now(), e.message, e.pre, e.post, function_nm
        ))
        raise e
    return output

placeholder = divide_values_better(100, numbers)
len(placeholder)
> 100
```

After logging the exception, we want to raise it manually so the function will alert a developer who is interfacing with it that they really should be passing a numeric type to this function for the base variable.

If the list sizes don't match, creates an object of our custom exception class

Logs our custom exception's details

Raises the custom exception

Gets the length of the input list "collection" and the post-for-loop length of the output list

Since we're replacing the failed zero-division error with 0.0 in the output list, our list lengths match (100).

Logs the TypeError exception before doing anything else (so we have visibility that it occurred)

At this point, when we run the function with either a valid collection (containing zero or not), we will get a log report of each instance that is replaced. When we call the function with invalid values, we will get an exception logged and also thrown (desirable behavior). Finally, when the lists don't match because of a future modification to this function (such as catching a new exception and not replacing a value or modifying the behavior of the logic), the person making those changes will be alerted in clear terms that their changes have introduced a bug.

The next listing shows the log results of running this on the original configuration for variable submission, testing an invalid string parameter being supplied as the base argument, and simulating the lengths not matching.

Listing 10.14 Logging results of caught and handled exceptions

```
def read_log(log_name):
    try:
        with open(log_name) as log:
            print(log.read())
    except FileNotFoundError as e:
        print("The log file is empty.")

read_log(log_file_name)
>
ERROR:root:2020-12-28 21:01:21.067276 -<class 'ZeroDivisionError'>- Couldn't
    divide 100 by 0 due to division by zero in divide_values_better
```

Very simple function to read in the log file

We're even handling the expected exception for the open() function so that if the log file hasn't been generated (because no issues occur with the usage of the function), we won't have a nasty exception thrown that isn't clear to the end user of the function. Instead, a simple explanation prints out that lets us know that the log hasn't been created yet.

The exception that we're expecting to get from passing in a collection list of integers containing the number 0

```
ERROR:root:2020-12-28 21:01:21.069412 The return size of the collection does
    not match passed in collection size. Input: 100 Output: 99 in
    divide_values_better
ERROR:root:2020-12-28 21:01:24.672938 -<class 'TypeError'>- Couldn't process
    the base value 'oops' (unsupported operand type(s) for /: 'str' and
    'int') in divide_values_better
```

The result of removing the "replace with 0.0" functionality in the catch block for handling the zero-division error

The logged result of passing in an invalid value as the base argument to the function (which would also throw an exception at runtime, but after having logged the exception into the log)

Logging even innocuous errors that may not seem important during development can be an invaluable tool for addressing issues in production. Whether you want to fix the root cause of nuisance issues or check on the health of a code base, without having logs and the appropriate data being written to them, you could be completely unaware of potential problems in your solution's code. When in doubt, log it out.

10.5 Use of global mutable objects

Continuing our exploration of our new team's existing code base, we're tackling another new feature to be added. This one adds completely new functionality. In the process of developing it, we realize that a large portion of the necessary logic for our branch already exists and we simply need to reuse a few methods and a function. What we fail to see is that the function uses a declaration of a globally scoped variable. When running our tests for our branch in isolation (through unit tests), everything works exactly as intended. However, the integration test of the entire code base produces a nonsensical result.

After hours of searching through the code, walking through debugging traces, we find that the state of the function that we were using actually changed from its first usage, and the global variable that the function was using actually changed, rendering our second use of it completely incorrect. We were burned by mutation.

10.5.1 How mutability can burn you

Recognizing how dangerous mutability is can be a bit tricky. Overuse of mutating values, shifting state, and overwriting of data can take many forms, but the end result is typically the same: an incredibly complicated series of bugs. These bugs can manifest themselves in different ways: *Heisenbugs* seemingly disappear when you're trying to investigate them, and *Mandelbugs* are so complex and nondeterministic that they seem to be as complex as a fractal. Refactoring code bases that are riddled with mutation is nontrivial, and many times it's simply easier to start over from scratch to fix the design flaws.

Issues with mutation and side effects typically don't rear their heads until long after the initial MVP of a project. Later, in the development process or after a production release, flawed code bases relying on mutability and side effects start to break apart at the seams. Figure 10.3 shows an example of the nuances between different languages and their execution environments and why mutability concerns might not be as apparent, depending on which languages you're familiar with.

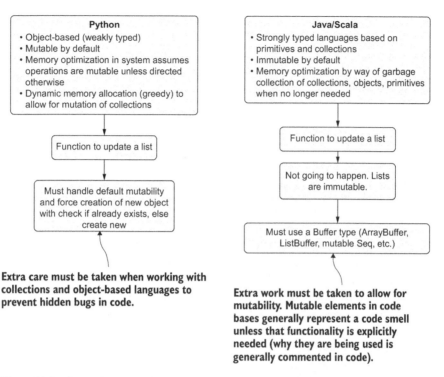

Figure 10.3 Comparing mutability in Python and JVM-based languages

For simplicity's sake, let's say that we're trying to keep track of some fields to include in separate vectors used in an ensemble modeling problem. The following listing shows a simple function that contains a default value within the function signature's parameters which, when used a single time, will provide the expected functionality.

Listing 10.15 An example utility function for maintaining a list of elements

Simple function for adding a list to a new list of elements
(not a realistic example for vector creation, but it's meant
to be simple for purposes of explanation)

Iterates through the supplied
list of elements and adds
to a new collection

```python
def features_to_add_to_vector(features, feature_collection=[]):
    [feature_collection.append(x) for x in features]
    return feature_collection
```

Returns the
new collection

The following is the output from a single use of this function. No real surprises here.

Listing 10.16 Usage of the simple listing function

```python
trial_1 = features_to_add_to_vector(['a', 'b', 'c'])
trial_1
> ['a', 'b', 'c']
```

Adds three string
elements into a new
collection by passing
it to our function

As expected, we have a list
containing those elements
that we passed in.

However, what happens when we call it a second time for an additional operation? The next listing shows this additional usage, including what the values are, but also what happens to the original variable declaration.

Listing 10.17   Object state mutation by repeated calls to our function

```
trial_2 = features_to_add_to_vector(['d', 'e', 'f'])     ◁──┐   Calls the function
trial_2                                                        again with a new list of
> ['a', 'b', 'c', 'd', 'e', 'f']   ◁──┐                        elements. We should
trial_1                                │  Uh, oh. The return still   expect the return to
 ▷ > ['a', 'b', 'c', 'd', 'e', 'f']    │  has values from when it    be ['d', 'e', 'f'], right?
                                       │  was called previously.
  And it updates the variable list from the   That's weird.
  first call that we made. This seems broken.
```

Now that's a bit unexpected, right? What if we were intending to build one model with fields a, b, and c, and then build another model with fields d, e, and f? Both of these models would have input vectors of all six columns. Utilizing mutation to override variables in this manner wouldn't break the project's code. Both models would execute without throwing exceptions. However, unless we validated everything very carefully, we would overlook that we just built two identically configured models.

Bugs like this are crippling to productivity. The time spent debugging to figure out why something doesn't work as intended can be large indeed; that's time that should be spent on building something new, instead of figuring out why our code doesn't work the way we intend.

All of this happens because Python functions are objects themselves. They maintain state, and as such, the language does not include the concept that the variables and operations that happen within them are isolable. Care must be taken, particularly when adding to code bases, that the original implementations are crafted in such a way so as not to introduce unexpected behavior (avoiding unintentional mutation, in this example).

The first and foremost goal when adding new functionality to a code base is to make sure that the code runs (exceptions aren't thrown). Correctness issues can arise if the changes are not validated, creating hard-to-diagnose bugs due to the inadvertent use of shortcuts such as unsafe mutation. How should we have written this code?

10.5.2 *Encapsulation to prevent mutable side effects*

By knowing that the Python functions maintain state (and everything is mutable in this language), we could have anticipated this behavior. Instead of applying a default argument to maintain isolation and break the object-mutation state, we should have initialized this function with a state that could be checked against.

By performing this simple state validation, we are letting the interpreter know that in order to satisfy the logic, a new object needs to be created to store the new list of values. The proper implementation for checking on instance state in Python for collection mutation is shown in the following listing.

Listing 10.18 A fixed implementation for the utility function

If nothing has been passed in to the feature_collection
argument, creates a new empty list (this triggers
Python to generate a new object in this case)

Changes the signature to default the second
argument to None instead of an empty list

```
def features_to_add_to_vector_updated(features, feature_collection=None):   ◄
    collection = feature_collection if feature_collection else list()
    [collection.append(x) for x in features]
    return collection
trial_1a = features_to_add_to_vector_updated(['a', 'b', 'c'])
trial_1a
> ['a', 'b', 'c']                                                          ◄
trial_2a = features_to_add_to_vector_updated(['d', 'e', 'f'])
trial_2a
> ['d', 'e', 'f']      ◄
trial_1a
> ['a', 'b', 'c']   ◄
```

As expected, we
get a new list with
the elements that
we passed in.

Now we get a new list with the repeated
call. This is the expected behavior.

The original variable has not been
changed with the reuse of the function.

Seemingly small issues like this can create endless headaches for the person (or team) implementing a project. Typically, these sorts of problems are developed early on, showing no issues while the modules are being built out. Even simple unit tests that validate this functionality in isolation will appear to be functioning correctly.

It is typically toward the midpoint of an MVP that issues involving mutability begin to rear their ugly heads. As greater complexity is built out, functions and classes may be utilized multiple times (which is a desired pattern in development), and if not implemented properly, what was seeming to work just fine before now results in difficult-to-troubleshoot bugs.

> **PRO TIP** It's best to become familiar with the way your development language handles objects, primitives, and collections. Knowing these core nuances of the language will give you the tools necessary to guide your development in a way that won't create more work and frustration for you throughout the process.

A note on encapsulation

Throughout this book, you'll see multiple references to me beating a dead horse about using functions in favor of declarative code. You'll also notice references to favoring classes and methods to functions. This is all due to the overwhelming benefits that come with using encapsulation (and abstraction, but that's another story discussed elsewhere in the text).

Encapsulating code has two primary benefits:

- Restricting end-user access to internal protected functionality, state, or data
- Enforcing execution of logic on a bundle of the data being passed in and the logic contained within the method

(continued)

While the first reason is largely inconsequential to the vast majority of data scientists (unless you're writing an open source project or utility libraries, or contributing to public-facing APIs), the second attribute of encapsulation can save ML practitioners no end of headaches. Through this bundling of data (the arguments of data being passed into a method) and the localized execution of logic upon that data, you can isolate behavior from other processes:

- A variable declared in a method is referenced only within that method.
- The only external-facing access that a method has to the outside world is in its return value.
- The operations that are performed cannot be influenced by the state of anything other than the arguments passed into it.

These attributes of encapsulation mean that you can ensure correctness of your code at any given time; for example, if you have a method whose sole purpose is to apply a sales tax offset to an item's price, you can pass in the item cost and the tax rate, and ensure that no matter what the underlying state of the system is external to that method, it's always just going to do one thing: apply a sales tax offset to the value passed in and return the adjusted value. These attributes also can help make your code more testable.

Encapsulation has many other benefits (particularly for ML work) that we will cover in part 3 of this book. For now, remember that mutability issues and the headaches that state management can bring can be completely removed by the proper application of encapsulation of data and logic through the use of functions and methods.

10.6 Excessively nested logic

Of all of the frequently coded parts of ML code bases, none bring more dread to those who must read and debug them than a large conditional logic tree. Most start relatively simply early in their utilization: a few if statements, a handful of elif, followed by a small number of catchall else statements. By the time the code has been in production for a few months, these monoliths of headache-inducing logic can span hundreds (if not thousands) of lines. These business logic rules generally evolve into a multilevel mess of complicated, confusing, and nearly impossible-to-maintain logic.

As an example, let's look at a frequent use case in the ML world: ensembles. Let's say that we have two models, and each is generating a probability per customer. Let's start with generating that dataset to represent the outputs of these two models.

Listing 10.19   Generating our synthetic probability data for the ensemble reconciliation

```
import random
def generate_scores(number, seed=42):
    def get_random():
        return random.uniform(0.0, 1.0)
    random.seed(seed)
```

Encapsulating function for generating our data

An encapsulated inner function that will have reference to the seed state of the random() function

Generates a random number based on the seed state supplied to random, using the uniform distribution between 0.0 and 1.0

```
        return [(get_random(), get_random()) for x in range(number)]
    generated_probabilities = generate_scores(100)
  > [(0.6394267984578837, 0.025010755222666936),
      (0.27502931836911926, 0.22321073814882275),
      (0.7364712141640124, 0.6766994874229113)]...
```

The synthetic data

Generates a tuple with our two simulated probabilities and iterates over number times to create a list of tuples

Now that we have some data generated, let's pretend that the business wants five levels of classification based on these different probabilities, combining their bucketed values into a single representative score.

Since Python doesn't (currently, as of Python 3.9) have switch (case) statements available to it, the approach to create this evaluated consolidated score might look something like the following.

Listing 10.20 Consolidation logic by way of `if`, `elif`, and `else` statements

```
def master_score(prob1, prob2):
    if prob1 < 0.2:
        if prob2 < 0.2:
            return (0, (prob1, prob2))
        elif prob2 < 0.4:
            return (1, (prob1, prob2))
        elif prob2 < 0.6:
            return (2, (prob1, prob2))
        elif prob2 < 0.8:
            return (3, (prob1, prob2))
        else:
            return (4, (prob1, prob2))
    elif prob1 < 0.4:
        if prob2 < 0.2:
            return (1, (prob1, prob2))
        elif prob2 < 0.4:
            return (2, (prob1, prob2))
        elif prob2 < 0.6:
            return (3, (prob1, prob2))
        elif prob2 < 0.8:
            return (4, (prob1, prob2))
        else:
            return (5, (prob1, prob2))
    elif prob1 < 0.6:
        if prob2 < 0.2:
            return (2, (prob1, prob2))
        elif prob2 < 0.4:
            return (3, (prob1, prob2))
        elif prob2 < 0.6:
            return (4, (prob1, prob2))
        elif prob2 < 0.8:
            return (5, (prob1, prob2))
        else:
            return (6, (prob1, prob2))
    elif prob1 < 0.8:
        if prob2 < 0.2:
            return (3, (prob1, prob2))
```

Function for processing the pair combination of two probabilities and resolving them through nested conditional logic

The nested logic structure (if first probability is less than 0.2, check conditions of second probability)

```
            elif prob2 < 0.4:
                return (4, (prob1, prob2))
            elif prob2 < 0.6:
                return (5, (prob1, prob2))
            elif prob2 < 0.8:
                return (6, (prob1, prob2))
            else:
                return (7, (prob1, prob2))
        else:
            if prob2 < 0.2:
                return (4, (prob1, prob2))
            elif prob2 < 0.4:
                return (5, (prob1, prob2))
            elif prob2 < 0.6:
                return (6, (prob1, prob2))
            elif prob2 < 0.8:
                return (7, (prob1, prob2))
            else:
                return (8, (prob1, prob2))
```

The caller function for evaluating the collection of paired tuples of probability values

```
def apply_scores(probabilities):
    final_scores = []
    for i in probabilities:
        final_scores.append(master_score(i[0], i[1]))
    return final_scores
scored_data = apply_scores(generated_probabilities)
scored_data
> [(3, (0.6394267984578837, 0.025010755222666936)),
   (2, (0.27502931836911926, 0.22321073814882275)),
   (6, (0.7364712141640124, 0.6766994874229113))]...
```

Calls the evaluation function for resolving the probabilities to a single score

Calls the function on the score data

First three elements of the resolved scores based on the conditional logic

This hierarchical logic chain is written out as a series of if, elif, and else statements. It's both difficult to read and would be a nightmare to maintain with additional real-world conditional logic embedded.

What would the experience be like if this needed to be modified? The person working on that ticket would have to meticulously read through this wall of conditional logic and make sure that each place is updated correctly. For this example, it's not overly onerous because of its simplicity, but in code bases that I've seen, the logic for business rules is rarely so simple and straightforward. Instead, nested conditional statements with and and or are typically within the conditional checks, further making this approach incredibly complicated.

If this approach were given to a traditional software developer, they would likely approach this problem in a completely different way: utilizing configuration structures to isolate the business logic from the processing of the consolidation of the scores. The next listing shows such a pattern.

> **Listing 10.21   A dictionary-based configuration approach to handling business logic**

```
threshold_dict = {
    '<0.2': 'low',
    '<0.4': 'low_med',
```

A lookup dictionary for removing the mapping logic from the processing logic (in an actual code base, these dictionaries would be in a different module from the processing logic that follows)

```
        '<0.6': 'med',
        '<0.8': 'med_high',
        '<1.0': 'high'
    }
    match_dict = {                    ◄──────   A resolver dictionary for converting
        ('low', 'low'): 0,                       the paired probability bucketed
        ('low', 'low_med'): 1,                   thresholds to a single score
        ('low', 'med'): 2,
        ('low', 'med_high'): 3,
        ('low', 'high'): 4,
        ('low_med', 'low'): 1,
        ('low_med', 'low_med'): 2,
        ('low_med', 'med'): 3,
        ('low_med', 'med_high'): 4,
        ('low_med', 'high'): 5,
        ('med', 'low'): 2,
        ('med', 'low_med'): 3,
        ('med', 'med'): 4,
        ('med', 'med_high'): 5,
        ('med', 'high'): 6,
        ('med_high', 'low'): 3,
        ('med_high', 'low_med'): 4,
        ('med_high', 'med'): 5,
        ('med_high', 'med_high'): 6,
        ('med_high', 'high'): 7,
        ('high', 'low'): 4,
        ('high', 'low_med'): 5,
        ('high', 'med'): 6,
        ('high', 'med_high'): 7,          Function for processing a
        ('high', 'high'): 8               single probability and mapping
    }                                     its value to a threshold bucket
    def adjudicate_individual(value):    ◄──┘
        if value < 0.2: return threshold_dict['<0.2']
        elif value < 0.4: return threshold_dict['<0.4']
        elif value < 0.6: return threshold_dict['<0.6']    Function for looking up and
        elif value < 0.8: return threshold_dict['<0.8']    evaluating the tuple of paired
        else: return threshold_dict['<1.0']                probabilities against the
    def adjudicate_pair(pair):                       ◄──   matching dictionary
        return match_dict[(adjudicate_individual(pair[0]),
            adjudicate_individual(pair[1]))]               Function for
    def evaluate_raw_scores(scores):           ◄───────    iterating through
        return [(adjudicate_pair(x), x) for x in scores]   each tuple in the
    dev_way = evaluate_raw_scores(generated_probabilities)  ◄──  total score set and
    dev_way                                                      applying the
    > [(3, (0.6394267984578837, 0.025010755222666936)),         resolution logic
      (2, (0.27502931836911926, 0.22321073814882275)),
      (6, (0.7364712141640124, 0.6766994874229113))]...     Calls the main function
                                                            for resolving the
                                                            probabilities to scores
```

First three
elements of
the data

While this approach is far easier to read than that of the earlier implementation from listing 10.20, it's still far from ideal. Let's suppose that, during the development of the project's solution, a decision was made to increase the number of models generating probability scores from two to eight.

How would this affect either of these two structures? The next listing illustrates how many lines of code we would have to write for eight models to resolve to a single score for both of these implementation patterns.

> **Listing 10.22   A function to calculate just how many lines of code we'd have to write**

A fun little function to calculate how many lines of code we'd have to write for the if, elif, else pattern

```
import math
def how_many_terrible_lines(levels):
    return ((5**levels) * 2) + math.factorial(levels)
how_many_terrible_lines(8)
> 821570
```

A very scary number! This is just not realistic to attempt.

Clearly, this isn't an option. Even if we were to attempt to use this method (the "dev way" with configuration dictionaries to handle the mappings), if we tried eight probabilities to merge into a single score, we'd have 32,768 conditions to create within the tuple-8 key for the dictionary. That's just a truly ridiculous number of lines of configuration to write.

A note on sticking with a poor design pattern

While the example of the `if/elif/else` pattern may seem a bit ridiculous to some readers, I've found it to be the most common approach in ML code bases that I've seen in the wild. The dictionary approach may also seem a bit ridiculous when thinking of how many permutations for a configuration control structure might be created when we're talking about eight different elements.

This example isn't intended to be hyperbolic. I've seen similar configuration files, with dictionaries that are well in excess of 10,000 keys to handle logic like this. Most of these are not hand-typed (that would be ridiculous), but rather are a result of machine-generated code and some copying and pasting into an IDE.

The problem isn't that there are tens of thousands of keys; Python hash tables can easily handle without too much hassle a unique key identifier count of 2^{26} before performance becomes a bottleneck in the lookup function (67,108,864 entries). Python can handle it. Your keyboard and your peers can't.

The real problem exposed with approaching business logic or feature-engineering work in this way is that it's even attempted in the first place. Approaching problems like this with the `if/elif/else` pattern or the dictionary pattern is akin to the old adage, "When all you have is a hammer, everything looks like a nail." There are better ways of solving problems like this that break a complex logical pattern into smaller, more manageable pieces.

If you ever find yourself having to copy and paste large chunks of logic over and over again, it's best to walk away from the keyboard, think about how to solve it more efficiently, and then return to test out some theories that can help not only save your code base from becoming an unmanageable mess, but also make it easier to modify and troubleshoot in the future.

Listing 10.23 shows a much better approach to this problem. In this block of code, we're going to adapt the data generator to support an arbitrary number of probabilities as part of the model return tuple, and then convert the lookup function from a dictionary to a direct mathematical representation of the scores. From this point, the code reduces the complexity to a much more manageable state, allowing easier resolution of the business rules by scaling, mapping to a new resolved score, and creating a code base that can be easily modified in the future.

Listing 10.23   A better solution that effortlessly scales

Generates a tuple-8 collection of probabilities to resolve to a single score

```
def generate_scores_updated(number, elements, seed=42):          ◁──  Function to generate
    def get_random():                                                 an arbitrary number of
        return random.uniform(0.0, 1.0)                               elements within each tuple
    random.seed(seed)
    return [tuple(get_random() for y in range(elements)) for x in range(number)]
larger_probabilities = generate_scores_updated(100, 8)
larger_probabilities
```

Example of the first tuple-8 generated

```
> [(0.6394267984578837, 0.025010755222666936, 0.27502931836911926,
    0.22321073814882275, 0.7364712141640124, 0.6766994874229113,
    0.8921795677048454, 0.08693883262941615), ...
def updated_adjudication(value):         ◁──   Adapts the score-resolving function to
    if value < 0.2: return 0                    mathematical bucketing. To return the space of
    elif value < 0.4: return 1                  this value to the range of the original 2-tuple
    elif value < 0.6: return 2                  ensemble design would be as trivial as creating
    elif value < 0.8: return 3                  a ceiling or floor function on the sum of the
    else: return 4                              values, divided by half of the tuple length.
def score_larger(scores):
    return sum(updated_adjudication(x) for x in scores)
def evaluate_larger_scores(probs):
    return [(score_larger(x), x) for x in probs]
simpler_solution = evaluate_larger_scores(larger_probabilities)
simpler_solution
> [(15, (0.6394267984578837, 0.025010755222666936, 0.27502931836911926,
    0.22321073814882275, 0.7364712141640124, 0.6766994874229113,
    0.8921795677048454, 0.08693883262941615)),
   (10, (0.4219218196852704, 0.029797219438070344, 0.21863797480360336,...
```

Function that sums the resolved scores of the buckets for each element within the probability tuple

Sample of a portion of the first two elements of the score resolver

The main function that iterates over the collection of all the tuple probabilities

We've solved the scalability and complexity problem in a small number of code lines. We've reduced the complexity (getting rid of dictionaries, mappings, and chained logic) and made the code much simpler. The pursuit of simplicity when writing code should always be the goal of any developer, particularly one who has to deal with the breadth of DS work.

Learning more, and the most frequent question I get asked

By far, the most frequent question I get asked by junior DS people is, "How can I get better at learning all this software development stuff?" It's a valid question. However, it's typically a rather misguided one.

Software development for ML is very, very different from pure software development. It's a laser-focused microcosm of all the elements that a developer will need to know, focused more on creating maintainable and stable code that performs the functions required of DS work. Certainly, common ground with pure software development fundamentals exists. Knowing the basics of good software design, abstraction, encapsulation, comprehension, inheritance, and polymorphism are critical to being successful as an ML engineer and as a developer. However, the similarities begin to diverge after these fundamentals.

What I try to tell junior data scientists when they ask this question is that they don't need to become a seasoned DS as well as a seasoned developer. That's simply untenable (akin to mastering two separate professions simultaneously) for the vast majority of people.

The constructive answer that I give them is rather open-ended, though. It's all about how much they want to know beyond the fundamentals and the specific skills needed to become a well-rounded ML engineer.

Software development skills aren't something that you *just learn.* You won't gain them from reading this book, or any other. You're also not going to learn them by taking an expensive class or scanning through repositories on the internet. These skills are learned by deliberately taking time to focus on new ways of solving problems with code while referring to how others who are more skilled than you have solved them in the past. They're learned by failing, rewriting, learning from your mistakes, testing, and working to creating code that breaks less frequently than the code you wrote last week. It is a *journey*—one that, in my opinion, is worthwhile.

The issues covered in this chapter are merely things that I see a lot of data scientists do in their code that cause their code to be complicated and hard to troubleshoot. These topics are most certainly not an exhaustive list, but rather a group of examples to help you to think about why certain code that you write might be challenging for you or others to troubleshoot, maintain, or even explain.

There's a reason that they call programming interfaces *languages.* As with any language that you learn, basic syntax rules, grammar, and structural components need to be understood and adhered to in order to make your thoughts and intentions understood by others. Some of the nuances of programming languages share those of spoken and written languages as well. There are well-crafted examples of perfect syntax, and there are also shorthand "slang" compositions that are unintelligible to all but a small inner circle of those in the know.

It's never a good idea to write code like you're texting a friend with an inside joke, just as it's not advisable to speak in that manner when at a job interview. Without the knowledge and standards of a language, though, even well-intentioned developers who are ignorant of such standards will produce code that is as unintelligible as a first-week student non-native speaker of a language, or, more damaging, as unrefined and amateurish as someone who delivers a speech in internet shorthand memetic idioms.

Once moving past the point of learning those foundational concepts (and the first language is the hardest to learn, for what it's worth), a vast gulf separates basic competency and artful mastery.

I like to think of *mastery* of a language as a corollary to comparing different authors writing poetry and prose. At the beginning, after learning the basics, your code may be at, perhaps, a children's book level. There are sentences, to be sure, and a plot, but a Pulitzer Prize is likely not in the cards. However, with time, practice, and fixing a lot of mistakes, eventually you'll get to the point where you're writing ML solutions that have all of the refinement and nuance of a David Foster Wallace novel.

The process of getting better with coding takes time. A lot of it. It is fraught with so many errors and frustrations that it may seem as though you'll never get very good at it. However, like anything else that you've learned to be good at, you'll eventually find that at some point, things become easier. The basic implementations that you struggled with in the past will become so commonplace and easy to do "perfectly" that you may not realize the gains that you've made. It all comes down to learning and practicing.

Summary

- Being able to identify common problematic implementation patterns (code smells) can help create a more legible, easier-to-debug, and extensible ML code base.
- Simplifying implementations in order to enhance legibility and reduce the cognitive burden of understanding how a code base functions is time well spent.
- Currying data with standard structures dramatically reduces the amount of refactoring needed to extend a code base, as well as reducing the complexity of troubleshooting failures.
- Safe applications of try/catch (exception handling) will create a more production-stable code base. Ensuring that only specific exceptions are caught will aid in investigating issues in production.
- Side effects and improper use of global variables can create potential deterministic problems in a code base. Knowing when to use them effectively and never to use them outside of those few required times can enhance code resiliency.
- Even if the logical process to execute intended behavior could lend itself to nested and complex recursive behavior, trying to refactor this logic into something more understandable should be a priority in ML code bases.

Model measurement and why it's so important

This chapter covers

- Methodologies for determining the impact of a model
- A/B testing approaches for attribution data collection

In part 1, we focused on aligning ML project work to business problems. This is, after all, the most critical aspect for making the solution viable. While those earlier chapters focused on communication before, during, and immediately up to a production release, this chapter focuses on the project communication *after release*. We'll cover how to present, discuss, and accurately report on the long-term health of ML projects—specifically, in language and methodologies that the business will understand.

Discussions about model performance are complex. While the business is focusing on measurable attributes of business performance, the ML team is focused on measurements of model efficacy as it relates to strength of correlation to a target variable. Even though a language barrier is implicitly defined in these differing goals, a solution is available. By focusing communications to the business around its metrics, you can answer the question the business leaders really want answered: "How is this solution helping the company?" Ensuring that analytics are performed on those business metrics that the internal customer really cares about, a DS team can avoid the situation that figure 11.1 illustrates.

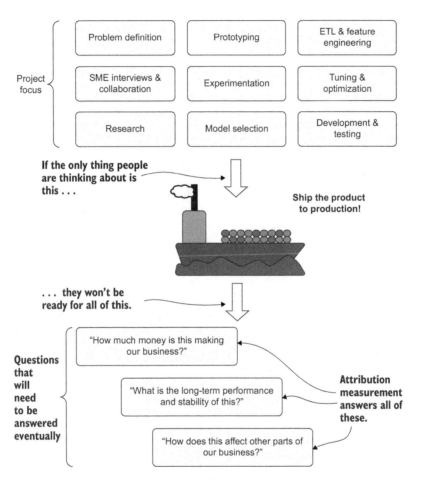

Figure 11.1 ML project myopia

This ML team has project myopia. By focusing on their own requirements in order to get a solid solution into production, the ML team members are ill-prepared to answer their customer's inevitable questions. Showing correlation metrics, after all, will mean absolutely nothing to the customer. Nor should it.

The solution to this problem is available. It involves a bit of work outside the core solution development code, but it is well worth it to keep the business involved and informed about the status of the project. It all starts with measuring those business attributes.

11.1 Measuring model attribution

We're moving on to ice cream. Specifically, we're a group of DSs working at an ice cream company. A few months ago, the sales and marketing teams approached us, asking for a model that will help identify when to send coupons to customers to increase the chance of them seeing those coupons in their inboxes. The marketing group's standard behavior is to send out a bulk mailing every Monday morning at 8 a.m. Our project aims to generate a day-and-hour combination to send the emails out on an individualized (personalized) basis.

The top of figure 11.2 shows the components and examples of our prior state. The bottom of the figure shows what the model output fashions as part of an image component generator, personalized to each of our members.

We've built this MVP and have shown some promising results based on our shadow runs. Through tracking our pixel data (a 1 × 1 pixel embedded in our emailed coupon codes that show the open and click rates for our marketing ads), we're finding shockingly accurate results from our model based on our monitoring of actual open and usage rates of our coupons.

While this news is exciting, the business isn't convinced by our delta error in minutes from prediction to actual opening time of the emails. What they really want to know is this: "Does this increase sales?" To begin to answer that question, we should analyze that metric, shown in figure 11.3.

How can we determine whether a causal relationship exists between sending targeted coupons to customers at times that they are most likely to see the coupons, and the customers' use of those coupons? It all begins with determining what to measure, who to measure it on, and what tools to utilize to determine if the model has a causal influence.

11.1.1 Measuring prediction performance

The first step that we need to think about in measuring our model's performance is the same as we would engage in for any design of experiments (DOE) exercise. We start by talking to the experts who engage in the email marketing campaigns (our internal customers for this project) well before the production release date of our solution. This team, after all, has a fundamentally deep understanding of both our customers and their interactions with our product line.

During these discussions, we'll want to focus on the marketing team's knowledge of our customer. That deep understanding of the customer base will aid us in determining which data that we collect about them can be used to limit the latent effects in order to minimize variance in our results. Table 11.1 shows the conjectures that the SME groups and the DS team have, along with the results of the analysis.

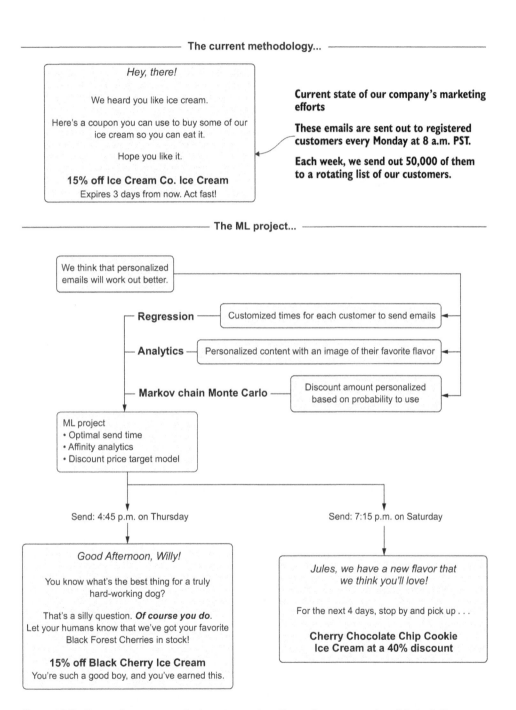

Figure 11.2 For our ice cream project, we have a baseline and a new experiment to test. How can we measure its success?

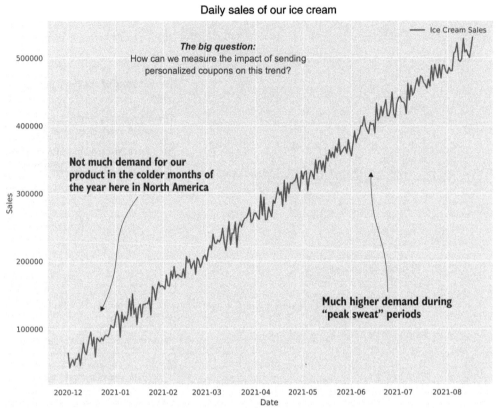

Figure 11.3   Sales: the real target metric for our model

Table 11.1   Hypothesized differentiators vs. actual prior evidence in our data

Hypothesis	Significant?	Stratification candidate?
Customers in hotter climates buy more ice cream.	No	No
Customers who live in rural areas buy more.	Yes	Maybe*
Customers over the age of 30 buy more.	No	Maybe*
Customers who open emails buy more.	Yes	Yes
Customers who have a long history with us buy more.	Yes	Maybe**
Customers with children buy more.	Yes	No***

* Possibility of introducing massive skew in our analysis. Potentially high-risk stratification value.
** Could be combined with purchase amount and recency of purchases.
*** Insufficient data and potentially hard to keep track of.

The analytical process of evaluating different customer base groupings on our historical data will help isolate behavior patterns to minimize within-group variance. Figure 11.4 illustrates what we're going to be doing with the optimal stratification methodology that we found in our analytical tests.

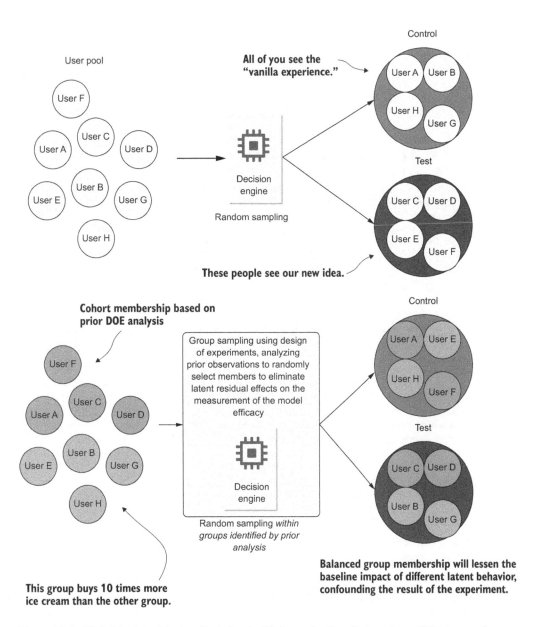

Figure 11.4 Minimizing latent factor effects by stratified grouping in order to reduce within-group variance

We know that we need to minimize the latent variable effects that are causing behavior imbalance. We can't get the data that conclusively identifies the behaviors that we're seeing (multimodality), but we certainly can improve our attribution if we control for it. But how can we do that? How do we group our users most effectively?

Based on our discussions with the SME group, we set about analyzing approaches that can reduce the inherent variability within our population. By listening to the marketing team, we find that its tried-and-true methodology for evaluating customer cohorts is the most optimal solution. By combining the recency of purchases, the number of historical purchases, and the total amount of spending sent our way by customers, we can define a standard metric to classify our cohorts (see the following sidebar regarding RFM for the power of this segmentation technique).

RFM: A great way to group humans if you're selling things to them

RFM, an acronym for *recency, frequency, and monetary value*, is a direct marketing term coined by Jan Roelf Bult and Tom Wansbeek. In their article "Optimal Selection for Direct Mail," they postulated RFM as a significantly powerful means of assigning value to customers. The pair estimated that 80% of a company's revenue actually comes from 20% of its customers.

While prescient in the extreme, the success of this methodology has been proven time and again in many industries (not relegated to only business-to-consumer companies, either). The principal concept is to define five quantile-based buckets of customers on each of these three observational variables. Customers with a high value in monetary value, for instance, would be the top 20% of spenders, receiving a value of 5 for M. Customers with a low value in frequency (the number of total purchases over the lifetime of the account), typically consisting of one-time purchasers, would have an F value of 1.

When combined, RFM values create a matrix of 125 elements ranging from the lowest-value customer (111) to the highest-value (555) customer. Applying business-specific and industry-specific meta-groupings atop these raw 125 matrix entry values allows for a company (and a DS team) to have points of latent-variable-lessening stratification points for the purposes of hypothesis testing.

I once was a bit incredulous at this technique of grouping human behavior in such a simplistic way—until I analyzed it for a third time at a third company. I'm now a pretty firm believer in this seemingly simplistic but wondrously powerful technique.

Using our RFM calculation to generate customer cohorts is shown in figure 11.5.

This RFM example isn't exclusive to humans (or dogs, for that matter). In the percentile analysis of our customer base, we run the gamut from the most valuable (555, having very recent purchases, frequent historical purchases, and high spending over their lifetime) to the least valuable (111, the inversion of the preceding). This gives us the ability to generally estimate the massive number of latent factors that influence customer behavior. This, in turn, gives us the ability to stratify when doing analyses to

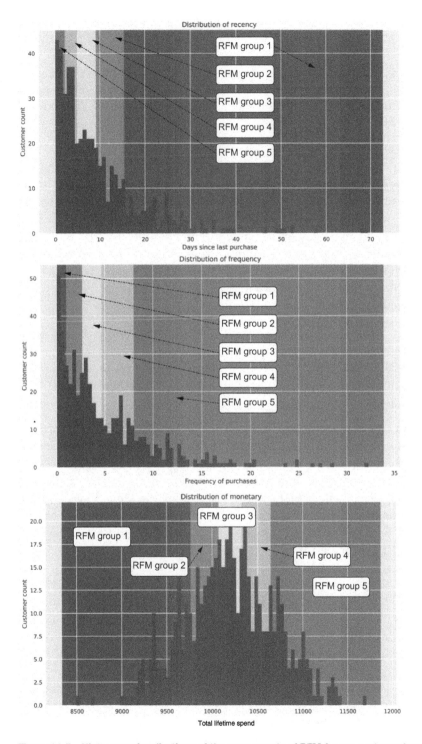

Figure 11.5 Histogram visualizations of the components of RFM for our customer base

ensure that we're exposing tests to relatively uniform groups of people who behave similarly. It allows us to reduce variance through controlling our experiments.

> **THOUGHT EXERCISE** If we did population sampling and 90% of the 555 members were selected into the control, while only 10% were in testing, what would the results of a causation validation be for our model? We would likely conclude that our model isn't very good, which would be misleading. Conversely, what dangers does the opposite situation pose?

While the 125 combinations of RFM that occur from these three attributes are interesting, they're not particularly helpful for analyzing our model's performance as it relates to the business metrics of concern. With a collaborative effort from the marketing SMEs, we're able to collapse these 125 groups into three primary meta-groups for our analysis: the high-value, medium-value, and low-value groups.

This results in a general separation of our customer base, shown in figure 11.6. The charts show a clear separation of each component's contribution to our baseline revenue, the statistical significance in these differences, and a winning formula for us to use when engaging in hypothesis testing.

> **NOTE** For further information about how these plots are generated (and the code), the statistical packages within Python that are employed to get these significance values, and the data generators involved, please see the companion code base to this book on GitHub at https://github.com/BenWilson2/ML-Engineering.

WHY CAN'T I JUST USE MY SCORING METRICS TO TELL HOW WELL THE MODEL IS DOING?

Let's temporarily set aside the fact that the business is likely not familiar with the concept of prediction error metrics that we use for estimating the goodness of fit of our models. The primary reason that we can't just use the scoring metrics to indicate how well the model is doing is that we aren't evaluating the same things when we're measuring business influence. Regardless of how well our models perform against holdout validation data, the metric performance is simply not guaranteed to have an effect on the targeted goal of any project.

It may seem as though we have completely solved a problem based on looking at metric performance against holdout data. However, claiming victory for an entire project solution based on these metrics is a bit preemptive and highly misleading. The problem with using correlation scores to estimate the quality of our models is that collected features don't encompass all of the factors that influence an outcome.

We are, in the process of generating a feature vector, looking to optimize the correlation of our observations to the response variable. We can never really be certain that the predictions will do anything at all to influence what we're trying to influence because of this fact.

For our scenario, the only way to determine influential effect of the predictions is to use *hypothesis testing*, measuring the revenue impact between those who see the

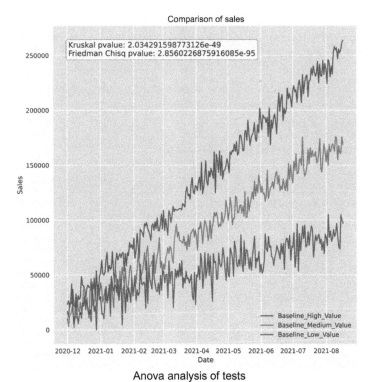

Figure 11.6 Analyzing homogeneity among the three meta-groups that we defined as part of our RFM calculations collectively with the marketing SME group

model's output and those who do not. The difference in revenue between these sample populations can give us confidence that our model has a probabilistic effect when applied to the entire population.

Before we get into a larger discussion of why this is (correlation versus causation), let's look at some differences in common supervised learning problems: ML metric scores compared to what a business metric for that same project would look like. Table 11.2 gives a few examples.

Table 11.2 Examples of project metrics vs. business metrics

Project	ML metric	Business metric
Fraud detection	Area under PR, area under ROC, F1	Fraud loss dollars, number of fraud investigations
Churn prediction	Area under PR, area under ROC, F1	Recency of purchases, login events for high-churn risk
Sales forecasting	AIC, BIC, RMSE, etc.	Revenue
Sentiment analysis	BLEURT, BERTScore	Number of users of tool, engagement rate
Ice cream coupons	MAE, MSE, RMSE	Revenue, coupon usage

This focus aligns the DS team's perspective on what matters to the business, rather than solely on applicable loss metrics. While loss metrics are incredibly important for training, the possibility exists that an optimized loss metric (particularly in the case of an optimization to a spurious correlation within the dataset) does not equate to favorable conditions in the target business metric. Utilizing both the loss metrics and the business metrics throughout the lifetime of an ML-powered project will greatly reduce the risk of not meeting business expectations.

The most important point to remember in presenting evidentiary results to the business at large is to never conflate the ideas of correlation and causation. Allowing people to infer causality from your results is a slippery slope to traverse. This becomes only more dangerous if the metrics being monitored are company-wide critical attributes such as revenue.

An A/B test can provide an evidence-based determination of a model's impact based on observed differences in behavior, but that's as far as you can go with making a declaration. It's never a certainty. The best thing to do is to never allude to the correlation-based features of the model or the grouping characteristics utilized in a stratified analysis as being the actual cause of a driving force. We simply just don't have the whole picture to make such claims.

A note on ML metrics

I would be remiss if I didn't clarify that I don't have any problem with ML metrics. They're incredibly useful, absolutely critical for the proper construction of models, and provide a wealth of information regarding the empirical quality of the correlation-focused predictions we're able to do. If anything, I generally find myself collecting too many of them throughout the process of building a solution. (I'm a "just in case" sort of mathematical hoarder.)

That being said, ML metrics are utterly useless to a business unit. They're irrelevant to internal and external customers.

They don't guarantee that you're going to be solving the problem that you're trying to solve. They are, by virtue of their design and purpose, nothing more than an informative tool to gauge the relative quality of how well you can match a target, provided the limited amount of data that you collect about reality.

What I'm arguing in this chapter (and, generally, in many parts of the book) is that our focus should always be on the end state. We, as ML practitioners, should be focused on what it is that we're building—not in the sense of which algorithms we're using, which statistical models we're employing, or in how elegant and clever our feature-engineering work is. The model and all of its supporting infrastructure and data feeds is employed to solve a problem.

Any project that is tackled by a DS team has intrinsic measurable qualities. If the project didn't, the chances that it will go beyond the experimentation phase is rather limited. The underlying problem being solved in any project has its own metrics that are generally defined by the team requesting that the DS team solve the problem.

Are we trying to increase sales? Then measure revenue, units sold, customer retention, repeat purchases, and length of sessions.

Are we trying to increase viewing of our content? Then measure percentage watched, time on platform, repeat visits, and consumption of recommendations.

Are we trying to detect fraud? Then measure successful identification rates, loss reduction, and customer satisfaction rates.

Are we predicting equipment failure? Then measure post hoc equipment-inspection health checks, catastrophic repair-cost levels, and equipment replacement spending.

The project's directive includes a certain aspect of the business that has been measured and that is being closely scrutinized to warrant devoting the DS team's efforts at fixing. The expectation from the business is that the application of ML will make things better.

If you're not measuring whether you're making things better, but instead using as justification of the predictive power of your implementation some esoteric statistical measure of correlation quality, you're doing yourself and your team a disservice.

Keep the project's terms in the metrics that the business is familiar with—the very reason the business leaders picked up that phone and gave you a ring about potentially being a hero for them. This focus will increase their faith in your team's abilities, keep the team honest about the project's impact on the business, and help everyone clearly recognize when things are no longer going as well as they once were (and, as you will see in the next section, this is an inevitability).

11.1.2 *Clarifying correlation vs. causation*

An important part of presenting model results to a business unit is to be clear about the differences between correlation and causation. If there is even a slight chance of business leaders inferring a causal relationship from anything that you are showing them, it's best to have this chat.

Correlation is simply the relationship or association that observed variables have to one another. It does not imply any meaning apart from the existence of this relationship. This concept is inherently counterintuitive to laypersons who are not involved in analyzing data. Making reductionist conclusions that "seem to make sense" about the data relationships in an analysis is effectively how our brains are wired.

For example, we could collect sales data for ice cream trucks and sales of mittens, both aggregated by week of year and country. We could calculate a strong negative correlation between the two (ice cream sales go up as mitten sales increase, and vice versa). Most people would chuckle at a conclusion of causality: "Well, if we want to sell more ice cream, we need to reduce our supply of mittens!"

What a layperson might instantly state from such a silly example is, "Well, people buy mittens when it's cold and ice cream when it's hot." This is an attempt at defining causation. Based on this negative correlation in the observed data, we definitely can't make such an inference regarding causation. We have no way of knowing what actually influenced the effect of purchasing ice cream or mittens on an individual basis (per observation).

If we were to introduce an additional confounding variable to this analysis (outside temperature), we might find additional confirmation of our spurious conclusion. However, this ignores the complexity of what drives decisions to purchase. As an example, see figure 11.7.

It's clear that a relationship is present. As temperature increases, ice cream sales increase as well. The relationship being exhibited is fairly strong. But can we infer anything other than the fact that there is a relationship?

Let's look at another plot. Figure 11.8 shows an additional observational data point that we could put into a model to aid in predicting whether someone might want to buy our ice cream.

With the cloud cover plotted against sales, we're getting an even stronger correlation than with temperature. What does this tell us? It simply says that a strong relationship (correlation) exists between these observed variables. We can't infer anything other than that. We most certainly can't make a logical leap of saying that high-temperature, cloudless days will guarantee ice cream purchases. Temperature and cloud cover certainly seem to have an influential effect on the purchase rate, but we can't definitively say that these are the causes of the choice to either purchase or not purchase our ice cream.

In the world of ML models, we're dealing with optimizing a cost function among the relationships of observed variables to achieve the best reasonable estimate of (a) prediction variable(s) based on the data that we have. This does not, under any circumstances, imply causation.

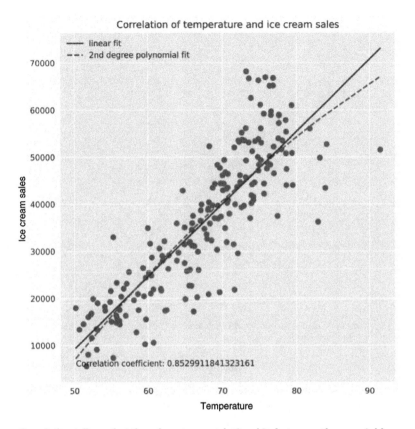

Correlation tells us that there is a *strong relationship between these variables.*

It doesn't tell us that one *causes* the other, though.

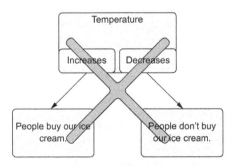

Figure 11.7 Correlation doesn't imply causal associations.

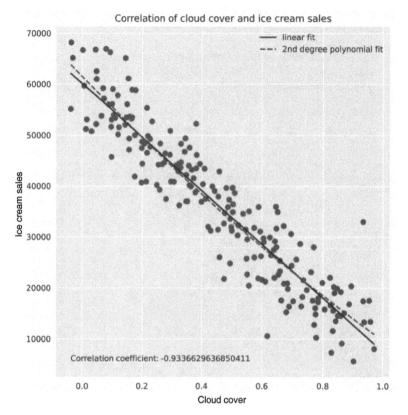

What if we analyzed cloud coverage percentage by ice cream sales and found an even stronger correlation?

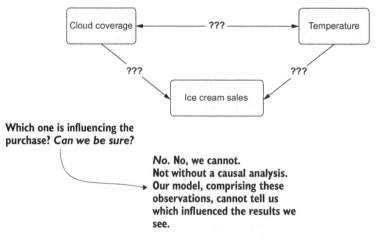

Figure 11.8 A confounding correlation, when we think of the relationship of temperature to sales. Which one is driving the sales? Is it the temperature or the cloud cover? Is it a mixed effect?

There's a simple reason for this: we're not omnipotent. We simply don't capture all of the reasons a decision is made. Since we're not observing *all* of the reasons, our model is certainly ignorant of them as well. If we were able to capture all of the influences, we would all be out of a job as data scientists anyway, as people would be able to directly state expected outcomes with flawless precision and near-zero uncertainty.

Let's imagine that we're trying to figure out whether someone is going to purchase ice cream. Figure 11.9 shows a composite of influencing factors that may drive

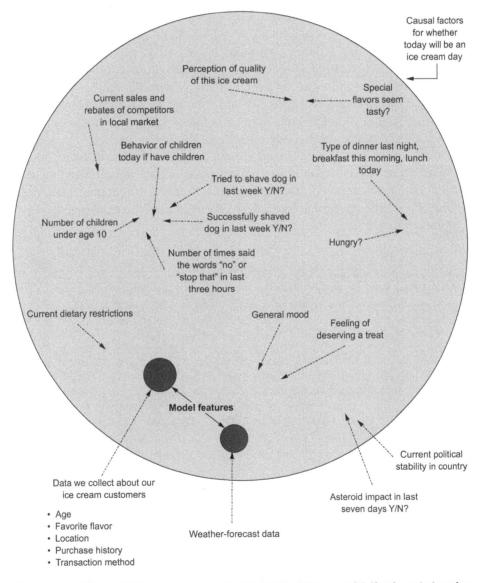

Figure 11.9 **The sea of influences to events that is unknowable to a model. If we're not observing all of those elements, we can't ever imply causation; we simply *don't have all of the information.***

someone's decision to purchase our product. In this vast sea of reasons, we are collecting a limited amount of data about this person. For the other influences that could be affecting the decision to buy, we simply can't collect this information. The model likely wouldn't be very generalizable if we did collect all of that information. We'd be crippled by the curse of dimensionality, and to make a useful model from this many features would require many billions of rows of data to be even remotely accurate.

It's always best to not attempt to assign a causal relationship to any ML model's results. Remember, we're dealing with correlation and a best-effort attempt to draw a conclusion from correlated values in order to build predictions. We're not set up for assigning meaning or motivation (causality) based on this myopic view of the myriad of forces that actually cause something to happen or not happen.

Similarly, we can't directly infer a causal relationship just because of a statistically significant result to an A/B test. We can only reject an equivalency in results between testing groups. However, what we are able to do with A/B tests is to validate through a causal experiment whether our predictions are useful.

It's important to understand these concepts as a data scientist. It's even more important, however, to reinforce them when speaking with your internal customers in the business that you're building projects for. Failing to communicate these principles has created a staggering amount of confusion and frustration in groups that I've worked with.

A note on causal analysis (inference)

Certain techniques, such as DOE and causal modeling, can arrive at causal relationships between features and a target. Unlike supervised learning, which focuses solely on minimization of error terms, causal relationships that are discovered through DOE modeling can be confidently determined.

We can determine the magnitude and direction of effects on a target variable through the careful construction of directed acyclic graph (DAG) relationships in DOE, something that traditional supervised learning is incapable of doing. For further reading on the topics of causal modeling and DOE, I highly recommend reading *Elements of Causal Inference: Foundations and Learning Algorithms* by Jonas Peters et al. (MIT Press, 2017).

11.2 Leveraging A/B testing for attribution calculations

In the previous section, we established the importance of attribution measurement. For our ice cream coupon model, we defined a methodology to split our customer base into different cohort segments to minimize latent variable influence. We've defined why it's so critical to evaluate the success criteria of our implementation based on business metrics associated with what we're trying to improve (our revenue).

Armed with this understanding, how do we go about calculating the impact? How can we make an adjudication that is mathematically sound and provides an irrefutable assessment of something as complex as a model's impact on the business?

11.2.1 A/B testing 101

Now that we have defined our cohorts by using a simple percentile-based RFM segmentation (the three groups that we assigned to customers in section 11.1.1), we're ready to conduct random stratified sampling of our customers to determine which coupon experience they will get.

The control group will be getting the pre-ML treatment of a generic coupon being sent to their inbox on Mondays at 8 a.m. PST. The test group will be getting the targeted content and delivery timing.

> **NOTE** Although simultaneously releasing multiple elements of a project that are all significant departures from the control conditions may seem counterintuitive for hypothesis testing (and it is confounding to a causal relationship), most companies are (wisely) willing to forego scientific accuracy of evaluations in the interest of getting a solution out into the world as soon as possible. If you're ever faced with this supposed violation of statistical standards, my best advice is this: keep patiently quiet and realize that you can do variation tests later by changing aspects of the implementation in further A/B tests to determine causal impacts to the different aspects of your solution. When it's time to release a solution, it's often much more worthwhile to release the best possible solution first and then analyze components later.

Within a short period after production release, people typically want to see plots illustrating the impact as soon as the data starts rolling in. Many line charts will be created, aggregating business parameter results based on the control and test group. Before letting everyone go hog wild with making fancy charts, a few critical aspects of the hypothesis test need to be defined to make it a successful adjudication.

HOW MUCH DATA DO WE NEED TO COLLECT?

When designing hypothesis testing, a critical part of the process is to determine appropriate sample sizes for the evaluation. The following listing shows a relatively straightforward method of determining an appropriate sample size based on the needs of the business.

Listing 11.1 Minimum sample size determinator

Someone was gracious enough to wrap the power solver from SciPy in statsmodels with a high-level API.

Generates a list of "lift" deltas between control and test (percentage difference between metrics)

```
from statsmodels.stats.power import tt_ind_solve_power
x_effects = [0.01, 0.05, 0.1, 0.15, 0.2, 0.25, 0.5]
```

```
sample_sizes = [tt_ind_solve_power(x, None, 0.2, 0.8, 1, 'two-sided') for x
    in x_effects]
sample_sizes_low_alpha = [tt_ind_solve_power(x, None, 0.01, 0.8, 1,
    'two-sided') for x in x_effects]
```

Solves for sample sizes for alpha 0.2 by setting effect_size to None

Solves for sample sizes for alpha of 0.01 (99% certainty in not having a type I error)

Figure 11.10 shows the result of running this code (the visualization code can be seen in the companion repository to this book). In both cases, we're leaving the power value at 0.8, which can and should be adapted if the risk of type II errors is detrimental to the business for this use case.

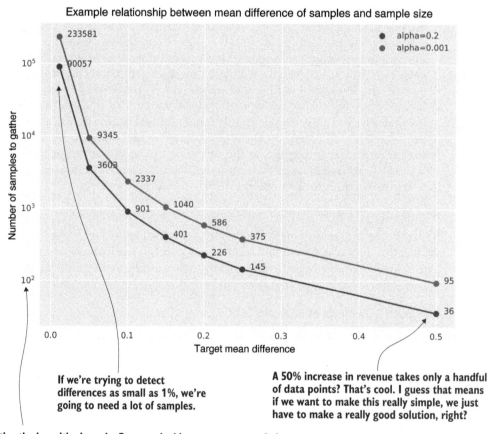

If we're trying to detect differences as small as 1%, we're going to need a lot of samples.

A 50% increase in revenue takes only a handful of data points? That's cool. I guess that means if we want to make this really simple, we just have to make a really good solution, right?

Notice the logarithmic scale. For marginal improvements made by a model, this should tell you something. If you're not really affecting the thing that you're working to influence, this is an indication that it's time to go back to the drawing board and rethink your approach.

Figure 11.10   Sample size determination based on confidence requirements

As the alpha value (the significance level of our measurements) decreases, the number of recorded samples to determine a difference between test and control increases. Having the ability to communicate the amount of time required to collect enough data in order to make a conclusive judgment is absolutely essential before a model enters production. Without these expectations set, the business will simply be wondering when, and more depressingly, if, it will ever see promising results from the project.

The preceding estimation is based entirely on statistical tests that require a normal distribution and homogenous sample group sizes. We will discuss in the remaining sections how to not only test parametric data, but also appropriate significance tests for nonparametric data and unbalanced sample sizes.

WHAT NOT TO DO

Figure 11.11 illustrates the way many companies evaluate attribution early in their journeys of using ML project work to impact business. Without proper analytics applied to the attribution measurement using sound statistical processes, a great deal of frustration can be felt by the business.

The best way to combat this is to set established rules about how data will be evaluated and how much time it's going to take to adjudicate impacts, and to have a monitoring system in place to test for statistical significance of the monitored parameters.

With our RFM cohorts defined, our sample size estimates understood, and an automated monitoring job to retrieve our attribution data for measurement, we're ready to start on the evaluation of our project. We're ready to see if all of the hard work was worth it.

11.2.2 *Evaluating continuous metrics*

For our ice cream coupon optimizations, one of the primary measures that the business is concerned with is revenue. In many cases when dealing with measures of monetary value, the distributions associated with spending are generally highly *non-normal*. Figure 11.12 shows an unbounded purchase plot of spending associated with variable priced goods and infinite basket situations (such as in e-commerce).

If you're dealing with distributions that look like this plot, you won't be using the standard parametric tests. For our use case, however, we have a fixed-price set of items (all of our ice cream is the same price), and the coupons that we're issuing are for a single item. We've done our homework with statistical analysis, though, validating that we're going to have data that is relatively normally distributed.

When conducting our experimental test of our solution, we're going to define the parametric tests as shown in listing 11.2. We'll be applying these to a standard plot that can show not only a specific cohort's sales data over time, but the equivalency test p-values for each of these tests. In actual practice, not all of these would be included as a report (displaying and calculating both parametric and nonparametric tests here are for demonstration purposes only). You should use only the one that is most applicable to your data.

ME 365 9802

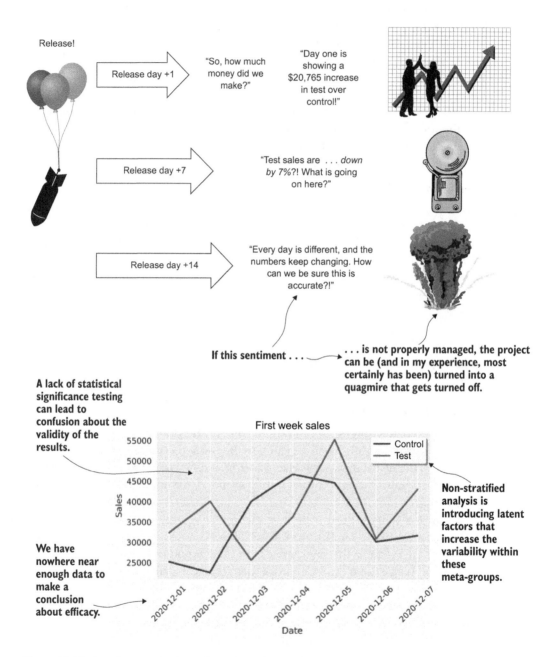

Figure 11.11   Ignoring hypothesis testing creates frustration.

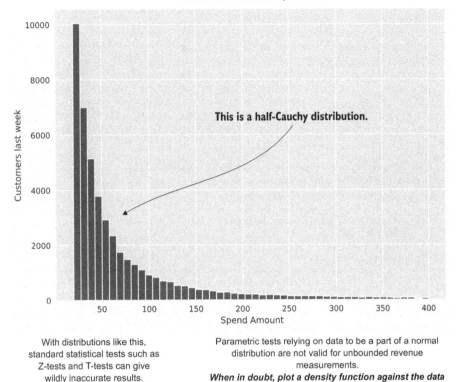

Figure 11.12 A normalcy validation check on revenue by customers

Listing 11.2 Line plot with statistical tests

```
from statsmodels.stats import anova
from scipy.stats import f_oneway, mannwhitneyu, wilcoxon, ttest_ind
from collections import namedtuple
import matplotlib.pyplot as plt
DATE_FIELD = 'Date'
TARGET_FIELD = 'Sales'
def calculate_basic_stats_df(series):
    StatsData = namedtuple('StatsData', 'name mean median stddev variance sum')
    return StatsData(series.name,
                     np.mean(series),
                     np.median(series),
                     np.std(series),
                     np.var(series),
                     np.sum(series)
                     )
def series_comparison_continuous_df(a, b):
    BatteryData = namedtuple('BatteryData', 'left right anova mann_whitney_u
        wilcoxon ttest')
```

Simple function to get critical stats about each series

Function that calls the SciPy and statsmodels modules for calculating parametric and nonparametric equivalency tests

```
        TestData = namedtuple('TestData', 'statistic pvalue')
        anova_test = f_oneway(a, b)
        mann_whitney = mannwhitneyu(a, b)
        wilcoxon_rank = wilcoxon(a, b)
        t_test = ttest_ind(a, b, equal_var=False)
        return BatteryData(a.name,
                           b.name,
                           TestData(anova_test.statistic, anova_test.pvalue),
                           TestData(mann_whitney.statistic, mann_whitney.pvalue),
                           TestData(wilcoxon_rank.statistic, wilcoxon_rank.pvalue),
                           TestData(t_test.statistic, t_test.pvalue)
                           )

def plot_comparison_series_df(x, y1, y2, size=(10,10)):
    with plt.style.context(style='seaborn'):
        fig = plt.figure(figsize=size)
        ax = fig.add_subplot(111)
        ax.plot(x, y1, color='darkred', label=y1.name)
        ax.plot(x, y2, color='green', label=y2.name)
        ax.set_title("Comparison of Sales between tests {} and
      {}".format(y1.name, y2.name))
        ax.set_xlabel(DATE_FIELD)
        ax.set_ylabel(TARGET_FIELD)
        comparison = series_comparison_continuous_df(y1, y2)
        y1_stats = calculate_basic_stats_df(y1)
        y2_stats = calculate_basic_stats_df(y2)
        bbox_stats = "\n".join((
            "Series {}:".format(y1.name),
            "    Mean: {:.2f}".format(y1_stats.mean),
            "    Median: {:.2f}".format(y1_stats.median),
            "    Stddev: {:.2f}".format(y1_stats.stddev),
            "    Variance: {:.2f}".format(y1_stats.variance),
            "    Sum: {:.2f}".format(y1_stats.sum),
            "Series {}:".format(y2.name),
            "    Mean: {:.2f}".format(y2_stats.mean),
            "    Median: {:.2f}".format(y2_stats.median),
            "    Stddev: {:.2f}".format(y2_stats.stddev),
            "    Variance: {:.2f}".format(y2_stats.variance),
            "    Sum: {:.2f}".format(y2_stats.sum)
        ))
        bbox_text = "Anova pvalue: {}\nT-test pvalue: {}\nMannWhitneyU pvalue:
          {}\nWilcoxon pvalue: {}".format(
          comparison.anova.pvalue,
          comparison.ttest.pvalue,
          comparison.mann_whitney_u.pvalue,
          comparison.wilcoxon.pvalue
          )
        bbox_props = dict(boxstyle='round', facecolor='ivory', alpha=0.8)
        ax.text(0.05, 0.95, bbox_text, transform=ax.transAxes, fontsize=12,
          verticalalignment='top', bbox=bbox_props)
        ax.text(0.05, 0.8, bbox_stats, transform=ax.transAxes, fontsize=10,
          verticalalignment='top', bbox=bbox_props)
        ax.legend(loc='lower right')
        plt.tight_layout()
```

Calls to the series comparison function for acquiring the significance test values for in-plot display

Calls to the basic stats calculations for each series

Figure 11.13 shows the result of executing this code; the first 150 days of testing results are depicted for the high-value customer cohort.

The datasets being compared here are nonparametric. This is due to the trend over time of sales causing our distributions to shift as a function of time. The only condition that would allow us to use comparisons such as ANOVA, T-tests, and Z-tests would be if our data had stationarity (a trend of 0).

Showing a time-series display in this fashion is but one part of illustrating test results. As we focused on in part 1, the ability to communicate clearly with the business is incredibly important for any ML project. It's even more important when the topic of attribution and measurement comes into the conversation. Having the full picture involves more than a single presentation of the data results, as we will cover next.

Do I really have to do this?!

In short, no.

ML project work has varying levels. Each level of business-impacting criticality has a corresponding level of urgency with regards to implementing attribution (and drift) measurements. Let's take a look at a few examples:

- *Internal tooling model for generating labeled data for other projects*—Standard ML metrics are fine.
- *Internal-to-the-company predictive model designed to assist another department with repetitive tasks*—Attribution modeling not applicable, periodic ad hoc drift detection could be worthwhile.
- *Internal-to-the-company project that directly affects critical business operations* (helping to influence major business decisions)—Absolutely critical to have drift detection, and attribution modeling is a good idea to build.
- *External customer-facing model*—Attribution measurement, drift detection, and bias detection (evaluation of prejudicial predictions that have real-world consequences of amplifying systemic societal issues based on the nature and type of data collected) are absolutely required.

The last element is what the majority of production ML is focused on: the critically important projects that affect the profitability or efficiency of a company. Of particular note in this list is the bias measurement, a topic of active research at the time this writing. I don't go into this topic in this book, but it is a critical aspect of what we do. (Entire books are written on this topic, and I encourage all professional ML practitioners to read at least one of them.)

Bias measurement becomes very important when our models are affecting people's lives: credit card applications, home loan approvals, police patrol recommendations, urban funding, and human behavior risk detection are but a small sampling of some of the applications of ML that are being discovered as having severe bias based on prior behavior reflected in our datasets. Keeping an eye on the results is always going to save you from difficult conversations down the line.

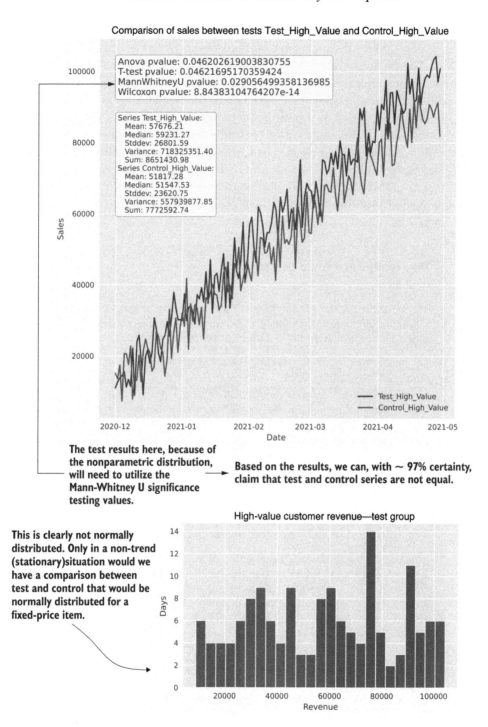

Comparison of sales between tests Test_High_Value and Control_High_Value

Anova pvalue: 0.046202619003830755
T-test pvalue: 0.04621695170359424
MannWhitneyU pvalue: 0.029056499358136985
Wilcoxon pvalue: 8.84383104764207e-14

Series Test_High_Value:
    Mean: 57676.21
    Median: 59231.27
    Stddev: 26801.59
    Variance: 718325351.40
    Sum: 8651430.98
Series Control_High_Value:
    Mean: 51817.28
    Median: 51547.53
    Stddev: 23620.75
    Variance: 557939877.85
    Sum: 7772592.74

The test results here, because of the nonparametric distribution, will need to utilize the Mann-Whitney U significance testing values.

Based on the results, we can, with ~ 97% certainty, claim that test and control series are not equal.

This is clearly not normally distributed. Only in a non-trend (stationary)situation would we have a comparison between test and control that would be normally distributed for a fixed-price item.

High-value customer revenue—test group

Figure 11.13 Plotting test and control groups over time, showing the nonparametric nature of the data

11.2.3 *Using alternative displays and tests*

To accompany any temporal-referenced hypothesis test, presenting a box plot of the results to the business can be useful. While these charts are incredibly useful for distilling information in an approachable way, the vast majority of laypersons are not familiar with seeing these plots accompanied by the critically important statistical summaries that help guide interpretability.

Without a reference of statistical significance, a judgment can be made too easily on insufficient (or high-variance) data. The next listing shows an ANOVA plot for parametric data and the required `DataFrame` manipulations to conduct the test.

Listing 11.3 Generation of ANOVA box plot report for parametric data

```
from statsmodels.formula.api import ols
from statsmodels.stats import anova
def generate_melted_df(series_collection, dates, date_filtering=DATA_SIZE):
    series_df = generate_df(series_collection, dates)
    melted = pd.melt(series_df.reset_index(), id_vars='Date',
      value_vars=[x.name for x in series_collection])
    melted.columns = [DATE_FIELD, 'Test', 'Sales']
    return melted[melted[DATE_FIELD] > max(melted[DATE_FIELD]) -
      timedelta(days=date_filtering)]
def run_anova(data, value_name, group_name):
    ols_model = ols('{} ~ C({})'.format(value_name, group_name),
      data=data).fit()
    return anova.anova_lm(ols_model, typ=2)
def plot_anova(melted_data, plot_name, figsize=(16, 16)):
    anova_report = run_anova(melted_data, 'Sales', 'Test')
    with plt.style.context(style='seaborn'):
        fig = plt.figure(figsize=figsize)
        ax0 = fig.add_subplot(111)
        ax0 = sns.boxplot(x='Test', y='Sales', data=melted_data,
          color='lightsteelblue')
        ax0 = sns.stripplot(x='Test', y='Sales', data=melted_data,
          color='steelblue', alpha=0.4, jitter=0.2)
        ax1 = fig.add_subplot(211)
        ax1.set_title("Anova Analysis of tests", y=1.25, fontsize=16)
        tbl = ax1.table(cellText=anova_report.values,
                        colLabels=anova_report.columns,
                        rowLabels=anova_report.index,
                        loc='top',
                        cellLoc='center',
                        rowLoc='center',
                        bbox=[0.075,1.0,0.875,0.2]
                        )
        tbl.auto_set_column_width(col=list(range(len(anova_report.columns))))
        ax1.axis('tight')
        ax1.set_axis_off()
        plt.savefig("anova_{}.svg".format(plot_name), format='svg')
```

Normalizing (melting) the DataFrame to support the ANOVA calculation in statsmodels

Creates the linear model needed for ANOVA

Superimposes the ANOVA result statistics to the chart for easy reference

The result of executing this code on an alternative dataset (one that is stationary and has no seasonal effects) is shown in figure 11.14. For details on the differences of this

Anova analysis of tests

	sum_sq	df	F	PR(>F)
C(Test)	80833089089.18445	1.0	3735.9011945872767	1.7073328996246434e-147
Residual	5149567454.058764	238.0	nan	nan

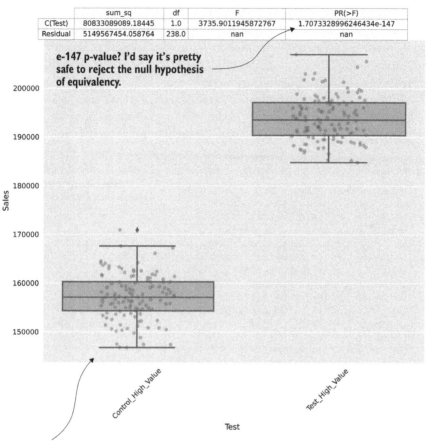

e-147 p-value? I'd say it's pretty safe to reject the null hypothesis of equivalency.

There is just a *slight difference* between these groups.

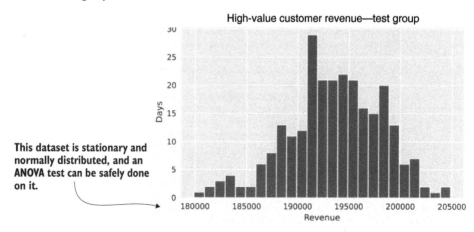

This dataset is stationary and normally distributed, and an **ANOVA** test can be safely done on it.

Figure 11.14   Stationary parametric test example

dataset's generation as compared to the one we have been using, see the companion repository to this book.

With these parametric tests, we can get a far more accurate determination of the magnitude of differences in our testing. This is mostly because of the foundation upon which parametric student tests are built (requiring that the sample mean follows a normal distribution, and the standard error of the mean follows a chi-squared distribution with $n - 1$ degrees of freedom). In our original problem, with several groups being tested at the same time, it might have been a bit onerous to plot each of the ANOVA tests as paired tests. With merely three groups being split between test and control, this might not be too punishing to look through. But 25 groups under test are a different story.

Enter Tukey HSD tests (*HSD* stands for *honestly significant difference*). These are another type of parametric test with the main difference from the student family of tests being that pairwise comparisons between each of the groups can be conducted all at once. The following listing shows an implementation of this test and the accompanying visualization report.

Listing 11.4 Tukey HSD hypothesis testing and plot

Defines the structure of the return
type from pairwise_tukeyhsd

```
from statsmodels.stats.multicomp import pairwise_tukeyhsd
def convert_tukey_to_df(tukey):
    STRUCTURES = [(0, 'str'), (1, 'str'), (2, 'float'),
      (3, 'float'), (4, 'float'), (5, 'float'), (6, 'bool')]
    fields = tukey.data[0]
    extracts = [extract_data(tukey.data[1:], x[0], x[1]) for x in STRUCTURES]
    result_df = pd.concat(extracts, axis=1)
    result_df.columns = fields
    return result_df.sort_values(['p-adj', 'meandiff'], ascending=[True, False])
def run_tukey(value, group, alpha=0.05):
    paired_test = pairwise_tukeyhsd(value, group, alpha)
    return convert_tukey_to_df(paired_test._results_table)
def plot_tukey(melted_data, name, alpha=0.05, figsize=(14,14)):
    tukey_data = run_tukey(melted_data[TARGET_FIELD], melted_data[TEST_FIELD],
      alpha)
    with plt.style.context(style='seaborn'):
        fig = plt.figure(figsize=figsize)
        ax_plot = fig.add_subplot(111)
        ax_plot = sns.boxplot(x=TEST_FIELD, y=TARGET_FIELD, data=melted_data,
          color='lightsteelblue')
        ax_plot = sns.stripplot(x=TEST_FIELD, y=TARGET_FIELD,
                                data=melted_data, color='steelblue',
                                alpha=0.4, jitter=0.2)
        ax_table = fig.add_subplot(211)
        ax_table.set_title("TukeyHSD Analysis of tests", y=1.5, fontsize=16)
        tbl = ax_table.table(cellText=tukey_data.values,
                             colLabels=tukey_data.columns,
                             rowLabels=tukey_data.index,
                             loc='top',
```

Extracts the data
from the payload
result from the
Tukey HSD test

Runs the
pairwise
Tukey
HSD test

Returns the
pairs, sorted by
significance and
mean delta

Creates a display table on top of the box plots that shows the relationships among all of the paired groups under evaluation

```
        cellLoc='center',
        rowLoc='center',
        bbox=[0.075, 1.0, 0.875, 0.5]
    )
    tbl.auto_set_column_width(col=list(range(len(tukey_data.columns))))
    ax_table.axis('tight')
    ax_table.set_axis_off()
    plt.tight_layout()
    plt.savefig('tukey_{}.svg'.format(name), format='svg')
```

Executing this code against our stationary full sample test group results in the plot shown in figure 11.15. As you can see by looking at the medium-value and low-value

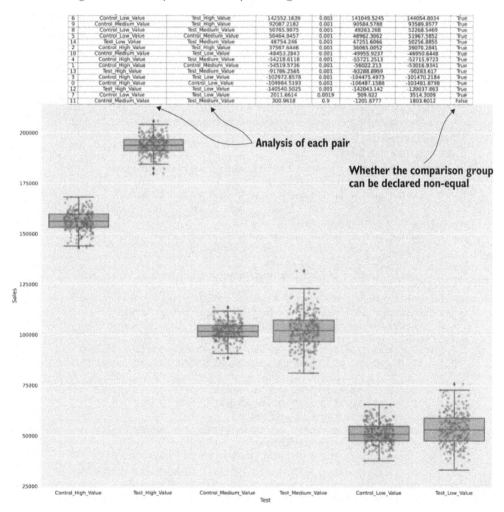

A pairwise comparison test gives a simple, comprehensible comparison in a single snapshot. It's highly useful, *but use an approach like this only if the base criteria for the test are met.*

Figure 11.15 Tukey HSD pairwise comparison test, showing each group to every other group and whether the null hypothesis can be rejected for the paired comparisons of equivalency

groups, visually discerning differences between seemingly similar data is incredibly difficult. Setting aside that making visual or simple aggregation evaluations is incredibly dangerous, having the statistical validation tests as part of any comparison chart that you display to the business can help solidify the conclusions.

This straightforward graph is easy enough for the business units to interpret. It helps prevent anyone from making a judgment on the success (or failure) of the project until sufficient data exists to endorse that conclusion, whatever it may be. In the graph, we see that there is no appreciable difference between the test and control group for our medium-value cohort. This can help identify which groups may need a different approach (opening the door to the next iteration of the model and further tests) and which should be handled carefully (the high-value group's test condition seems to be working splendidly; why change it now?).

11.2.4 *Evaluating categorical metrics*

We've been discussing revenue up to this point, but it's not the whole story in our ice cream consumption optimization project. While the executives are concerned about the model's influence on sales figures, the marketing team (our internal customer) wants to know the uptake rate for coupon usage.

We can't use the same approach that we used with continuous data for nominal data, unfortunately. Gone are the ANOVA tests, the Tukey HSD comparisons, or any other such technique. Instead, we need to delve into the world of categorical tests. We need to start thinking in the realm of *happen* versus *not happen* in regard to events that we're measuring.

Listing 11.5 shows a simplistic mock-up of data measuring the ratios between our test and control groups for an example 50,000 coupons issued during the first 50 days of testing. To keep the visualizations simple, we'll put all of our cohorts into a single group (but in practice, you would have a different chart and set of statistical tests for each cohort).

Listing 11.5 Categorical significance testing

```
from scipy.stats import fisher_exact, chi2_contingency
def categorical_significance(test_happen, test_not_happen, control_happen,
        control_not_happen):
    CategoricalTest = namedtuple('CategoricalTest',
                                 'fisher_stat fisher_p chisq_stat chisq_p
                        chisq_df chisq_expected')
    t_happen = np.sum(test_happen)
    t_not_happen = np.sum(test_not_happen)
    c_happen = np.sum(control_happen)
    c_not_happen = np.sum(control_not_happen)
    matrix = np.array([[t_happen, c_happen], [t_not_happen, c_not_happen]])
    fisher_stat, fisher_p = fisher_exact(matrix)
    chisq_stat, chisq_p, chisq_df, chisq_expected = chi2_contingency(matrix)
```

For each of the series data (event happens, event does not happen) for both test and control, gets the sum of these events

Runs a Fisher's exact test on the matrix of happen/not happen for each group

Runs a chi-square contingency test on the matrix

```
    return CategoricalTest(fisher_stat, fisher_p, chisq_stat, chisq_p,
        chisq_df, chisq_expected)

def plot_coupon_usage(test_happen, test_not_happen, control_happen,
    control_not_happen, name, figsize=(10,8)):
    cat_test = categorical_significance(test_series, test_unused,
        control_series, control_unused)
    with plt.style.context(style='seaborn'):
        fig = plt.figure(figsize=figsize)
        ax = fig.add_subplot(111)
        dates = np.arange(DATE_START,
                        DATE_START + timedelta(days=COUPON_DATES),
                        timedelta(days=1)).astype(date)
        bar1 = ax.bar(dates, test_series, color='#5499C7', label='Test
            Coupons Used')
        bar2 = ax.bar(dates, test_unused, bottom=test_series,
            color='#A9CCE3', label='Test Unused Coupons')
        bar3 = ax.bar(dates, control_series, bottom=test_series+test_unused,
            color='#52BE80', label='Control Coupons Used')
        bar4 = ax.bar(dates, control_unused,
            bottom=test_series+test_unused+control_series,
            color='#A9DFBF', label='Control Unused Coupons')
        bbox_text = "Fisher's Exact pvalue: {}\nChisq Contingency pvalue:
            {}\nChisq DF: {}".format(
            cat_test.fisher_p, cat_test.chisq_p, cat_test.chisq_df
            )
        bbox_props = dict(boxstyle='round', facecolor='ivory', alpha=1.0)
        ax.set_title("Coupon Usage Comparison", fontsize=16)
        ax.text(0.05, 0.95, bbox_text, transform=ax.transAxes, fontsize=12,
            verticalalignment='top', bbox=bbox_props)
        ax.set_xlabel('Date')
        ax.set_ylabel('Coupon Usage')
        legend = ax.legend(loc='best', shadow=True, frameon=True)
        legend.get_frame().set_facecolor('ivory')
        plt.tight_layout()
        plt.savefig('coupon_usage_{}.svg'.format(name), format='svg')
```

Gets the statistical tests from the categorical significance function

Stacks the bar charts atop one another for easily viewable rates of interaction over time

Constructs the statistical test reporting box for the plot

When we run this code (after having our sent and utilized ETL done for the coupons setup), we'll end up with a chart that looks like figure 11.16.

Figure 11.16 may not be applicable to all ML projects. The continuous value-based measurements in the earlier sections of this chapter are far more common. However, should you need to evaluate event-based data and provide a conclusive declaration about whether the test conditions are different, having this methodology as a tool is indispensable.

GENERAL APPLICATIONS OF ATTRIBUTION MEASUREMENT

We've discussed model attribution measurement for ice cream coupon issuance. Not to be dismissive of any ice-cream companies out there (I promise you, my dog loves you), but what about slightly *more serious* endeavors?

The key regarding the monitoring of business attributes is to select a measurement metric that is useful. The utility of these metrics is, for lack of a better phrase, focused

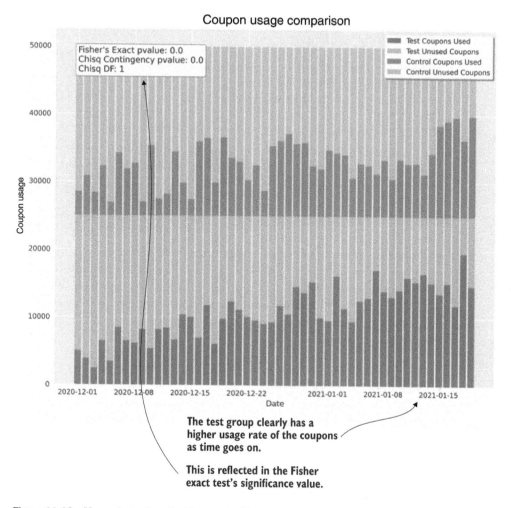

Figure 11..16 Measuring categorical happen/not happen events in a hypothesis test analysis

entirely on the concept of "the devil is in the details." The measurement of business success has nuances that can range from useful to pointless. It is critical to select measurable attributes that incorporate the nuances of the business. Having discussions with the business unit SME group that is responsible for that aspect of the business is incredibly helpful to ensure that your attribution analysis is relevant.

The devil is in the details

Business metrics are, to an outsider, seemingly wrought from common sense. If we're trying to measure revenue effects from a model, we just look at sales, right? If we're calculating engagement lift, we just look at login events. Optimization of flight routes to international airports would look at airplane occupancy rates, correct?

(continued)

While defining these rules may seem trivial, I can assure you that it is not. For each use case, the details surrounding how to calculate which metric and the details about how those metrics are calculated have proven to be both complex and highly specific to the ways in which the company decides to run its business. Therefore, it is incredibly important to discuss any attribution metrics with your colleagues who otherwise calculate these metrics for reporting purposes for the company.

If you're building a solution that is attempting to target revenue for the company, talk to the finance team. If you're working on efficiency optimizations for logistics, talk to the operations department. If the model is aiming to reduce defect density on manufactured parts, you should be talking to the quality assurance and metrology departments.

Having a series of metrics that are consistent with the way the company defines its success in the realm that you're interacting with will ensure that little to no confusion occurs when presenting the impact of the model to the business. With this consistency, faith in the solution is fostered, securing ML solutions as a key critical aspect to the operations of the company, and helping to grow innovation and generate further interesting projects for the DS team to solve.

How can I figure out which business metrics to monitor?

The short answer: ask.

Often the DS team is the one coming up with a great idea for ML project work—though the majority of the time, a business unit sponsor or executive approaches the team to solve a problem. Still, I can count on one hand the number of novel problems that I've been involved with.

I'm not understating the work that was done, simply being honest in saying that the problem existed before an ML solution was built. The difference is that it was being handled by humans rather than algorithms and code. Revenue maximization? That's marketing. Fraud detection? That's the fraud department. Pricing optimization? Demand prediction? Humans that have been doing that for a long time before you were called in to help out.

These people know their craft. They'll know more about the nuances of the data, the realm of what they're responsible for, and the nature of customers or processes far better than you will. The best source for determining which aspects of the business can be used to create a measurable metric for the performance of what you're going to be building is these people.

Every time I begin work on a new project—aside from the first few solutions that I built in a vacuum and that failed quite spectacularly—I get to know these people. I invite them to discussions, to lunch, to meetings, and generally just listen to everything they say. I ask them pointed questions about how their own jobs are measured for success (if the department's goals are the things that your model is measured against, it will be easier for everyone to understand the effects, after all). I ask them what queries they utilize to determine the success for their department. I ask what the team's objectives and key results (OKRs) are.

Perhaps they'll tell you that they're measured not by the number of correct fraud events that they detect, but more on the detection of novel fraud events that haven't been seen before. Maybe they'll say that they're focused on catching enough fraud but never wanting to falsely flag fraud on a legitimate customer. These can influence the construction of your model, but they can also be used as the very metrics to gauge the health of your implementation.

By doing this alignment and involving the people who know about the topic so deeply, you'll be preparing the project for a greater level of success upon release, but more important, for the ability to measure the production release model in the same way that the company at large will be viewing it. This will help ensure that you're aware of degradation and issues (hopefully) before the company is aware of them, increasing the levels of stability in the project.

Now that we've covered how we're going to measure an ML experiment for attribution analysis, focusing on answering the critical questions that the business will want to have answered about the project, it's time to face the other elephant in the room. We need to figure out how to detect drift, what to do about it, and when to take action when the inevitable deterioration of our model happens. Having the statistics established for measuring it with our attribution analysis, paired with our internal DS-focused loss metrics, we're prepared to face it head-on. It's time to think about model drift.

Summary

- Attribution analysis enables a DS team to communicate clearly about how its solution solves the problem that it was intending to solve for the business. Leveraging proper statistical methods and controlled testing can provide objective declarations of the status of the solution.
- By utilizing the correct statistical tests for evaluating A/B testing data, a statement regarding the status of a solution's performance can be made, providing a data-driven declaration of the impact.

Holding on to your gains by watching for drift

12

This chapter covers

- Identifying and monitoring for drift in production solutions
- Defining responses to detected drift

In the preceding chapter, we established the foundations for measuring the effectiveness of an ML solution. This solid base enables a DS team to communicate to the business about the performance of a project in terms that are relevant to the business. To continue making (hopefully) positive reports about the effectiveness of a solution, a bit more work needs to be done.

If proper attribution monitoring and reporting to the business are the bedrock and foundation of a project, entropy is the buffeting storm seeking to continuously tear down the project. We call this chaotic shift in performance *drift*, and it takes many forms. Combatting against it requires continuous monitoring and a suspicious distrust of everything going into and coming out of a model.

Throughout this chapter, we will look at the types and causes of, and solutions for, the major types of model drift. Fighting against drift will help ensure that the gains that you're making for your company continue to prove fruitful.

12.1 Detecting drift

Let's pretend that we've just shipped our ice cream recommender from chapter 11 to production. We've used sound engineering practices throughout development, and our internal SME testing has looked promising. Attribution measurement is set up, A/B testing is defined, and we're ready to start collecting the results. We release the proverbial kraken upon the world.

It isn't until about six weeks into the model running swimmingly in production that we are notified by the marketing group about some worrying trends in its analysis of the customer base. In one area of the country, the issuance and rebate rates for coupons have increased to such a degree that product shortages are occurring, while in a different area the imbalance in product purchase types has become so egregious that a massive overabundance of scrap product arises. *It may be time to panic a little bit.*

We collectively scramble, digging into the feature data in an ad hoc manner, putting all our other project work on hold as we fight this immediate fire of trying to investigate whether the root cause of the issues is the model. After a few days of exploratory analysis bearing little fruit with respect to a root cause, we're left with an ultimatum from the business: either fix the model or shut it off. The profit attribution lift, although offsetting the cost of product scrap, isn't a compelling enough story to placate the business.

We cross our fingers, close our eyes, and hope for the best as we initiate a new training run of the model. Based on the results of the holdout validation scoring metric during the training, it seems like the problem has resolved itself. For now.

What is going on here? Why did the model all of a sudden start behaving like this? Why was the business affected so heavily by something so seemingly innocuous? Most important, what should we have done differently before we released this model to production?

The simple answer is that *entropy is all around us.* Feature-measurement data, along with the latent factors that influence causality, are constantly shifting. In many cases, the actions we're taking on the output of models causes shifts in that data. Hidden feedback loops of influence can introduce new correlations that the model wasn't exposed to during training. What had once been a valuable relationship for target optimization can either deteriorate or strengthen to a point that the predictions coming out of a model are no longer solving the problem that the project was intended to address.

These impacts can, for some use cases, be rather severe and rapid (fraud detection, for instance, is highly susceptible to this because criminals are clever and will adapt to creative pursuits to defeat your model's ability to detect their activity), while others are gradual and easy to miss if not monitored algorithmically. Being aware of and controlling for these inevitable shifts is a part of ML project development. We need to expect them, have systems in place to discover them, and know how to recover from them.

12.1.1   *What influences drift?*

Model drift can take six primary forms. Some are obvious to detect, while others require a great deal of research and analysis to discover. Table 12.1 gives a brief overview of these mechanisms of model degradation.

Table 12.1   Prediction drift types and corrective actions

Drift type	Measurement method	Corrective actions
Feature drift	Feature distribution validation	Retrain model on new data
	Prediction post hoc error calculation	Revisit feature engineering
Label drift	Post hoc analysis of predictions	Retrain on new data, tune
Concept drift	Attribution measurement	Perform feature engineering work
	Feature distribution validation	Retrain model
	Post hoc prediction analysis	Revisit solution (new algorithm or approach)
	Ad hoc analysis	Evaluate solution relevance
	Causality models (simulations)	
Prediction drift	Post hoc prediction analysis	Analyze impact on business
	Attribution measurement	
Reality drift	You'll just know. Everything is on fire.	Shift to human intervention
		Reevaluate features
		Create hard-stop boundary in training data
		Retrain model
Feedback drift	Time spent improving model	Evaluate efficacy of solution
	Performance during retraining	Determine if new solution is needed

These measurement methods are relatively common, captured in greatest detail within concept drift detection. Each one of these measurement methods should be employed for any model that is pushed to production. The reasons for constant measurement are many, but chief among them are the following:

- Models will drift. There is no such thing as a static implementation.
- Gradual degradations are incredibly challenging to identify by attribution measurement alone. Monitoring the performance in multiple ways can alert you to issues that manifest themselves over a long period of time.
- Rapid degradations are challenging to respond to if historical measurement is not in place. Repairing a model with no data to define what went wrong is incredibly time-consuming.

- Alerting can buy you precious time to fix an eminent problem before it becomes a larger issue. This helps with the mission of the project and increases the business's faith in DS work.

To explore each of these mechanisms of drift, we'll be sticking with our ice cream scenario throughout this chapter for simplicity's sake (and for fun).

> **NOTE** Some of the techniques described in section 12.2 for setting up monitoring for these effects, particularly for feature-based drift, can be difficult to scale for models that use a kitchen-sink approach. (I've seen people try to implement massive vectors, consisting of thousands of features, in the hopes of improving accuracy.) This is definitely something to think about when designing predictive solutions. Taking the easy way, by just throwing a ton of data into a model and hoping for the best, can end up being a nightmare for monitoring the health of such an implementation.

FEATURE DRIFT

Let's imagine for a moment that our ice cream propensity-to-buy model uses weather-forecast data in multiple regions. Let's also pretend that we have no monitoring set up on our model and are using a passive retraining of the model each month.

When we were originally building the model, we did a thorough analysis of our features. We determined correlation values (Pearson's and chi-squared) and found an astonishingly strong relationship between temperature and ice cream sales. For the first several months, everything is going well, with emails going out at defined intervals based on a propensity-to-open score of greater than 60%.

All of a sudden, midway through June, the attribution models start to fall off a cliff. The open and utilization rates are abysmally low. From a revenue lift of 20%, the test group is now showing a 300% loss. We continue to operate like this, with the marketing team trying different approaches to its campaigns. Even the product development team starts trying new flavors under the mistaken impression that customers are getting tired of the flavors that are on sale.

It's not until a few months go by, when the DS team is informed that the project will likely get cancelled, that an in-depth investigation is undertaken. Upon investigation of the model's predictions for the week starting in mid-June, we find a dramatic step-function shift in the probabilities for propensity-to-use coupons. When we look into the features, we find something a bit concerning, shown in figure 12.1.

Even though this is a comical example of feature drift, it's similar to many that I've seen in my career. I've rarely come across a DS who hasn't had a data feed change unexpectedly without being notified, and many of those that I've experienced or heard about are as ridiculous as this example.

Many times, shifts like these will be of such a magnitude that prediction results become so unusable that it's known within a short period of time that something substantial has changed. In some rare cases, such as the one shown in figure 12.1, a shift

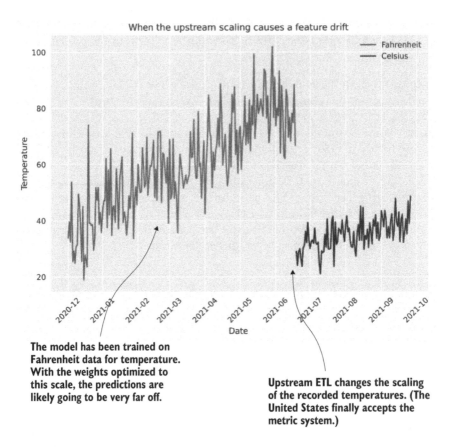

Figure 12.1   Feature drift by way of numeric scaling changes

can be nuanced and difficult to detect for a longer period of time if automated monitoring is not in place.

For this use case, the prediction outputs would be making recommendations for customers enduring a new modern ice age event. The probabilities coming out of the model would likely be very low for most users. Since the post-prediction trigger for sending out recommendations from the model is set at 60% propensity, the much lower probabilities would result in the vast majority of customers in the evaluation test no longer receiving emails. With feature monitoring in place that is measuring the mean and standard deviation, simple heuristic control logic would have caught this.

Another form of feature drift is *feature ignorance*. This sort of drift comes into play when our inference data is arriving to a trained model that is beyond the bounds of what the model was trained on. If, for instance, our model was trained on temperatures between 60°F and 95°F (Southern California), and the imputation features drift down to 20 because of the conversion to a Celsius scale, tree-based models will handle that just fine. They will bucket these new values within any decision criterion that captures temperatures in the lowest range (around 60).

Linear models, though? Not so much. The model's artifact is, after all, an equation in a linear model. The temperature value from the inference feature vector will be multiplied with a coefficient and either added to or subtracted from the remainder of the feature computations that were determined during training. With values far outside the range seen during that training estimation, the predictions could behave in wildly unexpected ways.

LABEL DRIFT

Label drift is a pretty insidious issue to track down. Typically caused by a shift in the distribution of several critical (high-importance) features, a drift in the label can work at cross-purposes to the desires of the business.

Let's imagine that some aspect of our model for ice cream propensity starts to be affected by a latent force that we don't fully understand due to a lack of data collection. We can see in the correlation what seems to be driving it, as it is universally reducing the variance of one of our feature values. However, we can't conclusively tie one of our collected data features to the effects that we're seeing. The main effect that we see is shown in figure 12.2.

With this distribution shift, we could be looking at dramatic impacts to the business. From an ML perspective, the model's accuracy (loss) could, theoretically, be better in the bottom scenario of figure 12.2 than it was during initial training. This can make discovering events like this incredibly challenging; from a model training perspective, it could appear to be much better and ideal. However, from a business perspective, a drift event like this could prove disastrous.

What would happen if the marketing team had a threshold for sending the customized email coupons out only if the probability for using one was above 90%? Restrictions like this are usually in place because of costs (bulk sends are cheap, while customized solutions are far more expensive for services). If the marketing team based its threshold for sending on this level, having analyzed the results of the model's predictions during the first few weeks of running, it would have selected an optimal cost-to-benefit ratio for these customized sends. With the label drift occurring over time in the second chart, this would mean that basically all of the test group customers would be entered into this program. This massive increase in cost could quickly make the project less palatable for the marketing department. If it were egregious enough, the team might just abandon its utilization of the project's output entirely.

Paying close attention to the distribution of a model's output over time can bring visibility to potential problems and ensure a certain degree of consistency to the output. When the results shift (and they will, let me assure you), be it in a seemingly positive or negative way, there could be follow-on effects from the results that the internal consumers of the model might not be prepared for.

It's always best to monitor this. The impact to the greater scope of the business, depending on the sort of problem that you're solving, could be severe if you're not

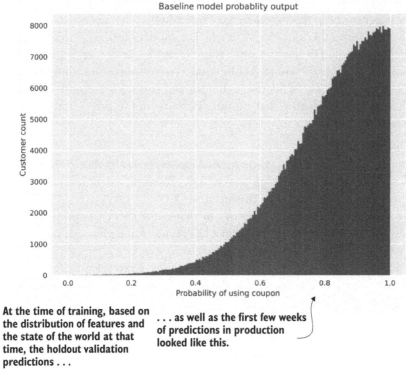

At the time of training, based on the distribution of features and the state of the world at that time, the holdout validation predictions . . .

. . . as well as the first few weeks of predictions in production looked like this.

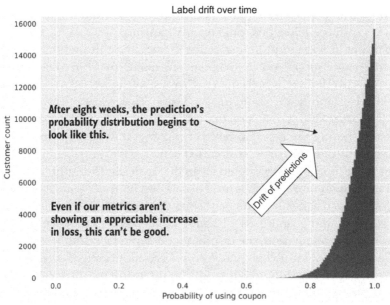

After eight weeks, the prediction's probability distribution begins to look like this.

Even if our metrics aren't showing an appreciable increase in loss, this can't be good.

Drift of predictions

Figure 12.2   Label drift is a shift in the prediction distribution.

continually monitoring the state of the predictions coming out of the solution. An implementation of label drift monitoring should focus on the following:

- Collection and storage of predictions
- For classification problems
  - Define a time window for aggregation of prediction class values and store the counts of each.
  - Track the ratio of label predictions over time and establish acceptable deviation levels for the ratio values.
  - Perform a comparison of equivalency, utilizing an algorithm such as Fisher's exact test with a very low alpha value (< 0.01), between recent values and the validation (test) metrics calculated during model generation.
  - (Optionally) Determine the probability mass function (pmf) of recent data and compare to the pmf of the validation predictions generated by the model during training. Comparison of pmf discrete distributions can be done with an algorithm such as Fisher's noncentral hypergeometric test.
- For regression problems
  - Analyze distribution of recent predictions (number of days back, number of hours back, depending on the volume and volatility of predictions) by capturing mean, median, stddev, and interquartile range (IQR) of the windowed data.
  - Set thresholds for monitoring the values of interest from the measured aggregated statistics. When a deviation occurs, alert the team to investigate.
  - (Optionally) Determine the closest distribution fit to the continuous predictions and compare the similarity of this probability density function (pdf) through the use of an algorithm such as the Kolmogorov-Smirnov test.

CONCEPT DRIFT

Concept drift is a challenging issue that can affect models. In simplest terms, it is an introduction of a large latent (not collected) variable that has a strong influence on a model's predictions. These effects typically manifest themselves in a broad sense, changing most, if not all, of the features used for imputation by a trained model. Continuing with our ice cream example, let's look at figure 12.3.

These values that we measure and use for correlation-based training (weather data, our own product data, and event data) have been used to build strong correlations to propensities to buy ice cream during the week for individual customers. As we discussed in chapter 11, the latent variables that are beyond our ability to collect have a stronger influence over a person's decision to buy than the data that we collect.

When unknown influences positively or negatively influence a model's output, we may get a dramatic shift in either our predictions or in the attribution measurements for the model, which is the case here. Tracking down the root cause can be either quite obvious (a global pandemic) or insidious and complex (social media

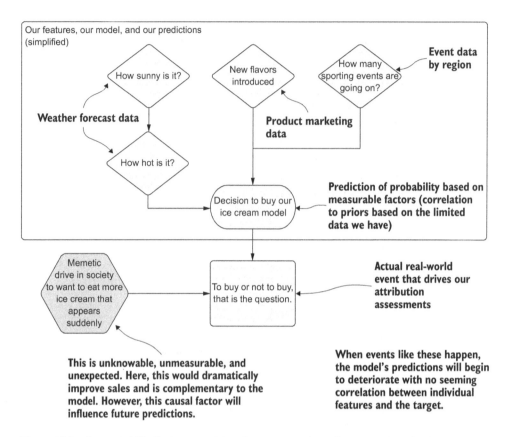

Figure 12.3 Concept drift effects on model performance, business impact, and attribution measurement

effects on brand image). We can go about monitoring this type of drift for our scenario as follows:

- Implement metric logging for
  - Primary model error (loss) metric(s)
  - Model attribution criteria (the business metric that the project is working to improve)
- Collect and generate aggregated statistics (over an applicable time window) for predictions:
  - Counts (number of predictions, predictions per grouped cohort, etc.)
  - Mean, stddev, IQR for regressors
  - Counts (number of predictions, number of labels predicted) and bucketed probability thresholds for classifiers
- Evaluate trends of aggregated statistics on predictions and attribution measurement over time. Unexplained drifts can be grounds for model retraining or a

return to feature-engineering evaluation (additional features may be required to capture the new latent factor effects).

Regardless of the causes, it is important to monitor both potential symptoms of this issue: the model metrics associated with training for passive retraining, and the model attribution data for active retraining. Monitoring these shifts in model efficacy can help with early intervention, explainable analytics reports, and the ability to resolve the issue in a way that will not cause a disruption to the project as a whole.

The answer may not be readily apparent as with other types of drift (namely, feature and prediction drift). The critical aspect of production monitoring for this type of unexplained drift is that it is captured in the first place. Being blind to this potential impact to a model's performance can have staggering effects on a business if left unchecked, depending on the use case. Creating these monitoring statistics through a simple ETL is always time well spent.

PREDICTION DRIFT

Prediction drift is highly related to label drift but has a nuanced difference that makes recovery from this type of drift follow an alternate set of actions. Like label drift, it affects the predictions greatly, but instead of being related to an outside influence, it's directly related to a feature that is part of the model (although sometimes in a confounding manner).

Let's imagine that our wildly successful ice cream company had, at the time of training our model solution, a rather paltry showing in the Pacific Northwest region of the United States. With a lack of training data, the model wasn't well suited to adapt to the extreme minority of feature data associated with this region. Adding to this lack of data issue, we were unaware of whether potential future customers in this region would like our product, because of the same dearth of information for exploratory data analysis (EDA).

After the first few months of running the new campaign, raising awareness through word of mouth, it turns out that not only do people (and dogs) in the Pacific Northwest thoroughly enjoy our ice cream, but their behavior patterns turn out to match quite well with some of our most highly active customers. As a result, our model increases the frequency and rate at which coupons are issued to customers in this part of the country. Because of this increased demand, the model begins to issue so many coupons to customers in this region that we create an entirely new problem: a stock issue.

Figure 12.4 shows the effect on the business that our model has inadvertently helped to create. While this isn't a bad problem per se (it certainly drives up revenue!), an unexpected driver to the foundation of the business's operation can introduce problems that will need to be solved.

The situation shown in figure 12.4 is a positive one indeed. However, the model's impact in this case will not show up in modeling metrics. In reality, this would likely show as a fairly equivalent loss score, even if we were to retrain the model on this new

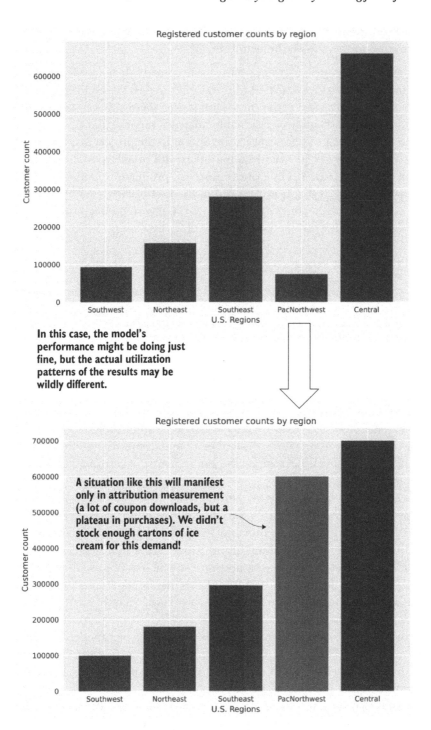

Figure 12.4   A highly beneficial impact to the business from a model's output. This can create other problems and might need rapid adjustment (particularly if the opposite condition happens).

data. The attribution measurement analysis is the only way to detect this and account for the underlying shifts in the customer base moving forward.

Prediction drift, in general terms, is handled through the process of feature monitoring. This set of tooling involves many of the following concepts:

- Distribution monitoring of priors for each feature compared to recent values, lagged by an appropriate time factor:
  - Calculate mean, median, standard deviation, IQR for the feature as it was at training time.
  - Compute recent feature statistical metrics that are being used for inference.
  - Calculate the distance or percentage error between these values.
  - If the delta between these metrics is above a determined level, alert the team.
- Distribution equivalency measurement:
  - Convert continuous features to a probability density function (`pdf`) for the features as they were during training.
  - Convert nominal (categorical) features to a probability mass function (`pmf`) for the features as they were during training.
  - Compute the similarity between these and the most recent (unseen-to-the-model through training) inference data utilizing algorithms such as the Wasserstein metric or Hellinger distance.
- Specifying statistical process control (SPC) rules for basic statistical metrics for each feature:
  - Sigma-based threshold levels whereby a smoothed value of each continuous feature over time is measured (typically, through a moving average or window aggregation) and alerted on when selected rules are violated. Western Electric rules are generally used for this.
  - SPC rules based on scaled percentage membership of categorical or nominal values within a feature (aggregated as a function of time).

Whichever methodology you choose to utilize (or if you'd like to choose to do all of them), the most critical aspect of collecting information about the state of the features during training is that it allows for monitoring and having advance notice of feature degradation.

To aid in tracking these statistical metrics, many (including myself) rely heavily on the tracking server of MLflow. Logging the values as part of a model-training event can help ensure that the historical record of what that model utilized for training is preserved, as well as keeping you from having to do an expensive (computationally and temporally) historic calculation of these values each time a validation of drift is executed.

REALITY DRIFT

I'm writing this sentence on January 20, 2022. It's been a rough past year in the ice cream business. It's arguably been a rough year for humanity in general. What once had been our company's primary means of selling our tasty treats (ice cream trucks trolling about neighborhoods, community parks, sporting events, and dog parks) hasn't been working out so well for us. We've had to reevaluate our distribution strategy and our marketing messaging and work through an incredibly tough economic climate due to the impacts of Covid-19.

Reality drift is a special case of concept drift: while it is an outside (unmeasured and unforeseen) influence, these foundational shifts can have a much more profound and large-scale impact on the effectiveness of a model than general concept drift. Not only pandemics cause reality drift, though. Horseshoe manufacturers, after all, would have had similar issues with predicting demand accurately during the first few decades of the 20th century.

Events such as these are foundationally transformative and disruptive, particularly when they are *black swan events*. In the most severe cases, they can be so detrimental to businesses that a malfunctioning model is the worst of their worries; the continued existence of the company is far more pressing of a problem.

For more moderate disruptive reality drifts, the ML solutions that are running in production are generally hit pretty heavily. With no ability to recognize which new features can explain the underlying tectonic shifts in the business, adapting solutions to handle large and immediate changes becomes a temporal problem. There simply isn't enough time or resources to repair the models (and sometimes, not even the ability to collect the data needed).

When these sorts of foundational paradigm-shifting events happen, models affected by the change in the state of the world should face one of two fates:

- Abandonment due to poor performance and/or cost-savings initiatives
- Model rebuilding after extensive feature generating and engineering

What you absolutely should never do is quietly ignore the problem. The predictions are likely to be irrelevant, retraining on original features blindly is not likely to solve the problem, and leaving poor-performing models running is costly. At the bare minimum, a comprehensive assessment of the nature and state of the features going into models needs to be undertaken to ensure that the validity is still sound. Without approaching these events in this thorough manner of validation and verification, the chances that the model (and other models) is allowed to continue to produce unvetted results for very long are slim.

FEEDBACK DRIFT AND THE LAW OF DIMINISHING RETURNS

A form of drift less spoken of is *feedback drift*. Imagine that we're working on a modeling solution for estimating a defect density on a part manufactured in a factory. Our model is a causal model, with our production recipes being built in such a way that it reflects a directed acyclic graph that mirrors our production process. After running through this Bayesian modeling approach to simulate the different effects of changing parameters to the end result (our yield), we find ourselves with a set of seemingly optimal parameters to put into our machines.

At first, the model shows relationships that do not result in optimal outcomes. As we explore the feature space further and retrain our model, the simulations more accurately reflect the expected outcome when we initiate tests. Our yields stabilize to nearly 100% over the first few months of running the model and utilizing the simulation's outputs.

By controlling for the causal relationships present in the system that we're modeling, we've effectively created a feedback loop in the model. The variances of allowable parameters to adjust shrink, and were we to build a supervised machine learning model for validation purposes on this data, it wouldn't learn very much. There simply isn't a signal to learn from anymore (at least not one worth much).

This effect isn't present in all situations, as causal models are more heavily affected by this than correlation-based traditional ML models are. But in some situations, the results of the predictions of a correlation-based model can contaminate our new features coming in, thereby skewing the effects of those features that were collected with the observed result that actually occurred. Churn models, fraud models, and recommendation engines are all highly susceptible to these effects (we are directly manipulating the behavior of our customers by acting on the predictions to promote positive results and minimize negative results).

This is a risk in many supervised learning problems, and it can be detected by evaluating the prediction quality over time. As each retraining happens, the metrics associated with the model should be recorded (MLflow is a great tool for this) and measured periodically to see if degradation occurs on the inclusion of new feature data to the model. If the model is simply incapable of returning to acceptable levels of loss metrics based on the validation data being used for recent activity, you may be in the realm of diminishing returns.

The response to this occurrence is to either revisit feature-engineering work (adding data that can assist in helping the model learn the new data paradigm) or revisit the project. Revisiting the project can mean, sometimes, that it's best to turn it off. Some problems can be completely solved over time by utilizing ML to discover the patterns present in behavior of systems (or people) and can be supplanted by modifying the manner in which the business operates.

12.2 Responding to drift

We've covered how to calculate model impacts by using appropriate statistical tests on attribution metrics, and we've discussed the types of model-affecting entropy that make our models less stable over time. If we were to see our ice cream coupon model deteriorate in any of the six ways defined in section 12.1, what process would we use to correct it?

12.2.1 What can we do about it?

It all starts with monitoring. For our ice cream coupon scenario, that involves building ETL processes for not only our predictions (safely storing each batch of predictions for analytics use cases), but also basic statistical measurement attributes to use for setting triggered alerts about model health.

Let's revisit the outside temperature measurements that are being fed as a feature into our model from chapter 11. Figure 12.5 shows a visual example of how, by setting three separate checks on the temperature feature, we could detect issues in the underlying data.

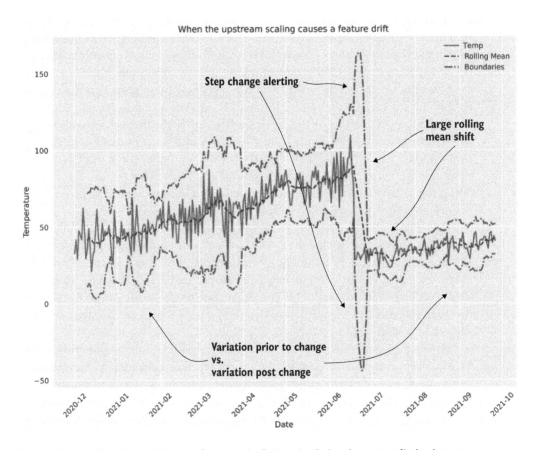

Figure 12.5   Setting threshold boundaries around a feature to alert on large-magnitude changes

This plot is intended to be a visual aid only. In practice, alerts would be configured through calculations performed on the data, triggering if the boundary shift magnitude crosses a predetermined threshold purely based on logic written in code. The three regions identified in this plot, though, are examples of rules that should be embedded in monitoring code that can alert the team to an issue in the input features to the model.

The first identified detection (step change alerting on the mean) is useful for detecting large, unexpected deviations that may prove problematic for a model's predictive capability. Rules like this are relatively trivial to implement, can have configured thresholds, and are an effective early-warning system for the ML team to intervene immediately when the new data arrives.

The second detection type (step change in the values of data variance) generally requires a bit more time to trigger. The variance of the same value (temperature) on different scales (Celsius versus Fahrenheit) is intrinsically different. As such, the total variance of the data will show a marked difference. However, to reduce the chances of false-positive warnings on discrete periods of time, alarm conditions concerned with variance monitoring generally require longer periods to trigger.

The third indication type, although coinciding with the shift in the mean, is a dramatic increase in variation that has not been historically observed. When large peaks occur in variation measurements (typically far larger than the changes that would be monitored by the second case in this example), an investigation is warranted into the state of the data being measured.

At the very least, to protect against both the slow entropic decay of model effectiveness and the foundational disruptive events seen in figure 12.5, we need to be measuring aspects of our models. Feature monitoring, training label drift measurement, model validation metrics, and attribution metrics are all elements that make up an effective strategy to identify drift.

Table 12.2 illustrates common types of modeling that I've seen and worked on in different industries and a general estimate of how long stability held before a retraining event was required, for perspective.

Table 12.2 Model stability and robustness to drift

Application	Attribution metric	Retraining periodicity (approximate)
Churn prediction	Purchase event after action taken on customer with high probability	Monthly
Customer lifetime value (CLV)	% of continued CLV group membership	Weekly
	Stability	
Transportation Industry	Revenue	Monthly
Demand/pricing	Purchase rate	
Recommendation engine (personalization)	Purchase rate or viewership rate	Hourly or daily
Image content labeling	% error in classification	Two to six months
Fraud detection	Loss event count	Biweekly
	Loss amounts	
	Undetected fraud event count	
Equipment failure	Maintenance costs (replacement)	Semiannually or annually
Prediction (survivability)	Count of unrequired maintenance	
Sales forecasting	Backtesting accuracy in projection	Daily or weekly

As you can see, the projected retraining periodicity varies quite widely across applications. Table 12.2 doesn't reflect what happens outside these plans. Even with a system in place for active retraining to trigger a new model to be created upon a degradation in model attribution performance, continued success is not guaranteed for that new model. Drift effects could have influenced both the old and new models (and most of the time, they do) to the point that just retraining on new data will not repair the model's performance to an acceptable level.

For a passive scheduled retraining paradigm, the problem can take longer to realize if the attribution measurements are not closely monitored. With the periodicity mentioned in table 12.2 (which is loosely approximated), the first scheduled retraining after a drift event will generally uncover an issue that requires manual intervention to solve. It could be revisiting feature-engineering stages for the project, including new features that can help the model adapt to the new state of the world in the existing features, or a complete overhaul of the approach used to build the project in the first place.

It is through monitoring the elements that impact a model, from feature metrics and model metrics, all the way to attribution measurement, that we can identify an issue that exists in the predictions. Once we identify it, though, what can we do about it?

12.2.2 *Responding to drift*

For our example of temperature drift shown previously in figure 12.5, the response to repairing the drift condition is trivial. We can apply a feature conversion to the older data to bring it in line with the new scaling of the temperature values. Identifying, isolating, and repairing issues that are obvious and trivial to correct is, well, obvious. Just fix it and move on.

Unfortunately, not every problem is so simple. What if we can't readily identify what is causing a degradation in the model? We have four primary means of responding to drift:

- Scheduled or triggered retraining, with validation of results against the prior model, and new model against new validation data. Keep the best one.
- For obvious issues (for example, ETL errors, explosions in cardinality, or shifts in variance of features), either repair or scale the features, retrain the model, validate its performance on new holdout data, and continue running as before on the new model.
- For prediction degradation issues that are not related to the obvious factors mentioned in the preceding list item, revisit feature engineering, and conduct exploratory data analysis and correlation analysis. Determine if any new features need to be added or existing features need to be removed. Attempt to retrain and release a new validated model to production.
- If the model shows a negative business impact that is statistically significant, stop using the model immediately. Attempt to perform root cause analysis and repair the issue (if possible). If the benefit of the model is no longer present, shut it down permanently.

The latter three elements in this list are relatively self-explanatory. However, the first one has a degree of nuance, principally in the mechanism used for retraining. There are two primary means of initiating a retraining event: passive and active, illustrated in figure 12.6.

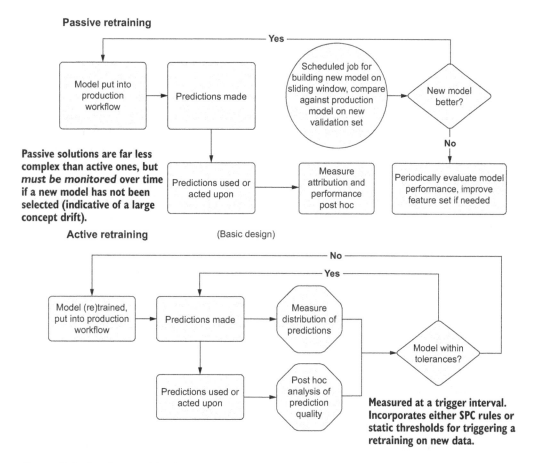

Figure 12.6 Passive retraining (scheduled) and active retraining (triggered) to respond to model drift

These two mechanisms for initiating a model retraining are remarkably different. In *passive retraining*, we set up a scheduled job that will take either a sliding window of our feature data to train a new model (this approach is useful for highly dynamic datasets predicting values that change rapidly over periods of time) or all data from the beginning of time, including new data that the previous production model has not seen. We then take a holdout validation set from the most recent data and run a model evaluation of the current prior model (our production model) and the new model against the same new holdout validation data. The winner, based on our model metrics, is the one selected for production.

For this passive retraining approach, we typically have alerting set up to notify us in the event that a new model is not selected for replacement for too many iterations. This is to warn us that a fundamental shift could occur in the recent data that may indicate a need to rebuild the feature-engineering set (which would be an activity removed from the passive retraining cycle).

For the *active retraining* implementation shown in the lower portion of figure 12.6, a constantly monitored, automated solution is used that measures attributes associated with the model's business impact and prediction quality (distribution, variance, mean, etc.). If the attribution monitoring detects a degradation in performance, an automated retraining event takes place. Like the passive implementation, a comparison of the new triggered model event against recent holdout data to the current running model against the same data is conducted. If the new model is better, it is selected for promotion into production (typically automated through CI/CD). As with the passive approach, repeated failures to succeed an earlier generation of model iteration will trigger an alert for the DS team to investigate.

Whether a passive or active implementation is chosen is entirely applicable to the size of the ML team working on the project, the stability of the implementation, the nature of the business use case, and the capabilities of the team. It doesn't matter which of these solutions is chosen for an ML project. The only important thing to understand is that one of them needs to be chosen.

Leaving a model to its own devices, assuming that it will go on predicting as well as it did when first trained with no further action, is a recipe for disaster. Projects that do not account for retraining, health checks, monitoring, and attribution measurements are doomed to failure, due to irrelevance or actively poor results negatively impacting a business.

Summary

- Monitoring for the primary types of drift—feature, label, concept, prediction, reality, and feedback—are incredibly important to ensure a solution's health.
- Retraining through passive or active means is an effective way to counteract drift. When these attempts fail, revisiting the implementation is critical to introduce new features that deal with drifts in order to ensure that the solution continues to serve its purpose.

ML development hubris

13

This chapter covers

- Applying refactoring to overengineered implementations to increase development velocity
- Identifying code to target for refactoring
- Establishing simplicity-driven development practices
- Adopting new technologies via sustainable means
- Comparing build, buy, and prior art in implementations

The preceding chapter focused on critical components used to measure a project's overall health from a purely prediction-focused and solution efficacy perspective. ML projects that are built to support longevity through effective and detailed monitoring of their inputs and outputs are certainly guaranteed to have a far higher success rate than those that do not. However, this is only part of the story.

Another major factor in successful projects has to do with the human side of the work. Specifically, we need to consider the humans involved in supporting, diagnosing

353

issues with, improving, and maintaining the project's code base over the lifespan of the solution.

> **NOTE**   When a project is released to production, that is merely the beginning of its life. The real challenge of ML is to keep something running well over a long period of time.

This human element comes in the following form:

- *How the code is crafted*—Can other people read it and understand it?
- *How the code performs*—Is it deterministic? Does it have unintentional side effects?
- *How complex the code is*—Is it over- or under-engineered for the use case?
- *How easy it is to improve*—ML code is in a constant state of refactoring.

Throughout this chapter, we'll look at signs to watch out for that define patterns making an ML code base a nightmare to maintain. From fancy code flexing (show-off developers) to empire-building framework creators, we'll be able to identify these issues, see alternatives, and understand why the most effective design pattern for ML project code development is the same as for all of the other aspects of the project.

> **TIP**   Build something only as complex as it needs to be to solve the problem at hand. People have to maintain this code, after all.

Why "hubris," though? That's a bit insulting.

I chose the term *hubris* as a component of this chapter's title after a long deliberation held between two temporally distinct versions of myself. On the one side was my current self, having felt the sting of crushing failure due to an overconfidence in my own skills, a builder of hopelessly confusing ego-driven solutions in the pursuit of prideful vanity, and a braggart-in-code who measured the success of a project in the cleverness of its implementation. The other side was a much younger version of myself, just getting started in the field and feeling as inadequate and as much an imposter as I could imagine a person to be.

I debated whether to use the term *arrogance* instead of *hubris*, but felt that would be disingenuous and inapplicable to what we'll be talking about in this chapter (and what I wish I could have a long, hard chat with my younger self about). *Hubris* is much more applicable. By definition, it is the possession of excessive pride and self-confidence. Note that it isn't about having pride (we all should be proud when we solve a complex problem in our profession), but rather the overabundance of it.

When we, as data scientists, exhibit hubristic tendencies, we tend to build overly complex solutions to problems. Whether because of ego, vanity, or a simple desire to prove to peers that our skills are sufficiently high (typically due to imposter syndrome or having been burned by some hot garbage that we've written in the past), the end result is the same: regret. We end up building unmaintainable, confusing, overly complex, and unextendable solutions that have a high probability of derailing projects or frustrating our peers, and fearing the day that we have to troubleshoot a failure in the code.

This chapter covers many of the dangerous ways that I've learned the lesson of pursuing simplicity in code, defining patterns of sustainable ML development that can, hopefully, save you from some painful mistakes I've made over the years.

13.1 Elegant complexity vs. overengineering

Imagine for a moment that we're starting a new project. It's not too much of a departure from the last two chapters (spoiler alert: it has to do with dogs). We have some data about the dogs. We know their breed, age, weight, favorite food, and whether they're generally of a favorable disposition. In addition, we have labeled data that measured whether each dog was exhibiting signs of hunger when they walked into our pet store franchise.

Armed with this data, we'd like to build a model that predicts, based on the registered data of our canine consumers, whether we should offer them a treat when they pass through the checkout line.

> **NOTE** Yes, I'm fully aware of how silly this is. It makes my wife chuckle, though, so the scenario is staying.

As we begin working on investigating the data, we realize that we have a truly enormous amount of training data. Billions upon billions of rows of data. We'd like to utilize it all in the training of the model, though, so our platform decision leaves a simple choice for running this: Apache Spark.

Since we've been using Python so extensively throughout this book, let's use this chapter to delve into another language used extensively for large-scale (in terms of training row count volume) ML projects: Scala. Since we'll be using Spark's ML library, in order to effectively build a feature vector from our columnar data, we'll need to identify any noncontinuous data types and convert them to indexed integer values.

Before we get into code examples that show the differences between the topic of this section, let's discuss the scales of ML coding practices. I like to think of development style (with regards to code complexity) as a delicate balancing act, illustrated in figure 13.1.

On the right side of this scale, we have very lightweight code. It's highly declarative (almost script-like), monotonous (statements copied and pasted many times over with slight changes to the arguments), and tightly coupled (changing one element means scouring through the code and updating all of the string-based configuration references).

These lightweight code bases often can seem like they are written by groups of people all working for different companies. In many cases, they are, as entire functions and snippets of code are lifted in their entirety from popular developer Q&A forums. An additional feature that many of them share is a reliance on heavily popular frameworks and tooling that are well-documented (or, at least, are complex enough that a sufficient density of questions and answers has been provided on the aforementioned

The scales of ML coding practices

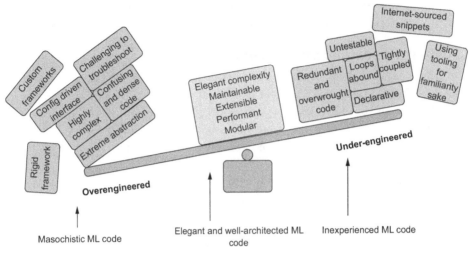

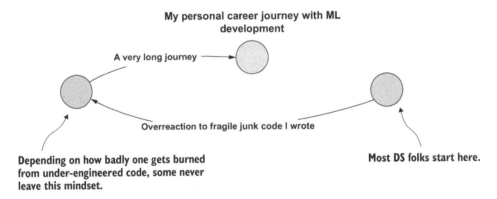

Figure 13.1   Striking a balance between these two extremes of software development practices can lead to more effective and production-stable project work.

developer forums to liberally borrow from), regardless of how well suited the use case is. Here are some key identifiers of this behavior:

- Using a framework intended for large-scale ML when the training dataset is in the thousands of rows and dozens of columns. (Instead of using SparkML, for example, stick to pandas and use Spark for training in broadcast mode.)
- Building real-time serving atop large-scale serving architecture when the request volume will never hit more than a few requests per minute. (Instead of using Kubernetes with Seldon, build a simple Flask app in a Docker container.)
- Setting up a streaming ingestion service for large-scale microbatch predictions when there are a few hundred predictions to be made per hour and the SLA

can be measured in minutes. (Instead of using Kafka, Spark Structured Streaming, or Scala user-defined functions, use the Flask app.)

- Building a time-series forecasting model using an LSTM running on GPU hardware with Horovod multi-GPU gang scheduling mode for a univariate time series that can be predicted with single-digit RMSE values with a simple ARIMA model. (Use an ARIMA model and choose the far cheaper CPU-based VMs instead).

On the left side of the scale, however, is the polar opposite. The code is dense, succinct, highly abstract, and typically complex. The left side can work in some groups and organizations, but by and large, it's unnecessary, confusing, and limits the number of people who can contribute to the project by virtue of the experience required in understanding advanced language features. Some ML engineers will, after having dealt with a sufficiently large and complex project using the lightweight scripting style of ML development, pursue the left side's heavy code approach on subsequent projects. The struggles that they had maintaining the scripted style and all of the extensive coupling that was present might lead to an explosion of abstracted operators that rapidly borders on building a generic framework. I can quite honestly say that I was that very person, reflected in my journey at the bottom of figure 13.1.

Sitting pleasantly in the middle of the figure is the balanced approach that has the greatest probability for long-term success of a team's development style. Let's take a look at examples of how our code might look when getting started with these two competing polar opposites.

13.1.1 Lightweight scripted style (imperative)

Before we get into the code of the minimalistic declarative style of writing our prototype ML model, let's take a brief look at what our data looks like. Table 13.1 shows a sample of the first five rows of the dataset.

Table 13.1 Sample of data from our hungry dog dataset

Age	Weight	Favorite food	Breed	Good boy or girl	Hungry
2	3.05	Labneh	Pug	No	True
7	20.44	Fajitas	Dalmatian	Sometimes	False
5	11.3	Spaghetti	German Shepherd	No	True
3	17.9	Hummus	Estrela	Yes	False
8	55.6	Bolognese	Husky	Yes, when food is available	True

We can clearly see that the majority of our data will need to be encoded, including our label (target) of `hungry`.

Let's take a look at how we could handle these encodings by building a vector and running a simple `DecisionTreeClassifier` by using the Pipeline API from SparkML.

The code for these operations is in the following listing. (See the "Why Scala?" sidebar for why I'm choosing to show these examples in Scala rather than Python.)

Listing 13.1   Imperative model prototype

```scala
import org.apache.spark.ml.feature.{StringIndexer,
 VectorAssembler,
 IndexToString}
import org.apache.spark.ml.classification.DecisionTreeClassifier
import org.apache.spark.ml.evaluation.BinaryClassificationEvaluator
import org.apache.spark.ml.Pipeline
val DATA_SOURCE = dataLarger
val indexerFood = new StringIndexer()
  .setInputCol("favorite_food")
  .setOutputCol("favorite_food_si")
  .setHandleInvalid("keep")
  .fit(DATA_SOURCE)
val indexerBreed = new StringIndexer()
  .setInputCol("breed")
  .setOutputCol("breed_si")
  .setHandleInvalid("keep")
  .fit(DATA_SOURCE)
val indexerGood = new StringIndexer()
  .setInputCol("good_boy_or_girl")
  .setOutputCol("good_boy_or_girl_si")
  .setHandleInvalid("keep")
  .fit(DATA_SOURCE)
val indexerHungry = new StringIndexer()
  .setInputCol("hungry")
  .setOutputCol("hungry_si")
  .setHandleInvalid("error")
  .fit(DATA_SOURCE)
val Array(train, test) = DATA_SOURCE.randomSplit(
  Array(0.75, 0.25))
val indexerLabelConversion = new IndexToString()
  .setInputCol("prediction")
  .setOutputCol("predictionLabel")
  .setLabels(indexerHungry.labelsArray(0))
val assembler = new VectorAssembler()
  .setInputCols(Array("age", "weight", "favorite_food_si",
    "breed_si", "good_boy_or_girl_si"))
  .setOutputCol("features")
val decisionTreeModel = new DecisionTreeClassifier()
  .setLabelCol("hungry_si")
  .setFeaturesCol("features")
  .setImpurity("gini")
  .setMinInfoGain(1e-4)
  .setMaxDepth(6)
  .setMinInstancesPerNode(5)
  .setMinWeightFractionPerNode(0.05)
val pipeline = new Pipeline()
  .setStages(Array(indexerFood, indexerBreed, indexerGood,
    indexerHungry, assembler, decisionTreeModel,
```

dataLarger is a Spark DataFrame containing the full dataset from the sample in table 13.1.

Indexes the first String-typed column (breed) and creates a new 0th ordered descending-sort based on occurrence frequency

Builds the indexer for the next categorical (String) column (good thing that there are only four of them, right?)

Builds the indexer for the target (label) column

Creates the train and test splits

Defines the fields (columns) that will be used for the feature vector

Builds a decision-tree classifier model (hyperparameters hardcoded for brevity)

```
        indexerLabelConversion))
val model = pipeline.fit(train)
val predictions = model.transform(test)
val lossMetric = new BinaryClassificationEvaluator()
  .setLabelCol("hungry_si")
  .setRawPredictionCol("prediction")
  .setMetricName("areaUnderROC")
  .evaluate(predictions)
```

Fits the pipeline against the training data (performs all stages of the pipeline, returning the processing steps along with the model as a single object of staged operations)

Calculates the scoring metric (in this case, areaUnderROC) and returns the metric value

Defines the order of operations to take and wrap in a pipeline (heavily modified during experimentation)

Predicts against the test data for scoring purposes

This code should look relatively familiar. It's what we all see when we look at API documentation for a particular modeling framework. In this case, it's Spark, but similar examples exist for any particular framework. It's of an imperative style, meaning that we're providing the execution steps directly in our code, preserving the manner in which we would do this step by step. While it makes the code incredibly easy to read (which is why examples in Getting Started guides use this format), it's a nightmare to modify and extend as we work through different tests during experimentation and MVP development.

Why Scala?

Well, we're working with Scala predominantly because of Spark. Python is a first-party language, fully supported by Spark, but the backend of Spark (the low-level guts of how the sausage gets made) is written in Scala. The Python API is merely a wrapper (interface) to the Scala APIs, and as such, if anything lower level than the `DataFrame` API is required to be interfaced with, we must do so in either Scala or Java.

The choice of whether to use Python in Spark or Scala in Spark usually comes down to a short list of factors:

- Prior familiarity with Java (or Scala) versus Python
- The need to perform complex data manipulations not supported directly through the `DataFrame` API's functions module—through the use of user-defined functions, resiliently distributed dataset (RDD) operations, or the development of custom estimators and transformers
- The need to use custom distributed algorithms to solve a particular problem (for example, at the time of writing this book, XGBoost is available as a only a Scala/Java library)

"But why are you using Scala in this book?"

That's an excellent question. It's mostly because there is a largely silent group of ML engineers in the industry who prefer it for their ML tasks, particularly when they're dealing with extremely massive datasets. (Not a lot of questions can be found regarding use of Scala and Java on internet search results because of the higher barrier to entry for using the code than for a more forgiving language such as Python.) I'm including Scala in this chapter to showcase a slightly different approach to developing

(continued)

ML code than what most people are familiar with in an effort to pique curiosity and broaden your horizons. Although the language might seem foreign to you if you're accustomed to only Python, let me assure you that learning it can be a rewarding endeavor and can help expand your technical repertoire as a professional ML engineer (giving you another set of tools to solve problems that might otherwise be incredibly arduous to solve in Python).

Numerous other, much more low-level and engineering-focused reasons exist for using Scala over Python in Spark. These reasons are related to topics—concurrency, thread management, and utilizing on-heap memory directly on the JVM—that are reserved for algorithm developers in the ML space. For the end user of Spark, performing ML-related work, Python is by far the widely accepted standard. However, that being said, it's always good to know an additional language for the 5% of use cases where you have no other choice than to use Scala (plus, it's an elegant and fun language for writing code!).

I never realized how much of a struggle writing code in this imperative style would be when I first started working on ML projects. Much of my code looked like listing 13.1. So why am I harping on this, if it's something that I admit freely to having done for dozens of projects early in my career as a data scientist?

What happens if, during our experimentation and testing, we find that we have to add more features to this model? What if we go through extensive EDA and find that there are 47 additional features that we can include that might make the model perform better? What if they're all categorical?

Then our code, if built in the imperative design style shown in listing 13.1, will become an unmanageable wall of text. We'll be using the Find functionality in our browser or IDE in order to know where to go in the code to update things. The Vector-Assembler constructor alone will start to be a massive array of strings that will be hard to maintain.

Writing complicated code bases in this fashion is error-prone, fragile, and headache inducing. While the reasons stated previously are bad enough during the experimentation and development phases of a project, think about what happens if the source data changes (a column gets renamed in a source system). How many places in the code base would we have to update? Could we get to them all in time while we're on call? Would we find them all and be able to recover the job before we have a service disruption for the predictions?

I've lived that life. My success rate for fixing things (adjusting the code base to support a fundamental change that happened upstream in the data) before the lack of new predictions became obvious and a problem was, at that time, just under 40%.

So, what I applied myself to, after suffering these frustrations, was to dance along that teetering plane of balance to the entire opposite side. I became my own (and my teams') worst enemy by embracing extreme abstraction and object-oriented principles, and truly thought I was doing the right thing by producing incredibly complex code.

13.1.2 An overengineered mess

So, what did a younger Ben build? He built something like the following listing.

Listing 13.2 Overly complex model prototype

Class containing the model generation code. At an early phase in a project (as this level of complexity would be), this is unnecessary to generate. Refactoring dependencies within the methods will be far more complex than imperative scripting.

Case class definition for currying data from the main method return signature (returns both the pipeline and the scoring metric)

Externalizes the constants from the methods utilizing them (final production code would have these in their own module)

Maps over the contents of the DataFrame's schema and applies a StringIndexer to any field that is of String type and is not the label (target) field.

Method for generating a String indexer if the label (target) is of String type. Note that other values are not handled here, so a full generic implementation has not been built.

Label inverter that converts the label back into the original values. In this implementation, there are no checks for handling if the target value does not meet the criteria for indexing. In that case, this code will throw an exception.

```scala
case class ModelReturn(
                    pipeline: PipelineModel,
                    metric: Double
                    )
class BuildDecisionTree(data: DataFrame,
                        trainPercent: Double,
                        labelCol: String) {
  final val LABEL_COL = "label"
  final val FEATURES_COL = "features"
  final val PREDICTION_COL = "prediction"
  final val SCORING_METRIC = "areaUnderROC"
  private def constructIndexers(): Array[StringIndexerModel] = {
    data.schema
      .collect {
        case x if (x.dataType == StringType) & (x.name != labelCol) => x.name
      }
      .map { x =>
        new StringIndexer()
          .setInputCol(x)
          .setOutputCol(s"${x}_si")
          .setHandleInvalid("keep")
          .fit(data)
      }
      .toArray
  }
  private def indexLabel(): StringIndexerModel = {
    data.schema.collect {
      case x if (x.name == labelCol) & (x.dataType == StringType) =>
        new StringIndexer()
          .setInputCol(x.name)
          .setOutputCol(LABEL_COL)
          .setHandleInvalid("error")
          .fit(data)
    }.head
  }
  private def labelInversion(
    labelIndexer: StringIndexerModel
  ): IndexToString = {
    new IndexToString()
      .setInputCol(PREDICTION_COL)
      .setOutputCol(s"${LABEL_COL}_${PREDICTION_COL}")
```

> **Dynamic means of generating a feature vector by manipulating the column listing and types to include. This doesn't include other types of data aside from numeric and string types, which would not include those other column types into the feature vector.**

```scala
          .setLabels(labelIndexer.labelsArray(0))
    }
    private def buildVector(
      featureIndexers: Array[StringIndexerModel]
    ): VectorAssembler = {
      val featureSchema = data.schema.names.filterNot(_.contains(labelCol))
      val updatedSchema = featureIndexers.map(_.getInputCol)
      val features = featureSchema.filterNot(
        updatedSchema.contains) ++ featureIndexers
        .map(_.getOutputCol)
      new VectorAssembler()
        .setInputCols(features)
        .setOutputCol(FEATURES_COL)
    }
    private def buildDecisionTree(): DecisionTreeClassifier = {
      new DecisionTreeClassifier()
        .setLabelCol(LABEL_COL)
        .setFeaturesCol(FEATURES_COL)
        .setImpurity("entropy")
        .setMinInfoGain(1e-7)
        .setMaxDepth(6)
        .setMinInstancesPerNode(5)
    }
    private def scorePipeline(testData: DataFrame,
  pipeline: PipelineModel): Double = {
      new BinaryClassificationEvaluator()
        .setLabelCol(LABEL_COL)
        .setRawPredictionCol(PREDICTION_COL)
        .setMetricName(SCORING_METRIC)
        .evaluate(pipeline.transform(testData))
    }
    def buildPipeline(): ModelReturn = {
      val featureIndexers = constructIndexers()
      val labelIndexer = indexLabel()
      val vectorAssembler = buildVector(featureIndexers)
      val Array(train, test) = data.randomSplit(
  Array(trainPercent, 1.0-trainPercent))
      val pipeline = new Pipeline()
        .setStages(
          featureIndexers ++
          Array(
            labelIndexer,
            vectorAssembler,
            buildDecisionTree(),
            labelInversion(labelIndexer)
          )
        )
        .fit(train)
      ModelReturn(pipeline, scorePipeline(test, pipeline))
    }
  }
```

The hyperparameters for this decision-tree classifier are hardcoded. While just a placeholder, the refactoring that will be needed in this coding style for tuning will be extensive. Since this is a private method, the main method signature will either need these values passed in as arguments, or the class constructor will need these values to be passed in at instantiation. This is a poor design.

While this is a somewhat flexible design for building a pipeline based on the data passed in, it can be challenging for others to contribute to, involving paying close attention to the orders of operations that need to happen should additional stages be inserted into the pipeline constructor.

```
object BuildDecisionTree {
  def apply(data: DataFrame,
            trainPercent: Double,
            labelCol: String): BuildDecisionTree =
    new BuildDecisionTree(data, trainPercent, labelCol)
}
```

Companion object to the class. This certainly should wait until the finalized API design is complete for the project.

This code might not look too absurd at first. It does, after all, greatly minimize verbosity when considering what would occur if we added additional features to the model's feature vector. In point of fact, if we were to add even 1,000 additional features to the model, the code would stay the same. That might seem to be a distinct bonus to approaching writing ML code in this manner.

What would happen if we needed different behavior for some fields than others for the `StringIndexer`? Suppose that some fields could support having the invalid keys (categorical values that were not present during training) appended to a catchall index value, while others could not. In that case, we'd have to modify this code extensively. We'd need to abstract the method `constructIndexers()` and apply a case and match statement to generate indexers for different types of columns. We would then likely need to modify the passed-in signature argument to the wrapper methods to include a tuple (or a case class definition) of the field name and how to handle the validation of key existence.

While this approach scales well, it's a cumbersome act to undertake during experimentation phases. Instead of focusing on validating the performance of different experiments to run against a model type, we're spending a great deal of time refactoring our class, adding new methods, abstracting complexity away, and potentially all in the pursuit of an idea that might not work out well at all.

Approaching prototyping work in this manner (high abstraction and generalization) is a recipe for disaster when considering productivity. In the early phases of a project, it's best to adopt a less complex style of coding that supports rapid iteration and modification. Moving toward the style exhibited in listing 13.2 is much more applicable to the final pre-release phases of a project (code hardening), specifically when the components for producing the final project solution are known, defined, and can be identified as necessary for the code base. As an example of how I approach these phases of development work, see figure 13.2.

Because of the highly variable nature of prototyping (everything is quite fluid and elements need to change quickly), I typically stick to minimal imperative programming techniques. As the development successively moves toward a production build for the project, more and more of the complex logic is abstracted to maintainable and reusable parts in separate modules.

Building an overengineered and overly complex code architecture early in the process will, as shown in listing 13.2, create walled-in scenarios that make refactoring for feature enhancements incredibly complex. Pursuing an overengineered development approach early in a project will only waste time, frustrate the team, and eventually lead to a far more complex and difficult-to-maintain code base.

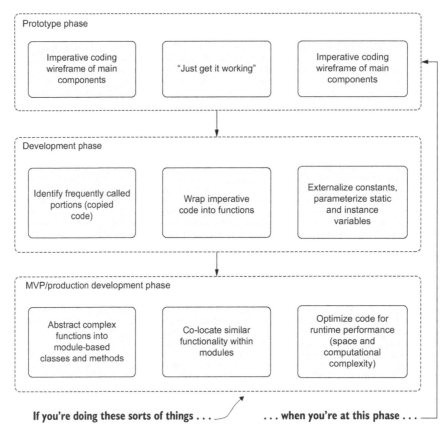

Figure 13.2   Avoiding refactoring hell by phased ML development

Don't do as I did. Fancy-looking code, particularly early in development, can only bring you problems. Choosing to pursue the simplest and most minimalistic implementation opens the door for extensibility when you need it, cohesive code structure for when you're writing production code, and a far easier-to-troubleshoot code base that isn't filled with technical debt (and dozens of TODO statements that will never get fixed).

13.2   Unintentional obfuscation: Could you read this if you didn't write it?

A rather unique form of ML hubris materializes in the form of code development practices. Sometimes malicious, many times driven by ego (and a desire to be revered), but mostly due to inexperience and fear, this particular destructive activity takes shape through the creation of unintelligibly complex code.

For our scenario, let's take a look at a common and somewhat simplistic task: recasting data types to support feature-engineering tasks. In this journey of comparative examples, we'll take a dataset whose features (and the target field) need to have their types modified to support the pipeline-enabled processing stages to build a model. This problem, at its most simplistic implementation, is shown in the next listing.

> **Listing 13.3 Imperative casting**

Encapsulates the modifications of the passed-in DataFrame by returning a DataFrame

Converts the age column to Double from its original Integer type (for demonstration purposes only)

Ensures that the weight column is of type Double

```
def simple(df: DataFrame): DataFrame = {
  df.withColumn("age", col("age").cast("double"))
    .withColumn("weight", col("weight").cast("double"))
    .withColumn("hungry", col("hungry").cast("string"))
}
```

Casts the target column from Boolean to String for the encoders to work

From this relatively simple and imperative-style implementation of casting fields in a `DataFrame`, we'll look at examples of obfuscation and discuss the impacts that each might have for something as seemingly simple as this use case.

> **NOTE** In the next section, we'll look at bad habits that some ML engineers have when writing code. Listing 13.3, it must be mentioned, is not intended to be disparaging in its approach and implementation. There is *nothing wrong with an imperative approach* when building ML code bases (provided the code base doesn't have tight coupling requiring dozens of edits if one column changes). It becomes a problem only when the complexity of the solution makes modifying imperative code a burden. If the project is simple enough, stick with simpler code. You'll thank yourself for the simplicity when you need to modify it and add new features.

13.2.1 The flavors of obfuscation

This section progresses through a sliding scale of complexity, with code examples that become progressively less intelligible, more complex, and increasingly harder to maintain. We'll analyze bad habits of some developers to aid you in identifying these coding patterns and to call them out for what they are—crippling to productivity and absolutely requiring refactoring to be maintainable.

If you find yourself going down one of these rabbit holes, these examples can serve as a reminder to not follow these patterns. But before we get to the examples, let's look at the personas that I've seen with respect to development habits, shown in figure 13.3.

These personas are not meant to identify a particular person, but rather to describe traits that a DS may go through during their journey of becoming a better developer. A nearly overwhelming number of people I've met (as well as myself)

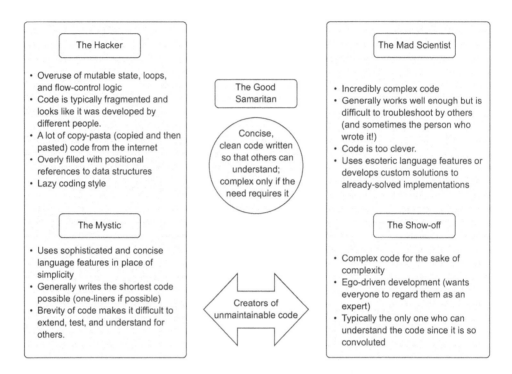

Figure 13.3   The different personas in ML code development. Moving away from the central region has a high probability of creating a lot of problems for the team in the future.

started off writing code as the Hacker. We'd find ourselves stuck on a problem that we'd never encountered before and instantly move to search online for a solution, copy someone's code, and if it worked, move on. (I'm not saying that looking on the internet or in books for information is a bad thing; even the most experienced developers do this quite frequently.)

As coding experience becomes deeper, some may lean toward one of the other three coding styles or, if they're mentored properly, move directly to the center region. Some people have something to prove—usually only to themselves, as most people just want their peers to write the sort of code that comes from a Good Samaritan developer. Others may feel that the least number of lines of code is an effective development strategy, though they're sacrificing legibility, extensibility, and testability in the process. Figure 13.4 shows the patterns that I've come across (and personally experienced).

This circuitous path leads to increasingly complex and unnecessarily complicated implementations before landing on the pinnacle of wisdom-fueled experience. The best we can hope for while making this journey is to have the ability to recognize and learn the better path—specifically, that the simplest solution to a problem (that still meets the requirements of the task) is always the best way to solve it.

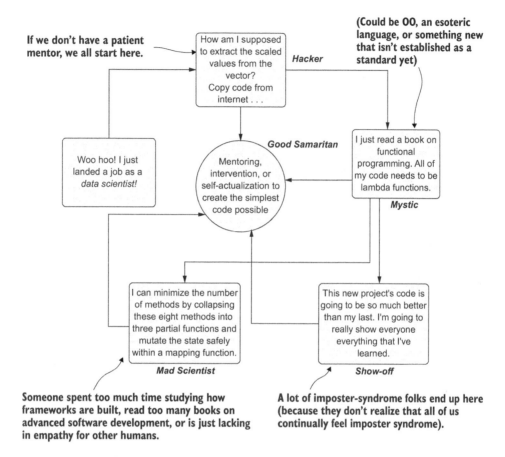

Figure 13.4 The paths of becoming a better developer

My personal history of growth as a developer

My own growth path throughout my career has touched on nearly every aspect of the journey shown in figure 13.4. Mostly driven by hubris, but also due to learning how to solve problems with code outside of a software engineering-focused company, it's been a case of learning things the hard way by screwing up constantly along the journey. I have been a Hacker (not the cool kind shown so famously in the 1995 movie *Hackers* with a "too cool for school" Jonny Lee Miller, a brief Mystic, a Show-off for too many years, a Mad Scientist on a few too many projects (much to the chagrin of my future self who had to fix code that I could no longer understand), and finally, a constant struggle to stay as a centrist Good Samaritan developer.

I mention this to illustrate that this journey is precisely as I said: a constant and Sisyphean struggle to strive for simple design and coherent code. It is, perhaps, one of the worthiest struggles to endure. The pursuit of writing cleaner and simpler code is

> **(continued)**
>
> not only to the benefit of your team and company, but also perhaps the most gener-ous gift you can give to your future self who has to troubleshoot or improve the code base later. All of the clever tricks, concise one-liners, ego-placating flexing with complex design patterns, and impossibly convoluted implementations that, in the moment of writing them, seem like a good idea, are actually not.
>
> I've had to learn this the hard way. *Repeatedly.* My only advice is to learn from my examples and be able to recognize when you or others you work with are treading toward any of these caustic development patterns. Light the beacon to bring people back to simplicity, and your projects will be more successful.

In the following sections, we'll look at versions of listing 13.3, wherein we are trying to recast some columns in a Spark `DataFrame` in order to prepare for feature-engineering transformations. It's a seemingly simple task, but by the end of this section, hopefully you'll be able to see just how "clever" someone can be by creating different types of confusing (and potentially very broken) implementations.

THE HACKER

A *Hacker* mentality is, for the most part, simply born from inexperience and a feeling of being completely overwhelmed with the concepts of software development (ML or not). Many people in this mode of development feel nervous about asking for help in building solutions or in understanding how other team members' solutions are built. Crippling feelings of inadequacy, known as *imposter syndrome*, may limit this person's growth potential if they are not provided effective mentoring and acceptance by the larger team.

Many of their projects or contributions to projects may feel completely disjointed and tonally dissonant. It may seem like different people were involved in crafting the code within the pull request that they submitted. It's likely true that there were: anon-ymous contributors to Stack Overflow.

Figure 13.5 summarizes many of the thoughts I had when I started writing full proj-ect code many years ago. I've asked other junior DS folks, after particularly rough peer reviews of their code, what motivated them to copy code from Stack Overflow, and their thought processes are paraphrased here as well.

A Hacker's code looks like a patchwork quilt. The lack of coherent structure, inconsistent naming conventions, and varying degrees of code quality is likely to get flagged repeatedly in a code or peer review submission. A test of the code (if any unit tests are written) will likely show many points of fragility in the implementation.

Listing 13.4 shows an example of what the Hacker type of developer might come up with for a solution to the column-recasting problem. While not directly indicative of a cobbled-together state, it's definitely full of antipatterns.

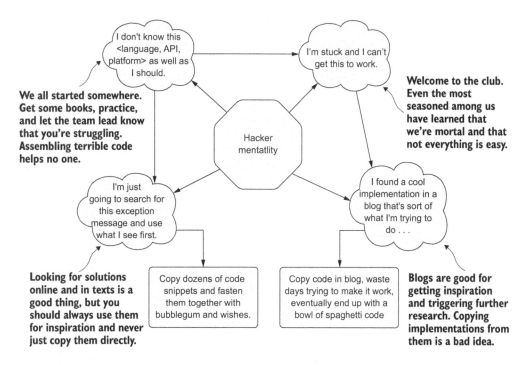

Figure 13.5 The Hacker thought pattern, creating chaotic and unstable code bases, is where we all start in ML.

Listing 13.4 Hacker's attempt at casting columns

The function argument castChanges is strange. What does the list of tuples represent?

Mutating objects is not considered a good practice in this instance. The DataFrame is immutable by nature, but declaring it as a var allows mutation to support this hacky method chaining in the foreach iterator.

Iterates over the List of tuples that are passed in

```
def hacker(df: DataFrame,
    castChanges: List[(String, String)]): DataFrame = {
  var mutated = df
  castChanges.foreach { x =>
    mutated = mutated.withColumn(x._1,
    mutated(x._1).cast(x._2))
  }
  mutated
}
val hackerRecasting = hacker(dogData, List(("age", "double"),
  ("weight", "double"),
  ("hungry", "string")))
```

Returning the mutated DataFrame will still preserve encapsulation, but it's a code sniff.

Positional notation for tuples is confusing, highly error prone, difficult to understand, and opens the door for frustration in API usage. (What happens if the data type and column names are switched?)

Example usage with the cumbersome definition of a List of tuples for the castChanges argument

In this code, we can see that the logic displayed is similar to the inherently mutable nature of Python. Instead of researching how to safely iterate over a collection to apply chained methods to an object, this developer implements a strong antipattern in Scala: mutating a shared state variable. In addition, because the function's argument castChanges has no concept of what those String values should be (which one should be the column name and which the data type is being cast to), the user of this function would have to look at the source code to understand which one goes where.

Recognizing these code smells in your peers' work is critical. Whether those people are brand-new to the team (or the profession), or have a great deal of experience and are simply "phoning it in," an effort should be made to help them. This is a perfect opportunity to work with a fellow member of the team, help them increase their skills, and in the process, build a stronger team full of engineers who are all creating more maintainable and production-stable code.

THE MYSTIC

As we progress in gaining skill and exposure to new concepts in ML software development, the next logical journey is to learn FP techniques. Unlike traditional software development, a great deal of DS coding work lends itself to functional composition. We ingest data structures (typically represented as array collections), perform operations on them, and return the modified state of the data in an encapsulated fashion. Many of our operations are based on applying algorithms to data, whether through direct calculation of values or through a transformation of structure. To a large degree, much of our code bases could be written in a stateless FP fashion.

At its core, many tasks in ML are functional. There is definitely a strong case to apply functional programming techniques to many of the operations that we do. The *Mystic* developer persona is not someone who selectively chooses appropriate places to use FP paradigms, however. Instead, they dedicate their time and effort to making the entire code base functional. They pass around configuration monads to functions in a semblance of weak state, sacrificing composition in favor of an almost fanatical zeal for the adherence of FP standards. To illustrate, figure 13.6 shows my thought processes when I discovered FP and all the wonders that it can bring to a code base.

When I first began learning FP concepts, trying my hardest to convert all of my code into this standard, I found its conciseness liberating, efficient, and elegant. I enjoyed the simplicity of stateless coding and the purity of pure encapsulation. Gone were the side-effect problems of mutating state in my earlier hacky code, replaced with slick and stylistic map, flatmap, reduce, scan, and fold. I absolutely loved the idea of containerizing and defining generic types as a way to reduce the lines of code I had to write, maintain, and debug. Everything just seemed so much more elegant.

In the process of refactoring code in this way, I managed to enrage the other people who were looking at each heavy-handed refactoring. They were right to call me out for increasing the complexity of the code base, decoupling functions in ways that didn't need decoupling, and generally making the code harder to read. To get a good

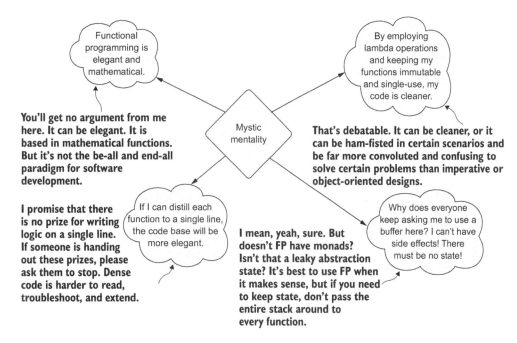

Figure 13.6 Inside the mind of an FP purist (the Mystic)

sense of what this implementation style would look like for our column casting, see the following listing.

Listing 13.5 A pure functional programming approach

The function signature's castChanges argument is safer than the Hacker's implementation. By requiring a DataType abstract class to be passed in, the chances of introducing unintentional bugs via this function are reduced.

Using a foldLeft (mapping over the castChanges collection and applying an accumulator to the passed-in DataFrame df) allows for the mutated state of the DataFrame to be far more efficient than in the Hacker approach.

```
def mystic(df: DataFrame,
           castChanges: List[(String, DataType)]
  ): DataFrame = {
  castChanges.foldLeft(df) {
    case (data, (c, t)) =>
      data.withColumn(c, df(c).cast(t))
  }
}
val mysticRecasting = mystic(dogData,
  List(("age", DoubleType),
  ("weight", DoubleType),
  ("hungry", StringType)))
```

Case matching to define the structure of the passed-in argument castChanges allows for elimination of the complicated (and annoying) positional reference that was in the Hacker implementation. This code is far cleaner.

Using the function doesn't save much on typing versus the Hacker implementation, but you can see how having these defined types for the casting conversion type makes the use of this function better.

As you can see, this implementation has a distinct functional nature. Technically speaking, for this use case, this implementation is the best of all the examples in this section. The `DataFrame` object is mutated in a safe accumulator-friendly way (the mutation state of chaining operations on the `DataFrame` is encapsulated within `fold-Left`), the argument signature utilizes base types as part of the casting (minimizing errors at usage time), and the matching signature used prevents any confusing variable-naming conventions.

The only way that I would make this a bit better would be to utilize a monad for the `castChanges` argument. Defining a case class constructor that could hold the mappings of column name to casting type would further prevent misuse or any confusing implementation details for others who wished to use this little utility function.

The issue in listing 13.5 isn't the code; rather, it is in the philosophical approach of someone who writes code in this manner and enforces these patterns everywhere in the code base. If you detect these sorts of development patterns everywhere in a code base, replete with highly convoluted and confusing state currying that ships the entire stack around to each function, you should have a chat with this person. Show them the light. Let them know that this pursuit of "purity" is as much a fool's errand as tilting at windmills. They're not the only one who has to maintain this, after all.

A word on functional programming

I know it might seem like I'm hating on FP. I'm not. You'll see in this chapter and in any code base that I contribute to that I choose to do loads of FP things. It's a wonderful programming style for what it is designed to do. In some languages, such as Python and Scala, it has performance benefits as well (using accumulators is far more efficient than using mutation).

However, what I am retroactively beating myself up for is the purist approach. In so many areas of ML development, using FP techniques simply doesn't make sense. Attempting to shoehorn an FP design pattern into deterministic state-controlled hyperparameter tuning is a recipe for disaster, for instance.

I do encourage all ML practitioners to learn FP concepts for places that make a great deal of sense. Do you need to iterate over a collection and apply a function to it? Don't use a `for` loop; use a `map` function (list comprehension in Python). Do you need to update the state of an object based on a large collection of tasks? Use a map-reduce paradigm (folding in Scala, list comprehension, again, in Python). These language features are incredibly helpful, are frequently far more performant than alternative iterators (such as `for` loops and `while` loops), and make for much cleaner code.

The only downside to using FP is if your team isn't familiar with it. That can always be addressed through training, though. Take a little bit of time to introduce the topic to your team and you'll find that iterations over collections will be easier to read, easier to write, and will run more cheaply.

THE SHOW-OFF

The *Show-off* persona can come in several forms. It can be an incredibly advanced independent contributor who has a lengthy history of developing software with no ML components. They may look at an ML project and try to build a custom implementation of an algorithm that otherwise exists in a popular open source library. They could also be a person who has graduated from being a Hacker type of developer, and armed with a deeper understanding of the implementation language and software design patterns, chooses to show everyone on the team how good they are now.

Regardless of why this sort of person builds complexity into their implementations, it will impact the team and the projects that the team must maintain in the same manner. The person who built it will end up owning it if the code isn't refactored.

There's absolutely nothing wrong with complexity in code if the use case and the problem being solved warrant that complexity. However, the Show-off type builds in complexity simply for the sake of overengineering the solution to appear skilled to others on the team. I imagine the mental state of people who fit the Show-off persona to look like figure 13.7.

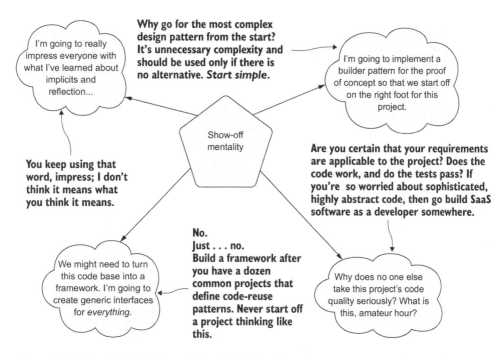

Figure 13.7   The unhelpful habits and thoughts of the Show-off

These habits and thinking patterns are significantly less than pleasant to endure when you're this person's coworker. The ideas that they're conveying aren't bad (except for the toxic one at the bottom right). Builder patterns, heavy abstraction, implicit typing, reflection, and well-crafted interfaces are all good things. However, they're tools to be used when the need arises.

The problem with the way this person thinks and writes code is that they'll start off implementing a project from the initial commit on the first branch with skeleton stubs for a grand project architecture that is completely unneeded. This is the sort of ML engineer who is focused solely on the code sophistication of the project and has little to no regard for the actual project's purpose. In this blindness, they typically strive toward writing very complex code that, to the rest of the team, seems intentionally obfuscated because of the overwhelming level of overengineering that they've done for the problem at hand.

> **TIP**   If you want everyone to think you're smart, sign up for *Jeopardy* and win some rounds. If you're flexing through your code, all you're doing is putting your team in jeopardy.

Let's take a look at our casting scenario function, this time written in the Show-off development style.

Listing 13.6   The Show-off's casting implementation

The mapping of the column name to the conversion type is odd. It's consumed in the next statement.

Defining the matching numeric types is fine for this particular implementation. What happens if integers need to be handled differently? The refactoring required to stick with this design pattern would be substantial!

```scala
val numTypes =
    List(IntegerType, FloatType, DoubleType, LongType, DecimalType, ShortType)
def showOff(df: DataFrame): DataFrame = {
    df.schema
      .map(
        s =>
          s.dataType match {
            case x if numTypes.contains(x) => s.name -> "n"
            case _                         => s.name -> "s"
          }
      )
      .foldLeft(df) {
        case (df, x) =>
          df.withColumn(x._1, df(x._1).cast(x._2 match {
            case "n" => "double"
            case _   => "string"
          }))
      }
}
val showOffRecasting = showOff(dogData)
```

The matching approach isn't bad on the data type of the passed-in DataFrame. That's the only good thing to say about this block of code.

Lazy passing of the map collection (x) from the first stage. Now position notation is required to access those values.

Once again, the wildcard match. An ArrayType or ListType column would present serious issues here.

Wildcard catch for all other conditions. What happens if the passed-in DataFrame contains a collection?

At least the instantiation of this function is pretty simple.

This code works. It behaves exactly as the three preceding examples did. It's just hard to read. By trying to show off skills and "advanced" language features, some pretty poor decisions were made.

First off, the initial mapping over the schema fields is completely unnecessary. Creating the Map type column that consists of a pseudo-enumeration of single character values to column name is not only useless, but also confusing. The collection generated from that first stage, which is then folded over in the accumulator action to the `DataFrame`, is instantly consumed, forcing the creation of a "temporary" `Map` object collection to apply the correct type casting. Finally, in the laziness of not wanting to fully write out all of the conditional matches that may occur, there's a wildcard match case in the final section. What happens when someone needs to handle a different data type? What are the steps for updating this to support binary types, integers, or Boolean values? Extending this is not going to be particularly fun.

Be wary of people who write code like this, particularly if they're a senior person on your team. A conversation about how important it is for everyone on the team to be able to maintain the code and troubleshoot it is a good approach. It's not likely that they're intentionally trying to make the code complex for others. With a request for a simpler implementation, they'll likely deliver and adjust their development strategy with this in mind for the future.

THE MAD SCIENTIST

The *Mad Scientist* developer is well-intentioned. They're also someone who has progressed on the path of knowledge of software development to a point far exceeding the fundamentals. With the amount of experience, number of projects, and sheer volume of code that they've written, they've begun to utilize advanced techniques within the languages (they typically are highly fluent in more than one) to reduce the amount of code that needs to be maintained.

These people typically think of how to tackle problems based on efficiency of development rather than from a position of wanting to be recognized for the sophistication of their code. They've learned a great deal over the years and have had to maintain (and refactor) less-than-optimal code enough that they choose to compose their implementations in ways that make it easier to troubleshoot and maintain.

These are noble goals when the rest of the team is of a similar level of technological competency as they are. However, most teams comprise a myriad of humans of differing levels of development competency. Crafting complex but highly efficient code can be a hindrance to the effectiveness of more junior people on the team. To illustrate these thought processes, figure 13.8 shows a bit of the Mad Scientist's mind.

Notice that the Mad Scientist's points are not bad ones. They're perfectly relevant and considered to be general best practices. However, the problem with this mentality arises when all the other humans working with the code aren't aware of these standards.

If code is written with these compositional rules in mind and just "thrown over the wall" by issuing a PR on a branch without the rest of the team being aware of why these standards are so important, the code design and implementation will be unintelligible to them. Let's look at our continuation of casting examples for how this Mad Scientist developer would potentially write this code in listing 13.7.

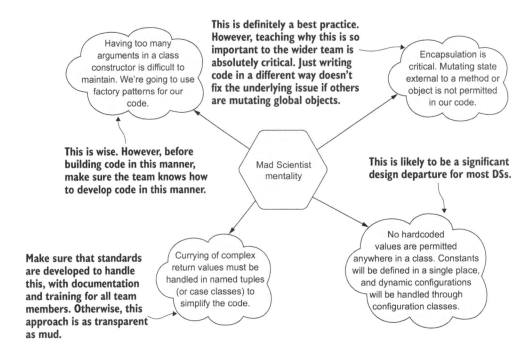

Figure 13.8   Without appropriate teaching and mentorship to the rest of the team, a more senior, highly advanced ML engineer may write code that's highly obscure and complicated.

Listing 13.7   A slightly more sophisticated casting implementation

Similar to the preceding examples, except we're iterating directly on the collection returned from the df.schema getter

Uses named entities from the return of the schema (variable s) to prevent unexpected bugs in the future

```
val numTypes = List(FloatType, DoubleType, LongType, DecimalType, ShortType)
def madScientist(df: DataFrame): DataFrame = {
  df.schema.foldLeft(df) {
    case (accum, s) =>
      accum.withColumn(s.name, accum(s.name).cast(s.dataType match {
        case x: IntegerType => x
        case x if numTypes.contains(x) => DoubleType
        case ArrayType(_,_) | MapType(_,_,_) => s.dataType
        case _                  => StringType
      }))
  }
}
```

By wrapping the decision logic within the casting statement, there are fewer lines of code. Matching directly to types from the metadata of the schema is going to be more future-proof as well.

Moves away from the confusing name reference df as in previous examples. Although it would be encapsulated here (and safe), naming it df is confusing to read.

Now, there's nothing wrong with this code. It's concise, covers the use case needed rather well, and is designed to not spontaneously detonate if complex types (arrays and maps) are in a column in the dataset. The only caveat here is to ensure that design patterns like this are maintainable by your team. If they're OK with maintaining and writing code in this manner, it's a good solution. However, if the rest of the team is used to imperative-style programming, this code design can be as cryptic as if it were written in a different language.

If the team is facing overwhelming mountains of imperative calls, it would be best to introduce the team to coding styles exemplified in listing 13.7. Taking the time to teach and mentor the rest of the team on more efficient development practices can accelerate project work and reduce the amount of maintenance involved in supporting projects. However, it is absolutely critical for more senior people to educate other team members as to *why* these standards are important. This does not mean throwing out a link to a language specification (someone linking the PEP-8 standard of Python to a PR is a pet peeve of mine), nor just firing off branches containing dense and efficient code at the team. Rather, it means crafting well-documented code, providing examples in the internal team documentation store, conducting training sessions, and sitting through pair programming with the less experienced members of the team.

If you happen to be one of these Mad Scientist types, writing elegant and well-constructed code that is misunderstood and opaque to the rest of your team members, the first thing that you should be thinking about is teaching. It is far more effective to help everyone understand why these paradigms of development are good than to write scathing PR review notes and reject merge requests. After all, if you're writing good code and submitting it to a team that doesn't have experience in the paradigms that you're utilizing, it's just as obfuscated as the mess of the Show-off code in listing 13.6.

A SAFER BET

Let's look at a safer, more legible, and slightly more standard method of solving this problem. Here's what a more maintainable implementation would look like.

Listing 13.8 A safer bet on invalid types casting

Uses an object for encapsulation and more efficient garbage collection by the JVM

Explicitly declares the data types that we want to convert to StringType

Explicitly declares the data types that we want to convert to DoubleType

Breaks out the schema reference purely to reduce the code complexity and make it more approachable to others reading it

```
object SimpleReCasting {
  private val STRING_CONVERSIONS = List(
BooleanType, CharType, ByteType)
  private val NUMERIC_CONVERSIONS = List(
FloatType, DecimalType)
  def castInvalidTypes(df: DataFrame): DataFrame = {
    val schema: StructType = df.schema
    schema.foldLeft(df) {
      case (outputDataFrame, columnReference) => {
        outputDataFrame.withColumn(columnReference.name,
          outputDataFrame(columnReference.name)
          .cast(columnReference.dataType match {
```

```
        case x if STRING_CONVERSIONS.contains(x) =>
          StringType
        case x if NUMERIC_CONVERSIONS.contains(x) =>
          DoubleType
        case _ => columnReference.dataType
      }))
}}}}
```

Converts only the numeric types that match our listing to DoubleType

Don't touch anything else. Just leave it be.

Converts the types that we declared to StringType if they're in our configuration listing

Notice the wrapping of the code in an object? This is to isolate references to those Lists that are defined. We don't want variables like that defined globally in a code base, so encapsulating them in an object serves that purpose.

In addition, the encapsulation makes it far easier for the garbage collector to remove references to objects that are no longer needed. SimpleRecasting, once used and no longer referred to within the code, will be removed from the heap along with all other encapsulated objects within it. The seemingly more verbose naming convention (which helps a new reader follow along with what is being acted upon within the foldLeft operation), enables this code to be read more clearly than the briefer code of listing 13.7.

A final note regarding this code is that the operations are entirely explicit. This is the largest hallmark of the difference in this code as compared to all previous examples, except for the original reference in listing 13.3 of the imperative casting. Here, as in that earlier example, we're changing only the typing of column types that we're explicitly commanding the system to change. We're not defaulting behavior to "just cast everything else as String" or anything else that would create fragile, unpredictable behavior.

This approach to thinking about coding will save you a lot of frustrating hours, days, and months of your life troubleshooting seemingly innocuous code that blows up in production. We'll revisit some of the ways that defaulting unknown state to a static value (or imputed values) can come back to bite us as ML engineers in the next chapter. For now, just realize that being explicit about actions is definitely a good design pattern for ML.

13.2.2 Troublesome coding habits recap

In the preceding section, we focused on several, shall we say, unfriendly ways to write code. Each is bad in its own way and for a myriad of reasons, but the worst offending reasons are in table 13.2.

The most important aspect of writing code to keep in mind is that the code that you create is not purely for the benefit of the system executing it. If that were the case, the profession would likely never have moved away from low-level code frameworks for writing instructions (second-generation languages such as assembly languages or, for the truly masochistic, first-generation machine code).

Table 13.2 Developer implementation sins

Sinful persona	Why it's so bad
Hacker	Fragile code is fragmented and stitched together, and breaks frequently.
Mystic	Complicated and dense code takes far too long to reverse engineer. Untestable nested code can silently introduce difficult-to-diagnose bugs.
Show-off	Intentionally complex code is intended to make others feel unworthy. Impossible to troubleshoot, repair, or expand upon. Nightmare code.
Mad Scientist	Too clever of an implementation for peers to understand (because of a failure to teach). Too rigid to allow for lightweight testing or extensibility.

Languages have advanced through higher-order generations not for the sake of computational efficiency for the processor and memory of the computers; rather, it has been for the sake of the humans writing, and more important, reading the code to figure out what it does. We write code, using high-level APIs when we can, and construct our code in ways to make it easy to read and maintain, solely for the benefit of our peers and future selves.

Avoid the habits listed in table 13.2 and move toward writing the code needed by you, your team, and the sort of technical talent that you're targeting to hire in the future for roles in your group. Doing so will help make everyone productive and able to contribute to building and maintaining solutions, and will prevent inefficient refactoring of horribly complex code bases to fix crushing technical debt wrought by unthinking developers.

13.3 Premature generalization, premature optimization, and other bad ways to show how smart you are

Let's suppose that we're starting a new project with a team of relatively advanced (from a software development perspective) ML engineers. At the start of the project, the architect decides that the best way to control the state of the code is to design and implement a framework for executing the modeling and inference tasks. The team is incredibly excited! Finally, the team members think, some interesting work!

In their collective giddiness, none of them realize that, aside from illegible code, one of the worst forms of hubris is that of spending time where time does not need to be spent. They're about to build useless framework code bases that serve no real purpose apart from being a justification for their own existence.

13.3.1 Generalization and frameworks: Avoid them until you can't

The first thing that the team does is work on a product requirements document (PRD) that outlines what they want their unique framework to do. A general design, based on a builder pattern, is drafted. The architect wants the team to do the following:

1 Ensure that custom default values are utilized throughout the project code (not relying on API defaults)

2 Enforce overriding of certain elements of the modeling process with respect to tuning hyperparameters

3 Wrap the open source APIs with naming conventions and structural elements that are more in line with the code standards at the company

Before experimentation is done, a plan of features is developed, as shown in figure 13.9.

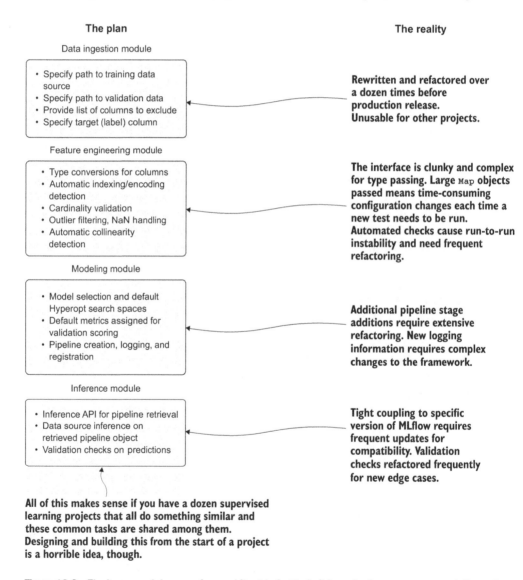

Figure 13.9 The hopes and dreams of an architect trying to build a cohesive wrapper around disparate frameworks to support all ML needs of the company. Spoiler alert: it doesn't end well.

This plan for critical features is more than a little ambitious. Were this to proceed, the Reality aspects shown at the right side of the figure would likely play out (they've always happened whenever I've seen someone attempt to do this). Full of rework, refactoring, and redesign, this project would be doomed.

Instead of focusing on solving the problem by using existing frameworks (such as Spark, pandas, scikit-learn, NumPy, and R), the team would be supporting not only a project solution, but a custom implementation of a framework wrapper—and all of the pain that goes along with that. If you're not staffed with dozens of software engineers to support a framework, it's best to think carefully about planning to construct one.

Adding to the immense workload of building and maintaining such a software stack is the simple fact that you'd be attempting to support a wrapper that is more generic than the framework that it is wrapping. Engaging in work like this never ends well for two primary reasons:

- *You now own a framework*—This means updates, compatibility guarantees, and a truly massive amount of testing to write (you *are* writing tests, right?). Functionality assurances are now in lockstep with the packages that you're using to build the framework.
- *You now own a framework*—Unless you're planning on making it truly generic, open sourcing it and having a community of committers involved in its growth, and committing to maintaining it, it's pointless work to engage in.

Pursuing generalized approaches truly makes sense only if a direct need for that exists. Does a critical new functionality need to be developed to make another framework for ML work more efficiently? Perhaps think about contributing to that open source framework, then. Is there a need to stitch together disparate low-level APIs to solve a common problem? This is likely a good case for the creation of a framework.

The *last thing* that you should be thinking about when starting a project, unlike our architect friend, is setting about building a custom framework to support that particular project. The premature generalization work involved (in time, distraction, and frustration) will detract heavily from the project's pending work, will delay and disrupt productive work that should be focused on solving the problem, and will inevitably need to be reworked many times over throughout the evolution of the project. It's simply not worth it.

Should I ever build a generic framework?
Of course! Well . . . maybe.

I'll list some considerations to think about and then leave you to determine whether building a framework is something you actually want to pursue (provided it's engaged in during designated time and not during a project delivery):

- How many people do you have on your team? If you can't devote at least 16 human hours per week to maintaining the framework, adding features, and troubleshooting it, you should reconsider whether it's worthwhile to start.

(continued)

- Are you planning on open sourcing it? How much of a community can you build around it? What are the company's legal rules around maintaining open source software? How much time can you devote to supporting the software?
- Does it solve a novel problem, or are you building functionality that already exists in another tool?
- Could you buy a tool or platform that does what you want your framework to do? If that's the case, I guarantee that buying that tool or using existing open source solutions will be cheaper than devoting your time and energy to building your own.
- How many dependencies will this framework have? For each additional package that you're bringing on, you're adding a factorial of headaches to its long-term maintenance. Software packages and dependencies change all the time with many deprecations that are little more than future threats that your framework is going to blow up in your face one day.
- What's the additional value that this planned framework brings? If it isn't accelerating your current and future project work by at least twice the amount of time you're going to spend building and maintaining this framework, it's a waste of time and energy.

Is the framework just a wrapper around another open source framework? The number of times I've seen people write a custom wrapper around pandas or Spark is truly shocking. Everything works well up until the next major release that has fundamental breaking changes (or the next minor critical feature addition that now requires implementing a wrapper for your custom APIs), forcing you to effectively rewrite your framework from scratch.

Those are just a few of the questions that I ask people who tell me that they're going to build a generic framework for ML work. I'm not trying to be dismissive of their lofty goals; it's just that I've been there and know firsthand the pains of maintaining something of this nature.

It makes perfect sense to build when you have hundreds of XGBoost models running in production to provide predictive insight into your business. But the business, and you, should understand the awfully large amount of work that you're getting yourself into. Pursue this path only when it would be foolish not to build a framework; a high-level API for building, monitoring, and inferring from hundreds of XGBoost models would be a good reason to build one.

13.3.2 Optimizing too early

Let's suppose we work for a different company—one without that architect from the previous section, preferably. This company, instead of an empire-building architect, has an advisor to the DS team who comes from a backend engineering background. Throughout this person's career, they've focused on SLAs that can be measured in milliseconds, algorithms that traverse collections in the most efficient way possible, and vast amounts of time eking out every available CPU cycle. Their world is entirely focused on the performance of discreet portions of code.

On the first project, the advisor wants to contribute to the DS team's work by helping to build out a load tester. Since the team is yet again dealing with determining whether dogs are hungry when entering the local pet supply store, the advisor guides the team on implementing a solution.

Based on their experience and knowledge of Scala for backend systems, the team members end up focusing on something that is highly optimized for minimizing the memory pressure on the JVM. They want to eschew mutable buffer collections in favor of explicit collection building (using only the minimum amount of memory needed) with a fixed predetermined size of the collection. Because of prior experience, they spend a few days building the code in order to generate the data needed to test the throughput of the modeling solution for inference purposes.

To start, the advisor works on defining the data structure that is going to be used for testing. Listing 13.9 shows both the data structure and the defining static parameters to generate the data with.

NOTE The Scala formatting in listing 13.9 is condensed for printing purposes and is not representative of proper Scala syntax design.

Listing 13.9 Configuration and common structures for data generator

Uses a case object to store
static values for data generation
(a pseudo-enumeration in Scala)

```scala
import org.apache.spark.sql.functions._
import org.apache.spark.sql.types._
import org.apache.spark.sql.{DataFrame, SparkSession}
import scala.collection.mutable.ArrayBuffer
import scala.reflect.ClassTag
import scala.util.Random
case class Dogs(age: Int, weight: Double, favorite_food: String,
                breed: String, good_boy_or_girl: String, hungry: Boolean)
case object CoreData {
  def dogBreeds: Seq[String] = Seq("Husky", "GermanShepherd", "Dalmation",
     "Pug", "Malamute", "Akita", "BelgianMalinois", "Chinook", "Estrela",
     "Doberman", "Mastiff")
  def foods: Seq[String] = Seq("Kibble", "Spaghetti", "Labneh", "Steak",
     "Hummus", "Fajitas", "BœufBourgignon", "Bolognese")
  def goodness: Seq[String] = Seq("yes", "no", "sometimes",
     "yesWhenFoodAvailable")
  def hungry: Seq[Boolean] = Seq(true, false)
  def ageSigma = 3
  def ageMean = 2
  def weightSigma = 12
  def weightMean = 60
}
trait DogUtility {
  lazy val spark: SparkSession = SparkSession.builder().getOrCreate()
  def getDoggoData[T: ClassTag](a: Seq[T], dogs: Int, seed: Long): Seq[T] = {
```

Defines the dataset
schema (with typing)
for testing

Uses a trait for multiple
inheritance to test
different implementations
and to keep the code
cleaner

We'll use a Spark
session reference in the
objects later, so having
it available in the trait
makes sense.

```
    val rnd = new Random(seed)
    Seq.fill(dogs)(a(rnd.nextInt(a.size)))
}
def getDistributedIntData(sigma: Double, mean: Double, dogs: Int,
                          seed: Long): Seq[Int] = {
  val rnd = new Random(seed)
  (0 until dogs).map(
    _ => math.ceil(math.abs(rnd.nextGaussian() * sigma + mean)).toInt)
}
def getDistributedDoubleData(sigma: Double, mean: Double, dogs: Int,
                             seed: Long): Seq[Double] = {
  val rnd = new Random(seed)
  (0 until dogs).map( _ => math.round(math.abs(rnd.nextGaussian() * sigma *
  100 + mean)).toDouble / 100)
}
}
```

Generates a random Gaussian distribution of Double values based on the mean and sigma

Uses a generic type to randomly fill in values (Strings or Booleans) into a fixed-size sequence

Generates a random Gaussian distribution of Integer values based on the passed-in mean and sigma values

Now that the helper code has been developed to control the behavior and nature of the simulation data, the advisor tests the performance of the methods defined in the trait DogUtility. The performance scales well to hundreds of millions of elements after a few hours of tweaking and refactoring.

It should go without saying that this implementation is a bit of an overkill for the problem at hand. Since this is at the start of the project, not only are the features required for the end-result condition of the model not fully defined, but the statistical distribution of the features hasn't been analyzed yet. The advisor decides that it's now time to build the actual control execution code for generating the data as a Spark DataFrame, as shown in the next listing.

Listing 13.10 An overly complex and incorrectly optimized data generator

Uses the trait DogUtility defined earlier to have access to the methods and SparkContext defined there

Uses implicits from Spark to be able to cast a collection of case class objects directly through serialization to a DataFrame object (cuts down on a lot of nasty code)

```
object PrematureOptimization extends DogUtility {
  import spark.implicits._
  case class DogInfo(columnName: String,
                     stringData: Option[Either[Seq[String],
                     Seq[Boolean]]],
                     sigmaData: Option[Double],
                     meanData: Option[Double],
                     valueType: String)
```

This is a mess. The Either type allows for a right-justified selection between two types and is challenging to extend properly. A generic type would have been better here.

The value type allows for optimized implementations of the generator below (for number of lines, not for ease of comprehension to the reader).

The Option type is here because these values are not needed for some of the configured method calls for the data generators (one doesn't need to define a sigma for a collection of Strings to be randomly sampled from).

An overly fancy and optimized (for code length) implementation for calling the data generators based on the configuration specified in the method dogDataConstruct (this implementation is fragile)

Builds the control payload for defining how the data generators will be called (and in which order)

```scala
def dogDataConstruct: Seq[DogInfo] = {
  Seq(DogInfo("age", None, Some(CoreData.ageSigma),
      Some(CoreData.ageMean), "Int"),
    DogInfo("weight", None, Some(CoreData.weightSigma),
        Some(CoreData.weightMean), "Double"),
    DogInfo("food", Some(Left(CoreData.foods)), None, None, "String"),
    DogInfo("breed", Some(Left(CoreData.dogBreeds)),
      None, None, "String"),
    DogInfo("good", Some(Left(CoreData.goodness)),
      None, None, "String"),
    DogInfo("hungry", Some(Right(CoreData.hungry)),
      None, None, "Boolean"))
}
def generateOptimizedData(rows: Int,
  seed: Long): DataFrame = {
  val data = dogDataConstruct.map( x => x.columnName -> {
      x.valueType match {
        case "Int" => getDistributedIntData(x.sigmaData.get,
                        x.meanData.get, rows, seed)
        case "Double" => getDistributedDoubleData(x.sigmaData.get,
                          x.meanData.get, rows, seed)
        case "String" => getDoggoData(x.stringData.get.left.get,
                          rows, seed)
        case _         => getDoggoData(
  x.stringData.get.right.get,
    rows,
    seed)
      }
    }
).toMap
    val collection = (0 until rows).toArray
      .map(x => {
        Dogs(
          data("age")(x).asInstanceOf[Int],
          data("weight")(x).asInstanceOf[Double],
          data("food")(x).asInstanceOf[String],
          data("breed")(x).asInstanceOf[String],
          data("good")(x).asInstanceOf[String],
          data("hungry")(x).asInstanceOf[Boolean]
        )
      })
      .toSeq
    collection.toDF()
  }
}
```

OK, so this is horrible for accessing a value. Two .get operations? You've got to be kidding me.

The root cause of the performance issues noticed below. This defaults to a Seq type but should be an IndexedSeq type to allow for O(1) access to individual values, instead of the current O(n).

Wraps each collection of data in a Map object to make accessing the values by name easier than doing positional notation

Major problem #2 with this code—mapping over the index positions of each collection to build rows. This is O(kn) in complexity.

Converts to a Spark DataFrame

After doing some testing on this code, the team members come to realize fairly quickly that the relationship between generated row size and runtime is far from linear. In fact, it's much worse than linear, being more akin to $O(n \times \log(n))$ in computational complexity. Generating 5,000 rows takes about 0.6 seconds, while a heavy load test-ing of 500,000 rows takes around 1 minute and 20 seconds. With the full load test of 50 million rows, the idea of waiting around for 2 hours and 54 minutes is a bit much.

What went wrong? They spent all of their time optimizing individual parts of the code so that, in isolation, each executed as quickly as possible. When the entire code was executed, it was a dismal mess. The implementation is just too clever in all of the wrong ways.

Why is it so slow, though? It's the last part that is so crippling. Although the mem-ory pressure is minimal for this implementation, the row count generation within the defined variable `collection` has to perform a non-indexed position lookup for each `Sequence` in the `Map` collection. At each iteration to build the `Dogs()` objects, the `Sequence` needs to be traversed to that point in order to retrieve the value.

Now, this example is a bit hyperbolic. After all, if this backend developer was really adept at their optimizations, they likely would have utilized an indexed collection and cast the data object from a `Sequence` to an `IndexedSeq` (which would be able to drive directly to the position being requested and return the correct value in a fraction of the time). This implementation, even with that change, is still *sniffing about in the wrong place*.

The performance is terrible, but that's only part of the story. What happens to the code in listing 13.10 if another data type needs to be added to be handled in the same manner as the `String` data? Is the developer going to wrap another `Either[]` state-ment around the first one? Is that then going to be wrapped in another `Option[]` type? How much of an unholy mess is this code going to become if a Spark `Vector` type needs to be generated? Because it was built in this manner, optimized excessively to an early state of a pre-MVP version of the solution, this code is either going to need to be modified heavily throughout the project to keep it synchronized with the DS team's feature-engineering work or will need to be rewritten completely from scratch when it becomes cumbersome and unmaintainable. The likeliest path for this code is that it is destined for the infinite well of trash that is an `rm -rf` command.

The following listing shows a slightly different implementation that utilizes a far simpler approach. This code is focused on reducing the runtime by an order of magnitude.

Listing 13.11   A far more performant data generator

Identical to the implementation in listing 13.10

To eliminate one stage of the iteration over the collection, we can just append each generated sequence of values (the eventual row data) to a Buffer.

Adds the first column's data (the integers generated randomly for age) to the Buffer

```
object ConfusingButOptimizedDogData extends DogUtility {
  import spark.implicits._
  private def generateCollections(rows: Int,
seed: Long): ArrayBuffer[Seq[Any]] = {
    var collections = new ArrayBuffer[Seq[Any]]()
    collections += getDistributedIntData(CoreData.ageSigma,
CoreData.ageMean, rows, seed)
```

Iterates over each row collection and
generates the Dogs case class structure
directly through position notation

```
    collections += getDistributedDoubleData(CoreData.weightSigma,
      CoreData.weightMean, rows, seed)
    Seq(CoreData.foods, CoreData.dogBreeds, CoreData.goodness,
      CoreData.hungry)
      .foreach(x => { collections += getDoggoData(
        x, rows, seed)})
    collections
  }
  def buildDogDF(rows: Int, seed: Long): DataFrame = {
    val data = generateCollections(rows, seed)
    data.flatMap(_.zipWithIndex)
        .groupBy(_._2).values.map( x =>
          Dogs(
            x(0)._1.asInstanceOf[Int],
            x(1)._1.asInstanceOf[Double],
            x(2)._1.asInstanceOf[String],
            x(3)._1.asInstanceOf[String],
            x(4)._1.asInstanceOf[String],
            x(5)._1.asInstanceOf[Boolean])).toSeq.toDF()
    .withColumn("hungry", when(col("hungry"),
      "true").otherwise("false"))
    .withColumn("hungry", when(col("breed") === "Husky",
      "true").otherwise(col("hungry")))
    .withColumn("good_boy_or_girl",  when(col("breed") === "Husky",
      "yesWhenFoodAvailable").otherwise(
        col("good_boy_or_girl")))
  }
}
```

Iterates through a collection
of all the String and Boolean
columns' data and passes their
configured allowable values to
the generator one by one

Calls the private method
defined above to get the
ArrayBuffer of randomly
sampled data for testing

Collapses the data to tuples that
contain the row values together
in the correct generated order

A husky will do
anything for
food. It will do
nothing for an
absence of food.

If you've ever known
a husky, you'll know
that they're always
hungry.

Might as well cast the Boolean
field to a String type to save a
processing step later

How did the code perform, once refactored? Well, it scales linearly now. The 5,000 rows of data took less than a second; 50,000 rows took 1 second; and 5 million rows returned in just under 1 minute and 35 seconds. The 50 million target that was tested from the previous implementation, however, returns that row count in approximately 15 minutes. That's quite a bit better than the more than 174 minutes from the earlier implementation.

While this scenario is focused on a load-testing data generator and is esoteric for most DS practitioners, much can be said for other aspects of more ML-centric tasks. What would happen if someone were to focus on optimizing for performance one of the least important (computationally, that is) aspects of an ML pipeline? What if someone focused all of their energy on a project into, as we were looking at in the first section of this chapter, the performance of casting columns to specific types?

Figure 13.10 shows a general breakdown of most ML workflows for a training cycle. Note the Fermi-level estimations for each listed execution action for a generic ML

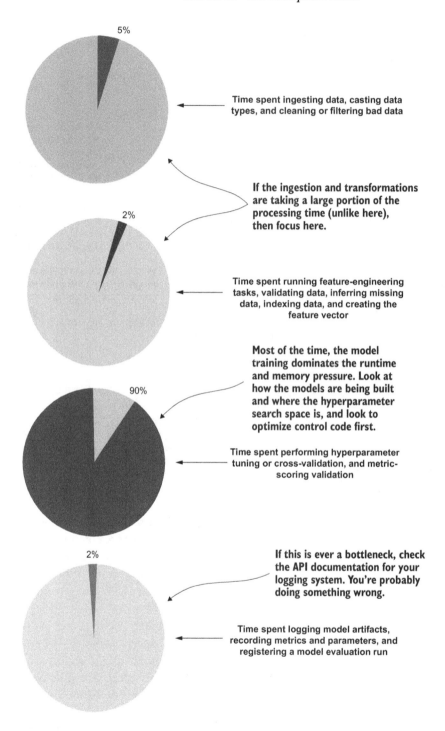

5%

Time spent ingesting data, casting data
types, and cleaning or filtering bad data

If the ingestion and transformations
are taking a large portion of the
processing time (unlike here),
then focus here.

2%

Time spent running feature-engineering
tasks, validating data, inferring missing
data, indexing data, and creating the
feature vector

Most of the time, the model
training dominates the runtime
and memory pressure. Look at
how the models are being built
and where the hyperparameter
search space is, and look to
optimize control code first.

90%

Time spent performing hyperparameter
tuning or cross-validation, and metric-
scoring validation

If this is ever a bottleneck, check
the API documentation for your
logging system. You're probably
doing something wrong.

2%

Time spent logging model artifacts,
recording metrics and parameters, and
registering a model evaluation run

Figure 13.10   A generic breakdown of wall-clock runtime for tasks within an ML pipeline

project. Where would you spend your effort if you were trying to optimize this job? Where should you look first for problems and address them?

As you can see, the vast majority of processing time for ML project code is primarily focused on data ingestion manipulations (loading data, joining data, calculating aggregations on data, and converting ordinal and categorical data to numeric representations) and hyperparameter tuning. If you notice that data ingestion is absolutely dominating the runtime of your project (provided that the platform you are utilizing can support massive parallel ingestion and the data storage format is optimal for rapid reading, as in Delta, Parquet, Avro, or a streaming source like Kafka), then look to either replatform your data to a more efficient storage paradigm or research more effective means of manipulating your data.

An incredibly small amount of time is spent on logging, model registration, and basic data manipulation tasks. Therefore, if these show a problem, the fix is likely going to be done relatively easily by reading the API documentation for the module that you're utilizing and correcting the errors in your code.

Knowing this, any optimization efforts should be primarily focused on reducing the total runtime and CPU pressure of these high temporal-bound stages of a job and not wasted on creating complex and clever code for insignificant portions of the solution. The key takeaway is that the process of optimizing ML code should focus on a few key critical aspects:

- *Wait until the entire code base functions end to end before spending time optimizing code.* The sheer number and frequency of changes that happen during development will likely make rework of optimized code a frustrating experience.
- *Identify the longest-running portions of the code.* Attempt to get clever to make these more performant before tackling the portions that are already comparatively fast.
- *Don't reinvent the wheel.* If a language construct (or similar functionality in a completely different language, for that matter) will remarkably speed up or reduce memory pressure of what you're trying to do, just use it. Implementing your own linked list abstract class or designing a new dictionary collection is the ultimate act of hubris. Just use what is out there and move on to solving a more worthwhile problem.
- *Explore different algorithms if the runtime is truly terrible.* Just because you really like gradient boosted trees doesn't mean that they're the ideal solution to every problem. Perhaps a linear model could get relatively close in performance at a fraction of the runtime. Is 0.1% accuracy worth a 50-times increase in budget to run the model?

Embodied within the collective DS-DNA of many teams that I see engage in premature optimization and generalization is the belief that the technical aspects of ML project work supersede the problems that they are trying to solve. They love the tools, the amazing new work being pushed out by large ML-focused organizations, and the rapid advancements being made continually in the ecosystem of ML. These groups care far more about the platforms, the toolkits, the frameworks, the algorithms, and the tech side of ML work than they do about making sure that their approach is going to help their business in the most efficient and maintainable way possible.

13.4 *Do you really want to be the canary? Alpha testing and the dangers of the open source coal mine*

Let's pretend for a moment that you are incredibly new to the field of DS. So new, in fact, that it's your first week on the job. In the office, you look around your desk. Not a single DS on the team has been employed in the profession for more than a month. The manager, an experienced software engineer, is busy with managing not only the DS team, but also the business intelligence team and the data warehousing group, and is busy interviewing additional candidates to fully round out the new DS team.

As a first task, a low-hanging fruit modeling project is generated for the team to tackle. Being told that no, you can't use your laptops to do the work as you did in school, the direction that the manager gives all of you is to select a framework for developing models.

Within the first few days of research and investigations into platforms and solutions, one of the team members catches wind of a new framework being discussed in blogs. It seems to be forward-thinking, feature-rich, and easy to use. The general discussion around what is planned to be built for it over the coming months is incredibly powerful. There is talk about supporting not only CPU tasks in a distributed massively parallel processing (MPP) system written in C++ that has a slick-looking Python API as an interface, but also GPU clusters and future plans to support a quantum computing interface (quantum oracle optimization of superposition of all possible solutions to least squares problems)!

If you've ever read the source code for an ML framework (one that's used by a majority of professionals in solving actual problems, that is), contributed to one, or built even a wrapper around the functionality exposed in one of the more popular open source ones out there, you'll realize how silly this "new and hot" framework is. If that describes you, you'd be in the right-hand section of figure 13.11 (not bitter, but rather, wise).

Let's agree that the team we're on is entrenched within the middle column of figure 13.11. The team members' naivete blinds them to the dangers that they're about to face in embracing this half-baked hubristic monstrosity that an overly ambitious developer is attempting to build. We try it out, we volunteer to be the canary, and our project pays with its life.

The end result of working in this new and heavily under-construction framework is inevitable: a complete and thorough failure. The failure of getting the project off the ground isn't because of the API they're using, nor is it in how they are tuning their solution. The real failure is in the hubris of the developer and the blog hype-o-sphere that surrounds bombastic claims of new functionality and frameworks.

The hype-o-sphere	What the innocent and naive take away	What the experienced (and possibly bitter) take away
Blog spam Hey Everyone! Check out the new ML framework that runs on remote quantum computers at a fraction of the cost of GPUs!	"Quantum computing! Wow! I bet that is *so fast*. Let me try the demo!"	"Excuse me, what did you say?"
Clickbait blog spam nonsense OMG! We just used this new quantum computing framework, and it helped us cure 37 types of cancer in one week!	"Well, I tried the demo. I didn't see anything about QC, but I like the APIs in the demo. It just feels more Pythonic than pandas and NumPy."	"What is this nonsense?"
Editorial review While still missing a few critical features, this new ML framework, utilizing Apache Arrow as the foundational data serialization format and highly optimized BLAS operators for algorithmic efficiency in a novel distributed system, shows some promise . . .	"Wow, a lot of people are talking about this framework! We really need to use this for our next project!"	"BLAS operators? Who cares? NumPy, Spark, and R all use those standards for basic linear algebra. That does not a good framework make."
Serious blog review While I like the features that are present right now, I feel like the backlog features need to be fully developed in order to make this a fully fledged solution for us. I'll be keeping an eye on the progress, though!	"It's decided. We're running with this if <insert tech influencer here> says that it's good."	"Half-baked. I'll evaluate it thoroughly at the 1.0 release, and if does what it says it does, I'll think about porting a few code bases over to it. Maybe."
Developer panic three months after 0.1 release Want to help contribute to the fastest-growing open source ML framework community? We're looking for skilled C++ developers, CUDA folks, and anyone with experience building production ML solutions!	"I don't know C++, but I'll contact them and offer my suggestions for features! I'll also file a few dozen issue tickets in GitHub to help them out!"	"Bit off a bit more than you could chew, eh? Feeling a bit overwhelmed? Maybe you shouldn't have flown so close to the sun."

Figure 13.11   The hype? It's real. It also usually means that the object of that hype is really bad (or at least not what it claims to be).

There is absolutely nothing wrong with trying things out. I frequently try out these newly announced packages to see if they're worthwhile. I do my testing on open source datasets, run them in isolated environments that won't contaminate my class path with flaky dependencies, and run them through their paces. I evaluate their claimed functionality, check for the ease of enhancing their functionality with custom implementations, and see how the system handles different modeling tasks. Is the memory utilization stable? Is the CPU usage on par (or, hopefully, better!) than comparable systems in widespread use? I ask all of these questions and more through my validations of their claims.

What I never do is attempt to build a project that a business depends on while using one of these packages in their early stages. There are several reasons for this:

- *The API's are going to change—a lot.* The entire interface will likely be completely refactored by the time a stable 1.0 release happens. You'll have to change your code to accommodate.
- *Things will be broken.* Maybe a few things, but usually a lot of things at the beginning of a project's alpha release phase. If you build something important on top of flaky code, you'll be dealing with an unstable project code base.
- *There's no guarantee that the project isn't going to become shelfware.* If a seriously strong community doesn't exist around the project with hundreds or thousands of contributors and buy-in by a significant portion of the ML community, the code base is likely going to become extinct and abandoned. You really don't want your project running on dead code.
- *Even at the first announced release, tech debt is in there.* Corners were cut, shortcuts were traversed, and bugs will be present. It may work great for the demos and be flawless for the prepackaged examples, but it likely won't work well for your highly specific custom logic that you need to implement to solve your predictive modeling task for your business. At least not until much later in its life cycle.
- *Just because it's new doesn't mean it's better.* Before deciding on something as critical as a framework or platform, you absolutely have to ignore the marketing hype from companies, blog posters, and the noisy buzz of advertisements. Test things out and perform a scientific study of your options. Select the solution that makes the most sense from a productivity, maintainability, stability, and cost perspective. The shiny new toy could be all of those things, but in my experience, it's almost never the case (although sometimes these projects do grow into exactly that eventually, so keep an eye on them).

Embracing another person's hubris is one of the most destructive tasks that can plague an ML team. By not doing proper testing and research of options about how and where to run your code, you run the risk of getting duped into a system that is fundamentally broken and will end up costing your team far more time and money in just keeping the lights on rather than innovating into new project solutions that you should be working on. Let your testing phase be your canary, not your ML projects.

13.5 *Technology-driven development vs. solution-driven development*

Let's shift gears from the newbie-crew of DS members in section 13.4 and take a look at working in a group filled with highly experienced ML engineers. Let's suppose that not a single person on the team has fewer than 20 years of software development experience, and each has grown bored and tired with building different flavors of deep learning models, gradient boosted trees, linear models, and univariate forecasts.

They all yearn to build something to automate away the tedium of the hundreds of predictive models that they are working on. What they want more than anything is a challenge.

When faced with their next major project, an association-rules-based implementation (were they to use a tried-and-true approach), they decide to get clever. They feel as though they could write a more performant version of the FP-growth algorithm on Apache Spark and set to work deriving an equation for an improved version of an FP-tree that can be mined dynamically in such a way as to eliminate one of the core scans of the tree for item collection retrieval.

While well-intentioned, they end up spending three full months working on their algorithm, testing it, and proving that it retains nearly identical results to the reference FP-growth implementation but at a fraction of the time to build and scan the tree. They've created a novel algorithm implementation and set to work on using it to solve the business use case that they agreed to develop.

They crack some beers, slap some backs, and get to work on writing their blog post and whitepaper, and prepare for some conference speaking engagements. Oh boy, everyone is going to know just how clever they are now!

They release the solution into production. Everything is working well, and the algorithm is, in their minds, paying for itself every day in cost savings of remarkably improved runtimes. That is, of course, until a major revision for the underlying framework is released. In this new runtime, significant changes are made to the way these trees are constructed in the open source framework, as well as a fundamental level of optimization in how antecedents are building the consequents.

The team is demoralized at the prospect of adjusting the model to fit in with the underlying changes in the developer-level APIs that they used to build their solution. Figure 13.12 illustrates their plight and what they should have done instead.

As you can see, the key decision that derailed the project was in not using preexisting standards that have been proven many times before. Not only did they have to build a solution to support the business use case, but they had to build an entirely new algorithm, integrate it to a framework's low-level design paradigms, and fully own the implementation to ensure that they can continue to support the business use case that drove the creation of their unique algorithm.

Because their algorithm leveraged so many of the internal structures of the framework to speed up development processes, the team is now left with a new quandary. Do they update their algorithm to work in the new framework version, hoping that it

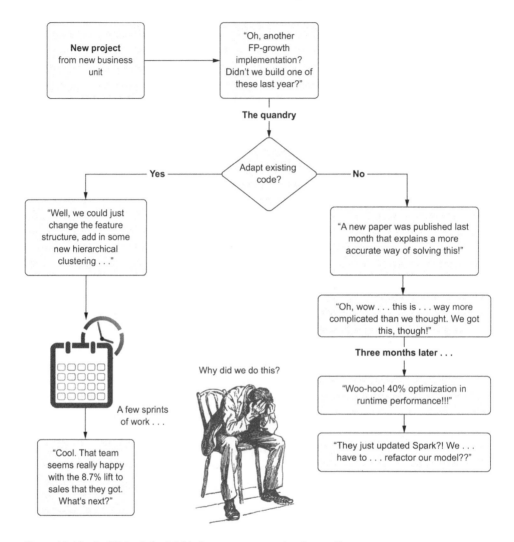

Figure 13.12   An ML technical debt choose-your-own-adventure path

will continue to outperform the provided FP-growth algorithm? Or do they refactor their entire solution to work with the standard algorithm?

There's no good answer here. Their custom framework is destined to either become shelfware or incur a few quarters' worth of conversion to make it work.

The principal problem with their attempt was building a custom implementation that they *weren't prepared to support*. They were building a solution not to solve the business problem, but rather for notoriety. They wanted to be noticed and appreciated for their skills. The team failed to realize that, while there is nothing really wrong with building new algorithms and advancing the state of the profession, the motivation behind building it should be centered on the necessity to solve a problem.

Had the team members approached the problem with a solution-driven mindset, they never would have entertained the possibility of creating a custom solution. Perhaps they would have contacted the maintainers of the existing popular open source framework and volunteered to create a new version that could be supported by that framework's community. If there was a distinct need to reduce runtime to meet an SLA and a novel algorithm needed to be built, that's fine. If you encounter that need, go build it. Just know that you need to maintain that code for as long as that business use case need exists.

I find myself increasingly more and more allergic to this concept of TDD, as it just adds more stress to an already stressful profession. By pursuing the easier (and, arguably, more boring) solution to a problem, particularly if you already have an existing solution to a nearly identical problem in place, you're leaving the business in better hands. You'll have less maintenance work to do and more time to creatively use your talents at solving more interesting future problems.

Summary

- Pursuing simple implementations that don't overreach the immediate needs of a project will save a great deal of refactoring later when the functionality needs to change. Less is more.
- While everyone is at a different stage of growth in software development skills, having a team focus on utilizing common design patterns that are easy to understand and read will ensure that everyone on a team can contribute to and maintain a code base.
- Building unnecessary functionality, complex interfaces, and clever unique implementations within an ML code base only means that you're having to support and maintain more code, providing no value to the organization. Keeping a code base only as complex as it needs to be to solve a problem is always a wise choice.
- Thoroughly investigating the capabilities, utility, and most important, the needs of any new technology to determine whether it is useful for a project is essential before deciding to integrate any such tooling into a project.
- Take care when working on a project for a business need to focus on implementing only what is needed to solve the problem. Anything apart from what is required for the project is vanity development and detracts from the maintainability of a solution.

Part 3

Developing production machine learning code

Once a project is ready to ship to production, a few final tasks remain before the implementation is ready to be scheduled for deployment. While it's tempting to see a test-passing build of an implementation as a complete and ready-for-the-real-world deployment, a few items need to be considered to ensure that people on call aren't getting paged every few hours.

From drift monitoring, to principles of code architecture (which will aid in performing final peer reviews), prediction-quality assurance, logging, and serving infrastructure, these last items are the most oft overlooked. When ignored, they are some of the most regrettable elements to forget for those who have lived without their proper design and implementation.

In this section, we'll go over these more advanced topics that can help make production deployment easier and help ensure that your models are explainable, able to be retrained, monitored, and (relatively) easy to update.

Writing production code

This chapter covers

- Validating feature data before attempting to use it for a model
- Monitoring features in production
- Monitoring all aspects of a production model life cycle
- Approaching projects with the goal of solving them in the simplest manner possible
- Defining a standard code architecture for ML projects
- Avoiding cargo cult behavior in ML

We spent the entirety of part 2 of this book on the more technician-focused aspects of building ML software. In this chapter, we'll begin the journey of looking at ML project work from the eyes of an architect.

We'll focus on the theory and philosophy of approaches to solving problems with ML from the highly interconnected, intensely complex, and altogether holistic view of how our profession functions. We'll look at case studies of production ML (all based, in one way or another, on things that I've messed up or have seen others mess up) to give an insight into elements of ML development that aren't frequently talked about. These are the lessons learned (usually the hard way) when we, as a profession, are more focused on the algorithmic aspects of solving problems, rather than where we should be focused:

- *The data*—How it's generated, where it is, and what it fundamentally is
- *The complexity*—Of the solution and of the code
- *The problem*—How to solve it in the easiest way possible

As we discussed in previous chapters, the goal of DS work is not merely in utilizing algorithms. It's not in a framework, a toolkit, or a particular model infrastructure that seems increasingly hot or popular.

> **NOTE** DS work should be solely focused on solving problems, using data, and applying the scientific method to our approach to ensure that we're solving them in the best way based on the data that we have available.

With this focus in mind, we're going to look at aspects of production development in the real world, specifically some uniquely destructive aspects of building solutions that might not seem obvious to the starry-eyed algorithm-focused practitioners who haven't been burned enough by poorly implemented solutions. Everyone who works in this profession long enough will learn these lessons, one way or another. The sooner you can learn from someone else's mistakes, the less of a chance that the learning will be as painful as it has been for some of us who have been doing this since before it was cool.

Where are all of the mentions of tools and frameworks?

As I've mentioned in many places throughout this book, successful ML is not about a set of tools. It's not about a particular platform either.

What sets a successful project apart from those that fail to continue solving their *raison d'être* isn't some clever API or hyped-up grandstanding framework or packaged solution. The four primary elements that make a project successful are simply these: the quality of the data, the minimum level of complexity employed to solve the problem, the ability of the solution to be monitored (and easily fixed), and, above all else, how well the solution solves the problem. Everything else, as a colleague of mine is wont to say often, is just fluff.

Throughout this chapter and the next, we'll focus on these essential elements—keeping data clean, monitoring the health of both data and models, and focusing on simplicity in solution development.

While frameworks, tools, platforms, and other quality-of-life utilities make the production process of ML solutions easier (and we'll delve into these topics in the last few chapters), those are not the be-all and end-all guarantors of success. They're all there if you need them (with the exception of platforms—you definitely need to select the one that works best for your team and company) and can help solve a lot of specific problems that some organizations will face, but they're not universal.

The tenets of successful ML most certainly are universal. If you don't get those figured out, it doesn't matter how fancy of a toolkit that you use. It doesn't matter if you have state-of-the-art CI/CD, a feature store, autoML, feature-generation factories, GPU-accelerated deep learning, or any other hyped tech term in the ML space. Those nifty tools won't save your project if your data sucks, your code is unmaintainable, and you're not making sure that your internal business customers are happy with the solution.

14.1 Have you met your data?

What I mean by *meeting* isn't the brief and polite nod of acknowledgment when passing your data on the way to refill your coffee. Nor is it the 30-second rushed socially awkward introduction at a tradeshow meetup. Instead, the meeting that you should be having with your data is more like an hours-long private conversation in a quiet, well-furnished speakeasy over a bottle of Macallan Rare Cask, sharing insights and delving into the nuances of what embodies the two of you as dram after silken dram caresses your digestive tracts: *really and truly getting to know it.*

> **TIP** Before writing a single line of code, even for experimentation, make sure you have the data needed to answer the basic nature of the problem in the simplest way possible (an if/else statement). If you don't have it, see if you can get it. If you can't get it, move on to something you can solve.

As an example of the dangers of a mere passing casual rendezvous with data being used for problem solving, let's pretend that we both work at a content provider company. Because of the nature of the business model at our little company, our content is listed on the internet behind a timed paywall. For the first few articles that are read, no ads are shown, content is free to view, and the interaction experience is bereft of interruptions. After a set number of articles, an increasingly obnoxious series of pop-ups and disruptions are presented to coerce a subscription registration from the reader.

The prior state of the system was set by a basic heuristic controlled through the counting of article pages that the end user had seen. Realizing that this would potentially be off-putting for someone browsing during their first session on the platform, this was then adjusted to look at session length and an estimate of how many lines of each article had been read. As time went on, this seemingly simple rule set became so unwieldy and complex that the web team asked our DS team to build something that could predict on a per-user level the type and frequency of disruptions that would maximize subscription rates.

We spend a few months, mostly using the prior work that was built to support the heuristics approach, having the data engineering team create mirrored ETL processes of the data structures and manipulation logic that the frontend team has been using to generate decision data. With the data available in the data lake, we proceed to build a highly effective and accurate model that seems to perform exceptionally well on all of our holdout tests.

It is upon release to production that we realize an issue, shown in figure 14.1. What we, as the DS team building the solution, failed to do was to check the conditions of the data that we were using for features.

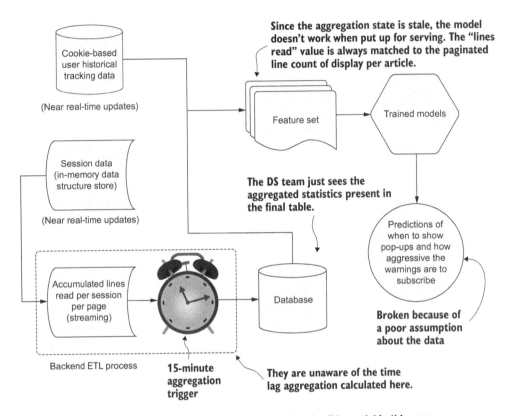

Figure 14.1   Failing to understand the data SLAs makes for a terrible model in this case.

Our model is trained from the data present in the lakehouse on object storage. What we didn't realize, when working on the extracted data during model development, was the mechanism of that data extract. We assumed that the features that we were using would be available directly within the data lake in near real-time. However, the data engineering team, to keep costs low and minimize the impact to production systems, developed its ETL from Redis to be a periodic dump on a 15-minute triggered window. From the data that we used for training, we saw consumption data from a session, split up into 5-second chunks of activity that we could use to readily create rolling aggregation statistics as a primary feature. It stands to reason that we could make the assumption that data would be loaded via a 5-second trigger continuously.

Once the solution entered production, it wasn't just that the effect wasn't personalized based on activity. Rather, the massive problem was that everyone was getting hit with the same prediction of "show all the ads and pop-ups" immediately upon seeing their first article. With a complete lack of relevant feature data, the model was rendered completely ineffective. We made a massive mess of the website for a full day, forced a complete re-architecting of the project, and ended up throwing away most of the solution that was based unknowingly around data that couldn't easily be made available to the model. Whoops.

Let's take a look at three primary guiding principles that I think about when starting DS projects and why they're important. If these three principles aren't adhered to, in my experience, the ability of a project to stay in production is slim to none—regardless at how cleverly implemented it is, how successful it is at solving a problem, or how much enthusiasm there is within the organization to use it.

14.1.1 *Make sure you have the data*

This example might seem a bit silly, but I've seen this situation play out dozens of times. Having an inability to get at the right data for model serving is a common problem.

I've seen teams work with a manually extracted dataset (a one-time extract), build a truly remarkable solution with that data, and when ready to release the project to production, realize at the 11th hour that the process for building that one-time extract required entirely manual actions by a DE team. The necessary data to make the solution effective was siloed off in a production infrastructure that the DS and DE teams had no ability to access. Figure 14.2 shows a rather familiar sight that I've borne witness to far too many times.

With no infrastructure present to bring the data into a usable form for predictions, as shown in figure 14.2, an entire project needs to be created for the DE team to build the ETL needed to materialize the data in a scheduled manner. Depending on the complexity of the data sources, this could take a while. Building hardened production-grade ETL jobs that pull from multiple production relational databases and in-memory key-value stores is not a trivial reconciliation act, after all. Delays like this could lead (and have led) to project abandonment, regardless of the predictive capabilities of the DS portion of the solution.

This problem of complex ETL job creation becomes even more challenging if the predictions need to be conducted online. At that point, it's not a question of the DE team working to get ETL processes running; rather, disparate groups in the engineering organization will have to accumulate the data into a single place in order to generate the collection of attributes that can be fed into a REST API request to the ML service.

This entire problem is solvable, though. During the time of EDA, the DS team should be evaluating the nature of the data generation, asking pointed questions to the data warehousing team:

- Can the data be condensed to the fewest possible tables to reduce costs?
- What is the team's priority for fixing these sources if something breaks down?
- Can I access this data from both the training and serving layers?
- Will querying this data for serving meet the project SLA?

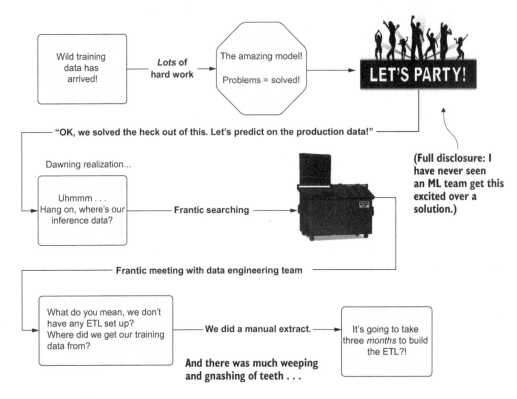

Figure 14.2   It's best to make sure you have data before shipping a solution to production.

Knowing the answers to each of these questions before beginning modeling work can help inform whether to engage in the project work. If the data isn't ready for consumption, the answers can give the DE team time to prioritize and asynchronously work on building these datasets while modeling is happening on a manually extracted copy of the final dataset.

14.1.2 *Check your data provenance*

Adding on to the basic questions surrounding data availability is the incredibly important question of *provenance of the data*. Specifically, by what mechanism does the data get into the data warehouse or data lakehouse? Knowing where the data comes from that's potentially going to go into your project helps you understand how stable it is, how clean it's going to be, and how risky it will be to include it in the model.

To illustrate the importance of provenance, let's suppose that we have three separate tables that we're sourcing the data from to solve a particular supervised learning problem. All three tables exist within a data warehouse backed by cloud object storage, and each is in parquet format. Each table, from the perspective of the end user of the data contained therein, appear to be similar. A bit of overlap occurs in each, as some data appears to be duplicated information of the same underlying information, but all the tables can be joined to one another based on foreign keys.

Figure 14.3 depicts the visible information when looking at the data in these three tables.

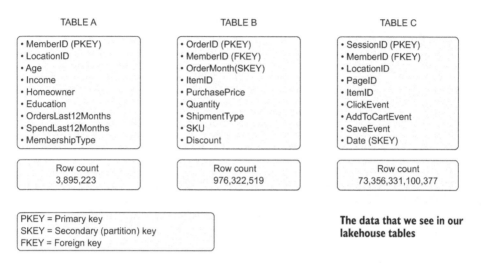

Figure 14.3   The three tables of data present in the lakehouse tables available for our project

By looking at the row counts and the field names, we can clearly see that we're looking at e-commerce data. Table A is our master members table, B our orders data, and C our site traffic data. If this is the end of our investigation into where the data comes from to populate these tables, we could be setting ourselves up for a bit of a rude awakening when utilizing this data for modeling purposes.

Before we start using this data to create a feature set, we need to know the ingestion mechanism. Without understanding when the data is loaded and at what frequency each table is updated, any joins that we do to create an imputation vector could have significant correctness issues.

Primarily because each of these datasets is produced and orchestrated by different engineering teams, but also because of the nature of the systems generating the data, there is a very low probability that there is agreement on recent data among them. For instance, on the most recent site activity data, the subsequent purchase event data may be delayed for more than an hour. Understanding these SLA considerations is absolutely critical to ensuring that feature data generated from these ETL processes is accurate. Figure 14.4 shows an expanded view of these tables, with some additional data obtained by questioning the DE team that owns the jobs that populate the data into the tables.

Having these new details from the DE team, we can make some fairly critical decisions about the data sources. We could then enter this information in our data catalog solution. Examples of this might look like table 14.1.

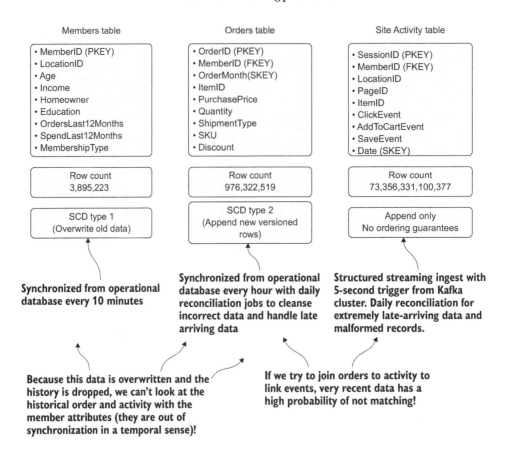

Figure 14.4   The additional information gained from chatting with the DE team about where the data comes from, how it gets there, and critical details about what can and can't be done with it

Table 14.1   Data catalog entries for our sample user-tracking data

Table name	Update frequency	Description/notes
Members table	10 minutes	Overwrite of existing data with changes. Historical changes reflected only in raw tables. If state change is needed for modeling, use Members_Historic table. Owned by frontend web team.
Order table	1 hour + daily reconcile	Orders data from live order and shipment source systems. To get latest state, must use Window function on version key value to get true natural key entries. Owned by backend marketplace engineering team.
Site Activity table	Real time + daily reconcile	Insertion order is not guaranteed to be correct. Data may be hours late when users are on a mobile device. Member use of VPN can cause bad location data. Changes to nested schema elements. Owned by DE team.

Based on these notes collected in the feature store, the DS team can understand the nuances of the data a great deal better. Thoroughly cataloguing the nature of source data systems can prevent one of the worst possible issues that can plague an ML solution: insufficient data available for generating quality predictions.

By taking extra time at the start of the production development phase to understand just where, when, and how data arrives at the source system used for both training and inference, a great many problems can be avoided. We can understand what data can and cannot be used for particular use cases (in this example scenario, the join between member attributes and either of the other tables for historical correlation purposes). We can identify a project's limitations based on the defined characteristics of end use; in our example, we would clearly not be able to use the activity data for an extremely low-SLA use case. If the project requires a freshness of data that's shorter in update frequency than that provided by the current ETL process, we can explore shortening that ETL process ahead of time to prevent a catastrophic production release issue.

With adequate time to prepare, the DE team can be working in parallel to the ML development work to provide the required data in the format needed to ensure that the implementation is acting upon recent-enough data to support the project's needs.

These issues of data provenance become compounded greatly when we start thinking of compliance issues. Here are some elements to think carefully about:

- Are there regulations surrounding the data that you want to use for modeling, such as the European Union's General Data Protection Regulation (GDPR), personally identifiable information (PII), or Health Insurance Portability and Accountability Act (HIPAA)? If so, please adhere to those requirements.
- Are there internal restrictions about visibility into the data that you're using?
- Is there an inherent bias in your data that could ethically compromise the model that you're building? (If you're interacting with data about humans, the answer is likely a resounding yes, and you should think carefully about the provenance of the data being collected.)
- How often do the source systems and processes feeding these tables go down for maintenance or fail outright? Is the ETL generally stable?
- How often does the schema change on these tables? Are there rules and processes for nested elements in the data structures (mostly applicable to web-based datasets) that govern whether they can be changed?
- Is the data that is generated coming from an automated process (an application) or from human input?
- Are data validation checks running to ensure that only clean data is allowed to be entered into these tables?
- Is the data consistent? Is the source durable? Is isolation involved in the writing of data to the tables to eliminate the chances of correctness issues?

We have an exhausting litany of other things to check for with regards to data quality when information comes from disparate systems. The important thing to keep in mind, above all others in regard to data, is to *trust nothing and verify everything* before using any dataset. Ask questions and get the information about your data before wasting time on building models that wouldn't work for a use case based on the nature of the data you're using to train on.

Throwing unknown and potentially incorrect data into a model is a surefire way to create total and completely unusable garbage for a solution. Trust me, I've learned this lesson more times than I'd care to admit.

14.1.3 *Find a source of truth and align on it*

I've yet to work at, with, or for a company that has immaculate data. While many organizations have nearly perfect data models, highly robust data engineering pipelines, and effectively flawless ingestion architecture, the concept of perfection in the data itself is a nigh-impossible goal to attain.

Let's imagine that we're in a business-to-business company, providing HR services to a wide breadth of industries. Our DE team is world-class and has employed from the very early days of the company a data model that has handled business changes over the years remarkably well. The information is laid out in a flexible relational star schema and allows for rapid access for analytics within the data warehouse.

Three years ago, things began to change with the advent of moving to cloud computing and the paradigm shift that a cost-effective data lake (cheaper than an on-premises solution) brought with it. Gone were the days when all new data source generation for analytics had to go through the DE team. Any group in the company could create data, upload it to the object store, register the source as a table, and utilize it for their purposes. The democratization of data access promised by the cloud vendor was surely to be a true revolution in the effectiveness and insights into our company!

It didn't quite work out that way, though. As the lake festered and became a swamp, multiple copies of similar-seeming data began to be birthed. Figure 14.5 shows a single hierarchal representation of industry types in multiple locations within the analytics layer of the data lake.

If we're about to work on our ML project by using these product hierarchies available in the data lake, which one do we choose from? With so much overlap and inconsistency, how do we figure out what is the most relevant?

There is simply no way to test all of them—particularly, as is mentioned at the bottom of figure 14.5, considering that multiple versions from the same group exist at various commit periods. What should be done?

The most successful approach that I've found is to *align the teams* on a process that provides a single source of truth that meets each of their needs. This doesn't imply that everyone needs to conform to the same definition of which groups of companies need to go in which aggregation bucket, though. Rather, it means the following:

- Maintaining a single copy of each department's definitions that supports its needs for interacting with the data (no _V2 or _V37 copies of the same data, adding confusion).

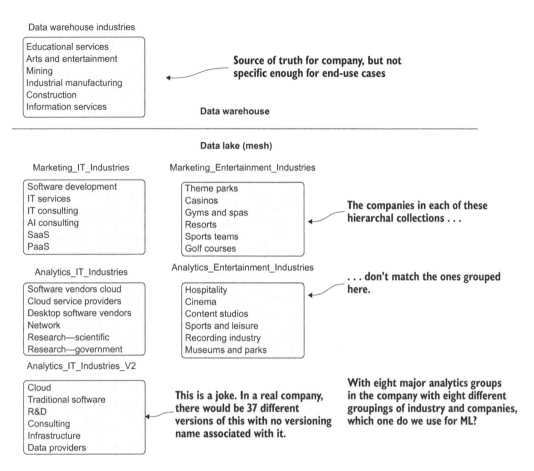

Figure 14.5 With self-service enabled on a data lake, having no unified source of truth can make everyone's lives more difficult.

- Choosing the correct type of slowly changing dimension (SCD) updates to accommodate the needs and uses of each team for this data. (Some teams may need historical references, while others may need only the most recent values.)
- Standardizing. If it's a duck, call it a duck. Calling things by unique and cute names like aquatic_avian_waterfowl_fun_plumage doesn't do anyone any favors.
- Periodic housekeeping. If the data isn't getting used, archive it. Keeping the lake healthy means that everyone can swim in it.
- Inventorying the data. Use entity-relationship (ER) diagrams in a knowledge repository, build or buy a data catalog, or maintain detailed documentation about each column in each table.

While all of these tasks may seem like an awful lot of work—and they are—they're the foundation on which modern businesses run. Having intelligible data doesn't just benefit ML projects, but allows for the same (mostly) clean data to be shared among the analytics groups and the DS group(s). It translates to everyone speaking the same language when conversing about the state of the business and the innovative future work that can leverage that data.

In the vein of data quality, one thing that you should never attempt to do as part of an ML project is to correct the data yourself (even if it is tempting to do so). The single-source-of-truth concept is far more important than you might believe.

14.1.4 *Don't embed data cleansing into your production code*

This is going to be a sensitive subject. Particularly for your data engineering friends.

Let's pretend that we're working on a project intended to estimate whether a customer should be automatically enrolled in a credit card offer that provides a higher limit than their current card. We've explored the data available in the data warehouse and have settled on the minimal number of features for building a prototype (keeping things simple to begin with) and the three tables required to source the data.

While doing data exploration and validation on the data, we encounter issues. From duplicate data, to inconsistent product descriptions, to scaling factor issues with the raw financial transaction historical data present, we have our work cut out for ourselves.

If we were to utilize the data-cleansing tools available in our ML platform to address these issues, we'd have an entire module in the code base devoted simply to data preprocessing tasks in order to fix the data. Running the data through the preprocessing stages, followed by feature engineering, and finally model training and validation, we'd have a process that works pretty well for generating a model.

What happens at prediction time, though? With the source data in such a poor state of quality, we have three options if we stick with this paradigm:

- Replicate the imputation, de-duplication, and regex code for a prediction job. (A bad idea because of maintainability concerns.)
- Create an independent utility preprocessing module that can be called from both the training and the inference jobs. (A better idea, but still not ideal.)
- Build the cleansing logic into a full pipeline object. (An even better idea, but potentially wasteful and expensive.)

Let's suppose that, in our rush to get the project out quickly, we completely forget to do any of these things. Our logic for data cleansing is built fully within our training code base, the model has been validated to work quite well, and we're ready to ship it to production.

While testing on an extremely small subset of the production data volume, we start to realize through our monitoring of model performance that multiple customers are getting contacted repeatedly, their credit limits being increased several times over.

Other seemingly well-qualified customers are getting credit-limit increase requests for cards and services that they don't currently have. Basically, we've built a great model that is predicting state on garbage data. Figure 14.6 illustrates the situation that has been created with this project.

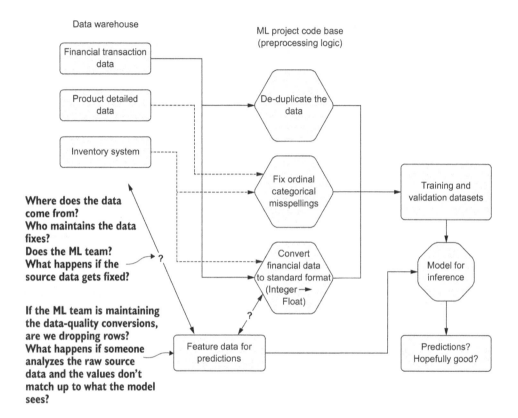

Figure 14.6 Fixing data-quality issues within ML code can create a great deal of chaos.

Figure 14.6, although an extreme case of forgetfulness and chaos, exposes the options that are listed as possible solutions when an ML team chooses to repair data-quality issues. When moving in this direction of fixing the data yourself, you now are responsible for that. Instead of building a solution with the data, you own a solution and the data-repair tasks.

While this particular scenario is unavoidable in certain organizations (such as small startups where a DS may be serving the role of DE as well as DS), the recommended course of action remains the same: specifically, that the data-cleansing code should never remain linked to a modeling solution. Figure 14.7 shows a better solution to data-quality issues.

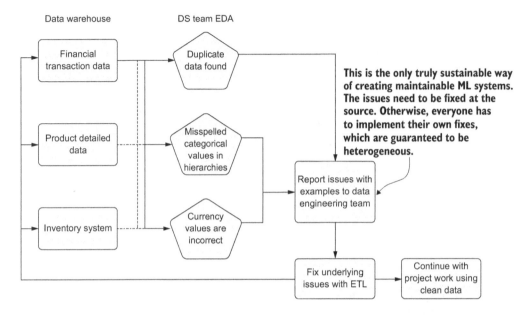

Figure 14.7 The better way forward for fixing data-quality issues: not embedding data repair tasks in ML code

The far more sustainable and preferred way of keeping data-repair tasks functional in a long-lasting manner is to fix the data at the source. This helps solve several problems:

- The data is cleaned for other use cases.
- Expensive de-duplication, correction of issues, interpolation, and complex joins are removed from model training and inference code (reducing complexity).
- The data is reliable for usage between training and inference (no risk for mismatched logic between training and inference).
- Feature monitoring (drift detection) is greatly simplified.
- Analytics and attribution measurement are greatly simplified.

Keeping a clean state for data used for modeling is a cornerstone of stable and production-grade ML solutions. While ML packages include a lot of tools for correcting issues in data, the most reliable manner of enforcing data correctness is doing it at the source: where the data is stored.

14.2 Monitoring your features

An often-overlooked part of production ML deployments is keeping a close watch on the features that are going into models. As professional DSs, we spend a truly obscene amount of time and effort analyzing each and every attribute associated with our features. Many times, solutions get shipped to production and the only thing that is monitored is the output of the model. This results in unexpected surprises when performance degrades, leaving us in a position of scrambling to diagnose what changed, why it may have changed, and how to go about fixing the problem.

There's a solution for this.

Let's suppose that we're working at our dog-food company from appendix A. We've shipped a model to production, have monitoring set up on the predicted dog-food demand, and the amount of product wastage is decreasing dramatically. We have a thorough and automated attribution-analysis system in place that is keeping track of the forecasting performance, showing a higher-than-anticipated performance result for the project.

Many weeks later, our predictions stop making sense. They're predicting far less inventory to order for each of the distribution sites. Luckily, we have humans in the loop to validate the order requests, so all is not lost. We watch, with growing concern over a period of days, as the order predictions for each product type drop to extremely low levels for all products.

We panic, retrain the model, and see the results become so nonsensical based on our understanding of prior demand for products that we turn off the prediction system altogether. It's not for another week of delving deeply into our feature data that we find the culprit. Figure 14.8 shows one of the key features that our model was using for predictions.

The graph at the top of figure 14.8 shows the sales figures for one of our regional distribution centers, while the graph at the bottom shows the newly adjusted sales figures that the finance team asked the DE team to create for the new, "more accurate" reporting paradigm for the company. During the period of overlap (the transition period), both of these columns of sales data were populated, but at the end of the transition period, data stopped feeding into the original column.

So, what happened with our model? Since the sales figures were such a critical part of the model, and because we were using imputation methods based on a recency window applied to the last seven days of data, the imputed values for missing data began to rapidly trend to zero. The model, having such a large weight applied to this feature, not only received data that it hadn't evaluated during training (zero sales, after all, is a bad thing and hadn't been present in our non-bankrupted company), but the impact of this value being so low effectively drove the demand predictions for all products to zero in a short period of time.

Setting aside the debate about null-value handling in ML (fill with 0, impute over the training set data's values, smoothing imputation, and so forth), how could we have caught this issue before it became a truly bad problem? Even if we had no prior warning of this change, how could we have had alerting established on the feature values so that the first day of values dropping to zero would have let us know that this particular feature had a problem?

The simplest solution is to collect basic statistics about each feature during training (alternatively, approximate statistics if you're on a distributed system with a large

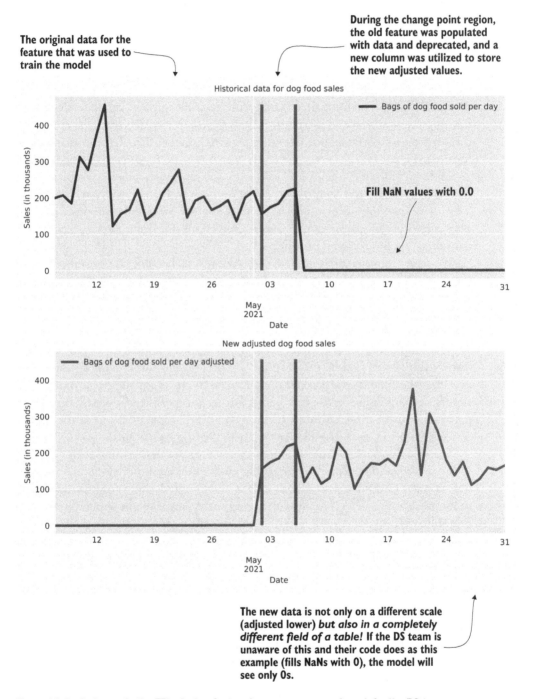

The original data for the feature that was used to train the model

During the change point region, the old feature was populated with data and deprecated, and a new column was utilized to store the new adjusted values.

Fill NaN values with 0.0

The new data is not only on a different scale (adjusted lower) *but also in a completely different field of a table!* **If the DS team is unaware of this and their code does as this example (fills NaNs with 0), the model will see only 0s.**

Figure 14.8   A change in the ETL of a key feature becomes a very sad week for the DS team.

training set). These statistics can be stored in a table that is versioned in accordance with each training iteration using a basic SCD type 2 methodology: append new rows for the features' data and increment the version with each subsequent run. A daily job can then be scheduled whose only purpose is to compare the values used for prediction for the last n hours or days to those of the features as they existed during the last training run. The following listing shows basic examples of this concept, run against the data shown in our scenario (the top graph in figure 14.8).

Listing 14.1 A simple feature-monitoring script

The prior-to-shift data from our scenario
(the original column of sales data)

```
import numpy as np
prior_to_shift = np.append(ORIGINAL_DATA,
BOUNDARY_DATA)
prior_stats = {}
prior_stats['prior_stddev'] = np.std(prior_to_shift)
prior_stats['prior_mean'] = np.mean(prior_to_shift)
prior_stats['prior_median'] = np.median(prior_to_shift)
prior_stats['prior_min'] = np.min(prior_to_shift)
prior_stats['prior_max'] = np.max(prior_to_shift)
post_shift = np.append(BOUNDARY_DATA,
np.full(ORIGINAL_DATA.size, 0))
post_stats = {}
post_stats['post_stddev'] = np.std(post_shift)
post_stats['post_mean'] = np.mean(post_shift)
post_stats['post_median'] = np.median(post_shift)
post_stats['post_min'] = np.min(post_shift)
post_stats['post_max'] = np.max(post_shift)
bad_things = "Bad things are afoot in our sales data!"
if post_stats['post_mean'] <= prior_stats['prior_min']:
    print(bad_things +
      " Mean is lower than training min!")
if post_stats['post_mean'] >= prior_stats['prior_max']:
    print(bad_things +
      " Mean is higher than training max!")
if ~(prior_stats['prior_stddev'] * 0.5
  <= post_stats['post_stddev'] <= 2.
  * prior_stats['prior_stddev']):
    print(bad_things + " stddev is way out of bounds!")
>> prior_stats
{'prior_stddev': 70.23796409350146,
 'prior_mean': 209.71999999999994,
 'prior_median': 196.5,
 'prior_min': 121.9,
 'prior_max': 456.2}
>> post_stats
{'post_stddev': 71.95139902894329,
 'post_mean': 31.813333333333333,
 'post_median': 0.0,
 'post_min': 0.0,
 'post_max': 224.9}
>> Bad things are afoot in our sales data! Mean is lower than training min!
```

A simple dictionary for safely storing our statistical values from the feature data

The as-trained feature statistics (standard deviation, mean, median, min, and max)

The post-shift data being used to compare against the trained statistics

A per validation run dictionary (health-check job script that measures these statistics on each feature)

Basic example checks for whether the mean of the feature now is below the minimum during training

Similar check for whether the mean is above the max of training values

A broad check on whether the variance of the feature has dramatically shifted

This code is intentionally simplistic and is intended to merely raise awareness of the need for monitoring relatively simple elements to calculate. The rules for a particular feature-monitoring toolkit that you may eventually develop can become as complex and feature rich as needed for your own use case or can stay relatively simple and built as a low-weight utility framework for monitoring basic statistics about any features used in your models.

In a real-world scenario, not only would we be retrieving data from all of our features, but we would be querying a table (or service that stores these statistics such as MLflow's tracking server). The alerting would clearly not be a simple `print` statement, but rather a notification through a pager duty alert, email, or similar mechanism to let the team know that a rather large problem and disruptive day is ahead. The architecture surrounding all of those needs is highly specific to the infrastructure that you might be running in, so we're keeping it simple here with `print` statements and dictionaries.

Active-in-development open source packages are being crafted at the time of this writing that are looking to solve this problem for the open source community. I highly encourage you to conduct some research to determine which one works well for your language, platform, and ecosystem. However, in the name of simplicity first, even building a simple validation script based on the logic in listing 14.1 can get the job done. The only thing that you don't want to do is to completely ignore the features after releasing a solution to production.

> **This might seem like a silly example, but . . .**
>
> I can imagine what you might be thinking: "This is ridiculous. Who would ever do something like this? This example is just far too much of a caricature!"
>
> Well, dear friend, I can assure you that this exact event has happened to me a total of six times in my career. I finally learned my lesson after that sixth one (probably because a serious, business-critical model was affected).
>
> As I've discussed, I don't always use a fancy implementation to check the health of features. Sometimes it's just a SQL-based script that's doing basic calculations over a period of time, joined to a stored table that contains the same basic metrics about the feature set as of the last time that it was trained. I don't spend a great deal of time fine-tuning what the thresholds should be, nor do I build complex logic utilizing statistical process-control rules or anything of that nature. Many times, it's as simple as described in the preceding example: What is the mean, the variance, and the general shape of the data? Is it in the same ballpark as the original data? Is the mean now above the previously recorded as-of-training maximum value? Is it below the minimum value? Is the variance an order of magnitude lower, or is it higher?

With these overly broad checks in place, you can monitor massive feature changes that could fundamentally break your model. That's usually a good step toward, if not identifying an imminent failure, at least identifying where to look when your more tightly monitored predictions and attributions start falling apart.

The end goal of this monitoring is to save time and mitigate the damage of a fundamentally broken model that is running in production. The faster that the problem can be diagnosed, fixed, and returned to a good state in production, the better off your day (or week, month, and year) is going to be.

14.3 Monitoring everything else in the model life cycle

In chapter 12, we talked at length about monitoring drift in features. That's incredibly important, but for a production ML solution, it's but one part of the full story around proper ML monitoring.

Let's imagine that we're working at a company that has an established ML footprint of projects in production: 14 major projects, all solving different use cases throughout the business. With our team of 10 DSs and 4 ML engineers, we're finding it difficult to scale the team to support additional workloads.

For all of us, large portions of our day are relegated to just keeping the lights on. On any given day, some model needs a bit of attention. Whether we're busy with a degradation in predictions that end users bring to our attention, or routine analytical maintenance required to check the health of a particular solution ourselves, we have precious little time to think about taking on another project. If we were to analyze our time spent on maintenance tasks for our solutions, we might see something similar to figure 14.9.

This daily life is a sad one. It's not that the models are bad, nor that the solutions that incorporate them are bad. The fact is that models will drift and performance will degrade. If we're not actively monitoring our models with automated solutions, we'll end up exhausting our team's resources in troubleshooting and repairing issues to such a degree that the only options available to take on new project work are to either hire more people (good luck with getting budget for that over a long period of time!) or to have visibility into the following:

- What is changing
- How it is changing
- What likely suspects are for drift (in features, model retraining, and predictions)

By having visibility into all aspects of our model life cycle, we can reduce the troubleshooting burden dramatically (and, at the same time, remove the manual act of

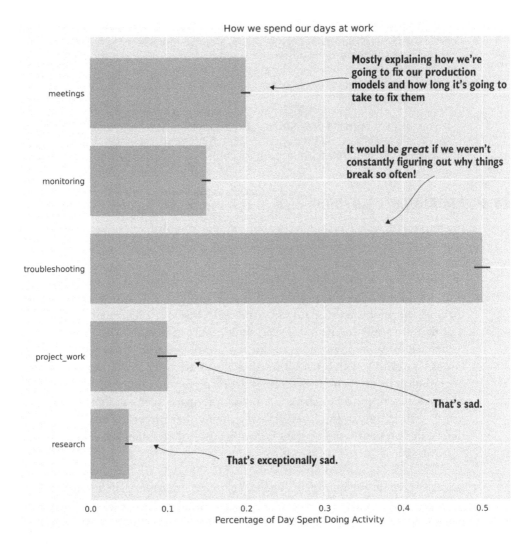

Figure 14.9 Even though we have a lot of models in production, we spend most of our time figuring out why they drift, how to fix them, meeting about why we're having to fix them, and doing repair work. This is "keeping the lights on" DS work.

monitoring altogether!). Figure 14.10 illustrates the portions of the model life cycle that should have some form of monitoring in place to alleviate the terrible burdens from figure 14.9.

The observations in many of these stages may seem like a bit of overkill. Why, for instance, should we be monitoring our feature-engineering data? Shouldn't the predictions be good enough?

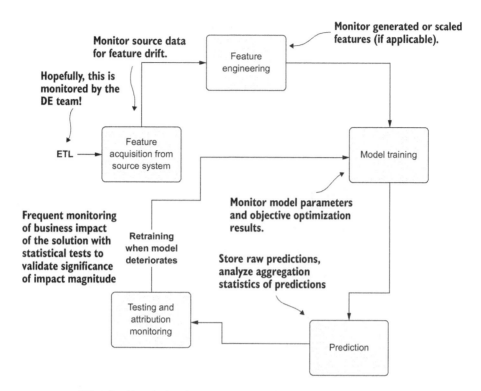

What should we be keeping an eye on in the ML life cycle? *Everything.*

Figure 14.10   The parts of ML projects that need monitoring

Let's take a look at why our bogged-down team should be monitoring features and any modifications that they might be doing to them. Figure 14.11 compares the same feature's distribution as seen during training (left) and later during production inference (right).

The model saw the feature within the confines of the range of data shown. Later, the feature drifts well outside the range that the model was exposed to during training. Depending on the model used, this could manifest itself in various ways, all equally bad (provided that the feature was at least somewhat significant to the model).

What would the process look like for the team members experiencing this, provided that they weren't monitoring for this shift in distribution? Let's keep it simple and say that their implementation was fairly pared down to begin with, having only 30 features. When the predictions start to suffer from incomprehensibly confusing results, an analytics process will have to be conducted on both the current state of the features and on the historical values as they existed during training. Many queries would be executed, references made to training events, graphs plotted, statistics

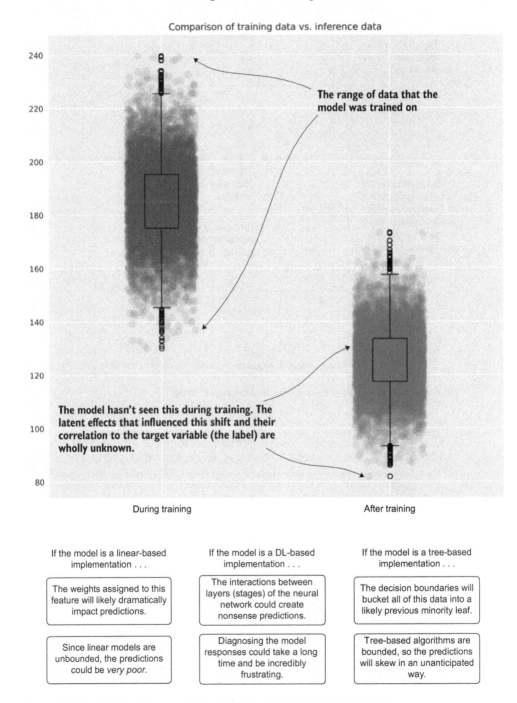

Figure 14.11   Significant feature drift and effects on different types of models

calculated, and a thoroughly time-consuming root cause analysis would need to be performed.

In the immortal words of Kimberly "Sweet Brown" Wilkins, "Ain't nobody got time for that." These post hoc investigations are lengthy. They're involved, monotonous, and draining. With 14 production projects running, a team of 14 supporting the ML needs of the company, and no monitoring of processes going on, this team is going to be absolutely swamped with zero value-add work. In a best-case scenario, they'd likely be looking at two to three investigations a week, each one taking at least one person's full workday to complete and another day to initiate a new training run and evaluate the test results.

By setting up monitoring on every aspect of the pipeline, however, the team could identify what shifted, by how much, and when the deviation began. This could save whole person-days of effort, freeing up the team to automate away this monotonous work of investigating why their model started to fall apart, giving them all time to work on new projects.

This monitoring system doesn't stop at simply looking at the features coming into the model. It also means looking at the following:

- *Generated features*—Interactions, scaling, and heuristics-based data manipulations
- *The model(s)*—Metrics for each training run
- *The predictions*—Distributions over time for either `pmf` or `pdf`, means and variance for regression, confusion matrices, and metrics for classification
- *The attribution*—Stability of business metrics that gauge the effectiveness of the solution for the problem it is trying to solve
- *Performance considerations*—For batch, job runtime; for online, response SLAs
- *Effectiveness of features over time*—Periodic recursive feature elimination and subsequent culling of unnecessary features

By focusing on monitoring each component throughout the life cycle of an ML-backed solution, you can help scale your team by eliminating drudgery-type work. When people aren't just keeping the lights on, they can focus more on new and innovative solutions that can prove greater business value over time. Another large part of responding to monitored health checks is keeping a solution as simple as possible while still solving the problem.

14.4 Keeping things as simple as possible

Simplicity is a unique form of elegance in ML applications. Scoffed at by many who are new to the field, because they initially believe that complex solutions are fun to build, the simplest solutions are the ones that endure. This is true for no greater reason than that they're easier to keep running than intensely complicated ones—mostly because of cost, reliability, and ease of upgrading.

Let's imagine that we're relatively new to a somewhat junior team. Each team member is steeped in the latest technological advancements in the field of ML, highly capable at developing a solution using these cutting-edge tools and techniques. Let's pretend for an instant that these coworkers of ours believe that people using "old" techniques like Bayesian approaches, linear algorithms, and heuristics in solving problems are mere Luddites who refuse to learn the technology of the future.

One of the first projects that comes along to the team is from the operations department. The senior vice president (SVP) of the retail group approaches the team in a meeting and asks for a solution that the operations department simply can't scale very well. The SVP wants to know if the DS team can, with only images as fodder for a solution, determine whether the people in the pictures are wearing a red shirt.

The DS team immediately goes to what they're experienced with in their toolboxes of latest and greatest solutions. Figure 14.12 illustrates the events that unfold.

A new project

"We need a system that will tell us whether people in photographs are wearing a red shirt."

Junior DS team

"We need to use either Mask R-CNN or YOLOv3."

"We will need a fully gender-, age-, and ethnicity-stratified training set of labeled images . . ."

". . . with bounding box coordinates around the shirts."

The business unit

"We have no idea what they're talking about, but it sounds really advanced."

"OK, we have the pictures . . . they're grouped in red shirt vs. not red shirt."

"We have no idea what you're talking about."

Months pass . . .

"We can successfully classify not only whether the person is wearing a red shirt, but also whether they're wearing long sleeves or short sleeves! It's 94% accurate!"

"We *did* notice that all of the images were of people at a front-facing view at around the same height."

"Wait a minute . . . you mean to tell us that all you wanted to determine was if the bottom one-third center point of each picture was red or not?"

"But . . . our employees' shirts are all short sleeves. See? All of the images are of people walking into the breakroom, and they're all wearing short sleeves."

". . . and?"

"Well, yes. The project was to figure out which locations needed to be issued the new blue color of our corporate retail uniforms and make sure that everyone had enough shirts to wear."

One week of work with Python's Pillow library later . . .

"We . . . uhmm . . . have a solution that is 100% accurate."

"Wow! That was fast! So, what was all that stuff that you were working on before?"

Figure 14.12 The discouraging results when advanced approaches are attempted before simpler ones

What happens in this scenario? The largest issue is in the complex approach that the team members take without validating simpler approaches. They choose to focus on technology over a solution. By focusing on a highly advanced solution to the problem and not entertaining a far simpler approach (grab a swatch of pixels at one-third of the way up in the center line of each image, determine the hue and saturation of those pixels, and classify them as either red or not red), they waste months of time and likely an awful lot of money in the process of solving the problem.

This scenario plays out remarkably frequently in companies—particularly those that are nascent to ML. These companies may feel a need to go fast with their projects because the hype surrounding AI is of such a deafening roar of cacophony that they think their businesses will be at risk if they don't get AI working at whatever the cost. In the end, our example team recognizes what the easiest solution could be and rapidly develops a solution that runs at massive scale with minimal cost.

The idea of pursuing simplicity exists in two main facets of ML development: defining the problem that you're trying to solve and building the most minimally complex solution to solve the problem.

14.4.1 Simplicity in problem definitions

In our preceding scenario, the problem definition was clear to the business and the ML team both. "Predict red shirts for us, please" couldn't get distilled to any more of a basic task than that. A fundamental breakdown still occurred in the discussion that was conducted, however.

The pursuit of simplicity in defining a problem centers around the elemental attributes of two important questions to be given to the internal (business unit) customer:

- *What do you want a solution to do?* This defines the prediction type.
- *What will you do with the solution?* This defines the decision aspect.

If nothing else aside from these two questions was discussed in the early-phase meetings with the business unit, the project would still be a success. Having the core need of the business problem addressed can more directly lead to project success than any other topic. The business simply wanted to identify whether employees were wearing the old company-branded red shirts in order to know to send them the new branded blue shirts. By fixating on the problem of red shirt versus blue shirt, a far simpler solution can be achieved.

Throughout the discussion that follows, we'd get the information about the nature of the photographs and their inherent homogeny. With these two fundamental aspects defined, the team can focus on a smaller list of potential approaches, simplifying the scope and work involved in order to solve the problem. Without these questions defined and answered, however, the team is left to an overly broad and creative exploration of possible solutions—which is risky.

The team members heard *image classification*, instantly went to CNN implementations, and for months on end locked themselves into a highly complex architecture.

Even though it eventually solved the problem fairly well, it did so in a way that would have been incredibly wasteful. (GPUs and DL models being trained on them are significantly more expensive than a pixel-hue-and-saturation bucketing algorithm that could run on a smart toaster oven.)

Keeping the problem definition for a particular prospective project to such simple terms will not only help guide initial discussions with the business unit requesting a solution, but also provide a path toward implementing the least possible complexity in whatever gets built.

14.4.2 *Simplicity in implementation*

If we were to continue on the path of analyzing our scenario for red-shirt classification, we could simply look at the end solution that the team came up with to illustrate what they should have done first.

I, and many others I've known in this profession over the years, have learned this painful lesson many times over. By building something cool for the sake of the cool, we often regret it terribly when we realize how difficult that cool implementation ends up being to maintain. We suffer through fragile code and highly complex coupling of processes that seemed like something really fun to build, but end up being a complete and total nightmare to debug, adjust, or refactor when the code fully breaks.

Instead of belaboring an example, I'll illustrate the way I think about problems that I'm asked to help solve. Figure 14.13 shows my thought process.

This flow chart isn't much of a caricature at all. I nearly *always* think through a problem at first as though I'm trying to solve it with basic aggregations, arithmetic, and case/switch statements. If that doesn't work, I move to Bayesian approaches, linear models, decision trees, and so forth. The last thing that I'm going to try to implement out of the gate is an adversarial network that requires hundreds of hours to train and, when it breaks, spend days (or weeks) troubleshooting mode collapse and how to adjust my Wasserstein loss to compensate for vanishing gradients. Thank you very much, but I'll use those only when I've exhausted all other approaches to solving a problem.

In its most pure form, figure 14.13 demonstrates a core component of my psyche: I'm lazy. Really, truly, and profoundly lazy. I don't want to develop custom libraries. I don't want to build insanely complex solutions (well, that's partly true; I love building them, I just don't want to *own them*).

I simply want to solve problems in a way that the code just works. I want to solve problems so effectively that people forget that my solution is running until someone freaks out that a platform service disruption happens and we all collectively remember what was actually running some critical part of the business. The only way that you get to achieve that penultimate version of laziness is by building something in the simplest way possible, having monitoring set up to alert you before anyone else notices that things are not OK, and having a clean code base that makes your repairs take hours instead of weeks.

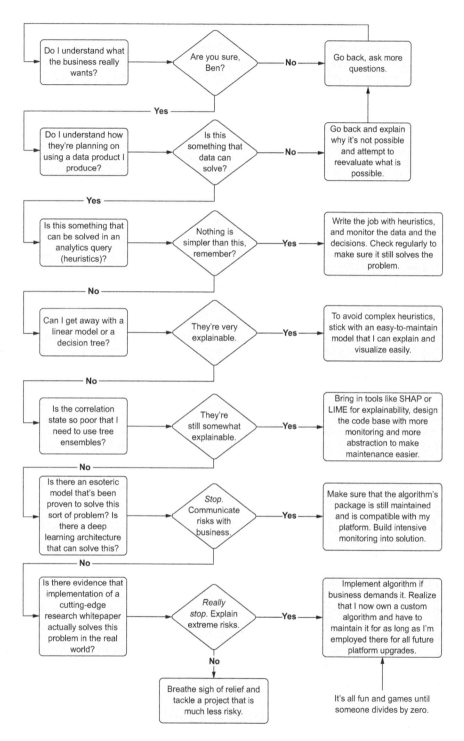

Figure 14.13 Author's thought process when evaluating ML approaches to problems

The other benefit of selecting a simple design to solve a problem is that the process of developing the solution (the nitty-gritty hands-on-keyboard part of the software engineering aspect) becomes much easier. The design becomes easier to architect, develop, and collaborate in. That all starts with building effective wireframes for code bases.

14.5 *Wireframing ML projects*

We all learn a truly painful lesson after our first real-world production ML project (universal, at least, to peers I've interacted with in my career). This truly painful lesson is experienced in a mild form during the development of a solution, but only after months of supporting a solution is the teaching fully complete. This is the lesson of code architecture and how a lack of it can generate a truly crippling level of technical debt so that in order to make even small changes to a code base, significant parts of it need to be refactored (or rewritten!).

Because of an aversion to having monolithic scripts weighing down maintenance and enhancements to a solution, the freshly enlightened typically go down a path of, during code development, working at separating major functionality of their code as they go.

Let's see how this plays out as we look at a team of newly wise ML practitioners. They've been supporting their first major (and arguably messy) code base for a few months and have identified multiple ways that they organized their code that didn't work well for maintainability.

They decide to, during various sprints, as new features need to be developed, split their code apart so that functionality is separated. Figure 14.14 illustrates their processes.

It takes a short time for them to realize that although their approach is worthwhile, it isn't the easiest way to go about building a project. Why is this the case with ML code?

- There are tight dependencies in scripts, particularly the hack-a-thon "just make it work" script.
- Experimental prototypes focus mostly on the algorithm, not on the data processing. Most of the eventually developed code base is in the realm of data processing.
- The code changes *frequently* during development (and after production release).

What the team ends up realizing by their third sprint is that refactoring all of their code into distinct modules as development progresses creates so much additional work and confusing code that new features become difficult to implement. Approaching code architecture in this way is simply not sustainable; managing code is hard enough with only a single person contributing, but nigh impossible if multiple people are working on a constantly refactored code base.

A better solution exists, and it involves setting up a basic wireframe for a project. While I balk at the term *template* when involving code, this is, in essence, essentially that, albeit a loose and mutable one.

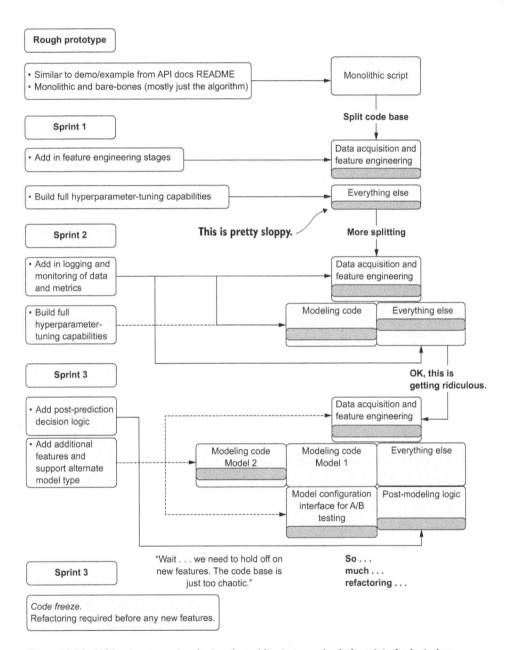

Figure 14.14 Without a general project code architecture, you're in for a lot of refactoring.

Most ML projects' architecture, at its most basic level, can be grouped into core groups of functionalities:

- Data acquisition
- Data validation
- Feature engineering, feature augmentation, and/or feature store interaction
- Model training and hyperparameter optimization
- Model validation
- Logging and monitoring
- Model registration
- Inference (batch) or serving (online)
- Unit and integration testing
- Post-processing prediction consumption (decision engines, if applicable)

Not every project is guaranteed to have all these components, while others might have additional requirements. (A deep learning CNN implementation might need a data serialization layer for batch-file processing and image augmentation, while an NLP project might need a module for ontological dictionary updating and interfaces, for example). The point is that distinct separations of functionality make up the wholly functioning part of the project. If they are all lumped haphazardly into modules where the boundaries of responsibility in the code become blurred (or, in the worst case, all in a single file), modifying and maintaining the code becomes a truly Herculean effort.

Figure 14.15 shows an alternative architecture that can be used immediately after the experimental prototype (the hack-a-thon-like rapid prototype is completed to prove the applicability of a model to the company's data). While the modules in this architecture may not contain much of anything to begin with, they serve as placeholders (stubs) based on what the team expects to need throughout the project. If new modules are needed, they can be created. If a stub is never populated during the final sprint before release, it can be removed.

This general template architecture enforces an encapsulation of concerns. It not only helps guide the sprint planning but also helps avoid merge conflicts in the code base at the end of sprints. It keeps the code organized from the beginning of the development period, makes searching for functionality easier, and helps make unit testing and troubleshooting far simpler.

While organizing stubs and creating abstraction may seem like excessive overkill for even simple projects, I can promise you, from having spent entire months of my productive working life doing nothing other than rewriting and refactoring fundamentally broken code architecture, it is anything but. It's far easier to collapse abstraction and remove placeholder modules than it is to translate a code base into some semblance of logical order from pure, distilled chaos.

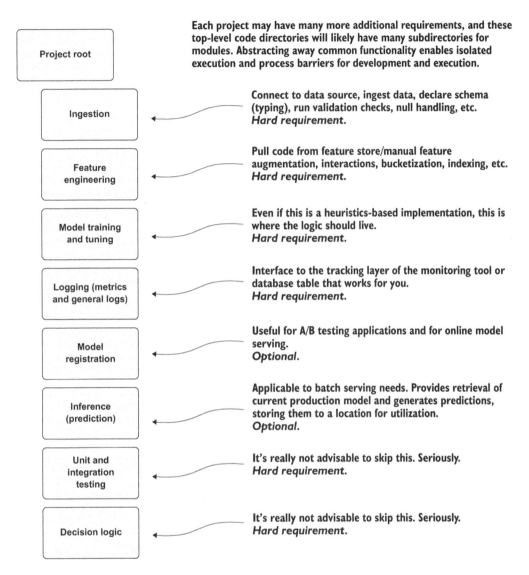

Project root

Each project may have many more additional requirements, and these top-level code directories will likely have many subdirectories for modules. Abstracting away common functionality enables isolated execution and process barriers for development and execution.

Ingestion

Connect to data source, ingest data, declare schema (typing), run validation checks, null handling, etc. *Hard requirement.*

Feature engineering

Pull code from feature store/manual feature augmentation, interactions, bucketization, indexing, etc. *Hard requirement.*

Model training and tuning

Even if this is a heuristics-based implementation, this is where the logic should live. *Hard requirement.*

Logging (metrics and general logs)

Interface to the tracking layer of the monitoring tool or database table that works for you. *Hard requirement.*

Model registration

Useful for A/B testing applications and for online model serving. *Optional.*

Inference (prediction)

Applicable to batch serving needs. Provides retrieval of current production model and generates predictions, storing them to a location for utilization. *Optional.*

Unit and integration testing

It's really not advisable to skip this. Seriously. *Hard requirement.*

Decision logic

It's really not advisable to skip this. Seriously. *Hard requirement.*

Figure 14.15 **A generic ML project code wireframe to keep code logically organized, easier to develop within, and easier to maintain**

As an example of what not to do, and just how bad an interconnected mess of a poorly designed ML code architecture can be, see figure 14.16. (Yes, it was one of mine.)

This example represents one of my first projects (details of the use case removed so I don't have a certain company's lawyers calling me) and allows me to convey the magnitude of the lesson that I learned from this. It was, shall we say, *substantial.*

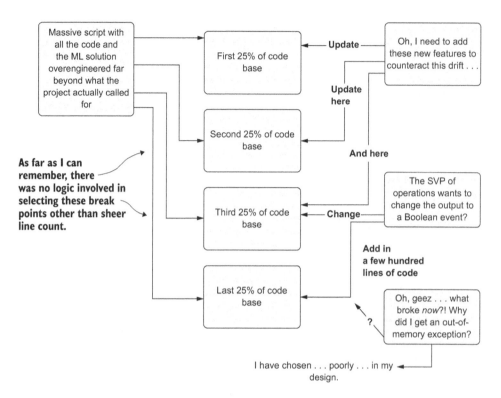

Figure 14.16   One of my earlier works of art before I knew what code design was and how abstraction, encapsulation, and inheritance work. Don't do this.

Having almost no logical design for a large code base does more than impact the initial development. It certainly is a major reason why providing a wireframe is important (particularly when an entire team is working on a project and needs to ensure that code merges aren't overwriting one another's changes). The lack of a logical design becomes acutely more painful when inevitable changes need to be made. Hunting through a massive script is incredibly time-consuming and frustrating even if you use clever naming conventions for variables and functions.

I learned to never underestimate the time savings that comes from proper code design. When framed properly, it enables the following:

- Stepping through modules for debugging or demonstration
- Writing isolated submodule unit tests and module-level unit tests to give peace of mind that large swaths of code are functional
- Driving directly to a place in the code in seconds (rather than searching for minutes or hours through a code base)
- Easily extracting common functionality from a code base and placing it in its own package for reuse by another project

- Significantly reducing the chances of having duplicated functionality in an ML code base, as it encourages abstraction and encapsulation from the start of development

Even for those who prefer to develop wholly within notebooks—which is OK, by the way, particularly if you're on a small team or a team of one—having such a separation of activities can make your development and long-term care of your project code orders of magnitude simpler than it otherwise would be. The alternative, after all, is what I did early in my career, continuing from the experimental scripts, bolting on functionality with reckless abandon until I was left with a Frankenstein's monster that I was as happy to look at as a villager with a pitchfork would be to see a real monster.

A note on frequent refactoring in ML code bases

Someone recently asked me, "How much should I refactor my code base when it becomes too complex, messy, or unmaintainable?" It stopped me for a bit, thinking of an appropriate answer. The framework developer in me wanted to call out, "Well, refactor early and often!," while the DS in me went through a series of painful flashbacks to intensely frustrating code refactoring that I've had to do over the years.

I finally answered as any noncommittal developer would who's written production ML code, with gravity, "As much as you're comfortable with in order to get your project maintainable again." It's not very good advice, unfortunately. There's a reason for that, though.

Technical debt in traditional software engineering (either FP or OO), incurred by hastily compromising standards in order to ship something out, can be paid down in a relatively straightforward way: you can refactor the code. It's likely already encapsulated and abstracted to the point that it won't be too challenging to refactor. Optimize the code for performance to your heart's content within the confines of your ability and skill level. Rewrite the entire thing from scratch if you prefer (module by module).

ML code is a bit different. Each of your decisions in how to write your code—from the perspective of performance, algorithmic complexity, data quality, monitoring, and validation—has far-reaching effects on not only the efficacy of the solution, but also the interconnectedness of the parts of the code as a whole. As opposed to traditional software engineering, all of these pieces of "Oh, we'll fix it later" sorts of tech debt that can be incurred have a *much higher* interest rate.

It's simply just not as easy to refactor our code. Some of it can be easily modified (adding a feature, removing a feature, changing how weights are applied, and so forth), but things like changing from a tree-based implementation to a generalized linear model, a machine vision approach to a CNN, or an ARIMA-based implementation to an LSTM, are basically full rewrites of our projects.

Changing the fundamental nature of the entire solution (for example, the API returns may change on the output of the model for different packages, necessitating rewrites to large swaths of the code) is incredibly risky and could delay a project by months. A final deprecation and removal of functionality in open source code may mean a complete reimplementation of a major portion of the code base and could mean a

> *(continued)*
>
> shift to a different execution engine. The greater the complexity that exists within a solution, the more ML technical debt that we accrue at a significantly higher interest rate than a software developer might for a similar type of decision.
>
> This is one of the primary reasons that we can't be fully agile when developing our software. We need to do a bit of pre-planning and architecture research, and, in the case of our code bases, to create a template of sorts that helps guide how each of the complex portions of our code interact with one another.

14.6   *Avoiding cargo cult ML behavior*

I've hammered quite heavily on avoiding hyped trends in ML throughout this book. In this section, I'm going to hammer away heavily on what I see as the most damaging form of the hype cycle: cargo cult behavior.

Let's imagine that we're in a company that has a relatively new ML footprint. Some key critical business problems have been solved, generally using proven and arguably unsophisticated statistical methods. The solutions are running well in production, they are monitored effectively, and the business is aware of the value of these solutions because of the thorough attribution determinations and testing that have been conducted. Then someone reads an article.

It's a blog post from a famous and successful tech company that walks through how it has solved a previously unsolvable problem that affects our company as well. The article's author mentions the newly open sourced solution that their company developed to solve the problem, provides a detailed explanation of how the algorithm works, and spends the vast majority of the post explaining the technical side of the implementation.

It's a great article, and it serves its purpose well as a recruiting tool for attracting top technical candidates to their company. What the reader at our company fails to realize is that the reason for writing the article is to recruit, not to let a small company pick up their open source tooling and magically solve this problem in a few weeks.

The desire for this solution to be tackled is so high, though, that everyone is on board with using this new software solution. A project plan is developed, experimentation is done, API documentation is thoroughly read and understood, and a basic prototype is built.

It seems as though things are progressing well in the early stages of the project, but after a month or so, cracks in the plan begin to emerge. The team realizes the following:

- The algorithm is incredibly complex and difficult to tune well.
- The company that invented the algorithm probably has a lot of internal tools that help make using it easier.
- The data formats required for many elements of the code are different from how they store their data.

- The tool requires expensive cloud infrastructure to run and the establishment of a great many new services that they are unfamiliar with.
- Not enough data has been collected to avoid some of the overfitting issues that they're seeing.
- Scalability concerns (with cost) restrict training times to days, slowing development.

It doesn't take too much additional time after these cracks appear for the team members to decide to try a different approach that is far less sophisticated. They find that their solution, although unable to match the purported accuracies shown by the creator of the tool, is still quite successful. The other chief benefit is that their solution is far less complex, orders of magnitude cheaper to run, and requires infrastructure that their platform for ML already supports.

This result is possible only if the team is lucky enough to abandon the path that they've started down early enough in the project timeline. I truly wish that I hadn't seen the alternative as many times as I have: teams spending months struggling to get something to work, spending a massive amount of time and money, with nothing to show for it in the end.

A cargo cult?

Cargo cult behavior originated in the post-WWII era on islands in the South Pacific. It was a tendency of certain indigenous people who, upon interacting with wartime military members who were using these isolated islands, received goods and services (medical, dental, technological, etc.) that they had never encountered before. In the years following the lack of return of these service members, groups on some islands began imitating the behavior, clothing styles, and caricaturizing of technology in the belief that if they mimicked the visitors, they would return one day. The islanders saw the outsiders (and their abundance of supplies, goods, and technology) as something beyond their understanding but beneficial to them.

While this term is highly prejudicial and antiquated, it endures to the modern day because of Richard Feynman's use of the term when describing inadequate scientific rigor displayed by some scientists during experimentation and validation of research. The term *cargo cult software engineering*, as applied to utilizing design principles, whole-cloth-lifted code samples from references, and the zealous adherence to standards that successful companies use without evaluating whether they are needed (or even relevant for the use case), was popularized by author Steve McConnell.

I use the term here in the vein of McConnell, as applied to the behavior of inexperienced teams and junior DSs who choose to latch on to every piece of technology, algorithm, framework, platform, and innovative advancement that comes out of big tech. Typically, this cargo cult ML behavior manifests itself in the form of using highly complex systems that were designed for highly complex problems with no regard to the applicability of those tools and processes for their own problems. They see that Massive Tech Company A developed a new framework for adjusting weights on neural networks, and they assume that, to be successful, they too must use this framework for all of their problem-solving projects (I'm looking at you, LSTM, for basic sales forecasts!).

(continued)

Teams who engage in this behavior fail to realize the very real reason these technologies were developed (to solve a specific set of problems at those companies) and the reason the source code was shared (to attract top talent to their companies). It was not shared so that everyone would latch onto a new paradigm and start using these technologies for even the most trivial and mundane ML task.

Following the hype-train of new technologies and assuming that the newest thing that comes out is a panacea to all problems is a recipe for disaster in terms of productivity, cost, and time. This approach frequently leaves less experienced groups at companies struggling to even get the technology to work in the first place.

What's more, some of the more experienced DSs and ML engineers at the companies that release these tools will readily admit that they don't use those tools for anything but what they were designed to solve (at least, the ones that I've known and have discussed this topic with do; I can't speak for everyone). They focus predominately on the simplest approaches to problems and move to more advanced approaches only when the need arises.

The thought processes that I've seen played out many times with this cargo cult behavior are exemplified in figure 14.17.

The team in this example erroneously believes that the new package is going to give them the same levels of success shown by the massive tech company's press release. The team equates the miraculous performance of this company with everything that comes out of the doors of that organization.

This isn't to say that these large companies are not successful. They generally employ some of the most profoundly innovative and clever software engineers in the world, in fact. The problem is that they're not releasing all the goods in order for others to leverage everything that makes them successful. Companies that try to copy these examples, expecting the same results, will almost always fail at replicating them. This is due to several critical factors:

- They don't have the same data.
- They don't have the same infrastructure and tooling.
- They don't have the same number of highly competent engineers available to support these complex solutions.
- They're likely not dealing with the exact same use case (different customers, different ecosystem, or a different industry).
- They don't have the same budget (in both time and money) to make it work.
- They don't have the same R&D budget to spend months iterating on solving a problem in a very advanced way.

I'm not in any way, shape, or form stating that new technologies shouldn't be used. I use them all the time—and most of the time, I enjoy doing so. My colleagues do as well with, similar to my own experience, varying success. New technology is great,

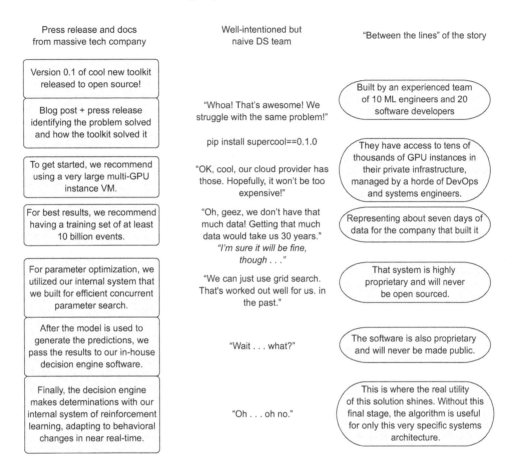

Figure 14.17 Blindly trusting the promises of a README and a blog post on a new package can waste a vast amount of time.

particularly when it solves previously unsolvable problems. What I am cautioning against, however, is placing blind faith in those technologies, assuming that they will magically solve all of your woes, and that if you copy the way some massive and innovative company does its ML, it will work out the same way for you.

The key to avoiding cargo cult behavior in ML can be distilled down to a few elemental steps covered in earlier parts of this book. Figure 14.18 shows a visual guide that has always worked well for me when evaluating new possible technologies.

I try to do my due diligence when evaluating new things that are announced in the field of ML. With the rapid pace of advancements and the seemingly never-ending megaphone-blast of hype coming out of the space, there simply isn't time to evaluate everything. However, if something does look promising, comes from an established and reputable source, and actually claims to solve a problem that I am struggling with (or have in the past), then it's a candidate for this rigorous evaluation.

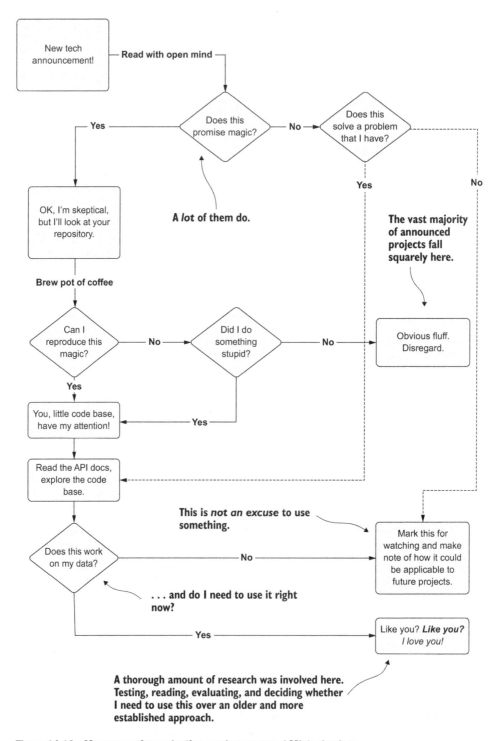

Figure 14.18   My process for evaluating newly announced ML technology

The sad state of affairs is that the vast majority of projects (even those espoused by large and successful tech companies) either never end up gaining community traction or aim to solve a problem that is far beyond the team's capabilities (or the current state of technology's capabilities) to be worthy of spending much time on. This becomes dangerous when teams don't evaluate the tech in the scope of their needs. Even if the technology is super cool and exciting, it doesn't mean that it's the right thing for your company to be using. Remember, using new tech is a high-risk activity.

Sticking to the simplest approach doesn't mean using the "new hotness." It means using the new hotness if, and only if, it makes your solutions easier, more maintainable, and easier to keep running. Everything else is, either to you or to everyone else in general, just fluff.

Summary

- Thoroughly vetting the provenance, characteristics, and properties of any data being considered for use in a model should be conducted before attempting to utilize it in a model. Time spent confirming its utility early on will save many frustrating investigations later in a project.
- Any data that is going to be used for an ML solution needs to be monitored fully with abnormalities handled in a predictable way. Unexpected behavior based on changes to both training and inference data can easily render a solution useless.
- Monitoring feature data is essential, but it is only one part of the model life cycle that should be watched. From ETL ingestion, to feature engineering, model training, model retraining, prediction, and attribution, each stage has metrics that should be collected, analyzed, and alerted upon if their behavior is unexpected.
- Focusing on simplicity in design and implementation, an ML project will get to production sooner, be easier to maintain, and likely cost far less, leaving any DS team free to solve additional problems that bring value to a company.
- By using a standard architecture for ML project code bases, refactoring can be kept to a minimum throughout development, team members can readily understand where abstracted logic resides, and maintenance will be far easier than if using custom designs for each project.
- Ensuring that any new technology that you take on as part of your repertoire is applicable to your team, your projects, and your company will help make all ML project work more sustainable and reliable. Evaluation, research, and skepticism will all benefit you.

15
Quality and acceptance testing

This chapter covers

- Establishing consistency for data sources used in ML
- Handling prediction failures gracefully with fallback logic
- Providing quality assurance for ML predictions
- Implementing explainable solutions

In the preceding chapter, we focused on broad and foundational technical topics for successful ML project work. Following from those foundations, a critical infrastructure of monitoring and validation needs to be built to ensure the continued health and relevance of any project. This chapter focuses on these ancillary processes and infrastructure tooling that enable not only more efficient development, but easier maintenance of the project once it is in production.

Between the completion of model development and the release of a project are four main activities:

- Data availability and consistency verifications
- Cold-start (fallback or default) logic development

438

- User-acceptance testing (subjective quality assurance)
- Solution interpretability (explainable AI, or XAI)

To show where these elements fit within a project's development path, figure 15.1 illustrates the post-modeling phase work covered in this chapter.

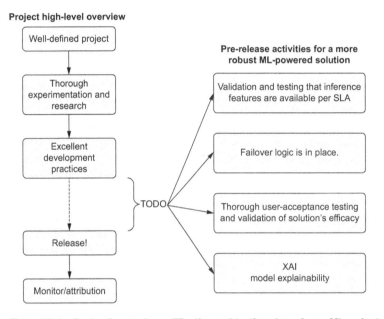

Figure 15.1 Production-grade qualification and testing phase for an ML project

These highlighted actions are generally seen as an afterthought or reactive implementation for many projects that I've had exposure to. While not applicable to every ML solution, evaluating each of these components is highly recommended.

Having their actions or implementations complete before a release happens can efficiently prevent a lot of confusion and frustration for your internal business unit customer. Removing those obstacles directly translates to better working relationships with the business and creates fewer headaches for you.

15.1 Data consistency

Data issues can be one of the most frustrating aspects of production stability for a model. Whether due to flaky data collection, ETL changes between project development and deployment, or a general poor implementation of ETL, they typically bring a project's production service to a grinding halt.

Ensuring data consistency (and regularly validating its quality) in every phase of the model life cycle is incredibly important for both the relevance of the implementation's output and the stability of the solution over time. Consistency across phases of modeling is achieved by eliminating training and inference skew, utilizing feature stores, and openly sharing materialized feature data across an organization.

15.1.1 *Training and inference skew*

Let's imagine that we're working on a team that has been developing a solution by using a batch extract of features for consistency throughout model development. Throughout the development process, we were careful to utilize data that we knew was available in the serving system's online data store. Because of the success of the project, the status quo was simply not left alone. The business wants more of what we're bringing to the table.

After a few weeks of work, we find that the addition of features from a new dataset that wasn't included in the initial project development makes a large impact on the model's predictive capabilities. We integrate these new features, retrain the model, and are left in the position shown in figure 15.2.

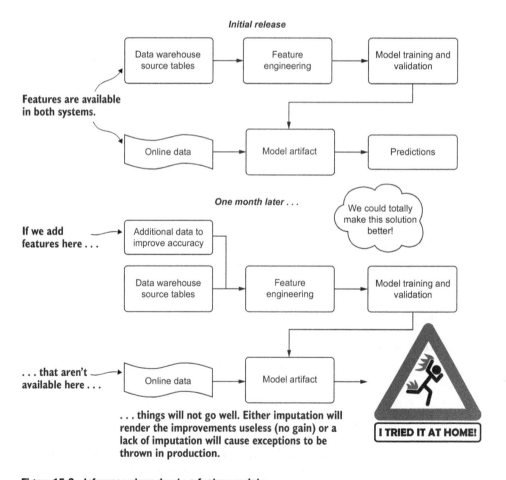

Figure 15.2   Inference skew due to a feature update

With the online feature system not able to access the data that was later included in the model revision, we have a training and inference skew problem. This problem manifests itself in two primary ways, as mentioned in figure 15.2:

- Null values are imputed.
  - If filling with a mean or median value of the feature space, the variance and potential information within the feature vector will be reduced, potentially leading to model degradation during retraining.
  - If filling with a placeholder value, the results may be worse than the original model.
- Null values are not handled. This may cause exceptions to be thrown, depending on the library used. This can fundamentally break the production deployment of the new model. The predictions will all be of the fallback heuristics "last hope" service.

Scenarios of mismatch between training and inference are not relegated to the presence or absence of feature data. These issues can also happen if the processing logic for creating the raw data is different between offline data in the data warehouse and the online systems. Working through these issues, diagnosing them, and repairing them can be incredibly costly and time-consuming.

As part of any production ML process, architectural validation and checks for consistency in offline and online training systems should be conducted. These checks can be manual (statistical validation through a scheduled job) or fully automated through the use of a feature store to ensure consistency.

15.1.2 *A brief intro to feature stores*

From a project's development perspective, one of the more time-consuming aspects of crafting the ML code base is in feature creation. As data scientists, we spend a great amount of creative effort in manipulating the data being used in models to ensure that the correlations present are optimally leveraged to solve a problem. Historically, this computational processing is embedded within a project's code base, in an inline execution chain that is acted upon during both training and prediction.

Having this tightly coupled association between the feature engineering code and the model-training and prediction code can lead to a great deal of frustrating troubleshooting, as we saw earlier in our scenario. This tight coupling can also result in complicated refactoring if data dependencies change, and duplicated effort if a calculated feature ever needs to be implemented in another project.

With the implementation of a feature store, however, these data consistency issues can be largely solved. With a single source of truth defined once, a registered feature calculation can be developed once, updated as part of a scheduled job, and available to be used by anyone in the organization (if they have sufficient access privileges, that is).

Consistency is not the only goal of these engineered systems. Synchronized data feeds to an online transaction processing (OLTP) storage layer (for real-time predictions) are another quality-of-life benefit that a feature store brings to minimizing the engineering burden of developing, maintaining, and synchronizing ETL needs for production ML. The basic design of a feature store capable of supporting online predictions consists of the following:

- An ACID-compliant storage layer:
  - *(A) Atomicity*—Guaranteeing that transactions (writes, reads, updates) are handled as unit operations that either succeed (are committed) or fail (are rolled back) to ensure data consistency.
  - *(C) Consistency*—Transactions to the data store must leave the data in a valid state to prevent data corruption (from an invalid or illegal action to the system).
  - *(I) Isolation*—Transactions are concurrent and always leave the storage system in a valid state as though operations were performed in sequence.
  - *(D) Durability*—Valid executions to the state of the system will remain persistent at all times, even in the event of a hardware system failure or power loss, and are written to a persistent storage layer (written to disk, as opposed to volatile memory).
- A low-latency serving layer that is synchronized to the ACID storage layer (typically, volatile in-memory cache layers or in-memory database representations such as Redis).
- A denormalized representation data model for both a persistent storage layer and in-memory key-value store (primary-key access to retrieve relevant features).
- An immutable read-only access pattern for end users. The teams that own the generated data are the only ones with write authority.

As mentioned, the benefits of a feature store are not restricted to consistency. Reusability is one of the primary features of a feature store, as illustrated in figure 15.3.

As you can see, implementing a feature store carries a multitude of benefits. Having a standard corpus of features throughout a company means that every use case, from reporting (BI) to analytics and DS research is operating on the *same set of source-of-truth data* as everyone else. Using the feature store eliminates confusion, increases efficiency (features don't have to be redesigned by everyone for each use case), and ensures that the costs for generating features are incurred only once.

15.1.3 *Process over technology*

The success of a feature store implementation is not in the specific technology used to implement it. The benefit is in the actions it enables a company to take with its calculated and standardized feature data.

Let's briefly examine an ideal process for a company that needs to update the definition of its revenue metric. For such a broadly defined term, the concept of revenue at a company can be interpreted in many ways, depending on the end-use case, the

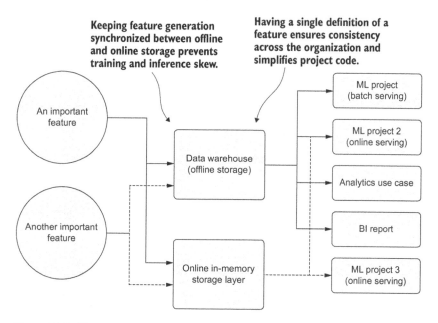

Figure 15.3 The basic concept of a feature store

department concerned with the usage of that data, and the level of accounting standards applied to the definition for those use cases.

A marketing group, for instance, may be interested in gross revenue for measuring the success rate of advertising campaigns. The DE group may define multiple variations of revenue to handle the needs of different groups within the company. The DS team may be looking at a windowed aggregation of any column in the data warehouse that has the words "sales," "revenue," or "cost" in it to create feature data. The BI team might have a more sophisticated set of definitions that appeal to a broader set of analytics use cases.

Changing a definition of the logic of such a key business metric can have far-reaching impacts to an organization if everyone is responsible for their group's personal definitions. The likelihood of each group changing its references in each of the queries, code bases, reports, and models that it is responsible for is marginal. Fragmenting the definition of such an important metric across departments is problematic enough on its own. Creating multiple versions of the defining characteristics within each group is a recipe for complete chaos. With no established standard for how key business metrics are defined, groups within a company are effectively no longer speaking on even terms when evaluating the results and outputs from one another.

Regardless of the technology stack used to store the data for consumption, having a process built around change management for critical features can guarantee a frictionless and resilient data migration. Figure 15.4 illustrates such a process.

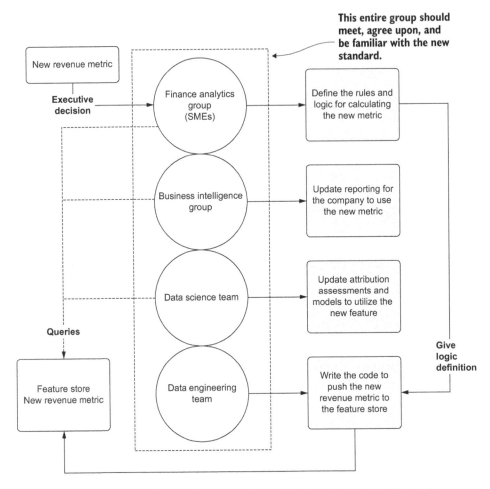

Figure 15.4   Setting a data change-point process for updating a critical feature store entry

As you can see, the new standard for reporting company revenue comes from the executive council. From this defining point, a successful feature store update process can begin. With the stakeholders present from each group that deals with company-wide utilization of this sort of data, a thorough evaluation of the proposed change can commence. Each of the producers and consumers of this data collectively agree on a course of action to ensure that the new standard becomes an actual standard at the company. After the meeting, each group knows the actions that it needs to take in order to make the migration to this new metric; the metric is defined, implemented, and synchronized through ETL to a common feature store.

Change-point processes are critical for ensuring consistency across an organization that relies on data to make informed decisions. By employing these processes, everyone is speaking the same "data language." Discussions around the veracity of analytics, reporting, and predictions can all be standardized on the same common definition of a data term. It also dramatically improves the stability of dependent production (automated) jobs and reporting that rely on this data.

15.1.4 *The dangers of a data silo*

Data silos are deceptively dangerous. Isolating data in a walled-off, private location that is accessible only to a certain select group of individuals stifles the productivity of other teams, causes a large amount of duplicated effort throughout an organization, and frequently (in my experience of seeing them, at least) leads to esoteric data definitions that, in their isolation, depart wildly from the general accepted view of a metric for the rest of the company.

It may seem like a really great thing when an ML team is granted a database of its own or an entire cloud object store bucket to empower the team to be self-service. The seemingly geologically scaled time spent for the DE or warehousing team to load required datasets disappears. The team members are fully masters of their domain, able to load, consume, and generate data with impunity. This can definitely be a good thing, provided that clear and soundly defined processes govern the management of this technology.

But clean or dirty, an internal-use-only data storage stack is a silo, the contents squirreled away from the outside world. These silos can generate more problems than they solve.

To show how a data silo can be disadvantageous, let's imagine that we work at a company that builds dog parks. Our latest ML project is a bit of a moon shot, working with counterfactual simulations (causal modeling) to determine which amenities would be most valuable to our customers at different proposed construction sites. The goal is to figure out how to maximize the perceived quality and value of the proposed parks while minimizing our company's investment costs.

To build such a solution, we have to get data on all of the registered dog parks in the country. We also need demographic data associated with the localities of these dog parks. Since the company's data lake contains no data sources that have this information, we have to source it ourselves. Naturally, we put all of this information in our own environment, thinking it will be far faster than waiting for the DE team's backlog to clear enough to get around to working on it.

After a few months, questions began to arise about some of the contracts that the company had bid on in certain locales. The business operations team is curious about why so many orders for custom paw-activated watering fountains are being ordered as part of some of these construction inventories. As the analysts begin to dig into the data available in the data lake, they can't make sense of why the recommendations for certain contracts consistently recommended these incredibly expensive components.

After spending months working through analyses, the decision is made to remove this feature from contract bidding. No one can explain why it is there, and they decide that it isn't worth it to continue to offer it. They are keener on offering automatic dog-washing stations (car-wash style), dog-poop robots (cleaners of, not made of), park-wide cooling fans, and automated ball-throwing apparatuses. As such, a large order is placed for those items, and the fountain-sourcing contracts are terminated.

A few months later, a competitor starts offering the exact same element on contracts that we have been bidding on. The cities and towns begin to go for the competitor's bid. When finally pressed about why, sales teams start hearing the same answer: the dogs just really love water fountains, particularly in areas that are far from people's homes and municipal dog-watering stations. What ends up happening here is shown in figure 15.5.

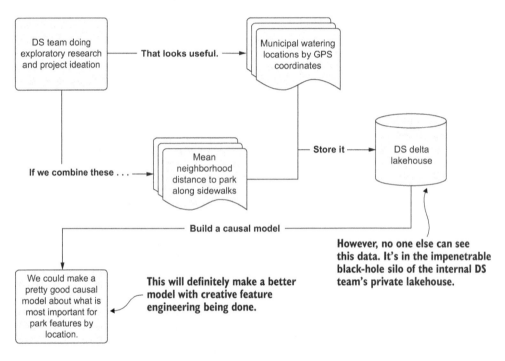

Figure 15.5 Storing critical data in a silo

With no visibility into these features that were collected and used for the amenities counterfactual-based simulation model that the DS team built, the business is unable to piece together the reasons for the model's suggestions. The data was siloed with no ill intentions, but it causes a massive problem for the business because critical data is inaccessible.

We're not farmers. *We should never be using silos.* At least not data ones. If farming's your hobby, don't let me stop you. We should, on the other hand, work closely with DE and warehousing teams to ensure that we're able to write data to locations that everyone can access—preferably, as we will discuss in chapter 17, to a feature store.

15.2 Fallbacks and cold starts

Let's imagine that we've just built an ML-powered solution for optimizing delivery routes for a pizza company. Some time ago, the business approached us, asking for a cheaper, faster, and more adaptable solution to optimizing the delivery routes of a single driver. The prior method for figuring out which addresses a certain driver would deliver the pizzas to was done by a pathing algorithm that generated optimal routes based on ArcGIS. While capable and quite fully featured, the business wanted something that considered the temporal nature and history of actual delivery data to create a more effective route.

The team worked on an LSTM-based approach that was trained on the last three years of delivery data, creating an adversarial network with reinforcement learning that rewarded optimal pathing based on timeliness of delivery. The project quickly advanced from a science project to something that was proving its worth in a handful of regions. It was far more adept at selecting delivery sequences than the brute-force pathing that their previous production system was capable of.

After reviewing several weeks' worth of routing data in the test markets, the business felt comfortable with turning on the system for all delivery routes. Things looked pretty good. Predictions were being served, drivers were spending less time stuck in traffic, and pizza was delivered hot at a much higher rate than ever before.

It took about a week before the complaints began pouring in. Customers in rural areas were complaining of very long delivery times at a frighteningly high rate. After looking at the complaints, the pattern began to emerge that every complaint was always with the last stop on a delivery chain. It didn't take long for the DS team to realize what was happening. With most of the training data focused on urban centers, the volume of drop-offs and the lower proximity between stops meant that an optimized stop count was being targeted in general for the model. When this delivery count was applied to a rural environment, the sheer distances involved meant that nearly all final-stop delivery customers would be greeted with a room-temperature pizza.

Without a fallback control on the length of routes or the estimated total delivery time, the model was optimizing routes for the minimal amount of time for the total delivery run volume, regardless of how long that total estimated time would be. The solution lacked a backup plan. It didn't have a fallback to use existing geolocation services (the ArcGIS solution for rural routes) if the model's output violated a business rule (don't deliver cold pizza).

A critical part of any production ML solution is to *always have a backup plan.* Regardless of the level of preparation, forethought, and planning, even the most comprehensive and hardened-against-failure solution will inevitably go wrong at some point. Whether the solution that you're building is offline (batch), near-real-time (micro-batch streaming), online, or edge deployed, some condition in the near or far future will result in the model just not behaving the way that you were hoping.

Table 15.1 shows a brief list of ways for a solution's model to malfunction and the level of impact depending on the degree of gravity of the model's use.

Table 15.1   When models don't play nicely

Condition	Comical example	Serious business example
Regression predictions outside of possible natural range	Predict that customer will spend -$8,745 today.	Withdraw reactor control rods to maximum height. Now.
Classifier predicting only a single class	Everything is a dog. Even that cat is a dog.	Self-driving car classifying a stop sign on an interstate highway.
Missed SLA on app/web	A blank void of empty IFrame elements.	Locking your accounts because of fraudulent activity.
No content filtering of chatbot	Starts reciting song lyrics.	Starts insulting the user.
No response from failure-detection system	Monitoring panel converted to Christmas display.	Shut off all power plants. On the Eastern seaboard.

While these examples are fairly ridiculous (mostly—some are based on real situations), they all share a common thread. Not a single one has a fallback plan. They allow bad things to happen if the single point of failure in the system (a model's prediction) doesn't work as intended. While purposefully obtuse, the point here is that all model-powered solutions have some sort of failure mode that will happen if a backup isn't in place.

Cold starts, on the other hand, are a unique form of model failure. Instead of a fully nonfunctional scenario that typical fallback systems handle, models that suffer from a cold-start issue are those that require historical data to function for which that data hasn't been generated yet. From recommendation systems for first-time users to price optimization algorithms in new markets, model solutions that need to make a prediction based on data that doesn't exist need a specific type of fallback system to be in place.

15.2.1 *Leaning heavily on prior art*

We could use nearly any of the comical examples from table 15.1 to illustrate the first rule in creating fallback plans. Instead, let's use an actual example from my own personal history.

I once worked on a project that had to deal with a manufacturing recipe. The goal of this recipe was to set a rotation speed on a ludicrously expensive piece of equipment while a material was dripped onto it. The speed of this unit needed to be adjusted periodically throughout the day as the temperature and humidity changed the viscosity of the material being dripped onto the product. Keeping this piece of equipment running optimally was my job; there were many dozens of these stations in the machine and many types of chemicals.

As in so many times in my career, I got really tired of doing a repetitive task. I figured there had to be some way to automate the spin speed of these units so I wouldn't have to stand at the control station and adjust them every hour or so. Thinking myself rather clever, I wired up a few sensors to a microcontroller, programmed the programmable logic controller to receive the inputs from my little controller, wrote a simple program that would adjust the chuck speed according to the temperature and humidity in the room, and activated the system.

Everything went well, I thought, for the first few hours. I had programmed a simple regression formula into the microcontroller, checked my math, and even tested it on an otherwise broken piece of equipment. It all seemed pretty solid.

It wasn't until around 3 a.m. that my pager (yes, it was *that long ago*) started going off. By the time I made it to the factory 20 minutes later, I realized that I had caused an overspeed condition in every single spin chuck system. They stopped. The rest of the liquid dosing system did not. As the chilly breeze struck the back of my head, and I looked out at the open bay doors letting in the 27°F night air, I realized my error.

I didn't have a fallback condition. The regression line, taking in the ambient temperature, tried to compensate for the untested range of data (the viscosity curve wasn't actually linear at that range), and took a chuck that normally rotated at around 2,800 RPM and tried to instruct it to spin at 15,000 RPM.

I spent the next four days and three nights cleaning up lacquer from the inside of that machine. By the time I was finished, the lead engineer took me aside and handed me a massive three-ring binder and told me to "read it before playing any more games." (I'm paraphrasing. I can't put into print what he said to me.) The book was filled with the materials science analysis of each chemical that the machine was using. It had the exact viscosity curves that I could have used. It had information on maximum spin speeds for deposition.

Someone had done a lot of work before I got there. Someone had figured out what the safe and unsafe thresholds were for the material, as well as the chuck drive motor.

I learned an important lesson that day. That lesson is illustrated in figure 15.6.

I was solidly in the top portion of figure 15.6. I rapidly learned, with no small amount of antagonistic reinforcement from my fellow engineers, to strive to be in the bottom portion of figure 15.6. I learned to think about what could go wrong in any solution and how important it is to have guardrails and fallback conditions when things did go wrong.

Many times, when building an ML solution, a DS can wrongly assume that the problem that they are tackling is one that has no prior art. There are certainly exceptions (the moon-shot projects), but the vast majority of solutions I've worked on in my career have had *someone* at a company fulfilling the role that the project is meant to automate.

That person had methods, practices, and standards by which they were doing that task. They understood the data before you came along. They were, for all intents and purposes, a living, breathing version of that three-ring binder that my boss threw at me in anger. They knew how fast the chuck could spin and what would happen to the lacquer if a technician tried to sneak a cigarette break in the middle of winter.

These individuals (or code) that represent prior art will know the conditions that you need to consider when building a fallback system. They'll know what the default conditions should be if the model predicts garbage. They'll know what the acceptable

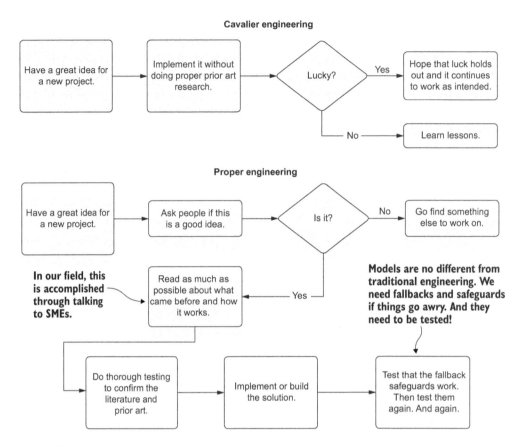

Figure 15.6   Figuring out the importance of safeguards and fallbacks in engineering work

range of your regressor's prediction can be. They'll know how many cat photos should be expected each day and how many dogs as well. They are your sage guides who can help make a more robust solution. It's worth asking them how they solved the problem and what their funniest story is of when things went wrong. It will only help to make sure you don't repeat it.

15.2.2 *Cold-start woes*

For certain types of ML projects, model prediction failures are not only frequent, but also expected. For solutions that require a historical context of existing data to function properly, the absence of historical data prevents the model from making a prediction. The data simply isn't available to pass through the model. Known as the *cold-start problem*, this is a critical aspect of solution design and architecture for any project dealing with temporally associated data.

As an example, let's imagine that we run a dog-grooming business. Our fleets of mobile bathing stations scour the suburbs of North America, offering all manner of services to dogs at their homes. Appointments and service selection is handled through an app interface. When booking a visit, the clients select from hundreds of options and prepay for the services through the app no later than a day before the visit.

To increase our customers' satisfaction (and increase our revenue), we employ a service recommendation interface on the app. This model queries the customer's historical visits, finds products that might be relevant for them, and indicates additional services that the dog might enjoy. For this recommender to function correctly, the historical services history needs to be present during service selection.

This isn't much of a stretch for anyone to conceptualize. A model without data to process isn't particularly useful. With no history available, the model clearly has no data in which to infer additional services that could be recommended for bundling into the appointment.

What's needed to serve *something* to the end user is a cold-start solution. An easy implementation for this use case is to generate a collection of the most frequently ordered services globally. If the model doesn't have enough data to provide a prediction, this popularity-based services aggregation can be served in its place. At that point, the app IFrame element will at least have something in it (instead of showing an empty collection) and the user experience won't be broken by seeing an empty box.

More-sophisticated implementations can be made, upgrading a global popularity ranking to one with more fine-grained cold-start pre-generated data. At a bare minimum, the geographic region can be used as a grouped aggregation to calculate popularity of services to create a pseudo-personalized failover condition. More-sophisticated grouping assignments can be made if additional data is available for the end user, referencing those aggregated data points across the user base for grouping conditions, ensuring that more refined and granular recommendations are served. A cold-start-enabled architecture is shown in figure 15.7.

Building a heuristics-based solution, leveraging the deep knowledge of the use case by collaborating with the SMEs, is a solid approach for solving the cold-start issue. When a user who doesn't have an order selection history of at least three appointments starts using the app, the model is bypassed entirely and a simple business rules pseudo-prediction is made. These cold-start solution implementations can take the following forms:

- Most popular items in user geographic location over the last month
- Most popular items bought today globally
- SME-curated collections of items
- High-inventory items

Regardless of the approach used, it's important to have something in place. The alternative, after all, is to return no data. This simply isn't an option for customer-facing applications that depend on some form of data to be produced from an API in order to populate elements in the interface with content. The benefit to having a cold-start alternative solution in place is that it can serve as a fallback solution as

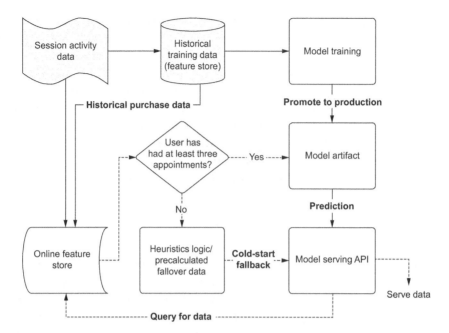

Figure 15.7   Logical diagram of a cold start solution

well. By a small adjustment of decision logic to check the veracity of the output coming from the model's prediction output, the cold-start values can be served in place of the problematic data.

It can be tempting to build something complex for this cold-start default value service, but complexity should be avoided here. The goal is to build something that is exceptionally fast (low SLA), simple to adjust and maintain, and relevant enough so as not to bring attention to the end user that something was not designed correctly.

Cold-start solutions don't apply exclusively to recommendation systems. Anytime a model is issuing predictions, particularly those with a low-SLA response requirement, some sort of value should be produced that is at least somewhat relevant to the task at hand (relevant as defined and designed by the business unit and SMEs, not by the DS team).

Failing to generate a value can, particularly for real-time use cases, break downstream systems that ingest that data. Failing to have a relevancy-dependent fallback for many systems can cause them to throw exceptions, retry excessively, or resort to system-protecting default values that a backend or frontend developer puts in place. That's a situation that neither the engineering department nor the end user wants to see.

15.3　*End user vs. internal use testing*

Releasing a project to production once the end-to-end functionality is confirmed to be working is incredibly tempting. After so much work, effort, and metrics-based quantitative quality checks, it's only natural to assume that the solution is ready to be sent out into the world for use. Resisting this urge to sprint the last mile to release is difficult, although it is absolutely critical.

The primary reasons it's so ill-advised to simply release a project based solely on the internal evaluations of the DS team, as we covered in part 1, are as follows:

- The DS team members are biased. This is their baby. No one wants to admit to having created an ugly baby.
- Quantitative metrics do not always guarantee qualitative traits.
- The most important influence over quality predictions may be data that is not collected.

These reasons harken back to the concept of correlation not implying causality, as well as creator bias. While the model's validation and quantitative metrics may perform remarkably well, precious few projects will have all of the causal factors captured within a feature vector.

What a thorough testing or QA process can help us do is assign a qualitative assessment of our solution. We can accomplish this in multiple ways.

Let's imagine that we work at a music streaming service. We have an initiative to increase customer engagement by way of providing highly relevant song choices to follow along after a queued listening session.

Instead of using a collaborative filtering approach that would find similar songs listened to by other users, we want to find songs that are similar based on how the human ear would interpret a song. We use a Fourier transformation of the audio file to get a frequency distribution and then map that distribution to a mel scale (a linear cosine transformation of the log power spectrum of an audio signal that closely approximates how the human ear perceives sound). With this transformation of the data and a plot, we arrive at a visual representation of the characteristics of each song. We then, in an offline manner, calculate similarities of all songs to all other songs through the use of a tuned tri-branch Siamese Network. The feature vector that comes out of this system, augmented by additional tagged features to each song, is used to calculate both a Euclidean and a Cosine distance from one song to another. We save these relationships among all songs in a NoSQL database that tracks the 1,000 most similar songs to all others for our serving layer.

For illustration, figure 15.8 is essentially what the team is feeding into the Siamese network, mel visualizations of each song. These distance metrics have internal "knobs" that the DS team can use to adjust the final output collections. This feature was discovered early in testing when internal SME members expressed a desire to refine filters of similar music within a genre to eras of music.

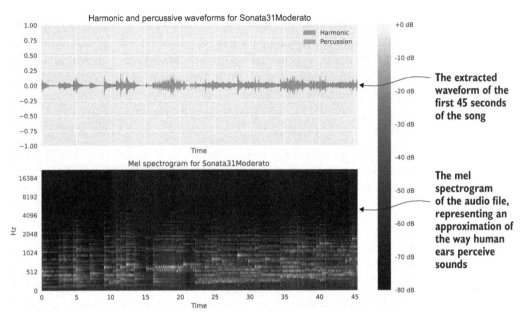

The extracted waveform of the first 45 seconds of the song

The mel spectrogram of the audio file, representing an approximation of the way human ears perceive sounds

The Siamese network will take these mel spectrographs into each CNN and generate a feature vector of the representation of what it "learns" about each audio file. These vectors are then fed into a distance measurement stage, which is used to update the weights during training. Once trained, the encoder can represent a uniqueness vector that can be used for new music.

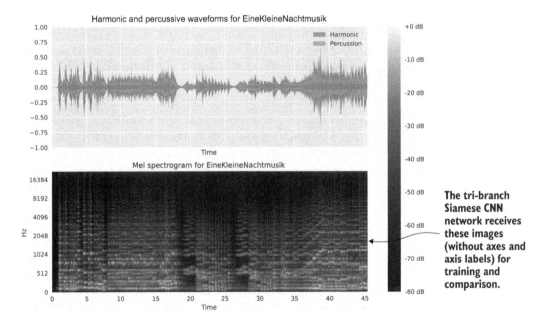

The tri-branch Siamese CNN network receives these images (without axes and axis labels) for training and comparison.

Figure 15.8 **Music file transformation to a mel spectrogram for use in Siamese CNN network**

Now that we can see what is going on here (and the sort of information the CNN would be creating from an encoded feature), we can delve into how to test this service. Figure 15.9 shows an overview of the testing.

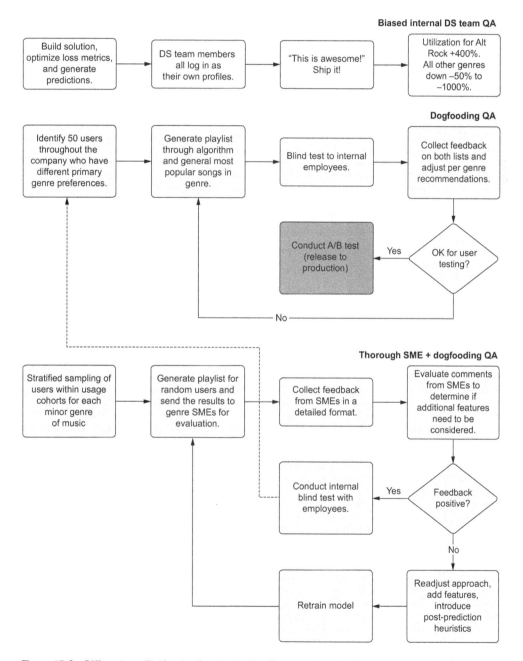

Figure 15.9 Different qualitative testing strategies. The one at the top is pretty bad as a practice.

Figure 15.9 compares three separate forms of preproduction QA work that can be done to make qualitative assessments on our service. The next three subsections cover each of these elements—internal biased testing, dogfooding (consuming the product of our own efforts), and thorough SME review—to show the benefits of the holistic SME evaluation approach over the others.

The end goal of performing QA on ML projects, after all, is to evaluate predictions on real-world data that doesn't rely on the highly myopic perspective of the solution's creators. The objective is to eliminate as much bias as possible from the qualitative assessment of a solution's utility.

15.3.1   *Biased testing*

Internal testing is easy—well, easier than the alternatives. It's painless (if the model works properly). It's what we typically think of when we're qualifying the results of a project. The process typically involves the following:

- Generating predictions on new (unseen to the modeling process) data
- Analyzing the distribution and statistical properties of the new predictions
- Taking random samples of predictions and making qualitative judgments of them
- Running handcrafted sample data (or their own accounts, if applicable) through the model

The first two elements in this list are valid for qualification of model effectiveness. They are wholly void of bias and should be done. The latter two, on the other hand, are *dangerous.* The final one is the more dangerous of them.

In our music playlist generator system scenario, let's say that the DS team members are all fans of classical music. Throughout their qualitative verifications, they've been checking to see the relative quality of the playlist generator for the field of music that they are most familiar with: classical music. To perform these validations, they've been generating listening history of their favorite pieces, adjusting the implementation to fine-tune the results, and iterating on the validation process.

When they are fully satisfied that the solution works well at identifying a nearly uncanny level of sophistication for capturing thematic and tonally relevant similar pieces of music, they ask a colleague what they think. The results for both the DS team (Ben and Julie) as well as for their data warehouse engineer friend Connor are shown in figure 15.10.

What ends up happening is a bias-based optimization of the solution that caters to the DS team's own preferences and knowledge of a genre of music. While perfectly tuned for the discerning tastes of a classical music fan, the solution is woefully poor for someone who is a fan of modern alternative rock, such as Connor. His feedback would have been dramatically different from the team's own adjudication of their solution's quality. To fix the implementation, Ben and Julie would likely have to make a lot of adjustments, pulling in additional features to further refine Connor's tastes in alt-rock music. What about all of the other hundreds of genres of music, though?

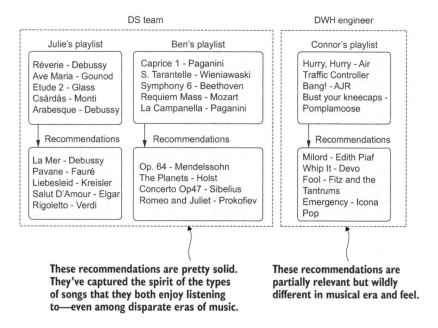

These recommendations are pretty solid. They've captured the spirit of the types of songs that they both enjoy listening to—even among disparate eras of music.

These recommendations are partially relevant but wildly different in musical era and feel.

Figure 15.10 Biased feedback in qualitative assessment of model efficacy

While this example is particularly challenging (musical tastes are exceptionally varied and highly specific to individuals), this exact problem of internal-team bias can exist for any ML project. Any DS team will have only a limited view of the nuances in the data. A detailed understanding of the complex latent relationships of the data and how each relates to the business is generally not knowable by the DS team. This is why it is so critical to involve in the QA process those in the company who know most about the use case that the project is solving.

15.3.2 *Dogfooding*

A far more thorough approach than Ben and Julie's first attempt would have been to canvass people at the company. Instead of keeping the evaluation internal to the team, where a limited exposure to genres hampers their ability to qualitatively measure the effectiveness of the project, they could ask for help. They could ask around and see if people at the company might be interested in taking a look at how their own accounts and usage would be impacted by the changes the DS team is introducing. Figure 15.11 illustrates how this could work for this scenario.

Dogfooding, in the broadest sense, is consuming the results of your own product. The term refers to opening up functionality that is being developed so that everyone at a company can use it, find out how to break it, provide feedback on how it's broken, and collectively work toward building a better product. All of this happens across a broad range of perspectives, drawing on the experience and knowledge of many employees from all departments.

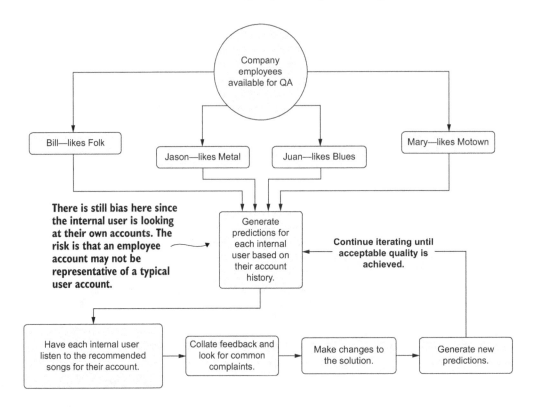

Figure 15.11 Dogfooding a project by utilizing volunteers to give subjective feedback as a user

However, as you can see in figure 15.11, the evaluation still contains bias. An internal user who uses the company's product is likely not a typical user. Depending on their job function, they may be using their account to validate functionality in the product, use it for demonstrations, or simply interact with the product more because of an employee benefit associated with it.

In addition to the potentially spurious information contained within the listen history of employees, the other form of bias is that people like what they like. They also don't like what they don't like. Subjective responses to something as emotionally charged as music preferences add an incredible amount of bias due to the nature of being a member of the human race. Knowing that these predictions are based on their listening history and that it is their own company's product, internal users evaluating their own profiles will generally be more critical than a typical user if they find something that they don't like (which is a stark contrast to the builder bias that the DS team would experience).

While dogfooding is certainly preferable to evaluating a solution's quality within the confines of the DS team, it's still not ideal, mostly because of these inherent biases that exist.

15.3.3 SME evaluation

The most thorough QA testing you can conduct while still staying within the confines of your own company leverages SMEs in the business. This is one of the most important reasons to keep SMEs within the business engaged in a project. They will not only know who in the company has the deepest knowledge and experience with facets of the project (in this case, genres of music), but they can help muster those resources to assist.

For the SME evaluation, we can stage this phase of QA beforehand, requesting resources who are experts in each of the music genres for which we need an unbiased opinion regarding the quality of generated song lists. By having experts designated, we can feed them not only their own recommendations, but also those of randomly sampled users. With their deep knowledge of the nuances of each genre, they can evaluate the recommendations of others to determine if the playlists that are being generated make tonal and thematic sense. Figure 15.12 illustrates this process.

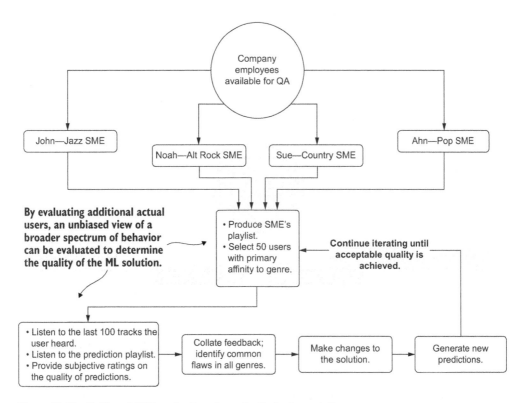

Figure 15.12   Unbiased SME evaluation of a project's implementation

With the far more thorough adjudication in place, the usefulness of the feedback is significantly higher than any other methodology We can minimize bias while also incorporating the deep knowledge of experts into actionable changes that can be iterated over.

While this scenario focuses on music recommendations, it can apply to nearly any ML project. It's best to keep in mind that before you start to tackle whichever project you're working on, some human (or many humans) had been solving that problem in some way before you were called in to work on it. They're going to understand the details of the subject in far more depth than anyone on the DS team will. You may as well try to make the best solution that you can by leveraging their knowledge and wisdom.

15.4 *Model interpretability*

Let's suppose that we're working on a problem designed to control forest fires. The organization that we work for can stage equipment, personnel, and services to locations within a large national park system in order to mitigate the chances of wildfires growing out of control. To make logistics effectiveness as efficient as possible, we've been tasked with building a solution that can identify risks of fire outbreaks by grid coordinates. We have several years of data, sensor data from each location, and a history of fire-burn area for each grid position.

After building the model and providing the predictions as a service to the logistics team, questions arise about the model's predictions. The logistics team members notice that certain predictions don't align with their tribal knowledge of having dealt with fire seasons, voicing concerns about addressing predicted calamities with the feature data that they're exposed to.

They've begun to doubt the solution. They're asking questions. They're convinced that something strange is going on and they'd like to know why their services and personnel are being told to cover a grid coordinate in a month that, as far as they can remember, has never had a fire break out.

How can we tackle this situation? How can we run simulations of our feature vector for the prediction through our model and tell them conclusively why the model predicted what it did? Specifically, how can we implement explainable artificial intelligence (XAI) on our model with the minimum amount of effort?

When planning out a project, particularly for a business-critical use case, a frequently overlooked aspect is to think about model explainability. Some industries and companies are the exception to this rule, because of either legal requirements or corporate policies, but for most groups that I've interacted with, interpretability is an afterthought.

I understand the reticence that most teams have in considering tacking on XAI functionality to a project. During the course of EDA, model tuning, and QA validation, the DS team generally understands the behavior of the model quite well. Implementing XAI may seem redundant.

By the time you need to explain how or why a model predicted what it did, you're generally in a panic situation that is already time-constrained. Through implementing

XAI processes through straightforward open source packages, this panicked and chaotic scramble to explain functionality of a solution can be avoided.

15.4.1 *Shapley additive explanations*

One of the more well-known and thoroughly proven XAI implementations for Python is the shap package, written and maintained by Scott Lundberg. This implementation is fully documented in detail in the 2017 NeurIPS paper "A Unified Approach to Interpreting Model Predictions" by Lundberg and Su-In Lee.

At the core of the algorithm is game theory. Essentially, when we're thinking of features that go into a training dataset, what is the effect on the model's predictions for each feature? As with players in a team sport, if a match is the model itself and the features involved in training are the players, what is the effect on the match if one player is substituted for another? How one player's influence changes the outcome of the game is the basic question that shap is attempting to answer.

FOUNDATION

The principle behind shap involves estimating the contribution of each feature from the training dataset upon the model. According to the original paper, calculating the true contribution (the exact Shapley value) requires evaluating all permutations for each row of the dataset for inclusion and exclusion of the source row's feature, creating different coalitions of feature groupings.

For instance, if we have three features (a, b, and c; original features denoted with $_i$), with replacement features from the dataset denoted as $_j$ (for example, a_j) the coalitions to test for evaluating feature b are as follows:

$$(a_i, b_i, c_j), (a_i, b_j, c_j), (a_i, b_j, c_i), (a_j, b_i, c_j), (a_j, b_j, c_i)$$

These coalitions of features are run through the model to retrieve a prediction. The resulting prediction is then differenced from the original row's prediction (and an absolute value taken of the difference). This process is repeated for each feature, resulting in a feature-value contribution score when a weighted average is applied to each delta grouping per feature.

It should come as no surprise that this isn't a very scalable solution. As the feature count increases and the training dataset's row count increases, the computational complexity of this approach quickly becomes untenable. Thankfully, another solution is far more scalable: the approximate Shapley estimation.

APPROXIMATE SHAPLEY VALUE ESTIMATION

To scale the additive effects of features across a large feature set, a slightly different approach is performed. The Python package shap utilizes this approximate implementation to get reasonable values across all rows and features without having to resort to the brute-force approach in the original paper. Figure 15.13 illustrates the process of this approximated approach.

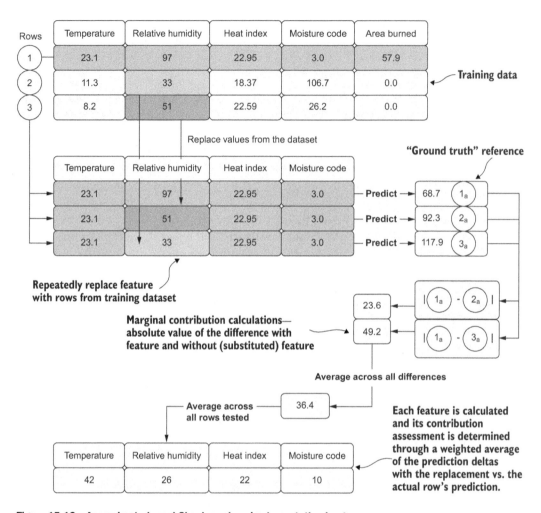

Figure 15.13 Approximate kernel Shapley values implementation in shap

The primary differentiator here as compared to the exhaustive search approach is in the limited number of tests conducted and the method of building coalitions. As opposed to the original design, a single row's feature vector is not used to generate a baseline prediction. Instead, a random sampling of rows is conducted, and the feature under test is swapped out with other values from the selected subset for that feature. These new synthetic vectors are then passed to the model, generating a prediction. For each of these synthetic predictions, an absolute difference is calculated, then averaged, giving the reference vector's feature contribution value across these coalitions. The weighting factor that is applied to averaging these values depends on the number of "modified" (replaced) features in the individual synthetic vector. For rows where more of the features are swapped out, a higher weight of importance is placed on these as compared to those with fewer mutations.

The final stage shown in figure 15.13 is in the overall per-feature contribution assessment. These feature-importance estimations are done by weighting each row's feature contribution margin and scaling the results to a percentage contribution for the entire dataset. Both calculated data artifacts are available by using the Python shap package (a per-row contribution estimation and an aggregated measurement across the entire dataset) and can help in explaining not only a single row's prediction but also in providing a holistic view of the feature influence to a trained model.

WHAT WE CAN DO WITH THESE VALUES

Simply calculating Shapley values doesn't do much for a DS team. The utility of having an XAI solution based on this package is in what questions these analyses enable answering. Some of the questions that you'll be able to answer after calculating these values are as follows:

- "Why did the model predict this strange result?" (single-event explanation)
- "Will these additional features generate different performance?" (feature-engineering validation)
- "How do ranges of our features affect the model predictions?" (general model functionality explanation)

The shap package can be used not only as an aid to solution development and maintenance, but also to help to provide data-based explanations to business unit members and SMEs. By shifting a discussion on the functionality of a solution away from the tools that the DS team generally uses (correlation analyses, dependence plots, analysis of variance, and so forth), a more productive discussion can be had. This package, and the approach therein, remove the burden from the ML team of having to explain esoteric techniques and tools, focusing instead on discussing the functionality of a solution in terms of the data that the company generates.

15.4.2 Using shap

To illustrate how we can use this technique for our problem of predicting forest fires, let's assume that we have a model already built.

> **NOTE** To follow along and see the model construction, tuning with the Optuna package (a more modern version of the previously mentioned Hyperopt from part 2), and the full implementation of this example, please see the companion GitHub repository for this book. The code is within the Chapter 15 directory.

With a preconstructed model available, let's leverage the shap package to determine the effects of features within our training data to assist in answering the questions that the business is asking about why the model is behaving a particular way. The following listing shows a series of classes that aids in generating the explanation plots (refer to the repository for import statements and the remainder of the code, which is too lengthy to print here).

Listing 15.1   `shap` interface

```
class ImageHandling:
    def __init__(self, fig, name):          ◄──┐  Image-handling class to handle
        self.fig = fig                           │  resizing of the plots and storing
        self.name = name                         │  of the different formats
    def _resize_plot(self):
        self.fig = plt.gcf()                ◄──┐  Gets a reference
        self.fig.set_size_inches(12, 12)       │  to the current plot
    def save_base(self):                       │  figure for resizing
        self.fig.savefig(f"{self.name}.png",
                         format='png', bbox_inches='tight')
        self.fig.savefig(f"{self.name}.svg",
                         format='svg', bbox_inches='tight')
    def save_plt(self):              Since this plot is generated      Unification of the
        self._resize_plot()            in JavaScript, we have to       required attributes
        self.save_base()                 save it as HTML.              coming from the shap
    def save_js(self):                                                 Explainer to enable
        shap.save_html(self.name, self.fig)   ◄──┐                     handling of all the
        return self.fig                           │                   plots' requirements
class ShapConstructor:                          ◄─┘
    def __init__(self, base_values, data, values, feature_names, shape):
        self.base_values = base_values
        self.data = data
        self.values = values
        self.feature_names = feature_names          Method called during class
        self.shape = shape                       instantiation to generate the shap
class ShapObject:                                 values based on the model passed
    def __init__(self, model, data):                in and the data provided for
        self.model = model                           evaluation of the model's
        self.data = data                                    functionality
        self.exp = self.generate_explainer(self.model, self.data)
        shap.initjs()
    @classmethod
    def generate_explainer(self, model, data):          ◄──────────┐
        Explain = namedtuple('Explain', 'shap_values explainer max_row')
        explainer = shap.Explainer(model)
        explainer.expected_value = explainer.expected_value[0]
        shap_values = explainer(data)
        max_row = len(shap_values.values)
        return Explain(shap_values, explainer, max_row)
    def build(self, row=0):
        return ShapConstructor(
base_values = self.exp.shap_values[0][0].base_values,
            values = self.exp.shap_values[row].values,
            feature_names = self.data.columns,
            data = self.exp.shap_values[0].data,
            shape = self.exp.shap_values[0].shape)
    def validate_row(self, row):
        assert (row < self.exp.max_row,
f"The row value: {row} is invalid. "              Generates a single row's
f"Data has only {self.exp.max_row} rows.")       waterfall plot to explain
    def plot_waterfall(self, row=0):        ◄──┤  the impact of each feature
        plt.clf()                                 to the row's target value
        self.validate_row(row)                    (composition analysis)
```

```
        fig = shap.waterfall_plot(self.build(row),
                                  show=False, max_display=15)
        ImageHandling(fig, f"summary_{row}").save_plt()
        return fig
    def plot_summary(self):
        fig = shap.plots.beeswarm(self.exp.shap_values,
                                  show=False, max_display=15)
        ImageHandling(fig, "summary").save_plt()
    def plot_force_by_row(self, row=0):
        plt.clf()
        self.validate_row(row)
        fig = shap.force_plot(self.exp.explainer.expected_value,
                              self.exp.shap_values.values[row,:],
                              self.data.iloc[row,:],
                              show=False,
                              matplotlib=True
                              )
        ImageHandling(fig, f"force_plot_{row}").save_base()
    def plot_full_force(self):
        fig = shap.plots.force(self.exp.explainer.expected_value,
                               self.exp.shap_values.values,
                               show=False
                               )
        final_fig = ImageHandling(fig, "full_force_plot.htm").save_js()
        return final_fig
    def plot_shap_importances(self):
        fig = shap.plots.bar(self.exp.shap_values,
                             show=False, max_display=15)
        ImageHandling(fig, "shap_importances").save_plt()
    def plot_scatter(self, feature):
        fig = shap.plots.scatter(self.exp.shap_values[:, feature],
                                 color=self.exp.shap_values, show=False)
        ImageHandling(fig, f"scatter_{feature}").save_plt()
```

Generates the full shap summary of each feature across the entire passed-in dataset

Generates a single row's force plot to illustrate the cumulative effect of each feature on its target value

Generates the entire dataset's combined force plots into a single displayed visualization

Creates the debugging plot for the estimated shap importance of each feature

Generates a scatter plot of a single feature against its shap values, colored by the feature in the remaining positions of the vector with the highest covariance

With our class defined, we can begin to answer the questions from the business about why the model has been predicting the values that it has. We can step away from the realm of conjecture that would be the best-effort attempt at explanation through the use of presenting correlation effects. Instead of wasting our time (and the business's) with extremely time-consuming and likely confusing presentations of what our EDA showed at the outset of the project, we can focus on answering their questions.

As an added bonus, having this game-theory-based approach available to us during development could help inform which features could be improved upon and which could potentially be dropped. The information that can be gained from this algorithm is invaluable throughout the model's entire life cycle.

Before we look at what these methods in listing 15.1 would be producing when executed, let's review what the business executives want to know. In order to be satisfied that the predictions coming from the model are logical, they want to know the following:

- What are the conditions that should cause us to panic if we see them?
- Why doesn't the amount of rain seem to affect the risk?

To answer these two questions, let's take a look at two of the plots that can be generated from within the shap package. Based on these plots, we should be able to see where the problematic predictions are coming from.

SHAP SUMMARY PLOT

To answer the question about the rain—as well as to provide an opportunity to understand which features are driving the predictions the most—the summary plot is the most comprehensive and utilitarian for this purpose. Because it combines all of the rows of the training data, it will do a per-row estimation of each feature's impact when run through the replacement strategy that the algorithm performs. This holistic view of the entire training dataset can show the features' overall magnitude of impact within the scope of the problem. Figure 15.14 shows the summary plot.

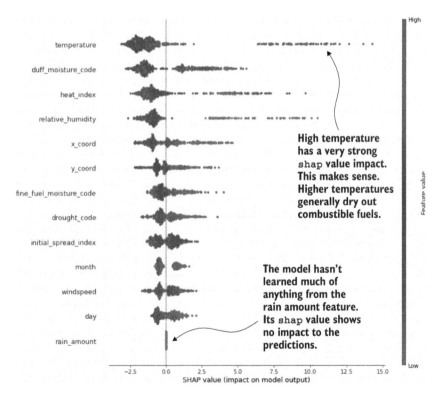

Figure 15.14 The shap summary plot, showing each feature's substitution and prediction delta for each row

Armed with this plot, a great deal of discussion can be had with the business. Not only can you jointly explore why the rain amount values clearly aren't making a difference in the model's output (the plot shows that the feature isn't even considered in the random forest model), but also how other aspects of the data are interpreted by the model.

> **NOTE** Make sure that you are very clear with the business on what shap is. It doesn't bear a relationship to reality; rather, it simply indicates how the model interprets changes to a feature within a vector on its predictions. It is a measure of the *model* and not on the reality of what you're trying to model.

The summary plot can begin the discussions about why the model is performing the way it is, what improvements might be made after identifying shortcomings identified by SMEs, and how to talk with the business about the model in terms that everyone can understand. Once the initial confusion is explained away regarding this tool, with the business fully understanding that the values shown are simply an estimation of how the model understands the features (and that they are not a reflection of the reality of the problem space you are predicting within), the conversations can become more fruitful.

It is, to be clear, *absolutely essential* to explain exactly what these values are before showing a single one of the visualizations that the tool is capable of generating. We're not explaining the world; we're explaining the model's limited understanding of correlation effects based on the data we actually collect. There is simply nothing more or less to it.

With the general discussion complete with the business and the issue of rainfall tackled, we can move on to answering the next question.

WATERFALL PLOTS

We can answer the second question, arguably the most important for the business to be worried about, with a series of visualizations. When the business leaders asked when they should panic, what they really meant was that they wanted to know when the model would predict an emergency. They want to know which attributes of the features they should be looking at in order to warn their people on the ground that something bad might happen.

This is an admirable use of ML and something that I've seen many times in my career. Once a company's business units move past the trough of distrust and into the realm of relying on predictions, the inevitable result is that the business wants to understand which aspects of their problem can be monitored and controlled in order to help minimize disaster or maximize beneficial results.

To enable this discovery, we can look at our prior data, select the worst-case scenario (or scenarios) from history, and plot the impact of each feature's contribution to the predicted result. This contribution analysis for the most severe fire in history for this dataset is shown in figure 15.15.

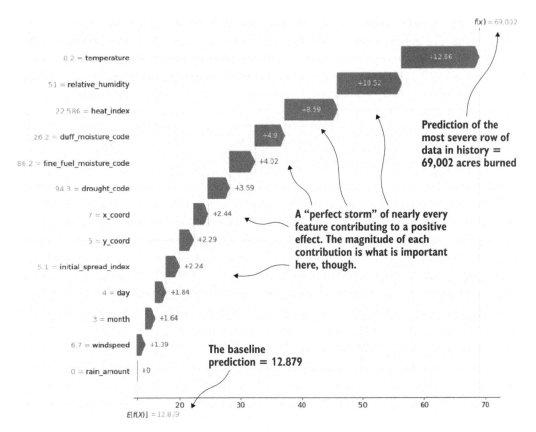

Figure 15.15 Waterfall plot of the most severe wildfire in history. The contribution margin of each feature can inform the business of what the model correlated to for high risk for fire.

While this plot is but a single data point, we can arrive at a more complete picture by analyzing the top *n* historical rows of data for the target. The next listing illustrates how simple this can be to generate with interfaces built around shap.

Listing 15.2   Generating feature-contribution plots for the most extreme events in history

Instantiates the shap package's handler to generate the
shap values by passing in a trained model and the training
data used to train it

```
shap_obj = ShapObject(final_rf_model.model, final_rf_model.X)
interesting_rows = fire_data.nlargest(5,
    'area').reset_index()['index'].values
waterfalls = [shap_obj.plot_waterfall(x) for x in interesting_rows]
```

Extracts the five most severe area
burn events in the training data to
retrieve their row index values

Generates the waterfall plots (as
in figure 15.15) for each of the
five most severe events

Armed with these top event plots and the contributions of each feature to these events, the business can now identify patterns of behavior that they will want to explain to their analysts and observers in the field. With this knowledge, people can prepare and proactively take action long before a model's prediction would ever make it to them.

Using shap to help educate a team to take a beneficial series of actions based on a model's inference of data is one of the most powerful aspects of this tool. It can help leverage the model in a way that is otherwise difficult to utilize. It helps to bring a much more far-reaching benefit to a business (or society and the natural world in general) from a model than a prediction on its own could ever do.

> **A personal note on XAI**
>
> Having explanations of how supervised (and unsupervised!) models arrive at their conclusions based on input features has helped me to craft more comprehensive solutions to problems. More than that, however, XAI enables me to conduct one of the most important tasks that a DS will ever engage in: winning the trust of the business.
>
> The building of trust and intrinsic faith in the ability of data to explain to and empower a business allows an organization to move more fully toward an objective and truly data-driven decision-making process. When evidence-based logic is used to guide a business, efficiency, revenue, and general employee well-being is increased. That, above all else, is reason to enable your business counterparts to take part in understanding the algorithms that you're employing to help them along their journey.

Many more plots and features are associated with this package, most of which are covered thoroughly in the companion notebook to this chapter within the repository. I encourage you to read through it and consider employing this methodology in your projects.

Summary

- Consistency in feature and inference data can be accomplished by using a rules-based validation feature store. Having a single source of truth can dramatically reduce confusion in interpretation of results, as well as enforcing quality-control checks on any data that is sent to a model.
- Establishing fallback conditions for prediction failures due to a lack of data or a corrupted set of data for inference can ensure that consumers of the solution's output will not see errors or service interruptions.
- Utilizing prediction-quality metrics is not enough to determine the efficacy of a solution. Validation of the prediction results by SMEs, test users, and cross-functional team members can provide subjective quality measurements to any ML solution.

- Utilizing techniques such as `shap` can help to explain in a simple manner why a model made a particular decision and what influence particular feature values are having on the predictions from a model. These tools are critically important for production health of a solution, particularly during periodic retraining.

Production infrastructure

This chapter covers

- Implementing passive retraining with the use of a model registry
- Utilizing a feature store for model training and inference
- Selecting an appropriate serving architecture for ML solutions

Utilizing ML in a real-world use case to solve a complex problem is challenging. The sheer number of skills needed to take a company's data (frequently messy, partially complete, and rife with quality issues), select an appropriate algorithm, tune a pipeline, and validate that the prediction output of a model (or an ensemble of models) solves the problem to the satisfaction of the business is daunting. The complexity of an ML-backed project does not end with the creation of an acceptably performing model, though. The architectural considerations and implementation details can add significant challenges to a project if they aren't made correctly.

Every day there seems to be a new open sourced tech stack that promises an easier deployment strategy or a magical automated solution that meets the needs of all. With this constant deluge of tools and platforms, making a decision on where to go to meet the needs of a particular project can be intimidating.

A cursory glance at the offerings available may seem to indicate that the most logical plan is to stick to a single paradigm for everything (for example, deploy every model as a REST API service). Keeping every ML project aligned in a common architecture and implementation certainly simplifies the release deployment. However, nothing could be further from the truth. Just as when selecting algorithms, there's no "one size fits all" for production infrastructure.

The goal of this chapter is to introduce common generic themes and solutions that can be applied to model prediction architecture. After covering the basic tooling that obfuscates the complexity and minutiae of production ML services, we will delve into generic architectures that can be employed to meet the needs of different projects.

The goal in any serving architecture is to build the minimally featured, least complex, and cheapest solution that still meets the needs of consuming the model's output. With consistency and efficiency in serving (SLA and prediction-volume considerations) as the primary focus for production work, there are several key concepts and methodologies to be aware of to make this last-mile aspect of ML project work as painless as possible.

16.1 Artifact management

Let's imagine that we're still working at the fire-risk department of the forest service introduced in chapter 15. In our efforts to effectively dispatch personnel and equipment to high-risk areas in the park system, we've arrived at a solution that works remarkably well. Our features are locked in and are stable over time. We've evaluated the performance of the predictions and are seeing genuine value from the model.

Throughout this process of getting the features into a good state, we've been iterating through the improvement cycle, shown in figure 16.1.

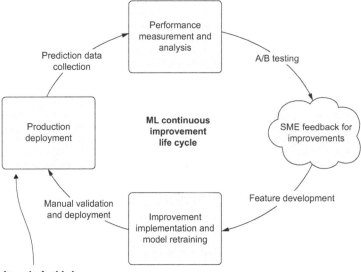

At cycle 1, this is easy.
At cycle 37, which code, training what model, is running in production right now?

Figure 16.1 Improvements to a deployed model on the road to production steady-state operation

As this cycle shows, we've been iteratively releasing new versions of the model, testing against a baseline deployment, collecting feedback, and working to improve the predictions. At some point, however, we'll be going into model-sustaining mode.

We've worked as hard as we can to improve the features going into the model and have found that the return on investment (ROI) of continuing to add new data elements to the project is simply not worth it. We're now in the position of scheduled passive retraining of our model based on new data coming in over time.

When we're at this steady-state point, the last thing that we want to do is to have one of the DS team members spend an afternoon manually retraining a model, manually comparing its results to the current production-deployed model with ad hoc analysis, and deciding on whether the model should be updated.

Oh, come on. No one does this manually.

From my own history as a DS, I didn't start using passive retraining for the first six years of solving problems. It wasn't due to a lack of need, nor a lack of tooling. It was pure and simple ignorance. I had no idea how big of a problem drift could be (I learned that the hard way several times over by having a solution devolve into irrelevance because of my neglect). Nor did I understand or appreciate the importance of attribution calculations.

Over years of repeatedly screwing up my solutions, I found techniques that others had written about through researching solutions to my self-imposed woes of inadequately engineered projects. I came to embrace the ideas that led me to DS work to begin with: automating annoying and repetitive tasks. By removing the manual activity of monitoring the health of my projects (via ad hoc drift tracking), I found that I had solved two primary problems that were plaguing me.

First, I freed up my time. Doing ad hoc analyses on prediction results and feature stability takes a lot of time. In addition, it's incredibly boring work.

The second big problem was in accuracy. Manually evaluating model performance is repetitive and error-prone. Missing details through a manual analysis can mean deploying a model version that is worse than the currently deployed one, introducing issues that are far more significant than a slightly poorer prediction performance.

I've learned my lesson about automating retraining (typically opting for passive retraining systems rather than the far more complex active ones if I can get away with it). As with everything else I've learned in my career, I've learned it by screwing it up. Hopefully, you can avoid the same fate.

The measurement, adjudication, and decision on whether to replace the model with a newly retrained one can be automated with a passive retraining system. Figure 16.2 shows this concept of a scheduled retraining event.

With this automation of scheduled retraining in place, the primary concern with this system is knowing what is running in production. For instance, what happens if a problem is uncovered in production after a new version is released? What can we do to recover from a concept drift that has dramatically affected a retraining event? How

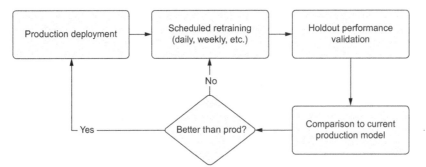

With an automated cadence to retraining, after some amount of time, a lot of versions of the model will be out in the wild.

Figure 16.2   Logical diagram of a passive retraining system

do we roll back the model to the previous version without having to rebuild it? We can allay these concerns by using a model registry.

16.1.1 MLflow's model registry

In this situation that we find ourselves in, with scheduled updates to a model happening autonomously, it is important for us to know the state of production deployment. Not only do we need to know the current state, but if questions arise about performance of a passive retraining system in the past, we need to have a means of investigating the historical provenance of the model. Figure 16.3 compares using and not using a registry for tracking provenance in order to explain a historical issue.

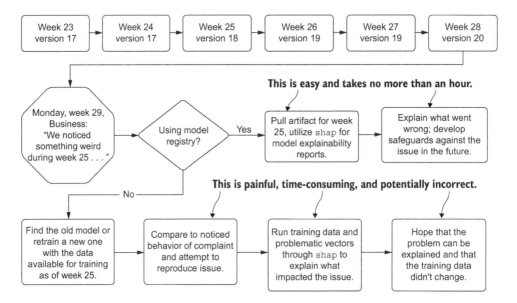

Figure 16.3   Passive retraining schedule with a historic issue found far in the future

As you can see, the process for attempting to re-create a past run is fraught with peril; we have a high risk of being unable to reproduce the issue that the business found in historical predictions. With no registry to record the artifacts utilized in production, manual work must be done to re-create the model's original conditions. This can be incredible challenging (if not impossible) in most companies because changes may have occurred to the underlying data used to train the model, rendering it impossible to re-create that state.

The preferred approach, as shown in figure 16.3, is to utilize a model registry service. MLflow, for instance, offers exactly this functionality within its APIs, allowing us to log details of each retraining run to the tracking server, handle production promotion if the scheduled retraining job performs better on holdout data, and archive the older model for future reference. If we had used this framework, the process of testing conditions of a model that had at one point run in production would be as simple as recalling the artifact from the registry entry, loading it into a notebook environment, and generating the explainable correlation reports with tools such as shap.

Is a registry really that important?

Well, in two words, "It depends."

I remember with a distinct spine-chilling horror one of my first major, real-deal, no-kidding, really serious ML implementations that I built. It wasn't by any means my first production release of a solution, but it was the first one that had serious attention being paid to it. It helped to run a rather significant part of the business, and as such, was closely scrutinized by a lot of people. Rightfully so, if I may add.

My deployment (if it could be called that) involved a passive-like retraining system that stored the last-known-good hyperparameters of the previous day's tuning run, using those values as a starting point to begin automated tuning. After optimizing to all of the new feature-training data available, it chose the best-performing model, ran a prediction on the new data, and overwrote a serving table with the predictions.

It wasn't until a full three months into the project's production run that the first serious question came up regarding why the model was predicting in an unexpected way with certain customers. The business leaders couldn't figure out why it was doing that, so they approached me and asked me to investigate.

Having no record of the model (it wasn't even saved anywhere) and realizing that the training data was changing consistently over time as the features updated made it completely impossible for me to explain the model's historical performance.

The business was less than pleased with this answer. Although the model didn't get shut off (it probably should have), it made me realize the importance of storing and cataloguing models for the precise purpose of being able to explain why the solution behaves the way it does, even if that explanation is months past the point at which it was being used.

16.1.2 *Interfacing with the model registry*

To get a feel for how this code would look to support an integration with the model registry service of MLflow, let's adapt our use case to support this passive retraining functionality. To start, we need to create an adjudication system that checks the current production model's performance against the scheduled retraining results. After building that comparison, we can interface with the registry service to replace the current production model with the newer model (if it's better), or stay with the current production model based on its performance against the same holdout data that the new model was tested against.

  Let's look at an example of how to interface with the MLflow model registry to support automated passive retraining that retains provenance of the model's state over time. Listing 16.1 establishes the first portion of what we need to build to have a historical status table of each scheduled retraining event.

> **NOTE**   To see all of the import statements and the full example that integrates with these snippets, see the companion notebook to this chapter in the GitHub repository for this book at https://github.com/BenWilson2/ML-Engineering.

Listing 16.1   Registry state row generation and logging

```
@dataclass
class Registry:                      ◁────┐  A data class to wrap
  model_name: str                          │  the data we're going
  production_version: int                  │  to be logging
  updated: bool
  training_time: str
class RegistryStructure:             ◁────┐  Class for converting the registration
  def __init__(self, data):                │  data to a Spark DataFrame to write a
    self.data = data                       │  row to a delta table for provenance
  def generate_row(self):
    spark_df = spark.createDataFrame(pd.DataFrame(
      [vars(self.data)]))            ◁────┐  Accesses the members of
    return (spark_df.withColumn("training_time",  │  the data class in a shorthand
F.to_timestamp(F.col("training_time")))           │  fashion to cast to a pandas
          .withColumn("production_version",        │  DataFrame and then a Spark
F.col("production_version").cast("long")))         │  DataFrame (leveraging
class RegistryLogging:                             │  implicit type inferences)
  def __init__(self,
              database,
              table,
              delta_location,
              model_name,
              production_version,
              updated):
    self.database = database
    self.table = table
    self.delta_location = delta_location
    self.entry_data = Registry(model_name,
                      production_version,     ┐  Builds the Spark
                      updated,                 │  DataFrame row at
                      self._get_time())  ◁────┘  class initialization
```

```
@classmethod
def _get_time(self):
    return datetime.today().strftime('%Y-%m-%d %H:%M:%S')
def _check_exists(self):
    return spark._jsparkSession.catalog().tableExists(
        self.database, self.table)
def write_entry(self):
    log_row = RegistryStructure(self.entry_data).generate_row()
    log_row.write.format("delta").mode("append").save(self.delta_location)
    if not self._check_exists():
        spark.sql(f"""CREATE TABLE IF NOT EXISTS
            {self.database}.{self.table}
            USING DELTA LOCATION
            '{self.delta_location}';""")
```

Method for determining if the delta table has been created yet

Writes the log data to Delta in append mode and creates the table reference in the Hive Metastore if it doesn't already exist

This code helps set the stage for the provenance of the model-training history. Since we're looking to automate the retraining on a schedule, it's far easier to have a tracking table that refers to the history of changes in a centralized location. If we have multiple builds of this model, as well as other projects that are registered, we can have a single snapshot view of the state of production passive retraining without needing to do anything more than write a simple query.

Listing 16.2 illustrates what a query of this table would look like. With multiple models logged to a transaction history table like this, adding df.filter(F.col("model_name" == "<project title>")) allows for rapid access to the historical log for a single model.

Listing 16.2 Querying the registry state table

```
from pyspark.sql import functions as F
REGISTRY_TABLE = "mleng_demo.registry_status"
display(spark.table(REGISTRY_TABLE).orderBy(F.col("training_time")))
```

Since we've registered the table in our row-input stage earlier, we can refer to it directly by <database>.<table_name> reference. We can then order the commits chronologically.

Executing this code results in figure 16.4. In addition to this log, the model registry within MLflow also has a GUI. Figure 16.5 shows a screen capture of the GUI that matches to the registry table from listing 16.2.

Now that we've set up the historical tracking functionality, we can write the interface to MLflow's registry server to support passive retraining. Listing 16.3 shows the implementation for leveraging the tracking server's entries, the registry service for querying current production metadata, and an automated state transition of the retrained model for supplanting the current production model if it performs better.

▸ (1) Spark Jobs

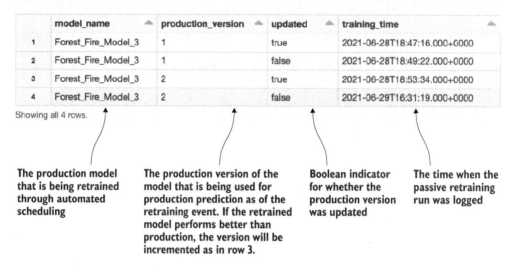

	model_name	production_version	updated	training_time
1	Forest_Fire_Model_3	1	true	2021-06-28T18:47:16.000+0000
2	Forest_Fire_Model_3	1	false	2021-06-28T18:49:22.000+0000
3	Forest_Fire_Model_3	2	true	2021-06-28T18:53:34.000+0000
4	Forest_Fire_Model_3	2	false	2021-06-29T16:31:19.000+0000

Showing all 4 rows.

The production model that is being retrained through automated scheduling

The production version of the model that is being used for production prediction as of the retraining event. If the retrained model performs better than production, the version will be incremented as in row 3.

Boolean indicator for whether the production version was updated

The time when the passive retraining run was logged

Figure 16.4   Querying the registry state transaction table

Forest_Fire_Model_3 ▾   Notify me about ⓘ   All new activity ▾

Registered Models > Forest_Fire_Model_3   **The project's name**

Details   Serving

Created Time : 2021-06-28 14:47:09   Last Modified : 2021-06-29 12:38:01   Creator : benjamin.wilson@databricks.com

▾ Description   Edit

Forest Fire Prediction for the National Park

▸ Tags

Each version's registration history   **Current production model's indication**

▾ Versions   All   Active 1   Compare

		Version	Registered at ▾	Created by	Stage	Pending Requests	Description
☐	⊘ 🔔	Version 3	2021-06-29 12:37:54	benjamin.wilson@databricks.com	Production	–	initial run
☐	⊘ 🔔	Version 2	2021-06-28 14:53:27	benjamin.wilson@databricks.com	Archived	–	initial run
☐	⊘ 🔔	Version 1	2021-06-28 14:47:10	benjamin.wilson@databricks.com	Archived	–	initial run

Figure 16.5   The MLflow model registry GUI for our experiments

Listing 16.3   Passive retraining model registration logic

```
class ModelRegistration:
    def __init__(self, experiment_name, experiment_title, model_name, metric,
                 direction):
        self.experiment_name = experiment_name
        self.experiment_title = experiment_title
        self.model_name = model_name
        self.metric = metric
        self.direction = direction
        self.client = MlflowClient()
        self.experiment_id =
          mlflow.get_experiment_by_name(experiment_name).experiment_id
    def _get_best_run_info(self, key):
        run_data = mlflow.search_runs(
          self.experiment_id,
          order_by=[f"metrics.{self.metric} {self.direction}"])
        return run_data.head(1)[key].values[0]
    def _get_registered_status(self):
        return self.client.get_registered_model(name=self.experiment_title)
    def _get_current_prod(self):
        return ([x.run_id for x in self._get_registered_status().latest_versions
          if x.current_stage == "Production"][0])
    def _get_prod_version(self):
        return int([x.version for x in
          self._get_registered_status().latest_versions
                  if x.current_stage == "Production"][0])
    def _get_metric(self, run_id):
        return mlflow.get_run(run_id).data.metrics.get(self.metric)
    def _find_best(self):
        try:
            current_prod_id = self._get_current_prod()
            prod_metric = self._get_metric(current_prod_id)
        except mlflow.exceptions.RestException:
            current_prod_id = -1
            prod_metric = 1e7
        best_id = self._get_best_run_info('run_id')
        best_metric = self._get_metric(best_id)
        if self.direction == "ASC":
            if prod_metric < best_metric:
                return current_prod_id
            else:
                return best_id
        else:
            if prod_metric > best_metric:
                return current_prod_id
            else:
                return best_id
    def _generate_artifact_path(self, run_id):
        return f"runs:/{run_id}/{self.model_name}"
    def register_best(self, registration_message, logging_location, log_db,
                      log_table):
        best_id = self._find_best()
```

Extracts all the previous run data for the history of the production deployment and returns the run ID that has the best performance against the validation data

Query for the model currently registered as "production deployed" in the registry

Method for determining if the current scheduled passive retraining run is performing better than production on its holdout data. It will return the run_id of the best logged run.

Utilizes the MLflow Model Registry API to register the new model if it is better, and de-registers the current production model if it's being replaced

```
try:
  current_prod = self._get_current_prod()
  current_prod_version = self._get_prod_version()
except mlflow.exceptions.RestException:
  current_prod = -1
  current_prod_version = -1
updated = current_prod != best_id
if updated:
  register_new = mlflow.register_model(self._generate_artifact_path(best_id),
                          self.experiment_title)
  self.client.update_registered_model(name=register_new.name,
                          description="Forest Fire
                          Prediction for the National Park")
  self.client.update_model_version(name=register_new.name,
                          version=register_new.version,
                          description=registration_message)
  self.client.transition_model_version_stage(name=register_new.name,
                                version=register_new.version,
                                stage="Production")

  if current_prod_version > 0:
    self.client.transition_model_version_stage(
      name=register_new.name,
      version=current_prod_version,
      stage="Archived")
  RegistryLogging(log_db,
        log_table,
        logging_location,
        self.experiment_title,
        int(register_new.version),
        updated).write_entry()
  return "upgraded prod"
else:
  RegistryLogging(log_db,
        log_table,
        logging_location,
        self.experiment_title,
        int(current_prod_version),
        updated).write_entry()
  return "no change"
def get_model_as_udf(self):
  prod_id = self._get_current_prod()
  artifact_uri = self._generate_artifact_path(prod_id)
  return mlflow.pyfunc.spark_udf(spark, model_uri=artifact_uri)
```

Acquires the current production model for batch inference on a Spark DataFrame using a Python UDF

This code allows us to fully manage the passive retraining of this model implementation (see the companion GitHub repository for this book for the full code). By leveraging the MLflow Model Registry API, we can meet the needs of production-scheduled predictions through having a one-line access to the model artifact.

This greatly simplifies the prediction batch–scheduled job, but also meets the needs of the investigation we began discussing in this section. Having the ability to retrieve the model with such ease, we can manually test the feature data against that model, run simulations with the use of tools like shap, and rapidly answer business questions without having to struggle with re-creating a potentially impossible state.

In the same vein of using a model registry to keep track of the model artifacts, the features being used to train models and predict with the use of models can be catalogued for efficiency's sake as well. This concept is realized through feature stores.

That's cool and all, but what about active retraining?

The primary difference between passive retraining and active retraining lies in the mechanism of initiating retraining.

Passive, scheduled by CRON, is a "best hope" strategy that attempts to find an improved model fit by incorporating new training data in the effort to counteract drift. Active, on the other hand, monitors the state of predictions and features to determine algorithmically when it makes sense to trigger a retraining.

Because it is designed to respond to unpredictable performance degradation, an active system can be beneficial if drift is happening at unpredictable rates—for instance, a model has been performing well for weeks, falls apart in the span of a few days, gets retrained, and performs well for only a few days before needing retraining. To create this responsive feedback loop to trigger a retraining event, prediction quality needs to be monitored. A system needs to be built to generate a retraining signal; this system ingests the predictions, merges the highly variable nature of ground-truth results that arrive at a later point (in some cases, seconds, at other times, weeks later), and effectively sets statistically significant thresholds on aggregated result states over time.

These systems are highly dependent on the nature of the problem being solved by the ML, and as such, vary in their design and implementation so much that even a generic example architecture is irrelevant for presentation here.

For instance, if you're trying to determine the success of a model's ability to predict the weather in the next hour in a certain location, you can get feedback within an hour. You could build a system that merges the hour-lagged real weather against the predictions, feeding the actual model accuracy into a windowed aggregation of accuracy rate over the last 48 hours. Should the aggregated rate of success in weather forecasting drop below a defined threshold of 70%, a retraining of the model can be initiated autonomously. This newly trained model can be compared against the current production model by validating both models through a standard (new) holdout validation dataset. The new model can then be used either immediately through a blue/green deployment strategy or gradually by having traffic dynamically allocated to it with a multi-bandit algorithm that routes traffic based on relative performance improvement compared to the current production model.

Active retraining is complex, in a nutshell. I recommend that people investigate it only after finding that passive retraining simply isn't cutting it anymore, rather than just because it seems like it's important. There are far more moving parts, services, and infrastructure to handle when autonomously handling retraining. The cloud services bill that you get when using active retraining will reflect the increase in complexity as well (it's expensive).

16.2   *Feature stores*

We briefly touched on using a feature store in the preceding chapter. While it is important to understand the justification for and benefits of implementing a feature store (namely, that of consistency, reusability, and testability), seeing an application of a relatively nascent technology is more relevant than discussing the theory. Here, we're going to look at a scenario that I struggled through, involving the importance of utilizing a feature store to enforce consistency throughout an organization leveraging both ML and advanced analytics.

Let's imagine that we work at a company that has multiple DS teams. Within the engineering group, the main DS team focuses on company-wide initiatives. This team works mostly on large-scale projects involving critical services that can be employed by any group within the company, as well as customer-facing services. Spread among departments are a smattering of independent contributor DS employees who have been hired by and report to their respective department heads. While collaboration occurs, the main datasets used by the core DS team are not open for the independent DS employees' use.

At the start of a new year, a department head hires a new DS straight out of a university program. Well-intentioned, driven, and passionate, this new hire immediately gets to work on the initiatives that this department head wants investigated. In the process of analyzing the characteristics of the customers of the company, the new hire come across a production table that contains probabilities for customers to make a call-center complaint. Curious, the new DS begins analyzing the predictions against the data that is in the data warehouse for their department.

Unable to reconcile any feature data to the predictions, the DS begins working on a new model prototype to try to improve upon the complaint prediction solution. After spending a few weeks, the DS presents their findings to their department head. Given the go-ahead to work on this project, the DS proceeds to build a project in their analytics department workspace. After several months, the DS presents their findings at a company all-hands meeting.

Confused, the core DS team asks why this project is being worked on and for further details on the implementation. In less than an hour, the core DS team is able to explain why the independent DS's solution worked so well: they leaked the label. Figure 16.6 illustrates the core DS team's explanation: the data required to build any new model or perform extensive analysis of the data collected from users is walled off by the silo surrounding the core DS team's engineering department.

The data being used for training that was present in the department's data warehouse was being fed from the core DS team's production solution. Each source feature used to train the core model was inaccessible to anyone apart from engineering and production processes.

While this scenario is extreme, it did, in fact, happen. The core team could have helped to avoid this by providing an accessible source for the generated feature data, opening the access to allow other teams to utilize these highly curated data points for

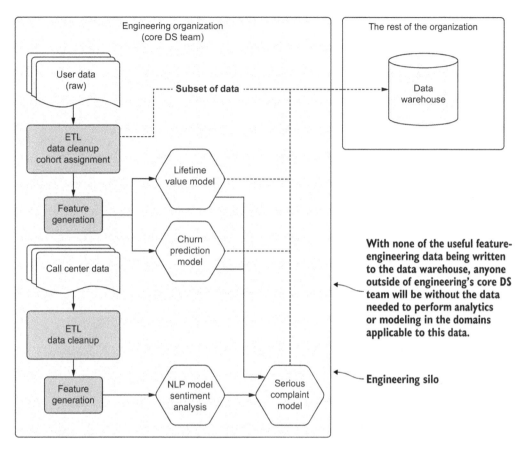

Figure 16.6 The engineering silo that keeps raw data and calculated features away from the rest of the organization

additional projects. By registering their data with appropriate labels and documentation, they could have saved this poor DS a lot of effort.

16.2.1 What a feature store is used for

Solving the data silo issue in our scenario is among the most compelling reasons to use a feature store. When dealing with a distributed DS capability throughout an organization, the benefits of standardization and accessibility are seen through a reduction in redundant work, incongruous analyses, and general confusion surrounding the veracity of solutions.

However, having a feature store enables an organization to do far more with its data than just quality-control it. To illustrate these benefits, figure 16.7 shows a high-level code architecture for model building and serving with and without a feature store.

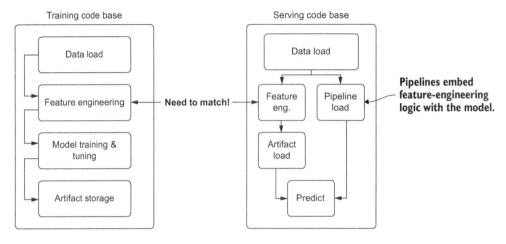

Traditional ML process for feature augmentation/engineering

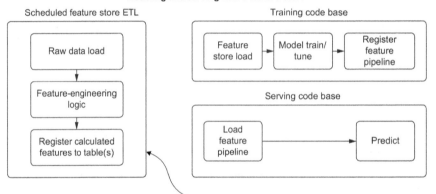

Modeling and serving with a feature store

These features are defined only once and can be used for any project or analytics use case.

Figure 16.7   Comparison of using a feature store versus not using one for ML development

The top portion of figure 16.7 shows the historical reality of ML development for projects. Tightly coupled feature-engineering code is developed inline to the model tuning and training code to generate models that are more effective than they would be if trained on the raw data. While this architecture makes sense from a development perspective of generating a good model, it creates an issue when developing the prediction code base (as shown at the top right of figure 16.7).

Any operations that are done to the raw data now need to be ported over to this serving code, presenting an opportunity for errors and inconsistencies in the model vector. Alternatives to this approach can help eliminate the chances of data inconsistency, however:

- Use a pipeline (most major ML frameworks have them).
- Abstract feature-engineering code into a package that training and serving can both call.
- Write traditional ETL to generate features and store them.

Each of these approaches has its own downsides, though. Pipelines are great and should be used, but they entangle useful feature-engineering logic with a particular model's implementation, isolating it from being utilized elsewhere. There's simply no easy way to reuse the features for other projects (not to mention it's nearly impossible for an analyst to decouple the feature-engineering stages from an ML pipeline without help).

Abstracting feature-engineering code certainly helps with code reusability and solves the consistency problem for the projects requiring the use of those features. But access to these features outside the DS team is still walled off. The other downside is that it's another code base that needs to be maintained, tested, and frequently updated.

Let's look at an example of interacting with a feature store, using the Databricks implementation to see the benefits in action.

NOTE Implementations of features of this nature that are built by a company are subject to change. APIs, feature details, and associated functionality may change, sometimes quite significantly, over time. This example of one such implementation of a feature store is presented for demonstration purposes.

16.2.2 Using a feature store

The first step in utilizing a feature store is to define a DataFrame representation of the processing involved in creating the features we'd like to use for modeling and analytics. The following listing shows a list of functions that are acting on a raw dataset to generate new features.

> **Listing 16.4 Feature-engineering logic**

```
from dataclasses import dataclass
from typing import List
from pyspark.sql.types import *
from pyspark.sql import functions as F
from pyspark.sql.functions import when
@dataclass
class SchemaTypes:
  string_cols: List[str]
  non_string_cols: List[str]
def get_col_types(df):
  schema = df.schema
  strings = [x.name for x in schema if x.dataType == StringType()]
  non_strings = [x for x in schema.names if x not in strings]
  return SchemaTypes(strings, non_strings)
def clean_messy_strings(df):        ◁──┐  General cleanup to strip out leading
  cols = get_col_types(df)            │  whitespaces from the dataset's string columns
```

```
     return df.select(*cols.non_string_cols, *[F.regexp_replace(F.col(x), " ",
       "").alias(x) for x in cols.string_cols])
def fill_missing(df):                          ◄─┐  Converts placeholder
  cols = get_col_types(df)                         │  unknown values to a
  return df.select(                                │  more useful string
*cols.non_string_cols, *[when(F.col(x) == "?",
"Unknown").otherwise(F.col(x)).alias(x) for x in cols.string_cols])
def convert_label(df, label, true_condition_string):     ◄─┐  Converts the target
  return df.withColumn(label, when(F.col(label) ==            │  from a string to a
true_condition_string,1).otherwise(0))                       │  Boolean binary value
def generate_features(df, id_augment):        ◄──────┐
  overtime = df.withColumn("overtime",                │
when(F.col("hours_worked_per_week") > 40, 1).otherwise(0))  │  Creates new encoded
  net_pos = overtime.withColumn("gains",                       features for the model
when(F.col("capital_gain") > F.col("capital_loss"), 1).otherwise(0))
  high_edu = net_pos.withColumn("highly_educated",
when(F.col("education_years") >= 16, 2)
.when(F.col("education_years") > 12, 1).otherwise(0))
  gender = high_edu.withColumn("gender_key",
when(F.col("gender") == "Female", 1).otherwise(0))
  keys = gender.withColumn("id",
F.monotonically_increasing_id() + F.lit(id_augment))
  return keys
def data_augmentation(df,
                      label,
                      label_true_condition,     ┌  Executes all the
                      id_augment=0):    ◄──────┤  feature-engineering
  clean_strings = clean_messy_strings(df)        │  stages, returning a
  missing_filled = fill_missing(clean_strings)   │  Spark DataFrame
  corrected_label = convert_label(missing_filled,
                                  label,
                                  label_true_condition)
  additional_features = generate_features(corrected_label,
                                          id_augment)
  return additional_features
```

Once we execute this code, we're left with a `DataFrame` and the requisite embedded logic for creating those additional columns. With this, we can initialize the feature store client and register the table, as shown in the next listing.

Listing 16.5   Register the feature engineering to the feature store

The library that contains
the APIs to interface with   Initializes the feature
the feature store   store client to interact
                                    with the feature store APIs   The database and
                                                                       table name where
                                                                       this feature table
```
    ┌─► from databricks import feature_store                          will be registered
    │   fs = feature_store.FeatureStoreClient()   ◄───┘
    │   FEATURE_TABLE = "ds_database.salary_features"   ◄─────
    ├─► FEATURE_KEYS = ["id"]
A primary │ FEATURE_PARTITION = "gender"   ◄───┐  Sets a partition key to make
key to  │   fs.create_feature_table(             │  querying perform better if
affect  │     name=FEATURE_TABLE,                 │  operations utilize that key
joins   │     keys=["id"],
        │     features_df=data_augmentation(raw_data,
```

```
                                    "income",
                                    ">50K"),
          partition_columns=FEATURE_PARTITION,
          description="Adult Salary Data. Raw Features."
      )
```

Specifies the processing history for the DataFrame that will be used to define the feature store table (from listing 16.4)

Adds a description to let others know this table's content

After executing the registration of the feature table, we can ensure that it is populated with new data as it comes in through a lightweight scheduled ETL. The following listing shows how simple this is.

Listing 16.6 **Feature store ETL update**

```
new_data = spark.table("prod_db.salary_raw")
processed_new_data = data_augmentation(new_data,
                                       "income",
                                       ">50K",
                                       table_counts)
fs = feature_store.FeatureStoreClient()
fs.write_table(
    name=FEATURE_TABLE,
    df=processed_new_data,
    mode='merge'
)
```

Reads in new raw data that needs processing through the feature-generation logic

Processes the data through the feature logic

Writes the new feature data through the previously registered feature table in merge mode to append new rows

Now that we've registered the table, the real key to its utility is in registering a model using it as input. To start accessing the defined features within a feature table, we need to define lookup accessors to each of the fields. The next listing shows how to do this data acquisition on the fields that we want to utilize for our income prediction model.

Listing 16.7 **Feature acquisition for modeling**

```
from databricks.feature_store import FeatureLookup
def generate_lookup(table, feature, key):
    return FeatureLookup(
        table_name=table,
        feature_name=feature,
        lookup_key=key
    )
features = ["overtime", "gains", "highly_educated", "age",
            "education_years", "hours_worked_per_week",
            "gender_key"]
lookups = [generate_lookup(FEATURE_TABLE, x, "id")
           for x in features]
```

The API to interface with the feature store to obtain references for modeling purposes

The list of field names that our model will be using

The lookup objects for each of the features

Now that we've defined the lookup references, we can employ them in the training of a simple model, as shown in listing 16.8.

NOTE   This is an abbreviated snippet of the full code. Please see the companion code in the book's repository at https://github.com/BenWilson2/ML -Engineering for the full-length example.

Listing 16.8   Register a model integrated with feature store

```
import mlflow
from catboost import CatBoostClassifier, metrics as cb_metrics
from sklearn.model_selection import train_test_split
EXPERIMENT_TITLE = "Adult_Catboost"
MODEL_TYPE = "adult_catboost_classifier"
EXPERIMENT_NAME = f"/Users/me/Book/{EXPERIMENT_TITLE}"
mlflow.set_experiment(EXPERIMENT_NAME)
with mlflow.start_run():
  TEST_SIZE = 0.15
  training_df = spark.table(FEATURE_TABLE).select("id", "income")
  training_data = fs.create_training_set(
    df=training_df,
    feature_lookups=lookups,
    label="income",
    exclude_columns=['id', 'final_weight', 'capital_gain', 'capital_loss'])
  train_df = training_data.load_df().toPandas()
  X = train_df.drop(['income'], axis=1)
  y = train_df.income
  X_train, X_test, y_train, y_test = train_test_split(X, y, test_size=TEST_SIZE,
                                                random_state=42,
                                                stratify=y)
  model = CatBoostClassifier(iterations=10000, learning_rate=0.00001,
    custom_loss=[cb_metrics.AUC()]).fit(X_train, y_train,
      eval_set=(X_test, y_test), logging_level="Verbose")
  fs.log_model(model, MODEL_TYPE, flavor=mlflow.catboost,
    training_set=training_data, registered_model_name=MODEL_TYPE)
```

Specifies the fields that will be used for training the model by using the lookups defined in the preceding listing

Converts the Spark DataFrame to a pandas DataFrame to utilize catboost

Registers the model to the feature store API so the feature-engineering tasks will be merged to the model artifact

With this code, we have a data source defined as a linkage to a feature store table, a model utilizing those features for training, and a registration of the artifact dependency chain to the feature store's integration with MLflow.

The final aspect of a feature store's attractiveness from a consistency and utility perspective is in the serving of the model. Suppose we want to do a daily batch prediction using this model. If we were to use something other than the feature store approach, we'd have to either reproduce the feature-generation logic or call an external package, processing on the raw data, to get our features. Instead, we must write only a few lines of code to get an output of batch predictions.

Listing 16.9   Run batch predictions with feature store registered model

```
from mlflow.tracking.client import MlflowClient
client = MlflowClient()
experiment_id = mlflow.get_experiment_by_name(EXPERIMENT_NAME).experiment_id
```

Retrieves the experiment registered to MLflow through the feature store API

```
run_id = mlflow.search_runs(experiment_id,
    order_by=["start_time DESC"]
    ).head(1)["run_id"].values[0]
feature_store_predictions = fs.score_batch(
                    f"runs:/{run_id}/{MODEL_TYPE}",
                    spark.table(FEATURE_TABLE))
```

Gets the individual run ID that we're interested in from the experiment (here, the latest run)

Applies the model to the defined feature table without having to write ingestion logic and perform a batch prediction

While batch predictions such as this one comprise a large percentage of historical ML use cases, the API supports registering an external OLTP database or an in-memory database as a sink. With a published copy of the feature store populated to a service that can support low latency and elastic serving needs, all server-side (non-edge-deployed) modeling needs can be met with ease.

16.2.3 Evaluating a feature store

The elements to consider when choosing a feature store (or building one yourself) are as varied as the requirements within different companies for data storage paradigms. In consideration of both current and potential future growth needs of such a service, functionality for a given feature store should be evaluated carefully, while keeping these important needs in mind:

- Synchronization of the feature store to external data serving platforms to support real-time serving (OLTP or in-memory database)
- Accessibility to other teams for analytics, modeling, and BI use cases
- Ease of ingestion to the feature store through batch and streaming sources
- Security considerations for adhering to legal restrictions surrounding data (access controls)
- Ability to merge JIT data to feature store data (data generated by users) for predictions
- Data lineage and dependency tracking to see which projects are creating and consuming the data stored in the feature store

With effective research and evaluation, a feature store solution can greatly simplify the production serving architecture, eliminate consistency bugs between training and serving, and reduce the chances of others duplicating effort across an organization. They're incredibly useful frameworks, and I certainly see them being a part of all future ML efforts within industry.

OK, feature stores are cool and all, but do I really need one?

"We got along just fine without one for years."

I'm usually a bit of a Luddite when it comes to new hype in technology. With a highly skeptical eye, I tend to take a rather pessimistic view of anything new that comes along, particularly if it claims to solve a lot of challenging problems or just sounds too

(continued)

good to be true. Honestly, most announcements in the ML space do exactly that: they gloss over the fine details of why the problem they're purporting to solve was difficult for others to solve in the past. It's only when I start road-testing the "new, hot tech" that the cracks begin to appear.

I haven't had this experience with feature stores. Quite the contrary. I most certainly did take a skeptical view of them at first. But testing out the functionality and seeing the benefits of having centralized tracking of features, reusability of the results of complex feature-engineering logic, and the ability to decouple and monitor features from external scheduled jobs has made me a believer. Being able to monitor the health of features, not having to maintain separate logic of calculated features for additional projects, and being able to create features that can be leveraged for BI use cases is invaluable.

These systems are useful during the development of projects as well. With a feature store, you're not modifying production tables that are created through ETL. With the speed and dynamic nature of feature-engineering efforts, a lightweight ETL can be performed on these feature tables that does not require the large-scale change management associated with changes to production data in a data lake or data warehouse. With the data fully under the purview of the DS team (still held to production code-quality standards, of course!), the larger-scale changes to the rest of the organization are mitigated as compared to changes to DE jobs.

Do you absolutely need a feature store? No, you don't. But the benefits of having one to utilize for development, production deployment, and data reuse are of such a large magnitude that it simply doesn't make sense not to use one.

16.3 *Prediction serving architecture*

Let's pretend for a moment that our company is working toward getting its first model into production. For the past four months, the DS team has been working studiously at fine-tuning a price optimizer for hotel rooms. The end goal of this project is to generate a curated list of personalized deals that have more relevancy to individual users than the generic collections in place now.

For each user, the team's plan is to generate predictions each day for probable locations to visit (or locations the user has visited in the past), generating lists of deals to be shown during region searches. The team realizes early on a need to adapt prediction results to the browsing activity of the user's current session.

To solve this dynamic need, the team generates overly large precalculated lists for each member based on available deals in regions that were like those that they've traveled to in the past. Fallback and cold-start logic for this project simply use the existing global heuristics that were in place before the project. Figure 16.8 shows the planned general architecture that the team has in mind for serving the predictions.

Initially, after building this infrastructure, QA testing looks solid. The response SLA from the NoSQL-backed REST API is performing well, the batch prediction and

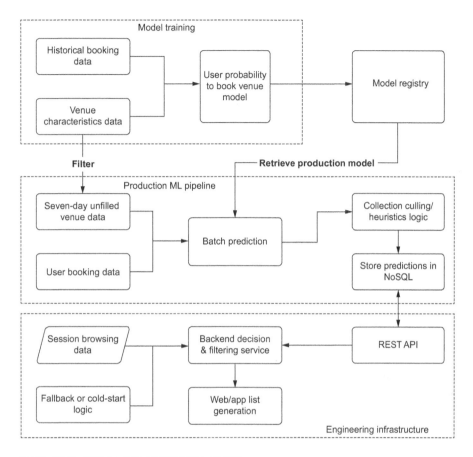

Figure 16.8 Initial serving architecture design

heuristics logic from the model's output is optimized for cost, and the fallback logic failover is working flawlessly. The team is ready to start testing the solution with an A/B test.

Unfortunately, the test group's booking rate is no different from the control group's rates. Upon analyzing the results, the team finds that fewer than 5% of sessions utilized the predictions, forcing the remaining 95% of page displays to show the fallback logic (which is the same data being shown to the control group). Whoops. To fix this poor performance, the DS team decides to focus on two areas:

- Increasing the number of predictions per user per geographic region
- Increasing the number of regions being predicted per user to cover

This solution dramatically affects their storage costs. What could they have done differently? Figure 16.9 shows a significantly different architecture that could have solved this problem without incurring such a massive cost in processing and storage.

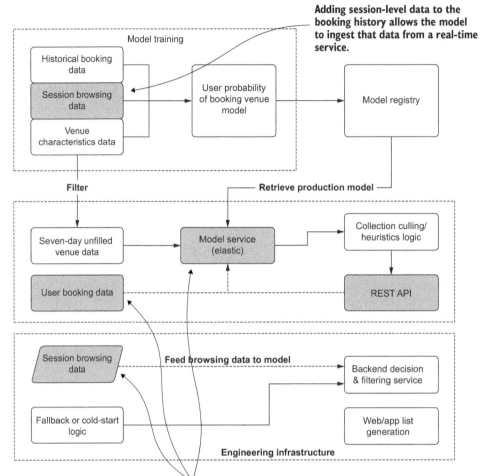

Figure 16.9   A more cost-effective architecture for this use case

While these changes are neither trivial nor, likely, welcome for either the DS team or the site-engineering team, they provide a clear picture about why serving predictions should never be an afterthought for a project. To effectively provide value, several considerations for serving architecture development should be evaluated at the outset of the project. The subsequent subsections cover these considerations and the sorts of architecture required to meet the scenarios.

16.3.1 Determining serving needs

The team in our performance scenario initially failed to design a serving architecture that fully supported the needs of the project. Performing this selection is not a trivial endeavor to get right. However, with a thorough evaluation of a few critical characteristics of a project, the appropriate serving paradigm can be employed to enable an ideal delivery method for predictions.

When evaluating the needs of a project, it's important to consider the following characteristics of the problem being solved to ensure that the serving design is neither overengineered nor under-engineered.

This sounds like a developer problem, not a "me problem"

It may seem like it's better to just have a software engineering group worry about how to utilize a model artifact. They, after all (in most cases), are better at software development than a DS group is, and have exposure to more infrastructure tools and implementation techniques than are applicable to the realm of ML.

In my experience, I've never had much success with "punting a model over the wall" to another team. Depending on the use case, the data manipulation requirements (those requiring specific packages or other algorithms that are highly esoteric to the DS realm), post-prediction heuristics needs, and artifact update velocity can be challenging for a developer to integrate. Without a close, collaborative effort with a production infrastructure development team, deploying a service that integrates with existing systems can be an exercise in frustration and a massive generator of technical debt.

Most times, after discussing a project's integration needs with development teams, we've come upon clever methodologies to store predictions, perform manipulations of data at massive scale, and collaborate on designs that serve the project's SLA needs at the lowest possible cost. Without input from the DS team on what it is that the model is doing, the development team is ill-prepared to make optimized architecture decisions. Similarly, without the advice and collaboration of the development team, the DS team is likely to create a solution that doesn't meet the SLA needs or will be too costly to be justified running for very long.

Collaboration is key when evaluating a serving architecture; many times, this collaboration helps inform the very structure and design of the ML solution's output. It's best to involve the "engineering consumers" of your model solutions early in the project design phase. The earlier that they're involved in the project (data engineers for batch bulk prediction solutions, software engineers for real-time serving solutions), the more of a positive influence they can have on the decision being made about how the solution is built.

SLA

The original intention of the team earlier in our scenario was to ensure that their predictions would not interrupt the end user's app experience. Their design encompassed a precalculated set of recommendations, held in an ultra-low-latency storage system to eliminate the time burden that they assumed would be involved in running a VM-based model service.

SLA considerations are one of the most important facets of an ML architecture design for serving. In general, the solution that is built must consider the budget for serving delays and ensure that for most of the time, this budget is not extended or violated. Regardless of how amazingly a model performs from a prediction accuracy or efficacy standpoint, if it can't be used or consumed in the amount of time allotted, it's worthless.

The other consideration that needs to be balanced with that of the SLA requirements is the actual monetary budget. Materialized as a function of infrastructure complexity, the general rule is that the faster a prediction can be served at a larger scale of requests, the more expensive the solution is going to be to host and develop.

COST

Figure 16.10 shows a relationship between prediction freshness (how long after a prediction is made it is intended to be utilized or acted upon) and the volume of predictions that need to be made as a factor of cost and complexity.

The top portion of figure 16.10 shows a traditional paradigm for batch serving. For extremely large production inference volumes, a batch prediction job using Apache Spark Structured Streaming in a `trigger-once` operation will likely be the cheapest option.

The bottom portion of figure 16.10 involves immediate-use ML solutions. When predictions are intended to be used in a real-time interface, the architecture begins to change dramatically from the batch-inspired use cases. REST API interfaces, elastic scalability of serving containers, and traffic distribution to those services become required as prediction volumes increase.

RECENCY

Recency, the delay between when feature data is generated and when a prediction can be acted upon, is one of the most important aspects of designing a serving paradigm for a project's model. SLA considerations are by and large the defining characteristics for choosing a specific serving layer architecture for ML projects. However, edge cases related to recency of the data available for usage in prediction can modify the final scalable and cost-effective design employed for a project.

Depending on a particular situation, the recency of the data and the end use-case for the project can override the general SLA-based design criteria for serving.

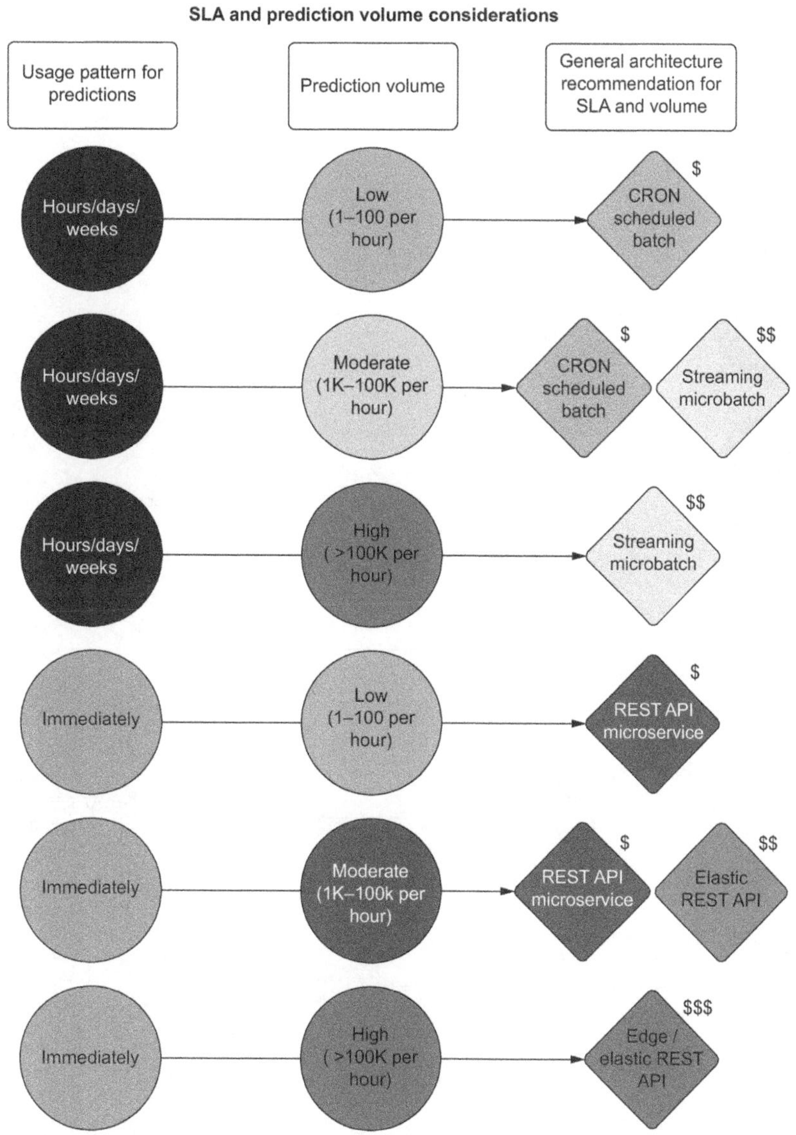

Figure 16.10 Architectural implications to meet SLA and prediction volume needs

Figure 16.11 illustrates a set of examples of data recency and consumption layer patterns to show how the architecture can change from the purely SLA-focused designs in figure 16.10.

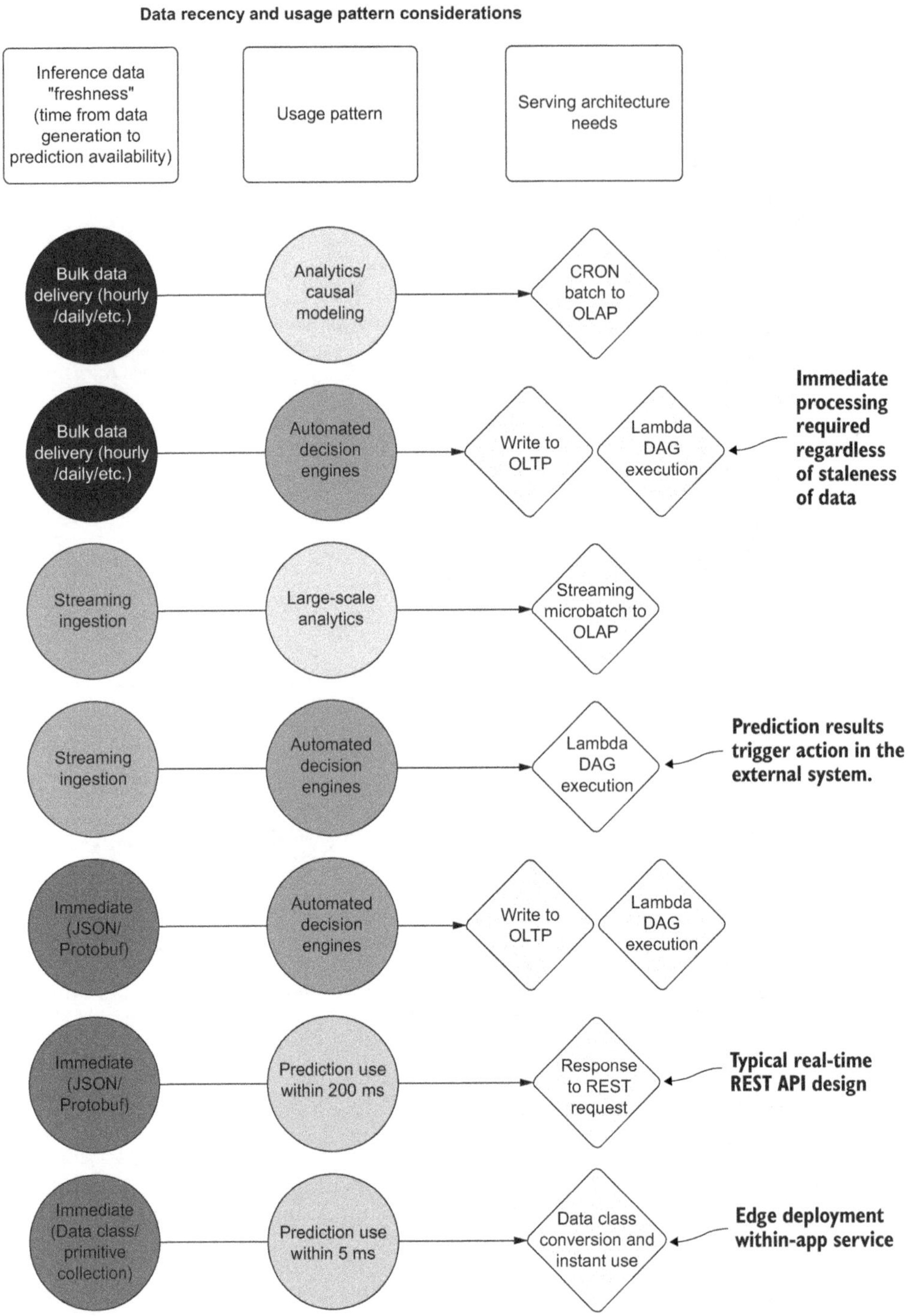

Figure 16.11   The effects of data recency and common usage patterns on serving architectures

These examples are by no means exhaustive. There are as many edge case considerations for serving model predictions as there are nuanced approaches to solving problems with ML. The intention is to open the discussion around which serving solution is appropriate by evaluating the nature of the incoming data, identifying the project's needs, and seeking the least complex solution possible that addresses the constraints of a project. By considering all aspects of project serving needs (data recency, SLA needs, prediction volumes, and prediction consumption paradigms), the appropriate architecture can be utilized to meet the usage pattern needs while adhering to a design that is only as complex and expensive as it needs to be.

But why don't we just build real-time serving for everything?

Simplifying ML deployments around a one-size-fits-all pattern may be tempting. For some organizations, reducing ML engineering complexity in this manner might make sense (for instance, serving everything in Kubernetes). It certainly seems like it would be easier if every single project just needed to use some form of framework that supported a single deployment strategy.

This does make sense if your company has only a single type of ML use case. If all your company ever does is fraud prediction on behalf of small companies, it might make sense to stick with Seldon and Kubernetes to deliver REST API endpoints for all your models. If you're focused on doing marketplace price optimizations based on asynchronous but low-traffic-volume models, a Docker container with a simple Flask server running inside it will do nicely.

Most companies aren't myopically focused on a single ML use case, though. For many companies, internal use cases would benefit from a simplistic batch prediction that's written to a table in a database. Most groups have needs that can be solved with far simpler (and cheaper!) infrastructures for some of their use cases that don't involve spinning up a VM cluster that can support hundreds of thousands of requests per second. Using such advanced infrastructure for a use case that's at most going to be queried a few dozen times per day is wasteful (in development time, maintenance, and money) and negligent.

It's critically important for the long-term success of an ML solution to choose an architecture that fits the needs of consumption patterns, data volume sizes, and delivery time guarantees. This doesn't mean to overengineer everything just in case, but rather to select the appropriate solution that meets your project's needs. Nothing less, and most certainly, nothing more.

When an ML project's output is destined for consumption within the walls of a company, the architectural burdens are generally far lower than any other scenario. However, this doesn't imply that shortcuts can be taken. Utilizing MLOps tools, following robust data management processes, and writing maintainable code are just as critical here as they are for any other serving paradigm. Internal use-case modeling efforts can be classified into two general groups: bulk precomputation and lightweight ad hoc microservice.

SERVING FROM A DATABASE OR DATA WAREHOUSE

Predictions that are intended for within-workday usage usually utilize a batch prediction paradigm. Models are applied to the new data that has arrived up until the start of the workday, predictions are written to a table (typically in an overwrite mode), and end users within the company can utilize the predictions in an ad hoc manner.

Regardless of the interface method (BI tool, SQL, internal GUI, etc.), the predictions are scheduled to occur at a fixed time (hourly, daily, weekly, etc.), and the only infrastructure burden that the DS team has is ensuring that the predictions are made and make their way to the table. Figure 16.12 shows an example architecture supporting this implementation.

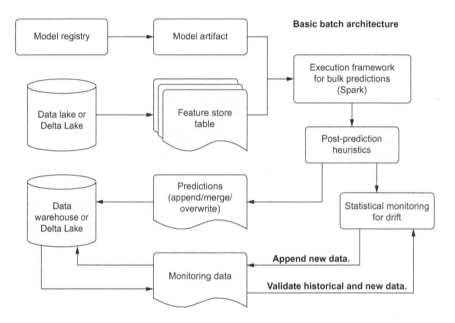

Figure 16.12 Batch serving generic architecture

This architecture is as bare-bones a solution as ML can get. A trained model is retrieved from a registry, data is queried from a source system (preferably from a feature store table), predictions are made, drift monitoring validation occurs, and finally the prediction data is written to an accessible location. For internal use cases on bulk-prediction data, not much more is required from an infrastructure perspective.

SERVING FROM A MICROSERVICE FRAMEWORK

For internal use cases that rely on more up-to-date predictions on an ad hoc basis or those that allow for a user to specify aspects of the feature vector to receive on-demand predictions (optimization simulations, for instance), precomputation isn't an option. This paradigm focuses instead on having a lightweight serving layer to host the model, providing a simple REST API interface to ingest data, generate predictions, and return the predictions to the end user.

Most implementations with these requirements are done through BI tools and internal GUIs. Figure 16.13 shows an example of such an architectural setup to support ad hoc predictions.

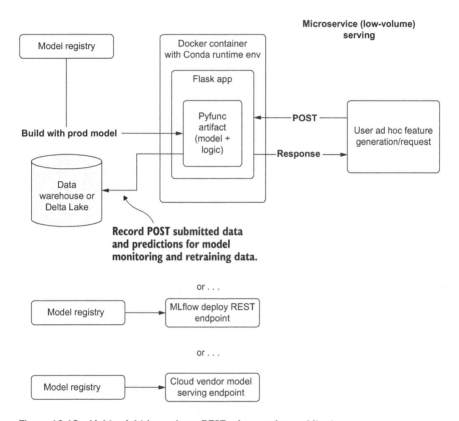

Figure 16.13 Lightweight low-volume REST microservice architecture

The simplicity of this style of deployment is appealing for many use cases of model serving for an internal use-case application. Capable of supporting up to a few dozen requests per second, a lightweight flask deployment of a model can be an attractive alternative to brute-force bulk computing of possible end-use permutations of potential predictions. Although this is technically a real-time serving implementation, it is of critical importance to realize that this is wildly inappropriate for low-latency, high-volume prediction needs or anything that could be customer-facing.

It's OK, we know that team

It can be rather tempting for internal-use projects to cut corners. Perhaps recording passive retraining histories seems like overkill for an internal project. It may be tempting to ship a code base to a scheduled job with a poor design that lacks appropriate refactoring that would have been done for a customer-facing model. Spending extra time optimizing the data storage design to support end-user query performance may seem like a waste of time.

After all, they're fellow employees. They'll understand if it doesn't work perfectly, right?

Nothing can be further from the truth. In my experience, the company's collective perception of a DS team is based on these internal use-case projects. The perceived capability, capacity, and competency of the DS team is directly influenced by how well these internal tools work for the users within departments in the company. It's critically important to build these solutions with the same level of engineering rigor and discipline as a solution that is used by customers. It's your reputation on the line in ways that you might not realize.

Perception of capability becomes important in internal projects for no larger reason than that these internal groups will be engaging your team for future projects. If these groups perceive the DS team as generating broken, unstable, and buggy solutions for their team's use, the chances that they will want to have your team work on something that is customer-facing is somewhere in the vicinity of zero.

The first customers that you have, after all, are the internal teams within the company. You'll do well to make sure your primary customers—the business units—are confident in your ability to deliver stable and useful solutions.

16.3.2 *Bulk external delivery*

The considerations for bulk external delivery aren't substantially different from internal use serving to a database or data warehouse. The only material differences between these serving cases are in the realms of delivery time and monitoring of the predictions.

DELIVERY CONSISTENCY

Bulk delivery of results to an external party has the same relevancy requirements as any other ML solution. Whether you're building something for an internal team or generating predictions that will be end-user-customer facing, the goal of creating useful predictions doesn't change.

The one thing that does change with providing bulk predictions to an outside organization (generally applicable to business-to-business companies) when compared to other serving paradigms is in the timeliness of the delivery. While it may be obvious that a failure to deliver an extract of bulk predictions entirely is a bad thing, an inconsistent delivery can be just as detrimental. There is a simple solution to this, however, illustrated in the bottom portion of figure 16.14.

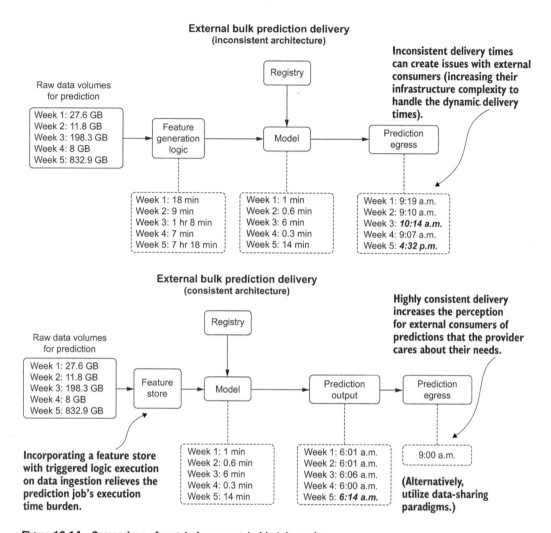

Figure 16.14 Comparison of ungated versus gated batch serving

Figure 16.14 shows the comparison of gated and ungated serving to an external user group. By controlling a final-stage egress from the stored predictions in a scheduled batch prediction job, as well as coupling feature-generation logic to an ETL process governed by a feature store, delivery consistency from a chronological perspective can be guaranteed. While this may not seem an important consideration from the DS perspective of the team generating the predictions, having a predictable data-availability schedule can dramatically increase the perceived professionalism of the serving company.

QUALITY ASSURANCE

An occasionally overlooked aspect of serving bulk predictions externally (external to the DS and analytics groups at a company) is ensuring that a thorough quality check is performed on those predictions.

An internal project may rely on a simple check for overt prediction failures (for example, silent failures are ignored that result in null values, or a linear model predicts infinity). When sending data products externally, additional steps should be done to minimize the chances of end users of predictions finding fault with them. Since we, as humans, are so adept at finding abnormalities in patterns, a few scant issues in a batch-delivered prediction dataset can easily draw the focus of a consumer of the data, deteriorating their faith in the efficacy of the solution to the point of disuse.

In my experience, when delivering bulk predictions external to a team of data specialists, I've found it worthwhile to perform a few checks before releasing the data:

- Validate the predictions against the training data:
  - *Classification problems*—Comparing aggregated class counts
  - *Regression problems*—Comparing prediction distribution
  - *Unsupervised problems*—Evaluating group membership counts
- Check for prediction outliers (applicable to regression problems).
- Build (if applicable) heuristics rules based on knowledge from SMEs to ensure that predictions are not outside the realm of possibility for the topic.
- Validate incoming features (particularly encoded ones that may use a generic catchall encoding if the encoding key is previously unseen) to ensure that the data is fully compatible with the model as it was trained.

By running a few extra validation steps on the output of a batch prediction, a great deal of confusion and potential lessening of trust in the final product can be avoided in the eyes of end users.

16.3.3 *Microbatch streaming*

The applications of streaming prediction paradigms are rather limited. Unable to meet the strict SLA requirements that would force a decision to utilize a REST API service, as well as being complete overkill for small-scale batch prediction needs, streaming prediction holds a unique space in ML serving infrastructure. This niche spot is firmly centered in the needs of a project having a relatively high SLA (measured in the range of whole seconds to weeks) and a large inference dataset size.

The attractiveness of streaming for high SLA needs lies in cost and complexity reduction. Instead of building out a scalable infrastructure to support bulk predictions sent to a REST API service (or similar microservice capable of doing paginated bulk predictions of large data), a simple Apache Spark Structured Streaming job can be configured to allow for draining row-based data from a streaming source (such as Kafka or cloud object storage queue indices) and natively running predictions upon the stream with a serialized model artifact. This helps dramatically reduce complexity, can support streaming-as-batch stateful computation, and can prevent costly infrastructure from having to run when not needed for prediction.

From the perspective of large data sizes, streaming can reduce the required infrastructure size that would otherwise be needed for large dataset predictions in a traditional batch prediction paradigm. By streaming the data through a comparatively smaller cluster of machines than would be required to hold the entire dataset in memory, the infrastructure burden is far less.

This directly translates into lower total cost of ownership for an ML solution with a relatively high SLA. Figure 16.15 shows a simple structured streaming approach to serve predictions at a lower complexity and cost than traditional batch or REST API solutions.

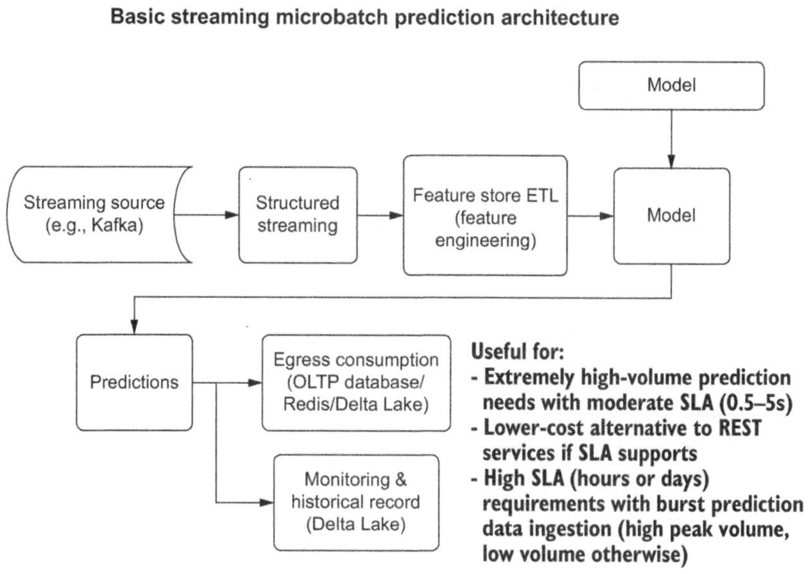

Basic streaming microbatch prediction architecture

Figure 16.15 A simple structured streaming prediction pipeline architecture

While not able to solve the vast majority of ML serving needs, this architecture still has its place as an attractive alternative to batch prediction for extremely large datasets and to REST APIs when SLAs are not particularly stringent. Implementing this serving methodology is worth it, if it fits this niche, simply for the reduction in cost.

16.3.4 *Real-time server-side*

The defining characteristic of real-time serving is that of a low SLA. This directly informs the basic architectural design of serving predictions. Any system supporting this paradigm requires a model artifact to be hosted as a service, coupled with an interface for accepting data passed into it, a computational engine to perform the predictions, and a method of returning a prediction to the originating requestor.

The details of implementing a real-time serving architecture can be defined through the classification of levels of traffic, split into three main groupings: low volume, low volume with burst capacity, and high volume. Each requires different infrastructure design and tooling implementation to allow for a high availability and minimally expensive solution.

LOW VOLUME

The general architecture for low volume (low-rate requests) is no different from a REST microservice container architecture. Regardless of what REST server is used, what container service is employed to run the application, or what VM management suite is used, the only primary addition for externally facing endpoints is to ensure that the REST service is running on managed hardware. This doesn't necessarily mean that a fully managed cloud service needs to be used, but the requirement for even a low-volume production service is that the system needs to stay up.

This infrastructure running the container that you're building should be monitored from not only an ML perspective, but from a performance consideration as well. The memory utilization of the container on the hosting VM, the CPU utilization, network latency, and request failures and retries should all be monitored in real time with a redundant backup available to fail over to if issues arise with fulfilling serving requests.

The scalability and complexity of traffic routing doesn't become an issue with low-volume solutions (tens to thousands of requests per minute), provided that the SLA requirements for the project are being met, so a simpler deployment and monitoring architecture is called for with low-volume use cases.

BURST VOLUME AND HIGH VOLUME

When moving to scales that support burst traffic, integrating elasticity into the serving layer is a critical addition to the architecture. Since an individual VM has only so many threads to process predictions, a flood of requests that come in for prediction and that exceed the execution capacity of a single VM can overwhelm that VM. Unresponsiveness, REST time-outs, and VM instability (potentially crashing) can render a single-VM model deployment unusable. The solution for handling burst volume and high-capacity serving is to incorporate process isolation and routing in the form of elastic load balancing.

Load balancing is, as the name implies, a means of routing requests in a sharded fleet of VMs (duplicated containers of a model serving application). With many containers running in parallel, request loads can be scaled horizontally to support truly staggering volumes of requests. These services (each cloud has its own flavor that essentially does the same thing) are transparent to both the ML team deploying a container and to the end user. With a single endpoint for requests to come into and a single container image to build and deploy, the load-balancing system will ensure that distribution of load burdens happens autonomously to prevent service disruption and instability.

A common design pattern, leveraging cloud-agnostic services, is shown in figure 16.16. Utilizing a simple Python REST framework (Flask) that interfaces with the model artifact from within a container allows for scalable predictions that can support high-volume and burst traffic needs.

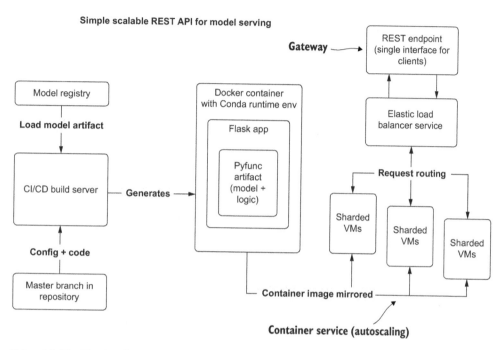

Figure 16.16 **Cloud-native REST API model serving architecture**

This relatively bare-bones architecture is a basic template for an elastically scaling real-time REST-based service to provide predictions. Missing from this diagram are other critical components that we've discussed in previous chapters (monitoring of features, retraining triggers, A/B testing, and model versioning), but it has the core components that differentiate a smaller-scale real-time system from that of a service that can handle large traffic volume.

At its core, the load balancer shown in figure 16.16 is what makes the system scale from a single VM's limit of available cores (putting Gunicorn in front of Flask will allow all cores of the VM to concurrently process requests) to horizontally scaling out to handling hundreds of concurrent predictions (or more). This scalability comes with a caveat, though. Adding this functionality translates to greater complexity and cost for a serving solution.

Figure 16.17 shows a more thorough design of a large-scale REST API solution. This architecture can support extremely high rates of prediction traffic and all the services that need to be orchestrated to hit volume, SLA, and analytics use cases for a production deployment.

BW 693 3462

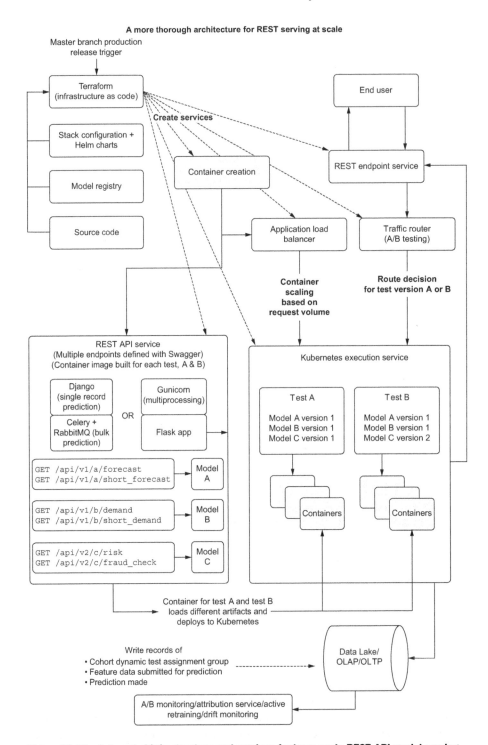

Figure 16.17   Automated infrastructure and services for large-scale REST API model serving

These systems have a lot of components. It's quite easy for the complexity to grow to the point that dozens of disparate systems are glued together in an application stack to fulfill the needs of the project's use case. Therefore, it is of the utmost importance to explain not only the complexity involved in supporting these systems, but the cost as well, to the business unit interested in having a solution built that requires this architecture.

Typically, because of this magnitude of complexity, this isn't a setup that a DS team maintains on its own. DevOps, core engineering, backend developers, and software architects are involved with the design, deployment, and maintenance of services like this. The cloud services bill is one thing to consider for the total cost of ownership, but the other outstanding factor is the human capital investment required to keep a service like this operational constantly.

If your SLA requirements and scale are this complicated, it would be wise to identify these needs as early in the project as possible, be honest about the investment, and make sure that the business understands the magnitude of the undertaking. If they agree that the investment is worth it, go ahead and build it. However, if the prospect of designing and building one of these behemoths is daunting to business leaders, it's best not to force them into allowing it to be built at the very end of development when so much time and effort has been put into the project.

16.3.5 Integrated models (edge deployment)

Edge deployment is the ultimate stage in low-latency serving for certain use cases. As it deploys a model artifact and all dependent libraries as part of a container image, it has scalability levels that outweigh any other approach. However, this deployment paradigm carries with it a large burden on the part of app developers:

- Deployment of new models or retrained models needs to be scheduled with app deployments and upgrades.
- Monitoring of predictions and generated features is dependent on internet connectivity.
- Heuristics or last-mile corrections to predictions cannot be done server-side.
- Models and infrastructure within the serving container need deeper and more complex integration testing to ensure proper functionality.
- Device capabilities can restrict model complexity, forcing simpler and more lightweight modeling solutions.

For these reasons, edge deployment might not be very appealing for many use cases. The velocity of changes to the models is incredibly low, drift impacts to models can render edge-deployed models irrelevant far more quickly than a new build can be pushed out, and the lack of monitoring available for some end users can provide such intense disadvantages to this paradigm as to leave it inapplicable to most projects. For those that don't suffer from the detractors for edge deployment, a typical architecture for this serving style is shown in figure 16.18.

Simple edge deployment architecture

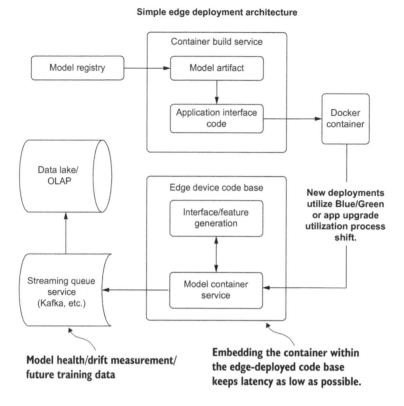

Figure 16.18   A simplified architecture of an edge-deployed model artifact container

As you can see, an edge deployment is tightly coupled to the application code base. Because of the large numbers of required packaged libraries involved in a runtime that can support the predictions being made by the included model, containerizing the artifact prevents the app development team from maintaining an environment that is mirrored to that of the DS team. This can mitigate many of the issues that can plague non-container-based model edge deployments (namely, environment dependency management, language choice standardization, and library synchronization for features in a shared code base).

The projects that can leverage edge deployment, particularly those focused on tasks such as image classification, can dramatically reduce infrastructure costs. The defining aspect of what can qualify for edge deployment is in the state of stationarity in the features being utilized by the model. If the functional nature of the model's input data will not be changing particularly often (such as with imaging use cases), edge deployment can greatly simplify infrastructure and keep total ownership costs of an ML solution incredibly low.

Summary

- Model registry services will help ensure effective state management of deployed and archived models, enabling effective passive retraining and active retraining solutions without requiring manual intervention.
- Feature stores segregate feature-generation logic from modeling code, allowing for faster retraining processes, reuse of features across projects, and a far simpler method of monitoring for feature drift.
- To choose an appropriate architecture for serving, we must weigh many characteristics of the project: employing the right level of services and infrastructure to support the required SLA, prediction volume, and recency of data to ensure that a prediction service is cost-effective and stable.

appendix A
Big O(no) and
how to think about
runtime performance

Runtime complexity, for ML use cases, is no different than it is for any other piece of software. The impact of inefficient and poorly optimized code affects processing tasks in ML jobs the same as it does any other engineering project. The only material difference that sets ML tasks apart from traditional software is in the algorithms employed to solve problems. The computational and space complexity of these algorithms is typically obscured by high-level APIs that encapsulate recursive iterations, which can dramatically increase runtimes.

The goal of this appendix is to focus on understanding both the runtime characteristics of *control code* (all the code in your project that isn't involved in training a model) and the ML algorithm itself that is being trained.

A.1 What is Big O, anyway?

Let's suppose we're working on a project that is set to release soon to production. The results are spectacular, and the business unit for whom the project was built is happy with the attribution results. However, not everyone is happy. The costs of running the solution are incredibly high.

As we step through the code, we discover that the vast majority of the execution time is centered around our feature-engineering preprocessing stages. One particular portion of the code seems to take far longer than we originally expected. Based on initial testing, shown in the following listing, we had imagined that this function wouldn't be much of a problem.

Listing A.1   Nested loop name-reconciliation example

```
import nltk
import pandas as pd
import numpy as np
client_names = ['Rover', 'ArtooDogTwo', 'Willy', 'Hodor',
    'MrWiggleBottoms', 'SallyMcBarksALot', 'HungryGames',
    'MegaBite', 'HamletAndCheese', 'HoundJamesHound',
    'Treatzilla', 'SlipperAssassin', 'Chewbarka',
    'SirShedsALot', 'Spot', 'BillyGoat', 'Thunder',
    'Doggo', 'TreatHunter']
extracted_names = ['Slipr Assassin', 'Are two dog two',
    'willy', 'willie', 'hodr', 'hodor', 'treat zilla',
    'roover', 'megbyte', 'sport', 'spotty', 'billygaot',
    'billy goat', 'thunder', 'thunda', 'sirshedlot',
    'chew bark', 'hungry games', 'ham and cheese',
    'mr wiggle bottom', 'sally barks a lot']
def lower_strip(string): return string.lower().replace(" ", "")
def get_closest_match(registered_names, extracted_names):
    scores = {}
    for i in registered_names:
        for j in extracted_names:
            scores['{}_{}'.format(i, j)] = nltk.edit_distance(lower_strip(i),
    lower_strip(j))
    parsed = {}
    for k, v in scores.items():
        k1, k2 = k.split('_')
        low_value = parsed.get(k2)
        if low_value is not None and (v < low_value[1]):
            parsed[k2] = (k1, v)
        elif low_value is None:
            parsed[k2] = (k1, v)
    return parsed
get_closest_match(client_names, extracted_names)
>> {'Slipr Assassin': ('SlipperAssassin', 2),
    'Are two dog two': ('ArtooDogTwo', 2),
    'willy': ('Willy', 0),
    'willie': ('Willy', 2),
    'hodr': ('Hodor', 1),
    'hodor': ('Hodor', 0),
    'treat zilla': ('Treatzilla', 0),
    'roover': ('Rover', 1),
    'megbyte': ('MegaBite', 2),
    'sport': ('Spot', 1),
    'spotty': ('Spot', 2),
    'billygaot': ('BillyGoat', 2),
    'billy goat': ('BillyGoat', 0),
    'thunder': ('Thunder', 0),
    'thunda': ('Thunder', 2),
    'sirshedlot': ('SirShedsALot', 2),
    'chew bark': ('Chewbarka', 1),
    'hungry games': ('HungryGames', 0),
    'ham and cheese': ('HamletAndCheese', 3),
    'mr wiggle bottom': ('MrWiggleBottoms', 1),
    'sally barks a lot': ('SallyMcBarksALot', 2)}
```

The list of registered names of dogs in our database (small sample)

The parsed names from the free-text field ratings that we get from our customer's humans

The $O(n^2)$ nested loop, going through each of the parsed names

Looping through every one of our registered names

Calculates the Levenshtein distance between the names after removing spaces and forcing lowercase on both strings

Loops through the pairwise distance measurements to return the most likely match for each parsed name. This is $O(n)$.

Runs the algorithm against the two lists of registered names and parsed names

The results of closest match by Levenshtein distance

On the small dataset used for validation and development, the execution time was in milliseconds. However, when running against our full dataset of 5 million registered dogs and 10 billion name reference extractions, we simply have too many dogs in our data to run through this algorithm. (Yes, there can be such a thing as too many dogs, believe it or not.).

The reason is that the computational complexity of this algorithm is $O(n^2)$. For each registered name, we're testing its distance to each of the name extracts, as shown in figure A.1.

The following listing shows an alternative approach to reducing the looped searching.

Listing A.2   A slightly better approach (but still not perfect)

Cleans up the names so that our Levenshtein calculation can be as accurate as possible (function defined in listing A.1)

Generates a static join key to support our Cartesian join we'll be doing

Generates the same static join key in the right-side table to effect the Cartesian join

Creates a pandas DataFrame from the client names list

```python
JOIN_KEY = 'joinkey'
CLIENT_NM = 'client_names'
EXTRACT_NM = 'extracted_names'
DISTANCE_NM = 'levenshtein'

def dataframe_reconciliation(registered_names, extracted_names, threshold=10):
    C_NAME_RAW = CLIENT_NM + '_raw'
    E_NAME_RAW = EXTRACT_NM + '_raw'
    registered_df = pd.DataFrame(registered_names, columns=[CLIENT_NM])
    registered_df[JOIN_KEY] = 0
    registered_df[C_NAME_RAW] = registered_df[CLIENT_NM].map(lambda x:
      lower_strip(x))
    extracted_df = pd.DataFrame(extracted_names, columns=[EXTRACT_NM])
    extracted_df[JOIN_KEY] = 0
    extracted_df[E_NAME_RAW] = extracted_df[EXTRACT_NM].map(lambda x:
      lower_strip(x))
    joined_df = registered_df.merge(extracted_df, on=JOIN_KEY, how='outer')
    joined_df[DISTANCE_NM] = joined_df.loc[:, [C_NAME_RAW, E_NAME_RAW]].apply(
        lambda x: nltk.edit_distance(*x), axis=1)
    joined_df = joined_df.drop(JOIN_KEY, axis=1)
    filtered = joined_df[joined_df[DISTANCE_NM] < threshold]
    filtered = filtered.sort_values(DISTANCE_NM).groupby(EXTRACT_NM,
      as_index=False).first()
    return filtered.drop([C_NAME_RAW, E_NAME_RAW], axis=1)
```

Calculates the Levenshtein distance by using the thoroughly useful NLTK package

Returns the rows for each potential match key that has the lowest Levenshtein distance score

Performs the Cartesian join (which is $O(n^2)$ space complexity)

Removes any potential non-matches from the DataFrame

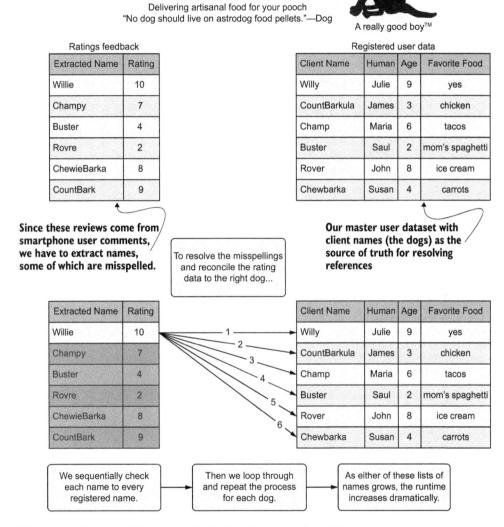

Figure A.1 The computational complexity of our feature engineering

NOTE if you're curious about the NLTK package and all of the fantastic things that it can do for natural language processing in Python, I highly encourage you to read *Natural Language Processing with Python* (O'Reilly, 2009) by Steven Bird, Ewan Klein, and Edward Loper, the original authors of the open source project.

Utilizing this DataFrame approach can remarkably speed up the runtime. Listing A.2 is not a perfect solution, since the space complexity will increase, but refactoring in this manner can dramatically reduce the runtime of the project and reduce costs. Figure A.2 shows the results of calling the function defined in listing A.2.

DataFrame representation of the name-resolution algorithm
(No dogs were harmed in the generation of this data.)

	extracted_names	client_names	levenshtein
0	Are two dog two	ArtooDogTwo	2
1	Slipr Assassin	SlipperAssassin	2
2	billy goat	BillyGoat	0
3	billygaot	BillyGoat	2
4	chew bark	Chewbarka	1
5	ham and cheese	HamletAndCheese	3
6	hodor	Hodor	0
7	hodr	Hodor	1
8	hungry games	HungryGames	0
9	megbyte	MegaBite	2
10	mr wiggle bottom	MrWiggleBottoms	1
11	roover	Rover	1
12	sally barks a lot	SallyMcBarksALot	2
13	sirshedlot	SirShedsALot	2
14	sport	Spot	1
15	spotty	Spot	2
16	thunda	Thunder	2
17	thunder	Thunder	0
18	treat zilla	Treatzilla	0
19	willie	Willy	2
20	willy	Willy	0

The parsed names from the free-text comments about how much the doggos liked their artisanal meals

Registered customer names in our database

Lowest scores found (the best match), returned by filtering the DataFrame in place

Figure A.2   Reducing computational complexity at the expense of space complexity

The important thing to remember about this example is that scalability is *relative*. Here we are trading computational complexity for space complexity: we originally were sequentially looping through two arrays, which takes a long time to do, but has a very low memory footprint; then, working with the matrix-like structure of pandas is orders of magnitude faster but requires a great deal of RAM. In actual practice, with the data volumes involved here, the best solution is to process this problem in a mix of looped processing (preferably in Spark `DataFrames`) while leveraging Cartesian joins in chunks to find a good balance between computation and space pressure.

Refactoring for performance and cost

Most refactoring of code bases is done to enhance their testability and extensibility. But in ML code bases, a frequent activity that prompts enhancements is runtime efficiency. This generally is focused more on the training and retraining of models than on prediction aspects of ML, but incredibly complex feature engineering is involved in these jobs. Many times, the root cause of nonperformant code in ML projects is in the feature-processing and control logic, rather than in the training of the model(s) (except for the case of extensive hyperparameter tuning, which will likely dominate the total runtime).

Primarily because of the long-running nature of these jobs, identifying and optimizing runtime performance can have a dramatic impact on the total cost of ownership of an ML solution. To effectively optimize, however, it's critical to analyze the computational complexity (affecting total runtime) and space complexity (affecting the size or number of machines required to run the code).

The analysis of runtime issues is, from both a practical and theoretical stance, handled through evaluating computational complexity and space complexity, referred to in shorthand as *Big O*.

A.1.1 A gentle introduction to complexity

Computational complexity is, at its heart, a worst-case estimation of how long it will take for a computer to work through an algorithm. *Space complexity*, on the other hand, is the worst-case burden to a system's memory that an algorithm can cause.

While computational complexity typically impacts the CPU, space complexity involves the memory (RAM) you need to have in the system to process the algorithm without incurring disk spills (pagination to a hard drive or solid-state drive). Figure A.3 shows how operating on a collection of data points can have different space and computational complexity, depending on the algorithm that you're using.

The different actions being performed on collections of data affect the amount of time and space complexity involved. As you move from top to bottom in figure A.3, both space and computational complexity increase for different operations.

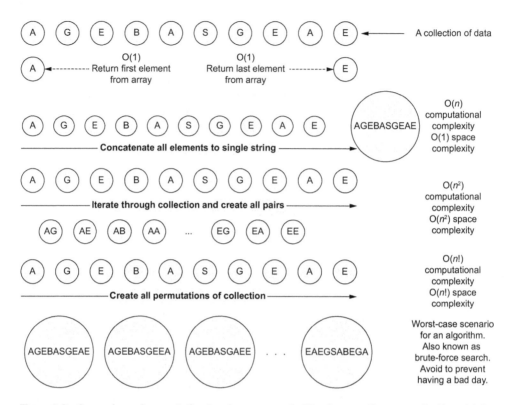

Figure A.3   Comparison of computational and space complexities for operating on a collection of data

Many other complexities are considered standard for assessing complexities in algorithms. Figure A.4 shows these standard assessments on a linear scale, while figure A.5 shows them on a logarithmic y-scale to illustrate just how much some of them should be avoided.

As figures A.4 and A.5 show, the relationship between collection size and algorithm type can dramatically affect the runtime of your code. Understanding these relationships (of both space and computational complexity) within the non-ML aspects of your code, outside of model training and inference, is absolutely essential.

Let's imagine what the costs would be for implementing something as simple as a collection traversal in project orchestration code. If we were trying to evaluate relationships between two arrays of numbers in a brute-force manner (looping through each in a nested fashion), we'd be looking at $O(n^2)$ complexity. If we were to merge the lists instead through an optimized join, we could reduce the complexity significantly. Moving from complexities like $O(n^2)$ to something closer to $O(n)$, as shown in figures A.4 and A.5, when dealing with large collections, can translate to significant cost and time savings.

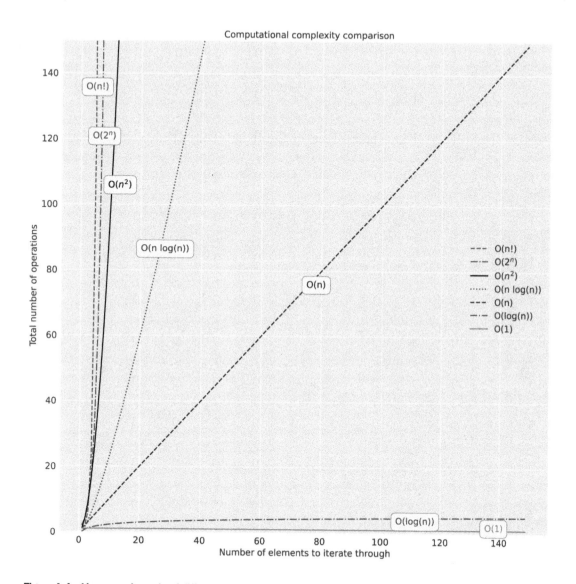

Figure A.4   Linear y-axis scale of different computational complexities filtered to 150 iterations

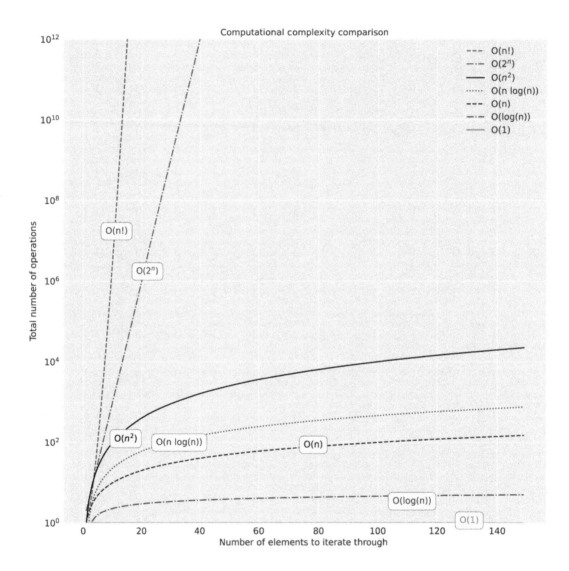

Figure A.5   Logarithmic y-axis scale of computational complexities. Pay close attention to the size of the y-axis toward the top of the graph. Exponential and factorial complexities can truly bring the pain.

A.2 *Complexity by example*

Analyzing code for performance issues can be daunting. Many times, we're so focused on getting all of the details surrounding feature engineering, model tuning, metric evaluation, and statistical evaluation ironed out that the concept of evaluating how we're iterating over collections doesn't enter our minds.

If we were to take a look at the control code that directs the execution of those elements of a project, thinking of their execution as a factor of complexity, we would be able to estimate the relative runtime effects that will occur. Armed with this knowledge, we could decouple inefficient operations (such as overly nested looping statements that could be collapsed into a single indexed traversal) and help reduce the burden on both the CPU and the memory of the system running our code.

Now that you've seen the theory of Big O, let's take a look at some code examples using these algorithms. Being able to see how differences in the number of elements in a collection can affect timing of operations is important in order to fully understand these concepts.

I'm going to present these topics in a somewhat less-than-traditional manner, using dogs as an example, followed by showing code examples of the relationships. Why? Because dogs are fun.

A.2.1 *O(1): The "It doesn't matter how big the data is" algorithm*

Let's imagine that we're in a room. A very, very large room. In the center of the room is a ring of food bowls. For dogs. And we've filled these bowls with some pasta Bolognese. It's been a torturous day of making it (for the dogs, smelling the entire time), but we've ladled the food into five separate bowls and are ready with our notepads to record data about the event. After all is said and done (bowls are cleaner than before they were ladled with pasta), we have collections of ordered lists representing different actions that our panel of dogs took.

When we wish to answer questions about the facts that we observed, we're operating on these lists, but retrieving a single indexed value associated with the order in which these events occurred. Regardless of the size of these lists, the O(1)-type questions are simply acquiring data based on positional reference, and thus, the operations all take the same amount of time. Let's take a look at this scenario in figure A.6.

O(1) doesn't care how big the data is, as figure A.6 shows. These algorithms simply operate in ways that don't traverse collections, but rather access positions of data within collections.

To show this relationship in a computational sense, listing A.3 illustrates a comparison of performing an O(1) task on two differently sized collections of data—with a similar runtime performance.

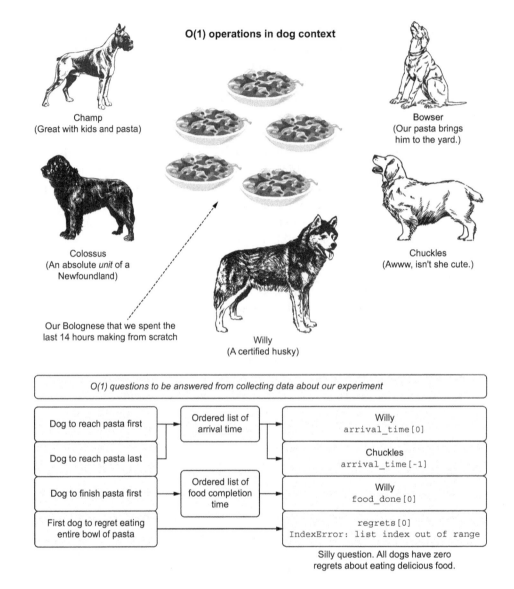

Figure A.6   O(1) search by means of hungry dogs

Listing A.3   Demonstration of O(1) complexity

Generates an array of integers between −100 and 100

Runs through 100,000 iterations of the operation to allow for per-run variance to be minimized to see the access speed

```
import numpy as np
sequential_array = np.arange(-100, 100, 1)
%timeit -n 1000 -r 100 sequential_array[-1]
>> 269 ns ± 52.1 ns per loop (mean ± std. dev. of
100 runs, 10000 loops each)
```

The absolute value of average speed per iteration is highly dependent on the hardware that the code is running on. 269 nanoseconds is pretty fast for using a single core from an 8-core laptop CPU, though.

Generates an array that is
just slightly larger than
the first one

261 nanoseconds. Even with
100,000 times more data, the
execution time is the same.

Quadratic equation to
illustrate mathematical
operations on a single
value

```
massive_array = np.arange(-1e7, 1e7, 1)
%timeit -n 10000 -r 100 massive_array[-1]
>> 261 ns ± 49.7 ns per loop (mean ± std. dev. of
100 runs, 10000 loops each)
def quadratic(x):
    return (0.00733 * math.pow(x, 3) -0.001166 *
math.pow(x, 2) + 0.32 * x - 1.7334)
%timeit -n 10000 -r 100 quadratic(sequential_array[-1])
>> 5.31 µs ± 259 ns per loop (mean ± std. dev. of 100 runs, 10000 loops each)
%timeit -n 10000 -r 100 quadratic(massive_array[-1])
>> 1.55 µs ± 63.3 ns per loop (mean ± std. dev. of 100 runs, 10000 loops each)
```

Executes 5.31
microseconds on a
single value from
the array

Executes 1.55 microseconds on a single value from the array
(less time than the previous due to indexing operations in
NumPy for accessing larger arrays)

The first array (sequential_array) is a scant 200 elements in length, and its access time for retrieving an element from its indexed c-based-struct type is very fast. As we increase the size of the array (massive_array, containing 2 million elements), the runtime doesn't change for a positional retrieval. This is due to an optimized storage paradigm of the array; we can directly look up the memory address location for the element in constant O(1) time through the index registry.

The control code of ML projects has many examples of O(1) complexity:

- *Getting the last entry in a sorted, ranked collection of aggregated data points*—For example, from a window function with events arranged by time of occurrence. However, the process of building the windowed aggregation is typically O($n \log n$) because of the sort involved.
- *A modulo function*—This indicates the remainder after dividing one number by another and is useful in pattern generation in collection traversals. (The traversal will be O(n), though.)
- *Equivalency test*—Equal, greater than, less than, and so forth.

A.2.2   *O(n): The linear relationship algorithm*

What if we want to know the status of our canine test subjects at a particular point in time? Let's say that we really want to find out the rate at which they are wolfing down their food. Suppose that we decide to collect data at 30 seconds into the feast to see the state of the food bowls for each dog.

The data that we collect for each dog would involve a key-value pairing. In Python, we would be collecting a dictionary containing the names of the dogs and the amount of food remaining in their bowls:

```
thirty_second_check = {'champ': 0.35, 'colossus': 0.65,
    'willy': 0.0, 'bowser': 0.75, 'chuckles': 0.9}
```

This operation, walking around and estimating the amount of food left in the bowls, recording it in this (key, value) pairing, would be O(n), as illustrated in figure A.7.

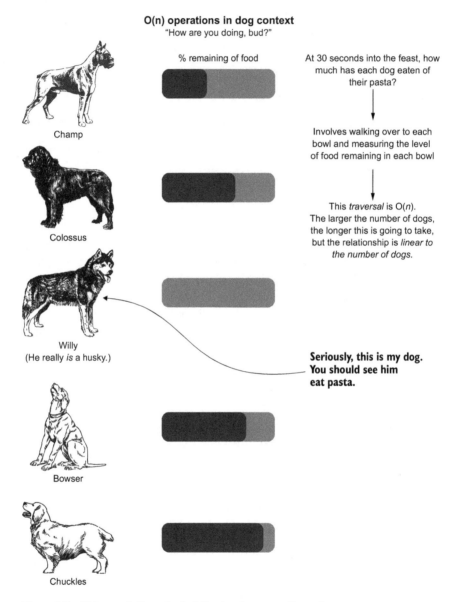

Figure A.7   O(n) search through all of the dogs' consumption rates

As you can see, in order to measure the amount remaining, we need to walk around to each dog and check the state of their bowl. For the five dogs we're showing, that may take a few seconds. But what if we had 500 dogs? That would take a few minutes of walking around to measure. The O(n) indicates a linear relationship between the algorithm (checking the amount of Bolognese eaten) and the size of the data (number of dogs) as a reflection of computational complexity.

From a software perspective, the same relationship holds true. Listing A.4 shows an iterative usage of the `quadratic()` method defined in listing A.3, operating over each element in the two NumPy arrays defined in that listing. As the size of the array increases, the runtime increases in a linear manner.

Listing A.4 Demonstration of O(n) complexity

Mapping over the small (–100, 100) array and applying a function to each value takes a bit longer than retrieving a single value.

Increases the size by a factor of 10 for the array, and the runtime increases by a factor of 10

```
%timeit -n 10 -r 10 [quadratic(x) for x in sequential_array]
>> 1.37 ms ± 508 µs per loop (mean ± std. dev. of 10 runs, 10 loops each)
%timeit -n 10 -r 10 [quadratic(x) for x in np.arange(-1000, 1000, 1)]
>> 10.3 ms ± 426 µs per loop (mean ± std. dev. of 10 runs, 10 loops each)
%timeit -n 10 -r 10 [quadratic(x) for x in np.arange(-10000, 10000, 1)]
>> 104 ms ± 1.87 ms per loop (mean ± std. dev. of 10 runs, 10 loops each)
%timeit -n 10 -r 10 [quadratic(x) for x in np.arange(-100000, 100000, 1)]
>> 1.04 s ± 3.77 ms per loop (mean ± std. dev. of 10 runs, 10 loops each)
%timeit -n 2 -r 3 [quadratic(x) for x in massive_array]
>> 30 s ± 168 ms per loop (mean ± std. dev. of 3 runs, 2 loops each)
```

Increases again by a factor of 10, and the runtime follows suit. This is O(n).

Increases by a factor of 10, and the runtime increases by a factor of 30?! This is due to the size of the values being calculated and the shift to an alternative form of multiplication in Cython (the underlying compiled C* code that optimized calculations use).

As can be seen in the results, the relationship between collection size and computational complexity is for the most part *relatively uniform* (see the following callout for why it's not perfectly uniform here).

When computational complexity breaks patterns at massive scale

In listing A.4, the final collection doesn't follow the same pattern as the preceding ones. Behavior such as this (a breakdown in assumed expected performance when dealing with massive data) is present in any system, particularly in distributed systems.

When some algorithms start processing data that is of a sufficient size, reallocation of memory may be a limiting factor in the performance of those algorithms. Similarly, garbage-collection operations in ML-focused languages (Python, or anything running in the JVM) can cause substantial disruptions to runtime performance because the system has to free space in memory in order to continue the operation that you are instructing it to perform.

O(n) is a fact of life in our world of DS work. However, we should all pause and reconsider our implementations if we're building software that employs our next relationship in this list: O(n^2). This is where things can get a little crazy.

A.2.3   *$O(n^2)$: A polynomial relationship to the size of the collection*

Now that our dogs are fed, satiated, and thoroughly pleased with their meal, they could use a bit of exercise. We take them all to a dog park and let them enter at the same time.

As in any social hour involving dogs, the first order of business is going to be formal introductions by way of behind-sniffing. Figure A.8 shows the combinations of greetings among our five dogs.

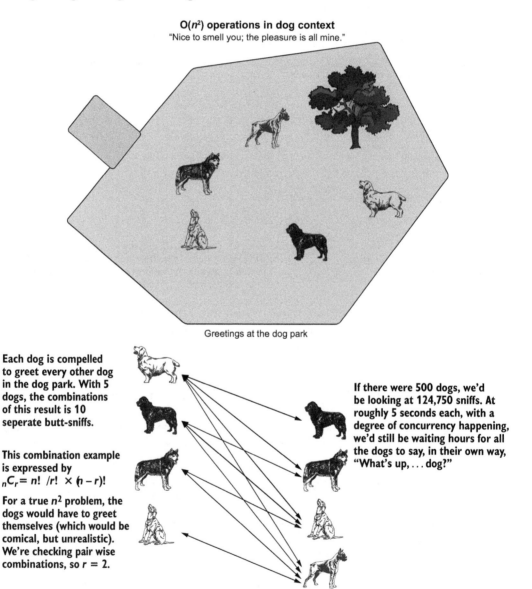

$O(n^2)$ operations in dog context
"Nice to smell you; the pleasure is all mine."

Greetings at the dog park

Each dog is compelled to greet every other dog in the dog park. With 5 dogs, the combinations of this result is 10 seperate butt-sniffs.

This combination example is expressed by
$_nC_r = n! / r! \times (n - r)!$

For a true n^2 problem, the dogs would have to greet themselves (which would be comical, but unrealistic). We're checking pair wise combinations, so $r = 2$.

If there were 500 dogs, we'd be looking at 124,750 sniffs. At roughly 5 seconds each, with a degree of concurrency happening, we'd still be waiting hours for all the dogs to say, in their own way, "What's up, . . . dog?"

Someone should let dogs know that there is a more efficient way of doing this.

Figure A.8   The dog park meet and greet. While not precisely $O(n^2)$, it bears a similar relationship.

NOTE Combination calculations are, in the strictest sense, O(n choose k) in complexity. For simplicity's sake, let's imagine brute-forcing the solution by interacting all possible permutations and then filtering, which would be O(n^2) in complexity.

This combination-based traversal of paired relationships is not strictly O(n^2); it is actually O(n choose k). But we can apply the concept and show the number of operations as combinatorial operations. Likewise, we can show the relationship between runtime duration and collection size by operating on permutations

Table A.1 shows the number of total butt-sniff interactions that will happen in this dog park based on the number of dogs let in through the gate (combinations), as well as the potential greetings. We're assuming the dogs feel the need for a formal introduction, wherein each acts as the initiator (a behavior that I have witnessed with my dog on numerous occasions).

Table A.1 Dog greeting by number of dogs

Number of dogs present	Number of greetings (combinations)	Potential greetings (permutations)
2	1	2
5	10	20
10	90	45
100	4,950	9,900
500	124,750	249,500
1,000	499,500	999,000
2,000	1,999,000	3,998,000

To illustrate what this relationship of friendly dog greetings looks like for both the combinations and permutations, figure A.9 shows the incredible growth in complexity as the number of dogs increases.

For the vast majority of ML algorithms (the models that are built through a training process), this level of computational complexity is just the beginning. Most are far more complex than O(n^2).

Listing A.5 shows an implementation of n^2 complexity. For each element of the source array, we're going to be generating an offset curve that rotates the element by the iteration index value. The visualizations for each section following will show what is going on in the code to make it clearer.

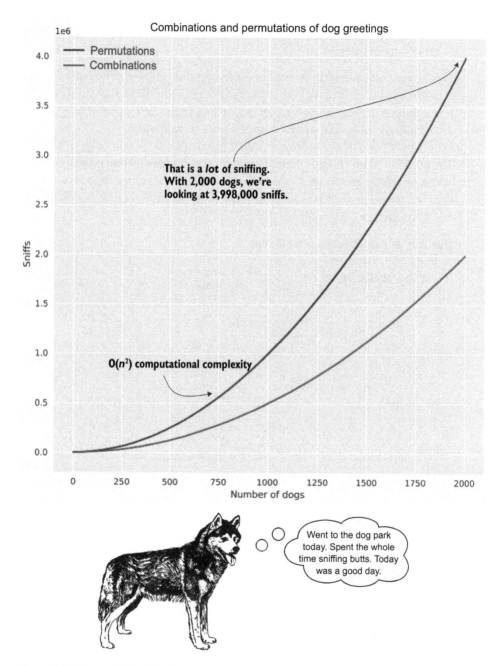

Figure A.9   **The explosion of sniffing as the number of dogs increases in our dog park. Exponential relationships in complexity are just as bad in code as they are for dogs when talking about efficiency.**

Listing A.5 An example of O(n^2) complexity

Function for modifying the quadratic solution to the array by a value from the array

Function for generating the collection of quadratic evaluation series values

Acquires the range around 0 for array generation (size + 1 for symmetry)

Catches warnings related to dividing by zero (since we're crossing that boundary of integers in the array)

```
import seaborn as sns
def quadratic_div(x, y):
    return quadratic(x) / y
def n_squared_sim(size):
    max_value = np.ceil(size / 2)
    min_value = max_value * -1
    x_values = np.arange(min_value, max_value + 1, 1)
    with warnings.catch_warnings():
        warnings.simplefilter("ignore")
        curve_matrix = [[quadratic_div(x, y) for x in x_values] for
                        y in x_values]
    curve_df = pd.DataFrame(curve_matrix).T
    curve_df.insert(loc=0, column='X', value=x_values)
    curve_melt = curve_df.melt('X', var_name='iteration', value_name='Y')
    fig = plt.figure(figsize=(10,10))
    ax = fig.add_subplot(111)
    sns.lineplot(x='X', y='Y', hue='iteration', data=curve_melt, ax=ax)
    plt.ylim(-100,100)
    for i in [ax.title, ax.xaxis.label, ax.yaxis.label] +
      ax.get_xticklabels() + ax.get_yticklabels():
        i.set_fontsize(14)
    plt.tight_layout
    plt.savefig('n_squared_{}.svg'.format(size), format='svg')
    plt.close()
    return curve_melt
```

Plots each curve with a different color to illustrate the complexity differences in the algorithm

The n^2 traversal to generate the array of arrays by mapping over the collection twice

Transposes and melts the resultant matrix of data to a normalized form for plotting purposes

For the algorithm defined in listing A.5, if we were to call it with different values for an effective collection size, we would get the timed results shown in the next listing.

Listing A.6 Results of evaluating an O(n^2) complex algorithm

With only 121 operations, this executes pretty quickly.

At 10 times the array size, 10,201 operations take significantly longer.

```
%timeit -n 2 -r 2 ten_iterations = n_squared_sim(10)
>> 433 ms ± 50.5 ms per loop (mean ± std. dev. of 2 runs, 2 loops each)
%timeit -n 2 -r 2 one_hundred_iterations = n_squared_sim(100)
>> 3.08 s ± 114 ms per loop (mean ± std. dev. of 2 runs, 2 loops each)
%timeit -n 2 -r 2 one_thousand_iterations = n_squared_sim(1000)
>> 3min 56s ± 3.11 s per loop (mean ± std. dev. of 2 runs, 2 loops each)
```

At 1,002,001 operations, the exponential relationship becomes clear.

The relationship to the input array size from listing A.5 and the results shown in listing A.6 can be seen a bit more clearly in figure A.10. If we were to continue increasing the size of the array generation parameter value to 100,000, we would be looking at 10,000,200,001 operations (while our first iteration of size 10 generates 121 operations). More important, though, is the memory pressure of generating so many arrays of data. The size complexity will rapidly become the limiting factor here, resulting in an out-of-memory (OOM) exception long before we get annoyed at how long it's taking to calculate.

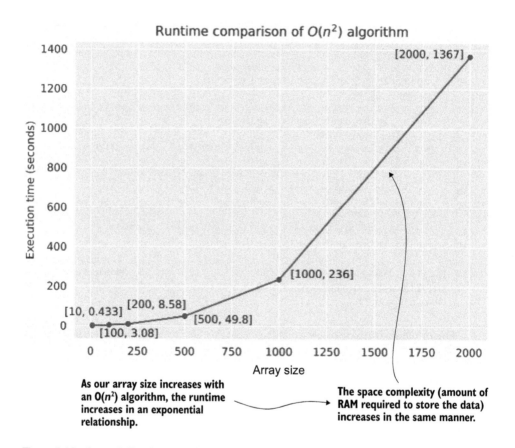

Figure A.10   Computational complexity of different collection sizes to the algorithm in listing A.5

To illustrate what this code is doing, we can see the result of the first iteration (using 10 as the function argument) in figure A.11.

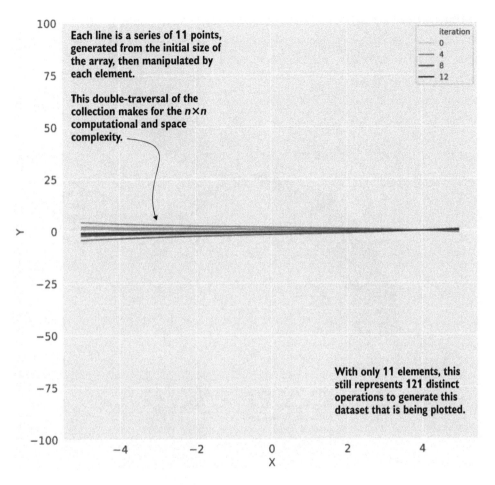

Each line is a series of 11 points, generated from the initial size of the array, then manipulated by each element.

This double-traversal of the collection makes for the $n \times n$ computational and space complexity.

With only 11 elements, this still represents 121 distinct operations to generate this dataset that is being plotted.

Figure A.11 The data generated from our $O(n^2)$ algorithm operating on an array of size 11 (execution time: 433 ms, ~26 KB space required)

Figure A.12 shows the progression in complexity from an array size of 201 (top) to a much more extreme size (2,001, at bottom) when run through this algorithm.

As you can see (keep in mind that these plots are generating a series that is plotted for each index position of the input array), a seemingly innocuous collection size can become very large, very quickly, when run through such an algorithm. It's not too much of a stretch to imagine how much this will affect the runtime performance of a project if code is written with this level of complexity.

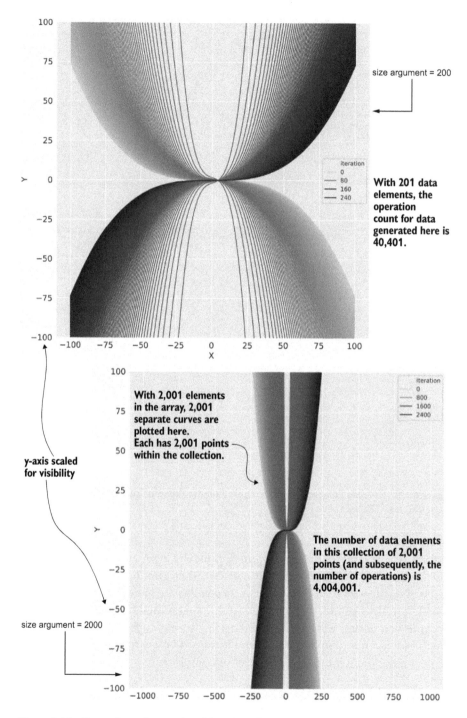

Figure A.12   Comparison of array sizes 201 (time: 8.58 s, space: ~5.82 MB) and 2,001 (time: 1,367 s, space: ~576.57 MB).

Complexity smells in code

In the grand scheme of code smells, computational complexity is generally one of the easier ones to spot. This complexity typically manifests itself in nested loops. Whether it be a declarative-style `for` loop that has additional `for` loops within it, a `while` loop with nested iteration or mapping within it, or a nested list comprehension, these structures in code stand out as potentially dangerous.

This isn't to say that the logic within nested loops and complex `while` statements is guaranteed to be worst-case scenarios of $O(n^2)$, $O(2n)$, or $O(n!)$, but these are places to spend more time when evaluating code. They're the smoke, so to speak, that needs to be investigated to ensure that a potential fire is not about to erupt when you run the code.

Seeing these in a code base simply means that you should spend extra time looking through the logic and running through scenarios. The best way to do that is to imagine what would happen if the collection being iterated over doubles in size. What if it increases by an order of magnitude?

Will the code scale? Will it take so long to run that an SLA is missed? Will the system that it's running on OOM? Thinking of how to identify, refactor, and change the logic of your code can help to prevent stability issues and cost considerations later.

A.3 *Analyzing decision-tree complexity*

Let's imagine that we're in the process of building a solution to a problem that, as a core requirement, needs a highly interpretable model structure as its output. Because of this requirement, we choose to use a decision-tree regressor to build a predictive solution.

Since we're a company that is dedicated to our customers (dogs) and their pets (humans), we need a way to translate our model results into direct and actionable results that can be quickly understood and applied. We're not looking for a black-box prediction; rather, we're looking to understand the nature of the correlations in our data and see how the predictions are influenced by the complex system of our features.

After feature engineering is complete and the prototype has been built, we're in the process of exploring our hyperparameter space in order to hone the automated tuning space for the MVP. After starting the run (with tens of thousands of tuning experiments), we notice that the training of different hyperparameters results in different completion times. In fact, depending on the tested hyperparameters, each test's runtime can be off by more than an order of magnitude from another. Why?

To explore this concept, let's step through how a decision-tree regressor works (in the sense of complexity) and evaluate how changing a few hyperparameter settings can affect the runtime. Figure A.13 shows a rather high-level view of what is happening in the algorithm when it is fit upon training data.

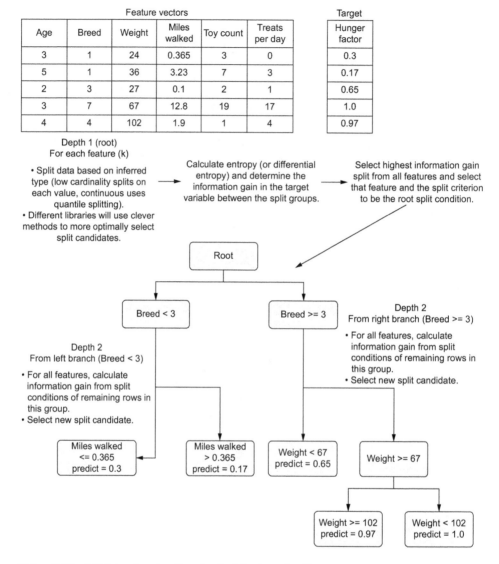

Figure A.13   A high-level explanation of a decision tree algorithm

This diagram is likely familiar to you. The basic structure, functionality, and behavior of the algorithm is covered in great detail in blog posts, other books, and as a foundational concept in learning the basics of ML. What is of interest to our discussion is what affects the computational and space complexity while training the model.

NOTE   Figure A.13 is an example only. This model is incredibly overfit and would likely do very poorly against a validation split. With a more realistic data-split volume and a depth restriction, the predictions would be the average of split-branch membership.

To start, we can see that the initial split at the root of the tree requires a determination of which feature to choose to split on first. A scalability factor exists right out of the gate with this algorithm. To determine where to split, we need to measure each feature, split it based on the criterion that the library's implementation chooses, and calculate the information gain between those splits.

For the purposes of computational complexity, we will refer to the number of features as k. Another component to the calculation of information gain involves the estimation of entropy, based on the size of the dataset being trained upon. This is the n in traditional non-ML complexity. To add to this complexity, we have to traverse each level of the tree. Once a split is realized as the best path, we have to continue to iterate on the features present in the subset of the data, repeatedly, until we hit the criteria set in the hyperparameter that equates to the minimum number of elements to populate a leaf (prediction) node.

Iterating through these nodes represents a computational complexity of $O(n \log(n))$, as the splits are restricted in size as we move closer to leaf nodes. However, because we are forced to iterate through all features at each of the adjudication nodes, our final computational complexity becomes more akin to $O(k \times n \times \log(n))$.

We can directly affect the real-world behavior of this worst-case runtime performance by adjusting hyperparameters (remember that $O()$ notation is *the worst-case*). Of particular note is that some of the hyperparameters can be beneficial to computational complexity and model efficacy (minimum count to create a leaf, maximum depth of tree), while others are negatively correlated (learning rate in other algorithms that utilize stochastic gradient descent, or SGD, for instance).

To illustrate the relationship between a hyperparameter and the runtime performance of a model, let's look at modifying the maximum depth of a tree in listing A.7. For this example, we're going to use a freely available open source dataset to illustrate the effect of hyperparameter values that directly influence computational and space complexity of a model. (My apologies for not collecting a dataset regarding dog characteristics and general hunger levels. If anyone wants to create that dataset and release it for common use, please let me know.)

> **NOTE** In listing A.7, in order to demonstrate an excessive depth, I break the rules of tree-based models by one-hot-encoding categorical values. Encoding categorical values in this manner risks a very high chance of preferentially splitting only on the Boolean fields, making a dramatically underfit model if the depth is not sufficient to utilize other fields. Validation of the feature set should always be conducted thoroughly when encoding values to determine if they will create a poor model (or a difficult-to-explain model). Look to bucketing, k-leveling, binary encoding, or enforced-order indexing to solve your ordinal or nominal categorical woes.

Listing A.7 Demonstrating the effects of tree depth on runtime performance

One-hot-encodes the month and day columns to ensure that we have sufficient features to achieve the necessary depth for this exercise. (See note preceding this listing.)

```
from sklearn.model_selection import train_test_split
from sklearn.tree import DecisionTreeRegressor
from sklearn.metrics import mean_squared_error
import requests
URL = 'https://raw.githubusercontent.com/databrickslabs
/automl-toolkit/master/src/test/resources/fire_data.csv'
file_reader = pd.read_csv(URL)
encoded = pd.get_dummies(file_reader,
columns=['month', 'day'])
target_encoded = encoded['burnArea']
features_encoded = encoded.drop('burnArea', axis=1)
x_encoded, X_encoded, y_encoded, Y_encoded =
    train_test_split(features_encoded,
target_encoded, test_size=0.25)
shallow_encoded = DecisionTreeRegressor(max_depth=3,
  min_samples_leaf=3,
  max_features='auto',
  random_state=42)
%timeit -n 500 -r 5 shallow_encoded.fit(x_encoded, y_encoded)
>> 3.22 ms ± 73.7 µs per loop (mean ± std. dev. of 5
runs, 500 loops each)
mid_encoded = DecisionTreeRegressor(max_depth=5,
  min_samples_leaf=3, max_features='auto',
  random_state=42)
%timeit -n 500 -r 5 mid_encoded.fit(x_encoded, y_encoded)
>> 3.79 ms ± 72.8 µs per loop (mean ± std. dev. of 5
runs, 500 loops each)
deep_encoded = DecisionTreeRegressor(max_depth=30,
  min_samples_leaf=1,
  max_features='auto',
  random_state=42)
%timeit -n 500 -r 5 deep_encoded.fit(x_encoded, y_encoded)
>> 5.42 ms ± 143 µs per loop (mean ± std. dev. of 5
runs, 500 loops each)
```

Pulls in an open source dataset to test against

Gets the train and test split data

A shallow depth of 3 (potentially underfit) reduces the runtime to a minimum baseline.

Moving from a depth of 3 to 5 increases runtime by 17% (some branches will have terminated, limiting the additional time).

Moving to a depth of 30 (actual realized depth of 21 based on this dataset) and reducing the minimum leaf size to 1 captures the worst possible runtime complexity.

As you can see in the timed results of manipulating the hyperparameters, a seemingly insignificant relationship exists between the depth of the tree and the runtime. When we think about this as a percentage change, though, we can start to understand how this could be problematic.

To illustrate the complexity of this tree-based approach, figure A.14 shows the steps that are being taken at each candidate split as the tree is being produced.

Not only do multiple tasks need to be accomplished in order to decide where to split and what to split on, but this entire block of tasks shown on the right side of figure A.14 needs to be completed for each feature on the subset of data that fulfills the

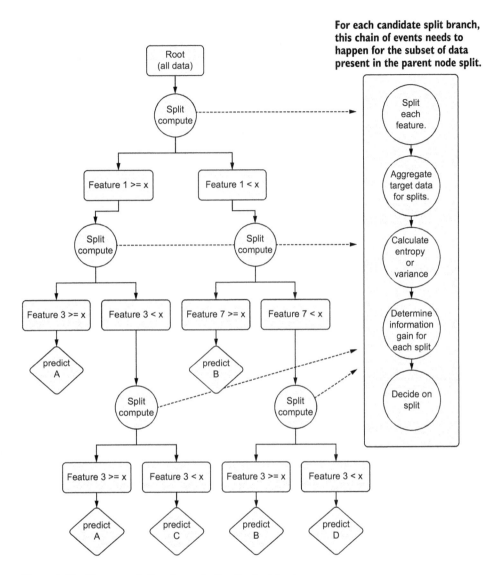

Figure A.14 The computational complexity of a decision tree

prior split conditions at each candidate node. With a tree depth of 30, 40, or 50, we can imagine that this tree becomes quite large rather fast. The runtime will increase comparatively as well.

What happens when the dataset is not, as in this toy example, 517 rows? What happens when we're training on 500 million rows of data? Setting aside the model performance implications (generalization capabilities) of running to too deep of a tree, when we think about a 68% increase in runtime from a single hyperparameter, the differences in training time can be extremely significant (and costly) if we're not careful about how we're controlling the hyperparameters of the model.

Now that you've seen how computationally expensive hyperparameter tuning is, in the next section we'll look at the computational and space complexities of different model families.

A.4   *General algorithmic complexity for ML*

While we won't be talking about the implementation details of any other ML algorithm (as I've mentioned before, there are books devoted to that subject), we can look at one further example. Let's suppose we are dealing with an incredibly large dataset. It has 10 million rows of training data, 1 million rows of test data, and a feature set of 15 elements.

With a dataset this big, we're obviously going to be using distributed ML with the SparkML packages. After doing some initial testing on the 15 features within the vector, a decision is made to start improving the performance to try to get better error-metric performance. Since we're using a generalized linear model for the project, we're handling collinearity checks on all features and are scaling the features appropriately.

For this work, we split the team into two groups. Group 1 works on adding a single validated feature at a time, checking the improvement or degradation of the prediction performance against the test set at each iteration. While this is slow going, group 1 is able to cull or add potential candidates one at a time and have a relatively predictable runtime performance from run to run.

The members of group 2, on the other hand, add 100 potential features that they think will make the model better. They execute the training run and wait. They go to lunch, have a delightful conversation, and return back to the office. Six hours later, the Spark cluster is still running with all executors pegged at >90% CPU. It continues to run overnight as well.

The main problem here is the *increase in computational complexity*. While the n of the model hasn't changed at all (training data is still the exact same size), the reason for the longer runtime is simply the increased feature size. For large datasets, this becomes a bit of a problem because of the way that the optimizer functions.

While traditional linear solvers (ordinary least squares, for instance) can rely on solving a best fit through a closed-form solution involving matrix inversion, on large datasets that need to be distributed, this isn't an option. Other solvers have to be employed for optimizing in a distributed system. Since we're using a distributed system, we're looking at SGD. Being an iterative process, SGD will perform optimization by taking steps along a local gradient of the tuning history.

To get a simplified sense of how SGD works, see figure A.15. This 3D plot represents a walk of the solver along a series of gradients in its attempt to find the global minima error for a particular set of coefficients for the linear equation being generated.

Gradient descent, visualized simplistically

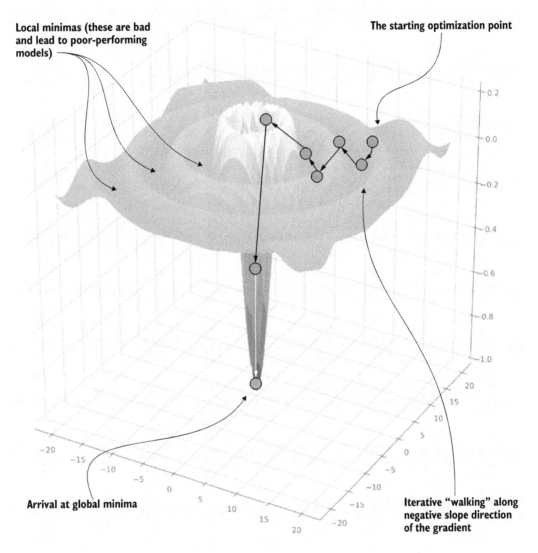

Local minimas (these are bad and lead to poor-performing models)

The starting optimization point

Arrival at global minima

Iterative "walking" along negative slope direction of the gradient

Figure A.15 A visual representation (with artistic liberties) of the SGD process of searching for minimization during optimization

NOTE Stochastic gradient descent will proceed along fixed-distance adjustments to attempt to arrive at the best fit to the test data (error minimization). It will stop when either the descent flattens to a slope of 0 and subsequent iterations within a threshold show no improvement or maximum iterations is reached.

Notice the iterative search that is occurring. This series of attempts to get the best fit of the equation to the target variable involves making adjustments to each of the coefficients for each element of the feature vector. Naturally, as the size of the vector increases, the number of coefficient evaluations grows. This process needs to occur for each iterative walk that is occurring.

However, a bit of a wrench is being thrown into this situation. SGD and iterative methodologies of its ilk (such as genetic algorithms) don't have a simple solution for determining computational complexity.

The reason for this (which is also true for other comparable iterating solvers, like limited memory Broyden-Fletcher-Goldfarb-Shanno, or L-BFGS) is that the nature of the optimization minima in both a local and global sense is highly dependent on the composition of the feature data (distributions and inferred structural types), the nature of the target, and the complexity of the feature space (feature count).

These algorithms all have settings for maximum number of iterations to achieve a best-effort optimization to a global minima state, but there is no guarantee that optimization will happen before hitting that iterator maximum count. Conversely, one of the challenges that can arise when determining how long training is going to take revolves around the complexity of optimization. If SGD (or other iterative optimizers) can arrive at a (hopefully, global) minima in a relatively short number of iterations, training will terminate long before the maximum iteration count is reached.

Because of these considerations, table A.2 is a rough estimate of theoretical worst-case computational complexity in common traditional ML algorithms.

Table A.2   Estimation of computational complexity for different model families

Model family	Training complexity	Prediction complexity
Decision trees	$O(kn\log(n))$	$O(k)$
Random forest	$O(kn\log(n)m$	$O(km)$
Gradient boosted trees	$O(knm)$	$O(km)$
Linear models (OLS)	$O(k2n)$	$O(k)$
Linear models (non-OLS)	$O(k^2n + k^3)$	$O(k)$
Support vector machines	$O(kn^2 + n^3)$	$O(km)$
K-nearest neighbors	$O(kmn)$*	$O(kn)$
K-means	$O(mni)$**	$O(m)$
Alternating least squares	$O(mni)$**	$O(ni)$

n = Number of rows in training set
k = Number of features in vector
m = Number of ensemble members
i = Number of iterations to converge
* m in this case is the restriction of number of neighbors to consider for definition of a boundary.
** m here refers to the number of k-centroids being considered.

The most common aspect of all of these complexities involves separate factors: the number of vectors used for training (row count in a DataFrame) and the number of features in the vector. An increase in the count of either of these has a direct effect on the runtime performance. Many ML algorithms have an exponential relationship between computational time and the size of the input feature vector. Setting aside the intricacies of different optimization methodologies, the solver of a given algorithm can have its performance impacted adversely as a feature set size grows. While each algorithm family has its own nuanced relationships to both feature size and training sample sizes, understanding the impact that feature counts have in general is an important concept to remember while in the early stages of a project's development.

As we saw in the previous section, the depth of a decision tree can influence the runtime performance, since it is searching through more splits, and thus taking more time to do so. Nearly all models have parameters that give flexibility to the application's practitioner that will directly influence the predictive power of a model (typically at the expense of runtime and memory pressure).

In general, it's a good idea to become familiar with the computational and space complexities of ML models. Knowing the impact to the business of selecting one type of model over another (provided that they're capable of solving the problem in a similar manner) can make a difference of orders of magnitude in cost after everything is in production. I've personally made the decision many times to use something that was slightly worse in predictive capabilities because it could run in a fraction of the time of an alternative that was many times more expensive to execute.

Remember, at the end of the day, we're here to solve problems for the business. Getting a 1% increase in prediction accuracy at the expense of 50 times the cost creates a new type of problem for the business while solving what you set out to do.

appendix B
Setting up a development environment

There are many reasons to start with a fresh slate when working on a new project. The following list shows a few of the more relevant ones with respect to ML project work:

- Dependency management is easier with a clean environment.
- Isolation of temporary files, logs, and artifacts is simpler.
- Scripted environment creation makes porting to production easier.
- Installation of libraries is less complex with fewer dependency collisions.

While many options exist for creating isolable environments for development of new projects, this appendix provides guidance on using Docker along with Conda's package management suite of tools, just as the companion repository to this book does.

B.1   *The case for a clean experimentation environment*

A major struggle that data scientists have once they've been building prototypes on their local computers for long enough is that older projects simply can't run anymore in the updated environments that subsequent projects have necessitated. As libraries evolve, the DSs upgrade library versions and add new packages with updated dependencies on other packages; dependencies change within this truly massive ecosystem comprising the large web of interconnected APIs

This incredibly complex and frustrating concept of maintaining compatibility among libraries is known as *dependency hell*, a moniker that is well-earned. Figure B.1 shows a typical scenario that happens with dependency struggles.

As you can see, the options for resolving library conflicts on a single local environment are quite dire. On one hand, you could be forced to refactor code bases

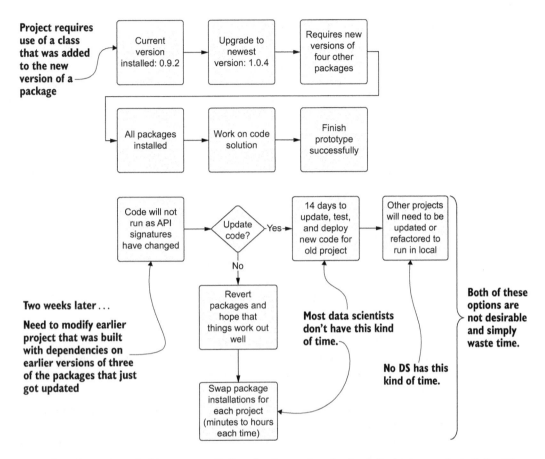

Figure B.1 Dependency hell in a common Python development environment. Package management struggles can waste a great deal of time.

and train runtime environments, both actions being untenable as the number of projects grows at a company. Alternatively, the DS team members would have to waste countless hours modifying their installed packages (reverting or upgrading) each time that they wanted to work on a new project. It's simply not a scalable solution.

Regardless of the operating system that you're running, if you have Python already installed on your machine, you're going to have some deep dependencies among the packages that are also installed. Some of the experimentation and testing will require library installations that could break either previously developed projects or utility applications that are available to you on the command line. Not to mention that each team member's computer likely has slight different versions of each of these critical packages, resulting in reproducibility issues if those team members run one another's code.

B.2   *Containers to deal with dependency hell*

This frustrating and time-wasting endeavor of making everything work together at all times has multiple solutions. One of the most popular is the prepackaged builds that are graciously provided as open source distributions (under a New BSD License) to the ML community by the company Anaconda. These tested and validated collections of packages are guaranteed to work well with one another, saving you from the arduous task of ensuring that behavior for yourself. There are three primary ways of creating a new, pristine environment with an Anaconda build of Python:

- *Conda environment manager*—Command-line tool that can create isolated Python environments locally from images that will not interfere with system Python installations
- *Anaconda Navigator*—GUI that allows for one-click setup of many popular development tools using isolated Conda environments on a local machine
- *Docker Container deployment of a Conda environment for use in a virtual machine (VM)*—Portable container definition that will create an isolated Python environment with the Conda package build that can run either on a local VM or in a cloud-based VM

Figure B.2 shows the first two approaches, which are applicable to ML experimentation in Python and use purely open source (free) solutions to isolate the runtime environments. The top portion can be done via the command-line interface (CLI) or through the Anaconda Navigator GUI.

These approaches solve the problem of having version conflicts within different project requirements, allowing for a massive savings in time and effort for the frustrating work that would otherwise be required to manage all of the packages for ML. For further explanation of what Docker is and why it is important, see the following sidebar.

What is Docker?

Docker is a containerization service. It is a platform that allows for operating system–level virtualization (think: a computer inside a computer) that can be configured with resources from the machine it's running on and can have full process-level isolation from other applications and operating system entities on the host machine.

This allows you to package up your software, libraries needed to run your software, and configuration files to run in different environments. You can even open up ports to communicate as if the container were its own computer.

Containerization for ML enables you to handle the dependency hell problem: each project can have its own set of libraries guaranteed to just work with your code in a repeatable and consistent manner. Containerization also gives you the ability to run the container in any environment—an on-premises server, a cloud-based server, or any virtual machine environment capable of running the container. This introduces portability to ML project work that is increasingly becoming not only more prevalent in the experimentation phases, but also absolutely critical for production-scale ML.

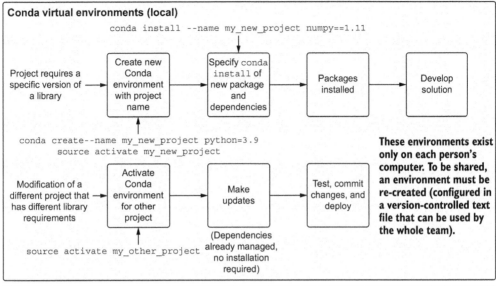

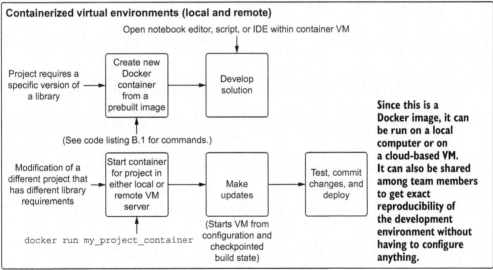

Figure B.2 Conda environment management vs. container service environment management. Both are good choices for streamlining experimentation, development, and production.

B.3 Creating a container-based pristine environment for experimentation

In this section, we're going to define and initiate a basic isolated runtime environment by using Docker. I'm rather partial to Anaconda for experimentation that doesn't require a paid service, so we're going to be using one of its preconfigured Docker containers that has a bootstrapped environment for Python 3 and the vast majority of core ML libraries already installed (well, at least the ones we'll need for this book, at any rate).

To ensure that we have the image on our system, we're going to run via the command line `docker pull continuumio/anaconda3`. This command will fetch the pre-built Docker container from Docker Hub, a repository of Docker images with both free and restricted images. The container includes a Linux operating system, the latest version of the Anaconda Python stack, and all of the configurations already completed for having a fully operable development environment for most DS work tasks with nearly no additional action required by the user.

> **NOTE** It's always advisable, particularly through the experimentation phase, to have an isolated environment where we can, as the kids say, "go absolutely nuts" with various packages, versions of those packages, and configurations that we might not want to have contaminating our computer's general environment. There is no more exquisite pain than realizing that your other project that you've been working on is now throwing dozens of exceptions because you updated to a newer version of NumPy.

To get a basic ML-enabled environment (a runnable VM image) built for us to perform the first phases of testing and research for a project, we can run the following (after ensuring that we install Docker, of course).

Listing B.1   Docker run command to create a basic ML environment

Feel free to name the container anything you'd like. If you omit this configuration, Docker will choose a fun name for you that makes it impossible to remember what is in the container.

Absolute path to local filesystem (you hopefully don't have a root users directory of benwilson)—change this.

```
docker run -i --name=airlineForecastExperiments
-v Users/benwilson/Book/notebooks:/opt/notebooks
-t -p 8888:8888
continuumio/anaconda3
/bin/bash  -c "/opt/conda/bin/conda install jupyter
-y --quiet && mkdir -p  /opt/notebooks &&
/opt/conda/bin/jupyter notebook --notebook-dir=/opt/notebooks
--ip='*' --port=8888 --no-browser --allow-root"
```

This is the image that we pulled from Docker Hub with the "docker pull continuumio/anaconda3" command.

Bash commands to allow us to install Jupyter and set it up to function with port forwarding so we can open up a local browser window and interface with the container's environment

---

Some slight modifications to this script—in particular, overriding the mount location (the first portion after the `-v` option that precedes the colon)—and a paste into the command line will have the container up and running. After the packages are collected and the image is built, the command line will give you a hint (a local host reference of `http://127.0.0.7:8888/?token=...`) that you can paste into your web browser to bring up Jupyter so you can start writing code in a notebook.

NOTE If you have a development environment hosted in the cloud somewhere that makes it remarkably easy for someone else to create this pristine environment for you, for a nominal fee, feel free to ignore this. This is for all my sisters and brothers of the maths who are on the laptop struggle bus with ML.

index